THE TRAVELER'S GUIDE
TO
JEWISH LANDMARKS
OF
EUROPE

THE TRAVELER'S GUIDE
TO
JEWISH LANDMARKS
OF
EUROPE

by

BERNARD POSTAL and SAMUEL H. ABRAMSON

FLEET PRESS CORPORATION
New York

To

Marge and Evelyn, whose patience, helpfulness,
and understanding were a lodestar that
kept us going from the first to
the last mile of this second
historical expedition

PREFACE

JEWISH TRAVELERS have left their imprint on history for more than three thousand years, but traveling for pleasure is a comparatively recent phenomenon among Jews. In earlier generations, Jews roamed far and wide on missions of mercy, to keep in touch with scattered Jewish communities, to find refuge from persecution, to seek greater economic opportunities, and to study.

The Diaspora—the Jewish community beyond the borders of ancient Palestine—came into being long before the first dispersion from Palestine, when intrepid Jews visited and settled in every corner of the then known world. The dispersions from the Holy Land, before and in the Christian Era, sent thousands of Jews traveling to the domains of the Mesopotamian, Greek, Roman, Byzantine, and Moslem empires. These wayfarers became the nuclei for the far-flung Jewish communities in North Africa, Asia Minor, the Near East, the Balkans, and Western Europe.

The fabulous Radanites, who introduced many standard commodities from the Orient to Europe, were traveling Jewish merchants whose caravans plied the land and sea routes from the south of France to China in the ninth century. Isaac the Jew was the sole survivor of a trade mission Charlemagne sent to the Caliph Harun-al-Rashid in Baghdad in the eighth century. The Jew Ibraham ibn Yakub was part of the deputation the Caliph of Cordoba, Spain, dispatched to Germany in the tenth century.

Jewish travelers from Byzantium paved the way for Jewish colonization in the Crimea, in Russia, and in Poland. Adventurous Jews from Spain, Portugal, Bohemia, Germany, and France crisscrossed Europe in medieval times, creating settlements as they went. Refugees from the Crusades and the Inquisition in Spain and Portugal crowded Europe's highways from the eleventh to the sixteenth century. In the seventeenth century Jews crossed the Atlantic to the New World, forerunners of the millions who were to follow in the nineteenth and twentieth centuries.

As late as 1933, however, Jewish travel literature was intended almost entirely for reading rather than for practical use. Like most travel books before the mid-nineteenth century, the works of Jewish travelers were largely for the armchair tourist who had neither the means nor the opportunity to see much of the world but could visit strange and romantic lands only through the eyes of those who had been there.

The earliest known Jewish travelogue was a collection of tales by Eldad Hadani, an itinerant ninth-century storyteller from Babylonia, whose fanciful yarns about Jewish kingdoms and tribes in Africa and Central Asia were the basis for the later Prester John legends. Benjamin of Tudela, a Spanish Jew, wrote an important book in Hebrew, describing the Jewish communities he visited in France, Italy, Greece, Palestine, Syria, Persia, and Mesopotamia, between 1165 and 1173. Petathiah of Regensburg, a German Jew, who started from Prague on a tour of Russia, the Crimea, Armenia, and the Near East, between 1178 and 1185, produced a similar work. Other medieval Jewish travelers gave accounts of holy places and tombs of Jewish scholars they had rediscovered or reported finding the ten so-called Lost Tribes of Israel. In the eighteenth, nineteenth, and early twentieth centuries, Jewish travel literature became more common, but in style and content it differed little from its predecessors.

The first comprehensive guide in any language to the old and bypassed seats of Jewish civilization in Europe and North Africa was compiled by Marvin Lowenthal. His delightful and authoritative work, *A World Passed By,* which appeared in 1933, was a treasure house of information. Many of the places he described are now gone, destroyed by Nazi vandalism and wartime bombing. More recently, the *London Jewish Chronicle* has been publishing an annual Jewish travel guide in the form of a directory of synagogues, communal institutions, kosher restaurants, and hotels throughout the world. Similar directories, confined entirely to Europe, have been published in French (by a Jewish weekly in Belgium) and in German (by a publishing house in Stuttgart).

None of these met the need for a practical, easy-to-use, readable book containing specific information about Jewish sights and sites in Europe, country by country, city by city, and town by town. But the demand for such data has been growing, because American Jews have contributed enormously to the postwar travel boom that now takes an estimated 750,000 Americans to Europe every year. Whether as businessmen or as pleasure-seekers, as students or as pilgrims come to honor parents and other kinfolk buried abroad, as World War II veterans who want to see the postwar Continent, or as former refugees from the Nazi terror visiting their old homes, American Jews are pouring into Europe by the tens of thousands annually.

More and more Jewish groups are regularly sponsoring organized tours of Europe. Virtually every American Jew who visits Israel spends some time in Europe. Jewish organizations, travel agencies, and government tourist bureaus have been besieged with requests for lists of places of Jewish interest in Europe. The American Jew going to Europe now wants to know all he can about the existence and location of Jewish landmarks of yesterday and today in Europe, so that he can plan to include them in an itinerary. He is eager to learn more about Jewish life in postwar Europe, to meet his fellow Jews, to visit their institutions, to see what is left of the great prewar Jewish communities, and to add another dimension to his trip by witnessing at first hand the work of the great American Jewish philanthropic agencies to which he has contributed.

When the first edition of this book appeared in 1962, it was the first to give on-the-spot, pinpointed information about everything Jewish there was to see in Europe on both sides of the Iron Curtain. It still is the only volume of its kind in the English language.

Designed primarily for use but also written to be read with enjoyment, it identifies, locates, and describes thousands of major and minor sites, landmarks, vestiges, shrines, memorials, buildings, institutions, monuments to catastrophe, and other places whose story is part of the chronicle of more than two thousand years of Jewish settlement, achievement, tragedy, and rebirth in Europe.

Alphabetically arranged by country, by city or town within each country, and by place within each city or town, the book is so organized as to make it an effective supplement to any general guidebook. By consulting this book before planning an itinerary, you can easily see exactly what there is of Jewish interest in any part of any country in Europe you intend to visit. But even if an itinerary is made without regard to places of Jewish interest, this book will be invaluable as a handy reference regardless of where you go in Europe.

Because we believe the traveler will welcome background information about the Jewish past and present in Europe, we have provided concise and up-to-the-minute histories of Jewish life in each country. Each country is dealt with separately.

The places described in this book fall into the following categories: Historically important or architecturally unique synagogues; modern synagogues; historic cemeteries; places and street names that recall old Jewries; monuments and memorials to Jews; places and streets named for Jews; concentration camp monuments and memorials; memorials to Jewish war heroes; birthplaces and graves of famous Jews; Jewish libraries and museums; Jewish historic vestiges and reminders of the Jewish past; Judaica collections in non-Jewish places; memorials to noted friends of Jews; works of art depicting Jewish themes or Jewish characters; Jewish historical objects in national and local museums; ancient Jewish buildings; famous institutions founded by or named for Jews; representative national Jewish institutions; representative local Jewish institutions; local Jewish press and entertainment; objects of Jewish interest in Christian institutions; selected kosher restaurants; miscellanea.

In the nine years since the first edition appeared, we have been assembling new material, checking and re-checking older material, and adding information provided by hundreds and hundreds of readers. We hope there will be other editions after this one and we will welcome corrections and additions.

We hope this book will make your trip to Europe more enjoyable. We know it will give your visit to Europe an extra dimension by enabling you to see for yourself how the philanthropic dollars you have contributed annually to the United Jewish Appeal through your local Jewish federation and welfare fund have made possible the reconstruction, rehabilitation, and revival of Jewish life and institutions in postwar Europe.

BERNARD POSTAL and SAMUEL H. ABRAMSON

New York
April, 1971

THANKS, IN EVERY LANGUAGE!

We are indebted to so many for so much in this book that there really is no adequate way of expressing our appreciation to all who assisted us even if we said it in all the languages of Europe.

Many years of independent research and on-the-spot investigation in a number of countries account for the bulk of the material, but a good deal of it was obtained through the unselfish efforts of hundreds of correspondents in many countries and in hundreds of cities and towns.

Librarians, scholars, municipal archivists, town and city functionaries, Jewish community officials, rabbis, churchmen, editors, museum curators, and university authorities cheerfully undertook extraordinary assignments and gladly met impossible deadlines to provide information, locate photographs, and verify facts.

The cooperation we received from the official government tourist bureaus in many countries was extraordinarily generous, remarkably understanding, and unfailingly helpful. Finally, we owe a unique debt to Ernest W. Michel, who translated hundreds of pages of raw data as a labor of love.

This listing of those who made distinctive contributions is divided into two parts: one records those abroad whose assistance was crucial, with the names classified under the country in which they reside or for which their aid was of particular significance; the other lists the names of those in the United States to whom we owe much.

AUSTRIA: Austrian Information Service; Egon Fink, Vienna; Wilhelm Krell, Vienna; Jonny Moser, Vienna; Dr. Josef Stummvoll, Vienna.

BELGIUM: Antwerp Tourist Bureau; Belgium Tourist Commission, Brussels; Brussels Information Center; Rabbi Robert Dreyfus, Brussels; Liège Tourist Office; Plantin-Moretus Museum, Antwerp.

BULGARIA: Dr. Asher Hannel, Sofia.

CANADA: Harold Alter, Downsview.

CYPRUS: Cyprus Ministry of Commerce and Industry, Nicosia.

CZECHOSLOVAKIA: Josef Bartoh, Prague; Cedok, Prague; K. Chaloupka, Prague; Jewish Museum, Prague; Pragopress, Prague.

DENMARK: Danish National Travel Office, Copenhagen; Dr. Rafael Edelman, Copenhagen; Harry D. Levitan, Copenhagen; Julian Margolinsky, Copenhagen.

FINLAND: Consulate General of Finland, New York; Rabbi Mika Weiss, Helsinki.

FRANCE: Basque Museum, Bayonne; Nissim de Camondo Museum, Paris; Carnavalet Museum, Paris; Maurice Chauvet, Montpellier; Chief Rabbi J. Cohen, Bordeaux; Embassy of Israel, Paris; Isidore Frank-Forter, Troyes; Jewish Art Museum, Paris; Albert Lévi, Bayonne; Malmaison Museum, Malmaison; Memorial to the Unknown Jewish Martyr, Paris; Roger Meyer, Paris; Municipal Museums, Nîmes; Municipal Museums, Strasbourg; Municipality of Arcachon; Municipality of Bruyères; Municipality of Lunel; Municipality of St.-Benoît-sur-Loire; ORT, Paris; André Pereyre, Bayonne; Léon Poliakov, Paris; Syndicat d'Initiative, Jouy-en-Josas; Syndicat d'Initiative, Lyons; Syndicat d'Initiative, Nancy; Syndicat d'Initiative, Nîmes; Syndicat d'Initiative, Pithiviers; Syndicat d'Initiative, Verdun.

GERMANY: Chaplain Alan Blustein, Bamberg; Central Council of Jews in Germany, Düsseldorf; Franconia Museum, Würzburg; Dr. Anneliese Schroder, Recklinghausen; Heinz Galinski, Berlin; German National Museum, Nuremberg; German Tourist Information Office; Hessian State Library, Darmstadt; Jewish Community of Berlin; Jewish Community of Cologne; Jewish Community of Mainz; Dr. Hans Lamm; Municipal Museum of Worms; Municipality of Borken; Municipality of Dessau (East Germany); Municipality of Dortmund; Municipality of Düsseldorf; Municipality of Frankfurt-am-Main; Municipality of Hamburg; Municipality of Hanover; Municipality of Heidelberg; Municipality of Heilbronn; Municipality of Munich; Municipality of Rothenburg; Municipality of Stuttgart; Municipality of Trier; Rabbi Martin Riesenburger, East Berlin; Society for Christian-Jewish Co-operation, Kassel; State Archives of Offenbach; State Museum of Regensburg; Benjamin Sternberg, Frankfurt.

GREAT BRITAIN: Board of Deputies of British Jews, London; British Museum, London; British Travel and Holidays Association, London; Coffee House Publicity Association, London; Canon A. M. Cook, Lincoln; G. P. V. Creagh, Bury St. Edmunds; S. Elliman, Edgware; Dr. B. Gatoff, Bradford; Samuel Goldsmith, London; Col. R. J. A. Hornby, London; Benny Isaacs, London; H. M. Jaffa, Cardiff; Jews' College, London; City Librarian, Cambridge; City Librarian, Leicester; London County Council; London Museum, London; Edward Mantus, London; A. S. P. Mason, Canterbury; Mayor's Office, Brighton;

Mayor's Office, Lincoln; Mayor's Office, Oxford; David Mellows, London; National Gallery, London; National Maritime Museum, Greenwich; National Portrait Gallery, London; The National Trust, London; Nottingham Municipality; St. Paul's Chapter House, London; S. D. Sassoon, Letchworth; Henry Shaw, London; Bernard Shillman, Dublin; Southborough Urban District Council; Rebecca Spivak, London; Sefton D. Temkin, London; Madame Tussaud's, London; University of Liverpool Library; University of London Library; University of Southampton; William Urry, Canterbury; Victoria and Albert Museum, London; Westminster Abbey Chapter House, London; York Cathedral Chapter House, York.

GREECE: Central Council of Jewish Communities of Greece, Athens; Lydia Eskenazi, Athens; National Tourist Organization of Greece, Athens.

HUNGARY: Dr. Alexander Scheiber, Budapest.

IRELAND: Irish Tourist Office, Dublin; Bernard Shillman, Dublin.

ITALY: Mrs. Pia Adad, Rome; American Jewish Joint Distribution Committee, Rome; Food and Agriculture Organization of the United Nations, Rome; Jewish Community of Florence; Jewish Community of Milan; *La Civiltà Cattolica,* Rome; Chief Rabbi Emanuele W. Levi, Verona; Fra J. Martin, Rome; Municipality of Alghero; Municipality of Cagliari; Municipality of Sassari; Municipality of Trani; Municipality of Turin; Olivetti, Milan; Vittorio Ovazza, Turin; Mrs. Ugo Piperno, Milan; Professor Cecil Roth, Oxford, England; the late Angiolo Treves, Turin; Professor Bruno Zevi, Rome.

LUXEMBOURG: Rabbi Charles Lehrman, Luxembourg City.

THE NETHERLANDS: Amsterdam Tourist Bureau; Anne Frank Foundation, Amsterdam; Bibliotheca Rosenthaliana, Amsterdam; L. Fuks, Amsterdam; International Court of Justice, The Hague; Jewish Historical Museum, Amsterdam; Mayor of Utrecht; P. J. Mijksenaar, Amsterdam; Municipal Archivist, The Hague; Rembrandt Museum, Amsterdam; Rijnsburg Municipality; H. Thien, Amsterdam; E. van Creveld, Amsterdam.

NORWAY: Norwegian National Travel Office.

POLAND: Akiva Kohane, Geneva; Abraham Kwartenko, Warsaw; Joseph Leftwich, London; Dr. Ber Mark, Warsaw.

SPAIN: Luis A. Blitz, Madrid; Edward Mantus, London; André Pereyre, Bayonne, France; Spanish Tourist Office.

SWEDEN: Daniel Brick, Stockholm; Jewish Community of Göteborg; Sweden National Tourist Office; Dr. Kurt Wilhelm, Stockholm.

SWITZERLAND: Bern Historical Museum; Federation of Swiss Jewish

Communities, Zurich; Bernard Fiszzon, London; Jewish Community of Geneva; Municipality of Basel; Swiss National Tourist Office.

TURKEY: Dr. Zvi Ankori, Jerusalem; Chief Rabbinate, Istanbul; Rabbi Isaac Jerusalmi, Paris; Edward Roditi, Paris; Rabbi Morris L. Rubinstein, Adana; Turkish Information Office.

YUGOSLAVIA: Federation of Jewish Communities in Yugoslavia, Belgrade; Yugoslav State Tourist Office.

UNITED STATES: Dr. Samuel Abrahamsen, New York; Dr. Arthur S. Abramson, Hartsdale, New York; Manuel Aguilar, New York; Harry Alderman, New York; American Jewish Joint Distribution Committee, New York; Austrian Information Service, New York; Hans J. Baumann, New York; Zev Baumgold, New York; Graenum Berger, New York; Edward L. Bernays, New York; Irving Bernstein, New York; Patricia Blake, New York; Roy Blumenthal, New York; B'nai B'rith Hillel Foundations, Washington, D.C.; Bordeaux Wine Information Bureau, New York; Rabbi Joseph M. Brandriss, Silver Spring, Md.; Dr. William W. Brickman, New York; British Information Services, New York; Dr. Winston E. Burdine, Atlanta; Rabbi David A. Jessurun Cardozo, New York; Mrs. John Cimino, New York; Roberta Cohen, New York; Mrs. Martin Cohn, Cincinnati; Mrs. Ida Cowen, New York; Clifton Daniel, New York; Peter A. De Maerel, New York; Irving Dickman, New York; Binyamin Eliav, New York; Mel Elfin, New York; Miriam R. Ephraim, New York; Dr. Morris Epstein, New York; Rabbi Chaim Essrog, New York; Mrs. Rose Fleischman, New York; Max Frankel, Washington, D.C.; French Government Tourist Office, New York; Harry Freud, New York; Daniel M. Friedenberg, New York; Abraham Gerbovoy, New York; Rabbi Joshua L. Goldberg, New York; Rabbi Philip Goodman, New York; Rabbi Harold H. Gordon, New York; Samuel Grand, New York; Rabbi David Greenberg, Scarsdale, New York; Alfred Grossman, New York; Edward E. Grusd, Washington D.C.; Rabbi Hugo Gryn, New York; Kurt Hampe, New York; Italian State Tourist Office, New York; Julian Jablin, Chicago; Murray Kass, New York; Dr. Abraham I. Katsh, Philadelphia; Rabbi Gilbert Klaperman, Lawrence, N. Y.; David Kosh, New York; Chaplain Marvin L. Labinger, Colorado Springs, Colo.; Dr. Sidney Licht, New Haven, Conn.; Seymour Liebman, Miami, Fla.; A. P. Lonek, Jr., New York; Ernest Maass, New York; Ernest W. Michel, New York; Rabbi Judah Nadich, New York; Ohrbach's, New York; Dr. Harry Orlinsky, New York; George Peabody and Associates, New York; George Perry, New York; Arnulf Pins, New York; Stojan Pudar, New

York, Jack Rader, New York; Rabbi Manfred Rechtshoffen, New York; John Henry Richter, Ann Arbor, Mich.; Rabbi William A. Rosenthall, New York; Harrison E. Salisbury, New York; Morris U. Schappes, New York; Dr. Joseph Schechtman, New York; Mrs. Charles Schulman, New York; Mrs. Irmgard Sherman, New York; S. I. Shneiderman, New York; Rabbi Matthew Simon, New York; Rabbi Henry F. Skirball, New York; Carl Sobin, New York; Henry B. Stern, New York; Yuri Suhl, New York; Chaim Suller, New York; Marc Tabatchnik, New York; United Synagogue of America, New York; Dr. Selman A. Waksman, New Brunswick, N. J.; Rabbi Martin M. Weitz, Lincoln, Pa.; Rabbi David H. Wice, Philadelphia; Yiddish Scientific Institute, New York; Thomas Yoseloff, New York; Rabbi Maurice L. Zigmond, Cambridge, Mass.

Many of the illustrations appearing in this book are from the personal collections of the authors. Grateful acknowledgment is hereby made to the following sources for their assistance in providing other illustrative material, (numbers below refer to the plates):

Alinari (19, 22); Joint Distribution Committee (31); Y. Berliner (27); Irving Bernstine (20); Cedok (1, 2, 4); Daniel Franck (28); German Tourist Information Office (18, 24, 26, 33, 34); Gilbert Klaperman (10); Harry Levitan (9); Netherlands National Tourist Office (5); Pressehuset (30); St. Paul's Chapter Office (23); Sopron (32); Spanish National Tourist Department (14); Studio Eve (25); Westminster Abbey Chapter Office (6); YIVO (16); Yugoslav Information Service (21)

CONTENTS

ALBANIA

The 230 Jews in this Communist state along the east coast of the Adriatic live mostly in Tirana and Valona, but there are also a few in Durrës (Durazzo) and in Shkoder (Scutari). Among these are five families of Greek origin who crossed into Albania to escape the Nazis but were never permitted to return by the Albanian government. Most of the Jews were well-off before their property was nationalized. They are now working as laborers or white collar workers, mostly in what were once their own enterprises.

All of the Jews are said to want to leave, but fear to apply for exit permits lest they lose their jobs. In 1952, Israel made visas available to all the 52 Jewish families but they were never used. In 1957, the Albanian authorities announced that exit permits would be granted to those wishing to go to Israel, but this policy was rescinded shortly afterwards.

There are no known Jewish institutions and no Jewish community life. The country's one synagogue, in Tirana, has been closed since the 1950s, but travelers reported that services were being held in a private home in Valona as late as 1956. Public celebrations of religious holidays are not permitted. The mosques in this largely Moslem country have been closed, but some churches are still open. Only for Passover are Jews allowed some measure of religious observance. JDC has managed to provide them with matzoth.

Benjamin of Tudela, medieval Jewish traveler, found Jews in what is now Albania, in 1170. Spanish Jews established themselves in Durrës and Valona in the sixteenth century, when Albania was a Turkish domain. A Torah Scroll that belonged to the Jews of Valona five hundred years ago is now owned by the Jewish community of Ioannina, Greece. Sabbatai Zevi, false messiah of the seventeenth century, spent his last days in exile at Berat, where a major Jewish center grew up.

In 1935, Jewish refugees from Germany and Austria were invited to settle in Albania as the result of the intercession of Herman Bernstein, who had been United States Minister there from 1930 to 1932. Official status was given to the Jewish community of Valona in 1937, but the colonization scheme died when Italy annexed Albania in 1939. Before King Zog fled, he admitted one hundred Jewish refugees and married the sister of Mrs. Michael Deutsch, wife of a Jewish physician from Senta, Yugoslavia. At a conference of representatives of resistance fighters' organizations from 12 countries, held in Vienna in 1965, the delegate from Albania reported that 40 Jews had taken an active part in the struggle against the Nazi occupation.

ANDORRA

There are 70 Jews in this tiny principality set high in the Pyrenees on the border of France and Spain. Most of them hail from Spanish Morocco. They make their living as bank clerks, shop employees, taxi drivers and merchants. Because this is a Roman Catholic country, births cannot be registered with the civil authorities without an accompanying certificate of baptism. The Andorran Jews, who have no community organization, register births in the nearest Spanish town. Burials also take place in Spain because there is no Jewish section in the Andorran cemetery. The unofficial Jewish leader is Elias J. Beniflah, who lives in the village of Les Escaldes.

AUSTRIA

A toll ordinance that set fees to be paid by Jewish merchants passing along the main trade route from Bavaria to the Balkans in 906 establishes the earliest known presence of Jews in Austria. Judenburg, one of the oldest towns in Austria, is believed to owe its name (Fortress of the Jews) to an eleventh-century Jewish colony. Vienna's first synagogue was opened in 1204.

For the next two centuries the Jewish position was tolerably good under the rule of the Holy Roman Emperors and their vassals, the Babenberg dukes. Mob violence was tempered by royal and ducal concern for the Jews as personal property, while onerous taxation was the price for pursuing business without too much hindrance. One duke employed a Jewish mintmaster. Frederick I entrusted his finances to Jewish agents. His charter of 1244 for the first time gave legal protection to Jewish lives, property, and communal institutions. Jews fleeing persecution in Germany in the thirteenth century were welcomed to Austria.

The first Hapsburg Emperor, Rudolph, confirmed Frederick's ordinance. Later Hapsburgs also sought to shield Jews from popular hatred and even invited harassed Jews from neighboring countries to settle in Austria. Jewish communities in Vienna, Judenburg, Krems, Wiener Neustadt, Tulln, Klosterneuburg and Innsbruck were permitted to unite into a national federation at the beginning of the fifteenth century.

Periodic pogroms between 1338 and 1406 were climaxed by mass expulsion in 1420 on the pretext that the Jews were aiding the revolt of the Hussite heretics against the Church. The Vienna synagogue was razed, its stones being used in the new buildings of the University of Vienna; all Jewish property was expropriated; many Jews were burned at the stake, and the survivors were banished from the whole of Lower Austria.

They never entirely disappeared, however, moving from province to province and city to city, as local conditions and the attitude of the nobles and the Church permitted. Midway through the sixteenth century the Emperor let a few return to Vienna as court-tolerated residents. These became the nucleus of the second Jewish community, which was legalized in 1624 with the establishment of the Vienna ghetto. A stiff annual fee to the city and to the Emperor was imposed for property and trade rights and a measure of self-rule. Outside Vienna, the Jews were allowed to live on the estates of the aristocracy, subject to an exorbitant levy. All through the country they remained subject to degrading restrictions and liable to momentary exile. The arrival of refugees from the Chmielnicki pogroms in Poland in 1648 enlarged the community and brought spiritual enrichment in the form of Talmudic learning and rabbinic leadership.

As the Jews became more dependent on royal favor, they were caught between the economic antagonism of the burghers and a rising tide of religious hatred. To placate the mob and to rid himself of heavy debts to the Jews, Emperor Leopold I banished them in 1670. This proved so economically disastrous that some Jews were invited to return as court bankers and imperial war purveyors. The first of these was Samuel Oppenheimer, who, with his associates and employees, laid the foundation for the third Jewish community, in 1676.

3

From the late seventeenth to the early nineteenth century, the new settlement consisted of two kinds of Jews: the rich and tolerated court Jews and their retinues, who were allowed to live outside the ghetto; and all the rest. Oppenheimer helped pay for the war against Turkey. His nephew, Samson Wertheimer, managed the government salt monopoly. Diego d'Aguilar, a Portuguese Jew, organized the tobacco monopoly. Other court Jews operated the imperial mint and the municipal bank and built up the copper and cotton industries and equipped the Hapsburg armies. Salomon Rothschild was the financial adviser to Prince Metternich.

Out of this financial complex developed a hierarchy of Jewish commerce and banking through which Jewish entrepreneurs enabled Vienna to penetrate the economically backward hinterland of the Hapsburg monarchy and to become the wholesale market for the entire Danube basin and southeastern Europe. By 1753 there were more than 1,000 Jews in Vienna and as many more in the provinces, making Austrian Jewry the largest in the German-speaking lands. While the privileged court Jews became entrenched, the ordinary Jew could own no property and remained subject to humiliating restrictions. Expansion of the Jewish population was controlled by forbidding more than one male descendant of a family to remain in the country and by strict curbs on Jewish marriages. Jewish public worship remained taboo.

A new era began in 1782 with the edict of tolerance by Emperor Joseph II, who abolished the Jewish poll tax and the requirement that Jews wear distinctive dress. Soon afterward they were permitted to adopt family names and became eligible for military conscription. A public synagogue was authorized in Vienna in 1811, the first in nearly 150 years.

The revolution of 1848 proclaimed religious freedom for all, abolished the ghetto and repealed the special Jewish taxes. Jews were among the leaders of the abortive rebellion, notably Ignaz Kuranda, who became the first Jew elected to the Austrian parliament, and Adolf Fischer, who headed the revolutionary police force. Though some anti-Jewish restrictions were re-enacted in the reaction that followed the short-lived liberal regime, complete emancipation was achieved in 1867.

Between 1875 and the start of World War I, the Jews made remarkable contributions to Austrian culture and industry. Jewish authors and composers helped make the literary and musical reputation of Vienna. The Jewish-owned and -edited *Wiener Neue Freie Presse* became one of the most influential newspapers in Europe. Simultaneously, anti-Semitism as a political force was born in Vienna and spread rapidly to the whole of Austria, whose pan-Germans made racism in its most rabid form their gospel even before Hitler was born. The election of the anti-Semitic leader, Karl Lueger, as mayor of Vienna in 1895, seriously weakened the liberal movement in which the Jews had played a significant role.

Some Jews, including many who had been ennobled by Emperor Francis Joseph, reacted by voluntary conversion to Christianity. Others turned to political Zionism, which Theodor Herzl founded in Vienna in the 1890s. A steady stream of immigrants from Moravia, Bohemia, Poland, Hungary, and Rumania after 1870 did much to preserve Jewish life and learning.

After World War I, during which Austria had more high-ranking Jewish army officers than any other country, the Jewish community was caught up in a series of disasters which ended in catastrophe. War refugees from Poland, Hungary, and Rumania swelled the Jewish population to 180,000 under the Austrian Republic.

While Jews enjoyed legal equality, their economic position was undermined by the postwar territorial changes which cut Vienna off from its natural markets in southeastern Europe.

The hatred of the nationalists for Viktor Adler and Otto Bauer, Jewish leaders of the Social Democratic party; the civil war between Fascists and Socialists; the whittling away of Jewish employment and cultural rights under the corporate state; anti-Jewish riots in the universities; the surge of Nazism and financial disasters touched off by the collapse of the Rothschild bank laid the ground for the tragedy which ensued when Hitler's armies overran Austria in March 1938.

Vienna, then Europe's third-largest Jewish community, owed much of its cosmopolitan character and musical and literary greatness to a galaxy of world-famous Jewish names. But this did not prevent the speedy introduction of the Nazi anti-Jewish laws and the beginning of an anti-Jewish terror immediately after the *Anschluss* with Germany. Many Jews, particularly among those who had intermarried or had been converted, committed suicide. About half of the Jewish population of 220,000—91 per cent of whom lived in Vienna—found temporary safety in France, Holland, Italy, Yugoslavia, Hungary, and Czechoslovakia, only to be trapped later by the Nazi occupiers. Those who did not flee were doomed by World War II, which found all of Austria's 70,000 remaining Jews concentrated in Vienna. Extermination camps in Poland claimed 50,000; another 15,000 died in concentration camps in Austria and Czechoslovakia. By 1942 the third Jewish community had been wiped out.

When the Russians entered Vienna in 1945, they found about 500 Jews—mainly half Jews—who had been hiding throughout the war. Slowly, survivors from concentration camps in Poland, Hungary, and Czechoslovakia came to Vienna, but few had lived there before. Between 1946 and 1949, more than 200,000 Jews passed through Vienna en route to Israel. Legally or illegally, with documents and without documents, they poured through the city, which became known as the gateway to freedom. An additional 125,000 came through Vienna after 1950 on their way from Hungary, Rumania, and Poland. American Jewish relief agencies, particularly the American Jewish Joint Distribution Committee, were of immense help to these survivors, as well as to those Jews who decided to stay in Vienna. Thousands of Jews fleeing Hungary in 1956 after Russian troops crushed an anti-Communist revolt, and thousands more who left Czechoslovakia after the Russian invasion of 1968 and the subsequent ouster of a liberal government poured into Vienna en route to Israel, the United States, Canada and Australia. For these refugees, and smaller numbers from Poland in 1969 and 1970, the JDC office was of immense help. Anti-Semitism emerged in the 1960s as an element of Austrian politics when Bruno Kreisky, a Jew, was foreign minister in a coalition government. In 1970 Kreisky became chancellor, the first Jew to achieve this post in Austria.

Today there are 12,000 Jews in Austria, 10,000 of them living in Vienna. Nearly half are dependent on Jewish communal services financed by community taxes, government reparations, and the American Jewish Joint Distribution Committee. Slowly the community is being rebuilt, and a network of Jewish religious, educational, cultural, and social-service agencies has been established once again.

BAD GASTEIN

KURHAUS BADER kosher restaurant, near the railroad station is usually open only in the summer, when this famous spa is thronged.

EDLACH

HERZL MEMORIAL, a tablet imbedded in a large concrete slab and inscribed in Hebrew and German, is on the grounds of an abandoned sanitarium in this mountain village where Dr. Theodor Herzl, father of political Zionism, died on July 3, 1904. The memorial was erected on the fiftieth anniversary of his death.

EISENERZ

MEMORIAL TO NAZI VICTIMS, in this Lower Austrian town is a simple plaque inscribed in Hebrew and German, and mounted on a stone wall topped by the Star of David. The memorial honors nameless Jews who died here.

EISENSTADT

JUDENGASSE (Jews' Street), in this capital city of Austria's easternmost province, near the Hungarian border, is a remnant of a mid-sixteenth-century ghetto in the shadow of the castle of Prince Esterházy. Crowded into thirty-one houses, the Jews of this town constituted an autonomous community for more than three centuries, with their own police and fire departments, judges and mayor. Dispersed by the Nazis in 1938, the Jewish community was never revived; only five of its prewar residents returned after the war. Today no Jews live in the Judengasse, which has only two new buildings. One is a trade-union headquarters, on the site formerly occupied by a synagogue that was erected in 1832. An old Hebrew inscription recording Samson Wertheimer as the founder and builder of the Jewish poorhouse, now the property of the Catholic hospital, can still be seen.

JEWISH CEMETERY dating from the seventeenth century, is dotted with plain markers carved with symbolic designs suggesting the occupations or names of the deceased. One stone is decorated with a pair of eyeglasses because beneath the stone lies Salomon Brille (*Brille* is the German word for eyeglasses). One of the Jews who returned after the war restored the cemetery, which had been damaged by the Nazis. The cemetery is reached via Wertheimgasse and what used to be Obergasse.

WERTHEIMER SYNAGOGUE built late in the seventeenth century by Samson Wertheimer, the Vienna court Jew, has also been restored.

WOLF MUSEUM on the Untergasse, founded in 1902 by Sandor Wolf, is now the County Museum occupying Wolf's house, which like other buildings in the old ghetto still have rooms with removal roofs for the time of Sukkot. Wolf was the last member of a well-to-do family of wine dealers. Some of the older houses on Untergasse have carved stone jars over their portals to indicate that the original occupants were Levites. In the museum are the scepter given to the ghetto's Jewish mayor in 1732 by Prince Esterhazy and the small Torah Scroll which Samson Wertheimer carried with him on his travels. The most unusual exhibit is a completely furnished Sabbath Room. The Wolf wine vaults, now owned by the government of Burgenland, run under the old houses in the Judengasse. One of the two pillars of the old ghetto gate still stands. Wound around it is a large iron chain which used to bar the ghetto to all traffic from Friday evening to Saturday night.

GRAZ

JEWISH COMMUNAL CENTER, 58 Grieskai. There is a small prayer house in the building, which is on the same street as the former main synagogue, burned by the Nazis.

PROVINCIAL MUSEUM preserves some old Sabbath lamps, silver Torah shields and other Jewish ritual objects that are more than four centuries old.

Near Graz is a little village called *Judendorf*, whose name indicates it was either founded by Jews or the home of a Jewish community in the Middle Ages.

INNSBRUCK

SYNAGOGUE, Zollerstrasse, was opened in 1961 to replace an older sanctuary on Sillgasse burned by the Nazis. The lay head of the Jewish community is Oskar von Lubomirsky, a former Polish prince who was converted to Judaism. This is Austria's smallest organized Jewish community. There are 100 Jews here.

JUDENBURG

POST HOTEL, on the Hauptplatz (Main Square), a building that is said to be more than five hundred years old, has, carved into the stone work on the south facade, the figure of a bearded Jew's head. This building is said to have been a synagogue before the Jews were expelled in 1496. There was an important Jewish colony here in the eleventh century. The town's name is said to mean Fortress of the Jews, but some scholars believe it is only a German form of the ancient Idunum of the Romans. But the visitor to this Styrian town on the right bank of the Mur at the foot of the Wenzelalpe will note that Judenburg's coat of arms bears the Austrian eagle and the Jew's head with pointed beard and peaked hat. In this part of southern Austria there were other towns with Jewish names in the thirteenth and fourteenth centuries—Judendorf, near Murau; Judenau near Tulln; Judenfurt; Judenhof; Judenweis; and Judenleithen. One of the gates of Judenburg is still called *Judenthurl* because a Jew strangled himself in it in his haste to flee in 1469.

KREMS

HEBREW-INSCRIBED TOMBSTONE of Rabbi Nehemiah of the fifteenth century has been preserved because it is built into the wall of the Piarist Church. Several other Jewish tombstones stand in the monastery garden.

LINZ

JEWISH COMMUNAL CENTER, 26 Bethlehemstrasse.

ST. ANDREWS CHURCH still displays an old tablet "in memory of four-year old Ursula Bock who was cruelly murdered by Jews on Good Friday, 1443."

MAUTHAUSEN

MAUTHAUSEN CONCENTRATION CAMP, a forty-five-minute drive from Linz, where 200,000 inmates perished, is maintained as a museum by an international alliance of survivors' committees. Half of those who died here were Jews, and most of the others were Russians, Greeks, and Yugoslavs. Preserved intact are the torture cells, the big gas chamber, underground execution room, crematory furnaces, and the peephole through which guards watched their victims die. The former laundry room is now a chapel. A small plaque at the camp's entrance resembles a simple gravestone on which an inscription relates how the first group of Dutch Jews sent to Mauthausen in 1942 were flung to their deaths from a cliff overlooking the granite quarry where thousands of them worked as slave laborers. The 186 steps leading from the quarry floor have been preserved. A special cemetery in the camp contains the remains of 2,800 nameless Jews whose corpses were exhumed from the camp's cellar. There are also monuments to Jewish, Russian, French, Polish, Italian and Yugoslav victims.

RINN

CHURCH TABLETS in the local Catholic church commemorating the "ritual murder" of "Holy Anderle," a nine-year old boy, by Jewish merchants in 1462 were removed in the late 1960s. A ceiling painting depicting the "sacrifice" of the child is still there.

SALZBURG

JEWISH COMMUNAL CENTER, 7 Mertenstrasse.

SYNAGOGUE, 8 Lasserstrasse. Right next door is a kosher restaurant. In the synagogue is an interesting mural in memory of the Holocaust victims.

Next to Vienna, Salzburg is Austria's number one tourist attraction because of its world-famed music festival from the last week in July through August. The festival was conceived by Hugo von Hofmannsthal, Austria's leading poet and lyric playwright, whose grandfather founded the first modern synagogue in Vienna. It was produced for many years after World War I by the late Max Reinhardt.

SEEFELD

JEWISH MARTYRS' MEMORIAL, a roughhewn red stone monument in the pine woods of this Upper Tyrol village, honors the sixty-three Jews from here who died at Dachau. A bronze plaque tells the simple story. The Jewish memorial is part of a larger area dedicated to the eighty Catholic soldiers from Seefeld who died in World War II.

VIENNA

VIKTOR ADLERPLATZ, a square in the Xth District, is named for the founder of the Austrian Social Democratic party, who played a leading role in securing universal suffrage in Austria.

PETER ALTENBERGGASSE, a street in the XIXth District, is named for a prominent poet and essayist whose real name was Richard Englander.

AMERICAN JEWISH JOINT DISTRIBUTION COMMITTEE, 3 Brahmsplatz.

ARNSTEINGASSE, a street in the XVth District, is named for Baron and Baroness Nathan von Arnstein, who in the late eighteenth and early nineteenth centuries were prominent philanthropists and art patrons. The Baron, whose grandfather was one of the early court Jews, was an important banker to the Austrian monarchy. The Baroness, better known as Fanny von Arnstein, presided over a famous Vienna salon where she was hostess to statesmen, artists, and writers.

AUSTRIAN NATIONAL LIBRARY, 1 Josefsplatz, has an immense collection of Judaica in many languages reflecting the history of the Jewish communities in all the countries that once were part of the Hapsburg monarchy. The library also owns a fine collection of Hebrew books and 227 Hebrew manuscripts.

BURGTHEATER, 5 Dr. Karl Lueger Ring, the best-known in Austria, has in its lobby busts of Adolf Sonnenthal, the greatest actor on the German stage in the late nineteenth century, and of Hugo von Hofmannsthal.

CENTRAL FRIEDHOF, Vienna's central cemetery, has a well-known Jewish memorial chapel at 11 Simmeringer Hauptstrasse, which has been completely restored after it was burned by the Nazis in 1938. In this chapel were held funerals for three generations of Vienna's Jews, including a virtual Who's Who in industry, art, science, music and literature. Along the tree-lined main avenue of the cemetery, leading from the chapel, are the tombs and mausoleums of the Rothschilds; Arthur Schnitzler, dramatist and novelist; Adolf Lieben, dean of the philosophy faculty at the University of Vienna; Ignaz Brüll, teacher of Gustav Mahler; and scores of others who helped to make Vienna's greatness. Here too is the monument to the late Dr. Tzvi Hirsch Chajes, last great chief rabbi of Vienna, whose remains have been removed to Israel. Scattered through the Jewish section of the cemetery are many small memorial tablets without tombstones, honoring victims of the Nazi terror not actually buried here.

CITY TEMPLE, 4 Seittenstettengasse, the only synagogue in Vienna not destroyed by the Nazis, is also the oldest extant Jewish public building. Dedicated in 1826, it replaced the first public synagogue permitted in Vienna, which had been opened on the same site in 1811, a stone's throw from the second Jewish settlement in the Leopoldstadt section. From the outside it doesn't look like a synagogue, because it is crowded between two other buildings as a result of the insistence of the government in 1826 that it not be erected as a detached structure. This discriminatory limitation saved the temple in 1938, when the Nazis wrecked twenty-two other synagogues and forty small prayer houses. Although the interior was badly damaged in 1938, the building escaped being burned because a fire in the synagogue might have ruined the adjacent buildings. Completely restored, the synagogue, with its unusual elliptical interior, is the center of Jewish life in Vienna. In this house of worship the famous Cantor Solomon Sulzer created modern cantorial music. Here too Vienna Jewry paid its last respects to the remains of Theodor Herzl when they were exhumed in 1949 before being sent to Israel for final burial.

The building next door, 2 Seittenstettengasse, also owned by the Jewish community, houses one of a number of small Jewish prayer houses, as well as several Jewish communal institutions. Visitors who get to Seittenstettengasse when no services are in progress in the synagogue, can be admitted to the synagogue by the porter at No. 2.

CUMBERLAND PALACE, on the Beckmanngasse, displays a bust of Max Reinhardt, the eminent Austrian theatrical producer who was known as the impresario of the Salzburg Music Festival. Above the entrance to the *Josefstadt Theater*, 26 Josefstädterstrasse, there is a sculpture of Reinhardt's head. In the XIVth District there is *Max Reinhardtgasse.*

DÖBLING CEMETERY, 65 Hartäckerstrasse, in the XIXth District, until August 14, 1949, was one of the great shrines of Jewish history, because Dr. Theodor Herzl was buried here. The tombstone over his now empty grave is still there. To the original inscription over the graves of Herzl and his parents have been added a few lines in German explaining that the bodies were removed to Israel in fulfillment of Herzl's wish.

FREUD'S HOUSE, 19 Berggasse, where Dr. Sigmund Freud lived and worked for forty-seven years, until he was driven out by the Nazis, is now a museum sponsored by the Sigmund Freud Society and the Vienna Municipality. The house and the study of the father of psychoanalysis have been restored and the building properly identified. Previously the only evidence that this was once Freud's home was a simple plaque, etched in pink marble, high above eye level, with this legend in German: "In this house lived and worked Professor Sigmund Freud from the year 1891 to 1938. He was the founder and father of psychoanalysis." The plaque was erected in 1953 by the Congress of the Federation for Mental Health. When the Nazis took over Austria, Freud and his family were in great danger, and heroic efforts were made to rescue them. Only the intervention of President Roosevelt enabled the Freuds to escape, after payment of a huge ransom. Until 1938 every Viennese boasted of Freud as a fellow citizen, and patients thronged to his office from all parts of the world, offering any price for his services.

DESIDER FRIEDMANN-HOF, 23 Ferdinandstrasse, is an apartment house named for the community's last president before the Nazi occupation, who died in the Auschwitz gas chambers. Owned by the Vienna Jewish Community, the building once housed a small synagogue which has now been replaced by a small museum. For lack of staff, the museum is not open to the public. Affixed to the front of the building is a large mosaic that recalls the famous Leopoldstädter Temple, which was destroyed in 1938. A memorial plaque on the inside honors the martyrs of the Warsaw ghetto uprising.

GESTAPO VICTIMS MONUMENT on Mortzinplatz, honors the hundreds of Austrians, including many Jews, who died on this spot, which was Gestapo headquarters during the Nazi occupation. The headquarters were in the Metropol Hotel, which was destroyed by bombing during the war. Nine other Gestapo victims, all Jews, who were murdered in 1945 a few hours before the Russians liberated the city, are memorialized by a plaque on a house in Ferstelgasse.

GOLDMARK HOUSE, 7 Gallgasse, corner of Backlinstrasse, where Karl Goldmark, one of the most eminent composers of nineteenth-century Europe, died in 1915, is marked by a memorial plaque. The Nazis removed the plaque, but it was restored in the 1950s when the house was reconstructed. Goldmark's brother, Joseph, was one of the leading figures of the abortive Austrian revolution of 1848. Karl's best-known opera, *The Queen of Sheba*, was not produced at the Vienna State Opera until 1875 because of his brother's revolutionary activities. Joseph Goldmark was the father-in-law of Justice Louis D. Brandeis of the United States Supreme Court, and of Dr. Felix Adler, founder of the Ethical Culture movement.

HEINEGASSE, in the IInd District, is named for the German-Jewish poet Heinrich Heine.

THEODOR HERZL-HOF, a municipal housing development between 13-15 Leopoldgasse and 7 Malzgasse, is named for the father of political Zionism. The block of apartments, occupying the site of a building used as a reception center for aged Jews before they were shipped to concentration camps, is in the heart of what used to be the Leopoldstadt area, which for more than two centuries was the ghetto. The naming occurred during the Herzl centennial in 1960. At 29 Haizingergasse is the house where Herzl lived in his last years. There was once a small plaque recording Herzl's association with the building, but it is no longer there. Herzl also lived at 16 Pelikangasse and on Türkenstrasse. At 12 Rembrandtstrasse is the house where final preparations were made for the first World Zionist Congress in 1897.

ISRAELI EMBASSY, 66 Peter Jordanstrasse.

JEWISH CEMETERY, 9 Seegasse, in the area of the medieval Jewish community, is the oldest surviving Jewish burial ground in Austria. It was first opened in the fifteenth century, and the oldest tombstone is dated 1450. It has not been used since 1783. One of those buried here is Samson Oppenheimer, the court Jew who founded the third Jewish community in Vienna. Still to be seen are thirteenth- and fourteenth-century gravestones from earlier cemeteries imbedded in the old cemetery wall.

Adjoining the cemetery and an old garden is the *Jewish Old Age Home and Hospital*. The second-oldest Jewish cemetery on the Währingerstrasse, which contains the tombs of most of Vienna's famous Jewish personalities of the early nineteenth century, is near the former Rothschild Hospital, which was heavily bombed during the war. In its ruins thousands of Jewish D.P.s found temporary refuge after the war. On the hospital site now stand an office building and an apartment house.

JEWISH COMMUNITY HEADQUARTERS, 25 Schottenring, is a large office building which houses the principal institutions of the Jewish community. It has a small collection of historical objects but it is not open to the public.

JEWISH SCHOOL, 16 Malzgasse.

JEWISH YOUTH HOME, 8 Krummbaumgasse.

JUDENPLATZ (Jews' Square), in the 1st District is a reminder of the thirteenth-century Jewish community that existed in this neighborhood. The city has posted a historical plaque on a building at one corner of the square. The ancient synagogue was at Nos. 7-8, the hospital at No. 9. Nearby there is still a *Judengasse* (Jews' Street). At 2 Judenplatz is a tablet recording in Latin the expulsion of the Jews in 1421. At 8 Judenplatz is a small Orthodox prayer house.

KAHAL ISRAEL JEWISH SCHOOL, 1 Gruenangergasse, is one of only three Jewish elementary schools in Vienna.

VIKTOR KAPLAN MEMORIAL in front of the Technical Museum on Mariahilferstrasse, honors the inventor of the turbine motor (1876-1934).

KOSHER RESTAURANT (The Weihburg), 10 Weihburggasse. A small room has been set aside here as an Orthodox prayer house.

LASSALLEGASSE, in the IInd District, is named for Ferdinand Lassalle, German-Jewish journalist and pamphleteer, who was the founder of the Social Democratic party of Germany.

LESSINGGASSE, in the IInd District, is named for Gotthold Ephraim Lessing, German critic, poet, and playwright, whose works on religious tolerance and brotherhood were influenced by his friendship with Moses Mendelssohn.

MARCUS MONUMENT in front of the Vienna Polytechnic School, in the IVth District, honors the Jewish mechanic and inventor Siegfried Marcus, who is credited with having invented the first benzine-driven vehicle in 1864. His failure to patent the pioneer self-propelled car cost him the right to be known as the inventor of the automobile. His other inventions included one of the first successful seismographs, underwater torpedos, and a variety of naval devices. The original model of Marcus's benzine car is preserved in the *Vienna Industrial Museum*, 12 Mariahilferstrasse. A memorial plaque citing his invention hangs on the wall of the house where he lived until his death in 1898.

MENDELSSOHNGASSE in the XXIst District, is named for Moses Mendelssohn, the German-Jewish philosopher.

MIZRACHI SCHOOL, 8 Judenplatz.

MUSEUM OF ETHNOLOGY, 19 Laudongasse, has a fine collection of material dealing with Jewish life in Austria.

OFNERGASSE, in the IInd District, is named for Julius Ofner, who, as a member of the lower house of the Austrian parliament from 1907 to 1919, fought for woman suffrage, for abolition of child labor, and for workmen's compensation laws. He also served on the Austrian Supreme Court and headed the Vienna Bar Association. A monument erected to him in this part of the city was destroyed by the Nazis.

ORT SCHOOL, 21 Ruthgasse.

REINHARDT THEATRE AND SEMINAR, a living memorial to Max Reinhardt, a world-famous school for stagecraft, is in the famed Schoenbrunn Castle, in the 13th District, between the Schoenbrunn and Hietzing subway stations. Reinhardt, who founded the school in 1929, was world-renowned as producer, director and teacher.

ST. STEPHEN'S CATHEDRAL, on Cathedral Square, the national cathedral, has a number of stained-glass windows depicting medieval Jews. Building blocks from the razed Rothschild palace on Prinz Eugenstrasse were used in repairing wartime damage to the cathedral.

ARTHUR SCHNITZLER-HOF, a large municipal housing development erected in 1959-60, at the corner of Döblinger Hauptstrasse and Währinger Gurtel, is named for the famous Jewish playwright. The development stands on a site that once formed part of the old Jewish Cemetery, which faces Währinger Park, on the site of the former Rothschild Hospital. The cemetery has not been cared for since World War II and is now a dense jungle of trees which have taken root. The caretaker's lodge is at 64A Semperstrasse on the side of the cemetery near the Arthur Schnitzler-Hof. The key to the cemetery gate is available there.

SONNENFELS STATUE in front of Vienna's Town Hall, honors Joseph von

Sonnenfels, the grandson of a German rabbi, who had an important part in drafting the 1782 Edict of Tolerance of Emperor Joseph II which paved the way for the emancipation of non-Catholics. Although Sonnenfels was baptized, he was always regarded as a Jew. He was responsible for the introduction of the public-school system, for the abolition of cruel and inhuman punishment, and for the beginnings of the liberal press. The statue, which stands in a kind of Honor Row, was removed during the Nazi occupation and ordered destroyed, but the official in charge stored the monument in the Town Hall basement, covering it with rugs. At the end of World War II it was restored to its former location. Nearby is the *Sonnenfelsgasse*.

SYNAGOGUE, 8 Schiffgasse, a small prayerhouse in a private home, is the temporary sanctuary of the congregation once known as the Schiffschul, a famous stronghold of Orthodoxy. The synagogue, on the old Judengasse, was destroyed by the Nazis in 1938 and after the war the adjoining Beth Hamidrash Torah Etz Chaim became the synagogue. But this building was destroyed by fire in 1965.

UNIVERSITY OF VIENNA, 1 Dr. Karl Lueger Ring, has in its great arcaded court a hall of fame among whose gallery of great professors are the busts and statues of a number of distinguished Jews. The best known of these is Sigmund Freud, whose bronze image is inscribed with a quotation from Sophocles: "Who divined the famed riddle and was a man most mighty." Other Jews memorialized in the hall of fame are Adolf Lieben, professor of chemistry; Leopold Oser, professor of anatomy; Ludwig Mauthner, professor of ophthalmology; Emil Zuckerhandel, professor of chemistry; Guido Goldschmiedt, professor of chemistry; Ernest von Fleischl-Marxow, professor of physiology; Leopold Eoves de Dittel, professor of surgery; Heinrich von Bamberger, professor of internal medicine; and Moritz Kaposi, professor of dermatology.

The University Library owns a substantial collection of Judaica.

VIENNA STATE HISTORICAL MUSEUM, in the Rathaus (Town Hall), preserves a number of Jewish tombstones from the seventeenth century. It also displays an etching of Baroness Fanny von Arnstein, mistress of Vienna's most important early nineteenth-century salon.

VIENNA STATE OPERA, 2 Opernring, has in its famed composers' foyer a bust of Gustav Mahler, who made musical history as a composer of nine great symphonies and as the musical director of the State Opera. There is a *Gustav Mahlerstrasse* in the IInd District.

ROBERT VON LIEBEN COMMEMORATIVE TABLET on the front wall of the Vienna Radio Building (Oesterreichischer Rundfunk), 30 Argentinierstrasse, is a bas-relief portrait of the celebrated inventor and physicist, who was a pioneer in research on the telephone, the electric phonograph, and the wireless. His improved model of the Wright airplane was adopted by the Austro-Hungarian government, and his discovery of the polarization of X rays led to the development of the amplifying tube, which made possible modern radio, television, and sound motion pictures. The original model of this tube is exhibited in the *Vienna Technical Museum*, 59 Waehringerstrasse. Before World War II, the Austrian government issued a memorial stamp in his memory.

BELGIUM

Jews first reached Belgium as traders who accompanied the Roman legions that occupied Belgica after Julius Caesar conquered Gaul in 50 C.E. Others came there as part of the dispersion that brought Jews to Western Europe following the destruction of the first Temple in Jerusalem in 70 C.E. Fourth-century records mention their presence in Tongeren and Tournai and indicate that they served in the armies of the Gauls. Jews were also among the earliest merchants and artisans in Brussels when that city was founded in the seventh century.

Treated decently during the Roman occupation and the first century of Frankish rule, the Jews played a significant role in importing essential goods from Asia Minor. Under the later Frankish kings and their successors, the Burgundians, the Jewish condition alternated between toleration and persecution. There were prominent Jewish physicians in Flanders in the ninth and tenth centuries and a flourishing Jewish community in Arras in the eleventh century. Jews expelled from England in 1290 and from France in 1300 found their way to Belgium.

Accusations of well poisoning and witchcraft during the Black Death led to sanguinary massacres of Jews in many cities of Belgium, as elsewhere in Europe. The slaughter of more than 500 Jews in Brussels in 1370, when they were falsely charged with desecrating a Christian religious symbol, marked the end of the Jewish communities in Belgium for more than a century. Streets still called Rue des Juifs in the French-speaking sections and Jodenstraat in the Flemish-speaking areas, in Antwerp, Ghent, Mons, Eupen, Tienen and Wasmes, are reminders of these Jewish settlements of the Middle Ages.

Marrano Jews from Spain and Portugal found temporary refuge in Belgium early in the fifteenth century when that country was part of the Spanish domains. The quasi-autonomous Belgian cities encouraged the settlement of the Marranos because of their invaluable mercantile and banking connections. Under the leadership of the Mendes brothers—Francisco and Diego—Antwerp became the world headquarters of the spice trade and an important center of international commerce and banking. The Rodriguez family introduced the diamond industry to Belgium. João Rodriguez, who later became one of Europe's most eminent physicians under the name of Amatus Lusitanus, and Martin Lopez de Villaneuva, an uncle of the French essayist Michel de Montaigne, were among the Marrano notables who lived in Belgium until they had to take flight again.

For a number of years Antwerp was the headquarters of an underground railway that enabled hundreds of secret Jews to get out of Spain and Portugal. The widows of the Mendes brothers masterminded this rescue system, which provided travel directions and transportation, information about safe hiding places, and even transmission of assets between Portugal and Turkey via Belgium, France, and Italy. Ultimately, most of the Marranos had to use this escape route themselves when they were compelled to leave Belgium.

A small Marrano community survived, with the aid of Dutch coreligionists who visited Belgium regularly on business. When Belgium became part of the Austrian Netherlands in 1714, the Marranos came into the open and were joined by a stream of Jews from Germany, Austria, and Holland. Belgium's annexation to the French Republic in 1794 brought religious equality and even larger numbers of Jews. A

Napoleonic decree of 1808 authorized the establishment of the Consistoire Central Israélite, now the oldest representative body of Belgian Jewry.

Under Dutch rule, following the fall of Napoleon, Jewish rights were confirmed and the first modern synagogue was erected in Brussels. By the time Belgium became independent in 1831, its 3,000 Jews were well established in Brussels, Antwerp, and Liège, and they enjoyed the same rights as all other citizens.

Russian and Polish Jews who began settling in the principal cities after 1880 revived the diamond trade and created the leather goods, textile, and clothing industries. Many of them became coal miners in the Charleroi region. In 1914 there were 25,000 Jews, more than half of them aliens and thus exempt from military service, yet thousands fought with the Belgian army. The first man taken hostage when the Germans entered Antwerp was Baron Léon Lambert of the Rothschild family. Chief Rabbi Armand Bloch defied the invaders by praying every Saturday for King Albert.

Between wars the Jewish population swelled to nearly 90,000 owing to heavy immigration from Eastern Europe and the admission of 35,000 refugees from Nazi Germany and Austria. When the Nazis overran the country in 1940, thousands of Jews fled to France and Switzerland, but 26,000 were deported to concentration camps. Ghettos were established in Brussels, Antwerp, Ghent, Liège, and Charleroi.

Hundreds of Belgians risked their lives during the occupation to befriend Jews by hiding them, by providing them with forged documents, and by temporarily adopting their children. The Belgian underground repeatedly published clandestine leaflets that described how to help Jews resist Gestapo raids. Queen Mother Elizabeth's personal intervention with Hitler spared the native-born Jews from deportation until 1943.

These efforts enabled 18,000 Jews to survive. In 1970, the Jewish population was 41,000. Brussels has replaced Antwerp as the largest Jewish community, the latter having become a stronghold of Orthodox Jewry. There are smaller communities in Arlon, Liège, Louvain, Ghent, Charleroi and Ostend.

ANTWERP

BEURS VOOR DIAMENTHANDEL (the Diamond Bourse), 78 Pelikaanstraat, is the largest of the city's four diamond exchanges where most of the dealers and a heavy proportion of the diamond cutters, polishers and setters are Jewish. The Diamond Bourse, which attracts 10,000 dealers from all parts of the world annually, is not only the world's biggest diamond market, but a unique social, cultural, and communal center. Members and visitors often spend the whole day here, engaging in communal affairs (mostly Jewish), planning collections for Jewish philanthropies, and exchanging news and information. The bulletin boards of all four exchanges contain notices of funerals, memorial services, and Jewish meetings. The restaurants in the diamond exchange include two that are kosher, Grosz in the Diamond Bourse, 78 Pelikaanstraat, and Oscar, in the Diamantkring, 86 Pelikaanstraat. Because the diamond industry is so heavily dominated by Jews, the term *"mazel and beracha"* is used by Jews and non-Jews to clinch a sale. The importance of the Jews in the diamond industry is indicated by the fact that after World Wars I and II, during which diamond dealers and workers fled the city, they were officially invited to return.

The diamond exchanges are closed on Saturday and on Yom Kippur. The banks that specialize in dealing with diamond dealers are also shut down on these days. At one end of the trading hall in the Diamond Bourse is a bronze bas-relief showing a German soldier using his rifle to strike a naked man lying on the ground behind barbed wire; this depicts the common experience of all the Antwerp Jews who were deported when the Nazis occupied the city. To visit one of the diamond exchanges you need an introduction by a member. The other three diamond exchanges are: Diamantclub, 62 Pelikaanstraat; Diamtantkring, 86 Pelikaanstraat, and Vrije Diamanthandel, 70 Pelikaanstraat.

B'NAI B'RITH HOME, 26 Charlottalei.

CZITRON KOSHER RESTAURANT, 37 Hovenierstraat.

EDEN KOSHER RESTAURANT, 10 Simonstraat.

GELKOP KOSHER RESTAURANT, 28 Van Leriusstraat.

ROMI GULDMUNTZ JEWISH YOUTH CENTRE, 10 Nervienstraat, named for the late diamond merchant and philanthropist, has an auditorium, library, conference rooms, workshops and a kosher snack bar.

ROMI GOLDMUNTZ SYNAGOGUE, 43 Oostenstraat, the city's principal synagogue, formerly known as the Machsike Hadath, was renamed for the late Romi Goldmuntz, one of the leaders of the diamond industry, whose generosity was in part responsible for the reconstruction of the building. Consecrated in 1893, it was almost entirely wrecked by the Nazis. One of the chief architects of the world diamond center, Goldmuntz was honored by the entire city on his seventy-fifth birthday, in 1957.

HOME FOR JEWISH AGED, 8 Marialei.

INSTITUTE FOR JEWISH LEARNING AND READING ROOM, 50 Plantin Moretuslei.

ISRAELIETENSTRAAT acquired its name in 1563 when Marrano Jews erected 12 houses here, each bearing the name of one of the twelve tribes of Israel.

JEWISH CULTURAL CENTER, 46 Consciencestraat.

JEWISH MARTYRS MEMORIAL, corner of Rue des Goujons and Rue Carpentier, in suburb of Anderlecht, was dedicated in 1970. Standing on a site donated by the municipal government, the memorial is a hexagonal structure surrounded by six walls symbolizing the 6,000,000 Jews killed by the Hitler regime. The architect was Andre Godart.

JODENSTRAAT is believed to be named for sixteenth-century Jewish residents, *Joden* being the Flemish word for "Jews." However, some feel the street may be named for the de Jode family of etchers and painters.

MACCABEE STADIUM, 53 Rue des Fortifications, erected through the generosity of Romi Goldmuntz, is the sports center for the Jewish community.

ORT TRAINING SCHOOL, 27 Belgielei.

PLANTIN-MORETUS MUSEUM, 22 Vrijdagmarkt, contains numerous sixteenth-century Hebrew Bibles printed by Christophe Plantin and Jan Moretus, famous printers of their day. In the museum, which preserves the original printing shop, press, and foundry, are on display the famous Biblia Polyglotta, an edition of the Bible in five languages—Hebrew, Latin, Greek, Syriac and Chaldaic. Also to be seen here are a notable collection of thirty Hebrew books printed in Venice between 1500 and 1548 by Daniel Bomberg, a Belgian Christian; old Hebrew grammars and handwritten Hebrew manuscripts; and a unique collection of Hebrew punches and matrices dating from the 16th century.

PORTUGUESE SYNAGOGUE, 31 Hoveniersstraat, uses the ritual of the Sephardic Jews.

HERMAN SCHAMISSO SYNAGOGUE (Cong. Shomre Hadath), Avenue Van den Nest, is in the new wing of the Antwerp Home for the Aged. It was the gift of the widow and children of Herman Schamisso, who escaped from Belgium during the Nazi occupation and while in England aided the Belgian underground. From 1946 to his death in 1957 he was president of the central Jewish welfare agency.

SOCIAL CENTRALE, 155 Lange Leemstraat, is the headquarters for all Jewish philanthropies. At 313 Lange Leemstraat is the *Tachkemoni School*, the principal Jewish educational institution, where both Hebrew and Flemish are taught. In this neighborhood is the city's Jewish quarter, which extends from Pelikaanstraat, on which all four diamond exchanges are located, to main boulevards and narrow streets in the vicinity of the Central Station. Here Yiddish and Hebrew are heard in the street as often as Flemish. Here too are a number of Chassidic synagogues.

TACHKEMONI JEWISH SCHOOL (day school), 313 Lange Leemstraat.

YESHIVA ETZ CHAIM, Rue Osy Kogels, in the Wilrijk suburb, is one of the most modern in Europe.

YESODEI HATORA AND JEWISH TEACHERS SEMINARY FOR GIRLS, 14-22 Lange Van Ruusbroecstraat.

ARLON

MEMORIAL TO JEWISH MARTYRS, near the city's communal cemetery, is a monument to the city's Jews who were deported by the Nazis. The memorial is a granite wall to which are affixed marble plaques listing the martyrs.

SYNAGOGUE, Rue de la Synagogue, is the oldest in Belgium, having been erected in 1866.

BANNEUX-NOTRE DAME

NOTRE DAME DES PAUVRES, a Catholic orphanage, has at its entrance gate a bronze memorial inscribed in Hebrew and French, honoring Albert van den Berg, a non-Jew, who was the leader of the anti-Nazi underground in Liège. Van den Berg saved fifty Jewish children from Liège by hiding them in the home. The marker was dedicated by the Liège Jewish community.

BASTOGNE

MARDASSON, the huge, star-shaped monument to the 76,890 Americans killed, wounded or missing in the World War II Battle of the Bulge, December 16, 1944-January 16, 1945, and particularly during the siege of Bastogne, contains three mosaic altars—Jewish, Protestant, and Catholic. It was in Bastogne that General Anthony C. McAuliffe gave his famous one-word reply, "Nuts!," to the German demand for the surrender of the 101st Airborne Division.

BRUSSELS

BERNHEIM MONUMENT in the Square Marie-Louise, honors General Louis Bernheim, one of Belgium's World War I heroes. The life-size bronze statue on a granite pedestal shows Bernheim in uniform. A professional soldier, Bernheim commanded the 7th Infantry at Antwerp when the German invasion began. Later he was given command of the 1st Army Division. At the time of the Allied counteroffensive he led the Northern Group of the Belgian Army. On his death in 1931, he was given a state funeral, with King Albert following the cortege.

BRUSSELS UNIVERSITY, 28 Avenue Paul Heger, has three buildings named for eminent Jews. The Institut de Botanique Errera is named for Abraham Leo Errera, who was professor of botany at the University of Brussels and later headed the institute that now bears his name. Errera was a member of a prominent family of Spanish and Portuguese Jews, one branch of which settled in Belgium. His son Jacques, a world famous molecular physicist, also taught at Brussels University until 1940. The *Spanjaard Gymnasium*, dedicated in 1938, and the *Institute of Physical Education* were gifts from Hugo Andriessen Spanjaard, a Jewish philanthropist and industrialist.

B'NAI B'RITH HEADQUARTERS (Fraternelle Henry Jones), 24 Rue aux Laines.

FOYER ISRAEL, 29a Rue Stas, is a lounge and meeting place for Jewish visitors. It was originally founded as an information bureau, employment agency, and forum for Jewish immigrants.

GREAT SYNAGOGUE, 32 Rue de la Régence, the city's chief synagogue, was consecrated in 1878. Except for minor damage on the outside, the structure was spared by the Nazis during the occupation. On the front interior wall of the synagogue there is a simple memorial plaque honoring the Brussels Jews who died on the field of battle during World War II or who were killed in Nazi death camps.

The *Brussels Jewish Community* and the *Consistoire Israélite* have their headquarters in the synagogue.

PAUL HYMANS CENTER, 13 Rue de Namur, national headquarters of the Liberal party, is a memorial to one of Belgium's greatest statesmen. For many years Foreign Minister, Hymans was one of the godfathers of the League of Nations. He was the president of its first Assembly in 1920 and represented Belgium at the Versailles Peace Conference.

ISRAEL EMBASSY, 40 Avenue de l'Observatoire.

JEWISH COMMUNITY CENTER, 89 Chaussée de Vleurgat, in the Borough of Ixelles, was opened in 1959 with the aid of funds from the Conference on Jewish Material Claims against Germany. The center is the headquarters for all Jewish youth organizations. There is a kosher snack bar but it is closed Friday evenings, Saturdays, holidays and during student vacations.

MACHZIKE HADATH SYNAGOGUE (Orthodox), 67a Rue de la Clinique, in the suburb of Anderlecht.

MONUMENT AUX FUSILLÉS, on the Boulevard Auguste Reyers, near the Military Cemetery (Tir National), memorializes the 342 members of the Belgian underground who were executed by the Nazis. Behind the monument are the graves of the martyrs, among whom were a number of Jews. They are identified by their names and portraits.

NATIONAL CENTER OF HIGHER JEWISH STUDIES (Centre National des Hautes Etudes Juives), 44 Avenue Jeanne, was founded in 1959 by a non-Jewish professor at the University of Brussels to make scientific studies of various aspects of Jewish life and problems.

NOR-KOR RESTAURANT, Avenue Marx, marked by a large Star of David, is not kosher but its menu is 'Jewish style.'

ST.-MICHEL AND STE.-GUDULE CHURCH, Place Ste.-Gudule, near Sabena Air Terminal, one of the city's chief religious shrines, was in effect also a monument to Jewish martyrdom in the 14th century until the Archbishop of Brussels ordered the removal in 1969 of paintings that had long aroused hostility towards Jews. In the church's Chapel du St.-Sacrament-de-Miracle there had been memorialized in stained-glass windows, paintings, and tapestries a medieval tragedy—the massacre of the Jews of Brussels in 1370 on the false charge of having desecrated a Christian religious symbol. The "miracle" in the chapel's name refers to the "rescue" of the symbol from its alleged Jewish defilers.

SEPHARDIC JEWISH COMMUNITY, 2 Rue Joseph Dupont.

TURKISH SYNAGOGUE, 2 Rue Joseph Dupont. Rue Joseph Dupont, is a side entrance to 32 Rue de la Regence, site of the Great Synagogue.

SEPHARDIC SYNAGOGUE SIMON ET LINA HAIM, 47 Rue du Pavillon, dedicated in 1964, was the first Sephardic house of worship in Brussels. It is named for Simon Haim, a prominent philanthropist, and his wife.

CHARLEROI

SYNAGOGUE, 56 Rue Pige-au-Croly. For years most of the Jews here were employed in the nearby coal mines.

JEWISH MARTYRS MEMORIAL in the Jewish cemetery at Marcinelle-Haye.

CRAINHEM-les-BRUXELLES

JEWISH CEMETERY, on Kerkhofstraat, in this village ten miles from Brussels, has a simple monument to the Jews who perished at the Breendonck concentration camp. The monument is a low concrete wall with a flat bronze plaque in front of it. Beneath the plaque is interred an urn containing the ashes of Jewish martyrs from Auschwitz.

FORT BREENDONCK

ONLY NAZI CONCENTRATION CAMP STILL INTACT IN WESTERN EUROPE is on the Antwerp-Brussels road, about fifteen miles from Brussels. Completely surrounded by barbed wire and lookout posts, the camp has been left almost exactly as it was in the Nazi era, when it housed 4,000 prisoners. You can still see the gallows and firing-squad posts. Outside the camp is a thirty-foot-high monument to the Unknown Political Prisoner, the work of Yudel Yankelevici, a Belgian-Jewish sculptor. The monument shows the figure of a kneeling man with his head turned defiantly toward the fortress. The fortress-camp was the assembly point for Jews being deported to Auschwitz. In the camp reliquary are urns with the ashes of victims of Nazism from other European concentration camps.

ENGHIEN

MAISON DE JONATHAS, 7 Rue Montgomery, a historic monument in the heart of the town, and a field on the outskirts called *Jardin de Jonathas* recall the medieval tale of Jonathas, the Jewish banker of Enghien who was falsely accused of desecrating a Christian religious symbol. This charge touched off the massacre of the Jews in Brussels in 1370.

GHENT

JODENSTRAAT recalls the ancient Jewish community here. Recently a small congregation was established in a rented building by the 70 Jewish families who now live here. The rabbi lives at 14 Savaenstraat.

JETTE-ST.-PIERRE

CHILDREN'S PLAYGROUND, École 3 bis, Chaussée de Wemmel 309, in this Brussels suburb is named in memory of Josette Linker, a local Jewish girl who at the age of ten was deported with her mother to Auschwitz, where both died.

KNOCKE

OFFICIAL TOURIST BUREAU in the Vuurtorenplaats, will refer visitors to kosher hotels, some with synagogues on the premises, in this resort community.

LIÈGE

JEWISH COMMUNAL CENTER, 12 Quai Marcellis.

MONTEFIORE MONUMENT in Montefiore Park, on the Square Notger, facing the left wing of the Palace of the Prince-Bishops, memorializes one of the founders of

Belgium's heavy industry, Georges Montefiore. He was born at Strijthem, near Brussels, in 1832. His name was Georges Lévi, but he took the name of Montefiore after his mother's family, which was related to the English Montefiores. A mining engineer, he invented many processes to improve coal mining, bronze casting, and the manufacture of heavy guns. At one time he employed thousands of workers in his foundries in Liège and in his power plants. Montefiore devoted much of his fortune to sponsoring medical institutes, scholarships, camps for convalescent children, and hospitals. From 1882 to 1902 he was a member of the Belgian Senate.

MONTEFIORE ELECTRO-TECHNICAL INSTITUTE, 33 Rue St.-Gilles, now a part of the University of Liège, was founded by Georges Montefiore to train engineers from all parts of the world. In the courtyard of the institute there is a bust of him. On the Plateau of Cointe there is a *Montefiore Boulevard*.

SYNAGOGUE, 71 Rue Fetinne.

MALINES

GENERAL BARON DOSSIN DE ST. GEORGES BARRACKS has on its front facade a large tablet erected by the Brussels Jewish community to memorialize the 24,000 Jews deported by the Nazis. The deportees were housed in the barracks pending their shipment to the death camps.

NAMUR

RESIDENCE OF ABBÉ ANDRÉ, 40 Rue de l'Ange, served as an assembly center for Jewish children during the Nazi occupation, when they were sent along to safety in Roman Catholic homes. Abbé André, who was the leader of this movement, unfurled a large blue-and-white Star of David flag on the front of his house after the liberation and threw his home open to Jews who had been in hiding. The Abbé still lives here.

OSTEND

SYNAGOGUE, 10 Place Philippe van Maestricht (behind the big church in the Rue Gand off the Boulevard Alphonse Pieters).

BULGARIA

Bulgaria was the only Nazi-occupied country whose Jewish population was spared the terrors of the death camps. Forcible protests by the church, the army, and the people compelled the pro-Nazi government to postpone the scheduled deportation of all Jews at the last moment in 1943. Many Jews were exiled to remote areas and the able-bodied were sent to labor camps, but the advance of the Russian army in the fall of 1944 saved the Jewish community. Under the postwar Communist government, anti-Jewish laws were abolished, confiscated Jewish property was restored, and Jews who wished to leave were permitted to go to Israel. Nearly 40,000 had left by 1950.

As early as 100 C.E., several centuries before the Bulgars conquered the country, there was a Jewish colony at Gigen, a Roman settlement along the Danube. The Byzantine conquest in the tenth and eleventh centuries brought an influx of Greek-speaking Jews, who founded a synagogue in 967 at Serdica (Sofia). By the end of the fourteenth century there were also Jewish communities at Philippopolis (Plovdiv), Stara Zagora, Nikopol, and Silistria.

A Jewess by the name of Sarah became Bulgaria's Queen Theodora in 1345 when she married Czar Ivan Alexander. Bulgarian folk songs still tell of Tamar (Mara), the Jewish Queen's daughter, who sacrified herself by becoming the wife of the Turkish Sultan when Bulgaria became a Turkish vassal. At the end of the fifteenth century, large numbers of Jewish refugees from Spain and Portugal, as well as emigrés from Italy, Bavaria, Poland, and France, were admitted to Bulgaria by the Turks.

During the four hundred years of Turkish rule, the Jews were left in peace. Their neutrality during the Russo-Turkish War created animosity against them despite the fact that they were responsible for saving Sofia from destruction by the retreating Turkish army. When Bulgaria regained its independence in 1878, it adopted a constitution that completely emancipated the Jews. But despite their distinguished record in the Serbo-Bulgarian War of 1885, the Balkan Wars, and World War I, the Jews again felt the sting of persecution after the fascist coup of 1923. A new era of anti-Semitism followed the Bulgarian alliance with Germany in the 1930s. In 1970, there were 6,000 Jews left in Bulgaria, more than half of whom lived in Sofia. There were smaller communities in Pleven, Plovdiv, Ruse, Stanke Dmitrov, Stara Zagora, Varna, Vidin and Yambol. The Social, Cultural and Educational Association of Jews in the People's Republic of Bulgaria, established in 1957, is the government-authorized national organization of Jews. This body gradually liquidated the religious, cultural, and philanthropic activities inherited from the Central Consistory of the Jews in Bulgaria. In 1961, the Association turned over to the government all community buildings, including synagogues, schools and hospitals, retaining only the Jewish Cultural House in Sofia and a few properties in other cities. The Central Religious Council of Israelites, which, like the association, is government-financed, administers the remnants of Jewish religious life, including the distribution of matzoth and the maintenance of Jewish cemeteries. Since 1966, the Association has published an annual volume entitled Annual Godishnik, which contains essays, articles and historical surveys of Jewish life in Bulgaria. It also publishes a fortnightly paper in Bulgarian called Evreiski Vesti (Jewish News).

NIKOPOL

JOSEPH CARO HOUSE where the compiler of the Shulhan Aruk lived from 1523 to 1536 while he was head of the famous Nikopol Yeshiva, is still standing.

PLOVDIV

SHOLOM ALEICHEM CULTURAL CENTER offers lectures and conducts a music school. There are four unused synagogues in this town, the birthplace of Queen Theodora, one dating from 1710.

RUSE

LEON TAGER-BEN DAVID OIL REFINERY a government plant, is named for a Jewish war hero who was hanged by the Germans after he sabotaged their oil depot.

SAMAKOV

SYNAGOGUE, an architecturally unique structure has been restored by the government as a museum.

SOFIA

ALADZAN STREET, one of the city's main thoroughfares, is named for Solomon Aladzan, a Jewish commander in the Bulgarian army who died in the fighting on the Yugoslav front in the closing days of World War II when Bulgaria switched sides and joined the Allies.

HAYYIM BIALIK LIBRARY, Rue Exarch Jossif 16, is named for the famed Hebrew poet. Founded in 1926 by young Zionists, who have since left for Israel, the library is now directed by Jewish Communists, who have retained the original name. The 18,000-volume library is housed in the Jewish Cultural Club.

GREAT SYNAGOGUE, Rue Exarch Jossif, 16, with its huge cupola, bell-shaped turrets and immense chandelier hanging from the interior of the 100-foot-high dome, is a massive monument to a once flourishing Jewish community. Its great ribbed dome was blasted by RAF bombers during World War II but was repaired in 1948 with the aid of funds from the Joint Distribution Committee. Now a national historical monument, the synagogue's main sanctuary is no longer used for worship. The wrought iron main gate, topped by a large Magen David, that leads into a court yard is rusting. Cobblestones in the yard sprout grass. The main door is padlocked. The handful of worshippers pray in a small chapel. The late Chief Rabbi Asher Hananel, who died in 1962 and has not been replaced, was arrested in 1961 when he refused to close the synagogue.

Across the hall from the chapel is the office of the Central Religious Council of Israelites. Cases lining the wall contain the records of 500 years of Jewish history. The Council's president, Isaac Moscona, who is paid by the state, has compiled an as yet unpublished dictionary of Ladino, the Spanish-Hebrew dialect used by Bulgarian Jews. In the synagogue lobby is a small display of old synagogue appurtenances, including richly embroidered garments worn by Jewish brides in medieval days.

ISRAELI LEGATION, 34 Luben Karavelov, has been closed since 1967 when Bulgaria broke relations with Israel. The Swedish Embassy represents Israeli interests.

JEWISH CULTURAL HOUSE, 50 Blvd. Stamboulinski, is named for Emile Shekerdjinsky, a war hero who fell in battle against the Germans in 1944. Supported by the government, the House contains a library, a permanent exhibit of Jewish history in Bulgaria, meeting rooms and a restaurant and is the headquarters of a Jewish choral group and dramatic company.

JEWISH SCIENTIFIC INSTITUTE, a section of the Bulgarian Academy of Science, Rue Exarch 61, is engaged in studying, translating and catologuing the large collection of old Hebrew and Ladino manuscripts the Academy acquired from the pre-war Jewish community. Eli Ashkenazi, former assistant to the late Chief Rabbi, has been commissioned by the government to work on the more than five thousand documents and unpublished books relating to the history of the Jewish communities in Bulgaria from the fourteenth century onward, as well as to the relations between the Khazars (a Russian tribe whose leaders adopted Judaism in the eighth century) and the Bulgars.

NATIONAL MUSEUM preserves a Latin inscription found at Gigen, the site of the Roman fort known as Colonia Ulpia. The inscription, all that remains of the Jewish colony, is from the tombstone of an "archi-synagogus Josephus."

VIDIN

SYNAGOGUE, an old building, has been converted by the government into a cultural museum.

CYPRUS

Cyprus, according to some scholars, is the Biblical Land of Kaphtor from which the Philistines came and from which King David recruited part of his bodyguard, the *Kerethi*. In Maccabean times, a century before the Christian Era, there was a Jewish colony on this Mediterranean island, whose copper mines were later worked by subjects of Judea's King Herod. The Apostle Paul reported preaching in the synagogues of Salamis and Paphos on his first missionary journey.

During the Jewish revolt against Rome in 115-17 C.E., the Jewish communities on Cyprus were exterminated by the Emperor Trajan, who ordered the permanent exclusion of Jews from the island. The community was apparently re-established, because in 610 Jews participated in a local rebellion against the Byzantine Emperor Heraclius. Benjamin of Tudela, who visited Cyprus in 1170, recorded the existence of a Jewish community that observed the Sabbath from daybreak to daybreak. The Jewish colony at Famagusta was well known during the years of Venetian rule in the Middle Ages. Joseph Nasi, the fabulous adviser to the Turkish Sultan Selim II, mapped the Turkish conquest of Cyprus in 1571, hoping to be made king of the island, where he planned to create a Jewish homeland. Thereafter little is known of the Jewish settlement on Cyprus until 1878, when a diplomatic coup by Benjamin Disraeli made England its master.

Between 1883 and 1900 several attempts were made to establish Russian and Rumanian Jews in agricultural colonies at Orides, Margo Chiflik, Kyklia, and Chomalki, but all failed. A small influx of German and Austrian Jews took place in the 1930s, and just before World War II Jewish industrialists from Palestine opened branch factories in Cyprus. There were 400 Jewish families living in Nicosia, the capital, and the port cities of Famagusta, Limassol, and Larnaca in 1941, when the German capture of Crete compelled their removal for safety to Palestine. Those who returned after the war made heroic efforts to ease the plight of the thousands of Jewish immigrants from Europe who were interned here by the British when the refugee ships on which they sought to reach Palestine were captured by British warships. The present Jewish population consists of 160 families.

FAMAGUSTA

JEWISH BRIDGE is the name still applied to the remains of an ancient span in the ruins of the city of Salamis, near Famagusta. The bridge was the site of a crushing defeat inflicted on a Jewish army commanded by Artemion in 117 C.E. when the forces of the Roman Emperor Trajan put down a Jewish revolt. In the ruins of Salamis, scholars believe, are stones from Jewish places of worship where the Apostle Paul appeared when he first set out to make converts.

JEWISH COMMUNITY OF CYPRUS the only Cypriote Jewish organization, has its headquarters here in the home of its chairman, Mrs. Ida Pershitz, a native of Israel, who owns an orange plantation.

REMAINS OF ESCAPE TUNNELS dug by the so-called illegal Jewish immigrants who were interned here by the British from 1946 to early 1949 in camps surrounded by barbed wire can still be seen. The British detained 53,000 of these refugees in camps on the seashore near Famagusta and up in the hills twelve miles away.

SQUARE OF THE JEWISH REFUGEES in the New Salamis quarter, contains a memorial to the Jewish refugees who were interned by the British at the Karaulis and Kasilotimbo camps. The memorial and the surrounding public garden and sports park were paid for by contributions from the former Jewish detainees.

LARNACA

OLD JEWISH CEMETERY now unused, was established by Jewish colonists from eastern Europe in the 1880s who were settled at Margo Chiflik, between Nicosia and Larnaca. Gaby Berdy, a native Cypriote and a descendant of one of those colonists, who lives here, is the secretary of the Jewish Community of Cyprus (P.O. Box 95). Periodic Jewish worship services are conducted in hotel lounges in Larnaca and Famagusta.

MARGO

JEWISH CEMETERY, opened in the 1890s, contains the graves of some of the nineteenth-century Jewish colonists. Most of the headstones, however, record the names of children who died in the refugee camps in 1946 and 1947. Also buried here is Paul Blattner, an English Jew who was chief inspector of Cyprus police at the turn of the century.

JEWISH COLONY SITE where a co-operative Jewish agricultural venture failed, is now privately owned by Jews who operate a successful dairy farm and a substantial orange plantation.

NICOSIA

ISRAELI EMBASSY, 27 Androcleus St. is the only Jewish building in Cyprus. Because the tiny Jewish community lacks a rabbi, a Jewish school, and a synagogue, it has made the Israeli Embassy a kind of cultural center. Religious services are held in a hotel. Cypriote Jews send their children to Israel—an hour's flight by plane—for schooling, and many of them go there for the major Jewish holidays. Israelis, on the other hand, who have developed close industrial, commercial, cultural, and athletic ties with Cyprus, come here for vacations. The conductor of the orchestra in Nicosia's leading hotel is an Israeli, as is the coach of the Cyprus soccer team. Hebrew newspapers from Israel are on sale at bookstalls here.

NICOSIA MUSEUM owns an inscribed stone recording the reconstruction of a fourth-century synagogue and preserves other inscriptions evidencing the early existence of Jewish settlements in Cyprus.

CZECHOSLOVAKIA

When Czechoslovakia was created in 1918 out of the ancient provinces of vanished empires, Jews had been living in the territories included in the new republic for more than a thousand years. Jewish settlement in Bohemia dates from 906. In that year, Jewish merchants whose caravans traversed the great trade highway leading from the Rhineland to the Near East founded at one of their principal stopovers—the left bank of the Vltava River at Prague—a community which is one of the oldest in continuous existence in Europe.

From Prague they spread into the hinterland of Bohemia and, in the twelfth and thirteenth centuries, to Moravia and Slovakia. By the middle of the fourteenth century, immigrants from Germany, Austria, and Poland—some invited by rulers who welcomed skilled Jewish artisans and merchants with international connections, and some who were refugees from persecution—had created 28 Jewish communities.

Except for occasional periods of toleration under the protection of enlightened rulers, Jewish history in this cockpit of Europe from the eleventh through the fifteenth century is largely a chronicle of humiliating restrictions, punitive taxes, enforced baptism, violent persecutions, and recurrent expulsions and readmissions. Notwithstanding their unstable and wretched lot, the Jews of Bohemia and Moravia created a unique spiritual and cultural life behind their ghetto walls, particularly in Prague.

For nearly two hundred years, beginning in the sixteenth century, Prague was the metropolis of European Jewish life. The Prague ghetto became virtually an autonomous Jewish town, with independent police and fire departments, and its own judges, town hall, mayor, and flag. Between 1576 and 1619 this self-contained community was a famous center of Jewish scholarship and rabbinical learning under the inspiration of the saintly Rabbi Loew, creator of the legendary Golem, and Rabbi Yom-Tov Lipmann Heller. Marcus Mordecai Meisel, banker and adviser to the Hapsburg emperor and the great patron of the ghetto, and David Ganz, co-worker of Kepler, were also products of this era.

Jewish heroism in the defense of Prague during the Thirty Years' War prompted Ferdinand III to mitigate some of the harsher restraints on the Jews, including the rigid limitation of the ghetto area. He also permitted large numbers of exiles from the Chmielnicki pogroms in Poland to settle in Bohemia. By 1708 Prague's 12,000 Jews constituted the largest Jewish community in Europe outside of Turkey.

All of Prague's Jews were expelled by Empress Maria Theresa in 1745, but the ban was lifted within three years because it had created economic havoc and increased the taxes of non-Jews. The edict of tolerance of Emperor Joseph II in 1781 for the first time enabled Jews to live outside the ghetto, to attend schools, and to enter the professions. Special levies on Jews remained in force, however, until two years before the ghetto was finally abolished in 1848. Full emancipation came only in 1867.

Pogroms in the wake of the abortive uprisings against the Hapsburgs in the 1840s caused many Jews to emigrate to the United States. Among them were Rabbi Isaac Mayer Wise, founder of Reform Judaism in America, and the parents of Louis D. Brandeis and of Abraham and Simon Flexner. In the last years of Hapsburg rule, Jews exerted a significant influence on German culture in Bohemia and made notable contributions to the professions, industry and commerce.

Thomas Masaryk, father of Czechoslovakian independence, who repeatedly defended Jewish rights in Bohemia and Moravia, had the support of leading Jews in his long struggle to liberate his country. In the republic born in 1918 there were more than 275,000 Jews, completely free for the first time. Between the two World Wars the Jews of Czechoslovakia were the happiest Jewish community in Central Europe. Jewish writers such as Franz Kafka, Egon Kisch, Max Brod, and Franz Werfel added luster to Czechoslovakian literature during this period. When the Nazis took over Germany and Austria, 50,000 Jewish refugees found a haven in Czechoslovakia.

Including the refugees, there were 360,000 Jews in Czechoslovakia when it was seized by the Nazis in 1939. Only 50,000 survived the Nazi occupation. By 1950 half of these had emigrated to Israel. The Soviet Union's reversal of its pro-Israel stand after 1949 moved the Stalinist regime in Prague to attacks on Zionism, the arrest of Jewish leaders, the expulsion of the JDC (in 1950) and the termination of all Jewish community activities except the strictly religious ones. This led to another mass exodus that reduced the Jewish population to 16,000 by 1951.

The anti-Semitic campaign erupted into the Slansky affair and the purges of 1952-54 during which eleven Jews accused of being "Zionist agents" were tried and executed. One of them was Rudolf Slansky, first secretary of the Communist Party. Soon after, Jewish emigration was banned and Zionist activity was forbidden.

Some liberalization occurred between 1963 and 1967 but the Six-Day War in the Middle East precipitated a new and violent official anti-Israel campaign and the breaking of diplomatic relations with Israel. The mysterious murder of Charles Jordan, director-general of JDC, in Prague in the summer of 1967, created widespread fear among the Jewish population. Popular and intellectual opinion objected so vigorously to the party line's pro-Arab policy that it became one of the elements in the struggle between Antonin Novotny's hardliners and the liberals of Alexander Dubcek in 1968. Under the short-lived Dubcek regime, Jews were readmitted to posts in the fields of culture and education as well as in foreign trade and the foreign service.

After the Russian invasion of August, 1968, and the subsequent overthrow of the liberal Dubcek regime, attacks on Jews intensified. Their role in the reform movement was magnified and the Dubcek government was assailed as a "Zionist conspiracy" to pry Czechoslovakia from the Soviet camp. In a new purge of authors, educators, economists and other pro-Dubcek figures, the brunt of the attack was borne by Professor Ota Sik, Dr. Eduard Goldstuecker, Eugene Loebl and Dr. Frantisek Kriegel. Sik was the father of the nation's economic reform. Loebl was a former president of the Czech National Bank. Goldstuecker, ambassador to Israel from 1942 to 1952 and vice-rector of Prague's ancient Charles University, had been elected president of the Writers' Union before the Soviet invasion. Kriegel, who had survived the Nazi regime, had been deputy minister of health in the Dubcek cabinet. Later he was a member of the presidium of the Communist Party's central committee and chairman of the National Front. He had been one of the four members of the National Assembly to vote against legalizing the Russian invasion.

Official figures published a few months before the invasion listed 14,000 Jews, 9,000 in Slovakia, the eastern part of the country. Only 1,500 of an estimated 5,000 were registered in the Prague Jewish community but many shunned religious affiliation. By early 1970, the population had fallen to about 12,000 after hundreds of Jews and those of Jewish origin has been blacklisted by the Communist Party.

The affairs of Czech Jewry are managed by two over-all agencies: the Council of Jewish Religious Communities in Bohemia-Moravia, which includes regional bodies in Prague, Brno, Usti, Pilsen and Ostrave, and the Central Association of Jewish Religious Communities in Slovakia. There are small communities in Bratislava, Karlovy Vary (Karlsbad), Holesov, Liberec, Kyjov, Nitra, Usti and Olomouc (Olmutz). Jewish religious life is vanishing. Only two synagogues in Prague are used for regular worship. There are only two rabbis left. Kashruth is still permitted. In Prague there is a kosher slaughterer, a communal butcher and a kosher restaurant in the headquarters of the Council of Jewish Communities. The government pays 90 percent of the cost of maintaining synagogues. There are three Jewish publications: a monthly, Vestnik Zidovskych Nabozenskychobciy Ceskosslovensku; a German language information Bulletin issued quarterly, and Judaica-Boehemiae, issued in French and German by the Jewish State Museum.

BOSKOVICE

GHETTO QUARTER in this medieval town has been restored by the state as a government museum.

BRATISLAVA

CHIEF RABBINATE OF SLOVAKIA, 7 Nesporova St.
FEDERATION OF JEWISH COMMUNITIES OF SLOVAKIA, 29 Smeralova St.
JEWISH MARTYRS MEMORIAL in the ceremonial hall of the new Jewish cemetery, memorializes 80,000 Slovakian Jews killed by the Nazis.
JEWISH SOUP KITCHEN, 49a Zamocka St., where Jews eat their meals and meet to talk. Next door is a newly-erected mikveh.
SYNAGOGUE, Heydukova St. is only one left in this once famous center of Jewish culture and religion. The synagogue has recently been restored. Next door is a small home for the aged.
UNDERGROUND JEWISH CEMETERY existed beneath the slope of the Bratislava Castle Hill, near the banks of the Danube, for more than three hundred years. Construction of a tunnel under the castle to link it with the Danube embankment resulted in the removal of the cemetery. But provision was made for preserving the tombs of some of the famed Talmudic scholars buried here. Their graves are pointed out by guides who open three iron covers beside the roadway just before the tunnel entrance and lead you down a stairway to an iron door. Behind this door is the last resting place of the rabbis, among them the Chatam Sofer and his pupils, who made the city a shrine of Jewish learning when it was known as Pressburg and belonged to Hungary. The key to the underground mausoleum is in the offices of the Federation of Jewish Communities.

BRNO (Brunn)

CHIEF RABBINATE OF BOHEMIA AND MORAVIA, 13 Namesty 28 Rijna.
MARTYRS MEMORIAL on Jewish cemetery, was dedicated in 1965 in memory of 10,000 Jewish victims of Nazis.
SYNAGOGUE, Tride kpt. Jarose 21.

CHEB

MARTYRS MEMORIAL on site of 19th century synagogue destroyed by the Nazis, honors Nazi victims of northern Bohemia.

DOLNI KOUNICE

SYNAGOGUE dating from 18th century, has been restored by the government as a museum piece in this town where there are no longer any Jews. The 15th century hillside Jewish cemetery also remains.

HOLESOV

SCHACH-SHUL, the synagogue of the famed Rabbi Sabbati Kohen, who was known as Schach, survived the Nazi occupation. The synagogue, which dates from 1560, and the old Jewish cemetery, have been converted into the Moravian branch of the Jewish State Museum in Prague. On the cemetery there is a tablet honoring the Schach and another memorializing Nazi victims. The whole town was once a semi-independent Jewish municipality with its own police, fire department and mayor.

KARLOVY VARY (Karlsbad)

SYNAGOGUE, 59 Vridelini St.
MARTYRS MEMORIAL on a public square, the former site of a synagogue burned by the Nazis.
KOSHER RESTAURANT, 59 Vridelni St., is in the same building with the synagogue.

KOMARNO

SYNAGOGUE here has a memorial tablet to victims of the Nazis. Another memorial, shaped like an old tombstone, stands in the local Jewish cemetery.

KOSICE

KOSHER RESTAURANT, 5 Zvonarska St., is in the rear of small Beth Hamedrash.
SYNAGOGUE, 5 Puskingasse, is last survivor of four Jewish houses of worship. One was recently sold to the municipality for a concert hall, and a third now serves as a newsprint warehouse for the local newspaper. The Hebrew letters spelling "Talmud Torah" can still be made out on the large Talmud Torah building, which is now used for non-Jewish purposes.

LIBEREC

SYNAGOGUE

MARIANSKE LAZNE (Marienbad)

BASCH MONUMENT memorializes Dr. Samuel Basch, the ghetto-born Jewish physician who in 1880 developed the first system for measuring high blood pressure. For a number of years he was private physician to the emperor of Mexico, Maximilian, who was the brother of Austria-Hungary's Emperor Francis Joseph.
JEWISH OLD FOLKS HOME, 2 Vrchlickeho, which is maintained by the government, also houses a synagogue and a kosher restaurant. Where the main synagogue, destroyed by the Nazis, once stood there is now a public park.
In the neighboring small town of Lazne Kynzvart, the government has erected a burial mound made of the stones from the Jewish cemetery which was desecrated by the Nazis. The stones were used to pave the town's main street, with the Hebrew inscriptions face up.

MIKULOV N. MORAVE

SYNAGOGUE is last Jewish house of worship in what was once spiritual capital of Moravian Jewry. An old Jewish cemetery also survives.

NOVE ZAMKY

SYNAGOGUE here has recently been restored.

OLOMOUC (Olmutz)

JEWISH COMMUNAL CENTRE, Namesti Rude Armady 4, also houses a synagogue.

OSTRAVA

SYNAGOGUE AND COMMUNAL CENTRE, 8 Zerotinova St. In the Jewish cemetery there is a memorial to concentration camp victims.

PILSEN

SYNAGOGUE, Leninova St., a massive structure with twin cupolas topped by the Tablets and Magen David, stands in a vast square in the center of the city. Its exterior is dilapidated while the interior is shabby from neglect.
COMMUNAL CENTRE, 5 Sadova St.

PODEBRADY

JEWISH OLD FOLKS HOME here also houses a synagogue.

PRAGUE

CHARLES BRIDGE, a historic crossing of the Vltava River linking the Old Town and the main part of the city, has, about one third of the way across, a monument to Jewish degradation in the form of a giant crucifix surrounded by huge gilded Hebrew letters spelling out the traditional Hebrew sanctification, "*Kodosh, Kodosh, Kodosh, Adonai Tzvuoth* (Holy, Holy, Holy Is the Lord of Hosts)". A plaque inscribed in Latin, German, and Czech, affixed to the base of the crucifix, explains this extraordinary sight. It appears that in 1609 a Jew was accused of desecrating the crucifix and as punishment the ghetto community was compelled to pay for affixing the Hebrew words in letters of gold. The gold has long since vanished, having been stolen during the German occupation.

GHETTO REMAINS, a medieval enclave in the heart of the city, are bunched in a sort of reservation in and around Maislova and Josefovska Sts. The ghetto grew up around the original tenth-century settlement on the banks of the Vltava River. After it was separated from the Old Town of Prague by a series of gates, it acquired the name of Judenstadt (Jewish Town). Greatly enlarged in the seventeenth century and renamed Josefstadt in 1790 in honor of the emperor who first allowed the Jews to live outside the ghetto, the Judenstadt remained the core of Prague Jewry until 1848.

In that year the municipality broke up the Jewish Town and converted it into the city's District V, now known as Josefov. During the massive rebuilding program that began in Prague in 1896, most of the ghetto was torn down. Left standing as national monuments were the Old-New Synagogue, Pinkas Synagogue, Klaus Synagogue, Meisel Synagogue, and the Jewish Town Hall. These historic buildings, restored by the government at great cost, are now part of the government-sponsored State Jewish Museum, whose exhibits are also displayed in buildings outside the former ghetto. The Old Jewish Cemetery and the State Jewish Museum are the most popular tourist sites in Prague.

JEWISH TOWN HALL, 18 Maislova St., was once the seat of the self-governing Jewish town. Built at the end of the sixteenth century by Marcus Mordecai Meisel, mayor of the ghetto, who was the banker of the emperor of Bohemia and who used his wealth to improve the ghetto and to foster Jewish learning, it was rebuilt in 1754 after a fire. At that time there was added a unique clock with Hebrew characters for numerals and with hands that run backward. High above this clock is another, with Arabic numerals. In the building is the so-called High Synagogue, also built by Meisel, but now unused. Today the Town Hall is the headquarters of the Council of Jewish Religious Communities. In the basement is a kosher restaurant. All the ancient documents recording the beginnings of the community are kept here.

KLAUS SYNAGOGUE adjoining the Pinkas Synagogue on Josefovska St. is the largest of the surviving ghetto synagogues. It was founded at the end of the sixteenth century by the famed Rabbi Judah Loew and rebuilt in 1694. A marvelous baroque structure, it now houses an exhibit called "Crimes Not Forgotten," which consists of documents, films, photographs, and other evidence of Nazi crimes in Czechoslovakia. It was in this building that the Nazis, agreeing to a Jewish suggestion, assembled tens of thousands of Jewish ritual objects, books, Torah Scrolls, Torah mantles, and other items from the 168 synagogues they destroyed in Bohemia, Moravia, and Slovakia, as the basis for a proposed international Jewish museum to be conducted by the Nazis. After the war, this huge collection was redistributed by the Czechoslovak authorities among a number of buildings as part of the State Jewish Museum.

LIBRARY OF JEWISH MUSEUM in the central building of the ghetto's former school, 3 Jachymova St., contains the prized 30,000-volume library of the Jewish community, and some of the ghetto archives. Here, too, is a collection of some five thousand unforgettable poems and drawings by Jewish children who passed through the Terezin concentration camp on their way to death at Auschwitz, and an equally touching collection of paintings by Jewish artists depicting life in Terezin.

MEISEL SYNAGOGUE, Maislova St., another 16th century edifice built by Mordecai Meisel, was rebuilt at the end of the 19th century. It now displays the silver treasures of the old Jewish community and of the destroyed synagogues. The collection of spice boxes, menorahs, Torah pointers and crowns, and other ritual objects is regarded as one of the largest in the world. In 1964, an anonymous buyer purchased from Artia, the Czech Foreign Trade Corporation, 1,500 Torah Scrolls which had lain unused in the Meisel Synagogue since 1939 when they were deposited there by the Nazis who collected them from synagogues throughout the country. The Scrolls are now housed in a museum at the Westminster Synagogue, London, which has donated some of them to synagogues throughout the world.

MUSEUM OF PRAGUE GHETTO, 3 Jachymova St., a romanesque structure originally erected as a mortuary, which separates the Klaus Synagogue from the Old Jewish Cemetery. Founded by the Jewish community in 1912 to house ghetto relics and liturgical articles from the synagogues that were torn down, the museum is now the core of the State Jewish Museum established by the government after World War II.

The exhibits in this museum provide a vivid historical panorama of the Jewish Town from its earliest times until the end of the eighteenth century. The entrance hall is devoted to maps, etchings, drawings, replicas, and other displays, which describe the beginnings of the Jewish quarter and its growth up to the middle of the fifteenth century. The main hall is given over to prints, maps, religious objects, portraits, and other memorabilia dealing with the ghetto during its greatest era—from the late sixteenth to the middle of the seventeenth century. Among the relics here are a number associated with the legend of the Golem and its creator, Rabbi Loew, including the latter's own kiddush cup; the caftan and banner of Solomon Molcho, the false messiah of the sixteenth century, who bequeathed his flag and robe to the Prague Jewish community before he was burned at the stake. A small room under the staircase contains a display of documentary and pictorial materials about the eighteenth-century community. The upper room is set aside for a fascinating exhibit of the economic and social life of the ghetto, with special emphasis on the development of Jewish trade and craft guilds.

OLD JEWISH CEMETERY at the edge of the old ghetto, Stareho Hubitova St., is crowded with a fascinating array of more than 10,000 tombstones, whose inscriptions constitute a history of the ghetto from the middle of the fifteenth century, when the cemetery was first opened, to the late eighteenth century, when further burials within the city walls were forbidden. Here are buried the most celebrated figures of the ghetto: Rabbi Loew; Marcus Mordecai Meisel; Rabbi David Oppenheim, whose famed library is now part of the Bodleian at Oxford University (see Great Britain); Josef Solomon Medigo, physician and mathematician, who was a pupil of Galileo; and David Ganz, historian and astronomer. The oldest stone that has been deciphered is dated 1439 and beneath it lies Rabbi Abigdor Karo, a beloved elegist.

There was an older cemetery on the same site which was sacked in 1389, and scholars believe that there are thirteenth- and fourteenth-century graves beneath those still covered by visible tombstones. In some places the upper edges of deeply buried stones appear above ground among the later tombs. Most of the visible tombs are of red marble or limestone, with raised inscriptions. Many of the stones are engraved with artistic symbols representing the Biblical tribe, family name, or profession of the deceased. Hands outstretched in blessing show that the tomb belongs to a member of the priestly tribe of Aaron; Levites are identified by a jug; the graves of tailors are decorated with a pair of scissors, printers and scribes with a book, musicians with a violin, and physicians with tweezers.

The best-known tomb, which looks like a sarcophagus, is that of Rabbi Loew. A rampant lion is carved on the tomb (*loew* meaning "lion") which is surrounded by the graves of his thirty-three disciples. The tiny cemetery, now timeworn, with mossgrown stones huddled amid creeping plants and bending alders, is as crowded as the ghetto must have been in its heyday.

OLD-NEW SYNAGOGUE (Alte-Neue Schul), 2 Cervana St., is the oldest Jewish house of worship in Europe still used for its original purpose. A gem of Czech Gothic architecture, it was originally erected in the mid-thirteenth century. The gloomy, legend-laden, high, narrow, gabled building was long regarded as the oldest existing synagogue in Europe, but recent finds give this distinction to the Pinkas Synagogue (*see below*). Most authorities attribute the name Old-New Synagogue to one of its periodic renovations. But there is a fascinating tale which says that the name is really Al-tenai Schul—the "on condition that" synagogue. According to this version, the synagogue was said to have been built by exiles from Jerusalem after the destruction of the Temple in 70 C.E., who brought with them Temple stones, which were used in the synagogue's foundations. The builders pledged themselves and their heirs to tear down the building when the Messiah came and to take the stones back to Palestine.

The untouched interior is designed like a double hall. The heads of the columns are richly decorated with plastic ornaments. The artistic doorway and the tympanum over the altar are part of the original construction. The synagogue is sunk below the street level and is dimly lit by twelve narrow windows. On the walls, it is claimed, one can still make out the bloodstains of Jews who perished in the synagogue during a pogrom in 1389. On the *bimah* (platform) hangs a scarlet flag embroidered with a Magen David and a Swedish hat. This banner was presented to the Jews of Prague by Ferdinand III in 1648 in appreciation of their role in the defense of the city against the Swedes. The emblem was customarily carried by the ghetto Jews at the head of processions on festive occasions. The always empty chair on the *bimah* is said to be the one used by Rabbi Loew in the sixteenth century, when he preached here.

The attic of the synagogue is supposed to house the remains of Rabbi Loew's

Golem. The synagogue seats one hundred men, and services are still held here daily. One of the tiny annexes, dating from the seventeenth century, is used by women worshipers who can hear the prayers through slits in the wall.

On the lawn of the synagogue stands a statue of Moses.

PINKAS SYNAGOGUE, on Josefovska St., next to the Old Jewish Cemetery and a stone's throw away from the Old-New Synagogue, is now accepted as being the oldest memorial of the Prague Jewish settlement. Recent excavations have established that the synagogue's foundations date from the tenth century. A marble plaque in the foyer states that it was built in 1535 by Aaron Meshullan Horowitz, but a detailed study completed in 1959 uncovered architectural proof that parts of the building are more than nine hundred years old. The main structure of the present synagogue was erected in the thirteenth century and enlarged by Horowitz as a private family synagogue in 1535. As of 1971, it is a perfect example of a medieval synagogue, complete with ritual appurtenances, but empty, except for tourists.

Part of the State Jewish Museum, this synagogue has been set aside as a memorial to the 77,297 Bohemian and Moravian Jews who perished at the hands of the Nazis. On the walls around the Ark of the Torah are engraved in tiny letters and figures in alphabetic order the names of the martyrs and all available data concerning their birth, date of deportation, and death. Artists worked five years to complete this memorial. At the beginning of 1970, the names were beginning to fade because of the poor quality of paint and cement used in affixing them to the walls.

SPANISH SYNAGOGUE on Dusni St., the first modern building in the former ghetto, was erected in 1867 on the site of what is believed to have been Prague's first synagogue. Today it is a treasure house of eight thousand synagogue textiles, rich in history and artistic value. Among them are two thousand *parochot* (Torah curtains) and Torah mantles formerly used in the now destroyed synagogues. The Torah mantles and *parochot* are shown to visitors in a kind of huge album placed in front of the unused Ark. Reflector lights show up the details of the embroidered patterns in a sort of "moving museum." The interior of the synagogue is an artistic gem, its decorations having been copied from the medieval synagogues of Spain—whence its name.

GOLEM TAVERN just outside the Old Jewish Cemetery, on Stareho Hubitova St., is not a Jewish restaurant but a popular wine tavern.

ISRAELI LEGATION, 10 Vorsilska, Xth District, has been closed since 1967.

JEWISH LIBRARY, a rebuilt synagogue in the suburb of Michle, displays more than one thousand Torah Scrolls assembled from synagogues throughout Bohemia and Moravia.

JUBILEE SYNAGOGUE, 7 Jerusalem St., is the only synagogue in the city still being used for worship, except for the Old-New Synagogue in the former ghetto area. It was built in the 1890s.

RABBI LOEW STATUE at the entrance to the Prague Town Hall, is Ladislas Saloun's towering, hewn-stone monument of the supposed creator of the legendary Golem. Known as Der Hohe Rabbi Loew because of his great height, he was the religious head of the Prague ghetto in the closing years of the sixteenth century and early in the seventeenth. The outstanding Jewish scholar of his generation, Judah Ben Bezalel Loew was greatly beloved by Jews and highly respected by Christians, among them men of science, and by the Hapsburg emperor, because of his towering reputation as philosopher, theologian, and cabalist. A host of legends are associated with his name but the best-known of these concerns the Golem, a medieval robot he is said to have fashioned out of clay and then infused with temporary life through an amulet bearing the name of God. The Frankenstein stories had their origin in this legend, which even in modern times has prompted investigators to search the surviving ghetto synagogues for the remains of the Golem. A tour called "Rabbi Loew and the Golem" is regularly conducted by the Czech Government Tourist Office, whose special guides conduct visitors around the former ghetto area.

NEW JEWISH CEMETERY, in the Strasnice section, outside the Greater City of Prague, is visited by many tourists who seek out the grave of Franz Kafka. His tombstone is adorned with fresh flowers almost daily by visitors.

OLSANY FIELDS, the second-oldest Jewish cemetery in Prague, is now a public park. Established in 1713 as a burial ground for ghetto victims of a plague, it was then far beyond the Old City's walls. When the Old Jewish Cemetery was barred to further interments, the Olsany Cemetery became the community's Jewish burial ground. From 1777 to 1890, when this cemetery too was closed, all Jewish dead were buried here. As the enlarged city grew up around Olsany Fields, the municipality, in consultation with the Jewish community, gradually converted it into a park. Historic tombs, including those of Rabbis Ezekiel Landau and Eleazar Flekeles, have been faithfully preserved.

NATIONAL MEMORIAL, on the Vitkov Hill, honors the late Egon Ervin Kisch, famed Czech-Jewish writer, by keeping his ashes in a place of honor. Kisch, who had been elected honorary chairman of the Council of Jewish Communities shortly before his death, is also honored by a Kisch Street.

PRAGUE TOWN HALL has on the ceiling of its great salon three heavy chains which were once used to close the gates of the ghetto. The city's coat of arms, incidentally, contains the six-pointed Star of David. In 1920, when Greater Prague was formed out of the surrounding suburbs and the older towns, the new coat of arms included the escutcheons of Prague and the former independent municipalities, including the Jewish Town.

ST. SIGISMUND CATHEDRAL preserves what is said to be a fragment of the seven-branched Menorah which once stood in the Temple in Jerusalem. It is said to have been brought to Prague by a king of Bohemia who obtained it in Milan. It may be seen in the third chapel, north aisle, as you enter.

STARE SINOGOGY is the name of a non-Jewish restaurant that you pass on the way to the Old Jewish Synagogue. "Stare" means old in Czech.

PRESOV

SYNAGOGUE

PRIBOR (Freiberg)

BIRTHPLACE OF SIGMUND FREUD in this Moravian village that used to be called Freiberg, is marked with a simple plaque showing his head in bas-relief and giving the year of his birth, 1856. Dedicated in 1931, on the seventy-fifth birthday of the father of psychoanalysis, the plaque is between the middle two of four upper windows of a simple two-story house opposite an old synagogue. The inscription reads: "Prof. Dr. Sigmund Freud, the founder of psychoanalysis, was a scientist of world renown." The Freud family left for Vienna when Freud was three years old. In 1968 the town council erected a small monument to Freud.

TEREZIN

THERESIENSTADT, the Nazis' so-called "model ghetto" concentration camp, was located in this former fortress town forty miles from Prague. It is now a shrine memorializing the 141,000 Jews who were imprisoned here at one time or another. Of these, 34,000 died here and 88,000 were sent to Auschwitz. The camp's most famous prisoner was the late Rabbi Leo Baeck, who survived. The entrance hall, where 200 bodies at a time were once stacked, is now adorned with Hebrew inscriptions. The cremating ovens can still be seen. The cemetery is dotted with memorials to the identifiable dead. A simple stone marks the spot where the ashes of 20,000 unknown Jews are buried. The stone is inscribed with the Czech word "Popel," which means ashes. Theresienstadt concentration camp was in use from

1941 until May 9, 1945 when it was liberated by the Russian army. An exhibit of 44 drawings by adult prisoners and 51 by children has been viewed throughout the world. Only 100 of the 15,000 child prisoners survived. A recently discovered document shows that Jews who once served in the Czech army organized a resistance movement in Terezin in 1942 to disrupt production of war material for the Germans. The Terezin prisoners were forced to manufacture ammunition boxes and to process mica. The cemetery of Ghetto Terezin is part of the National Terezin Memorial, an official state agency.

TRNAVA

SYNAGOGUE, 7 Kapitulska St.
MARTYRS MEMORIAL, 32 Halenarska St., in the courtyard of a former synagogue.

DENMARK

The Jewish community of Denmark is the oldest in Scandinavia. It had its beginnings in 1622, when a group of Sephardic Jews from Amsterdam and Hamburg accepted the invitation of King Christian IV to help him build up his newly founded city of Glückstadt in the then Danish province of Schleswig-Holstein. The King's Jewish physician, Dr. Jonah Charizi, influenced the monarch's action. In 1657 the Sephardic Jews were admitted to Denmark proper, where they were joined by coreligionists from Germany in the 1670s.

By 1684 there was a synagogue in Fredericia, East Jutland, another at Nakskov, and the nucleus of a Jewish community in Copenhagen. Seventeenth- and early eighteenth-century Jewish cemeteries in Fredericia, Nakskov, Aalborg, Randers, Aarhus, Faaborg, Horsens, Odense and Slagelse are reminders of the early Jewish settlements there.

Copenhagen's first synagogue was dedicated in 1766. Full religious toleration was granted the Jews in 1814, and complete civil and political equality came in 1849. Although never very numerous, the Danish Jews produced many famous figures. Among these were the Brandes brothers—Georg, an eminent historian and literary critic, and Edvard, leader of the Liberal party early in this century and twice minister of finance; Herman Trier, president of Parliament; Niels Bohr, father of atomic energy; Victor Borge, the pianist; Gen. C. J. de Meza, Commander of the Danish Army during the war with Germany in 1864, whose father converted to Christianity; Johanna Louise Heiberg, noted actress; Henry Gruenbaum, Socialist editor and Minister for Economic Affairs in the cabinet during the 1960s, and acting-premier; and Dr. Stephan Hurwitz, vice-chancellor of Copenhagen University, who conceived of the ombudsman idea and served as Denmark's ombudsman from 1955 on. Danish Jewry consists largely of two groups; the so-called Viking Jews who came before 1903, and those who arrived after the Czarist pogroms in Russia early in this century. Another infusion came after World War I, and a third in the 1930s when Jews from Nazi Germany were admitted. In 1969 and 1970 Jews fleeing Poland found a sanctuary in Denmark whose government provided generous grants for housing and maintenance and gave assistance in finding jobs.

The most extraordinary episode in the history of Danish Jewry occurred in 1943 when virtually the entire Jewish population was saved from deportation to the Nazi death camps through the heroic efforts of the Danish underground. In a period of ten days beginning on Rosh Hashana and ending on the eve of Yom Kippur, daring fishermen and resistance leaders ferried more than 7,000 Jews across Ore Sound to Sweden, a distance of 4 to 30 miles, in a motley fleet of fishing boats. This war-time escape began when G. F. Duckwitz, a German consular official in Copenhagen, leaked to Danish leaders the news of a plan to deport all the Jews. The underground informed Rabbi Marcus Melchior who sounded the alarm from his pulpit on the first day of Rosh Hashanah. Most of the Jews fled north to the area around Helsingor, where they were hidden in seaside inns, churches and woods along the beach until the Danish resistance forces and fishermen could carry them to safety in Sweden. Only 472 Jews were captured by the Nazis on Oct. 1 and 2, and they were shipped to the Theresienstadt concentration camp in Czechoslovakia. Of these 52 died. The others, along with those in Sweden, returned in 1945 to their homes, businesses, and even gardens that had been maintained by the Danes.

In 1970 there were 6,000 Jews in Denmark, almost all of whom live in Copenhagen. Most of the older generation have assimilated, but the younger people have given new vitality to the Jewish community. Nearly 200 children attend a Jewish day school in Copenhagen. The Jewish Youth Council has won the right to elect its own representatives to the board of deputies, the advisory body to the National Jewish Council. Rabbi Bent Melchior succeeded his late father in 1969 as chief rabbi.

COPENHAGEN

BENDIXGADE is a street named for the late Victor Bendix, noted Danish composer.

BOHR ALLE is a street named for Denmark's greatest scientist, Niels Bohr, who was half-Jewish. His mother Ellen Adler, was a member of a prominent Jewish banking family related to the Melchiors (*see below*). Bohr's standing in Denmark is only slightly less sacred than that of the royal family and Hans Christian Andersen. It was at Bohr's Institute for Theoretical Physics at the University of Copenhagen (on Amelienborg Square) that atomic physics had its great synthesis in the 1920s. Theoretical work done at the Institute by Lise Meitner, a half-Jewess, enabled Bohr to calculate that U 235 was the fissionable element involved in the discoveries of German scientists. Bohr, who won the Nobel Prize in Physics in 1922, and his family were rescued from the Nazis in 1943 when the latter planned to deport all Danish Jews. Before he left Sweden, he prevailed on King Gustav to accept all Jews from Denmark who could escape, and Bohr saw to it that the news was beamed to Denmark via the government-owned Swedish radio. Bohr, under the cover name of "Mr. Baker" directed a secret laboratory at Los Alamos, New Mexico, where the first atomic bomb was assembled and tested.

BRANDES ALLE is a street named for Dr. Ludwig Israel Brandes, one of Denmark's leading physicians and social workers of the nineteenth century.

CAROLINE SCHOOL, 34-36 Princess Charlottesgade, a Jewish primary school and kindergarten, is the second-oldest Jewish institution in Denmark. It was founded in 1805 as a boys' school and after World War II was consolidated with a Jewish girls' school that had been established in 1810. The school is named for Denmark's Princess Charlotte.

NATHAN JOSEF FRAENKELS JEWISH OLD FOLKS HOME, 7 Dyrkob, is the oldest of three Jewish homes for the aged in Copenhagen. Some of the Jews who were not saved by the Danish underground in 1943 were residents of these homes.

FREDERIKSBORG CASTLE in the western suburb of Frederiksberg, has among its collection of portraits of Danish notables a painting of Mendel Levin Nathansen, who is regarded as the father of Danish journalism. A leading member of the banking house of Meyer and Trier, he turned to economics and journalism in 1831. For nearly thirty years he was editor of the *Berlingske Tidende* of Copenhagen. He founded the Caroline School (*see above*) and was largely responsible for the grant of religious liberty achieved by the Danish Jews in 1814.

GOLDSCHMIDT MEMORIAL on the Allegade, in Frederiksberg, honors Meier Aron Goldschmidt, a mid-nineteenth-century novelist, journalist, and political essayist, who is one of the great names in modern Danish literature. Goldschmidtvej is a street named for him.

GREAT SYNAGOGUE, 12 Krystalgade, erected in 1833, is one of only two synagogues in Denmark. It was founded by the first Jewish settlers toward the end of the seventeenth century. The late King Christian X was among the congregation when the synagogue observed its centennial in 1933. Ten years later the same monarch defied the Nazi occupiers by refusing to acquiesce in the adoption of anti-Jewish decrees. King Christian and the entire royal family threatened to resign if the Danish Parliament were compelled to approve anti-Jewish laws. The story that King Christian promised to wear the yellow Star of David and to urge all Danes to do likewise if the Nazis compelled the Jews to wear it as a badge of shame is a widely current legend outside of Denmark, but it is not true. The yellow star was never introduced in Denmark. Nevertheless, King Christian's opposition to the Nazis deterred them from destroying the synagogue whose Torah Scrolls and other treasures were hidden by the Danish clergy in a neighboring church. In 1953 Christian's son, King Frederik, and Queen Ingrid, attended a special service in the Great Synagogue on the tenth anniversary of the rescue of Danish Jewry.

HAKOAH, Jewish sports club, 9 Bremensgade.

ISRAEL EMBASSY, 4 Trondhjems Plads.

ISRAELSPLAD or Israel Square, in the center of the city, was for 200 years known as Green Square because it was for 200 years the site of a vegetable market. The re-naming took place in 1968 on the 25th anniversary of the rescue of Danish Jewry.

JEWISH COMMUNITY CENTER, 7 Ny Kongensgade, is also the headquarters of the Jewish Community of Denmark (Det Mosaiske Troessemfund), the Jewish Youth Organization and the Jewish Choir. A museum of Jewish ceremonial objects and a Jewish library are also located here.

JEWISH OLD FOLKS HOME on Uterslev Mose, the newest of the city's three homes for the Jewish aged, was built with funds largely provided by the Danish Government and the Copenhagen County Council. On display here is a silver menorah presented by King Frederick IX. It was a gift to him in 1960 by the American Jewish community, and is inscribed "with everlasting thanks to the King and people of Denmark for saving the Jewish community of their country."

KOSHER RESTAURANT, 2 Rorholmsgade.

MACHZIKEI HADAS SYNAGOGUE (ultra-Orthodox), Ole Suhrsgade 12.

MELCHIOR'S PLADS is a street named for Moritz Gerson Melchior whose summer home, "Rolighed," was the second home of Hans Christian Andersen. The Melchiors and their kin, the Henriques, befriended the famed author in his declining years. It was at "Rolighed" on Melchior's Plads that Andersen died. Moritz Melchior was a member of the Danish Parliament and one of the founders of the Danish free-trade movement.

MELCHIORSVEJ is a street named for Moses Melchior, one of Denmark's leading merchants and bankers, who served on the Copenhagen City Council from 1869 to 1884. The Melchior family established itself in Denmark in 1760 and its members played an immense role in Danish industry, commerce, science, and public service, as well as in the Jewish community. The present chief rabbi of Denmark, Bent Melchior, is a member of this family.

MEYERSGADE is a street named for Ernest Meyer, one of Denmark's best-known nineteenth-century painters. His works hang in the Copenhagen Academy and in the Thorvaldsen museum.

MOSES STATUE in front of the Vor Frue Kirk (Our Lady's Church), the Copenhagen cathedral, in Norregade, is a life-size likeness of Moses holding the Ten Commandments. It is the work of the Danish sculptor, H. W. Bissen.

MUSEUM OF THE DANISH RESISTANCE on the Esplanaden, is a part of the National Museum and is devoted to the history and exploits of the Danish resistance during World War II; it has a department that displays a collection of photographs depicting the Nazi persecution of Danish Jews, the routes used by the underground in smuggling them out, the help provided by Sweden, and the return of the Jews in 1945.

NATHANSEN MEMORIAL, on the Allegade, honors Henri Nathansen, one of Denmark's great dramatists and novelists. His novels of Jewish life in Denmark and his plays were immensely popular.

NATIONAL GALLERY, Solvgade, has among its portraits one of Mendel Levin Nathansen (*see above*).

NY CARLSBERG GLYPOTEK, on Dante's Plads, which houses a great collection of old and modern sculpture, has a piece entitled "Bust of a Young Jew," acquired in 1891. It has been erroneously identified as a likeness of Flavius Josephus, the Jewish historian of Roman times.

OLD JEWISH CEMETERY, on the Moellegade, opened in 1693, is one of the oldest in northern Europe. Among its 5,500 well-preserved tombstones is one shaped like an obelisk, over the grave of Mendel Levin Nathansen.

PARLIAMENT (FOLKETING) BUILDING, in the restored Christiansborg Palace, has among its memorials to Danish notables a painting and a bust of Carl Edvard Cohen Brandes, leader of the Liberal party early in this century, twice minister of finance, and one of the most prominent dramatic critics of his time.

POSTS AND TELEGRAPH MUSEUM displays a bust and portrait of Joseph Michaelson, a 19th century editor and post office official, whose ideas led to the establishment of the Universal Postal Union.

ROUND TOWER, adjoining Trinity Church, on Kobmagergade, is one of a number of seventeenth-century Copenhagen buildings on whose facades the name of God is carved in Hebrew. God's name is also chiseled in big gold Hebrew letters over the gate-way to the *Holmen's Church*, on the Holmen's Kanal, the church of the Royal Navy and the royal family.

There are two attributions given for these Hebrew inscriptions–one to Christian IV, who first invited the Jews to Denmark, another to church architects of the post-Reformation era who were equally at home in Latin, Greek, and Hebrew, and used all three in their decorative scheme.

ROYAL LIBRARY, 9 Bremensgade, has a special Jewish department known as Bibliotheca Judaica Simonseniana, which is one of the great Jewish book collections in Europe. Its 50,000 volumes of Hebraica and Judaica, 400 manuscripts and 60 Hebrew incunabula, had their origin in the private library of David Simonsen, chief rabbi of Denmark from 1893 to 1902, for whom it is named. Rabbi Simonsen's family was among the first Jewish settlers in Denmark. The library includes some rare first prints.

Saved from destruction by the Nazis, the Simonseniana serves as the central information bureau for the Association of Libraries of Judaica and Hebrew in Europe. It is engaged in tracing and cataloguing all Jewish books in all European libraries. Dr. Rafael Edelmann, director of the Royal Library's Department of Judaica, occupies the chair of Jewish studies at the University of Copenhagen, the only professorship of its kind in Scandinavia.

A bust and a portrait of Georg Brandes, one of the great historians and literary critics of the late nineteenth and early twentieth centuries, are also in the Royal Library. A literary champion of cultural and political freedom, he helped introduce Ibsen, Strindberg, and Lagerlöf to the main stream of Western literature.

ROYAL THEATRE, on Kongens Nytorv, has a bust and a portrait of Henrik Hertz (considered by some the Danish Molière), who was one of Denmark's greatest nineteenth-century playwrights.

SCANDINAVIAN JEWISH HIGH SCHOOL, 5 Laderstrade.

TRIER'S PLADS is a street named for Herman Martin Trier, who served in the Danish Chamber of Deputies from 1884 to 1909 and was elected its president in 1901.

YIDDISH LIBRARY, Ny Kongensgade 10.

TUBORG HARBOR has a large commemorative stone inscribed in Danish with a brief legend recalling the heroism of the Danes who rescued their Jewish fellow-citizens.

HELSINGOR

JEWISH REFUGEE MEMORIAL in the Ferry Station of this city is a sculptured representation of a Danish fishing boat with Jewish refugees, recalling the heroism of the Danish underground in 1943. The monument is the work of Harald Isenstein, one of Denmark's leading sculptors, who was himself among those rescued in 1943.

ODENSE

HANS CHRISTIAN ANDERSEN MUSEUM in this town where the beloved writer of fairy tales was born, has a number of items of Jewish interest. One is Andersen's student examination certificate to the University of Copenhagen which lists Hebrew as one of the subjects he studied in 1828. A later document shows Hebrew crossed out in favor of history. Yiddish and Hebrew translations of Andersen's works are also on exhibit. As a boy, Andersen attended a school for poor Jewish children in Copenhagen. His childhood memory of an anti-Jewish riot was later incorporated in his best novel, *The Improvvisatore*. Many of his works contain sympathetic pictures of Jews and Jewish life.

FINLAND

The first Jews came to Finland about 1830 as conscripts in Czarist army units on garrison duty at Viipuri (Vyborg) and Helsinki. They were the so-called Cantonists who as adolescents had been forced into the Czar's army between 1800 and 1856 for a period of 25 years. These involuntary Jewish recruits were educated at special schools and then assigned to distant places such as Siberia and Finland. Barred from Finland while it was part of Sweden, Jews remained excluded when Finland became a Russian duchy in 1809. The earliest Jewish settlement resulted from the application to Jews of an imperial decree authorizing Russian soldiers to remain in Finland after completion of their army service.

The number of Jewish ex-soldiers and their families increased slowly in the 1840s and 1850s during which they successfully resisted official pressure for their conversion. By 1865 they had obtained the right to erect a synagogue in Helsinki, but lack of funds caused the project to be abandoned for forty years. Services were conducted in private homes in Helsinki, Turku (Åbo), and Viipuri.

Until Finland became independent in 1917, the Jews were denied the right to establish religious communities, were excluded from all trades and professions but peddling, were forbidden to live anywhere but in the three principal cities, and were required to obtain residence permits semi-annually. Meanwhile, the Jewish population grew through immigration from Poland and Lithuania in the 1880s and from Russia after the pogroms of the 1880s and the Russian Revolution. In 1938 Finland admitted 250 refugees from Germany and Austria and later welcomed a number of Jewish doctors and scientists who had fled from Norway and Denmark.

During the Russo-Finnish War in 1939, virtually every able-bodied Jew enlisted in the Finnish army. When Finland was compelled to cede Viipuri to Russia, the entire Jewish community abandoned homes and property rather than renounce Finnish citizenship and moved en masse to Helsinki and Turku and to the newest Jewish settlement in Tampere (Tammerfors). Although Finland became an ally of Nazi Germany in 1941 and declared war on Russia, she refused the Nazis' request to turn over to them the German-Jewish refugees and resisted all anti-Jewish measures. Some Jews in the Finnish army were for a time actually part of the German army on the Finnish-Russian border.

There are 1,700 Jews in Finland; 1,300 in Helsinki, 300 in Turku and 100 in Tampere. The leading Jewish family is the Jacobsons. Max Jacobson has headed Finland's UN delegation since 1965 and in 1969 was president of the UN Security Council. His mother, Mrs. Jonas Jacobson, heads Finland's Women's International Zionist Organization.

AHVENANMAA ISLANDS (Åland Islands)

These islands in the Gulf of Bothnia, famed tourist area, are known also for the ruins of Bomarsund, a Russian fortress built partly by Jewish military conscripts and destroyed by British and French naval forces during the Crimean War in 1854. Not far from the ruins are the graves of a number of Russian-Jewish soldiers.

HÄMEENLINNA (Tavastehus)

OLD CEMETERY in this town near Turku has graves of Russian-Jewish soldiers who came to Finland as conscripts. The earliest tombstones are dated 1835.

HELSINKI

HELSINKI UNIVERSITY LIBRARY, Rikhardinkatu 3, owns many original Russian documents on Jewish history not to be found anywhere else. It also has a collection of Hebrew and Yiddish books printed in Russia between 1825 and 1917.

ISRAEL EMBASSY, 5A Vironkatu.

KOSHER MEALS can be obtained by advance arrangement with Miss Sarah Smolar at 40A Kalevankatu.

SYNAGOGUE, Malminkatu 26, the only one in Finland's capital city, was opened in 1906, but its history goes back more than a century. It was founded by former soldiers in the Russian army. Attached to the synagogue is a Jewish Community Center, which houses a Jewish preparatory and day school, recreational facilities, a community library and the Hakoah Sports Club. Club members have represented in Finland in the Olympic Games and in the World Maccabiad. Preserved in a glass cage in the synagogue is wreath presented by Field Marshall Mannerheim on a visit to the synagogue in 1944. The wreath memorialized the 23 Jewish soldiers who had died in the Russo-Finnish War. There is a legend that the two gilded doves and gilded crown that decorate the Ark in the synagogue came from Czarist warships, having been lifted by Jewish seamen as a gift to the synagogue when it was dedicated.

TUOMIOKIRKO, the Lutheran cathedral located in the heart of the city between the university and the House of Parliament, has the Hebrew word *Adonai* chiseled over the western main entrance, and also on the eastern wall. The wording was carved when the cathedral was built between 1830-1852. Hebrew words can be found in many Lutheran churches in Finland, most often above the altar.

TAMPERE (Tammerfors)

JEWISH COMMUNAL CENTER, Nasilinnankatu 38. The building is also used for a synagogue and a kindergarten.

TURKU (Åbo)

JEWISH COMMUNITY CENTER adjoining the synagogue, was built in 1956 with the aid of funds from the Conference on Jewish Material Claims Against Germany. The community Hebrew school and kindergarten are in the same building.

SYNAGOGUE, Brahenkatu 17, erected in 1912, is the second oldest in Finland.

FRANCE

The earliest documents attesting to the presence of Jews in France date back to the fourth century, but there is good reason to believe that Jews had settled much earlier, in Roman times. In the sixth century Jewish communities were to be found in Marseilles, Uzès, Narbonne, Clermont-Ferrand, Orléans, Paris, and Bordeaux, most of these administrative centers on the great trade routes.

During this early period the Jews enjoyed equality with their fellow countrymen—as they had under Roman law. They built synagogues, they maintained organized communities, and their rabbis and other synagogue officials had legal status. While they were principally merchants and slave dealers, they were free to follow other occupations, among them those of tax collector, sailor, and physician.

With the triumph and establishment of Christianity in Gaul, the situation began to change. In an endeavor to consolidate its position, the Church began to press for limitations on the rights of the Jews. At a series of Church councils in the sixth century, one restriction after another was imposed on the Jewish community, gradually placing it in an inferior position to the Christian population. The Church was the dominant power, and the Merovingian kings were not unwilling to accept its authority. As a result, the clergy was prohibited from taking meals with Jews, intermarriage was forbidden, Jews could not serve as judges or tax collectors, they could not own Christian slaves, they were forbidden to proselytize, to appear among Christians four days after Good Friday, to exercise civic or administrative rights over Christians, or even to sing psalms at burials of their own people.

Coupled with these restrictions, a vigorous campaign for the conversion of the Jews was carried on. The campaign was conducted with such pressure that Pope Gregory the Great was impelled to enjoin more moderation and to counsel the employment of persuasion only.

Despite these restrictions, seldom enforced, the Jews seemed to prosper and even to enjoy the esteem of the populace. When Wamba, the Visigoth King, decreed conversion or expulsion for the Jews of his realm, the edict provoked an uprising. They were given protection by the Count of Nîmes, the Bishop of Maguelon, and others, but the rebellion was crushed and the Jews were expelled in 673. This was the first expulsion in a long series in the centuries ahead.

In the eighth and ninth centuries, under the Emperor Charlemagne and his successors, the Jews of France enjoyed a period of tranquillity and prosperity. Charlemagne himself displayed a tolerant and generous spirit toward his Jewish subjects. He had a Jewish physician, and he sent Isaac the Jew in 797 on an embassy to Harun al-Rashid. Many restrictions were eased or lifted, the rights and privileges of the Jews were confirmed, and their position was regulated by law. During the Carlovingian period, Jews traveled widely, and one writer, about 850, pictures them as voyaging as far as the Indies and China.

The period from the middle of the ninth to the twelfth century marked an epoch in French history. French society was transformed by the development of the feudal system and the organization of the guilds. The evolution of the new system, which restricted many occupations to Christians, had a serious effect on the position of the Jew in French society. At the same time this was the era when the great rabbis and rabbinical schools of France brought renown to French Judaism. This was also the period of the development of Hebrew literature in France.

During this period Jewish culture was awakening, and it soon blossomed into full flower. The tenth and eleventh centuries produced great scholars and poets, and the *Yeshivoth* of France attracted students from all over Europe. The eleventh century was dominated by two towering figures who profoundly influenced Judaism. The first was Gershon, called "the Light of the Exile," who prohibited polygamy among European Jews; the second was Rashi, the great commentator, founder of the school at Troyes. They and their pupils, many of whom achieved fame of their own, made French Judaism a paramount influence in the Jewish world.

While Gershon and Rashi were products of the Judaism of northern France, Provence in the south was undergoing its own renaissance of learning. If anything, it attained even greater heights than those attained in the north. Proximity to Spain and peaceful conditions in the district made Provence a chosen land for Jewish learning. The rabbinical schools of Arles, Béziers, Lunel, Marseilles, Narbonne, Nîmes, and other cities soon became famous. When Benjamin of Tudela visited the communities of Provence in 1160, he found renowned scholars teaching hundreds of students in busy schools. Maimonides, Aristotelian and ardent rationalist, was considered an oracle in Provence, and his opinion was sought in all matters. There was intense intellectual excitement as the liberalism of the southern schools struggled with the conservatism of the north. Never again was this moment of intellectual glory to be recaptured by French Jewry.

The ritual-murder libel in France was closely connected with the Crusades. The Jews of France do not seem to have suffered as much as other sections of Europe during this period, except perhaps during the First Crusade in 1096. During the Second Crusade, the Jews were accused of murdering Christians. In the latter part of the twelfth century, this libel cropped up time after time, with dire results. Finally King Philip Augustus decreed the expulsion of the Jews in April 1182. In July of that year, they were compelled to leave the royal domain of France and their synagogues were converted into churches. At that time the royal domains were reduced to the territory around Paris and Orléans.

In July 1198, King Philip Augustus recalled the Jews to Paris. He permitted them to engage in banking and pawnbroking, but their business was placed under control and taxed heavily, and a special account called "Produit des Juifs" was set up in the royal treasury. Furthermore, the Jews were made serfs of the King. The nobles followed the example of the King, and the status of the Jews was reduced to that of personal vassals of king and lords.

In 1306 the Jews were expelled again by King Philip the Fair. In the intervening century since their last expulsion, the kingdom of France had increased considerably, and the refugees, estimated at 100,000, could find asylum only in the few sections of the country that were not part of the kingdom. By this time the intellectual decay of the Jews of northern France was well advanced. They had not recovered from the terrible blow of the condemnation and burning of the Talmud in 1242. Their schools declined, and the great Rabbi Jehiel of Paris even sent an emissary to Palestine to collect money for his academy.

King Louis X recalled the Jews to the kingdom of France in 1315 for twelve years. While he imposed rigorous conditions on them, he took them under his protection. The twelve years extended to seventy-nine. This period of comparative calm was disrupted in 1394, when Louis XI once again decreed the expulsion of the Jews. The kingdom of France by this time covered most of the country and the Jews were expelled in succession from every new province acquired by the French Crown.

Soon the Comtat Venaissin, centering around Avignon, part of the Pontifical States, was the last refuge of Jews in France. They were banished from Provence in 1481. Portuguese and Spanish Marranos had settled in the sixteenth century in Bordeaux and Bayonne, but they were tolerated as "new Christians" and did not practice Judaism openly until after 1730. When Alsace-Lorraine was annexed in 1675, Louis XIV granted the Jews permission to remain, but they lived under cruel and restrictive legislation.

During the eighteenth century, a spirit of tolerance began to prevail. A colony of Portuguese and German Jews was tolerated in Paris. Enlightened Christians such as Dohm demanded justice for the Jews. The minister Malesherbes summoned a commission of Jewish notables which included Cerf Berr, an Alsatian Jew who was purveyor to the army, and eminent representatives of the Jews of Bordeaux and Bayonne such as Furtado, Gradis and Isaac Rodrigues.

As a result, in 1784 the poll tax was abolished, and permission was granted for Jews to settle in all parts of France. Shortly afterward the Jewish question was raised by two men who later became prominent in the French Revolution—Count Mirabeau and the Abbé Grégoire. When the Revolution broke out Abbé Grégoire demanded the emancipation of the Jews before the National Assembly.

In 1790, the National Assembly declared the Avignonese Jews and the Portuguese Jews of Bordeaux and Bayonne full citizens. In 1791 all Jews in France were proclaimed full citizens, a few days before the dissolution of the National Assembly.

The Jews of France thus achieved full emancipation. They immediately gave proof of their patriotism by serving in the Army of the Republic. However, when Napoleon's reign began, reactionaries attempted to undo the good work of the Revolution. Napoleon ordered the convocation of an assembly of 110 Jewish notables, which met in July 1806. In September of that year, the Emperor declared himself satisfied with the answers given to his questions by the notables and ordered the convocation of a Sanhedrin of seventy-one members. This body met in February 1807 to discuss the answers given by the Assembly of Notables, which it confirmed. Thenceforth these principles were to have legal force for all the Jews of the French Empire. To enforce these decisions, Napoleon instituted the consistorial system by a decree on March 17, 1808. This system is still in force in France today.

Under Louis XVIII further progress was made. In February 1831, Judaism was placed on an equal footing with Catholicism and Protestantism as regards support for the synagogue and rabbis from the public treasury. In 1846 the special Jewish oath (*More Judaico*) was abolished. From this time on, no legal barrier separated French Jews from their fellow citizens.

In the nineteenth century, Jews achieved eminence in every walk of life. They occupied high places in literature, art, science, jurisprudence, and the army. The Dreyfus Affair, with its evocation of virulent anti-Semitism, came as a great shock to many Jews who had believed this impossible in France, the country of *Liberté, Égalité, Fraternité*. After a great struggle, which almost tore France apart, Dreyfus was vindicated and the anti-Semitic forces were discredited, for the time being.

World War II brought martyrdom to France's Jewry. With the defeat of France and the division of the country into two zones, new travails began. From 1940 to 1944, the Jews of France suffered the tragic consequences of defeat. In occupied France they underwent the horror of persecution, degradation, seizure, and deportation. In the Unoccupied Zone, under Marshal Pétain, they suffered to a lesser degree, until the Germans occupied the whole of Metropolitan France in November 11, 1942. The Nazi terror reached into every part of the country in all its fury. Fascist Frenchmen carried out the orders of their Nazi masters. France was defaced with concentration camps at Drancy, Pithiviers, Compiègne, Gurs, Le Vernet, and a dozen other places. Assassination became the order of the day and the most eminent personalities fell victims to the slaughter, including Georges Mandel, former Minister of the Interior, and Victor Basch, octogenarian philosopher.

The Jews of France fought back wherever they could during this terrible period. Leaders of the Consistoire Central remained in the country to deal with the German conquerors and the Vichy government. Despite the dangers, they protested various repressive measures and attempted to carry on relief work to ameliorate the sufferings of the Jewish community. Many Jews took an active part in the resistance movements. There were a number of Jewish maquis groups, and several rabbis served as chaplains in the maquis. When liberation came, the Jewish community of France had paid a ghastly toll, with about 100,000 deported and 10,000 slain.

With liberation came the task of rebuilding a shattered community. Dispersed and impoverished, with many leaders gone, the Jews found it a difficult task, but gradually order came out of chaos. Communities were re-established, institutions were reopened, and, with the aid of the American Jewish Joint Distribution Committee, French Jewry rapidly began to approach a state of normalcy. Within a few years after the end of the war, the Jewish community established the Fonds Social Juif Unifié to look after its own needs.

Jews have taken their place in every facet of French life. Before World War II, one Jew, Léon Blum, had attained the eminence of Premier. Since the end of the war, two Jews, René Mayer and Pierre Mendès-France, have attained that distinction. After World War II the Jewish community of France numbered about 250,000, composed of about 100,000 members of the old community who survived the war and 150,000 newcomers from Eastern Europe. With the end of French rule in Algeria in 1962, there was a vast influx of Jews from North Africa, coming not only from Algeria, where the Jewish community dwindled to practically nothing, but also from Tunisia and Morocco. This created a tremendous change in the demographic composition of the Jewish community. Provincial communities, especially Marseilles, experienced tremendous growth overnight. Many dying communities in small towns were given a new lease on life, many new communities were established, and cities which had not had a Jewish community for four or five centuries had a new rebirth. The influx had a deep effect on religious life in France, since many of the newcomers are observant and need religious facilities. These were provided by the authorities as quickly as possible.

The Six Day War had a traumatic effect on French Jewry. The anti-Israel position of the late President de Gaulle created difficulties. Despite all the pressures, propaganda and veiled threats, French Jewry stood firm in its support for Israel. It refused to be intimidated and this stand had the support of many Frenchmen who did not forget that France had been Israel's firm friend for years. Despite many problems and difficulties ahead, French Jewry had good reason to look to the future with confidence. It is today a community of 535,000, active and viable, one of the largest in the world.

AGEN (Lot-et-Garonne)

RUE des JUIFS is a remnant of the medieval Jewry of Agen.
SYNAGOGUE AND COMMUNITY CENTRE, 28, rue de Montesquieu.

AIX-en-PROVENCE (Bouches-du-Rhône)

RUE VENAL, north of the Hotel de Ville, was formerly the Rue des Juifs, centre of the ancient Jewry of Aix.
SYNAGOGUE, avenue Darius-Milhaud prolongée. The synagogue is housed in a prefabricated building erected on land lent by the municipality. The old synagogue, dedicated in 1840, was sold in 1952 to a Protestant church. Darius Milhaud, the composer, was born in Aix in 1892. Many of his works have been inspired by the liturgy and songs of the old Jewish communities of Provence. His father served as head of the Jewish community and his great-grandfather organized the first synagogue in modern times.
In 1940 Milhaud composed a cantata for the centenary celebration of the synagogue founded by his great-grandfather. In June 1970 he performed the ground-breaking ceremony for the new Jewish community centre. When completed the centre will house the synagogue, library, classrooms and banquet hall.
RUE JULES ISAAC is a main street renamed after the famous historian and founder of the *Amitié Judéo-Chrétienne*.

AIX-les-BAINS (Savoie)

SYNAGOGUE, Pavillon Salvator, Rue Roosevelt.
YESHIVAH, route de Tresserve.

AMIENS (Somme)

CATHEDRAL Before the main portal may be seen a representation of the Synagogue Defeated, in the shape of a withered tree with an axe laid to its trunk. Above the portals, in a large gallery, there are niches containing twenty-two colossal statues of the kings of Judah. Also to be seen is a late Gothic wood carving of "Samson in Bonds."
SYNAGOGUE, 58, rue du Port d'Amont.

ANGERS (Maine-et-Loire)

SAINT-MAURICE CATHEDRAL contains several ancient Hebrew inscriptions.
RUE de la JUIVERIE is a reminder of the medieval Jewish community of Angers.
SYNAGOGUE, 3, rue Thomasseau.

ANNECY (Haute-SAVOIE)

SYNAGOGUE and COMMUNITY CENTRE, 18, rue de Narvik, was built through the initiative and generosity of Mr. Rudolphe Moos, a local industrialist, and with the aid of the American Joint Distribution Committee, the Fonds Social Juif Unifié and The Claims Conference, it was dedicated in 1963.

ANTIBES (Alpes-Maritimes)

SYNAGOGUE and COMMUNITY CENTRE, villa "La Monada", chemin des Sables, Juan-les-Pins. The villa was presented to the community by Mr. David Zagha of Cannes. Eventually a synagogue will be built on the grounds and Marc Chagall has agreed to supervise the building plans.

ANTONY (Hauts-de-Seine)

SYNAGOGUE, *See* MASSY
STUDENT'S HOUSE, 49, rue Croix-de-Berny.

ARCACHON (Gironde)

SYNAGOGUE on Avenue Gambetta, was the gift of Daniel Osiris, the famous philanthropist, and was built in 1877 on land given by the city. The synagogue is open only on the High Holy Days and during festival seasons, when services are conducted by a representative of the chief rabbi of Bordeaux, and during the summer months.

ARLES (Bouches-du-Rhône)

ARLÉSIEN MUSEUM, 42 rue de la République, founded by the famous Provençal poet Frédéric Mistral, preserves the relics of old Provence. It contains a collection of Jewish religious and cultural objects, presented by Armand Lunel, the historian of Provençal Jewry, and his grandson Albert Lunel.

LAPIDARY MUSEUM, Place de la République, has several tombstones of the early medieval period, removed from the ancient Jewish Cemetery, known as Montjuif, which was located near the Cemetery of Aliscamps. One of these stones records the memory of "our master Meier of Marni." These hoary stones are the only reminders of a community which flourished for almost a thousand years.

The former *Rue des Juifs* is now the Rue D. Fanton, one block north of the Place du Forum. In the vestibule of the chapel of the Blue Penitents may be seen the door of the ancient synagogue with the text of two biblical verses.

ASNIERES (Hauts-de-Seine)

SYNAGOGUE and COMMUNITY CENTRE, 73 bis, rue de Bas.

ASSY (Haute-Savoie)

CHURCH OF THE PLATEAU has two stained-glass windows by Marc Chagall, his first work in this medium, executed in 1957. Chagall presented these windows as a gift. (*See* METZ.)

CHURCH OF NOTRE-DAME-de-TOUTE-GRÂCE in the Plateau d'Assy, started in 1937 and completed during the war, is a treasure-house of modern art. In addition to Fernand Léger, Jean Lurçat, Henri Matisse, Georges Bracque, Pierre Bonnard, and Georges Rouault, two great modern Jewish artists are represented here.

Looming in front of the Rouault windows is Jacques Lipchitz's sculpture which he named Notre-Dame-de-Liesse (Our Lady of Joy). This sculpture, which Lipchitz considers one of his most important works, was commissioned in 1946 by ¡Père Couturier, the great pioneer of the revival of sacred art in Catholic churches, and was installed in the church in 1957. In accepting the commission, Lipchitz had set one condition, that the following inscription be set up in some visible spot. It appears on the base of the figure and reads: "Jacob Lipchitz, Jew, loyal to the faith of his ancestors, made this Virgin to further good will among men on earth so that the spirit may prevail."

In the baptismal vestry there may be seen a ceramic mural by Marc Chagall which portrays Moses leading the Israelites through the Red Sea. This Old Testament scene is flanked on both sides by two white plaster plaques by Chagall, depicting scenes of baptism.

AUVERS-sur-OISE (Seine-et-Oise)

This small town, where Vincent van Gogh worked and ended his life, is now a shrine for art lovers. A few paces from the small walled cemetery where Van Gogh lies buried beside his brother Théo, stands the monumental statue of Van Gogh (10½ feet, 880 pounds), the work of the Russian-born Jewish sculptor Ossip Zadkine. The statue was erected in the summer of 1961.

AUXERRE (Yonne)

In this small town there is a monument to the resistance martyrs, symbolizing the violation of human rights and the determination that freedom must be safeguarded.

AVIGNON (Vaucluse)

The Jews of Avignon, with those of Carpentras, Cavaillon and L'Isle-sur-Sorgue, formed the "four holy communities" of the Comtat Venaissin, part of the Pontifical States. These communities had a special liturgy of their own, called *Comtadin*, which greatly resembled the Portuguese.

ANCIENT GHETTO, known as Carrière des Juifs, lies in the tangle of narrow streets and alleys under the Palace of the Popes, which crowns a high hill. Street names such as Rue de Vieille-Juiverie and Rue Reille Juiverie recall its status of a thousand years ago. An ancient, battered building on the northeast corner of these two streets was reputed to have housed the synagogue. This ancient section of the city is being rebuilt and the house was demolished several years ago. Some of the ghetto streets are gone, only Rue de Vieille-Juiverie, Rue Pente-Rapide and Rue Petite-Reille remain. Near the Rue Pente-Rapide the foundations of a thirteenth-century synagogue have been found.

CALVET MUSEUM, 65 rue Joseph Vernet, has on display an eighteenth-century inscription which records the founding of a communal institution. In part it reads, "This house was founded at the expense of the community, through the efforts of four men . . . who made personal sacrifices in the building of it . . . 1st day of Elul, year 5505 [August 30, 1742]."

NEW GHETTO established in 1226, was located in the center of town. Its presence is recalled by some street names, *Rue Jacob* and *Place Jerusalem*. There was until some years ago a *Rue Abraham*. In the vicinity of the synagogue there are some old houses, high and congested, which are reminders of the Jewry of centuries ago. There is also a chemin de la Synagogue.

SYNAGOGUE, officially listed at 2, Place de Bir-Hakeim, is actually on the Place Jerusalem, a small square which runs off the Place de Bir-Hakeim. It is a modern, low, square building which stands on the site of its medieval predecessor, destroyed in a fire in 1844. Inside the vestibule of synagogue are a number of memorial plaques. One is to "Our Glorious Dead 1914-1918" listing 9 names. Another, placed in October 1948, is to the memory of "The Martyrs of the Faith of Israel" deported during World War II. It lists 75 names, headed by Chief Rabbi Joseph Sachs, and includes a family of 18, M. et Mme. Szafrajgen and their 16 children.

BAIGNEUX-les-JUIFS (Côte d'Or)

The medieval Jewish community occupied the section named "Pré de la Synagogue".

BAUGÉ (Isére)

RUE des JUIFS marks the location of the medieval Jewry of Baugé.

BAYONNE (Basses-Pyrénées)

ANCIENT CEMETERIES
See BIDACHE
See LABASTIDE-CLAIRENCE
See PEYREHORADE

BASQUE MUSEUM, 1 rue Marengo, one of the best-known museums devoted to regional art and folklore, has a Jewish Room (Salle Israélite). In addition to a collection of religious objects and articles relating to the history of the community, there is on display a chart showing the coats of arms of the ancient Jewish families of Bayonne.

CEMETERY currently used by the Jewish community, aside from occasional burials at Peyrehorade, is located in the St.-Étienne section of St.-Esprit. It was established in 1660 and has been in continuous use for three centuries, a unique record.

MEMORIALS TO WAR VICTIMS In the courtyard of the synagogue and at the cemetery of Peyrehorade, there are plaques commemorating the community's victims of two World Wars.

SYNAGOGUE, 35 rue Maubec, was dedicated September 24, 1837. Its construction was authorized by King Louis Philippe, in an ordinance signed April 22, 1836. The synagogue is located in the St.-Esprit quarter, across the river from Bayonne, where the Jews lived in that period.

SYNAGOGUE REMAINS Of the seven synagogues once maintained by Bayonne's Jewry, traces remain of only two—the *Temple de Gueldes*, which once occupied the building at 49 rue Maubec, and the *Temple Brandon*, once housed at 22 place de la République, which was closed August 28, 1872.

BEAULIEU-SUR-MER (Alpes-Maritimes)

On the other side of the bay of Villefranche, on which the winter resort of Beaulieu is located, is *Cap-Ferrat*, a promontory of splendid houses with spacious gardens.

On the crest of the promontory, at the narrowest part of the isthmus, stands the Villa-Musée Ile-de-France, bequeathed to the Academie des Beaux-Arts by Baroness Béatrice Ephrussi de Rothschild, in memory of her father, Alphonse de Rothschild and her mother Eléanora.

The Italian style two story villa was designed by an architect named Messiah and was built in 1912. Mme. Ephrussi called it Ile-de-France, after the region in France where she was born.

Mme. Ephrussi died in 1934 and her bequest included not only the pictures, furniture, porcelain and tapestries in Ile-de-France, but also the collections in her two villas at Monte Carlo.

Ile-de-France is modest in comparison to Waddesdon Manor, in Aylesbury, England, a gift to the nation by James de Rothschild but it is a veritable treasure house of all schools and periods. Mme. Ephrussi was a great traveller and she had a taste for mixing her purchases and putting them together—such as Chinese and Sienese. Room after room is filled with the treasures of many countries.

The garden is as eclectic as the villa. It was laid out at great expense. The ground, all rock, had to be flattened and tons of earth brought in. A Temple of Love is a reproduction of the Petit Trianon, and there are French, Spanish, English and Japanese gardens.

BEAUNE (Côte-d'Or)

RUE des JUIFS behind the cathedral recalls the medieval Jewry.

BELFORT (Territoire de Belfort)

A number of local streets bear the names of prominent Jewish citizens of Belfort: Marcel Bonneff, Pierre Dreyfus-Schmidt, Leon Schwob, Jacques Levy and Jules Levy. The old pavilion of the municipal hospital bears the name of a former mayor, Edouard Levy-Grunwald. Two monuments in the local Jewish cemetery memorialize the local Jewish soldiers killed in World War I and the 245 members of the community deported and killed by the Germans 1940-1945.

SYNAGOGUE, 6, rue de l'As-de-Carreau was built in 1862.

COMMUNITY CENTRE, 27, rue Stroltz.

BENFELD (Bas-Rhin)

SYNAGOGUE, Rue de la Dîme. This small synagogue, built in 1846, escaped destruction during the German occupation, because of the protection of the municipality. The chapel was badly damaged, but was restored after liberation.

BESANÇON (Doubs)

ANCIENT CEMETERY is located outside the Charmont Gate.

SYNAGOGUE, 2, rue Mayence, is a large structure, built in Moorish style in 1869.

TRISTAN BERNARD, eminent famous Franco-Jewish novelist and dramatist, was born in 1866 at 23 Grande-Rue. A memorial plaque marks the house. The same street produced another eminent literary figure, Victor Hugo, who was born at No. 138 in 1802.

BÉZIERS (Hérault)

In the Middle Ages Beziers was an important Jewish centre of learning, and was the home of many great scholars.

LAPIDARY MUSEUM contains the longest and finest Hebrew inscription in France. The stone commemorates the inauguration of a synagogue about the middle of the twelfth century, probably in 1144. The inscription relates that the ground was furnished and costs were paid by Rabbi Solomon Halafta, "one of the great and leading men of our city." Benjamin of Tudela gave high praise to the same Rabbi Halafta, whom he met when he visited Béziers in 1165.

RUE de la JUIVERIE recalls the ancient medieval Jewish community.

SYNAGOGUE and COMMUNITY CENTRE, 13, rue Viennet.

BIARRITZ (Basses-Pyrénées)

SYNAGOGUE, Corner Rue de Russie and Rue Pellot. The synagogue was built at the turn of the century through the generosity of the De Poliakoff family of Russia. Services are conducted only during the summer season.

BIDACHE (Basse-Pyrénées)

During the French Revolution the Jews of Bidache transformed their synagogue into a Temple of Reason. The old Jewish cemetery, on the Route du Port dates back to 1690. It was used by the Jews of Bayonne and is now in sadly neglected condition.

BERNAY (Eure)

RUE aux JUIFS is a remnant of the medieval Jewry of Bernay.

BISCHHEIM-SCHILTIGHEIM (Bas-Rhin)

Up to the French Revolution, was one of the most important Jewish communities of Alsace. This was the home of Cerf Berr, head of the Jews of Alsace and his brother-in-law, David Sintzheim, who presided at the Grand Sanhedrin of 1806 and became the first Chief Rabbi of France in 1808.

SYNAGOGUE, 41, rue des Abeilles. The synagogue was dedicated in 1959 to replace an older one which had been built in 1837 and was destroyed by the Nazis in 1944.

RITUAL BATH constructed in 1780 by Cerf Berr for his brother-in-law Rabbi David Sintzheim may be seen. Inquire at synagogue.

BLOIS (Loir-et-Cher)

This small town in the heart of the château country achieved infamy in Jewish history. On March 26, 1171, thirty-one Jews, including sixteen women and a new-born infant, were burned alive on a ritual-murder charge, the first of its kind in France. For centuries Blois was known as a "City of Blood"; the anniversary of the burning became a fast day, and the lament for the martyrs, written by Rabenu Tam, a grandson of Rashi, became part of the liturgy. Today the *Rue des Juifs* is the only trace left of this unhappy community.

BONDY (Seine-Saint-Denis)

AVENUE LEON-BLUM is named for the Socialist writer and political leader who was Premier of France just before World War II.

Synagogue, 28, avenue de la Villegeoise.

BORDEAUX (Gironde)

ANCIENT CEMETERIES, the oldest, dating back to 1725, is located at 74 Cours de la Marne. The smaller Avignonnais cemetery, used by the Jews who came from Avignon, is situated at 49 rue Sauteyron.

CHURCH OF ST.-SEURIN has a statue of the Synagogue Defeated, left of the south portal. This Synagogue Defeated is not as abject and degraded as her sister in Notre Dame of Paris—she still keeps her purse on her belt.

COMMUNAL INSTITUTIONS

La Maison de Retraite, formerly a home for the aged, is now mainly occupied by newcomers from North Africa. It has a library and is used as a meeting place by the Jewish students' organizations and other groups.

Le Répos Maternel, a rest home for pregnant women, is located in the nearby commune of Graqignan. It was founded by Madame Henry Deutsch de la Meurthe, a member of the Raba family of Bordeaux.

JEWISH CEMETERY is located on the Cours de l'Yser and dates back to 1764. In our first edition in 1962 we drew attention to the fact that Pauline and Hans Herzl, children of Theodor Herzl, were buried here side by side in unmarked graves. Since that time the situation has been rectified and a memorial stone has been placed on the graves reading: "Here Rest Hans and Pauline Herzl Children of the Creator of the Jewish State".

MARTYRS' MEMORIAL listing the hundreds of Jews of Bordeaux deported during the occupation is located in the courtyard of the synagogue. It bears the following inscription: "In this synagogue, savagely profaned and devastated and converted into a prison in January 1944 by Nazi barbarism, tears, laments, and moans covered the altar of the Lord. 'Have we not all one Father? Hath not the same God created us all?' (Malachi Ch. 2.)"

MONTAIGNE'S BIRTHPLACE The mother of Michel de Montaigne, philosopher and writer, was Antoinette Lopez, a member of a Jewish family of Bordeaux. Born and raised in the Jewish faith, she became successively a Protestant, a Catholic, then a Protestant again. Montaigne was born in 1533 in the Château de Montaigne in the St.-Émilion district near Bordeaux. He wrote his great *Essays* there, and for a time served as mayor of Bordeaux. His great-grandfather was Ramon Eyquem, a merchant of Bordeaux who purchased the Château de Montaigne and adopted the name; he was described as a dark man who spoke French with a Spanish accent, and may have been a Marrano.

In the section of the château known as La Tour de Montaigne may be seen his library and the room in which he died in 1592. It is a national historic monument and open to visitors.

MONTAIGNE'S TOMB is located in the Faculty of Letters of the University of Bordeaux.

ROTHSCHILD CHÂTEAUX Two of the greatest wines of France are produced at the Château Lafitte-Rothschild and the Château Mouton-Rothschild, both located in the nearby commune of Pauillac, in the Médoc district. Château Lafitte-Rothschild was acquired in 1867 by Baron James de Rothschild, and the present owner is Baron Élie de Rothschild. Château Mouton-Rothschild was acquired in 1853 by Baron Nathaniel de Rothschild, and its cellars are considered the most beautiful in France. The present owner, Baron Philippe de Rothschild, in 1961 created a wine museum, thus making the château the first oenological shrine in Europe. Both cellars are open to the public.

RUE JUDAÏQUE recalls the medieval Jewry which lay outside the city walls. Close by is the *Rue Porte-Dijeaux* (Jew's Gate), which commemorates the gateway to the Jewish quarter.

STREET NAMES commemorate a number of Jewish personalities.

Rue David Gradis is named for the shipping magnate whose vessels carried French commerce to the West Indies in the eighteenth century.

Rue Furtado is named for Abraham Furtado, merchant, supporter of the Girondist faction in the Revolution, chairman of the assembly of Jewish notables convened by Napoleon in 1806, and treasurer of the city of Bordeaux.

Rue Rodrique Péreire is named for Jacob-Rodrique Péreire, who devoted his life to the welfare of the deaf-mutes of France.

Avenue Georges Mandel is named for the former Minister of the Interior assassinated in 1944.

There is also a *Place Amélie Raba-Léon* and, in the suburban area, a *Rue Isaac Seba*, a *Rue Cardoze*, and several streets named for Léon Blum, former Premier of France.

SYNAGOGUE, 213 rue Ste. -Catherine, was dedicated on September 5, 1882, in an era when Bordeaux was the center of Sephardic Judaism in France. It replaced the first consistorial synagogue which was built in 1810 and destroyed in a fire in 1873. Previously, the Jewish community had been served by a number of smaller houses of worship; in 1806 there were no fewer than nine in Bordeaux.

The synagogue is noted both for its size and for the beauty of its interior, much of which survived the destruction sustained during the occupation. In a sense it is the cathedral synagogue of the Sephardic Jews of France; it has a seating capacity of 1,500 as compared to the 982 capacity of the Sephardic synagogue on the Rue Buffault in Paris, which was erected through the efforts of Daniel Osiris, native of Bordeaux.

During the occupation, gangs of French fascists wreaked havoc on the interior of the synagogue, destroying most of the precious furnishings. In 1944, the Germans turned it into a prison for deportees. When liberation came, the synagogue presented a scene of utter ruin, and the work of reconstruction was begun. It was a slow process, but after twelve years of labor the task was completed. With its fourteen massive columns of Carrara marble, the synagogue of Bordeaux once again presents a picture of serene beauty.

Bordeaux is the native city of two famous Jewish writers, both distinguished as poets, critics and dramatists. A plaque marks the house at 54, cours Victor Hugo, where Catulle Mendes was born in 1841. Georges de Porto-Riche was born in 1849 at 6, rue du Pont-de-la-Mauresque.

BOULAY (Moselle)

SYNAGOGUE, Route de Faulquemont.

RUE des JUIFS is a reminder of the medieval Jewish community. In 1671 the young Rabbi Raphael Levy, the "Martyr of Boulay" was burnt at the stake on a charge of raping and murdering a young girl of Glatigny for ritual purposes. The discovery of the girl's body led to his rehabilitation by the Court of Nancy. The rabbinate forbade any Jew to spend the night in Glatigny, an interdiction observed to this day. It is interesting to note that since the middle of the 19th century Jews have served on the Municipal Council of Boulay and several have occupied the post of Mayor.

BOULOGNE-BILLANCOURT (Hauts-de-Seine)

SYNAGOGUE, 43, rue des Abondances.

BOURGES (Cher)

BOURGES CATHEDRAL provides an illustration of the Christian version of the relationship between Judaism and Christianity. A group of scenes in a window in the Chapel of Notre-Dame-de-Lourdes tells the story, which is repeated in a number of French cathedrals and churches. According to the theory, the Old Testament merely presaged the New. A series of Biblical scenes all foretell the triumph of the Church and the degradation of the Synagogue. Both Church and Synagogue are portrayed by female figures, who stand on opposite sides of the crucified Christ. The Synagogue, blindfolded, her staff broken and her crown askew, bows her head in dismay, a picture of utter defeat. A moon in eclipse shines dimly over her head, while above the head of the Church the sun shines brightly. It is interesting to note that Judas wears a pointed, medieval Jewish bonnet.

RUE des JUIFS lies immediately behind the cathedral.

MUNICIPAL MUSEUM has on display several souvenirs of Jewish interest, especially a basin said to have come from the Temple in Jerusalem.

CAEN (Calvados)

RUE aux JUIFS at the foot of the château, is a reminder of the old Jewry of Caen.

SYNAGOGUE and COMMUNITY CENTRE, 46, avenue de la Liberation, was dedicated in 1966.

RUE du DR. PEKER commemorates a local physician who was deported by the Nazis.

CAMBRAI (Nord)

MUNICIPAL LIBRARY which was destroyed in 1944 but has since been reconstructed, has in its manuscript collection the medieval "Rituel hebreu". Microfilm copies are made available to scholars and students.

CANNES (Alpes-Maritimes)

SYNAGOGUE, 20 boulevard d'Alsace. Dedicated in 1955, the building of the synagogue was made possible by the generosity of an Egyptian Jew, Fernand Adda.

CARPENTRAS (Vaucluse)

ANCIENT CEMETERY in the La Fontrouse quarter, in the northeast section of the city near the aqueduct, probably dates from 1343. The old gravestones are bare, since inscriptions were forbidden by the papal authorities. Stones from an earlier cemetery were built into the town wall. Several are to be seen in the Municipal Museum.

CATHEDRAL OF ST.-SIFFREIN, an ancient building commenced in 1404, should be entered by the south portal on the left side, known as the Porte Juive. This is the door used by Jews in bygone days when they were forced to listen to proselytizing sermons.

MATZOTH BAKERY located in a low, vaulted cellar, may be entered from the courtyard of the synagogue. There are two ovens set deep in the wall and two huge stone kneading blocks. There are also a bread mixer and a millstone dating from the eighteenth century. A marble slab was, according to tradition, given to the Jews by a pope for the preparation of unleavened bread. Water was drawn from the well in the courtyard. In existence as early as 1625, these bakeries have long been out of use. One of the kneading blocks bears the name of its donor, "Gad of Digne—a gift—1652."

MIKVAH (Ritual Bath) located in a subcellar of the synagogue, is hewn out of the living rock. It is still fed by a natural spring, as in centuries past. It is of great depth, and the water level fluctuates. Steps cut into the stone provided access for users.

RUE de la VIEILLE JUIVERIE recalls the *carrière*, the ancient Jewish section of Carpentras.

SYNAGOGUE situated on the northeast corner of the town square, is regarded as a historical monument. The original synagogue was built in 1367, but it underwent radical changes in the enlargements and reconstructions of 1741, 1784, and 1899. With the decline of the Jewish community, the synagogue fell into a state of decay, and about 1930 Mrs. Peter J. Schweitzer, of New York, assisted in its partial restoration. In 1953, when there was danger of the imminent collapse of the building, Louis P. Schweitzer, a son of Mrs. Schweitzer, provided enough funds to begin some urgent repairs. The French government was sufficiently impressed by this interest to declare the synagogue a historical monument and undertake its restoration, which was completed in 1959.

The exterior of the synagogue is drab and uninteresting, a not unusual feature in an era when anonymity provided protection. The interior, however, is strikingly beautiful, and it is easy to see why this edifice is regarded as one of the architectural gems of France.

The Ark of the Law is situated on the east wall. To the right of the Ark, in a niche, there is a tiny, richly upholstered Louis XVI chair, which is known as the "Chair of Elijah." In the original structure the women's synagogue was housed in the cellar. At a later date the women were provided with narrow balconies on the sides of the Ark and along the north wall. The gallery on the west wall was reserved for the use of the synagogue officers and communal authorities.

An unusual feature is the raised platform in front of the west gallery, which is reached by two circular staircases. From here, facing the Ark and high above the worshipers, the officiating minister conducted the service. In all of Europe only the synagogue of Cavaillon shares this unique feature, apparently peculiar to the Comtat Venaissin. The remarkable collection of candelabra contains one in bronze from Holland, several in Venetian glass, and others in painted sheet iron.

An ancient community, Carpentras flourished for centuries. A twelfth-century document, attributed to Rabenu Tam, grandson of Rashi, refers to the learned rabbis of Carpentras. In 1789, the Jewish community numbered 1,000, almost 10 per cent of the population of the town. In the early years of this century it had almost ceased to exist. In recent years, the influx of Jews from North Africa has brought a revival of the community, which now comprises about forty families, and regular services are held every Friday evening. (*See* AVIGNON *and* CAVAILLON.)

THE INGUIMBERTINE LIBRARY has a Hebrew collection of great interest, known by the name of its donor, Garsin Cavaillon.

Two other streets bear the names of prominent Jewish citzens of Carpentras, Rue Naquet and Rue Garsin-Cavaillon.

Mlle. Mossé, daughter of a former rabbi of the community, was for years custodian of the synagogue keys. She relinquished this function upon the establishment of the new community after the North African influx in 1962. With her death in 1968, there is only one decendant of the original community left, Robert Crémieux, 70 years old and childless. With him, nearly 700 years of history in Carpentras will end.

CAVAILLON (Vaucluse)

ANCIENT CEMETERY of the Jewish community was for centuries located at the foot of St. Jacques hill near the Roman arch on Boulevard Carnot. In 1951 the bodies were disinterred and reburied in the municipal cemetery. The plaque marking the spot reads as follows: "Here was located the cemetery where the Israelites of the holy community of Cavaillon were buried since the 14th century".

JUDÉO-COMTADIN MUSEUM located in the annex of the synagogue, contains a fine collection of relics of the Jewries of the Comtat. Included are tombstones of great antiquity, religious objects, and documentation on the history of the community. Also to be seen there is the ancient matzoh bakery of Cavaillon fully equipped.

SYNAGOGUE, 14 rue Hébraïque, is regarded as a historical monument. It was rebuilt in 1772 on the site of an older synagogue and restored in 1930. It seems to be half suspended in air, as it rests on an archway which spans the Rue Hébraïque. This arch was probably once the gate to the ancient ghetto of Cavaillon.

The general appearance of the interior resembles the synagogue in Carpentras, but there is a greater air of elegance and artistry. The woodwork and ironwork, created by master craftsmen of the area, are truly works of art. The interior of the Cavaillon synagogue has been compared to "a precious casket carved like a jewel."

Here too, as in Carpentras, the minister officiated from a lofty platform. The ladies prayed in a separate room, on the ground floor, and the "Chair of Elijah" is perched on a bracket high in a corner of the east wall. Since there is no Jewish community in Cavaillon, the synagogue is no longer in use. Travelers interested in visiting the synagogue may apply to the custodian, 5, rue Chabran. (*See* AVIGNON *and* CARPENTRAS)

The last representative of the ancient community, Achille Astruc, passed away in 1932. The influx from North Africa in 1962 bypassed Cavaillon. It did not attract the newcomers, as Carpentras did, probably because Cavaillon, although advertised as the melon capital of the world, has little economic viability.

CHALONS-SUR-MARNE (Marne)

Two streets, *Rue des Juifs* and *Rue de la Petite Juiverie* mark the location of the medieval Jewry destroyed by a massacre in 1321.

SYNAGOGUE, located on Rue Lochet was built in 1874. Tombstones in the Jewish cemetery date back to 1850 when the modern Jewish community was re-established.

CHALON-SUR-SAONE (Saône-et-Loire)

MUNICIPAL MUSEUM contains several ancient tombstones dating back to the medieval Jewish community of the 13th century.

SYNAGOGUE, 8 rue Gemini, was originally built in 1882 by M. Diloff as a gift to the community. Damaged during World War II, it was restored by M. Gerschel.

CHAMPIGNY-SUR-MARNE (Val-de-Marne)

SYNAGOGUE and COMMUNITY CENTRE, 19 avenue du Général de Gaulle. Established about 1920, it originally was Ashkenazi, but in recent years it was turned over to Jews of Turkish and North African origin and now uses the Sephardi ritual.

CHAMPSAC (Vienne)

A section of the town bears the name *La Judée* and marks the location of the medieval Jewish community.

CHARLEVILLE (Ardennes)

See SEDAN

CHARTRES (Eure-et-Loir)

CHARTRES CATHEDRAL possesses a magnificent window (sixth on the north aisle) which tells the oft-repeated story of the relationship between Judaism and Christianity. (*See* BOURGES)

RUE aux JUIFS may be found along the river, below the town market place. It is a reminder of the medieval Jewish community which ceased to exist in the thirteenth century.

CHATEAUDUN (Eure-et-Loire)

RUE MARCEL PROUST is named for the famous French writer who mentions the chateau five times in his great work "A la Recherche du temps perdu".

CHAUMONT (Haute-Marne)

RUE des JUIFS records the memory of the ancient Jewish section of the city.

CLERMONT-FERRAND (Puy-de-Dôme)

RUE FONTGIÈVE was the centre of the medieval Jewish community which disappeared at the end of the 13th century. Jews lived in Clermont before Christians did. One of their early synagogues was destroyed on Ascension Day in the year 576.

In the courtyard of the *Museum of History and Art* may be seen an ancient tombstone which came from the Jewish cemetery of Ennezat.

SYNAGOGUE, 20, rue des Quatre-Passeports, was built after the modern community was re-established in 1860.

COMMUNITY CENTRE, 6, rue Blatin, was dedicated on the 9th of February 1969 and was named in honor of the late Jules Isaac, historian and philosopher and founder of the Amitié Judéo-Chrétienne. It occupies the 1st floor of a building in the heart of the city and offers educational and social facilities to the community.

COLMAR (Haut-Rhin)

The Jewish community of Colmar has a long and bloody history. In 1285 the Jews were expelled from the city and their great rabbi, Meir of Rothenburg, was taken into captivity. The Emperor Rudolph of Habsburg demanded an enormous ransom. Rabbi Meir forbade his people to pay the ransom and he died in captivity. There were many massacres during the centuries. In 1830 Colmar was designated at the seat of the Jewish Consistory of Haur-Rhin.

COMMUNITY CENTRE is located at 3, rue de la Cigogne.

DAS JUDENLOCH, located outside the city, is the place where the Jews of Colmar were burnt at the stake in 1349.

JEWISH CEMETERY, on the Rue du Ladhof, dates from the first half of the nineteenth century.

SYNAGOGUE, 1 rue de la Cigogne, is the seat of the Chief Rabbi of the Consistory. It was built in 1843, and was restored after being almost completely destroyed in World War II.

UNTERLINDEN MUSEUM, 1 place d'Unterlinden, has on display several tombstones from the ancient Jewish cemetery. Among other items of Jewish interest are the famous gargoyle from the church at Rouffach depicting the Devil in the act of seizing a Jew clinging to his purse; the original of the gargoyle known as "La Truie aux Juifs" from the exterior of the Church of St.-Martin in Colmar, now replaced by a copy; and a small collection of medieval Jewish jewels found shortly before 1870 in a house on the rue des Juifs, which is today the rue Berthe-Molly.

CORBEIL-ESSONES (Seine-et-Oise)

RUE de la JUIVERIE, a small street, is the only vestige of the medieval community which was famous for its yeshivoth.

CREHANGE (Moselle)

This village near Metz has a large Jewish cemetery which was used by communities in the area for several centuries. The tombstones date back to the seventeenth century and there is one to a victim of the Nazis. The keys to the cemetery may be obtained from Mr. René Loeb, president of the Jewish community in the nearby village of Faulquemont. *See* FAULQUEMONT.

DIJON (Côte d'Or)

ARCHAEOLOGICAL MUSEUM, 5 rue du Dr. Maret, contains a collection of several dozen fragments of twelfth and thirteenth-century Jewish tombstones.

CHARTREUSE OF CHAMPMOL, near Dijon, is renowned for the *Well of Moses,* a famous sculptural group created by the fourteenth-century Dutch sculptor Claus Suter. Moses, an imposing, majestic figure with horned head, guards the well with five other prophets, David, Daniel, Isaiah, Jeremiah, and Zechariah. The whole group illustrates a contemporary Passion play in which Mary pleads with the prophets that her son be spared his agony. According to the play, the prophets are adamant and the sculptured angels weep at their verdict.

SYNAGOGUE and COMMUNITY CENTRE, 5, rue de la Synagogue, was dedicated in 1879. During the occupation in World War II the Germans used the synagogue as a warehouse. They spared the beautiful and impressive building but removed the original pews. For years after the end of the war plain board benches were used until the complete restoration of the synagogue.

DRAGUINAN (Var)

RUE LA JUIVERIE was the heart of the ghetto of this ancient community. There may be seen the remains of the imposing thirteenth-century synagogue. The façade, twenty-three meters in length, has four symmetrically placed doors. A strange-looking stone gargoyle on the face of the building is known locally as the "Head of Moses." For the first time in over five centuries, Draguinan once again has a Jewish community of about 25 families from North Africa. There is as yet no synagogue, but community headquarters is located at 3, rue des Endronnes.

DRANCY (Seine-Saint-Denis)

CONCENTRATION CAMP was located in this town on the outskirts of Paris from 1941 to 1944. Here were interned 120,000 people, mostly Jews, who were deported to Nazi extermination camps. Avenue Jean Jaures leads to an area southeast of the town, Fer de Cheval, where large, grim buildings were used to house the unfortunate victims. There is a monument to their memory erected by the municipality.

SYNAGOGUE, 8, boulevard Saint-Simon.

DUN-SUR-AURON (Cher)

RUE des JUIFS is a reminder of the ancient Jewish community which dated to the 6th century and which flourished until the 13th century.

ELBEUF (Seine-Maritime)

SYNAGOGUE, 36, rue du Général de Gaulle

ENGHIEN-LES-BAINS (Val-d'Oise)

SYNAGOGUE and COMMUNITY CENTRE, 47, rue Malleville

EPERNAY (Marne)

This community was organized after the Franco-Prussian war of 1870 by emigrés from Alsace-Lorraine.

SYNAGOGUE, 2, rue Placet.

EPINAL (Vosges)

Epinal was the birthplace of Emile Durkheim, the celebrated sociologist (1858-1917), who was the son of the first rabbi of the community.

SYNAGOGUE, 9, rue Charlet, was burnt by the Nazis in 1944 and reconstructed in 1958.

ERSTEIN (Bas-Rhin)

SYNAGOGUE, 7, rue du Vieux-Marché.

EVREUX (Eure)

Evreux was noted as an intellectual centre of Judaism in the 12th century. Traces of the medieval Jewry may be seen in the former *rue aux Juifs.*

SYNAGOGUE, Place Saint-Taurin.

FAULQUEMONT (Moselle)

Until Napoleon's arrival as a conqueror in 1791, Jews were forbidden to live in Faulquemont by the Bishop of Metz to whom the village belonged.

On the outskirts of Faulquemont there is a road known as the *Judenweg.* Jews from communities in the area were permitted to travel along this road to transport their dead to the Jewish cemetery in the nearby village of Crehange, thus bypassing Faulquemont which was Judenrein.

The small Jewish community has a synagogue. Information and the keys to the ancient cemetery at Crehange may be obtained from the president of the community, M. René Loeb, rue de Metz.

See CREHANGE

FONTAINEBLEAU (Seine-et-Marne)

SYNAGOGUE, 38, rue du Parc. The original synagogue, dedicated in 1857, was destroyed by the Germans in World War II. The beautiful Sevres porcelain chandelier presented by Napoleon III was destroyed at that time. The officers of SHAEF have presented a new chandelier to the synagogue, which was rebuilt on the site of the old one and dedicated in April 1965. The cost of rebuilding was financed by the Consistoire and a war damage payment by the French government.

FORBACH (Moselle)

SYNAGOGUE and COMMUNITY CENTRE, this community was founded in the 18th century by Jewish inhabitants of surrounding villages. The synagogue was constructed about 1830, and was restored in 1950.

FREJUS-SAINT-RAPHAEL (Var)

SYNAGOGUE, Villa Ariane, Rue de la Pinede.

GARCHES (Hauts-de-Seine)

Henri Bergson (1859-1941), renowned philosopher is buried in the cemetery in this village on the outskirts of Paris near Saint-Cloud.

GRASSE (Alpes-Maritimes)

Since the fifteenth century, when 600 Jewish families from Spain found refuge in Grasse and subsequently converted and were absorbed in the general population, there has been no Jewish community in Grasse. Since 1962 a new community of North African Jews has been established, numbering about forty families.

SYNAGOGUE, 6, rue Mougins-Roquefort, was established in 1965 through the efforts of Mr. Michel Gordon, a pharmaceutical technician who has lived in Grasse for many years. It is located in an ancient building, near the town's thirteenth century ghetto, now known as the Place aux Herbes.

GRANVILLE (Manche)

RUE de JUIFS marks the location of the medieval Jewry of Granville.

GRENOBLE (Isère)

In the fourteenth century Grenoble was an important Jewish community. From 1394 until the French Revolution no Jews lived there. Alsatian refugees in 1871 and North African repatriates in 1962 were the two most important elements in the creation of the modern community.

SYNAGOGUE and COMMUNITY CENTRE, 11, rue André-Maginot.

GURS (Basses-Pyrénées)

In 1939 a camp for Spanish Republican refugees was established in this village.

During World War II it was used as a camp for Jews. Many thousands were imprisoned in this concentration and later deported. The cemetery is large, impressive and well-kept.

HAGUENAU (Bas-Rhin)

SYNAGOGUE, Rue des Juifs. The synagogue, built in 1821, was sacked by the Germans in World War II and was restored in 1959. Two inscriptions attached to the wall of the courtyard are memorials to two former synagogues of the community. The first, in Hebrew, is the dedicatory tablet of the first synagogue of Haguenau, built in 1252. The second, found in 1953 on the site of a second synagogue 98, rue du Sel, says in Hebrew and German that "The House of Prayer, burnt in 1676 with the rest of the city, was reconstructed in 1683".

JEWISH CEMETERY, one of the most ancient in Alsace, contains more than 3000 graves.

HAYANGE (Moselle)

SYNAGOGUE, Rue de Verdun, was built in 1957 on the site of the former synagogue, which dated from 1854 and which had been destroyed by the Germans in World War II.

HYERES (Var)

SYNAGOGUE, Chemin de la Ritorte.

JOIGNY (Yonne)

RUE des JUIFS is a remnant of the medieval Jewish community, which was large and the home of the famous Tossafist Yomtov de Joigny.

JOUY-en-JOSAS (Seine-et-Oise)

Léon Blum, former Premier of France, is buried in the municipal cemetery. Frequent pilgrimages are made to his grave by French Socialists.

JUAN-LES-PINS (Alpes-Maritimes)

See ANTIBES

LABASTIDE-CLAIRENCE (Basses-Pyrénées)

ANCIENT JEWISH CEMETERY was used for several centuries by the Jewish communities of Bayonne and in the area. Many tombstones bear Portuguese inscriptions. The long disappeared Jewish community here was once famous for its doctors.

See BAYONNE

LA COURNEUVE (Seine-Saint-Denis)

SYNAGOGUE and COMMUNITY CENTRE, 2, place Alfred-de-Musset.

LA REOLE (Garonne)

RUE des JUIFS is a vestige of the medieval Jewish community.

LA ROCHELLE (Charente-Maritime)

RUE de la JUIVERIE recalls the medieval community which once flourished in La Rochelle.

LE HAVRE (Seine-Maritime)

SYNAGOGUE and COMMUNITY CENTRE, 38, rue Victor-Hugo. The synagogue, built after the modern community was established in 1850, was burnt during World War II and rebuilt in 1950.
RUE LEON-MAYER bears the name of a former Deputy Mayor of the city who was Minister of Merchant Marine in 1932.

LE MANS (Sarthe)

RUE de la JUIVERIE and MARCHÉ aux JUIFS recall the location of the medieval Jewish community, which was renowned for its famous rabbis.
SYNAGOGUE and COMMUNITY CENTRE, 2, boulevard Paixhans.

LENS (Pas-de-Calais)

SYNAGOGUE, 87, rue Casimir-Beugnet, was dedicated in 1931.

LES LILAS (Seine-Saint-Denis)

SYNAGOGUE and COMMUNITY CENTRE, 1, rue de la Croix-de-l'Epinette.

LE VENTOUX (Bouches-du-Rhône)

See MONT SEREIN

LE VERNET (Ariége)

In 1939 the French authorities chose this obscure village as a site for one of the camps to house the flood of Republican refugees from Spain. The camp population reached 17,000. During World War II the Vichy authorities used the camp as a place of internment for Jews, as well as some foreigners. Liberated in 1944, Le Vernet became for a short time a camp for German prisoners of war.
Today little is left of the concentration camp of Le Vernet, beyond a few huts which have become a rural slum. Near the highway, forty miles south of Toulouse, a gray concrete slab stands barely visible when the corn is high. In tarnished copper, the legend reads: *"To the foreigners dead far from their fatherlands 1939."*
Visitors may see the register of births and deaths in the village hall on the unpaved village square. There are listed the names, countries and ages of the dead, starting first with Spanish names, followed later by names such as Hugo Weil and Paul Dreyfus of Germany, and Aron Sanger of Poland. The cause of death was never listed.

LIBOURNE (Gironde)

SYNAGOGUE and COMMUNITY CENTRE, 17, rue Lamothe.

LILLE (Nord)

SYNAGOGUE, 5, rue Auguste-Angellier, was built in 1871 and uses the Ashkenazi ritual. There is a Sephardi chapel in the same building.
CHAPEL using the Polish ritual is located at 7, rue du Cours-Debout.

LIMAY (Seine-et-Oise)

In the church of this village near Mantes may be seen a thirteenth-century tombstone embedded in the wall above the baptismal font. It commemorates "Rabbi Meier, son of Rabbi Elijah—died on the third day of the portion Tazriah, the year 5003 [March 17, 1243]."

LIMOGES (Haute-Vienne)

The ancient community which disappeared centuries ago suffered many persecutions, particularly in 994 and 1010. Here lived Rabbi Joseph Tov Elem, pupil of Rashi and illustrious leader of medieval Judaism.

SYNAGOGUE and COMMUNITY CENTRE, 27, rue Pierre-Leroux, was dedicated in December 1967.

LISIEUX (Calvados)

RUE aux JUIFS recalls the site of the medieval Jewry of Lisieux.

LOUDUN (Vienne)

CHEMIN des JUIFS is a vestige of the medieval Jewish community of Loudun.
MUNICIPAL MUSEUM has on display some ancient medieval tombstones.

LUNEL (Hérault)

Two vestiges remain of a community renowned from the eleventh to the thirteenth century. Its academy was called the "dwelling place of the Torah," and the "sages of Lunel" were famed throughout the Jewish world.

ANCIENT CEMETERY was probably located in the vineyard known as Cimetière des Juifs.

ANCIENT SYNAGOGUE vestiges may be found in the former Hôtel de Bernis, on Rue Alphonse Ménard. The building, now used for commercial purposes, is the property of Élie Rouvière, who will be happy to welcome visitors.

LUNÉVILLE (Meurthe-et-Moselle)

ÉMILE ERCKMANN MONUMENT was erected to the memory of the writer who, in collaboration with Alexandre Chatrian, was the author of many books about life in Alsace. Though not a Jew, he depicted Jewish characters with sympathy and understanding, particularly old Rabbi David Sichel, who became part of the folklore of the region.

ABBÉ GRÉGOIRE MONUMENT, in the Place des Carmes, immortalizes the French priest (1750-1831) who waged a long and successful fight for Jewish emancipation. The adoption of the Act of Emancipation by the National Assembly on September 27, 1791, was due in large measure to his efforts. Abbé Grégoire carried his struggle for Jewish rights to other countries; he was in Venice when the gates of the ghetto were burned, and he fought for Jewish emancipation in Holland. The house in which this great friend of the Jews was born may be seen in Veho, with a commemorative tablet placed on it in 1931, the centenary of his death.

MONUMENT TO WORLD WAR II VICTIMS located in the local Jewish cemetery, lists 6 members of the community "killed on the field of honor" and 138 who "died in deportation." The monument is in the shape of a tower built exclusively of Jewish tombstones desecrated and overturned by vandals.

SYNAGOGUE, 5 rue Costara, is a modern structure which replaces the ancient synagogue built in 1785, which was destroyed by the Germans in World War II.

Among the founders of this congregation were the ancestors of the writer André Spire.

RUE ALFRED LEVY was named in honor of a native son who was Chief Rabbi of France from 1907-1919.

LYONS (Rhône)

JEWISH COMMUNITY CENTER, 3 rue de Turenne, was dedicated on January 27, 1961. Modern in design, it is part of the projected civic center, *Place de l'Étoile*, of Lyons. The project received financial aid and technical assistance from the American Jewish Joint Distribution Committee, the Conference on Jewish Material Claims against Germany, and the Fonds Social Juif Unifié, the major French-Jewish social-welfare agency.

The Center, a five-story building, houses the communal offices, an auditorium seating four hundred, a library, meeting rooms, arts and crafts workshops, and other facilities. It will serve as a cultural center for the large Jewish community and several smaller ones which have been established in the area.

The dedication of the Center marked the climax of years of effort to rebuild the Jewish community of Lyons, which had numbered 7,000 before World War II. Lyons had served as the principal center of the Jewish refugee underground during the occupation, and three quarters of the community had been lost through deportation. With the postwar influx of Jews from Central and Eastern Europe and North Africa, the community has grown to 21,000. The new community center will serve to unite these diverse elements.

ORT TRADE SCHOOL, 3 rue de l'Harmonie, provides technical training for young people.

RUE JUIVERIE behind the Church of St.-Paul, recalls the old Jewry. As early as the ninth century, the Jewish quarter was located at the foot of the "Fourvière" hill, which faces the chief synagogue. There is a record that there was a synagogue here as early as the year 800, but no trace is left of either the synagogue or the cemetery which was also located here.

SAINT PIERRE MUSEUM A medieval tombstone may be seen in Arcade XVI, exhibit No. 267.

RUE du GRAND RABBIN ABRAHAM BLOCH, named in memory of the Chief Rabbi of Lyon who was killed at Taintrux in 1914, borders the Jewish cemetery.

SYNAGOGUES

Consistorial Synagogue, 13, quai Tilsitt, was dedicated on June 23rd, 1864. Located on the left bank of the Saône River, facing the Church of St. George.

Sephardi Synagogue, 47, rue Montesquieu, founded in 1919.

Synagogue de la Duchère, le Plateau, dedicated in 1966.

"Strictly Orthodox" Synagogue, 87, rue de Sèze

MACON (Saône-et-Loire)

MUNICIPAL MUSEUM exhibits several tombstones dating 1260, 1304 and 1310, found on the site of the ancient cemetery at a place called Pontjeu (Pont des Juifs). The medieval community, which dated to the ninth century, disappeared about five centuries ago. The new community of some twenty families maintains a small chapel at 7, rue Saint-Jean, where services are conducted by members of the congregation.

MALEMORT-DU-COMTAT (Corrèze)

There are remains of a medieval synagogue which is a vestige of the community which was massacred in 1348 and never re-established. Inquire at the Mairie for directions.

MARSEILLES (Bouches-du-Rhône)

There have been Jews in Marseilles since time immemorial. In the fifth century the Bishop of Marseilles mounted a great campaign to convert the local Jews. The Radanites, Jewish merchant adventurers, sailed to the Far East in the ninth century out of Marseilles. Benjamin of Tudela in the twelfth century found a community of 300 families. At the end of the eighteenth century there were only 200 families.

The Jewish community of Marseilles underwent a phenomenal growth in less than ten years, jumping from about 15,000 in 1962 to 65,000 in 1970. The early years of the vast influx from Algeria and other countries of North Africa brought many economic, social and cultural problems to the community. Overnight the facilities of the community were taxed to the breaking point and vigorous measures had to be taken to meet the needs of a growing and viable Jewish community.

The American Joint Distribution Committee, using funds provided by the United Jewish Appeal, gave financial aid through OSE-FRANCE, the national Jewish medical organization; through ORT, the organization which provides technical training, and through the Fonds Social Juif Unifié, the national federation of Jewish welfare agencies. With the help of the JDC, the FSJU set up a social service structure which was able to cope with the situation.

Within a few years the situation was stabilized, the newcomers were absorbed into the economy and the communal structure was broadened to involve the new elements, overwhelmingly Sephardi, to give them a voice in the administration of communal affairs. Today Marseilles is the second largest Jewish community in France and looks to the future with hope and confidence.

EDMOND FLEG COMMUNITY CENTER, 4, impasse Dragon, was dedicated in December 1968. The center, named for the late French Jewish writer and humanist, cost $185,000 to construct and was built through the aid of JDC, FSJU, Central British Fund, the Conference on Jewish Material Claims Against Germany, and the French Ministries of Youth and Sports, and Family Affairs. The project was initiated in 1963 by the local B'nai B'rith chapter which received a grant from American chapters.

In recognition of the late Charles H. Jordan's deep interest in the reconstruction of the French Jewish community and the role of the JDC in developing the synagogue/centre building program, the Marseilles community dedicated the main auditorium in Mr. Jordan's name. Mr. Jordan was the Director-General of the JDC who met a tragic and mysterious death in Prague in August 1967.

It is expected that the municipality will change the name of the Impasse Dragon to rue Edmond Fleg.

GRAND ARENAS, several miles from Marseilles, is the transit camp through which thousands of immigrants have passed en route to Israel. Originally a French army installation, the French government made it available for use as an immigrant staging area shortly after the establishment of the State of Israel.

JEWISH CHILDREN'S HOME is located in an old château in the hills on the outskirts of Marseilles, overlooking the rocky seacoast.

KOSHER RESTAURANTS

Fleurette, Rue Vincent Scotto.

Community Centre, 4, impasse Dragon.

ORT TRADE SCHOOL, 3 rue des Forges, was built in 1961 to replace the old school, which functioned for some years on Boulevard Notre-Dame. With the tremendous influx of newcomers since 1956 it was found necessary to provide greater opportunities for technical training. The new building enabled the school to double its enrollment of students.

ROND POINT de la PLAGE on the seashore, presents a replica of Michelangelo's heroic statue of David.

SYNAGOGUES The beautiful Sephardic synagogue at 117 rue Breteuil is the seat of the Consistoire of Marseilles, whose authority extends over the Jewish communities of southern France. Dedicated in 1865, it suffered great destruction during the occupation. The Germans burned its prayer books and Torah Scrolls, and wrecked the front wall by bombing. The sexton risked his life to rescue a Sefer Torah, which was returned to the synagogue after liberation. The damage has been repaired and the synagogue restored.

"Strict Observance" synagogue, 73, rue Saint-Ferréol.

Synagogue at 10, impasse Dragon, houses two congregations, Ozer Dalim which is Sephardi, and Hachnassat Orchim, which is Ashkenazi. In Ozer Dalim are housed eight very old Sifrei Torah brought from Algeria, five from Tlemcen and three from Algiers.

There are about fifteen other synagogues in Marseilles, large and small, mostly Sephardi or using rituals derived from specific localities in North Africa.

Information on the synagogues, schools and other local Jewish institutions may be obtained at the office of the Consistoire Israélite des Bouches-du-Rhône, 119, rue Breteuil.

MARVEJOIS (Languedoc)

RUE de la JUIVERIE is a remnant of the picturesque Jewish quarter of medieval times.

MASSY (Essone)

SYNAGOGUE and COMMUNITY CENTRE, corner of avenue Saint-Marc and rue des Anglais. Also serves the adjoining Jewish community of ANTONY. Massy-Antony is typical of the new communities which have mushroomed in the suburbs of Paris since the influx of repatriates from North Africa in 1962. It is located five miles south of the Porte d'Orleans, the southern gateway to Paris.

The synagogue, financed by the Consistoire of Paris, was dedicated in 1964. The local authorities have been very helpful and have allocated a plot of land for a Jewish cemetery, which Paris does not have. The new community has achieved a harmonious working relationship between the various elements. In many ways Massy-Antony is considered a blueprint for the many new communities which have developed in the past few years.

STUDENTS HOUSE, 49, rue Croix-de-Berny, Antony.

MEAUX (Seine-et-Sarne)

SYNAGOGUE, 67, rue de Fublaines

MENDE (Lozere)

MEDIEVAL SYNAGOGUE located at 17, rue Notre-Dame, is now in process of restoration. It is believed that Jews settled in Mende even before the common era. In 1306 Philip the Fair ordered the expulsion of all Jews from his kingdom. In Mende, the beautiful synagogue was converted into a monastery by the local bishop. Since 1789 it has been used either as a dwelling place or storehouse.

Rue Notre-Dame was the heart of the local Jewry up to the fourteenth century, and it is surrounded by a warren of ancient alleyways, narrow and tortuous. The entrance to the ancient synagogue is a lofty, imposing gate, surmounted with an ogival arch in the Gothic style. The gate gives on to a courtyard surrounded by a gallery supported by granite columns.

A stairway leads down into a crypt which was once the site of the synagogue itself.

There is a white marble washtub which was probably used for ritual purification. In a recess in the wall there is a double rectangular cupboard which may have served as the Ark. There are no inscriptions to indicate that this was once a house of prayer but the site has been thoroughly authenticated.

An ancient tombstone of this community may be seen in the Lapidary Museum in Narbonne. Armand Lunel, the historian and novelist, himself a descendant of the eighteenth century Carpentras rabbi and poet, Jacob of Lunel, has headed the efforts for the restoration of this ancient synagogue of a community which was once one of the most famous in Languedoc.

METZ (Moselle)

Jewish history in Metz goes back to the 9th century. The great Rabbenu Gershom was born here in 960. In 1829 the Minister of the Interior authorized the establishment of a national rabbinical school in Metz, which was transferred to Paris in 1859.

METZ CATHEDRAL Two stained-glass windows created by Marc Chagall are installed in the north apse of the cathedral. Chagall was commissioned in 1958 by the Director of French Historical Monuments to prepare the sketches. A portion of one of these, the Prophet Jeremiah (Chagall used Biblical themes), was shown at the great retrospective Chagall exhibition at the Museum of Decorative Arts in Paris in 1959. He took no payment for his labor—he has never accepted money for work for the Church, even though these windows were commissioned by the French government for this thirteenth-century cathedral, which is a national historic monument. (*See* ASSY.)

SYNAGOGUE, 39, rue du Rabbin-Elie-Bloch. In 1964 the street was renamed in memory of Rabbi Elie Bloch of Poitiers, a youth movement rabbi who was active in the Resistance, and was deported and killed by the Nazis.

The synagogue was dedicated in 1951 replacing the former synagogue which was built in 1840 and was destroyed during the German occupation, and which too was built on the site of an earlier synagogue. This street was at one time the rue des Juifs.

EN JURUE, a street in the centre of the city, recalls the location of the medieval Jewish community.

PLACE GUSTAVE-KAHN in front of the synagogue, is named in honor of the famous poet who was a native son of Metz.

MUNICIPAL LIBRARY has a very large collection of documents on the history of the Jews of Metz and of the region.

MOLSHEIM (Bas-Rhin)

A Hebrew inscription of the 14th century may be seen on the *Klaus*, an ancient schoolhouse.

MONTAUBAN (Tarne-et-Garonne)

SYNAGOGUE and COMMUNITY CENTRE, 14, rue Sainte-Claire.

MONTAIGU (Vendée)

RUE de la JUIVERIE recalls the medieval Jewish section of Montaigu.

MONTE-CARLO (Principauté de Monaco)

SYNAGOGUE, 14, quai Antoine I.

MONTPELLIER (Hérault)

ANCIENT MIKVAH (Ritual Bath) dating to the eleventh century, may be seen in the cellar of the building at 1 rue de la Barallerie. The cellar is kept locked; interested travelers may obtain permission to enter by applying to the owner's representative, M. Forat, 1 boulevard Bonne-Nouvelle.

COMMUNITY CENTRE, 3, avenue de Lodève.

MEDICAL SCHOOL of the University of Montpellier has a large marble plaque in the lobby listing the names of "the Masters of the University of Medicine at Montpellier 1200-1220." The list is headed by the name of "le Rabbin Samuel Yehoudah ben Tibbon de Lunel 1199." This early physician and philosophical writer, better known as Samuel ben Judah ibn Tibbon, was born in Lunel about 1150 and died in Marseilles about 1230. He was an enthusiastic adherent of Maimonides. His father, famed as a translator and for his ethical will, taught him medicine. Jews contributed largely to the establishment of the Montpellier Medical School in the 12th century and Jacob ben Mahir was named Dean of the Faculty in the year 1300. Montpellier retained a tradition of hospitality to Jewish students for centuries.

SYNAGOGUE, 5, rue des Augustins. The modern community began to develop in 1940.

MONTRICHARD (Loir-et-Cher)

RUE de la JUIVERIE is a vestige of the medieval Jewish community of Montrichard.

MONTROUGE (Hauts-de-Seine)

SYNAGOGUE, 90, rue Gabriel-Péri. In 1966 the synagogue was dedicated in a prefabricated building on the site of the medieval Jewish cemetery.

MONT SEREIN

In the winter of 1966 an ecumenical chapel was dedicated on the Mont Serein heights of Le Ventoux in southeastern France near Marseilles. Represented in the service of dedication were the Catholic, Protestant, Orthodox and Jewish faiths. The chapel, far up on the skiing slopes, is dedicated to ecumenism and in petition for unity. It was conceived, financed and built by an association known as Amis du Mont Serein.

Chief Rabbi Salzer of Marseilles represented the Jewish community in the dedication service. The chapel is triangular in shape and points northward with its vortex toward the mountains. The walls are of native Vendoux stone and the ceiling and beams of local wood. The upper facade is one great window, 175 feet long and weighing three tons. The architect was the Abbé Roy, formerly of the Beaux Arts.

The Jewish chapel is on the lower level. Simple in design, it contains an ark and a Star of David as the sole decoration.

MULHOUSE (Haut-Rhin)

Mulhouse was the birthplace of Alfred Dreyfus (1859-1935) the central figure of the celebrated Dreyfus Affair.

HISTORICAL MUSEUM, 4, place Guillaume Tell, has a collection of Jewish ritual objects from the area.

RUE de JUIFS is a reminder of the medieval Jewish community of Mulhouse.

SYNAGOGUE, 19, rue de la Synagogue, was built in 1849 and was damaged during World War II. It was requisitioned by the municipal theatre and thus saved from complete destruction.

NANCY (Meurthe-et-Moselle)

Jews lived in Nancy in the Middle Ages. Here was born Andre Spire (1868-1966), famous poet who was one of the greatest Jewish literary figures in France.

JEWISH CEMETERY is located in the Preville cemetery, on Rue Raymond Poincaré.

JOAN OF ARC STATUE in Place Lafayette was the gift of the philanthropist and art patron Daniel Osiris to the city of Nancy which bestowed upon him the freedom of the city.

MUSÉE HISTORIQUE LORRAIN, 64, Grande Rue, contains an important Jewish collection, mostly obtained through the René Wiener legacy. The collection is exhibited in a special room and is arranged in three themes: the Torah, Jewish life from the cradle to the grave, and Jewish holidays and festivals.

OSIRIS CRÈCHE, another gift from Daniel Osiris to the city, is operated as a municipal institution for children.

SYNAGOGUE, 16 rue du Grand-Rabbin-Haguenauer, was consecrated in 1788, enlarged in 1841 and 1861, and new facade added in 1935. During the German occupation in World War II the synagogue was used as a hospital supply depot. Before their retreat the Germans prepared to destroy the building, but it was saved by the arrival of American troops.

RUE du GRAND-RABBIN-HAGUENAUER was named in honor of Chief Rabbi Paul Haguenauer of Nancy, who was deported by the Nazis in 1944 with 700 Jews of the community.

RUE du PROFESSEUR-HIPPOLYTE-BERNHEIM was named in honor of Prof. Hippolyte Bernheim (1837-1919), a famous native son of Nancy.

(For additional information about Daniel Osiris, *see* PARIS, Montmartre Cemetery.)

NANTERRE (Hauts-de-Seine)

SYNAGOGUE and COMMUNITY CENTRE, 35, rue du Chemin-de-Fer.

NANTES (Loire-Atlantique)

In the Middle Ages Nantes was the centre of the Jews of Brittany. The community was massacred in 1235 by the Crusaders.

RUE de la JUIVERIE is a reminder of the medieval Jewry.

SYNAGOGUE, 5, impasse Copernic, was founded in 1870.

NARBONNE (Aude)

LAPIDARY MUSEUM, Place Lamourguie, contains the oldest known Jewish inscription in France. It is found on a tombstone dating from the year 689, inscribed in Latin, but unmistakably Jewish because of the Menorah and the Hebrew words for "Peace unto Israel." It reads, "Here rest in peace, of blessed memory, the three children of Master Paratorus, son of the late Master Sapaudus, namely, Justus, Matrona and Dulciorella, who lived, Justus thirty years, Matrona twenty years, Dulciorella nine years. *Shalom al Yisroel.* They died in the second year of our lord King Egicanus."

Also to be seen are two medieval tombstones and a dedicatory inscription from a synagogue saying, in part, "The synagogue, Holy Ark, and east wall were finished in the month of Tebet, the year 5000 [1239 or 1240] ... we also hope to see the Temple rebuilt when God shall have ended our captivity."

Nothing else remains of a community which was founded in the fifth century, and about which, in the twelfth, Benjamin of Tudela wrote, "Famous sages and princes are found here."

RUE BENJAMIN CREMIEUX commemorates a native son who achieved fame as a novelist and playwright. Benjamin Cremieux (1888-1944) was born in the rue du Pont-des-Marchands.

NEUILLY-SUR-SEINE (Hauts-de-Seine)

FOYER "LE REFUGE", 19, boulevard de la Saussaye, was founded in 1866 by Coralie Cahen (1832-1899) as a home for delinquent children. Coralie Cahen acquired fame as an ambulance driver in the Franco-Prussian war of 1870-71. After the war she went to Germany to work for the repatriation of French prisoners of war. She was awarded the Legion of Honor in 1899. Today the Foyer is a home for young Jewish men and women. Student travellers can be accommodated in July.

SYNAGOGUE and COMMUNITY CENTRE, 12, rue Ancelle, was dedicated in 1878.

NICE (Alpes-Maritimes)

The first reference to the presence of Jews in Nice dates to the fourth century. In 1723 the King of Sardinia obliged the Jewish community to re-establish the ancient ghetto (Giudaria). This lasted until the end of the century when French republican troops took the city and broke the ghetto chains.

ANCIENT GHETTO was situated in the heart of the old city, where the elegant houses of the rue Benoit-Bunico (formerly rue Giutaru) are located. The house at 18 rue Benoit-Bunico is said to have been the ancient synagogue.

CHAGALL MEMORIAL is being built in huge Olivetti Park in Cimiez, a hilltop quarter of Nice. Near it is the Matisse Museum. This will make the famous Jewish artist the second living artist to have an entire museum dedicated to his work. Picasso was the first. The museum will be built to Chagall's specifications. He has already made over to the French Republic 67 works, part of a series known as the "Biblical Message", on which the artist has worked for the last 15 years. Chagall will donate more of his works, notably engravings and designs, and he will also design stained-glass windows and ceramics for the museum. Chagall has asked that the building be in three sections, one the museum proper; then a cultural centre for musical and theatrical performances; finally a place reserved for meditation. Chagall was made an honorary citizen of Nice in 1970.

See SAINT-PAUL-DE-VENCE.

COMMUNITY CENTRE is located at 1, rue de Voltaire.

HOME FOR THE AGED, located at La Colline, quartier Saint-Antoine, was recently enlarged to 140 beds.

MARTYRS' MEMORIAL The Jewish community has erected a striking memorial in the Jewish cemetery to "The Heroes of the Resistance" and "The Martyrs of Persecution". On pedestals against an inscribed wall are two urns—one, on the left, containing ashes of the victims; another, on the right, containing soap made from human fat in the Nazi extermination camps.

SECONDARY SCHOOL is located in the Villa Jacob, petite avenue du Prince-de-Galles, Cimiez. This is the second Jewish secondary school operated by the Alliance Israelite Universelle and was dedicated in October 1964.

SYNAGOGUES

Sephardi Synagogue, 7 rue Gustave-Deloye, was dedicated in 1886.

Ashkenazi Synagogue, 1 rue Blacas, was built in 1954 to replace an older house of worship on boulevard Dubouchage.

KOSHER RESTAURANTS

Carmel, 8 rue de France

Poznanski, 1, rue Longchamp

NÎMES (Gard)

ARCHAEOLOGICAL MUSEUM, Boulevard Amiral Courbet, contains an ancient tombstone which for many years served as the lintel of the doorway to the house at 8 Rue des Greffes. Some years ago the municipal authorities had it removed to the museum. The tombstone, probably from the eleventh century, commemorates "The wise and venerable Rabbi Isaac."

BERNARD LAZARE MONUMENT stands in the public gardens. The city of Nîmes erected this memorial to the great liberal publicist who distinguished himself in the Dreyfus Affair, on October 4th, 1908. It was destroyed by the Germans in 1939. The municipality restored this memorial to this distinguished native son of Nîmes.

MONT DUPLAN, a hill in the city of Nîmes, was the site of the earliest Jewish cemetery. It was given to the Jewish community by Bishop Frotaire in the eleventh century and was known in various periods as *Poium Judicum, Podium Judeum,* and *Puech Jusieu* (the hill of the Jews).

MUNICIPAL LIBRARY, 19 Grande Rue, contains a collection of eighteen ancient Hebrew manuscripts. It also houses the Salomon Reinach collection of books on archaeology, philology, and history.

RUE FRESQUE, formerly the **Rue de la Juiverie,** has at one end (on the Place du Marché) an ancient archway, once one of the entrances to the *carrière,* as the Jewries were called in the southern lands. The archway at the other end of the street has long disappeared.

SYNAGOGUE, 40, rue Roussy, follows the old Comtadin ritual used by the Jews of the Comtat Venaissin (the former Papal States which centered around Avignon)

It is interesting to note that, during the French Revolution, the Jews of Nîmes, inspired the spirit of the times, closed their synagogue.

Another great native son of Nîmes, to whom no memorial has been erected, was Adolphe Cremieux (1796-1880). A famous political figure, he was also active in Jewish communal life in France, having held office as President of the Consistoire Central and the Alliance Israelite Universelle. As a young lawyer in 1827 he refused to take the oath *more judaico* in the court of Nîmes. As Minister of Justice in the Government of National Defense in 1870, he was responsible for the emancipation of the Jews of Algeria.

NIORT (Deux-Sèvres)

RUE de la JUIVERIE marks the location of the medieval Jewish community of Niort.

NOGENT-SUR-MARNE (Seine)

COMMANDANT FRANCHETTI MONUMENT commemorates the Jewish officer who was killed there in 1871 while leading his troops in the Franco-Prussian War.

SYNAGOGUE, 46, rue des Héros-Nogentais.

NYONS (Drôme)

RUE JUIVERIE, a short street running between the place aux Herbes and the rue Colonel Barillon, is the actual medieval Jewry of Nyons. The five houses on each side of the street, mostly four stories in height, date back to fifteenth century and earlier.

A souvenir of the ancient community was found recently when a merchant on the place aux Herbes, which was once occupied by a cemetery, broke through the wall of his house. In doing so he found a mezzuzah in a niche in the wall, in perfect condition. This mezzuzah will form part of the collection of the Nyonsais Museum being created by Mr. Charles Samuel, local notary and historian. Mr. Samuel will be glad to show it to visitors.

OBERNAI (Bas-Rhin)

SYNAGOGUE, route de Selestat, was built in 1848.

ORLÉANS (Loiret)

The second (533) and the third (538) Council of Orléans protested vehemently against mixed marriages between Jews and Christians. The Synod of Orléans (541) took restrictive measures against Jewish owners of slaves. In the thirteenth century Orléans was a famous centre of Jewish learning.

RUE JOYE and RUE aux JUIFS are two reminders of the medieval Jewish community.

SYNAGOGUE and COMMUNITY CENTRE is located on the Place de la Salle-des-Fêtes.

PARDAILHAN (Hérault)

Early in 1960, a group of 89 Parisians, comprising twenty families, established an Israeli-type *kibbutz* in the abandoned hamlet of Pardailhan, twenty-five miles northeast of Béziers. Situated on a high plateau in the Cévennes mountains, cold, arid and rocky, Pardailhan presented every conceivable obstacle. In 1900 an active village of 500 inhabitants, Pardailhan had sunk to a population of 8 old people in 1960. As of 1961, the village once more is alive with the sounds of work and happy voices.

This is all the result of the eighteen months which Vincent Thibaut, a Parisian engineer, and his wife Thérèse spent in an Orthodox *kibbutz* in Israel. His experiences convinced Thibaut that "the *kibbutz* way of life plus Judaism" offered an answer to modern man's problems. He became a convert to Judaism, returned home, and organized the group which settled at Pardailhan. The *kibbutz* is run along strict Israeli lines. Although they have embraced Judaism they have rejected many of its practices and traditions since they regard Judaism as an ethical creed only.

PARIS (Seine)

There is historical evidence that Jews lived in this area under the Romans who occupied Lutetia which became Paris in the fourth century. Under the Roman Empire Jews from Judaea and the Mediterranean colonies were at liberty to practice their religion. The Franks, pagan conquerors from the other side of the Rhine conquered Gaul in the fifth century, bringing about the fall of the Roman domination. Their chief, Clovis, was coverted to Christianity and from that time on began the vicissitudes of the Jews of Paris.

Persecuted and restricted, massacred and expelled from time to time, nevertheless the Jews of Paris managed to achieve intermittent fame, between periods of persecution. The talmudical academies of Paris were known throughout Europe, when they were permitted to exist. The kings Philip-Augustus, Saint-Louis, Philip IV le Bel, and Charles VI le Fou bear the odious distinction of being remembered by Jews as the chief instigators of the medieval genocide.

In the twelfth century, that indefatigable traveler Benjamin of Tudela wrote of Paris as *Ha-ir Hagedolah*, "that Great City." Through the centuries it has remained a great and unique city, to Jew and Christian alike. Because of long enforced absences of the Jewish community, it may lack Jewish architectural monuments, but Paris contains innumerable relics of the Jewish past.

ALLIANCE ISRAÉLITE UNIVERSELLE, 45, rue de la Bruyère, is headquarters of an organization, founded in 1860, which is responsible for the maintenance of almost 150 schools in France and various countries of the Mediterranean area. The Alliance Library has 100,000 volumes of Judaica. It was founded in 1868 and had as its nucleus the libraries of Salomon Munk, Bernard Lazare, Lazard Isidore, Zadok Kahn and Senior Sachs.

AMERICAN JOINT DISTRIBUTION COMMITTEE, 23, rue la Boetie, is the French headquarters of this famous Jewish relief organization founded in 1914.

BELLEVILLE SECTION in the east of Paris, is more North African than French. About 10,000 Jews have crowded into the ancient houses of this quarter. A walk through the streets is an exciting experience. Poor though it is, life is intense and pulsating, the people friendly. This section has always been a haven for newcomers, once it received Jews from Eastern Europe.

SARAH BERNHARDT MONUMENT, on the south side of the Place Malesherbes, was erected in 1926. The sculpture, by F. Sicard, represents the great actress in her famous role of Phèdre.

Paris has many other reminders of the Divine Sarah: a plaque on her birthplace at 5 Rue de l'École-de-Médecine, which reads, "Sarah Bernhardt, glory of our theatre, was born in this house on October 25, 1844"; her grave in Père-Lachaise; and finally the *Square Sarah Bernhardt*. For decades the Théâtre Sarah Bernhardt was a landmark on the Place du Châtelet. In 1965 her name disappeared from the marquee. It was the last of the city's eighty playhouses to be named for a star. It is now the Theatre of the City of Paris.

NISSIM de CAMONDO MUSEUM, 63 rue de Monceau, was founded by Count Moïse de Camondo in memory of his son Nissim, killed in aerial combat September 5, 1917. An admirer and collector of French art of the eighteenth century, Count de Camondo presented his house, built in 1910, and his art collection, to the Union Centrale des Arts Décoratifs in 1935, to form an annex of the Museum of Decorative Arts.

CARNAVALET MUSEUM, 23 rue de Sévigné, has on display a number of personal souvenirs of the great actress Rachel. These are the remains of a larger collection, much of which was lost during the evacuation of the Museum in World War II.

In the courtyard may be seen three Hebrew tombstones dating from the thirteenth century.

CLUNY MUSEUM, Place Paul Painlevé. The Strauss-Rothschild collection of Jewish ritual objects has been the property of this museum for many years. Once displayed in a "Jewish Room," the collection was removed during World War II, when the Museum was closed. It remained in storage until 1957, when about a hundred priceless objects were loaned to the Jewish Museum in New York for its tenth-anniversary exhibition. A few pieces may be seen in the Cluny Museum today; it is hoped that the entire collection will soon be exhibited again. Private arrangements to see the collection may be made with the museum administration.

Adjoining the Cluny Museum are the remains of the thermae, the ancient Roman baths. Attached to the walls are a series of slabs, thirteenth-century tombstones which once covered the graves of medieval French Jews in a cemetery now buried under the foundations of the great publishing house of Hachette.

In remarkably clear Hebrew lettering, the oldest records the memory of "Solomon, son of the scholar Rabbi Judah, who departed for the Garden of Eden the year 1230; may his soul be bound in the bundle of life."

CONSISTOIRE OF PARIS, 17, rue Saint-Georges, is the headquarters of the Jewish community of Paris, known officially as the Association Consistoriale Israelite de Paris. It was created by an ordinance of May 25, 1844, which fixed the composition of the consistories. The law on the separation of church and state, December 9, 1905, changed the functions of the consistoire. It became the representative organ of French Jewry and was consulted by the public authorities whenever a legislative or administrative measure affected the Jewish community.

CEMETERIES Why, then, in writing of the "City of Light," as it is known to those who love it, should so much attention be paid to its cemeteries? The place of ancient Jewish cemeteries in this work is obvious. But need so much be said of modern cemeteries? Surely this is inconsistent in writing of a city known for its beauty and gaiety and *joie de vivre*. However, there is no inconsistency; the great cemeteries are designed for the use of the living as well as the dead. Travel guides, from *Baedeker* a century ago to the *Guide Bleu* today, have paid detailed attention to them.

In the cemeteries lie many of the great men and women of France. The French are a sentimental people and treasure the memories of their past. Jews, we hope, are no less sentimental. There are no specifically modern Jewish cemeteries in Paris. Sectarian cemeteries are forbidden under the French law of 1905 on separation of Church and State. This has resulted in the dispersion of the Jewish dead, although, in truth, their dispersion in the cemeteries of Paris began long before 1905.

This guide, while concerned primarily with the resting places of Jewish celebrities, has included some non-Jewish friends, such as Émile Zola, and in one case, the tomb of a notorious enemy of the Jews, Édouard Drumont. It is good to remember.

Ashkenazi Cemetery is located at Montrouge, between 94 and 96 rue Gabriel Péri south of the Porte d'Orléans. It was opened in April 1785, and the last burial was in September 1809. Originally purchased by Cerf Berr, a leading Jew of his day, it was presented by him to the community in 1792. Permission to visit may be obtained at the office of the Paris Consistoire, 17 rue St.-Georges.

Bagneux Cemetery, Avenue Marx-Dormoy. Monument to the "foreign Jewish volunteers who died for France" was dedicated in 1948. The monument is the work of the famous Jewish sculptor N. Rapoport. It rests on the common grave of seventy Jewish heroes of the last war.

Montmartre Cemetery, entrance on the Avenue Rachel.

3rd Division. Daniel Osiris (d. 1907), philanthropist and art patron, born in Bordeaux in 1825. A replica of Michelangelo's *Moses* which he commissioned before his death, marks his grave. Osiris built synagogues in Paris and a number of other places, presented the Château de Malmaison to the State, gave statues and fountains to a number of French cities, established scientific prizes, and restored many famous tombs in Père-Lachaise cemetery.

9th Division. Jacques Offenbach (d. 1880), the composer, lies under a rich marble monument, decorated with a lyre and bronze palm.

19th Division. Émile Zola (d. 1902), writer and valiant fighter in the Dreyfus Affair. Originally buried here, Zola's ashes were transferred to the Panthéon on June 4, 1908.

27th Division. Heinrich Heine (d. 1856) and his wife, Mathilde (d. 1883) lie here. This is probably the most celebrated grave in Paris. On the tombstone is a harp entwined by a garland of flowers, and under it the names: "Heinrich Heine—Frau Heine." A marble slab has the following engraved on it: "To the Memory of Heine—liberal-minded Vienna." Above the tombstone is a marble bust by the Danish sculptor Hasselriis, commissioned by Empress Elizabeth of Austria. Occasionally pebbles are placed on the grave by visitors, following an old custom; others leave their cards.

Jewish Section. Jacques François Fromental Élie Halévy (d. 1862), the composer, member of the French Academy. The marble statue by Duret was erected by the French government.

Montparnasse Cemetery, Boulevard Edgar-Quinet.

2nd Division. Abbé Henri Grégoire (d. 1831), fighter for Jewish rights in France. Through his efforts, the National Assembly, during the Revolution, decreed the emancipation of French Jewry. He was one of the first of the clergy to swear fealty to the new constitution in 1790. On his death the Archbishop of Paris refused his remains Christian burial, as he had declined to retract his oath.

5th Division. Adolphe Crémieux (d. 1880), French statesman, born in Nîmes in 1796, defender of the rights of his fellow-Jews. Through the "Crémieux Law" he was instrumental in extending rights of French citizenship to the Jews of Algeria.

9th Division. General Louis Binger (d. 1936), explorer of the mouth of the Niger, which gave the Ivory Coast to France.

22nd Division. Catulle Mendès (d. 1909), noted writer and critic.

28th Division. Colonel Alfred Dreyfus (d. 1935), central figure of the Dreyfus Affair.

30th Division. Jewish cemetery. Gustave Kahn (d. 1936), one of the great names of symbolist poetry.

Passy Cemetery, Place du Trocadéro, entrance on Avenue Georges-Mandel. Near the terrace on the Avenue Paul-Doumer, is the tomb of Dinah Félix (d. 1909) actress, sister of the great Rachel. In the southeast corner of the cemetery will be found the grave of the writer Tristan Bernard (d. 1947).

On the terrace dominating the Place du Trocadéro is the tomb of Georges Mandel, former Minister of the Interior, who was assassinated in 1944.

The *Avenue Georges-Mandel* (since 1944) is one of the most attractive streets in Paris, has a central island, and is bordered with fine homes and mansions, all with front gardens.

Père-Lachaise Cemetery, Boulevard de Ménilmontant, is the largest cemetery in Paris, the most frequently visited, and one of the most famous in the world. The following tombs may be of interest to the Jewish traveler.

4th Division. Achille Fould (d. 1867), Minister of Finance under Napoleon III.

7th Division (known as the Jewish cemetery). There may be seen the tomb of the great tragedian Rachel (d. 1858), the mausoleum of the Rothschild family, the strange tomb of Jacob Robles (d. 1893) totally unknown, born in Port-au-Prince, and tombs of distinguished members of the Jewish community.

The striking mausoleum of the unhappy lovers, Héloïse and Abelard, is located in this section. Originally erected at the Abbey of Paraclet in 1779, it was transferred to Paris during the Revolution, and finally moved to Père-Lachaise in 1817.

25th Division. Adolphe Philippe d'Ennery (d. 1898), dramatist, who founded the D'Ennery Museum of Oriental Art.

29th Division. Karl Ludwig Börne (d. 1837), German liberal writer and politician. The grave is marked by a bust of Börne and bas-relief by David d'Angers, representing France and Germany extending their hands under the blessing of Freedom.

44th Division. Sarah Bernhardt (d. 1923), the greatest actress of her time.

74th Division. Rosa Bonheur (d. 1899), famous animal painter.

89th Division. Oscar Wilde (d. 1900), with a controversial monument by Sir Jacob Epstein. The statue representing an angel of death was completed by Epstein in 1912. It was found indecent and hidden under a tarpaulin for some years. It was quietly uncovered shortly after World War I began and there were no incidents.

94th Division. Édouard Drumont (d. 1917), notorious anti-Semitic writer, who played a prominent role in the Dreyfus Affair.

97th Division. Jean-Richard Bloch (d. 1947) well known writer. Also in this section are two memorials to the memory of French dead in deportation camps. The monument to 10,500 known to have died at Mauthausen concentration camp was unveiled on May 5, 1951; a twenty-ton granite monument, it depicts a cadaverous inmate carrying a heavy stone. The other is dedicated to the martyrs of Neuengamme concentration camp.

Sephardi Cemetery, 44 rue de Flandres, was purchased through the efforts of Jacob-Rodrigue Péreire, a native of Bordeaux, in 1780. The first burial was on March

8, 1780, and the cemetery was closed in February 1810. Péreire, famous for his work on behalf of the deaf-mutes of France, was buried in September 1780, exhumed in 1876 and transported to the family mausoleum in Montmartre Cemetery. His sons became the great railroad builders of France. Salomon Perpignan, founder of the Royal Free School of Design, was buried here in 1767.

The cemetery is small, about thirty graves, and neglected. To reach it one must pass through the yard of an old coach house and through a gate. Permission to visit may be obtained at the office of the Paris Consistoire, 17 rue St.-Georges.

CHURCH OF ST. JEAN-ST. FRANCOIS since about 1800 was the center of the cult of the Billettes, the original desecration of the host legend of 1290. For centuries the "miraculous" wafer was harbored in the Church of St. Jean-en-Greve. When the church was destroyed around 1800, a number of the relics found a refuge at the Church of St. Jean-St. François. Until the middle of 1969 a group of eight tapestries running the length of the nave were on exhibit, "relating the scenes of the crime of the Jew Jonathas, perpetrated on Easter Sunday, 1290." There was also a painting outside the Virgin's chapel, depicting nine gruesome acts of Jonathas. The church had on the door, in white letters on a black background, an invitation "to pray, adore, expiate, in reparation of the outrages done to the Living Jesus in the Host".

The cult of the Billettes has apparently come to an end. At the command of the Catholic hierarchy of Paris, the tapestries and other artifacts depicting the medieval legend of the desecration of the Host were removed from the church. The hierarchy had to overcome opposition to removal of the relics. As late as 1954, a monsignor of the Paris diocese excitedly announced the discovery by a Catholic scholar of "decisive, irrefutable" authentication of the crime of the Jew Jonathas. Upon examination it was found utterly without foundation, and the Church authorities finally put to rest a vile slander for which so many Jews had paid with their lives through the centuries.

CHURCH OF SAINT-ROCH has a Chapel of the Deportees, where ashes from the crematoria of ten concentration camps are preserved. Special ceremonies are held there from time to time.

D'ENNERY MUSEUM, 59 avenue Foch, was founded by Adolphe Philippe d'Ennery (1811-1899) the famous dramatist. He willed his home and his great collection of Oriental art to the State, which established the museum bearing his name.

FLEA MARKET, Avenue de la Porte-de-Clignancourt, consists of a great collection of booths, where an enormous assortment of articles is offered for sale. Some of the booth owners are Jews, and Yiddish will be helpful in striking a bargain.

FONDS SOCIAL JUIF UNIFIÉ (F.S.J.U.), 19, rue de Teheran, is the national Jewish social-welfare organization of France. It was founded in 1949 to co-ordinate the social, cultural and education work being done by a multitude of organizations. It has played the dominant role in the of the great new Jewish community which has grown up since World War II and particularly since the great influx from North Africa in 1962. The F.S.J.U. derives its funds from monies raised by the Appel Unifié Juif de France (United Jewish Appeal of France), which raises funds both for local needs in France and for Israel.

FOYER des ISRAÉLITES RÉFUGIÉS, 5, rue de Varize, founded in 1934 by Mme. Tauba Lewine, for Jewish refugees, was installed in its present quarters after World War II, with the financial aid of the government, the United Nations and private gifts. With sixty-four beds, it is a home for aged Jews, and also maintains a canteen for non-residents, a loan fund, a social service department and a library of 4000 books in French and Russian.

HALÉVY, FATHER AND SON No. 26, place Dauphin, was the home of Ludovic Halévy (1834-1908) who died there. He was famous as the librettist for Jacques

Offenbach, the composer. His son, Daniel Halévy (1872-1962) lived and died in the house. He acquired fame as a left-wing sociologist.

HEINRICH HEINE More than a century after his death, Heine's memory is still as fresh as his lyrics in the city he loved above all others. Although he wrote

Keine Messe wird man singen
Keinen Kadosch wird man sagen
(No mass will be sung
No Kaddish will be said)

he has not been forgotten. His grave in Montmartre Cemetery is still visited by thousands. *Rue Henri Heine* bears his name in Gallicized form. And for those who are interested, his progress through Paris can be traced in the houses in which he lived during his troubled and tragic career.

The ancient furnished rooming house at 52, rue de Vaugirard, was his home upon his arrival in Paris in 1831. From 1832-1834 he lived on the second floor of 38, rue de l'Echiquier, on the court. In 1834 he moved to 3, Cité Bergère, where he lived on the third floor. Then at 25, rue Bleue, from 1840-1841. He moved to 21, rue des Grands-Augustins, in 1841, to a house over three centuries old. At 50, rue d'Amsterdam, from 1848-1854, third floor back, he lay on his "mattress grave" for years, coughing out his life, and there he wrote his lovely "Hebrew Melodies". Until a few years ago, when it was demolished to make way for a housing development, it was possible to see the ancient hotel at 3, avenue Matignon, where he came in November 1854, and where, on the fifth floor, he drew his last painful breath on February 17th, 1857. The site is marked by a tablet. The poet made his summer residence at 64, rue de Passy, and it was there that his wife, Mathilde, died in 1884.

THEODOR HERZL MEMORIAL PLAQUE was placed on the Hôtel de Castille, 37 rue Cambon, in May 1961. It reads, "Here in 1895, Theodor Herzl, founder of the Zionist movement, wrote *The Jewish State*, a prophetic book which foretold the resurrection of the State of Israel."

BARONESS CLARA de HIRSCH STATUE may be seen in the Square Boucicaut, in the rear of the Bon Marché department store. It forms part of a group of two figures, representing two great benefactresses of the city of Paris. The other statue is that of Mme. Boucicaut, founder of the Boucicaut Hospital. Baroness de Hirsch shared in the many benefactions of her husband, Baron Maurice de Hirsch, and after his death she carried them on. She was responsible for the building of the Institute of Biological Chemistry in 1900. The inscription on the monument reads: "Madame de Hirsch, 1833-1899—Madame Boucicaut, 1816-1887. Two women of good will symbolizing kindness and charity. Monument erected by the City of Paris."

LUCIEN de HIRSCH SCHOOL is a Jewish primary school at 70 avenue Secrétan. On the school wall is a plaque in memory of former teachers and pupils of Jewish schools of Paris who died in active service or were martyred by the Nazis. On the night of July 24, 1944, all the children and teachers of this school—107 persons—were taken by the Gestapo and deported to Auschwitz. One teacher, Mlle. Bloch, survived and attended the unveiling ceremony in March 1954.

HOSTEL FOR JEWISH STUDENTS (LE TOIT FAMILIAL), 9 rue Guy Patin, through most of the year is occupied by students registered in the University and other educational institutions in Paris. From July to October, it will accommodate students visiting Paris.

HÔTEL des JUIFS, beautiful old sixteenth-century house, still stands in the rear of the courtyard of 20 rue Ferdinand Duval, formerly the Rue des Juifs. It is a relic of the old Jewry around Rue St.-Denis and Rue de Rivoli, composed of Jews from Alsace, Lorraine, and Germany who came to Paris in the eighteenth century.

IMPRESSIONISM MUSEUM, Terrasse du Jeu de Paume, was established in 1947 as a branch of the Louvre to house French art of the second half of the nineteenth century. In it there are two Camondo rooms, which contain part of the valuable collection of modern art presented by Count Moïse de Camondo to the Louvre in 1911.

INSTITUTE OF BIOLOGICAL CHEMISTRY, Rue du Dr.-Roux, facing the Pasteur Institute, was built in 1900 through the generosity of Baroness Clara de Hirsch. A statue to her memory may be seen in the Square Boucicaut.

INSTITUTE OF OPHTHALMOLOGY, 29 avenue Mathurin-Moreau, erected in 1905, was founded by Baron Edmond de Rothschild.

INTERNATIONAL INSTITUTE FOR HEBRAIC STUDIES, 20 rue Servandoni, is France's first school for the training of liberal rabbis and educators. It was established in late 1956. The Institute was founded by the World Union of Progressive Judaism.

INSTITUTE OF PHYSICO-CHEMICAL BIOLOGY, Rue Pierre Curie, was founded in 1931 by Baron Edmond de Rothschild. The Institute was erected at a cost of fifteen million francs. It is part of a group of scientific institutions in the area.

LES INVALIDES The marble plaque commemorating the war service of 12,000 foreign Jews who joined the French army as volunteers during World War I was restored, in February 1955, to its place in the vast barracks square of the Invalides. First affixed in 1932, the plaque was removed by the Germans in 1940 and exhibited as a war trophy in Berlin.

JEWISH STUDENTS' CLUB (CENTRE HILLEL), 11 rue de Vaugirard, is the gathering place of Jewish students in Paris.

JEWISH STUDENTS' UNION, 6 rue Lalande, is the headquarters of the Jewish students' organization, Union des Etudiants Juifs de France.

JEWISH YOUTH CENTER, 4 rue Notre Dame-des-Victoires. The first community center for youth in France set up on the American pattern was opened November 1955. The four-story building, purchased with a grant from the Ford Foundation, contains meeting rooms, game rooms, snack bar, classrooms and social hall. Original sponsor was the Joint Distribution Committee, which provided the necessary furniture and equipment in conjunction with the Conference on Jewish Material Claims against Germany.

KAHN GARDENS, Quai du Quatre-Septembre, at the Pont de St.-Cloud, created about 1900 by the banker Albert Kahn and acquired in 1936 by the Department of the Seine. These superb gardens have rare trees and plants, and an authentic Japanese house in a Japanese setting. There is also a photograph collection founded by Mr. Kahn, which is composed of 72,000 pictures of horticultural interest from all parts of the world.

KOSHER RESTAURANTS
A la Bonne Bouchée, 1 rue des Hospitalières Saint Gervais (Jewish quarter)
Community Centre, 19, boulevard Poisonnière
Eden, 36 boulevard Bonne-Nouvelle
Chez Sadia, 8, rue Cadet (Oriental)
Sabrinna, 5, boulevard Montmartre
Le Foyer Israélite, 5 rue de Médicis (simple meals, patronized by Jewish students)
THE LOUVRE

The Louvre's Department of Oriental Antiquities is a vast collection which contains relics of the great civilizations of Biblical times. Babylon, Assyria, Egypt, and other contemporaries of ancient Israel tell vivid stories through their stones and artifacts. It is in the Palestine Room of the Sully Crypt, however, that the Jewish traveler will find a series of objects which are a direct link with the Israel of the Bible.

The famous Moabite stone, a black basalt stele erected in 842 B.C.E. by Mesha, King of Moab, tells of his victory over Ahab, King of Israel. The thirty-four lines of the Phoenician inscription constitute the earliest record of any Hebrew dialect. It is the most valuable monument for the study of ancient Palestinian history.

Also to be seen are a series of articles excavated at Jericho by Garstang; the great sarcophagus of Queen Helena of Adiabene, who embraced Judaism with her family, who endowed the Temple with lavish gifts, whose sons built the Tomb of the Kings, and whose grandsons died in the defense of Jerusalem; and a number of ancient Jewish ossuaries. Also to be seen there are doors from the burial chambers of the Tomb of the Kings in Jerusalem, carvings from the Tomb of the Judges, and one of the jars which contained portions of the Dead Sea Scrolls.

In the Art and Furniture Department of the Louvre may be seen the Adolphe de Rothschild Room, containing the collection of antique furniture and jewelry given by Baron Adolphe de Rothschild in 1900; and the three Camondo Rooms, housing the collection presented by Count Moïse de Camondo.

In the Department of Paintings there are a number of works of Jewish interest. In the Van Dyck Room, Peter Paul Rubens is represented by "The Sacrifice of Abraham," "Abraham and Melchizedec," and "The Family of Lot Fleeing Sodom." In the Holland Gallery, Rembrandt's "Bathsheba at the Bath" may be seen. In the Croy Room is "Sarah Presenting Hagar to Abraham," by Van der Werff. In Room 3 of the Salles de la Colonnade (XVIII-Century Art), there is a portrait of John Julius Angerstein and his wife. Angerstein, one of the founders of Lloyd's, created a great art collection, which was the nucleus of the National Gallery in London. (*See* GREAT BRITAIN, *section on* LONDON.)

The Louvre has had many Jewish benefactors. One of the greatest gifts was Baron Edmond de Rothschild's bequest of his collection of 30,000 engravings and 3,000 drawings. In 1954, the Louvre held an exhibition at the Orangerie in which 200 masterpieces from the collection were exhibited. The exhibit included engravings by Leonardo da Vinci and the earliest known woodcut, dating from the fourteenth century. Subsequent public exhibitions were held in 1959, 1960, and 1961. While the Edmond de Rothschild Collection is not on public view, private arrangements to see it may be made with the museum administration.

Of particular interest is the room dedicated to the work of Chaim Soutine, who died in Paris during the German occupation. Soutine, a native of Russia, led a hard life and died in misery, leaving behind a great legacy of artistic works which hark back to his *shtetl* origin. A section of the lintel of the facade of the second century synagogue in Bar'am in Israel is to be seen. It bears the Hebrew inscription, "May there be peace in this place, and in all places in Israel. This lintel was made by Jose the Levite. Blessings upon his works. Shalom."

LUXEMBOURG GARDENS   There may be seen, to the south of the fountain, a statue of Scheurer-Kestner, Christian senator for Alsace, who played a vital part in the defense of Captain Dreyfus. Appropriately, his statue is flanked by figures of Justice and Truth.

MAZARINE LIBRARY, 23 quai de Conti, affiliated with the Institute of France, was founded in 1643. It contains a large collection of books and manuscripts dealing with the ancient Jewish history of France, Italy, and Spain.

MARCEL PROUST
The famous writer spent his infancy (1890-1900) at 9, boulevard Malherbes in the bourgeois home of his parents. After the death of his mother, toward the end of 1906, he went to live at 102, boulevard Haussmann in a house belonging to his aunt. When he was forced in 1919 to leave his apartment on the boulevard Haussmann, he moved to an apartment in a building at 8 bis rue Laurent-Pichat. It was placed at his disposal by the actress Rejane who owned the building. Proust was a friend of Jacques Porel, son of the actress. He lived there several months. The building is marked with a   plaque. Late in 1919 Proust moved to 44, rue Hamelin, in an apartment on the fifth floor, thinking it was a temporary dwelling. He lived here until his death in 1922, surrounded by the great mass of manuscripts of his life's work.

The building is marked with a plaque. As long as his health permitted Proust went each year to visit the tomb of his Jewish ancestors Weil, his mother's family, in the small Jewish cemetery on the rue du Repos.

MEDICAL SCHOOL, Rue des Saints - Pères, bears a plaque of Maimonides on the facade.

MEMORIAL TO DEPORTEES of the 11th Arrondissement was unveiled in June 1965 by M. Jean Sainteny, French Minister for Veterans. A plaque on the Japy secondary school in the Arrondissement reads "to the memory of the men, women and children of the 11th Arrondissement who were assembled here on August 2, 1941 and July 16, 1942, whose destination was Auschwitz because of their Jewish religion."

MEMORIAL TO THE DEPORTEES OF FRANCE A moving memorial to the estimated two hundred thousand French of all faiths, who were deported during World War II to Nazi extermination camps, was dedicated in April 1962 behind Notre Dame. It was paid for by public subscription and is located across the street from the cathedral, on the easternmost tip of the Ile de la Cité. The monument is an underground crypt of extraordinary architectural inspiration and of great physical and spiritual beauty. It is entered through a garden, by two staircases that descend to an open court. At one side of the court is a narrow, tall doorway into the crypt. Inside are a series of small rooms with phrases from French poets picked into the wall like carved graffiti. A brass disc on one of the floors bears the inscription, "They went to the other end of the earth and did not return". From the central room, behind a grating that guards a symbolic sarcophagus, there extends a long narrow corridor with a single distant bare lamp at its end and the black corridor walls are studded with rows of small glass-headed nails, perhaps two hundred thousand of them. On one of the walls is the simple, unsigned phrase, "Pardon. Do not forget". The architect of this unforgettable memorial crypt is Georges-Henri Pingusson.

MEMORIAL TO THE UNKNOWN JEWISH MARTYR, 17 rue Geoffroy-l'Asnier. This impressive and moving memorial to the Jewish victims of Nazism was dedicated in October 1956. It brought to fruition an idea initiated by Isaac Schneersohn, the founder and president of the Center of Contemporary Jewish Documentation, which was created in the underground period of 1943, in France. The idea took hold and received support in France and abroad. Great financial assistance for the project was given by the Conference on Jewish Material Claims against Germany, and contributions came from various countries. The Paris City Council presented the site, located in the Jewish quarter, the "Pletzel."

The memorial is a four-story building in a large paved courtyard, with granite walls along two sides. The front of the building is a blank stone wall, bearing inscriptions in Hebrew and French.

A huge bronze cylinder in the center of the courtyard is shaped to recall a crematorium urn. It bears the names of the death camps and the Warsaw ghetto. Two flights down lead to the Hall of Remembrance, where six chests, built into the walls, contain the books in which are inscribed the names of thousands of martyrs.

The crypt contains a symbolic tomb of black marble, shaped as a Star of David. In the tomb are ashes of martyrs collected from various death camps and the Warsaw ghetto.

The memorial also contains the archives and library of the Center of Contemporary Jewish Documentation and a museum.

MERKAZ de MONTMARTRE, 12 rue des Saules. Youth center dedicated May 1953, aimed primarily at countering the activities of a Catholic mission in the Montmartre district which proselytizes among the youth of North African origin who have settled in the area. It houses kindergarten, club, Talmud Torah, and hostel for thirty university students.

ADAM MICKIEWICZ MUSEUM, 6 quai d'Orléans, is devoted to the memory of

Poland's national poet, particularly the years he spent in France. Mickiewicz was Poland's greatest champion of Jewish rights. His wife was reputed to have been of Jewish descent. He was the author of *Pan Tadeusz*, in which he referred warmly to the patriotism of Polish Jewry. The house in which he wrote *Pan Tadeusz* may be seen at 63 rue de Seine. A bronze monument to Mickiewicz is located on the Place de l'Alma. (*See* POLAND, *section on* CRACOW)

MINISTRY OF THE INTERIOR, Place Beauvau. In the court of honor there is a plaque in memory of Georges Mandel, Minister of the Interior in 1940, who was assassinated by French fascists in 1944.

MONT VALÉRIEN, on the outskirts of Paris, is crowned by a large fort built in 1830. During the German occupation in World War II, Mont Valérien was the site of many executions of groups of hostages. In the first large group of sixty-six hostages shot on December 19, 1941, there were forty-eight Jews. They were later buried in Père-Lachaise Cemetery. Services in their memory are held from time to time, and wreaths are placed on the execution site. Every year de Gaulle visited the "Crypt of the Resistance," where other martyrs are buried, to commemorate the anniversary of the liberation of Paris on June 18, 1944. Plans are now underway to erect a suitable memorial on Mont Valérien. From 1941 to 1944 a total of 1,500 to 1,800 martyrs of the resistance were killed here by the Germans.

MUSEUM OF DECORATIVE ARTS, 17 rue de Rivoli, has a tapestry in the great gallery on the third floor which, in five panels, depicts the story of Esther. It was executed in 1738-1740 by Jean François de Troy.

MUSEUM OF FRENCH MONUMENTS, Place du Trocadéro, has an excellent reproduction in Salle XI of the beautiful "Synagogue Defeated" of the Cathedral of Strasbourg.

MUSEUM OF JEWISH ART, 12 rue de Saules, was founded in 1948. It has on exhibition collections of Jewish ritual art, models and reproductions of synagogues from the twelfth century to the present, and the work of Jewish artists.

NATIONAL LIBRARY, 58 rue de Richelieu, has a collection of Hebrew manuscripts and a large Judaica library. A special staff is assigned to handle Hebrew and Jewish books. A group of Jewish specialists is preparing a catalogue to cover the large Jewish collection ranging from the sixteenth to the twentieth century.

NATIONAL MUSEUM OF MODERN ART, Avenue Président-Wilson, has a room devoted to the work of Marc Chagall, established in 1950. In the museum may be seen the work of other famous Jewish artists, including Pissarro, Modigliani, Kisling, and Pascin.

NORMAL SCHOOL OF THE ALLIANCE ISRAÉLITE UNIVERSELLE, 59 rue d'Auteuil, is a teachers' training school for young Sephardic Jews, mostly of North African origin.

NOTRE DAME CATHEDRAL On either side of the central portal, in tall niches, are figures representing the Church Triumphant and Synagogue Defeated. The Church wears, with queenly pride, the crown she has taken from her enemy. The Synagogue is blinded by a coiling serpent, her staff is shattered, and from her hand slips the Tablet of the Law.

The great northern rose window, dating to about the year 1250, contains some eighty subjects from the Old Testament. In the innermost circle of medallions are sixteen prophets, in the second circle are thirty-two kings. In the outermost circle are thirty-two patriarchs and high priests.

THE OPERA, Place de l'Opéra, has a bust of Ida Rubinstein, the great actress, in the museum and library. It is located in the vestibule on the first floor. (Enter from Rue Auber on Place Charles-Garnier.) The actress is represented in the role of Scheherazade. A bust of Giacomo Meyerbeer, the composer, may also be seen here. The new ceiling of the Paris Opera painted by Marc Chagall was unveiled on

September 23rd, 1964. The great artist accepted the commission to paint a new ceiling in July 1962 from André Malraux, French Minister of Culture. Chagall conceived of his work as a "mirror" to reflect "in a bouquet of dreams the creation of the performers and composers." He has taken the floral image literally. The circular ceiling painting of some 600 square feet is divided into five petal-like sections, each with its dominant color, white, red, blue, yellow and green. The painting is filled with many figures and symbols suggested by ballet and opera, but not literally drawn from them. "There is nothing precise in it," Chagall has said. "One cannot be precise and still be true". The decision to repaint the Paris Opera ceiling caused a long debate in French artistic circles. However, Marc Chagall's monumental painting has received universal acclaim.

ORT (ORGANIZATION FOR REHABILITATION THROUGH TRAINING), 10 Villa d'Eylau, is the French headquarters of this organization.

ORT VOCATIONAL TRAINING CENTER, 4 bis rue des Rosiers, is in the heart of the Pletzel, the Jewish section of Paris.

ORT TRADE SCHOOL, 43-45 rue Raspail, Montreuil, was opened in September 1948. The ceremony was attended by ex-Premier Léon Blum and David Dubinsky, president of the International Ladies' Garment Workers Union, which financed the building of the school.

THE PANTHÉON, Place du Panthéon, has several items of Jewish interest. In the main rotunda there are two large marble plaques. One is in memory of the "writers who died for France 1914-1918," and there are eight or nine names of Jewish writers among those listed. The other says, "Here homage was rendered on July 2, 1949, to the writers who died for France during the war of 1939-1945." Most of the thirty Jewish names inscribed are of writers who perished in Nazi concentration camps or were murdered in France. Among those listed are the names of Marguerite Aron, Victor Basch, J. Lévi-Valensi, Georges Mandel, Irene Nemirowski, Georges Politzer and Jean Wurmser.

In the crypt may be seen the tomb of Émile Zola, great writer and leading figure in the Dreyfus Affair, whose ashes were transferred to the Panthéon on June 4, 1908 from Montmartre Cemetery, where he was buried in 1902.

The philosopher Henri Bergson is memorialized on the walls of the Panthéon.

PLACE de COLOMBIE To the southeast of the Place de Colombie, near the Porte de la Muette, is located the last piece of the ancient royal domain of la Muette. The kings of France maintained a hunting lodge here in the seventeenth and eighteenth centuries. Baron Henri de Rothschild, doctor and playwright, built a modern mansion on the remains of the royal property. The house and extensive grounds (about five and a half acres) have, since 1948, been considered international territory and are the property of the European Organization for Economic Co-operation. It contains a collection of beautiful ancient tapestries and six modern tapestries by Lurçat. Visitors are welcome.

PLACE D'ISRAËL was named in an impressive ceremony in March 1960. The Embassy of Israel is located nearby at 143 avenue Wagram.

PLACE du PALAIS-ROYAL has a white marble monument of Alfred de Musset by Antonin Mercié, presented to the city of Paris in 1906 by Daniel Osiris. Mercié executed the replica of Michelangelo's *Moses* which rests on the grave of Osiris in the Montmartre Cemetery.

PLACE NAMES

Paris has many streets, avenues and squares named for Jews. The following listing, not complete, giving names and dates, will give some idea of the Jewish influence on the topography of Paris, which has been most generous in recognizing the contributions of her Jewish sons and daughters, native and adopted.

Quai André-Citroën (1958)
Place Albert-Kahn (1966)
Rue du Capitaine-Olchanski (1907)
Rue Catulle-Mendes (1926)
Rue Crémieux (1897)
Rue Darmesteter (1932)
Avenue Docteur-Arnold-Netter (1962)
Place du Docteur-Hayem (1935)
Rue Edouard-Colonne (1912)
Avenue Erlanger (1908)
Villa Eugene-Manuel (1929)
Rue Furtado-Heine (1897)
Square Georges-Cain (1925)
Rue Georges-de-Porto-Riche (1932)
Avenue Georges-Mandel (1945)
Rue Halévy (1864)
Place Henri-Bergson (1946)
Rue Henri-Heine (1866)
Rue de l'Interne-Loeb (1927)

Place d'Israël (1960)
Rue Jacques-Bingen (1946)
Rue Jacques-Mawas (1926)
Place Léon-Blum (1957)
Rue Léon-Maurice-Nordmann (1944)
Rue Maurice-Loewy (1935)
Rue Mendelssohn (1932)
Rue Meyerbeer (1867)
Rue Michel-Bréal (1932)
Rue Paul-Strauss (1911)
Boulevard et place Péreire (1862)
Rue Pierre-Masse (1961)
Rue Pissarro (1932)
Avenue Rachel (1899)
Rue Rosa-Bonheur (1900)
Rue Spinoza (1885)
Place Tristan-Bernard (1953)
Place Victor-Basch (1944)

THE PLETZEL, located in the Fourth District (*Arrondissement*) is a conglomeration of narrow streets and alleys centering around the *Rue des Rosiers*. The houses are ancient and dilapidated, with walls leaning at crazy angles. Once only Yiddish was heard on the streets of the quarter and Yiddish signs advertised kosher restaurants, butchers, delicatessens and bakeries. The influx of North African Jews has changed this and they mingle in harmony with the older settlers from Eastern Europe. Their signs are in French rather than Yiddish, their kosher food seems more exotic.

The name Pletzel is probably derived from the Yiddish (German) *platz* which is so similar to the French *place* and simply means the "Little Place." It is a term of affection for an area East Europeans have inhabited for many years. Actually, the Pletzel is located on the site of the thirteenth-century ghetto of Paris, known as the *Juiverie*. In 1281 a large building in the vicinity was bought from the Templars by a Jew, Dieudonne de Brie. The Jews had their own flour mills, cemeteries, and synagogues. For hundreds of years, no Jews lived in this section until Jews from Eastern Europe began to settle here again in the early years of this century.

There are no ancient Jewish monuments to be seen here. During World War II, the Jews were removed, and after the liberation some returned and fought legal actions for homes and shops. Soon they were joined by others, and the area became a center of Jewish life again.

The Pletzel has one large and seven small synagogues. The large synagogue on the Rue Pavée was dynamited by the Germans on Yom Kippur 1940. It has been restored and is of modern-style architecture. It has been declared a National Monument by the Government.

There is a well-known Jewish bookshop, reopened by Madame Rottenberg-Libermann after the war. The area has its own Chassidic rabbi, Reb Itzhakl, a descendant of the great Rabbi Elimelech. He gives board and lodging to the poor, is reputed to eat one meal a day, and spends his nights reciting psalms.

RABBINICAL SEMINARY (Séminaire Israélite de France), 9 rue Vaquelin, is located in the Latin quarter, a few minutes walk from the Sorbonne. It was founded in Metz in 1829 and was moved to Paris in 1883, when its present building was consecrated. The seminary provides living quarters for most of the students and has a synagogue seating 200. Most of the present students are Sephardim from North Africa.

The library of the seminary consists of about 20,000 volumes and also many manuscripts. This library was enriched by the legacy of Albert Cohn, a great bibliophile. Many of its treasures were lost when they were transferred to Frankfort-am-Main during the German occupation. Others were destroyed but some priceless Hebrew manuscripts and incunabula were saved.

A plaque on the entrance commemorates former rabbis and pupils who were deported by the Nazis or who died fighting in the resistance.

RACHEL STATUE may be seen in the vestibule of the Théâtre Français, on the Place du Palais Royal. She is shown here in the role of Phèdre and represents Tragedy. The great actress, born Elisa Rachel Félix, became the toast of Paris in 1838, at the age of seventeen. She was the reigning queen of the city until her premature death at thirty-seven. She died a loyal daughter of her people with the "Shema" on her lips and was buried with great ceremony in the Père-Lachaise Cemetery. Avenue Rachel records her memory, and visitors may still see the magnificent mansion in which she lived and died, at 9 rue de Birague, now occupied by the New York School of Fine and Applied Art. A collection of her personal mementoes is on display at the Carnavalet Museum.

ROTHSCHILD BANK, largest private bank in France, is located at 19 rue Laffitte, where it was established by the founder, Baron James de Rothschild in 1835. The bank also includes the buildings at 21, 23, and 25 rue Laffitte. After 150 years, the private banking firm now run by Barons Guy, Elie and Alain de Rothschild is to become a public company, an organization believed to be better suited to modern conditions. The headquarters of the bank are to be demolished and a new building will rise on the same spot, which will no longer house "Messieurs de Rothschild Frères" but an incorporated company.

ROTHSCHILD FOUNDATION, 76, rue de Picpus. This foundation was created in 1852 and later turned over to the Consistoire Central of Paris to serve ill and aged Jews. At this time it maintains a hospital and old people's home of 540 beds at 76, rue de Picpus (south side of the Picpus cemetery). It also maintains a home for aged or incurable women at Villeneuve-Saint-Denis (120 beds), and also several other institutions, including a hospital for defective children at 41, rue Joseph de Maistre. Members of the Rothschild family still head the foundation and sit on its board.

RUE du FAUBOURG-ST.-HONORÉ, long the most fashionable street in Paris, has many Jewish associations, particularly of the Rothschild family, whose homes dotted this elegant street for many years.

No. 33, now occupied by the Cercle Interallié, a diplomatic club, is the former residence of Baron Henri de Rothschild. It was built in 1714 and purchased in 1856 by Baron Nathaniel de Rothschild, where he began to assemble his celebrated collection of Greuze paintings. (A completely preserved eighteenth-century *salon* may be seen on the main floor.)

No. 35 became the property of Émile and Isaac Péreire, the railroad builders, in 1855, and was occupied by members of the family.

No. 41, built in 1835, was later acquired by Baron Edmond de Rothschild and was his residence for many years. Now occupied by the American Documentation Center of the United States Embassy. (Library open to visitors.)

No. 45 is today the home and private business headquarters of the present Baron Edmond de Rothschild.

No. 49 was purchased in 1860 for one million francs by Émile Péreire.

In the vicinity, other historic houses may be seen. At *23 Avenue de Marigny* is another former Rothschild mansion. It was built by Baron Gustave de Rothschild and was designed by Alfred Philibert Aldrophe, the architect of the Great Synagogue on the Rue de la Victoire. On the capstone over the front door may be seen a carved figure of the Wandering Jew.

At *19 avenue Foch* is the residence of Baroness Édouard de Rothschild, widowed mother of the present head of the French House of Rothschild. The number plate is not blue on white like the others on the street, but blue and gold, the Rothschild colors.

The Artists' House, founded by Baron Salomon de Rothschild, is located at his former residence at *11 rue Berryer.* President Doumer was assassinated in this house on May 6, 1932, while opening a bazaar. Part of the extensive gardens of the house is now a playground for children, the gift of Baroness Salomon de Rothschild. Balzac, the great French writer, died on August 20, 1850, in a small house once located in the garden. This is marked by a plaque at *25 rue Balzac,* on one side of the property.

SYNAGOGUES

This is only a partial listing of the synagogues of Paris, of which there are about fifty. The following are the best known and most historic.

Temple Nazareth, 15, rue Notre-Dame-de-Nazareth was dedicated in March 1852. It was built on the site of an older synagogue which was demolished in 1848. It was the first synagogue in Paris to use an organ. It was the seat of the Chief Rabbi of France and the Chief Rabbi of Paris until the dedication of the synagogue on the rue de la Victoire in September 1874. Chief Rabbi Joseph Saks, rabbi of the synagogue, was deported to his death with his wife in World War II. In the peristyle there are plaques recording the names of congregants who disappeared in deportation.

Temple Tournelles, 21 bis, rue de Tournelles, is the second largest synagogue in Paris, seating 1500. It was built before the Franco-Prussian war of 1870, was burnt during the Commune and was reconstructed by the architect Varcollier and rededicated in 1876. It followed the Ashkenazi ritual until 1958, when the Consistory turned it over for the use of Jews from North Africa and now follows the Sephardi ritual. During World War II the rabbi of the congregation, Nathan Levy, was deported to his death with his wife from their refuge in Auvergne.

Temple Victoire, 44 rue la Victoire, is considered the "cathedral" synagogue of Paris and indeed, of all France. It is also sometimes called the "Rothschild" synagogue. Consecrated on the 9th of September 1874, it is an imposing structure, built in neo-Romanesque style. It was designed by Alfred-Philibert Aldrophe, one of the foremost French architects of the period, who was then chief architect of the city of Paris. The building is the property of the city of Paris and was built with funds provided by the city and by the Consistoire Israelite of Paris. The interior is impressive, with a huge silver menorah standing before the Ark and cadelabra hanging from the lofty Roman arches. On the right of the Ark is the chair reserved for the Chief Rabbi of France and on the left that of the Chief Rabbi of Paris. In the courtyard are marble tablets memorializing the victims of two wars. On February 27th, 1949, Vincent Auriol, President of the Republic presided at the ceremony dedicating the memorial to the martyrs of World War II. After extensive renovation, the synagogue was rededicated on April 20th, 1967.

Oratoire Vauquelin, 9, rue Vauquelin, is the chapel of the Seminaire Israélite de France. It was founded in 1880 and seats 250. The Director of the Seminary, Chief Rabbi Henri Schilli is the rabbi of the congregation, and services are conducted by students at the Seminary.

Synagogue Rachi, 6, rue Ambroise-Thomas, was founded in 1936 and it houses an Ashkenazi congregation. It seats 450.

Temple Berith-Shalom, 18, rue Saint-Lazare, seating 700, serves a congregation the majority of whom originated in Salonika and Constantinople.

Temple Buffault, 28-30, rue Buffault, was until recent years the only Sephardi synagogue to be a part of the Consistoire of Paris, to which it affiliated in 1906. It was consecrated on September 3rd, 1877, and can seat about 1500. The building was constructed through the help of the philanthropist Daniel Osiris, who was the largest contributor to the building fund. Mathieu Wolf, rabbi of the congregation, was deported to his death in World War II.

Temple Don Isaac Abravanel, 84, rue de la Rquette, was designed by architects Heaume and Persitz, and consecrated on April 1st, 1962. It houses a Sephardi congregation and has seating capacity of 600. To the left of the entrance to the synagogue is a memorial to the memory of Sephardi volunteers of two wars.

Temple Chasseloup-Laubat, 14, rue Chasseloup-Laubat, is the only synagogue on the Left Bank. It was a gift of the late Baron Edmond de Rothschild to the Consistoire.

Temple de Montmartre, 13, rue Saint-Isaure, was also the gift of the late Baron Edmond de Rothschild for the use of Russian Jews settled in the Eighteenth Arrondissement.

Temple de l'Union Liberale Israelite, 24, rue Copernic, has since 1906 housed a liberal congregation. It is also the office of the Union Libéral Israélite, the organization of French Liberal Judaism.

UNIVERSITY CITY, Boulevard Jourdan, is a great residential center for students in Paris. In addition to the buildings housing students from various countries, there is an International House, the gift of John D. Rockefeller, Jr., in 1935.

The Fondation Deutsch de la Meurthe, erected in 1921, was the first house built and is considered the mother of the University City. It is now the administrative center. Since then thirty other buildings have been erected.

Émile Deutsch de la Meurthe was among the first to sponsor the creation of a University City in Paris. A monument to his memory has been erected in the garden. It depicts him in bas-relief and bears the following inscription: "Émile Deutsch de la Méurthe, who, with a magnanimous gift, made it possible to realize the idea of the University City of Paris." The banker David David-Weill also helped greatly in its creation.

VAUX de CERNAY is a lovely valley in the suburbs which has long been popular among Parisian artists. The valley contains the Abbey of Vaux de Cernay, which was founded in 1128. Suppressed during the Revolution, it fell into ruins. Baroness Nathaniel de Rothschild acquired the property and restored the ruins. Her grandson, Baron Henri de Rothschild, carried on her work and preserved the natural beauty of this area which has inspired the work of such painters as Corot, Pelouse, and Français.

VÉLODROME d'HIVER (Palais des Sports), 6 boulevard de Grenelle, the Parisian sports arena, has a plaque commemorating the 30,000 Jews of Paris who were rounded up on July 16, 1942, and after several days' imprisonment, were deported to Nazi concentration camps.

WORLD JEWISH CONGRESS, 78, avenue Champs-Elysées, is French headquarters for this organization. The World Jewish Congress is concerned with the defense of the rights of Jewish individuals and communities.

PAU (Basses-Pyrénées)

SYNAGOGUE, 8, rue des Trois-Frères-Bernadac, was built about 1850.

PAVILLONS-SOUS-BOIS (Seine-Saint-Denis)

SECONDARY SCHOOL, 35-37, allée Robert-Estienne, was opened by the Alliance Israelite Universelle in September 1963.

PERIGUEUX (Dordogne)

The Jews were expelled from the city in 1302. A new community was created when the Jewish community of Strasbourg was evacuated to Dordogne in 1939. After World War II when the Jews of Alsace returned to their homes, a few remained. These were reinforced in 1962 by newcomers from North Africa.

RUE JUDAIQUE and RUE MOSAIQUE recall the medieval Jewry of Perigueux.
SYNAGOGUE and COMMUNITY CENTRE, 2, rue Paul-Louis-Courrier (parc Gamenson) was dedicated in December 1967.

PERPIGNAN (Pyrénées-Orientales)

Perpignan was a great centre of Jewish learning in medieval times. The community was renowned for its physicians, astronomers and rabbis, among them Don Vidal Solomon (1249-1306), one of the greatest Talmudists of his time.
SYNAGOGUE and COMMUNITY CENTRE, 10, rue Jean-Payra.

PEYREHORADE (Basses-Pyrénées)

There are three cemeteries here, two of them very old. The oldest, located in the centre of the village on rue des Chapons, was dedicated Jan. 6th, 1628. The second, dating to 1737, faces the Home for the Aged and bears a commemorative plaque. The third is still in use.
See **BAYONNE**

PÉZENAS (Hérault)

RUE JUIVERIE is the location of the medieval Jewry of Pézenas.

QUIMPER (Sud-Finisterre)

Max Jacob, the poet, was born in this small town in Brittany in 1876, in the rue du Parc, in the building in which the Café de Bretagne is located. His father was a tailor and antique dealer.
See **SAINT-BENOIT-SUR-LOIRE**

PITHIVIERS (Loiret)

A monument to Jewish victims of Nazi persecution in France was dedicated in June 1957, in this small town near Orléans, on the site of the concentration point established by the Germans in May 1941. From here tens of thousands of Jews were deported to extermination camps in Eastern Europe. An urn containing ashes from Auschwitz was bricked into the monument by a former death camp inmate. The French government contributed funds toward the erection of the memorial.

RHEIMS (Marne)

RHEIMS CATHEDRAL has two figures on its walls representing the Synagogue Defeated, one above the left portal on the west front and the other above the portal of the south front.
SYNAGOGUE, 49, rue Clovis, is over 100 years old. Rheims had a Jewish community of 350 families when it was built. Just before World War II there were 200 Jewish families; 100 families were still in the city when the Germans arrived in 1941. The Nazis rounded up all the Jews in a single day and deported them all. Only one of the deported families survived and returned to the city. A plaque on the outside wall of the synagogue lists the families who never returned. There are now about 150 families in the new community.
WAR MEMORIAL is located on the Boulevard Général-Leclerc. It takes the form of a sunken garden, in the center of which is an urn containing ashes from concentration camps. One panel of the memorial is dedicated to "Civilian Victims of Nazi Repression," and most of the names listed are Jewish.

RIQUEWIHR (Haut-Rhin)

The *Judenhof* recalls the medieval Jewry of this city.

ROANNE (Loire)

SYNAGOGUE and COMMUNITY CENTRE, 9, rue Beaulieu. The Jewish community of Roanne was established in 1933 by a group of Jews of Polish origin.

ROSENWILLER (Bas-Rhin)

This village has a celebrated Jewish cemetery dating to the fifteenth century, one of the oldest and largest in Alsace. It contains the tomb of Cerf Berr, the "prevot" of the Jews of Alsace, who died in 1794.

ROUEN (Seine-Maritime)

The record of Jewish presence in Rouen goes back to the Roman era. In the medieval era the Jews of England looked to Rouen as a centre of Jewish learning.

AVENUE des JUIFS recalls the site of the Jewry of the Middle Ages.

MUNICIPAL LIBRARY, 3 rue de la Bibliothèque, contains a number of Hebrew manuscripts.

ROUEN CATHEDRAL has a window in the farthest right bay of the apse which tells the story of the new alliance, the Christian version of the relationship between Judaism and Christianity. (*See BOURGES*)

SYNAGOGUE and COMMUNITY CENTRE, 55, rue des Bons-Enfants, was reconstructed in modern style in 1950. The original synagogue on this site was built in 1860 and was destroyed in World War II.

RUEIL-MALMAISON (Seine-et-Oise)

The *Château of Malmaison* was the residence of the Empress Josephine. It had fallen into decay when it was acquired in 1896 by the philanthropist Daniel Osiris, who restored it and presented it to the State. It was accepted by the French government in a decree signed by President Émile Loubet on January 16, 1904.

Malmaison is now a national monument, visited by thousands every year. A pavilion, erected since the restoration of the château, is dedicated to Daniel Osiris. It bears an inscription recording his great service in saving Malmaison for the nation.

SAINT-BENOIT-SUR-LOIRE (Loire)

BASILICA OF ST. BENOIT contains a plaque which reads, "March 5, 1944—Max Jacob, penitent poet of St.-Benoit, died in the camp at Drancy." This memorializes the poet and artist who was a central figure and outstanding influence in avant-garde art and literature in the early years of this century. He numbered among his friends Modigliani, Picasso and Lipchitz. Born a Breton Jew, he was baptized a Catholic on February 18, 1915, with Picasso as godfather, after seeing an apparition of Christ on his studio wall. Jacob spent fifteen years in St.-Benoit. He wore the yellow badge with pride during the occupation and was taken to Drancy from the Basilica.

FLEURY CEMETERY where Jacob is buried has a simple tombstone reading "Max Jacob—1876-1944." The Association of Friends of Max Jacob plans to erect a more imposing memorial and to place a plaque on the house in which he last lived.

RUE MAX-JACOB was formerly the Rue de la Poste.

See **QUIMPER**

SAINT-DENIS (Seine-Saint-Denis)

SYNAGOGUE and COMMUNITY CENTRE, 43, rue Lesne.

SAINT-DIÉ (Vosges)

A monument to the memory of Chief Rabbi Abraham Bloch, a French army chaplain of World War I, was unveiled in September 1958 on the former battlefield of St.-Dié. It is located in the section near the Col d'Anozel, at the foot of the Kemberg Mountain. This monument replaced the first memorial, which had been destroyed by the Germans during World War II.

Abraham Bloch, Chief Rabbi of Lyon and Chaplain of the Fourteenth French Army Corps, was killed on the battlefield on August 29, 1914, one month after he had left his home to join the army. At the moment of his death he was holding the crucifix to the lips of a dying Catholic soldier. Dressed in ecclesiastical robe and hat, he was hit by a bursting shell, which killed him instantly.

Rabbi Bloch had served as a rabbi in Algeria, where two squares, one in Constantine and the other in Algiers, were named "Place du Grand Rabbin Abraham Bloch." The first monument to his memory was dedicated in September 1934 in an impressive ceremony attended by high officials of the government and the army.

SYNAGOGUE, 16, rue Dauphine, was built in 1963 to replace the former synagogue destroyed by the Germans in 1944.

SAINT-ÉTIENNE (Loire)

SYNAGOGUE and COMMUNITY CENTRE, 34, rue d'Arcole, was built in 1880 and restored in 1966.

SAINT-FLORENTIN (Vaucluse)

RUE des JUIFS is a reminder of the medieval Jewry of Saint-Florentin.

SAINT-FONS-VENISSIEUX (Rhône)

This community was founded in 1920 by Jews from Algeria and Morocco.
SYNAGOGUE, 3, place Durel.
YOUTH CENTRE, 20, allée Picard.

SAINT-GERMAIN-EN LAYE (Seine)

RUE REINACH commemorates the three Reinach brothers, Joseph, Salomon and Theodore, famous archaeologists and literary men. A plaque marks the house in which they were born on this street.

MUNICIPAL MUSEUM has on exhibit the oldest Jewish tombstone in France, the stone of Auch. With Latin inscription it has on it a shofar, menorah and *lulav*. Also in this museum may be seen a tombstone, of the medieval period, found between Mantes and Lemay. The inscription is entirely Hebrew and it records the memory of Benia, the daughter of a certain Salomon.

SAINT-REMY-DE-PROVENCE (Bouche-du-Rhône)

Remains of the ancient cemetery is the only vestige of the medieval community. Inquire at the *mairie*.

SARCELLES (Val-d'Oise)

Sarcelles is one of the dormitory towns north of Paris, which have grown up since 1962. The Jewish community now numbers 5,000.

MUNICIPAL LIBRARY was named in memory of Anna Langfus in 1966. Mme. Langfus, who lived in Sarcelles, was awarded the Goncourt literary prize in November 1962 for her novel on Jewish life in occupied Poland, "Les Bagages de Sable".

SYNAGOGUE AND COMMUNITY CENTRE, 74, avenue Paul-Valery, was dedicated in April 1964.

SAINT-PAUL-DE-VENCE (Alpes-Maritimes)

Marc Chagall moved here from Vence, three miles away, in the winter of 1966 to a new house he had built in a secluded wood behind the Fondation Maeght. He lived for many years in Vence on a small estate "Les Collines" but was driven away by the increasing building in the town which cut off the views he loved. Although an honorary citizen of Vence he was forced to seek the quiet of Saint-Paul-de-Vence. There he continues his work and from there can keep an eye on the museum "Chagall Memorial" now under construction in Nice.

SARREBOURG (Moselle)

This small community gave two mayors to the city of Sarrebourg, Jules Levy in 1873 and Sylvain Beer several years later. In World War II the community lost 75 members through deportation, of whom 68 died in Auschwitz.

SYNAGOGUE, 1, rue du Sauvage, was built in 1858, replacing an older, smaller synagogue on the site. During the German occupation in World War II it was used as a warehouse.

MEMORIAL TO THE DEPORTEES is located in the Jewish cemetery.

RUE LAZARD commemorates a prominent Jewish citizen of Sarrebourg.

SARREGUEMINES (Moselle)

SYNAGOGUE, Rue de Verdun.

SAVERNE (Bas-Rhin)

RUE des JUIFS recalls the medieval Jewish community.

SYNAGOGUE, Rue de Lutzelbourg, an attractive small building set in a garden on the edge of the town, was built in 1950 to replace the older synagogue destroyed by the Germans during the occupation in World War II.

SCHILTIGHEIM (Bas-Rhin)

See BISCHHEIM

SEDAN et CHARLEVILLE (Ardennes)

SYNAGOGUE, 18, avenue Philippoteaux, Sedan, was built in 1950 to replace the old synagogue which was destroyed by the Germans in World War II.

SÉLESTAT (Bas-Rhin)

ANCIENT CEMETERY contains fifteenth-century Jewish tombstones.

ANCIENT SYNAGOGUE dating from the fourteenth century, now a private building. It has served various purposes through the centuries, including an arsenal for the French army. Building is located on Rue Ste.-Barbe.

COMMUNITY CENTRE, 4, rue Sainte-Barbe

MUNICIPAL MUSEUM contains a collection of Jewish ritual objects.

SYNAGOGUE, Place Vanolles, was rebuilt in 1960 after its destruction by the Germans during World War II.

SENS (Yonne)

RUE de la GRANDE and RUE de la PETITE JUIVERIE marks the location of the medieval Jewry of Sens. In 1012, Renaud, Count of Sens, converted to Judaism and ordered that he be called "King of the Jews". The medieval talmudic academy of Sens was famous throughout Europe. Among its heads were Samson ben Abraham de Sens (1150-1230) important tosafist and the great polemist Nathan l'Official who conducted debates with the bishops of Vannes, Meaux, Poitiers and Angoulême.

SOULTZ (Haut-Rhin)

ANCIENT CEMETERY dating to the fourteenth century and one of the largest in Alsace, is located at Jungholtz, on the outskirts of Soultz.

SYNAGOGUE and CHAPEL, 7, rue des Bouchers, was built in 1838, to replace two other synagogues which had become too small. The synagogue was devastated during the Nazi occupation in World War II and has remained unusable. The small chapel was restored in 1945 and removed to the community house, an historic building which once housed a convent. It is adequate for the use of the small Jewish community of Soultz today.

STRASBOURG (Bas-Rhin)

Jewish history in Strasbourg goes back at least to the twelfth century when Benjamin of Tudela visited the community there. There were savage persecutions during the Crusades, and many massacres during the centuries. From the fourteenth century to the French Revolution, Jews were not permitted to live in Strasbourg but could visit during the day for business purposes. In 1770, Cerf Berr, the "prevot general" of the Jews of Alsace obtained for his family and 68 other Jews the right to reside in Strasbourg. This was the beginning of the modern community.

Today Strasbourg is a vibrant community of 13,000 souls, with many active Jewish institutions. It is a centre for Jewish learning for the area.

ALSATIAN MUSEUM, 23 quai St.-Nicolas, has a rich collection of Jewish ritual objects displayed in three rooms on the main floor. This collection is the property of the Jewish Museum, founded in 1905 by an organization interested in preserving the records of the Jews of Alsace and Lorraine.

AKIVA SCHOOL, 9 quai Zorn, a secondary school recognized by the State.

CEMETERIES The ancient cemetery at Koenigshoffen was acquired in 1795. In 1900 a new cemetery was dedicated in Cronenbourg.

HOME FOR AGED JEWS known as the Hospice Elisa, is located in a magnificent château in the countryside near Strasbourg. It was founded in 1853 by Louis Ratisbonne, president of the Consistory, in memory of a cousin.

JEWISH HOSPITAL, Hospital Hadassa, is located at 13, place de Haguenau.

KOSHER RESTAURANTS

Chalom, 16a, avenue de la Paix.

Universitaire, 11, rue Sellenick.

NATIONAL LIBRARY, 6 place de la République, has a number of Hebrew manuscripts and a large collection of books on topics of Jewish interest.

NOTRE DAME MUSEUM, 3 place du Château, contains a thirteenth-century statue representing the Synagogue Defeated. Here may also be seen a statue of "Samson the Tree-Uprooter", a medieval figure removed from a ruined Benedictine monastery in Alspach.

ORT TRADE SCHOOL, 14 rue Sellenick, is housed in a historic structure. It is the property of the École de Travail Israélite du Bas-Rhin, founded in 1832 by Louis Ratisbonne, for the purpose of teaching "manual work to poor Jewish children of the Bas-Rhin department." For years it was a hostel where young people who learned trades in private workshops lived during the three years of their apprenticeship. In 1947 the building of the Ecole de Travail, constructed in 1903, was transformed by ORT into a modern technical school.

ORPHANAGE, "Les Violettes" is located at 23, rue Sellenick.

ROHAN MUSEUM, 2 place du Château, has on display several Jewish tombstones dating to the Middle Ages.

RUE des JUIFS behind the cathedral, marks the location of the medieval Jewry. Benjamin of Tudela found the Jewish community living in this area around the synagogue, which disappeared long ago.

RUE BRULEE memorializes the martyrdom of Friday, February 13th, 1349, the eve of St. Valentine's Day, when about 2000 Jews were burnt in a huge bonfire for refusing to accept baptism. The Prefecture building stands on the site of the Jewish cemetery where the tragedy occurred. Three Strasbourg Christians, Gossedturm, Guntze de Wintertur and Peter Schwarber, who protested the massacre, were deprived of their possessions and reduced to poverty.

STRASBOURG CATHEDRAL has a very finely sculptured Synagogue Defeated in the south portal. She is represented blindfolded and shorn of her mantle.

STUDENTS' HOSTEL Cité Universitaire Laure Weill, 11, rue Sellenick, is used by students at the famous University of Strasbourg, and come from all parts of Europe and abroad. Tourists are acommodated during the summer months.

SYNAGOGUES, There are three main synagogues in Strasbourg.

Synagogue de la Paix, 1A, rue du Grand Rabbin Rene-Hirschler, is the chief synagogue, seating 1600. It was consecrated in 1958 and it stands in the heart of a lovely park provided by the municipality about a mile from the centre of the city. The name "Synagogue de la Paix" was indicative of the community's hope for peace. The building, of contemporary design, has a huge menorah visible for miles. It houses the community centre, Hebrew day school, yeshivah and a kosher restaurant. The Youth Chapel is dedicated to the memory of Rabbi Sammy Klein who was killed by the Nazis in 1944. It also houses the small Reform congregation of Strasbourg, in true ecumenical spirit. Construction was made possible by funds provided by the French Government, the Conference on Jewish Material Claims Against Germany and local contributors.

RUE du GRAND RABBI RENE-HIRSCHLER which leads to the synagogue was renamed in April 1962 in memory of Rabbi Rene Hirschler who was Chief Rabbi of the Lower Rhine (Bas Rhin) District, who was killed, together with his wife and children in a Nazi concentration camp in 1943. Pierre Pfimlin, Mayor of Strasbourg and former Prime Minister of France, presided at the dedication ceremony.

Ets Haim synagogue, 28A rue Kageneck, was founded in 1882. It is the only synagogue in Strasbourg to survive the German occupation in World War II. All others were destroyed.

Adath Israel synagogue, 2, rue Saint-Pierre-le-Jeune, is a Hassidic congregation.

UNIVERSITY OF STRASBOURG has a chair in modern Hebrew, established in 1955. The incumbent is Professor André Neher. Hebrew is also taught in the high schools of the city.

YOUTH HOSTEL is located at 42, avenue de la Fôret-Noire.

STRUTHOF (Bas-Rhin)

CONCENTRATION CAMP at Struthof, not far from Strasbourg, was the only one of its kind on French soil. It was specially designed by the Nazis for the extermination of Jews, political prisoners, and members of the resistance. The camp has been preserved as a permanent memorial to those who perished there. Visitors may see the prisoners' barracks, the thousands of graves, and the gas chamber, the only one in France. The impressive memorial to the martyrs is a shaft which points like a giant sword into the sky; it rises from a great boat with a white sail and stands out starkly against the forest-covered hills. Erected in 1950, it was designed by architect B. Monnet. The sculptor L. Fennaux carved the ghostly shadow of a hunger-ridden prisoner on the interior surface. Rising to a height of 40.5 metres and towering above barracks, barbed wire and graves, the effect is overwhelming.

TARBES (Hautes-Pyrénées)

SYNAGOGUE and COMMUNITY CENTRE, Cité Rothschild, 6 rue de Pradeau.

THIONVILLE (Moselle)

SYNAGOGUE and COMMUNITY CENTRE, 31, avenue Clemenceau. In January 1964 unknown vandals tried to burn down the century old synagogue of Thionville, in the vicinity of Metz. The local fire brigade managed to put out the fire before much damage was done.

TOULON (Var)

In 1348 the Jews of Toulon were accused of poisoning the wells and forty were massacred.
SYNAGOGUE, 6, rue de la Visitation, was built in 1945.

TOULOUSE (Haute-Garonne)

Toulouse Jewish history is one of the most ancient in France. The community flourished during the Middle Ages. In 1217 all the Jews of Toulouse were thrown into prison and ordered to choose between baptism and death. Their young children were turned over to priests and baptized. Simon de Montfort released the adult Jews on payment of a heavy ransom but their baptized children were never returned. The community ceased to exist in 1685.

During World War II the Jewish resistance organization, which played an important role in the fight against the Germans, was organized in Toulouse. Since 1960 a new community has grown and today, with 18,500 Jews, Toulouse is one of the most important communities in France.

COMMUNITY and YOUTH CENTRES, 14, rue de Rempart-Saint-Etienne and 36, rue de Pech.

MUSEUM OF ANTIQUITIES has on display the medieval tombstone of Don Vidal Salomon Nathan and the dedicatory inscription of a synagogue dated 1240.

MUNICIPAL LIBRARY, 1 rue de Périgord, contains a number of old Hebrew books.

ORT SCHOOL, chemin du Cabirol à Colomiers.

PLACE du TEL-AVIV was given its name in October 1962 as part of the ceremony at which Toulouse and Tel Aviv were declared "twin cities". The entire city was decked out with French and Israeli flags. A highlight of the festivities was a concert given by the noted cellist Pablo Casals.

ST.-RAYMOND MUSEUM, Place St.-Serrin, contains two items of Jewish interest. The first is an ancient amulet, engraved with the Hebrew words for "accident of sleep" followed by the first line of Genesis 49:24. The second is a block of marble from the city of Berenice, on the coast of Cyrenaica, from the days of Caesar Augustus. It records a vote of thanks by the Jewish community of Berenice to the ex-Governor Marcus Titius for his justice and benevolence; it promises to sing his praises in their synagogue and to set up this tablet in the best place in the town amphitheatre.

SYNAGOGUE, 2, rue Palapret, follows the Portuguese Sephardi ritual. It is the largest in the city.

ADATH YECHOUROUN, 3, rue Jules-Chalande, the only Ashkenazi congregation, was founded in 1956.

There are several more small congregations, all Sephardi.

TOURS (Indre-et-Loire)

The community dates back to the sixth century and its talmudists enjoyed a great reputation during the Middle Ages. The modern community was re-established at the end of the nineteenth century.

SYNAGOGUE and COMMUNITY CENTRE, 37, rue Parmentier.

TROYES (Aube)

Troyes was one of the most important centres of medieval Judaism. Here Rashi (1040-1105), dominant personality in Judaism, greatest commentator on the Bible, and illustrious Talmudic exegetist, was born, lived and died. The academy headed by his grandson, Rabbenu Tam (1100-1171) attracted students not only from France but from all parts of Europe, as far away as Bohemia and Russia. Three great synods, which had an indelible effect on European Judaism, were held in Troyes.

No trace remains of the medieval community. It is possible that the parish of Saint Frobert occupies the ground covered by the ancient Jewry, and it is also possible that the old Church of Saint Frobert, long in ruins and now demolished, and the Church of Saint Pantaleon, were originally synagogues. For years it was said that a local butcher-shop was located on the site of Rashi's own synagogue and that flies were never to be found in that shop. The shop has long since gone and the story is now legend.

RUE des MAURES was formerly the rue de la Juiverie.

RACHI SYNAGOGUE and COMMUNITY CENTRE, 5, rue Brunneval. The modern community was constituted in the late nineteenth century.

TROYES CATHEDRAL has on a side wall a gargoyle in the form of a grotesque Jew. He wears a pointed hat and carries a fat purse slung from his belt. One hand thrusts forth his beard and the other is pressed behind his neck.

VALENCE (Drôme)

RUE de la JUIVERIE is a reminder of the medieval community of Valence.

SYNAGOGUE, 1, place du Colomonbier was built in 1964 and dedicated in 1966.

VALENCIENNES (Nord)

SYNAGOGUE, 36, rue de l'Intendance.

VERDUN (Meuse)

SYNAGOGUE, Impasse des Jacobins, suffered great damage during the occupation. The Germans stripped the synagogue and turned it into a mess hall. They also destroyed the marble tablet on the synagogue wall inscribed with the names of sons of the community, headed by the name of the beloved Rabbi Jules Ruff, who had given their lives in World War I. After the liberation, American Jewish soldiers helped restore the synagogue.

JEWISH WAR MEMORIAL The huge granite monument to the Jewish soldiers of the French army and to the foreign Jewish volunteers who died in World War I was unveiled in June 1938, on the twenty-second anniversary of the Battle of Verdun. The monument lies in the shadow of the great Ossuary of Fort Douaumont.

Built in the shape of an arched wall, the monument is one hundred feet long and twenty-three feet high. It is intended to represent the Wailing Wall in Jerusalem, and it is bare except for reproductions of two Tablets of the Law in the center. The sole inscription reads, *"Aux Français Alliés et Volontaires Étrangers Israélites morts pour la France 1914-1918."* During World War II the Germans painstakingly covered the inscription with concrete, but this was removed by American troops when they captured the town in 1945.

VARENGEVILLE-SUR-MER (Seine-Maritime)

Georges de Porto-Riche, the eminent dramatist, is buried in the local "cimetière marin".

VERSAILLES (Yvelines)

Admiral Louis Kahn 1895-1970 was born in Versailles and is buried there. He was an active leader of French Jewry and occupied the post of president of the Consistoire Israelite de France from 1963 to his death.

SYNAGOGUE, 10, rue Albert Joly, was designed by Alfred-Philibert Aldrophe, the famous Jewish architect who designed the Great Synagogue on rue de la Victoire in Paris. It was dedicated in 1866.

VICHY (Allier)

There was a Jewish community in Vichy in the thirteenth century.
SYNAGOGUE, 2 bis, rue du Maréchal-Foch.

VILLEJUIF (Val-de-Marne)

Villejuif, a shabby industrial suburb of Paris, on the road to Orly airport, has nothing more than its name (Jew Town) to recall the medieval Jewish community which once existed there. It now has a Jewish community of some 500 families, which has not, as yet, created any institutions of its own. The local church has a painting of Moses being rescued from the water, attributed to Fragonard.

VILLEURBANNE (Rhône)

SYNAGOGUE de la FRATERNITÉ, 4, rue Malherbe, was dedicated in May 1964. The synagogue is the pride of this industrial city near Lyons. It is a synagogue built and paid for by German Christian young people to atone for the guilt of their elders. The story began after World War II when a group of German Jews turned to the German consul in Lyons, Count Paul Yorck von Wartenburg, for assistance in repairing the ramshackle house in which they met for worship. Count von Wartenburg enlisted the help of a German group that does volunteer work in countries that suffered under Nazi rule, Aktion Sühnezeichen (Action Atonement).

Soon the first group of young Germans arrived in Villeurbanne to begin work. They were housed by a local priest in a former Catholic church. Raymond Carpe, a local Catholic architect, designed the three story building. The synagogue is a gray stone rectangular shell with floor-to-roof clear windows framed by red concrete ribbing. Mr. Carpe designed the entire facade like a door, to symbolize the synagogue as a place of refuge for the Jewish people. The pews were presented by a German Evangelical church. Action Atonement contributed $80,000 to the project. The West German Government provided an additional $20,000, through its restitution payments for Jewish victims of the Nazis.

VILLIERS-LE-BEL et GONESSE (Val-d'Oise)

SYNAGOGUE and COMMUNITY CENTRE, 23, rue Alexis-Varagne, dedicated in 1962.

VINCENNES (Val-de-Marne)

SYNAGOGUE and COMMUNITY CENTRE, 30, rue Céline-Robert, founded in 1905.

VITTEL (Vosges)

SYNAGOGUE, rue Croix-Pierrot, open July and August only.

VIVIERS (Mayenne)

RUE de la JUIVERIE marks the location of the medieval Jewry.

CORSICA

BASTIA

Bastia, the largest city on the island, has a small Jewish community of about 35 families. Most are Sephardim who emigrated from Syria and Palestine before World War II. The synagogue, 3, rue du Castagno, is located in an out of the way building in the old town. The Haham, Rabbi Meyer Toledano, who performs his functions as spiritual leader in a voluntary capacity, is a merchant with a small shop on rue Napoleon.

Ajaccio has a community of ten families. Some Jews also live in Corte, Ile Rousse and Porto-Vecchio. The total Jewish population of Corsica is about 300.

GERMANY

Jewish history in Germany began in the first two centuries of the Common Era, when Jewish soldiers and traders who accompanied the Roman legions into Gaul settled down permanently in the Rhineland, where towns were growing up around the garrisons. As early as 300 C.E. there were Jewish communities at Cologne, Mainz, and Trier. A decree of the year 321 by Constantine the Great, the first Christian emperor of Rome, gave the Jewish citizens of Cologne specific civic responsibilities. Before the Romans were driven out by the Germanic tribes in the fifth century, there were eight Jewish communities in western Germany, but nothing is known of them for the next three hundred years.

Between the ninth and eleventh centuries, the medieval kings, nobles, and churchmen vied for Jewish settlers. Rhineland Jewish merchants and international traders were an important economic asset because they brought essential goods from the Slavic east and the Orient to the raw communities of Germany and advanced the funds needed to promote trade and carry on government. In 1084, the bishop of Speyer explained the significance of Jewish enterprise when he said, "Desiring to make a town out of the village of Speyer, I thought to raise its dignity many times by getting Jews to settle there."

The privileges, self-rule, and good relations with the German masses enjoyed by these early Jewish communities were short-lived. They came to an end in 1096, when religious hatred, inspired by church bigotry and inflamed by the First Crusade, touched off a series of persecutions and massacres that continued with increasing violence into the fifteenth century. Scores of Jewish communities were destroyed by mob violence and pillaging during these centuries of martyrdom. A horrible picture of the Jew as an enemy of the home, religion, and the state, which found its way into German folklore and literature, was built up by libelous accusations of blood ritual murder, well poisoning, and desecration of Christian images. Encouraged by the rising class of German burghers and artisans, who were eager to eliminate Jewish competition, this hatred pushed the Jews out of almost every means of livelihood but money lending, which only exacerbated public feeling against them as usurers.

Emperors and princes added to their income by selling charters of protection to the Jews and then subjecting them to exorbitant levies. When the towns and local lords rebelled against the crown, they ignored royal warnings to protect the Jews and periodically expelled them as enemies of God. Only the fragmentation of Germany spared the Jews from the kind of mass expulsion they suffered in England, France, and Spain. Ousted from one town or barony, they found temporary haven in another city or principality. Barons and princes regularly rid themselves of debts to the Jews by driving them out and then inviting back only those who still had assets. In this process, the Jews were gradually impoverished, reduced to peddling, confined to ghettos, and deprived of all civic rights.

Martin Luther's rebellion gave hope that his assaults on the Church for its role in the oppression of the Jews might end the anti-Jewish violence. When Luther found the Jews resisted his efforts to convert them, he outdid the Catholic clergy in his anti-Semitic utterances and writings. From the early fifteenth to the middle of the seventeenth century the Jews were gradually expelled from most German cities and states, except in Worms and Frankfurt-am-Main, where Jewish communities existed almost continuously from the tenth century. Many fled east to Poland, Lithuania, and Hungary, taking with them their Judaeo-German dialect, which became the Yiddish language, and their piety and love of learning. The few who remained eked out a hazardous existence in the smaller towns of Germany under the uncertain protection of local princelings.

The resettlement in Mergenthau, Fürth, and Mainz in the sixteenth century and an invitation by Danish rulers to Marrano Jews from Holland and Portugal to colonize in Hamburg early in the seventeenth century ushered in a more favorable era that continued into the eighteenth century. When the Holy Roman Empire broke up into a loose federation of independent states under absolute rulers, the German princes invited Jews back to help them repair the destruction wrought by the Thirty Years' War. Jewish merchants, bankers, and entrepreneurs were in great demand to equip and pay armies, create government machinery, establish credit, promote commerce, and introduce industry. Employed as court purveyors, financiers, and royal counselors, some of these court Jews became wealthy and influential and were able to provide a measure of security for their less privileged coreligionists. Around these court Jews grew up the modern Jewish communities in every corner of Germany. Anti-Jewish violence came to an end, and some minor relaxations of curbs were permitted, but the majority of Jews still had few rights of residence or occupation and no civic or political status and were strictly limited as to numbers.

The well-to-do court Jews and their mercantile associates, who were the first to acquire secular education, launched the struggle for Jewish emancipation in the hospitable climate of eighteenth-century Enlightenment. Moses Mendelssohn was the most significant figure in the effort to lift the German Jew out of his cultural ghetto. He translated the Hebrew Bible into German, launched a magazine to transmit general culture to Hebrew-reading Jews, organized schools for Jewish children where German was taught in addition to Jewish subjects, and pressed for the whole-hearted participation of Jews in all realms of society.

Mendelssohn's wide contacts with leaders of liberal thought and politics and his important role in German cultural life enabled him to pave the way for the era of greater Jewish freedom that began after the French Revolution. His advocacy of a happy synthesis of German culture with Jewish loyalty as the way to wipe out the legal disabilities and social indignities under which German Jews smarted met with bitter opposition. Many Jewish leaders feared Mendelssohn's reforms as a threat to Judaism and as the road to conversion. In the generation after Mendelssohn, thousands of German Jews, including his own children, did accept baptism. Other Jewish leaders succeeded in adapting religious forms to German life in a series of radical steps that gave birth to Reform Judaism and to an age of Jewish scholarship and scientific study.

The French Revolution brought speedy emancipation to Jews living in the western German areas incorporated into France and gave impetus for similar equality in other states. In the reaction that followed Napoleon's defeat in 1815, many of these gains were lost and had to be won all over again, slowly and piecemeal. Heinrich Heine, the poet, and Ludwig Börne, the journalist, were typical of the culturally emancipated Jews who found the continuing legal disabilities and political handicaps so unbearable that they accepted baptism as the ticket of admission to European culture. Regarded as Jews despite their conversion, they exercised a great influence on the Young Germany Movement, which tried to introduce French ideas of liberalism into reactionary Germany. Gabriel Riesser and Johann Jacoby, who remained stanch Jews, fought for the emancipation of all Germans as the road to Jewish equality. In the Frankfurt Parliament of 1848, called to create a united and democratic Germany, the president was Eduard von Simson, a baptized Jew, while Riesser was one of the vice-presidents. Both were on the delegation that offered the imperial crown to Frederick William IV in 1849. When the 1848 revolution ended in failure, thousands of German Jews became part of the famous migration of '48ers to the United States.

Not until the unification of Germany in 1871 under Bismarck did the Jews win formal equality throughout the country under the first national constitution, one of whose authors was Eduard Lasker. He and Ludwig Bamberger, the two Jewish leaders of the National Liberal party, were allies of Bismarck in creating a united Germany. William I accepted the crown of the German Empire from the Reichstag of the North German Confederation, of which Eduard von Simson was president.

The brief era of German liberalism from the 1860s to 1880 enabled Jews to make notable contributions in the professions, industry, science, commerce, journalism, and the arts, in the face of a new wave of politically-inspired, anti-Jewish agitation. The landed and military aristocracy made it almost impossible for an unbaptized Jew to be a judge, an army officer, a professor, or an administrative official. The average German still couldn't bring himself to accept the Jew as an equal. When Bismarck split with the Liberals, who had heavy Jewish support, and began his struggle with the Socialists, whose founder and first political organizer were both baptized Jews, the Iron Chancellor's new conservative allies adopted anti-Semitism as a political weapon.

Between the 1870s and 1900, the country was flooded with anti-Semitic literature whose underlying theme was the racial superiority of Aryans and the inferiority of Semitic peoples. This concept became the rallying cry to combat liberalism and democracy as "Jewish and un-German." Neither patriotism in the Austro-Prussian and Franco-Prussian Wars, in which more than 8,000 Jews distinguished themselves, nor the brilliant achievements of Jews who helped establish Germany's reputation in science, technology, and industry, allayed the growth of the anti-Semitic movement. World War I halted the anti-Jewish campaign only temporarily, despite the enormous role of Jews in the war effort. Fritz Haber and Richard Willstätter headed the chemical services; Max Warburg and Carl Melchior helped provide the financial sinews; Walther Rathenau mobilized industrial production; and Albert Ballin built the merchant marine. More than 100,000 Jews, one out of every six in the country, were in uniform, and 12,000 gave their lives for the Fatherland.

The overthrow of the Hohenzollern monarchy in 1918 and the establishment of the German Republic in 1919 marked the high tide of Jewish equality with the admission of Jews to the civil service, the judiciary, academic posts, and even major public offices. The interim Socialist regime that governed Germany after the end of the war included two Jews; Hugo Preuss, principal author of the Weimar Constitution, was one of thirteen Jews who sat in the national constituent assembly of 423 Socialists, Liberals, and Catholic Centrists that proclaimed Germany a democratic republic.

The prewar anti-Semitic tradition and exploitation of the widespread bitterness against the burdens imposed by the Versailles Peace Treaty enabled foes of the republic to discredit and undermine it by identifying it with Jews who were prominent in the Liberal and Socialist parties that came to power under the new constitution. Big industrialists hostile to trade unions, Junkers plotting to restore the monarchy, and right-wing political parties opposed to democracy made common cause in blaming Germany's defeat on an "international Jewish conspiracy" and a Jewish "stab in the back." Postwar inflation, unemployment, and reparations payments, for which the Jews were held responsible, smoothed the road for Hitler and his Nazi party to come to power in 1933.

Beginning with economic boycotts, book burnings, and cultural and social ostracism, the Nazi campaign to liquidate the Jews moved swiftly to economic despoliation, political disfranchisement and ghettoization, and finally total annihilation through deportation and mass murder. Before November 10, 1938, when 187 synagogues were destroyed by fire or looting mobs and thousands of Jewish places of business were wrecked in a nationwide pogrom, almost half of Germany's Jews had fled, leaving their property behind. World War II cut off escape for the remainder, most of whom died in gas chambers and concentration camps. At the end of the war 90 per cent of German Jewry had been exterminated. As part of the Nazis' "final solution" of the Jewish problem, 6,093,000 of the 8,300,000 Jews who had lived in Nazi-occupied Europe were murdered or died as a result of Nazi barbarity.

Hilter lost the war but won his *Kampf* against the German Jews, who have been reduced to a tiny remnant of the once great and distinguished Jewish community. As of 1971, there were 33,000 Jews, mostly old people, in Germany. The average age was 48. Births were rare. Some 10,000 lived in 80 communities of West Germany and 2,000 were scattered among nine communities in East Germany. In West Germany another 10,000 are not registered as Jews and not affiliated with Jewish communities. Some 10,000 Jews in West Germany lived on government pensions, either as payment for confiscated property or as compensation for persecution. About 7,000 Jews were returnees from Israel and other countries. Most of the Jews were former displaced persons from Russia, Poland, Hungary, Rumania and Czechoslovakia, who remained in Germany after their release from concentration camps.

In West Germany there are 70 Jewish congregations, 45 synagogues, most of them built with government funds, but only two Jewish elementary schools. The largest Jewish communities are in West Berlin, Frankfurt-am-Main, Munich, Duesseldorf, Hamburg and Cologne. All are united in a Central Council of Jews in Germany. There are 15 rabbis in West Germany. There is a major Jewish weekly, the Allgemeine Judische Wochenzeitung, and a few smaller weeklies. In East Germany, where there are some 3,000 Jews not officially registered as such, the largest Jewish communities are in East Berlin, Leipzig, Magdeburg, Erfurt, Dresden and Karl Marx Stadt. The state maintains 120 Jewish cemeteries and pays annual subventions to the Jewish communities. There is only one rabbi who lives in East Berlin.

The postwar government of West Germany not only has done much to expiate Nazi crimes through economic restitution, reparations to Israel, and many forms of moral penance, but is trying hard to root out all vestiges of anti-Semitism. Scores of Nazis have been tried and imprisoned. Government funds have been made available to finance Jewish cultural and religious activities, to rebuild synagogues and to restore cemeteries, to honor great Jewish personalities repudiated by the Nazis and to replace Jewish names on war memorials. Christian good will movements are widespread; Anne Frank has become a national heroine; young people regularly make pilgrimages of atonement to concentration camp sites and to Israel and the government is making zealous efforts to educate youth about the grisly events of the Nazi era.

In 1952 West Germany signed an agreement with Israel providing for a collective restitution payment of $825,000,000 by West Germany to the Jews, to be spread over 14 years. Seven-eights of this went directly to Israel and the rest was allocated to the Conference on Jewish Material Claims Against Germany to help restore communities and institutions destroyed during the Nazi occupation of Europe. Other large sums were paid to surviving victims of the Holocaust. In 1965 West Germany and Israel established diplomatic relations. Economic, cultural, social and trade relations between the two countries have grown steadily. East Germany, however, which has paid no reparations to Jews, follows a militant anti-Israel line.

The rise of a neo-Nazi movement in West Germany and periodic anti-Semitic incidents indicated that Nazism had not been entirely uprooted. Nevertheless, Jews again sat in the parliaments of the two Germanys. Herbert Weichmann, who was burgomaster of Hamburg and president of the Bundesrat, upper house of West Germany's parliament, declined an offer to become president of Germany. Joseph Neuberger served as minister of justice in the Social Democratic government of North Rhine-Westphalia. Ludwig Rosenberg was head of the Federation of Trade Unions of West Germany. In East Germany, the government included Jews who were alienated from the Jewish community, among them Otto Winzer, minister of foreign affairs; Alexander Abusch, minister for cultural affairs; Herbert Grunstein, minister of interior, and Alexander Norden, head of propaganda. Jews again serve as judges and are prominent in the press, arts and radio and television.

FEDERAL REPUBLIC OF GERMANY
(West Germany)

AACHEN

JUDENGASSE (Jews Street), which runs along what was once the western wall of the city's Roman rampart, is a reminder that Jews lived here as early as the ninth century.

MARTYRS' MEMORIAL honoring Jews who lost their lives here during the Nazi holocaust, stands at the entrance to the *Jewish Cemetery* at Lütticherstrasse.

REUTER MEMORIAL, 117 Pontstrasse, a three-story red brick building, is a memorial to Paul Julius Reuter, who in 1850 launched the pioneering Reuter's News Agency by flying pigeons from the roof. At No. 13 Pontstrasse, the *International Museum of Journalism*, there are displayed files of early Jewish newspapers in several languages.

SYNAGOGUE, 50 Oppenhoffallee, erected in 1957, replaced one burned down by the Nazis in 1938. The synagogue also houses a communal center.

AMBERG

SYNAGOGUE, 5 Salzgasse, was one of the few Jewish houses of worship that escaped destruction at the hands of the Nazis. It suffered minor damage in 1939, and during the war the Nazis used it as a warehouse.

ANSBACH

18TH CENTURY SYNAGOGUE that survived Nazi era as grain warehouse has been restored and converted into a state museum from which an annual Hanukah service is broadcast over the government radio and TV.

AROLSEN

INTERNATIONAL TRACING SERVICE, on Grobe Allee, in this town near Kassel, is the repository of nearly 20,000,000 documents, including the records of more than 8,000,000 victims of the Nazis. The records and card index of the I.T.S. are in constant use for determining compensation claims by victims of the Nazis as well as for ascertaining the fate of millions of families. Originally established by the United Nations Relief and Rehabilitation Agency and operated under the direction of the International Relief Organization and the Allied High Commission, the "archives of terror" are now administered by the International Red Cross. On entering the main doorway, the visitor sees on one of the walls a large mural inscribed with the names of 30 towns associated with the Hitler terror. Another mural, in many languages, including Yiddish, consists of the words "never again." The building's dedication mural reads: "The purpose of this building is to house the archives of horror and so preserve the records of mass destruction, torture and slavery under the National Socialist dictatorship."

AUGSBURG

SYNAGOGUE, 8 Halderstrasse. At 80 Hummelstrasse (Kriegshaber) is a seventeenth-century cemetery. There is a memorial to World War I soldiers in the cemetery at 64 Haunstetterstrasse, and in nearby Kempten, on Memmingstrasse, is a memorial to Jewish and non-Jewish residents who died in concentration camps.

BADEN-BADEN

JEWISH MILITARY CHAPEL FOR FRENCH TROOPS, Jägerweg, about one and a half hours' ride from the center of the city, is a permanent installation for Jewish servicemen on duty with the French forces.
SYNAGOGUE, 2 Werderstrasse.

BAD-GODESBERG

ISRAEL EMBASSY, 78 Ubierstrasse, is in this suburb of Bonn, the capital of West Germany.

BAD HOMBURG

ADULT EDUCATION CENTER, on Rande der Alstadt, a former Jewish school that was attached to a synagogue built in 1867 and destroyed in 1938, is now a public educational institution. Above the entrance are inscribed the words, "Think of the teaching of Moses My servant." Inside, on a simple marble tablet, are these words: "Jewish citizens built this school behind the synagogue in 1877. Generations of young people were educated here. Crime and stupidity destroyed the synagogue on November 9, 1938 and damaged the school. On January 22, 1956, the Adult Education Center took over this building to work in it for understanding and tolerance." Opposite this tablet is a large photograph of the old synagogue.
JEWISH COMMUNAL HEADQUARTERS, 28 Hölderlinweg.

BAD KREUZNACH

MICHEL-MORTSTRASSE is named for a Jewish family that lived here for several generations until the Nazi era. The home of Jakob Michel, at 6 Mannheimerstrasse, one of the oldest buildings in the city, has been declared a public monument. A descendant of this family, Ernest Michel, who survived the Auschwitz death camp, is now executive vice-president of the United Jewish Appeal of New York.

JEWISH CENTER, 11 Gymnasialstrasse.

BAD NAUHEIM

SYNAGOGUE, 24 Karlstrasse.

BAMBERG

BAMBERG CATHEDRAL, on the Domplatz, has a statue of the "Synagogue Defeated." It is just to the right of the central portal. Below it is a representation of a medieval Jew with pointed bonnet on which is perched a devil in the form of a monkey with wings. Jews lived in this ancient town before the cathedral was completed in 1237.

JEWISH COMMUNITY CENTER, 7 Willi Lessingstrasse, replaced the synagogue on the same street which was burned to the ground by the Nazi in 1938. The street is named for Willi Lessing, a Bamberg Jew who was killed in a vain effort to halt the anti-Semitic rampage. On the site of the synagogue, Bamberg has erected a stone memorial. In June, 1965, Bamberg sprang into headlines around the world when the monument was daubed with a swastika in red paint. This outrage was the first of scores of similar incidents that occurred not only in Germany but throughout the world in 1965.

MUNICIPAL HISTORICAL MUSEUM, 7 Domplatz, preserves the painted walls and ceiling from an early-eighteenth-century log-cabin synagogue in the Lower Franconian hamlet of Horb. The painting is the work of Eliezer Sussman ben Solomon, a Jewish artist, who devoted himself to converting tiny rural synagogues into gaily decorated buildings. The Horb paintings contain many ancient Jewish symbols, Hebrew inscriptions and heraldic designs.

REMNANTS OF THIRTEENTH-CENTURY SYNAGOGUE are incorporated into the Turnhalle, 1 Judenstrasse. More than a century after the Jews were driven out of Bamberg during the 1349 massacres, part of the walls and ceiling of the synagogue were incorporated into a church. The Nazi used the building as a sports arena. A group of Protestant congregations now owns it. Between Bamberg and Nuremberg archeologists have uncovered what is believed to be the oldest Jewish cemetery in Germany. Scholars are exploring its several levels.

BAYREUTH

SEVENTEENTH-CENTURY SYNAGOGUE, 10 Grunewaldstrasse, wrecked on the inside by the Nazis, has been rebuilt on the original foundation.

BERCHTESGADEN

GENERAL WALKER HOTEL, built by Hitler as an inn for Nazi bigwigs and personal guests, houses a kosher kitchen as part of the facilities established by the United States Army for American military personnel seeking recreation. From this hotel overlooking the ruins of Hitler's private retreat, the Berghof, the visitor can often hear Yiddish singing and Hebrew prayers, for it is the scene, several times a year of religious retreats and Torah convocations for Jewish military personnel and chaplains serving with the United States forces in Europe. The brick and rubber-lined tunnels that led to Hitler's bunker have been completely stripped.

BERGEN

BERGEN-BELSEN CONCENTRATION CAMP SITE, now a peaceful area of winding walks, trees, grass, and flowers, two hours by train from Hamburg, has two major memorials recalling the once notorious Nazi death camp, the only major one that has been completely razed. One memorial, standing where the extermination furnaces once did their deadly work, honors the dead of all the nations whose people lived and died here. It is a tall obelisk made of great hewn stones and bears only the dates of the camp. The imposing shaft faces a 50-by-200 foot concrete platform and wall of similar size. On the wall are inscriptions in Russian, Dutch, Czech, Polish, French, English, Yiddish, and Hebrew, an epitaph to the nameless thousands who died here. At the foot of the monument there are always flower wreaths, many of them honoring Anne Frank, the young Dutch-Jewish girl whose diary has become a memorial to faith and spirit. She is buried here.

Not far from this international memorial is a separate monument to the 30,000 Jews who died at Bergen-Belsen. This is a simple square of stone standing upright on a small shaft, with smaller stone and a stone globe on top. A Star of David and some carved broken tree stumps are the only decoration. The inscription reads: "Israel and the world shall remember thirty thousand Jews exterminated in the concentration camp of Bergen-Belsen at the hands of the murderous Nazis. Earth conceal not blood shed on thee." This memorial was erected on April 15, 1946, on the first anniversary of the camp's liberation by the British.

Scattered over the grounds are simple black-and-white markers near mounds that break the flat earth at irregular intervals. "Here lie buried 800 bodies," one marker reads. Another says, 1,000, a third mentions 2,500, and a fourth records 5,000. Near the Jewish memorial is a sign that reads: "The gravestones in this area have only a symbolic meaning. They do not mark graves." There are also markers erected to individuals who died in the camp. At the entrance to the camp the Federal State of Lower Saxony has erected a House of Documents which displays photographs, documents and other material shedding light on the horrors committed here. The one-story building, sponsored by the Association for Christian-Jewish Cooperation, has a room in memory of Anne Frank. Members of a German youth group, Aktion Sühnezeichen, helped construct the building which has become a center for youth pilgrimages from all over Europe.

BERLIN (West)

LEO BAECK HOUSE, 11-13 Baselerstrasse, a co-operative residential home and old folks home, is named for the late Rabbi Leo Baeck, the last great spiritual leader of German Reform Jewry who stayed at his post in Berlin until he was shipped to the Theresienstadt concentration camp in Czechoslovakia. *Leo Baeckstrasse* in the Zehlendorf district was named for him in 1961.

MARTIN BUBERSTRASSE one of the main streets in the Zehlendorf district, is named for the late Dr. Martin Buber, world-famed Jewish religious philosopher.

CHURCH AND JEWRY INSTITUTE of the Evangelical Church, located in the new main building of the Ecclesiastical University, in Berlin-Zehlendorf, seeks to counter latent anti-Semitism in and out of the church through research, publications, films and seminars.

EICHMANN'S HEADQUARTERS, 116 Kurfurstenstrasse, the secret base of operations of Department IV-B4 of the Main Office for Reich Security, the official name of the Nazi agency that planned the extermination of 6,000,000 Jews, was torn down in 1965.

"FINAL SOLUTION" HOUSE, a villa at 56-58 Am Grossen Wannsee, now a student dormitory, was the address where Hitler and his highest officials assembled on Jan. 20, 1942 to map plans for the implementation of the "final solution"—the extermination of European Jewry.

ANNE FRANK HOUSE, 5 Brabanterstrasse, is a community youth center sponsored by the Senate of West Berlin. In the lobby there is a portrait of the now famous young martyr whose name is venerated by German youth. Young people use the building for discussion groups, exhibits and meetings.

GOLLANCZSTRASSE a street in the suburb of Frohnau, is named for Victor Gollancz, the English publisher and eminent Jew, who was a leader of the Save Europe Now movement, which did extensive relief work in Germany after World War II. He also worked for reconciliation between Germany and the western Allies.

INTERNATIONAL CENTER FOR DOCUMENTATION AND RESEARCH INTO NAZISM AND ITS CONSEQUENCES occupies a 20-room building on Limonenstrasse in the Dahlem district.

JEWISH COMMUNITY CENTER, 79-80 Fasanenstrasse, off the Kurfürstendam, is the principal institution of the Jewish community of 6,000, the largest in Germany. Opened in 1959 on the site once occupied by the Great Synagogue, which the Nazis destroyed in 1938, the Center has a large auditorium used as a synagogue during the High Holy Days, a kosher restaurant open to the public, a modern library, recreation rooms and religious-school classrooms. In front of the modern structure, toward which the West Berlin municipality contributed $476,000, stands the cornerstone pillar from the Fasanenstrasse Synagogue. Affixed to the pillar is a tablet on which are inscribed, in Hebrew and in German, the words, "Thou shalt love thy neighbor as thyself." Framing the doorway of the Center is the old stone archway from the wrecked synagogue. In the courtyard is a memorial wall on which are inscribed the names of the Nazi concentration camps.

JEWISH COMMUNITY HEADQUARTERS, 13 Joachimstalerstrasse, is the building occupied by the official Jewish body for the city. It includes offices, a library, a kindergarten, a kosher canteen, and the reception hall for the rabbinate. In the same building is the rebuilt Joachimstalerstrasse Synagogue.

KAFKA MEMORIAL, 13 Grunewaldstrasse, is a tablet marking the entrance to the house where Franz Kafka, world-famous Jewish author, lived from 1923 to 1924. Erected in 1954, the thirtieth anniversay of Kafka's death, it is inscribed with some lines from his writings.

MEMORIAL TO JEWISH CITIZENS, 7-8 Levetzowstrasse, corner of Fagosstrasse, is an inscribed tablet erected by the West Berlin municipality on the now empty site where once stood a synagogue. From this spot many of Berlin's Jews were assembled for deportation to the death camps. On either side of the plaque affixed to a brick wall are weeping willow trees.

MEMORIAL TO VICTIMS OF 1933-45 at Teltower Damm-an der Dorfaue, is a simple piece of field stone inscribed "to the victims 1933-1945."

MONUMENT AGAINST DESPOTISM, on Holzhauserstrasse, in front of the town hall of the suburb of Wittenau, is a striking stone monument of a human being tied to a wheel shaped like a broken swastika. The inscription reads, "Each ideology based on force tortures the people on its symbols."

MONUMENT TO VICTIMS OF HITLER, in the Plötzensee prison, in Stauffenbergstrasse, formerly Bendlerstrasse, is West Berlin's official memorial to all of Hitler's victims. Located at the spot where Hitler had the participants in the Generals' Plot of July 20, 1944, shot, the monument is a tall stone wall on which are inscribed the words, "To the Victims of the Hitler Dictatorship, 1933-45." Off to the side of the wall is a large stone urn containing soil from all the concentration camps. Behind the wall, the city has preserved the original execution chamber where 2,000 people were killed.

MEMORIAL TO BURNED SYNAGOGUE, 34-38 Munchenerstrasse, on the site of a synagogue burned by the Nazis in Nov., 1938, is a tall, austere geometric procession of heavy stone blocks, with a huge Menorah carved in relief on the top-most stone.

OLD FOLKS HOME, 3 Iranischestrasse, cares for many aged survivors of the Nazi era, including those who still wear German decorations won in World War I. Across the street, at No. 2, is the once famous Jewish Hospital, which in 1962 was taken over by the West Berlin government. The municipality reimbursed the Jewish community and operates the hospital as a memorial to Jewish victims of Nazism.

PESTALOZZISTRASSE SYNAGOGUE, 14-15 Pestalozzistrasse, survived the Nazi era despite heavy damage. It was rebuilt in 1947 by the Senate of West Berlin. Over the entrance is a plaque with these words: "Six million Jewish souls have been lost."

WALTHER RATHENAU HOUSE, 65 Koenigsallee, now a workers' youth hostel, is the former villa of the noted industrialist, philanthropist, and statesman who became Germany's foreign minister in 1922. Bitterly attacked by anti-Semites because he signed the Treaty of Rapallo with Russia, Rathenau was assassinated by anti-Semitic nationalists on June 24, 1922, while riding to his office. His assassin became one of the Nazi heroes, but Rathenau was hailed as a martyr to German democracy. A memorial tablet erected by the German Republic on the spot where he was killed, Koenigsallee at the corner of Erdenerstrasse, was removed by the Nazis but has now been restored.

HEINRICH STAHL HOUSE, 11 Baselerstrasse, a community-sponsored cooperative residence for old folks, is named for the man who became president of the Berlin Jewish Community in 1933 when the Nazis came to power. He refused to emigrate when he had the chance and stayed in office until 1942, when he was deported to the Theresienstadt concentration camp in Czechoslovakia, where he died.

SYNAGOGUE, 10-16 Fraenkelufer, was completely rebuilt after the war by the West Berlin municipality.

SPANDAU FORTRESS where the Nazi war criminals sentenced at the Nuremberg Trials were confined, was built in the sixteenth century in part with tombstones from a fourteenth-century Jewish cemetery which was razed in the sixteenth century. On the 725th anniversary of Spandau some of these stones, still bearing Hebrew inscriptions, were turned over to the Berlin Jewish community "as a symbol of a new and common future in peace and freedom." The stones are now preserved in the Jewish Cemetery at Heerstrasse-Rupenhorn.

SYNAGOGUE MEMORIAL, in Steglitz district, is a stone shaft memorializing the synagogue and Jewish Society for the Blind which once occupied the site.

WOLFENSTEINDAM, an access street at the Handel square in the Steglitz district, is a memorial to Moses Wolfenstein, founder of the Berlin-Steglitz synagogue.

BIELEFELD

JEWISH COMMUNITY HEADQUARTERS, 35 Stapenhorststrasse. In the local Jewish cemetery is a memorial to the 400 Jews from this city who died in concentration camps. At the entrance to the cemetery is a replica of a monument to the city's Jewish World War I dead, which was destroyed when the synagogue was wrecked.

RATHENAUSTRASSE is named for Walther Rathenau, the noted industrialist and statesman.

BINGEN

SYNAGOGUE FACADE and remains of synagogue burned in 1938 are still preserved.

BISINGEN

CONCENTRATION CAMP CEMETERY in the Hechingen district, has a memorial to the 1,158 unknown victims who are buried here in a common grave.

BONN

SYNAGOGUE, 2-4 Wörthstrasse, corner of Koblenzerstrasse, directly across the street from the Federal Ministry of Foreign Affairs, is the only Jewish house of worship in the capital of the Federal Republic of Germany. Erected in 1959, the building has a memorial on the inside to the Jews of Bonn who died at the hands of the Nazis.

BREMEN

JEWISH CEMETERY, 14 Deichbruchstrasse, has some very old and remarkable tombstones dating from the early seventeenth century. In the chapel there is a memorial to Jewish soldiers of World War I. Nearby is a monument to the victims of Nazism.

SYNAGOGUE AND JEWISH COMMUNITY CENTER, 117 Schwachhauser Heerstrasse, is a brand-new structure, with marble floors and stained-glass windows, erected by the municipal authorities. It replaces the Gartenstrasse Synagogue, which the Nazis destroyed.

ROSENAKSTRASSE in West Bremen, is named for Dr. Leopold Rosenak, one of the city's early rabbis.

BRUNSWICK (Braunschweig)

CATHEDRAL OF ST. BLASIUS, on the Burkplatz, displays a fifteen-foot-high, seven branched candelabrum which is said to be an exact reproduction of the one that stood in King Solomon's Temple in Jerusalem. It weighs 772 pounds.

JEWISH COMMUNITY HEADQUARTERS AND SYNAGOGUE, 4 Steinstrasse.

CELLE

JEWISH COMMUNITY HEADQUARTERS, 48 Brunkhorststrasse.

COBLENZ

JEWISH COMMUNITY HEADQUARTERS, 5 Schlachthofstrasse.

COLOGNE (Köln)

COLOGNE CATHEDRAL preserves in its archives an inscribed tablet dated 1266 which contains the promise of Archbishop Engelbert II to guarantee the safety of the local Jews and to protect them from competition by Christian moneylenders.

GERMANIA JUDAICA, 97 Hansaring, is a library on the third floor of a red brick building housing a growing collection of books, old and new, about the role of Jews in German history and on Jewish history. The library is sponsored by Cologne publishers, writers and book-dealers.

JEWISH CEMETERY, at Cologne-Bocklemund, has a recently built mausoleum in which are preserved a number of tombstones, including several that date from early medieval times, from the oldest Jewish cemetery. In the newer cemetery was the grave of Moses Hess, one of the first Jews in the last century to project the idea of a Jewish national home in Palestine through his famous volume, *Rome and Jerusalem*, published in 1862. His remains were transferred to Israel in 1961.

MEDIEVAL GHETTO REMAINS is an open space south of the Town Hall, are a last link with one of the oldest Jewish communities in Europe. The remnants include the walls, part of the foundation and staircase, a piece of the well of a thirteenth-century ritual bath, and a part of the wall of a fourteenth-century synagogue. These evidences of the ancient Jewish settlement, founded in the fourth century, were uncovered during construction work for Cologne's new city hall. A municipal office building is being erected on the site of these finds, which once included the old ghetto, but plans have been made to preserve the parts of the ritual bath by enclosing them in glass and keeping them on permanent exhibit.

MOTHER AND CHILD MONUMENT, at Anlagen am Hansaring, is a simple memorial to seven members of a Jewish family who were martyred on this spot by the Nazis, as well as to all victims of the Nazis. Nearby is the newer Jewish cemetery.

MUNICIPAL DEPARTMENT OF CULTURAL AFFAIRS, 2 Merlostrasse, has the original mss. of the 900-page catologue describing the immense array of historical materials assembled for the Monumenta Judaica, an exhibit of 2,000 objects depicting Jewish history in Germany for nearly 2,000 years, that was displayed in the city's ancient arsenal in 1964.

OFFENBACHPLATZ is a street named for Jacques Offenbach, the Cologne-born composer and musical director, whose operattas are still widely heard. His *Tales of Hoffmann* is an international favorite. Offenbach's father was a cantor in the Cologne synagogue, but the composer lived in France most of his life.

SYNAGOGUE, 50 Roonstrasse, the only one in this ancient Jewish community, was opened in 1959 to replace an older one destroyed in 1938. On part of the site of the former synagogue in the Glockengasse the new Opera House has been erected. The new synagogue, which was dedicated by Chancellor Adenauer, a former mayor of Cologne, was the scene of a Christmas Eve desecration by vandals in 1959 which touched off a world-wide epidemic of swastika daubings on synagogues. The building also houses a kosher restaurant and a community center in which there is a memorial hall honoring martyrs to Nazism.

STATE MUSEUM OF COLOGNE, 1-3 Streitzzeughausstrasse, exhibits on the second floor a permanent display of Jewish ritual objects presented by German citizens who hid them for their Jewish friends in homes, churches, and cemeteries from 1933 to 1945. Among the pieces are many that go back to the fifteenth century.

WALLRAF-RICHARTZ MUSEUM, the city's leading art gallery, gives the works of Max Liebermann, one of Germany's greatest nineteenth- and early-twentieth-century painters, a place of honor. Liebermann, who was president of the Prussian Academy of Art before World War I, was forbidden by the Nazis to paint or exhibit.

EDITH STEIN SCHOOL, a girls high school, is named for a prominent Jewish educator who died in Auschwitz.

DACHAU

DACHAU CONCENTRATION CAMP MEMORIAL on site of one of the most infamous Nazi camps, is just outside this town, a short drive from Munich. After turning into the second entrance gate on the road from Dachau, the visitor approaches a small park area in front of which, set on a marble base, is a bronze statue of a concentration camp victim. The base is inscribed, "To honor the dead; to admonish the living." In this landscaped sector, containing a grove of pine trees, grassy areas, and flower-bordered walks, is a connected complex of buildings that housed the crematorium, the gas chamber (completed just before the camp's liberation and, so, never used), and rooms used for gruesome medical experiments and torture. Nearby are markers noting the location of the "hanging tree," where prisoners were hanged, and the pistol range, where victims were lined up and shot.

Some of the torture rooms have been converted into a museum where there are preserved many articles used in daily life by the prisoners, torture instruments, photographs of crematorium operations, and documents. On the crematorium walls can be seen inscriptions of names and bitter accusations and many Stars of David. In the park area are two mounds beneath which are buried the ashes of thousands who died at Dachau. A stone marker, inscribed in French, German, and English, identifies the spot as the "grave of thousands of unknown." Nearby is a wooden box labeled "ASHES STORED HERE." Behind the mounds are international monuments containing the emblems of the nations whose citizens died here. One of them, representing "the thousands of unknown Jews who died here," is a simple vault of basalt blocks, half sunk in the ground to symbolize the death platform and the concentration camp bunker, topped by a Menorah and a text from Psalms in Hebrew and German.

The Catholic memorial is the Convent of Atonement founded by Carmelite nuns who live there. The Evangelical Church erected a simple monument to Protestants in the form of a small chapel.

The main monument, erected by the International Dachau Committee and designed by a Yugoslav sculptor, depicts the suffering of the prisoners whose elongated, emaciated bodies are pierced by barbed wire. The inscription reads: "May the example of those who perished here between 1933 and 1945, on account of their fight against Nazism, unite the living in their common defense of freedom and security and their respect for the dignity of man."

All of the prison barracks have been torn down but their site has been marked by concrete blocks and numbered gravel beds. The museum is housed in what used to be supply and laundry rooms. The guard towers have been restored. It is estimated that 207,000 prisoners passed through Dachau, the Nazis' first concentration camp, and some 27,800 are known to have been killed there. Thousands of these are buried at Leitenberg Cemetery in the town of Dachau.

DARMSTADT

HESSIAN STATE LIBRARY in the Castle, a famous local landmark, is the repository of the Darmstädter Passover Haggadah, one of the most precious of all Jewish ceremonial objects extant. Written on parchment sometime during the fourteenth century by Israel ben Meier of Heidelberg, the Haggadah's art work was created by two different artists. For centuries this masterpiece belonged to various Jewish families. In 1780 it was acquired by a Baron Hopsch for his private collection. Subsequently, it came into the possession of the State Library. During the Nazi era, the Haggadah was secreted in the Offenbach Leather Museum where its costly leather binding served as perfect camouflage.

JEWISH COMMUNITY HEADQUARTERS, 11 Osannsstrasse.

DEGGENDORF

CATHOLIC CHURCH, here in 1961 covered up and made unreadable the medieval anti-Jewish captions on pictures of a "desecration of the Host" attributed to local Jews in 1337. The pictures, which also depicted a massacre of Jews here as "a God-willed act," were removed entirely in 1969 on orders from the Vatican.

DETMOLD

JEWISH COMMUNITY HOUSE, 13 Alleestrasse.

DORTMUND

MEMORIAL TO NAZI VICTIMS, a tall stone shaft, is situated in the Jewish section of the East Cemetery.

SYNAGOGUE, 9 Prinz Friedrich Karl Strasse, was the first Jewish house of worship built in the Ruhr since the end of World War II. The funds were provided by the North Rhine-Westphalia State.

DUISBURG

JEWISH COMMUNAL CENTER AND SYNAGOGUE, 24 Koehnenstrasse.

DÜSSELDORF

BÖRNESTRASSE is named for the eighteenth-century German journalist, pamphleteer, and patriot, Ludwig Börne, who was one of the prime movers of the 1848 revolution.

CENTRAL COUNCIL OF JEWS OF GERMANY, the national representative body of Jews in West Germany, has its national headquarters at 49 Fischerstrasse.

DUMONT-LINDEMANN ARCHIVES, 3 Ehrenhof, is a famed collection of German theatre memorabilia founded and donated by Gustav Lindemann and his wife, who managed the Düsseldorf Theatre from 1905 to 1932.

ANNE FRANK ELEMENTARY SCHOOL, Freiligrathplatz, is named for the author of the famous diary.

HEINE ARCHIVES in the Heine Room of the City and County Library, 3-7 Grabbeplatz, is the largest collection of the original manuscripts of Heinrich Heine, one of Germany's greatest literary personalities, who was born in Düsseldorf in 1797. Among the more than 3,700 pages of his work, much of it in the poet's own handwriting, is the original manuscript of "Die Lorelei," Heine's most famous poem, which during the Nazi era was ascribed to "an unknown author." The collection also includes a part of Heine's famous Passover narrative, *Rabbi of Bacharach*. The room also houses much of Heine's personal library, his death mask, and an important collection of books by and about Heine. The Archives are being converted into a Heine literary museum.

HEINE'S BIRTHPLACE, 53 Bolkerstrasse, in the old part of the city, was wrecked by bombs during World War II, but the front has been restored and a plaque affixed to it, even though the restored house, occupied in part by a baker's shop, is not the one in which Heine was born. That building was torn down in 1890. The plaque shows Heine's head and gives the date of his birth.

HEINE BUST stands in the Zum Goldenen Kessel restaurant, 44 Bolkerstrasse, on the site of a building where Heine's father was in business when the poet was born.

HEINE MEMORIAL in the Ehrenhof (court of honor) at the end of the Hofgarden by the side of the Rhine River, is a larger-than-life-size figure entitled "Ascending Youth," which in 1932 won first prize for the sculptor Georg Kolbe in a competition for a Heine Memorial. The statue was bought by the city of Düsseldorf but could not be exhibited during the Nazi regime, when everything associated with Heine was taboo. After World War II it was put on permanent display together with a little marker indicating that it was meant as a Heine memorial.

HEINE MONUMENT on Napoleon's Hill in the Hofgarten, is Aristide Maillol's sculpture of an armless girl standing at the top of a flight of steps. Along the wall on the right of the steps is a carved inscription containing a quotation from the poet's works and a head of Heine in bas-relief. The statue is called *Harmony*.

HEINE PLAQUE is affixed to the wall of the entrance hall of the Düsseldorf City Hall.

HEINRICH HEINE SCHOOL, 186 Heerdter Landstrasse, has a bust of the poet in the entrance lobby.

There is also a *Heinestrasse* in Düsseldorf, as well as a Heinrich Heine Allee, one of the city's most attractive boulevards. There is a movement afoot to rename Düsseldorf University as Heinrich Heine University.

KLEINSTRASSE, a new street near the site of the former synagogue, is named for the community's late Rabbi Siegfried Klein, who died in Auschwitz.

LASSALLESTRASSE is named for Ferdinand Lassalle, the political organizer of the German Socialist party.

FELIX MENDELSSOHN-BARTHOLDY MEMORIAL is a tablet affixed to the house at 1 Jan Wellemplatz, where the beloved composer and musician lived and worked from 1833 to 1837, while he was Düsseldorf's musical director. In this house, which was destroyed during World War II, he composed his *St. Paul* oratorio. Mendelssohn-Bartholdy was the grandson of Moses Mendelssohn, the philosopher and Jewish reformer. A bust of Mendelssohn-Bartholdy by Ivo Beucker stands in the foyer of the Düsseldorf Opera House, 16a Alleestrasse. The city also has a *Mendelssohnstrasse.*

NEW SYNAGOGUE, 50 Zietenstrasse, dedicated in 1958, is an unusual, circular structure with a series of memorial stained-glass windows facing the street. A community center in the building is called Leo Baeck Hall in honor of the great Jewish scholar and hero of the Nazi era. In the same building are the editorial offices of the *Allgemeine Wochenzeitung der Juden in Deutschland,* German Jewry's weekly journal.

NORTH CEMETERY, a municipal burial ground that includes the new Jewish cemetery, has an imposing memorial to all of Düsseldorf's war victims. The old Jewish cemetery, now closed, is at 187 Ulmenstrasse, a short walk from the new one.

OLD SYNAGOGUE MEMORIAL, an inscribed stone marking the site of the Great Synagogue on Kasernenstrasse, was erected in 1946 by the city. The old synagogue was burned down by the Nazis in 1938. On its ruins there was erected a one-story air-raid shelter during the war. The shelter was replaced by the City of Düsseldorf Hotel, and the memorial stone is on a side wall of the hotel. The inscription reads: "Here stood the synagogue of the Jewish community of Düsseldorf. On November 9, 1938, it became a victim of race hatred. Of its proud congregation of 3,500, 55 Jewish citizens are still alive. To the dead in honored memory, to the living in vigilance. The City of Düsseldorf, November 9, 1946."

SCHLOSSMANN FOUNTAIN on the grounds of the City Hospital, 5 Moorenstrasse, memorializes Dr. Arthur Schlossmann, eminent German-Jewish pediatrician. There is also a *Schlossmannstrasse.*

BERNHARD SOPHER GALLERY, 5 Ernst Pönsgen Allee, a permanent memorial exhibit of the works of the late Jewish sculptor, who lived in and worked in Düsseldorf from 1909 to 1936 before emigrating to the United States, is housed in the home of Werner Sack, an industrialist, who established it.

EMDEN

JEWISH COMMUNAL CENTER AND SYNAGOGUE, 48 Petkumerstrasse.

ENDINGEN

ST PETER'S CHURCH recently removed the anti-Semitic relics, the remains of two children described as victims of a "ritual murder" by Jews in 1470. For 500 years the relics were enshrined in the church. A hill outside the town still bears the name "Judenbuck" (Jew Knoll) because it was there that three Jews were burned after the "ritual murder."

ENSINGEN

VAIHINGEN-ENZ CONCENTRATION CAMP where 1,500 people died, among them 300 Jews, is marked by a memorial inscribed, "In eternal memory to the victims of the Nazi tyranny who died in the Vaihingen-Enz Concentration Camp. Their remains were buried here in 1956."

ESSEN

NEW SYNAGOGUE, 46 Sedanstrasse, is housed in a metal-clad dome perforated by circular lights, and is linked across a walled garden to the Community Center.

OLD SYNAGOGUE, 29 Steelerstrasse, one of the most beautiful in Germany, was gutted by Nazi incendiaries in 1938. The exterior has been retored to look like a synagogue, but the building is now an exhibition hall. Behind the building is a tomb memorializing the 2,500 Essen Jews killed by the Nazis. At the nearby Parkfriedhof there is another memorial to Nazi victims.

ESSLINGEN

EBERSHALDEN CEMETERY has a memorial to 85 Jewish victims of the Nazis. It is shaped like a huge Star of David, and on it is inscribed: "Here rest the remains of 85 Jews of unknown nationality, victims of Nazi barbarity. Their death is a reminder to humanity for the living generation—1947." Near the town's inner bridge, there is another memorial to Nazi victims in the form of a small chapel.

FLOSSENBURG

FLOSSENBURG CONCENTRATION CAMP victims are memorialized in a tiny park in the middle of which stands a crematorium chimney on which are listed the number of dead from each country.

ANNE FRANK VILLAGE

SETTLEMENT FOR EUROPEAN D.P.s who cannot emigrate because of age or sickness, is one of six such villages in Germany and Belgium founded by Father Dominique Georges Pire, a Belgian priest, who won the Nobel Peace Prize in 1958 for his work among refugees. The village named for Anne Frank is outside the city of Wuppertal and houses twenty families. In the village's cornerstone is a handful of earth from the Bergen-Belsen concentration camp where Anne Frank died and is buried.

FRANKFURT-AM-MAIN

BÖRNESTRASSE the present name for the street that used to be known as the Judengasse (Jews' Street) in the ancient ghetto, honors Karl Ludwig Börne, the first German journalist, who was born at 118 Judengasse. Börne, whose articles and pamphlets set the stage for the Young Germany Movement that led to the revolutionary year of 1848, was originally named Löb Baruch but took the name Börne when he was baptized. The conversion was a formality, since he always regarded himself as a Jew. A vigorous champion of political liberty, he was one of the heroes of the German literary *salons* and in his last years waged war against reactionary forces in Germany from his home in Paris. A marble monument to Börne erected in 1877 in the Bockenheimer Anlage no longer exists, but the city has erected a memorial plaque affixed to the Nebbien'schen Gartenhausen in the Bockenheimer Anlage.

BÖRNEPLATZ SYNAGOGUE destroyed in 1938, is memorialized by a marble plaque attached to the wall of the old Jewish cemetery behind the Blumen-Grosmarkthalle. The first burials here took place in 1272 and the last in 1828, but most of the old gravestones have vanished. Entrance to the cemetery is through the Dominikanerplatz. Keys to the closed gates may be obtained at Jewish Community Headquarters, 5-7 Baumweg. This historic cemetery was the second in the eight hundred-year history of Frankfurt Jewry.

MARTIN BUBER HIGH SCHOOL, a secondary school opened in 1967, is named for the eminent German-born Jewish philosopher.

HENRY AND EMMA BUDGE HOME, houses the city's newest synagogue, which was opened in 1970.

CATHEDRAL OF FRANKFURT on Domplatz, built in the thirteenth century and heavily damaged during World War II air raids, was found, during postwar restoration work, to have Jewish tombstones with Hebrew inscriptions dating from the middle of the thirteenth century as part of its substructure. During the removal of the cathedral's stone base, slabs used in one layer of the foundation were identified as Jewish gravestones, probably from the first Jewish cemetery, which was sacked during an attack on the Jewish community in 1241.

Subsequently, the front of the cathedral's altar was also identified as a Jewish tombstone. The northern wing of the cathedral, containing the famed Anna Altar, was consecrated in 1353, four years after the Jews were expelled from Frankfurt during the Black Death persecutions when their second cemetery was vandalized. These stones can be seen next to the walls of the cathedral's so-called Kreuzgangs. This is usually closed, but keys are obtainable at the Catholic Dompfarramt, 1 Domplatz.

CITY HISTORICAL MUSEUM, 31 Saalgasse, contains a small exhibit of Jewish ritual and art objects, remnants from the destroyed Jewish Museum in the vanished ghetto and from Jewish libraries looted by the Nazis and assembled in Frankfurt as a central institute for Nazi propagandists. The museum is planning a new building which will house a large and permanent Jewish exhibit.

CITY AND STATE LIBRARY, 14-15 Untermainkai, has 150,000 volumes of Judaica and Hebraica, about a fourth of the prewar collection. Much of the valuable Hebraica collection was destroyed during air raids.

PAUL EHRLICH INSTITUTE, 42-44 Paul Ehrlichstrasse, on the campus of Frankfurt University, is named for Dr. Paul Ehrlich, whose research led to the discovery of "606," the cure for syphilis, and to other major chemical breakthroughs, which earned him the Nobel Prize in Medicine in 1908. Adjoining the Institute is *Georg Speyer House*, the world's first scientific institute for chemotherapy research, which was founded in 1909 by the widow of Georg Speyer, Frankfurt banker and philanthropist. It was created to encourage Ehrlich's research. Ehrlich's former laboratory is preserved intact. On the wall are two memorial tablets and Ehrlich's death mask. In the lecture hall used by the Institute and Speyer House is a bronze bust of Ehrlich. Mrs. Speyer also contributed 1,500,000 gold marks, an unprecedented sum by pre-World War I standards, to convert the Academy of Frankfurt into a university.

FELDERBERGSTRASSE SYNAGOGUE, 22-26 Altkönigstrasse, was badly damaged inside by the Nazis, but the exterior was unharmed. On the wall of the synagogue is a plaque memorializing, in Hebrew, "the honest and pious souls of our community . . . who were cut off in their youth by the bloodthirsty Nazis, 1933-1945. Their memory will last forever in the heart of the whole house of Israel." It was in this building that the Nazis had planned to establish a permanent museum to house Jewish religious treasures taken from destroyed synagogues throughout Europe.

ANNE FRANK'S BIRTHPLACE, 24 Ganghoferstrasse, is marked with a memorial tablet as the house where the martyred Jewish youngster was born in 1929. Erected by the youth of Frankfurt, the tablet notes that "she died as a victim of Nazi persecution in 1945 in the Bergen-Belsen concentration camp. Her life and death—our obligation."

FRANKFURT UNIVERSITY, one of the country's best institutions of higher learning, has in its library a "Literature in Exile" section that displays portraits of such world-renowned authors, thinkers, composers and dramatists as Max Reinhardt, Kurt Weill, Arnold Schoenberg and Albert Einstein. In the main lobby of the university is a bust of Dr. Max Horkheimer, one-time rector of the university, who was driven from his post by the Nazis. The university was founded by Wilhelm Mertin, a Jewish philanthropist who later embraced Christianity.

JOACHIM GOTTSCHALK BUST in the lobby of the Grossen Hauses, 1-3 Am Schauspielhaus, recalls one of the tragedies of the Nazi era. Gottschalk, a prominent German actor who was married to a Jewess, was ordered to divorce his wife, who with her children were to be deported to a concentration camp. A few days later the entire family committed suicide.

HEINRICH HEINE MONUMENT in the Taunusanlage, is a marble pedestal to which Heine's name and head are affixed on a bronze tablet. On the pedestal are bronze figures of a young boy and girl.

HOME FOR THE AGED, 36 Gagernstrasse, also houses a synagogue.

NEW JEWISH CEMETERY, on Ratbeilstrasse, contains the graves of most of the celebrated Jewish figures of nineteenth- and early-twentieth-century Frankfurt, among them the Rothschilds, Paul Ehrlich, Georg Speyer, and members of the Schiff and Warburg families. A newer Jewish cemetery, on Eckenheimer Landstrasse, contains the graves of Franz Rosenzweig and other Nazi martyrs.

JEWISH COMMUNITY CENTER, 5-7 Baumweg, also houses a synagogue and a home for the Jewish aged.

JEWISH COMMUNITY HEADQUARTERS, 17 Hebelstrasse, also houses a synagogue.

JEWISH SCHOOL, Friedrichstrasse, opened in 1966, was the first Jewish school to be established in post-war Germany. Still the only Jewish school in the country, it is not a religious school but a regular elementary school that teaches Hebrew and Jewish culture.

KOSHER RESTAURANT in the Hebraica Club, 17 Bronnerstrasse.

LESSING MONUMENT, at the corner of the north end of the Obermain Bridge, erected in 1882 on the centennial of the birth of Gotthold Ephraim Lessing, recalls the great non-Jewish German writer, who championed tolerance and freedom of thought in the eighteenth century and vigorously defended the Jews. A close friend of Moses Mendelssohn, Lessing used the Jewish philosopher as the hero of his principal work, *Nathan the Wise,* which is entirely devoted to tolerance.

MEMORIAL TO NAZI VICTIMS in Taunus Park, is a bronze sculpture by Benno Elkan depicting a woman mourning over a dead child.

STAUFENMAUER a thirteenth-century wall that once surrounded the ghetto, was uncovered by Allied bombing during World War II, and a piece of it can be seen where the Tongesgasse enters the Fahrgasse. Behind the wall are now modern apartments but the ancient archway that was a passageway to the ghetto still exists. The first Jewish cemetery in Frankfurt was near this wall, but, like the whole former ghetto area, it was destroyed by World War II air raids. Nothing remains of the *Judengassen,* the generic name for the streets in the ghetto, where Mayer Amschel Rothschild launched his business as financial adviser to several German princes and as a dealer in antique coins and established a banking dynasty that spread to France, England, Austria, and Italy. The Rothschild House at 26 Börnestrasse, the famous Jewish Museum at 146 Fahrgasse, and all the other landmarks of the ghetto were razed by Allied bombers during World War II. On the site of the Rothschild house there is now an office building. Only a *Rothschild Park* and some old records in the City Archives recall the Rothschilds' beginnings here.

STERLINGSTRASSE, a new street in the northern district, is named for the late Dr. Eleonore Sterling, German-Jewish sociologist.

SYNAGOGUE, 30 Freiherr vom Steinstrasse, is the largest of six synagogues in Frankfurt, which has 6,000 Jews.

SYNAGOGUE, 29 Roederberg Weg.

FREIBURG

CATHEDRAL CHURCH on Münsterplatz, has on its exterior a Gothic statue depicting the Sacrifice of Isaac.

JEWISH COMMUNITY HEADQUARTERS, 25 Holbeinstrasse.

NAZI VICTIMS MEMORIAL is affixed to the site of the synagogue destroyed in 1938. A new synagogue, built on stilts, was opened in 1970 in the heart·of the city.

FRIEDBERG

JEWISH RITUAL BATH, dating from 1260 can still be seen at 20 Judengasse. Built by the medieval Jewish community, it was lost to sight until 1903. It is now the property of the municipality, which has restored it completely. You can still see the steps that lead down seventy-five feet to the subterranean bath in whose well fresh water still runs. An inconspicuous plaque in a nook of the mikveh commemorates the destruction of the Friedberg synagogue in 1938. The bath is now protected by the municipality as a historical monument.

FULDA

JEWISH CEMETERY on Edelzellerstrasse, has a memorial to local Jewish victims of Nazi persecution.

JEWISH COMMUNITY HEADQUARTERS, 10 Von Schildeckstrasse.

STATE LIBRARY, 12 Heinrich von Bibraplatz, has a substantial collection of old Hebrew manuscripts.

FÜRTH

JEWISH CEMETERY here, 350 years old, is believed to be burial place of Joseph Oppenheimer, the famed "Jew Süss," court financier of Württemberg in the early eighteenth century, who was executed in 1738. He was the hero of Lion Feuchtwanger's popular novel and also the subject of many anti-Semitic plays and movies.

SYNAGOGUE, 2 Julienstrasse, is in the courtyard of what was once a Jewish orphanage founded in 1763 as the first of its kind in Germany. The synagogue was the only one of seven in Furth that escaped destruction in 1938.

JEWISH COMMUNITY HEADQUARTERS, 31 Blumenstrasse.

GAILINGEN

SYNAGOGUE MEMORIAL, a bronze plaque affixed to a chunk of rock in the center of a carefully tended garden, marks the spot where the synagogue stood from 1836 to 1938.

GELSENKIRCHEN

SYNAGOGUE, 9 Von der Reckestrasse, was dedicated in 1958. At Gelsen-kirchen-Horst there is a memorial to 250 Jewish women who died in the Gelsenberg-Benzin concentration camp.

GÖTTINGEN

ALBERT EINSTEINSTRASSE, between Ewaldstrasse and Düster-Eichenweg, was named for the celebrated physicist in 1953.

HEINRICH HEINESTRASSE runs from Schillerstrasse to Durrstrasse.

JUDENGASSE in the suburb of Weende, runs into the main Hannöverschestrasse.

JUDENSTRASSE is in the heart of the oldest section of this famed university town.

MEMORIAL TO NAZI VICTIMS is at the Gewerkschaftshaus on Oberen Maschstrasse.

GOSLAR

JEWISH COMMUNITY HEADQUARTERS, 1 Doktorswiese. There was a Jewish settlement here as early as 1252.

HAGEN

CITY HALL has on permanent display in its Memorial Book the names of the 600 Hagen Jews who lived here before the Nazis began their war on the Jews.
SYNAGOGUE, 16 Pottshofstrasse, was built in 1960 to replace one on the same site wrecked by the Nazi.

HAMBURG

ALTONA JEWISH CEMETERY, on Königstrasse in Altona, is a historical picture gallery in stone of the notables of the early Jewish community, which was founded at the end of the sixteenth century by Marranos from Holland and Portugal. The tombstones are all lavishly sculptured with art symbols and Jewish emblems.
BALLINDAM, a main street on one side of the Binnen-Alster, one of the two lakelike extensions of the Alster River, near the Lombard Bridge, is named for Albert Ballin, one of the leading figures in German economic life before World War I. Friend and adviser of Wilhelm II, Ballin resisted the Kaiser's repeated offers of a title of nobility if he would accept baptism. Born in Hamburg in 1857, Ballin expanded his father's travel agency into a world-wide shipping service that carried tens of thousands of European immigrants to America in the 1880s and 1890s in German ships. As general manager of the Hamburg-Amerika Line, he pioneered in building the first big ocean liners, including the ships that became the *Berengaria*, the *Leviathan*, and the *Majestic*. Before World War I he was the key figure in the expansion of the German merchant marine. Ballin died of an overdose of sleeping pills on November 9, 1918 when he heard that the Kaiser had fled to Holland. At the time it was erroneously reported that he had committed suicide. In 1957, on the centennial of Ballin's birth, the Hamburg municipality honored him by a special stamp and memorial exercises at his tomb.
HAMBURG TEMPLE, 120 Oberstrasse, now used by the German Radio Network, was so solidly built that it withstood all efforts of the Nazis to wreck it in 1938. A plaque on the building, which was erected in 1931, recalls that it was originally a synagogue. This congregation, founded in 1817 as the Israelitischer Tempelverein, became the cradle of Reform Judaism.
INSTITUTE FOR THE HISTORY OF GERMAN JEWS, a branch of the Hamburg Science Foundation, located in Hamburg University, collects and publishes material about the history of Jews in Central Europe. It is supported by the municipality.
JEWISH COMMUNITY CENTER, 29 Schaeferkamps Allee.
JEWISH CEMETERY, at 68 Ilandkoppel, Ohlsdorf, has a memorial to Jewish victims of Nazism.
JEWISH HOSPITAL AND OLD FOLKS HOME, 25-27 Schäferkampsallee, was opened in 1960 to replace the old Jewish hospital, which had been founded early in the nineteenth century by Solomon Heine, wealthy merchant and uncle of Heinrich Heine. The older hospital was destroyed by the Nazis.
KUNSTHALLE (Art Museum), 1 Glockengiesswall, owns the Oscar Troplowitz Collection of art masterpieces donated in 1920 by Dr. Oscar Troplowitz, noted industrialist.
MUSEUM OF ART AND COMMERCE, 1 Steintorplatz, has a collection of Jewish art and ritual objects.

MENDELSSOHN ELEMENTARY SCHOOL, 86 Mendelssohnstrasse, is named for Felix Mendelssohn-Bartholdy, the famous composer, who was the grandson of Moses Mendelssohn. The composer, who was born in Hamburg in 1809, was the author of the beloved *Midsummer Night's Dream* and is regarded as one of the great musical geniuses of the nineteenth century.

RATHAUS (City Hall) has in its main foyer an honor gallery on which notable Hamburgers are memorialized by portrait medals. Solomon Heine, Mendelssohn-Bartholdy, Heinrich Hertz, and Gabriel Riesser are the four Jews whose portraits are to be seen here.

Hertz discovered the electromagnetic wave which made possible radio and modern tele-communications. Although he did not identify himself with the Jewish community, the Nazis regarded him as a Jew and persecuted his relatives and sought to obliterate his name. This was quite impossible since the Hertzian Wave, by which the electromagnetic wave is known throughout the world, was in common use in Germany as the *kilohertz*, the equivalent of the kilocycle everywhere else. Hertz died in 1894 at the age of 37. The *Heinrich Hertz High School* is at 23 Vossberg.

Riesser, the celebrated champion of Jewish emancipation, was the author of memoranda and articles that helped arouse German liberals in support of Jewish equality. He served in the 1848 parliament and in 1859 became the first professing Jew named a judge in Germany. There is a Gabriel Riesserstrasse in the Borgfelde section. His tombstone is in the Ohlsdorf Jewish Cemetery. There is a plaque honoring Heinrich Heine in the building of the Hoffmann & Campe Publishing Co., 14 Havestehuderweg. A marble statue of Heine that used to stand in the Barkhof survived the war and was purchased by the Hoffmann family and taken by their heirs to Marseilles, France.

SYNAGOGUE, 34 An der hohen Weide, a modern octagon-shaped structure dedicated in 1960, is now the center of Jewish life in Hamburg. It is part of a complex of buildings that includes a community center and homes for rabbis and community officials. The badly damaged synagogue at 24 Kielortalee is no longer used.

HANOVER

JEWISH COMMUNITY CENTER AND SYNAGOGUE, 10 Haeckelstrasse, was dedicated in 1961. It is next door to the *Jewish Old Folks Home*.

JEWISH SOLDIERS MEMORIAL in the undamaged chapel of the Jewish cemetery at 55 Strangriede, lists the Hanover Jews who died for Germany in the Franco-Prussian War and in World War I.

MARKTKIRCHE, one of the city's oldest churches, has an inscription in its vestry recording the expulsion of Jews from the city in 1350 on a charge of well poisoning.

JEWISH CEMETERY, at Judenkirchhof, which was opened in 1600 and closed in 1865, is situated on a hill in the center of the city. It is protected as a historical monument. Among those buried here are Joseph Hameln, whose daughter-in-law, Glückel, wrote an important volume of memoirs on seventeenth-century Jewish life in Germany, and Heinemann Heine, grandfather of Heinrich Heine.

MEMORIAL TO NAZI VICTIMS in the New Jewish Cemetery, 90 Burgwedelerstrasse, consists of two plaques in the rebuilt Jewish chapel. The one on the left reads: "In memory of our dead comrades of the Muhlenberg, Ahlem and Stocken concentration camps." The one on the right reads: "Remember the twelve million victims of the Nazi terror from all nations." There is also a monument here in memory of Jewish victims of the Bergen-Belsen concentration camp.

RATHENAUPLATZ in the heart of the city between the Opera House and Georgsplatz, is named for Walther Rathenau, industrialist and statesman. (*See* BERLIN *above.*)

SYNAGOGUE MEMORIAL, on the administrative building of the Protestant Church for the Greater Hanover area, is a plaque memorializing Hanover's famous synagogue which fell victim to the Nazi terror in 1938.

HECHINGEN

JEWISH CEMETERY now maintained by the city, escaped desecration during the Nazi era. In the chapel, the city has erected a memorial to the Jews who died during the Nazi holocaust. The cemetery is on a mountainside.

SYNAGOGUE, on Goldschmiedsstrasse, formerly the Judengasse, was built at the end of the seventeenth century. The exterior escaped damage during the Nazi era; after the war, when only one Jew returned to the city, the building was turned over to him and he is using it for business purposes.

HEIDELBERG

HEIDELBERGER CASTLE RUINS, on the slopes of the Königstuhl mountain overlooking the city and the Neckar River, have still visible an inscription, in Hebrew and in Latin, from Psalm 118: "This is the gate of the Lord. Let the righteous enter."

JEWISH CEMETERY, on Klingenteichstrasse, near the castle ruins, dates from the fourteenth century. It is now closed.

JEWISH COMMUNITY HEADQUARTERS, 10-12 Häusserstrasse.

MEMORIAL TO NAZI VICTIMS is located in the new Jewish cemetery at the Bergfriedhof, a municipal cemetery.

SYNAGOGENPLATZ is the new name of the street on which the old Heidelberg synagogue stood until 1938. A memorial tablet has been erected on the site of the synagogue. No new synagogue has yet been built.

UNIVERSITY OF HEIDELBERG LIBRARY owns a large collection of Judaica and the originals of agreements between twelfth-century Jews and local princes.

HEILBRONN

ANCIENT JEWISH TOMB in the basement of a house where a synagogue once stood has been preserved and will be marked as a historical site.

HERFORD

JEWISH COMMUNITY HEADQUARTERS, 57 Hansastrasse.

HERZOGENRATH

MOSES STATUE in the village square of this town on the Dutch border, depicts the lawgiver as a heavy-set figure with a crown of thorns on his head and a loincloth about his waist. This odd representation was dedicated in 1962 to replace an earlier statue, a traditional depiction of Moses erected in 1852 but destroyed by the Nazis in 1934.

HILDESHEIM

JEWISH COMMUNAL CENTER, 32 Mellingerstrasse.

JUDENSTRASSE, near the old market place, a remnant of the Jewish settlement that goes back to 1347, was virtually destroyed by Allied bombings in World War II.

HOF

SYNAGOGUE AND COMMUNAL CENTER, 13 Karolineanstrasse.

ISRAELSDORF

VILLAGE, near Lübeck has no known Jewish connection but the Nazis changed its name to Walddorf in 1933. The old name, which appears in records going back to 1163 as Israelistorpe, and later as Isrelosdorpe and Israelsdorpe, was restored in 1946.

JULICH

JEWISH CEMETERY in this Ruhr town has a ten-foot high memorial in memory of 60 Jews from the community who were killed during the Nazi regime.

KARLSRUHE

JEWISH CEMETERY, Kriegsstrasse, contains seventeenth-century tombs.
SYNAGOGUE AND JEWISH COMMUNITY HOUSE, 154 Kriegsstrasse, opened in 1970, is designed like a Star of David. Building funds were provided by the municipality and the Baden-Wuerttemberg Landtag.

KASSEL

ASCHROTT PARK AND FOUNTAIN, near City Hall, is named for one of the city's leading prewar citizens.
HESSIAN COUNTY MUSEUM exhibits three of Rembrandt's famous paintings of Jewish subjects. These are "The Blessing of Jacob," "Study of a Head of an Old Jew," and "Study of a Head of an Elderly Jewish Man with Fur Cap."
JEWISH CEMETERY, on the Fasanaweg, has in its chapel a monument erected by the city of Kassel to Nazi victims. In the older part of the cemetery are some interesting tombstones dating to the early 1700s.
JEWISH COMMUNITY HEADQUARTERS, 19 Heubnerstrasse.
LUDWIG MONDSTRASSE is named for Ludwig Mond, chemist, inventor, and industrialist, who was born here but settled in England in 1867, where his discoveries led to major developments in industrial chemistry. His son became the first Lord Melchett.
NUSSBAUM PLAYGROUND, a municipal recreation center named for the late Sara Nussbaum, occupies the site on which the main synagogue stood before the Nazi destroyed it.

KIEL

JEWISH COMMUNITY HEADQUARTERS, 101 Muhliusstrasse.

KONSTANZ

JEWISH COMMUNITY HOUSE, on ground floor of a multi-story building, occupies site where the old synagogue destroyed by the Nazis stood until 1938.
CATHEDRAL, contains a number of building blocks which are former Jewish gravestones, including those of some of the famed Kolynomus family.
SYNAGOGUE MEMORIAL, a plaque originally erected on the site of the synagogue destroyed in 1938, has been removed to the Jewish Cemetery, which is part of the municipal cemetery. A small Jewish prayer house has been erected on the site of the synagogue.

KREFELD

JEWISH COMMUNAL CENTER, 2 Rheinstrasse.

LÜBECK

JEWISH CEMETERY which has some tombstones that are three hundred years old, has two monuments memorializing Jews who died en route to the Belsen concentration camp.

SYNAGOGUE AND JEWISH COMMUNAL CENTER, 11-13 St. Annenstrasse, is the only one in northern Germany that escaped destruction by the Nazis.

LUDWIGSBURG

SYNAGOGUE MEMORIAL, Alleenstrasse, corner Solitudestrasse, marks site of synagogue wrecked in 1938. The inscription reads: "Here stood the synagogue erected in 1884. Its deliberate destruction on November 10, 1938, should be a reminder to our conscience to cherish humanity and justice." In this town is the headquarters of the official German government agency investigating Nazi war crimes.

MAINZ

JEWISH CEMETERY, 85 Mombacherstrasse, on a hillside in this ancient Rhine River town, is a direct link with the tenth-century Jewish community. Recently restored by the municipality, the cemetery has at least two hundred gravestones that go back to the thirteenth century or earlier. They had been scattered around the burial ground for hundreds of years after it had been desecrated during the expulsion of the Jews in 1348. These old stones are now numbered. No. 164 is the stone of Rabbenu Gershom ben Jehudah, known as the Light of the Exile, who died in 1028. He was the recognized religious leader of western Jewry; his decrees were accepted by all European Jews. No. 1, also dated in the eleventh century, is the gravestone of Rabbi Meshullam ben Kolynomus. No. 2 commemorates Rabbi Jacob ben Yakar, teacher of Rashi, who died in 1064.

STATE ALTERTUMSMUSEUM, at Grosse Bleiche, preserves other links with the ancient Jewish community in the form of remnants of a stone house believed to have been built around 1000 by members of the Kolynomus family who founded the Jewish community here in the tenth century. Many of the Kolynomus family were great scholars, poets, and philosophers. One saved the life of Emperor Otto II after the Battle of Cotrone in 982. Another was the first to chant the celebrated Yom Kippur hymn, "Unethanneh Tokef," the author of which was Rabbi Annon, also of Mainz. According to Jewish legend, Rabbi Annon composed the hymn in his dying hours, when he was carried into the synagogue on Rosh Hashana after having been tortured because of his refusal to accept baptism.

JEWISH COMMUNITY HEADQUARTERS, 2 Forsterstrasse. The three synagogues that stood here before the war were destroyed by the Nazis and by Allied bombers.

MANNHEIM

MEMORIAL TO NAZI MARTYRS, in the Jewish Cemetery, is shaped like an urn and bears the inscription, "To those who found no grave."

SYNAGOGUE, 6 Maximilianstrasse.

MARBURG

JEWISH COMMUNAL HEADQUARTERS, 7 Alter Kirchhainer Weg.

MICHELSTADT

SYNAGOGUE, oldest in the state of Hesse, has been restored by Hessian State Indemnification Commission. It was originally built in 1791.

JEWISH CEMETERY contains the grave of the Baal Shem of Michelstadt.

MINDEN

SYNAGOGUE AND JEWISH COMMUNAL CENTER, 6 Kampstrasse.

MÜNSTER

SYNAGOGUE AND JEWISH COMMUNAL CENTER, 6-8 Klosterstrasse, a tiny sanctuary seating barely 100, was built in 1957. Judenfelderstrasse (Jews' Fields Street) was the site of the pre-Nazi synagogue.

MULHEIM

JEWISH COMMUNAL HEADQUARTERS, 7 Kampstrasse.

MULDENAU

ST. BARBARA CATHOLIC CHURCH, near Cologne, has engraved on its church bell the Einstein equation that formed the basis for the atomic bomb. The church's pastor explained the engraving by saying the bell should give a picture of modern times and the equation is part of them. As inscribed on the bell, the equation is garbled because someone substituted an R for the C in "$E = MC^2$."

MUNICH

BAVARIAN STATE LIBRARY, 16 Ludwigstrasse, has 420 Hebrew manuscripts and 18 Hebrew incunabula dating from the Middle Ages. It also owns a unique collection of old Judaeo-German writings, a fifteenth-century Haggadah, and one very ancient Babylonian Talmud manuscript.

EINSTEINSTRASSE is named for Dr. Albert Einstein.

HEINE MEMORIAL, 7 Hackenstrasse, is a plaque noting that Heinrich Heine lived there from 1827 to 1828. The poet was in Munich while serving as editor of a publishing company and waiting for an academic appointment that never came.

JEWISH COMMUNITY CENTER AND HOME FOR AGED, 27 Reichenbacher Street. A fire attributed to anti-Semitic arsonists took the lives of seven elderly Jews on the night of Feb. 14, 1970.

KOSHER RESTAURANT, 27 Reichenbach Street, is in same building as Jewish Community Center.

MEMORIAL TO VICTIMS OF NAZIS, in the old Jewish cemetery in the Perlacher Forest, is a parklike area in the center of which is a marble-lined ground-level tomb containing the ashes of 4,000 Jews. In the new Jewish cemetery, 217 Ungererstrasse, is another memorial to Nazi victims and a monument to Jewish soldiers of World War I. Still another memorial is on the Platz der Opfer des Nationalsozialismus. A national education center to be erected on the site of the former Wittelsbach Palace is also planned as memorial to the victims of Nazism.

MOSES FOUNTAIN, a fountain-statue representing Moses in the desert striking a rock to bring forth water, stands in the courtyard at Lenbachplatz created by new office buildings, the new Justice Building, and a line of elegant shops. Commissioned by the city council and sculpted by Professor Joseph Henselmann, head of Munich's Academy of Fine Arts, it was erected in 1958 not far from where the Nazis burned the city's oldest synagogue twenty years earlier. The sculpture consists of a twelve-foot-high, rough, slender rock, on top of which is a bronze figure of Moses holding a rod from which an arch of water sprays out into a pool below.

OFFENBACHSTRASSE, in the western part of the city, is named for the composer, Jacques Offenbach.

SHERMAN FIELD, a little-league baseball diamond, in the Perlacher Forest behind the United States Army hospital, is named for the late Pfc. Alvin I. Sherman, of Linden, New Jersey, who was killed in a plane crash in 1960. Sherman, a military policeman, earned the gratitude of the local residents by organizing and coaching little-league teams.

SPANIER MEMORIAL, in the Children's Hospital on Lachnerstrasse, is a bronze medallion honoring Dr. Julius Spanier, a prominent pediatrician and one of the founders of the hospital.

SYNAGOGUE, a newly-erected structure, was dedicated during the city's celebration of its 2,000th anniversary in 1964.

SYNAGOGUE MEMORIALS, plaques at 1 Herzog-Rudolfstrasse and 3 Herzog-Maxstrasse, memorialize the city's two synagogues which were destroyed in 1938. At 7 Herzog-Maxstrasse is a *Jewish Communal Center.* The plaques were erected by the municipality of the city where Hitler staged his first putsch in 1923 and which in the 1940s was the staging area for thousands of Jews en route to nameless tragedy at the nearby Dachau concentration camp. The most impressive memorial is in a small park and occupies the site of the former chief synagogue of Munich.

NEUENGAMME

CONCENTRATION CAMP MEMORIAL, walled-in site of the Hamburg-Neuengamme Concentration Camp, where 55,000 people, most of them Jews, were exterminated by the Nazis, is an 81-foot granite pillar and a bronze sculpture depicting a dying camp inmate lying on the ground and making one last desperate effort to rise. At the foot of the memorial are 22 stone plaques with the names of the nations whose citizens died here.

NEUSS

NELLY SACHS SCHOOL FOR GIRLS, a secondary school in this town near Duesseldorf, is named for the German-Jewish poetess who in 1966 shared the Nobel Prize in Literature with Shmuel Yosef Agnon, Israeli author.

NEUSTADT

SYNAGOGUE, Wienerstrasse, is a post-war structure. There is also a new Jewish Home for the Aged here.

NEUSTADT AN DER WEINSTRASSE

JEWISH COMMUNITY CENTRE, 119 Karolinenstrasse.

NEUSTADT-HOLSTEIN

INTERNATIONAL MEMORIAL for victims of a bombing attack killed when three ships loaded with concentration camp inmates were sunk is situated here. Nearby, in a small Jewish cemetery, is a memorial to Jews who survived the concentration camps but died shortly after liberation.

NUREMBERG

GERMAN NATIONAL MUSEUM, 1 Kornmarkt, preserves four tombstones from a thirteenth-century Jewish cemetery wrecked during the 1349 massacres after which the stones were used for building materials. One stone, dated 1282, once covered the grave of the young son of Rabbi Joseph. Another is dated 1313, and two are dated 1477 and 1448, respectively, the latter from a later burial ground. The museum also has a collection of early-eighteenth-century prayer books, prayer shawls, Torah covers, mezuzoth, and Sabbath lamps. Two famous illuminated Haggadoth that once formed part of this collection were sold to the Jewish National Museum in Jerusalem. In 1970, four ancient tombstones taken in 1372 from the Nuremberg Jewish cemetery and converted into building blocks for the spiral staircase in the south dome of the church of St. Lorenz, the local castle, were returned to the Jewish community. The 600-year old Hebrew lettering on the stones, which have been set up in the new Jewish cemetery, can still be read.

JEWISH COMMUNITY HEADQUARTERS, 6 Wielandstrasse, serves the handful of Jews who returned to this ancient city where the Nazi party rallies were held, where the infamous Nuremberg racial laws were adopted, where Julius Streicher's notorious Jew-baiting paper, *Der Stuermer*, was published, and where the Nuremberg war criminals trials of 1945-46 were held in the old Palace of Justice. The cells where the Nazi prisoners were housed during the trials can still be seen. All of the buildings erected for the Nazi party rallies except the Party Congress Hall have been razed. There is still a Judengasse outside the old castle walls.

OBERHAUSEN

ATONEMENT HALL, a memorial to the town's Jewish citizens murdered by the Nazis, was built by the volunteer labor of high school students.

JEWISH COMMUNAL HEADQUARTERS, 10 Trachebergstrasse.

OFFENBACH

NEW SYNAGOGUE, 109 Kaiserstrasse, in a garden area, was dedicated in 1956. A plaque bearing the name of local Jews killed by the Nazis stands in the lobby.

OLD SYNAGOGUE, built in the early 1800s, escaped destruction during the Nazi era, but after the war it was sold to the city and has since been converted into a theatre.

NEW JEWISH CEMETERY, on Friedhofstrasse, next to the old cemetery, was opened in 1861. The old cemetery, which has been converted into a grassy field, is said to have been the burial ground of Jacob Frank, an eighteenth-century pseudo messiah.

OLDENBURG

JEWISH COMMUNAL HEADQUARTERS, 5 Lambertistrasse.

SYNAGOGUE MEMORIAL, on the site of the synagogue destroyed by the Nazis, is a stone slab with an inscription in Hebrew and German.

OSNABRUCK

SYNAGOGUE AND JEWISH COMMUNAL HEADQUARTERS, 14 Schnatgang.

PADERBORN

SYNAGOGUE, 27 Theodorstrasse, was erected in 1959.

PASSAU

ILZSTADT CHURCH has a series of stained-glass windows depicting the alleged desecration of Christian images by Jews in 1477.

JEWISH COMMUNAL CENTER, 2 Brunngasse.

RECKLINGHAUSEN

JEWISH COMMUNAL CENTER, 3 Am Polizeipräsidium, which survived the Nazi era, has been rebuilt and now includes a small synagogue that serves the 90 Jews in this city and in the neighboring towns of Bochum and Herne. The Recklinghausen synagogue was burned in 1938, and most of the 3,000 Jews from this area were sent to a death camp at Riga, Latvia. Thomas Grochowiak, in whose father's house a few Jews were hidden during the Nazi period, is the director of the local art museum where in 1960 there was staged one of the greatest exhibitions of Jewish sacred art and displays dealing with Jewish cultural life ever shown. It was called "Synagoga" and included objects from 130 museums, galleries, and libraries in many countries.

OLD JEWISH CEMETERY, on the edge of the town amid farm land, has two memorials: one honors Jews from this area who died in concentration camps; the other lists the names of thirteen Jews who died for the Fatherland in World War I.

REGENSBURG

AM JUDENSTEIN, one of the old streets here, is named for a Jewish tombstone dated 1347 and bearing the name of Moses ben Joseph. It is set into the wall of a school on this street. This stone was one of thousands in the medieval Jewish cemetery which were used for building purposes or plastered into house fronts after 1519, when the Jews were expelled. The Jewish settlement here began in the tenth century, and it escaped the tragedies that befell other German Jewish communities in the thirteenth, fourteenth, and fifteenth centuries.

EVANGELICAL HOSPITAL, 135 Emmeransplatz, also has a Jewish tombstone set into its walls.

JUDENGASSE, a street inside the walls of the oldest part of the city, was the location of the tenth-century Jewish community whose members were active traders between Germany and Turkey via the Danube.

MUNICIPAL MUSEUM, 2-4 Dachauplatz, owns at least forty of the Hebrew-inscribed tombstones from the cemetery, which was wrecked in 1519. Most of the stones are from the thirteenth and fourteenth centuries.

JEWISH COMMUNITY HEADQUARTERS, 2 Schäffnerstrasse.

ROTHENBURG

CHURCH OF ST. JACOB has a stained-glass window depicting the wanderings of the ancient Israelites in the desert, with manna, in the form of bread rolls and pretzels, falling from heaven.

CORN EXCHANGE BUILDING, in the northern corner of the newer section of the city, was built in 1588 and includes among its stone blocks many Hebrew-inscribed tombstones from the thirteenth-century Jewish cemetery. The tombstones can be seen in the east and west sections of the building. Three times Jews were driven out of Rothenburg; once in 1298, again in 1348-49, and finally in 1519. They were not allowed to return until the nineteenth century. This medieval town on the River Tauber is famed in Jewish history as the seat of the great Rabbi Meir of Rothenburg.

JUDENTANZHAUS (Jewish Dance House), a timber-framed building of medieval construction that has recently been restored, is attached to the Weisse Turm (White Tower), a gate of the ancient city fortification, at the top of the Judengasse, where it runs into Pfargasse. A low stone wall has been built in front of the tanzhaus around a small garden. Inside the wall are imbedded 10 ancient Jewish tombstones dating to the 13th century.

Houses were first erected in the Judengasse, which runs downhill in the northeastern part of the old town, in 1204, and ends at the Klingengasse. On the left hand corner is a large old house with an old Jewish tombstone imbedded in the wall.

In 1397, when the Jews suffered one of their periodic expulsions from the city, the town council sold the synagogue and the Jewish dance hall for 2,000 gulden to one Peter Creglinger, who built a chapel to the Virgin on the site of the synagogue.

TOWN MUSEUM, preserves many tombstones from the thirteenth-century Jewish cemetery. One contains an inscription referring to the burning of Jews in 1295 in the citadel just outside the town. The Historical Conservation Society, which is restoring old buildings damaged during the war, has identified and preserved a stone building that was attached to the medieval synagogue on the Georgengasse. Another medieval Jewish structure, a Jewish hostel that stood in the upper eastern corner of the Judengasse, was one of the town's showplaces until it was wrecked by Allied bombers. It has now been rebuilt in accordance with the old plans but not their dimensions.

ST. GOAR

LORELEI, a 430-foot cliff above the Rhine between St. Goar and Oberwessel, recalls Heinrich Heine's famous poem based on the German legend of an enchantress who, by her singing, lured sailors to disaster on her rock in the Rhine. The Nazis failed in their efforts to expunge Heine's name from any link to the Lorelei poem.

SAARBRÜCKEN

SYNAGOGUE AND JEWISH COMMUNAL CENTER, 8 Lortzingstrasse.

SANDHAUSEN

SYNAGOGUE here was restored with the help of Chancellor Adenauer and the government of Baden-Württemberg. The building escaped serious damage because the Nazis thought it was a church. The building had been a Protestant church since 1700, but was converted into a synagogue in 1866.

SCHWABISCH HALL

OLD WOODEN SYNAGOGUE with interior painted walls is preserved here as a historical monument.

SEESEN

JACOBSONSTRASSE, the city's main business street, is named for Israel Jacobson, the last of the court Jews, who was both a rabbi and a merchant. In 1810 he built a synagogue here, where he introduced prayers, hymns, and sermons in German, and an organ, thus being the first to establish a substantial reform in the synagogue liturgy. He also built a private school on the synagogue grounds, which became the first nonsectarian school in Germany. The school is now owned by the state; the synagogue was destroyed in 1938. On its site is a memorial, inscribed in German, Hebrew, and English. There is also an orphanage founded by and named for Jacobson next to the Jewish cemetery on Debnestrasse.

JEWISH COMMUNITY HEADQUARTERS, 9 Jacobsonstrasse.

SPEYER

JEWISH WOMEN'S RITUAL BATH, dating from the eleventh century, on the Judenbadgasse (Jews' Bath Street), just off the medieval Judengasse, has been preserved almost exactly as it was originally built. It escaped destruction in 1689, when the French sacked the town, as well as later disasters, because it is underground. A long flight of stone steps leads to a dressing room with stone benches and the pool. The bath is in what used to be a garden behind the remnants of the old synagogue. The key to the bath may be obtained at the nearby police station on Maximilianstrasse. There is a fading stone tablet that records the fact that documents going back to 1340 mention the bath.

SYNAGOGUE REMNANT, the east wall of the medieval sanctuary still stands. The niche for the Ark is still visible.

STUTTGART

HIRSCH BRIDGE, an important access highway in the Neckar Harbor of Stuttgart, is named for Dr. Otto Hirsch, the prime mover in developing the canal which the bridge spans. Until the Nazis came to power, Hirsch served on various government commissions in Wüttemberg. He was chairman of the executive committee of the central organization of German Jews until his deportation to the Mauthausen concentration camp, where he died in 1941. A plaque at the bridge approach tells his story.

JEWISH CEMETERY, 44 Friedhofstrasse, has a monument to the local Jews killed by the Nazis.

SYNAGOGUE AND COMMUNAL CENTER, 36 Hospitalstrasse, was built in 1952. There is a small kosher restaurant in the building. Two stone tablets of the Ten Commandments, salvaged from the ruins of the synagogue erected in 1861 and destroyed by the Nazis in 1938, are built into the interior of the synagogue. Also salvaged from the old synagogue is a memorial listing the names of 90 Stuttgart Jews who died fighting for Germany during World War I.

WORLD WAR II MEMORIAL, in the heart of the city, is a monument to the victims of the Nazi terror, erected by the municipality. On the monument are these words: "1933-1945—Outlawed, Rejected, Tortured, Massacred, Hanged, Gassed. Millions of victims of the National Socialist tyranny beg you: Never Again!"

THALICHTENBERG

OLD JEWISH CEMETERY below the castle, which was built with Jewish money, has stones marked with names of Jewish victims of Nazis.

TREUCHTLINGEN

JEWISH CEMETERY, corner of Uhlbergstrasse and Oettingerstrasse, which dates from 1773, was partially destroyed by the Nazis and further damaged by Allied air attacks. It was restored in 1950 by the Bavarian Restitution Office. The site of the former synagogue is now a fenced off grassy plot.

TRIER

ALTMANSTRASSE is named for Dr. Adolf Altman, prewar chief rabbi of Trier, who perished at Theresienstadt concentration camp.

BISHOPS MUSEUM (Gotik Room), 6 Banthusstrasse, displays figures of the Synagogue Defeated and of Noah, Jacob, and Abraham, pieces of statuary from the thirteenth-century Church of Our Lady, which was almost ruined in World War II.

JUDENGASSE, remnant of a medieval ghetto, still exists near the market place. Jews first settled here early in the eleventh century, when the town was still known as Trevisum. An inscription on the tombstone of Archbishop Eberhard, who died here in 1066, the year he intended to expel the Jews, alleges that the Jews killed him by magic, having burned his effigy. Trier is also known as Treves, from its original Latin name. There are Jewish families in Italy and France named Treves whose ancestors came from this Rhineland city. The common Jewish name, Dreyfus, is a variation of Treves. Karl Marx was born here in 1818.

KARL MARX HOUSE, 10 Bruckstrasse, where Karl Marx was born in 1818, had been turned into a museum in 1932 on the 50th anniversary of Marx's death. The Nazis tore the building down, but in 1968, during the celebration of Marx's 150th birthday, it was rebuilt and converted into a permanent exhibition of his letters, works and related materials.

LOEBSTRASSE, memorializes Siegfried Loeb, a member of the city council when he died in 1950.

NEW JEWISH CEMETERY, on the Ruwererstrasse, has a memorial to the city's Jews who were deported by the Nazis.

OLD JEWISH CEMETERY, on the Weidegasse, dates from about the fifteenth century. The first Jewish cemetery, no longer in existence, was near the Judemauerstrasse (Jewish Wall Street).

RHINE COUNTY MUSEUM, 44 Ostallee, preserves a number of tombstones from the fifteenth-century Jewish cemetery.

SYNAGOGUE, Kaiserstrasse, corner Hindenburgstrasse, a tiny square sandstone edifice, was dedicated in 1957 to replace the one destroyed by the Nazis in 1938. The old synagogue, erected in 1859, was a continuation of the medieval Jewish colony.

ULM

SYNAGOGUE MEMORIAL, next door to City Savings Bank, is a tablet on the site of the former synagogue, honoring 600 Jews killed by the Nazis.

WEINHEIM

SYNAGOGUE SITE has memorial plaque affixed to site of old synagogue destroyed by Nazis in 1938.

WIESBADEN

SYNAGOGUE, 33 Friedrichstrasse, was dedicated in 1966, to replace an older sanctuary on the same site which had survived the Nazis' Kristallnacht, Nov. 8-9, 1938. The Nazis spared the old synagogue because it was located in the midst of and tangential to other buildings in the heart of the city, and to have put it to the torch would have meant burning down much of the city's center.

WILDBAD

MEDIEVAL JEWISH RITUAL BATH can still be seen here.

WIMPFEN

OLD HOUSE with Jewish inscription is believed to have been former synagogue.

WORMS

OLD JEWISH CEMETERY, at Andreasring, between the old and new city walls, where the oldest gravestone dates from 1076, has survived Crusaders, emperors, wars, and Nazis. There are some two thousand tombstones here, most of them sagging and battered. One, not far from the entrance gate, marks the grave of Rabbi Meier of Rothenburg, who died in prison in 1293, refusing to permit the community to ransom him. His body was released after his death, when the ransom was paid by a man who asked the honor of being buried alongside the rabbi. This man lies in Grave No. 88, in a section known as the "Rabbinertal" because so many Jewish sages of the Middle Ages are buried there. The Nazis wrecked the cemetery in 1938, scattering stones and destroying old gates and walls, but complete destruction was prevented through the efforts of Dr. Friedrich M. Illert, curator of the State Museum and Cultural Institute. Allied bombs did further damage, but the surviving stones have been set back in place, the entrance has been rebuilt, and the outer walls have been restored. The historic ground is now maintained by the Worms municipality. Ancient documents refer to the cemetery as "the holy sand" because of a tradition that the earth in it came from Palestine. A new Jewish cemetery, at the Hocheimer Hohe, escaped damage in 1938.

OLD SYNAGOGUE, in the back section of the Judengasse, which runs along the inner city wall north of the city, between the Martins Gate and the Bärengasse, is a faithful reconstruction of a sanctuary built in 1034 by the same artisans who created the famous Worms Cathedral. Between 1096, when the Jewish community was massacred by Crusaders, and 1842, the synagogue was repeatedly damaged and restored. In 1185 a ritual bath was added and a women's annex was built in 1212. When the French burned Worms, in 1689, they used the synagogue for a stable. The Nazis turned it into rubble in 1938. Only the foundation stones, the doorway, and the ritual bath survived the Nazi onslaught, despite Dr. Illert's desperate attempt to save this historical treasure.

He did manage to save some of the inscribed stones from the synagogue—a chair believed to have been used by Rashi, the famed Talmud commentator; the community's priceless archives, a thirteenth-century manuscript prayer book; and a collection of religious objects of great historical importance. These he hid in the Worms Cathedral until after the war, when they were taken to the City Museum. The original archives, manuscripts, and much of the ritual collection were sent to Israel, but photostatic copies and photographs, together with the so-called Rashi Chair, are now on permanent exhibit in the Rashi Chapel. This was originally built in 1642 as an annex to the synagogue. Incorporated in the rebuilt synagogue are some of the original momumental stones, moldings, ornaments, and a stone from a Jerusalem quarry. The synagogue was rebuilt at a cost of $125,000, contributed by the Federal government, and was reconsecrated in December of 1961.

In the Middle Ages, Worms symbolized the spiritual glory of German Jewry. Together with Speyer and Mainz, Worms formed a historic trio of cities renowned among Jews everywhere as centers of learning and wealth. Rashi, when he was a young man, was among the scholars who studied in Worms. Martin Luther, who made his great declaration of faith in Worms, used commentaries from Rashi in his German translation of the Hebrew Bible.

WUPPERTAL

ELSE LASKER-SCHULER MEMORIAL, a plaque on a house in Elberfeld-Sadowstrasse, honors the late German-Jewish poetess, who was born here in 1869. A street in Elberfeld, a suburb of Wuppertal, is named for her.
SYNAGOGUE AND COMMUNITY HEADQUARTERS, 73 Friedrich Eberstrasse.

WÜRZBURG

ANNE FRANKSTRASSE is named for the famed Dutch-Jewish girl diarist.
JEWISH COMMUNITY HEADQUARTERS, 11 Valentin-Beckerstrasse.
JEWISH CEMETERY has a memorial tablet in honor of local Jewish victims of Nazism. It was erected by the youth council of the Metal Workers Trade Union.
MAIN-FRANCONIA MUSEUM housed in the Marienberg Fortress, preserves a Torah Ark from a medieval synagogue at Westheim and fragments of tombstones from Würzburg's fourteenth-century Jewish cemetery. Paintings of eighteenth-century wooden synagogues that used to be on display in the museum were destroyed during the war when the old museum building was bombed.

SYNAGOGUE AND COMMUNITY HEADQUARTERS, 11 Valentin-Becker-strasse, was erected in 1965 to replace an 1841 structure burned to the ground by the Nazis in 1938. The site of the latter building is marked by a memorial plaque.

GERMAN DEMOCRATIC REPUBLIC
(East Germany)

BERLIN (East)

ALBERT EINSTEIN SUMMER HOME in the suburb of Caputh, has been converted into a national memorial by the Monuments Commission. The Nazis had confiscated the property.

CHILDREN'S MEMORIAL in front of the Old People's Home, in Berlin-Niederschoenhasuen, honors the 150 Jewish children, 71 of them infants in arms, who were never seen again after being taken away by the Nazis in a furniture van.

HEINRICH HEINESTRASSE named for the poet, is right on the edge of the border between West and East Berlin.

JEWISH CEMETERY, 2 Lothringerstrasse, in the Weissensee section, is the newest and biggest in the Greater Berlin area. Opened in 1880, it contains more than 115,000 graves, including those of most of the great personalities in German-Jewish history between 1890 and 1939. Besides tombs and mausoleums of the famous, there are also long rows of tiny graves containing the ashes of concentration camp victims brought here in urns by relatives in the early years of the Nazi terror when the Gestapo still handed over the ashes of their victims on the payment of five marks.

Jewish funeral processions from West Berlin are halted at "Checkpoint Charlie" of the divided city which is as far as mourners are permitted to go. Only the hearse is allowed to proceed into East Berlin. Non-Germans, however, are permitted to visit the cemetery which was restored and reconstructed after the war. A card index of all the graves, available in the office of the cemetery secretary, provides leads to the location of most of the graves.

The street leading to the cemetery is known as *Herbert Baumstrasse*, in honor of the young Jew, Herbert Baum, leader of a group of Jewish resistance fighters, who was executed by the Nazis in 1943. The German Democratic Republic exhumed the remains of Baum and his colleagues and reinterred them in front of the Jewish Heroes Row, where the 366 Berlin Jews who died in World War I are buried. At the entrance to the cemetery, in front of the chapel, is a simple monument to the victims of Nazism.

A short walk from this cemetery is another, the Adath Israel Cemetery, once owned by the Orthodox Jews of Berlin. Here there is a memorial marker over the burial place of the remnants of Hebrew manuscripts and books destroyed by the Nazis between 1933 and 1945.

JEWISH COMMUNITY CENTER, 28 Oranienburgerstrasse, is next door to the empty Oranienburgerstrasse Synagogue, once the largest in Germany. The Nazis tried to burn it in 1938 but after the inside was destroyed they put out the flames because of the danger to adjacent buildings owned by non-Jews. In the synagogue's annex the Nazis tortured Jews.

MARTYRS' MEMORIAL on Grosse Hamburgstrasse, where a huge Jewish Home for the Aged once stood, is a monument honoring the 55,000 Berlin Jews deported to death camps by the Nazis. In 1942 the Gestapo took over the Home and converted it into a detention camp, where Berlin Jews were held before being shipped to Auschwitz, Treblinka and Theresienstadt.

Karl Marxallee is the new name of *Stalinallee,* East Berlin's principal thoroughfare. It was changed late in 1961 when the statue of Stalin on this street was torn down.

MOSES MENDELSSOHN GRAVE is in the oldest Jewish cemetery, 26 Grosse Hamburgstrasse. There is a bust of Mendelssohn near the entrance. His grave is No. 751 near the south wall.

ROSA LUXEMBOURG GRAVE in the Friedrichsfelde section, is a Communist shrine where East Berliners annually assemble for ceremonies on the anniversary of her assassination in 1919. She and Karl Liebnecht, a non-Jew, were the founders of the German Communist party.

SYNAGOGUE, 53 Rykestrasse, the only one in East Berlin, was gutted by the Nazis, but it has been restored by the German Democratic Republic. It stands behind a high gate in a courtyard in which there is a sign reading FRIEDENSTEMPEL (Freedom Temple). Dr. Edmund Singer, the rabbi of this congregation, is the only rabbi in East Germany. He serves not only the 900 Jews in East Berlin but also the 600 Jews who live in Leipzig, Magdeburg, Erfurt, Dresden, Halle, Karl Marx Stadt, Schwerin and Weimar.

DESSAU

MENDELSSOHNSTRASSE, near the Schiller Gardens in the northern part of the city, was named for Moses Mendelssohn, the famous philosopher, who was born in Dessau in 1729. The memorial plaque once affixed to the house at 10 Askanischestrasse, where Mendelssohn was born, is now preserved in the City Museum. The old house was torn down to make way for a new row of buildings on what is known as August Bebelstrasse. The monument to Mendelssohn, that once stood outside the Dessau railroad station, was carted away to the Jewish cemetery by the Nazis and later demolished. The original Mendelssohnstrasse is now known as Johann Sebastian Bachstrasse.

DRESDEN

SYNAGOGUE AND JEWISH COMMUNITY HEADQUARTERS, 20 Bautzenerstrasse.

CHAPEL AT JEWISH CEMETERY, Fiedlerstrasse, was badly damaged by the Nazis but has now been rebuilt.

ERFURT

SYNAGOGUE AND JEWISH COMMUNITY HEADQUARTERS, 16 Mao-Tse-Tung-Ring.

HALLE

JEWISH COMMUNITY HEADQUARTERS, 13 Grosse Markerstrasse.

KARL MARX STADT

JEWISH COMMUNITY HEADQUARTERS in city formerly known as Chemnitz, 28 Stollbergerstrasse. This is probably the only city in Europe named for a Jew.

LEIPZIG

MARTYRS' MEMORIAL in the local Jewish cemetery, honors 5,000 local Jews who died at the hands of the Nazis.

PUBLIC LIBRARY has on display the famous 14th century illuminated Machzor Lipsia.

SYNAGOGUE AND JEWISH COMMUNITY HEADQUARTERS, 10 Loehrstrasse, was rededicated in 1962 after its renovation by the local authorities. The Nazis had used it as a storeroom.

LWEIMAR-SCHOENDORF

LUTHERAN CHURCH, a post-war modern structure in this town near the site of the infamous Buchenwald Concentration Camp, has a memorial to those who suffered under the Hitler regime. The memorial has a barbed-wire motif, clear glass windows and bare light bulbs, a reminder of Christianity responsibility.

MAGDEBURG

SYNAGOGUE AND JEWISH COMMUNITY HEADQUARTERS, 1A Groeper-strasse.

POTSDAM

EINSTEIN TOWER, Am Telegraphenberg, a combination of cupola observatory and astro-physical laboratory, was designed in 1921 by the late Eric Mendelsohn. It was intended to be used for the investigation of spectroanalytic phenomena in relation to Albert Einstein's Theory of Relativity. It is now a scientific laboratory.

RAVENSBRÜCK

CONCENTRATION CAMP MEMORIAL is a twelve-foot-high bronze statue of a female figure carrying in her arms an emaciated camp victim. The statue memorializes the 92,000 women from many countries who died in the Ravensbrück concentration camp, where 132,000 women prisoners were used as guinea pigs in Nazi medical experiments.

SACHSENHAUSEN

MONUMENT TO CONCENTRATION CAMP VICTIMS is a towering, three-cornered obelisk bearing the red triangle signs of the concentration camps; it stands on the site of the huts into which more than 100,000 Nazi prisoners were crammed before being killed. The camp site is now laid out as a memorial park, with a simple structure occupying the site of the crematorium. There is also a museum depicting life and death at Sachsenhausen and a museum of the anti-Nazi resistance movement.

SCHWERIN

JEWISH COMMUNITY HEADQUARTERS, 3 Schlachterstrasse.

STUTTHOF

MUNICIPAL MUSEUM contains a permanent exhibit of documents and other memorabilia connected with life and death in the Sutthof concentration camp, where 85,000 people, many of them Jews, were murdered.

TESSIN

ANNE FRANK SCHOOL, named for the famous Dutch Jewish girl diarist, has a monument to her on the school grounds.

WEIMAR

BUCHENWALD CONCENTRATION CAMP just outside this city via Etterbergstrasse, has been preserved by the German Democratic Republic as the most elaborate death camp memorial in Europe. The memorial is dominated by a great round bell tower atop the 1,560-foot forested Etterberg hill, which is reached by a road built by concentration camp prisoners. The eight-story tower contains a bell with a metal wrapping of entangling barbed wire. The bell tolls three times daily. The four concentration camp buildings that remain include: the crematorium with its six ovens; the main building, where there is a plaster model of the original camp in precise detail; the former execution room, which now contains a museum of weapons of torture, lamp shades made from human skin and a scarf woven from human hair, the metal-lined carts in which bodies were piled thirty at a time and then dumped via chutes into a basement before being taken to the crematorium; and the prison laundry. Everywhere are signs and memorial plaques and flower wreaths. The original camp gate still stands. Over it in iron letters are the words *"Jedem das Seine"* (To each what he deserves).

On the side of the hill are a series of landscaped plazas marked by formal memorials for the citizens of eighteen nations who died at Buchenwald. Sculptured figures symbolize the victims of Buchenwald, where 60,000 died. There are also three mass graves marked by great circular monuments of hewn stone blocks.

CASTLE OF WEIMAR displays a beautiful bronze bust of Heinrich Heine by Johannes Friedrich Rogge of Dresden. It has been there since 1954.

WITTENBERG

CASTLE CHURCH, 54 Collegienstrasse, to the doors of which Martin Luther nailed his famous 95 theses in 1517, was also the first church on which the notorious *Judensau* sculpture, the figure of a sow giving suck to a piglet and two young Jews, first appeared, in the middle of the fifteenth century. It can be seen on the outside near the roof. Behind the hog is the figure of a rabbi holding up the sow's tail. Below the sculpture are carved the meaningless words, "Rabini Shem Hamphorash." (In Hebrew the words *Shem ha-Meforash* stand for "the ineffable name of God.") This insulting representation in wood carvings and stone later appeared in church buildings in Germany, Austria, and Belgium.

GIBRALTAR

Although the present Jewish community, numbering about 700, dates from 1704, when England occupied this fortified promontory off the southern coast of Spain, Jews lived here in the days of the Romans. They were also at Gibraltar in the eighth century as part of the army of Tarik, the Moorish invader who landed in 711. In 1492, when Spain expelled Jews and Moslems from Granada, the last Moorish stronghold in Spain, Gibraltar became a refuge for Marrano Jews who escaped with the aid of smugglers. For a time there was a plan to turn Gibraltar over to Spanish and Portuguese Jewish refugees.

The Treaty of Utrecht, by which Spain ceded Gibraltar to Britain in 1713, forbade Jews or Moslems to live there. But this ban was honored in the breach, because the Jews were major factors in trade between Gibraltar and North Africa and between the Rock and England. There were only 100 Jews in Gibraltar in 1713, but by the middle of the eighteenth century they accounted for a quarter of the civilian population. They distinguished themselves by their heroism during the sieges of 1727 and 1779-1783. A Dutch ship captured by Jewish privateers from Gibraltar helped alleviate famine during the second siege. Later, Gibraltar Jews served as intermediaries between the British and the Moslem rulers in North Africa. One Jewish envoy, Aaron Cardozo, was a friend of Lord Nelson, who lent a frigate to the Jewish emissary when he went on a diplomatic errand to Morocco.

The Gibraltar Jews are mostly of North African origin, descendants of the fifteenth- century exiles from Spain who poured through Gibraltar en route to the Moslem lands on the African shore of the Mediterranean. Some are of English ancestry and a few hail from eastern Europe. They are almost all Sephardic, and they speak both English and the Andalusian dialect of Spanish. During World War II, most of the Jews were evacuated for safety to England, the British West Indies, and the Portuguese islands in the Atlantic. In 1971, Sir Joshua Hassan, a native of the Rock, and vice-president of the largest of Gibraltar's four synagogues, was both mayor of this self-governing British crown colony, an office to which he was first elected in 1955, and prime minister. Gibraltar's Jews are unanimously opposed to Spain's effort to gain control of the Rock.

The community is served by two rabbis. What used to be the communal Jewish school is now a government school, but all of the pupils are Jewish. All Jewish-owned shops are shut tight on Friday night, on Saturday, and on Jewish holidays. British seamen can often be seen waiting patiently in front of these stores for the first evening star on Saturday night that will enable them to begin their shopping. There are no performances in Gibraltar theatres on Friday night. A walk through the city reveals the extensive Jewish impact on Gibraltar as evidenced in streets with names such as Ben-Zimrah Ave., Benoliel Passage, Sarfatti Passage and Serraya Ramp.

ABUDARHAM SYNAGOGUE, Parliament Lane, is the youngest of the four synagogues, having been founded in 1820.

ES HAYYIM SYNAGOGUE, 91 Irishtown, was founded in 1759 and its building is the oldest Jewish structure on the Rock.

GIBRALTAR MUSEUM has among its permanent exhibits photos of Jewish types of Gibraltar and an old printing plate on which is engraved the Kiddush for the Friday evening service.

HEBREW SCHOOL on Bomb House Lane, is now a government school.

ISRAELI CONSULATE, 3 City Mill Lane, is the headquarters of the famed Benaim family, which has been identified with Gibraltar for two centuries. David Benaim, the grand old man of the family, was the honorary Israeli consul here in 1962. His son, M. E. Benaim, welcomes visitors and helps arrange for a tour of the Rock.

JEWISH CEMETERY in the neighboring Spanish city of La Linea, has been used by the Gibraltar Jews for generations but it only came into Jewish ownership in recent years, when the Spanish authorities sold the Jewish section of the old graveyard to the Hebrew Community of Gibraltar.

JEWISH SOCIAL AND CULTURAL CLUB, 10 Bomb House Lane, is the headquarters of the Hebrew Community. Visitors are always welcome. The club is host to Jewish military and naval personnel serving with the British forces on Gibraltar, and it aids Jews from North Africa on their way to Israel. Visitors may obtain kosher meals here.

NEFUSOT YEHUDAH SYNAGOGUE, 65 Line Wall Rd., is known as the 'Flamenco Synagogue'—i.e. Flemish Synagogue—because it was founded by Jews from Flanders and Holland in 1799. Largest of the four synagogues on the Rock, the present building dates from 1951 after the older building was badly damaged during an explosion of a munitions ship in the harbor. Located behind a lovely garden in a cool-looking courtyard, this synagogue is of typical Moorish architecture.

PUBLIC LIBRARY contains many archives recording the role played by Jews in Gibraltar's history. On file here are copies of a Ladino paper called "Cronica Israelite," that was published during the 1840s.

SHAAR HASHAMAYIM SYNAGOGUE, 47-49 Engineer Lane, oldest of the four synagogues, was founded in 1749, when Jews first acquired a legal right to live in Gibraltar. Rebuilt in 1768, it is known as the "Cathedral Synagogue." It can easily be missed because it is almost concealed by a facade which appears to be part of the row of buildings on the lane. Inside is a typical Sephardic synagogue like those to be found in all countries where Sephardic Jews lived.

TOWN HALL has a memorial plaque commemorating the heroism of a young Jewish officer from Gibraltar who was killed in action during World War II.

GREAT BRITAIN

Recorded Jewish History in Great Britain begins soon after the Normans invaded England in 1066. William the Conquerer encouraged the migration of Jewish merchants and artisans from Rouen in Normandy, and they settled in London, Oxford, and Cambridge before the end of the eleventh century. There were individual Jews in Britain in Roman and Anglo-Saxon times, as traders and slaves; but no organized Jewish community existed until the last decade of the eleventh century. The first written mention of Jews is a reference to "fil Manasse" (son of Manasses) in the Domesday Book, which William the Conquerer had compiled in 1086 to record the ownership and extent of landed property.

The first three Norman kings protected the Jews. Under their successors, however, the Jews were robbed, pillaged, massacred, and finally expelled in 1290 by Edward I. There were then said to be 16,000 Jews in England. Thereafter England had no Jewish community for more than 350 years, but there were individual Jews in a number of cities even during this era. There were converts in London, crypto-Jews from abroad who came on medical and diplomatic missions, and even a few practicing Jews who managed to eke out a secret existence.

Henry VIII and Elizabeth I tolerated the handful of Spanish and Portuguese Marranos who worshiped secretly as Jews in London and Bristol. One of these, Dr. Hector Nunes, earned England's gratitude by being the first to warn that the Spanish Armada had sailed. Another was Elizabeth's physician, Dr. Rodrigo Lopes, who died on the gallows, victim of a false charge of treason.

Repeated petitions for the legal readmission of the Jews and for their right to worship publicly failed until 1656, when Oliver Cromwell's oral guarantees and the approval of the Council of State enabled those already in England to proclaim their Judaism openly and permitted others from Holland to enter the country in safety. Cromwell's historic action was influenced by the writings and personal appeals of Menasseh ben Israel, the chief rabbi of Amsterdam, as well as by the Puritans' interest in the Jews as the people of the Bible and by the government's appreciation of what Jewish merchants could do for British trade.

In 1657 the Portuguese and Spanish Jews of London opened the first synagogue in modern England. Jewish immigrants from Germany established the second congregation in 1690. Between the religious toleration of the mid-seventeenth century and complete civil and political emancipation more than two centuries elapsed. Not until 1858 was Baron Lionel Nathan de Rothschild seated as the first professing Jew in the House of Commons. His son Nathan Meyer had the same distinction in the House of Lords in 1885.

Since 1858 there have been one or more Jews in every Parliament. Until the end of the 19th century all were Liberals but thereafter they divided along Liberal and Conservative lines. Emanuel Shinwell was the first Jewish Labor MP, having been elected in 1922. The majority of Jewish MPs in the last decade have been Laborites. In 1971 there were 45 Jewish MPs and more than a score of Jewish members of the House of Lords.

Jews have held the highest offices in Britain. Herbert Samuel, who became postmaster general in 1909, was the first professing Jew in the cabinet. Shinwell and

Leslie Hore-Belisha were ministers of defense. Samuel was home secretary and head of the Liberal Party. Lord Reading served as chief justice, ambassador to the United States, viceroy of India and foreign secretary. Sir Keith Joseph was minister of housing in the last Conservative government. Harold Lever and John Diamond were postmaster general and chief secretary of the treasury, respectively, in the Labor Government of Harold Wilson.

London has had seven Jewish lord mayors and Leeds, Manchester, Liverpool and Glasgow have also had Jewish lord mayors. Jews are prominent in the world of science—Sir Solly Zuckerman, nuclear expert, Sir Ernst Boris Chain, Nobel prize winner—in the arts—Harold Pinter, playwright, and Herbert Lyons, head of the Shakespeare festival—Sir Isaiah Berlin, philosopher; Sir Isaac Wolfson and the Marks and Lyons families in business and philanthropy.

When Britain observed the 900th anniversary of Westminister Abbey, part of the celebration included a unique exhibit of Anglo-Jewish history in the Abbey.

In 1971 there were 450,000 Jews in Great Britain, 280,000 of whom lived in Greater London, and all but 15% of whom were concentrated in London, Leeds, Liverpool, Birmingham, Manchester and Glasgow. Until 1880, British Jewry numbered 60,000, and was already well-rooted in the life of the country to which it had contributed many distinguished figures. In that year, large numbers of Jewish immigrants began arriving from Russia, Poland and Rumania. The older Jewish community—represented by such great families as the Rothschilds, Montefiore, Samuels, Salamons, Sassoons, Mocattas, Goldsmids, Henriques, Monds and Jessels—created a vast network of social and cultural institutions to meet the needs of the newcomers.

Ultimately, the immigrants and their descendants radically altered the social, economic and cultural character of the community while making their own distinctive and substantial contribution to every facet of British society. Gradually they took over the leadership of the Jewish community as they produced a new generation of Jewish notables. The East European Jews at first formed Yiddish-speaking ghettos in the East End of London and other large cities but they have long since coalesced with the older community and spread out into the suburbs. A new but smaller wave of immigrants after World War II from Eastern Europe and from Britain's former Asiatic and African colonies added a new dimension of Orthodoxy to the community.

The great majority of synagogues are Orthodox and recognize the chief rabbi as their ultimate spiritual authority. He has the same status as the archbishop of Canterbury and the Catholic primate. Eighty synagogues in Greater London and the provinces are banded together in the United Synagogue, which elects the chief rabbi. The smaller Federation of Synagogues is more militantly Orthodox, and the Union of Orthodox Hebrew Congregations even more so. There are also federations of Reform synagogues (more like the American Conservative congregations) and Liberal synagogues (like the American Reform congregations).

The major central Jewish organization beyond the religious sphere is the Board of Deputies of British Jews, dating back to 1760. There is also the younger Anglo-Jewish Association. The stalwart identification of British Jewry in every generation with all efforts to defend and rescue their persecuted brethren abroad and to further Jewish settlement in Palestine led logically to frequent intervention by the British government on behalf of oppressed Jews in many parts of the world and to the issuance of the Balfour Declaration in 1917.

(Detailed information about Jewish institutions and kosher restaurants and hotels in Great Britain is available in the *Jewish Year Book*, published by the *Jewish Chronicle*, 25 Furnival St., London, E.C.4.)

ENGLAND

AYLESBURY

WADDESDON MANOR, six miles northwest of Aylesbury, is a national museum containing one of the most magnificent private art collections ever given by its owner to the public in any country; it was bequeathed in 1957 to the National Trust (public custodian of landmarks and art treasures) by James de Rothschild. The collection of eighteenth-century paintings, tapestries, porcelain, furniture, snuff boxes, miniatures, and illustrated books is regarded as one of the most sumptuous ever put together. It was assembled by Baron Ferdinand de Rothschild, a great-grandson of the original Rothschild from Frankfurt-am-Main, and grandson of Salomon Rothschild, who started the Austrian branch of the celebrated family of bankers, philanthropists, and art patrons. The collection is housed in a vast Renaissance château set in a 200-acre park. Ferdinand left the collection, in 1898, to his sister, Miss Alice de Rothschild, who in turn passed it on to her great-nephew, James de Rothschild. The latter also provided a $1,500,000 bequest as a maintenance fund for the château and its art objects and the model village in Waddesdon Manor which Ferdinand had built. (Check with The National Trust, 23 Caxton St., London, S.W.1, for admission fees and visiting hours.)

BANBURY

UPTON HOUSE, the former home of the oil and transportation magnate Walter Horace Samuel, second Viscount Bearsted, was bequeathed to the National Trust, together with its collection of noted paintings, which includes works by Tintoretto, Brueghel, El Greco, Goya, and Rubens. Among the latter's work is the final sketch for "Judas Maccabeus Praying for the Dead," the finished work being in the museum at Nantes, France.

BIRMINGHAM

CENTRAL SYNAGOGUE, 133 Pershore Road.

HILLEL HOUSE, 26 Somerset Road, is an international Jewish student residential house, and the center for Jewish student activities.

SINGERS HILL SYNAGOGUE on Ellis Street, oldest and largest of four synagogues in a community whose beginnings go back to 1720, replaced the city's first synagogue, which had been erected in 1791 in a slum area known as the Froggery. Four years earlier the Jews of Birmingham acquired much notoriety because of the presence in their midst of Lord George Gordon, an erratic nobleman who had become a convert to Judaism. A godson of King George II, Gordon was a bitter foe of Catholic political emancipation until he became an Orthodox Jew. Some writers have mistakenly said that he was circumcised in the Birmingham synagogue, but he had left the city four years before it was opened. In his cell in Newgate Prison, where he served a term for criminal libel, he practiced the minutiae of Judaism. Known as "the Moses of Birmingham," he signed his letters in prison with the name Israel Bar Abraham Gordon and refused to see any Jewish visitors who did not abide by every jot and tittle of Jewish religious observances.

BLACKPOOL

This seaside resort, north of Liverpool, is one of England's most popular vacation spots. There are a number of kosher hotels here.

JEWISH SOCIAL CLUB AND YOUTH CENTRE, headquarters in the Hippodrome Building on King Street, is the rendezvous of the younger Jewish element.

PROGRESSIVE JEWISH CONGREGATION, Raikes Parade.

UNITED HEBREW CONGREGATION, Leamington Rd.

BOURNEMOUTH

BOURNEMOUTH HEBREW CONGREGATION, Wootton Gardens, and *Reform Congregation,* 53 Christchurch Rd., serve Jewish vacationists in this popular English Channel resort community. There is a large number of kosher hotels and guest houses.

BOVEY TRACY

JEW'S BRIDGE, a "fair stone" bridge erected during the reign of King Edward II (1307-27), by Sir Roger Jew and Sir Walter Jew, across the River Bovey, between Exeter and Plymouth, is still in use and still called by that name. "Jew" as a family name was fairly common in Devonshire, old records also listing John Jew, Thomas Jew and William Jew, but none has any connection with the real name of Jew. They are probably derived from "le Jeu," a Norman-French name.

BRADFORD

HEBREW CONGREGATION, Springhurst Road, is a new building dedicated in 1970.

BRIGHTON

This resort city and its suburb, Hove, have a large number of kosher hotels and guest houses.

THE BOMBAY BAR, St. George's Rd. and Paston Place, in what is known as the Kemptown section of this English Channel resort community, is now what the British call a high-class public house, or bar, but this solidly built structure with a pagoda-like roof was once a Jewish mausoleum built in the 1890s by Albert Sassoon, a member of the noted family of Jewish industrialists, traders, statesmen, poets, and entrepreneurs. Sassoon was buried in this building in 1896, as was his son in 1912, but their remains were removed in 1933. During World War II the old mausoleum was used as an air-raid shelter.

HEBREW CONGREGATION, Middle St., is one of the loveliest small synagogues in all of Europe. It is famed for its lavish ornamentations, designs of its stained glass windows and the clusters of fruit in gilded metal, representing all the fruits mentioned in the Biblical texts.

SYNAGOGUE, Holland Rd., Hove.

SYNAGOGUE (Liberal), 6 Lansdowne Rd., Hove.

REFORM SYNAGOGUE, Palmeira Rd., 65 Holland Rd., Hove.

BRISTOL

CHURCH OF ST. GILES on a corner of Small St., occupies part of the site of a twelfth-century synagogue, the only remains of which are the vault beneath the church. Until the expulsion of Jews in 1290, Bristol was one of the major Jewish communities in England. In 1210 the whole of British Jewry was imprisoned in Bristol Castle until it raised a huge ransom demanded by King John.

SYNAGOGUE, Park Row, was erected in 1870, but the modern Jewish community originated in the middle 1700s.

BURY ST. EDMUNDS

MOYSES HALL on the Cornhill, is one of the oldest surviving Norman buildings in England and is believed to have been an eleventh-century Jewish residence. There is also a tradition that it was once a synagogue, because its interior architectural detail corresponds in some features to the ancient Old-New Synagogue in Prague. In 1190 the only Jewish residents who escaped a massacre here found refuge in this building, now a museum containing material on the history of the town dating from the seventh century.

ABBEY OF BURY ST. EDMUNDS has two large Stars of David high above its main gate. The ancient Jewish symbols can be seen just below the turrets. There is a story that the Stars of David were built into the gate because local Jews contributed to the rebuilding of the abbey after it was destroyed by fire in 1327. But the present gate was erected in 1347, when there were no known Jews in the town. In this abbey the Magna Charta was drawn up for presentation to King John in 1215.

CAMBRIDGE

ALPHABET MUSEUM, 7 Mortimer Rd., in the garden of its founder and owner, Dr. David Diringer, lecturer at Cambridge University, includes scripts of 350 different modern and ancient alphabets.

CAMBRIDGE MILITARY CEMETERY at Madingly, a few miles outside of Cambridge, has engraved along a high wall leading to the chapel the names of many Jews who were among the 5,100 United States dead and missing who were lost in and around the United Kingdom during World War II. This is an American military cemetery.

BENNO ELKAN CANDELABRA in King's College Chapel, Cambridge University, is a magnificent bronze sculpture on which Hebrew Biblical characters are carved.

CAMBRIDGE UNIVERSITY LIBRARY has in its twenty-five miles of shelves not only thousands of Hebrew-printed books and Judaica but also a treasure house of more than a thousand Hebrew manuscripts and the renowned Schechter-Taylor Geniza Collection of tens of thousands of fragments of historic writing that shed new light on the life of the Jews who lived along the banks of the Nile, Tigris, and Euphrates rivers from the ninth to the eleventh century. Among this collection is the complete text of the Book of Ecclesiasticus (Sirach), one of the books of the Apocrypha.

The discovery of these fragments in 1897-98 by Dr. Solomon Schechter, then a lecturer in rabbinics at Cambridge and later president of the Jewish Theological Seminary in New York, created the same stir then as did the Dead Sea Scroll finds in the twentieth century. Dr. Schechter made his discovery in an old synagogue in Egypt. In 1961 the Jewish Theological Seminary in New York completed the microfilming of these fragments and made them available to scholars in the United States.

Cambridge's Hebrew collection originated in 1647, when Parliament appropriated five hundred pounds to buy the collection of an Italian rabbi.

CAMBRIDGE UNIVERSITY has a portrait of Sir Isaac Wolfson in Wolfson Hall at Churchill College. Sir Isaac, one of the great philanthropists of his day and an observant Jew, provided the funds for the University Centre overlooking the River Cam, and half of the funds for Britain's first Institute of Theoretical Astronomy at Cambridge.

MARY FRERE HEBREW LIBRARY at Girton College, a part of Cambridge University, has an important collection of 41 Hebrew manuscripts and 150 Hebrew books.

SYNAGOGUE, Ellis Court and Thompson's Lane, was built in 1938, and the present congregation, founded in 1888, has no link with the thirteenth-century Jewish community that flourished here. Until 1939, when the new Guildhall was built, remains of an ancient stone house built by Rabbi Benjamin in the thirteenth century next to the medieval synagogue could still be seen at Market Square. The contemporary synagogue contains the Herbert Loewe Memorial Library of Judaica. The synagogue was built for Jewish students and is administered by the Jewish Students' Society. It houses a kosher restaurant.

CANTERBURY

CANTERBURY CATHEDRAL, mother church of the Church of England, has in one of its thirteenth-century windows a stained glass representing the figure of Moses and a female figure of the Synagogue, the latter bearing on her left arm the Tablets of the Torah. In the Cathedral Archives and Chapter Library are records of the twelfth-century Jewish community. In those days only London and Lincoln had larger Jewish communities.

The newest unit of the Cathedral's chapter library is named for Sir Isaac Wolfson. It occupies the rebuilt Cheker, a medieval name for the monk's counting house, which was destroyed in 1860 and rebuilt around its old pillars.

WESTMINSTER COLLEGE, a theological school, has two artistic figures showing the Synagogue with the Scroll of the Law, and the Church with her Chalice, a modern representation that is a return to the pre-medieval era when Christian art depicted the Church and the Synagogue as complementary.

COUNTY HOTEL on High St., corner of Stour St., occupies the site where in the twelfth century stood the house of Jacob of Canterbury, "the Rothschild of the twelfth century." Fragments of Jacob's house are incorporated in the hotel's masonry, including some stones in the wine cellar. There is no physical trace of the medieval synagogue which stood behind Jacob's house.

JEWRY LANE right behind the County Hotel, leading off to Stour St., has borne this name since the thirteenth century, when there were at least twenty-one houses on this street occupied by Jews.

ST. DUNSTAN'S STREET RAILROAD CROSSING is the site of a synagogue erected in 1762 but torn down in the 1840s to make way for a railroad. The two-hundred-year-old Jewish cemetery near where the synagogue stood is still maintained.

NINETEENTH-CENTURY SYNAGOGUE on King St., near Palace St., is now the social hall of a church, but its odd-looking Egyptian architecture has been maintained. It was opened in 1848, a year after its cornerstone was laid by Sir Moses Montefiore. There is now no Jewish community in Canterbury, but if you buy Leon-Hart rum, which is still made here, you are drinking a liquor named for the family of the late Alderman Hart, who was mayor of Canterbury three times in the nineteenth century.

EXETER

SYNAGOGUE on Mary Arches St., erected in 1763, escaped destruction during the Nazi air raids when most of the city was wrecked. It remains unused because there is only a handful of Jews here, except for students at the University of Exeter. During the university term services are held for the High Holy Days and on Friday evenings. The synagogue has been decreed as hallowed ground by the town council, together with the adjacent Synagogue Place. Among the memorial tablets on the interior wall is one erected by Jews who served with the United States armed forces in Britain during World War II, expressing appreciation for the local community's hospitality. There was a Jewish community here in the twelfth century. Services are held only during High Holy Days and on Friday evening during the University term.

JEWISH CEMETERY on Magdalen St., right behind the famed Exeter Cathedral, has graves with inscriptions dating back more than two hundred years. The casual visitor gets the impression that the Jewish tombstones are in the Cathedral churchyard.

There was a Jewish community here in the 12th century but no trace of it remains.

UNIVERSITY COLLEGE OF EXETER has a Lopes Hall, commemorating Sir Menassah Lopes, member of an old Sephardic Jewish family, who represented this district in the House of Commons.

FALMOUTH

OLD SYNAGOGUE SITE, now a warehouse. It has not been used as a synagogue for nearly a century since the 18th century Jewish settlement in this one-time flourishing port city moved away. On the outskirts of the city there is an old Jewish cemetery, too.

GATESHEAD

YESHIVA, at 179 Bewick Rd., is the focal point of a modern East European *shtetl* which Orthodox Jews have re-created in this seaport town. There are 165 full-time students at the Yeshiva. At No. 50 Bewick Rd. there is a training school for teachers. At No. 180 Bewick Rd. is a synagogue and another at 22 Claremont Pl. A modern dormitory for Yeshiva students was erected in 1963 by the family of Charles Wolfson. There are also a Jewish boarding school and a Jewish bookshop.

TALMUDICAL ACADEMY, 88 Windermere St.

GREENWICH

NATIONAL MARITIME MUSEUM in Greenwich Park, displays Hogarth's painting of Sir Alexander Schomberg, Jewish naval officer who distinguished himself during England's conquest of Canada. He took an active part in the capture of Quebec. His son, Sir Alexander Wilmot Schomberg, was a vice-admiral in the British Royal Navy during the Napoleonic Wars.

One of the galleries in the Museum's annex, *Flamsteed House*, which used to be part of the old Royal Observatory, is named the *Herschel Gallery* in honor of Sir William Herschel, the famous astronomer, who some authorities claim was of Jewish origin. In 1781 he discovered the planet Uranus and subsequently made many important contributions to astronomy. The gallery contains parts of Herschel's great forty-foot telescope and the lathe on which he ground his reflectors, as well as relics of his son, Sir John Herschel, and his sister, Caroline, who were also noted astronomers.

GUNNERSBURY PARK

PUBLIC MUSEUM, former estate of the English Rothschilds, now owned by the borough councils of Brentford, Chiswick, Ealing, and Acton, suburbs of London, contains portraits of all the English members of the famed family since the acquisition of the estate in 1835. Among the items on display are family heirlooms such as dolls' beds, wedding gowns, property deeds, carriages, cameos. There are also scrapbooks, documents, and other memorabilia relating to the history of the

Rothschilds in England since the first member of the family, Nathan Meyer Rothschild, arrived in 1798 on behalf of his father's Frankfurt-am-Main bank.

HIGH WYCOMBE

DISRAELI MEMORIAL, or, as it is officially known, Hughendon Manor, the home of the Earl of Beaconsfield, who is better known to history as Benjamin Disraeli, the favorite Prime Minister of Queen Victoria. Born a Jew of a family which had fled from the Spanish Inquisition to Italy, Disraeli was baptized when he was thirteen, but his enemies and his friends never regarded him as other than a Jew. Carlyle called him "Hebrew conjurer," and Bismarck, at the Berlin Congress of 1878, said of Disraeli, "the old Jew, that's a man." Twice Prime Minister and for a generation leader of the Conservative party, Disraeli also was a novelist of note. Among his books are several in which he deals sympathetically with Jews.

Disraeli acquired Hughendon Manor in 1848 and lived there until his death. In 1939 it was converted into a memorial and museum under the administration of the National Trust. The Manor House is full of all sorts of relics of Disraeli's literary and political career and of his travels to the Middle East. The Disraeli memorial consists of Disraeli's portrait, his insignia from the Order of the Garter, and a quotation from Proverbs, 16:13. Among the art on display is a life-size portrait of the Queen presented to him by "his grateful sovereign and friend."

Disraeli and his wife are buried in the churchyard on the grounds of the Manor House.

SYNAGOGUE, 33 Hampden Rd.

HORSHAM

HERBERT SAMUEL EDUCATIONAL CENTRE at Eder Farm, is the first country center in Britain devoted entirely to Jewish education. It is named for Sir Herbert Samuel, late leader of the Liberal Party and the first professing Jew to be named a member of a British Cabinet.

HOVE

See BRIGHTON

HULL

OLD HEBREW SYNAGOGUE, Osborne St., was erected in 1955 to replace an 1826 structure destroyed during Nazi air raids. This congregation was founded by immigrants from western Germany.

CENTRAL SYNAGOGUE, Cogan St. is also a new building. Its former synagogue was wrecked by Nazi bombs during the blitz.

KENDAL

MUSEUM, near the bus and coach station in this small town in the Lake District on the direct route to Scotland, has a mixed collection of objects among which the visitor finds to his surprise a glass case containing an unwound portion of an old Torah Scroll, said to date from the 15th century and supposedly presented to the museum by a non-Jewish Army colonel who acquired it in Aden.

LANCASTER

LANCASTER UNIVERSITY, one of England's new universities, boasts of an inter-denominational chaplaincy center which houses Catholic, Protestant and Jewish chapels as well as a kosher restaurant. The Jewish student community has become the first Jewish settlement here since pre-expulsion times. Over the university entrance is a soaring tri-dimensional spire that reflects the inter-faith nature of the chaplaincy center.

LEEDS

BETH HAMIDRASH HAGODOL SYNAGOGUE, 21 Newtown Park View, is the oldest of the eleven Jewish congregations in Leeds, which has 25,000 Jews, making it the third-largest Jewish community in Great Britain. Some Jews lived here in the closing years of the eighteenth century, but the community was founded in 1804. The first synagogue was erected in 1860. A key center for the British clothing industry, Leeds owes much of its economic growth to Jewish manufacturers, among them Sir Montague Burton.

B'NAI B'RITH HILLEL FOUNDATION, 2 Springfield Mount, is the cultural and religious center for Jewish students at Leeds University, and also an international Jewish students hostel.

SELIG BRODETSKY JEWISH PRIMARY SCHOOL, 17 Sandhill Lane, is named for the late Dr. Selig Brodetsky, professor of mathematics at Leeds University and president of the Board of Deputies of British Jews.

GREAT SYNAGOGUE, 3 Belgrave St.

JUDEAN CLUB, 420 Street Lane, sometimes known as the Sam Lyons Center, is an important youth center.

LEEDS UNIVERSITY in its department of Semitics displays an important collection of Jewish manuscripts assembled by Frederick Kahn, a refugee from Germany, and acquired for the university by Stanley H. Burton and I. Arnold Ziff.

LOUIS STREET SYNAGOGUE, 1 Louis St., a mosquelike structure, is said to be the most beautiful in England.

QUEENSHILL JEWISH HOUSING ESTATE is a garden housing development established by the Jewish Housing Association on a 13-acre site. Among its facilities is the Bernard Lyons Community Center.

REFORM SYNAGOGUE, Roman Ave., off Street Lane.

LEICESTER

ISRAEL HART PUBLIC LIBRARY (Garendon St. Branch Library), at Garendon and Upper Kent Sts., a branch of the Leicester City Libraries, was erected and presented to the city in 1883 by Sir Israel Hart, who was Lord Mayor in 1885, 1886, and 1893.

JEWRY WALL, the west end of St. Nicholas Church, has had this name since the thirteenth century, but its origin remains in doubt. One theory is that the thirteenth-century Jewish community was located near the wall, which dates from Roman times. Later studies challenge this explanation and claim that the wall is named for some link to the twenty-four jurats (aldermen) of Leicester who used to meet in the town churchyard.

JEWISH YOUTH CENTRE on Highfield St., is directly across the street from the synagogue mentioned below.

LIBERAL SYNAGOGUE, 19 Hannam Court.

SYNAGOGUE on Highfield St., which was erected in 1896 under the leadership of Israel Hart, is a striking reminder of the futility of an edict issued in 1253 by Simon de Montfort, Earl of Leicester, banishing the Jews from the city "in my time or in the time of any of my heirs, to the end of the world." A memorial tablet to the 6,000,000 victims of the Holocaust was erected in the synagogue in 1962.

LETCHWORTH

RABBI SOLOMON DAVID SASSOON HOME, 15 Sollershott East, houses the world's greatest private collection of Hebrew manuscripts, priceless Scrolls of the Law, many incunabula and 1,290 Hebrew and Samaritan manuscripts, including many unpublished writings that cover a period of nearly 1,000 years. There is hardly a facet of Jewish thought that is not represented in the Sassoon collection.

LINCOLN

JEWS' HOUSES, a cluster of three buildings on the hillside of Steep Hill, just below the ancient Cathedral, are among the most important surviving Jewish relics in Great Britain. All three structures are of Norman design, date from the twelfth century, and are believed to be the oldest private stone dwellings in England. Best known of the three is *Aaron's House,* a fortresslike structure with walls two feet thick and a cellar strong enough to withstand twentieth-century bombs. It was built by Aaron the Jew, one of the great figures in English Jewish history. Next to the king, Aaron was the richest man in the England of his day. As the head of a chain of money-lending offices, he provided the funds that built the cathedrals in Lincoln and Peterborough. When he died in 1186, his estate was so vast that a special "Aaron's Exchequer" was created to administer it on behalf of the king. The second Jew's house is said to have belonged to a Jewess named Bellaset. Next door to Bellaset's house is *Jews' Court,* which historians believe was the synagogue before the Jews were expelled.

SHRINE OF "LITTLE ST. HUGH " in the south aisle of Lincoln Cathedral, is the tomb of an eight-year-old boy named Hugh whom the medieval Jews of Lincoln were accused of murdering for ritual purposes. Chaucer, in his "Prioresse's Tale," gives the ancient version of this libelous accusation, which in 1255 touched off massacres of Jews in many British cities. For years over the tomb of "Little St. Hugh" there was an inscription recording the martyrdom of Hugh, his burial in the cathedral, and the fact that the ritual murder charge against medieval Jews was a common superstition. In 1959 a new version replaced the old inscription (the old story was removed from guidebooks to Lincoln in the 1930s) and it now reads:

"The Shrine of 'Little St. Hugh.' Trumped-up stories of 'ritual murders' of Christian boys by Jewish communities were common throughout Europe during the Middle Ages and even much later. These fictions cost many innocent Jews their lives. Lincoln had its own legend and the alleged victim was buried in the Cathedral. A shrine was erected above and the boy was referred to as 'Little St. Hugh.' A reconstruction of the shrine hangs near. Such stories do not redound to the credit of Christendom, and so we pray: REMEMBER NOT LORD OUR OFFENSES NOR THE OFFENSES OF OUR FOREFATHERS."

LINCOLN CATHEDRAL LIBRARY, in its remarkable collection of broadsheets collected in Holland by an English clergyman who lived there during the English Civil War, has a large sheet containing an illustration of a giant model of the Temple of Solomon in Jerusalem. The nine-foot model was the work of Rabbi Jacob Leon, a noted scholar and heraldic expert who taught Talmud in Amsterdam, where he died in 1678. He had presented it to Queen Henrietta Maria. The broadsheet of the Temple model was published in English, French, Spanish, Dutch, German, Latin, and Hebrew editions.

One of the carvings outside the Judgment Porch, the great south door of the entry to the Angel Choir, in the Cathedral, depicts a medieval Jew. He appears on a corbel beneath an angel, and on his chest is carved the Tablets of the Law.

LIVERPOOL

ALLERTON SYNAGOGUE, Mather Ave. was erected in early 1950s with government funds as compensation for another synagogue destroyed in Nazi air raids.

CHILDWALL SYNAGOGUE, Dunbabin Rd.

HAROLD COHEN LIBRARY of the University of Liverpool, on Ashton Street, is named for its donor who died in 1936, two years before it was opened. The inscription in the entrance hall recalls that Cohen's "noble benefaction . . . enabled the University to build this library henceforth to bear his name." In the main reading room there is a life-size portrait of Cohen, who also furnished the library in the Students' Union, which is known as "the Little Cohen Library." Cohen's father, Louis S. Cohen, who was mayor of Liverpool in 1900, endowed at Liverpool University the first chair in dentistry in Great Britain.

GREENBANK DRIVE SYNAGOGUE, Greenbank Drive.

HILLEL HOUSE, 25 Arundel Ave., opened in 1970, is a university center named for Morris Datnow.

JEWISH YOUTH CENTRE, 15 Dunbabin Rd., opened in 1965, is said to be largest of its kind in England.

LIBERAL SYNAGOGUE, 28 Church Road North.

OLD HEBREW CONGREGATION, Princes Rd., was founded about 1780 by Jewish emigrants from Germany and Austria who were headed for the United States by way of this west-coast seaport but then changed their minds. An earlier community existed in the 1750s, when Sephardic Jews from London doing business with Ireland settled here. The present synagogue, architecturally once considered the handsomest in England, was opened in 1874. It lost its title some years ago when much of the facade was removed as a dangerous structure. This was the first synagogue in England from whose pulpit sermons were preached in English. It was also the first to have a choir.

LONDON

ADLER ST., in Whitechapel (see below) is named for Dr. Herman Adler, chief rabbi of the British Empire from 1891 to 1911.

ADLER HOUSE, Tavistock Sq., also named for Rabbi Adler, is the seat of the Chief Rabbi and his Beth Din.

ASSOCIATION FOR JEWISH YOUTH, 33 Henriques St., is the headquarters of the national association of Jewish youth clubs, British counterparts of the American Y.M.H.A.s and Jewish Community Centers.

LEO BAECK COLLEGE, 33 Seymour Pl. in the West End, a rabbinical college sponsored by the Reform Synagogues of Great Britain and the Union of Liberal and Progressive Synagogues, memorializes the late Dr. Leo Baeck (Bäck), spiritual leader of German Reform Jewry from 1922 to 1933. Under the Hitler regime, Rabbi Baeck became the head of the representative national organization of German Jews. Despite many opportunities to leave, he remained at his post and with his congregation until its liquidation. In 1943 the Nazis put him in the Theresienstadt concentration camp, where he was found alive in 1945. He later taught at the Hebrew Union College in the United States and was the prime mover in the establishment of the World Union for Progressive Judaism.

LORD BALFOUR STATUE in the House of Commons, memorializes the World War I Foreign Secretary whose name is associated with the Balfour Declaration which was issued over his name by the British Government on Nov. 2, 1917.

BASEVI HOUSE, 17 Savile Row, the residence of Joshua George Basevi, one of England's most famous architects of the mid-nineteenth century and a cousin of Benjamin Disraeli, is marked with one of the London County Council's blue-and-white plaques which identify 206 of London's historic homes.

BAYSWATER SYNAGOGUE, Kilburn Pk. Rd. and Andover Pl., was one of Anglo-Jewry's ecclesiastical landmarks from 1863, when it was dedicated on Chichester Pl. and Harrow Rd., until 1965, when it was torn down to make way for an access road to a new housing development. Its pulpit was occupied by some of the greatest names in Anglo-Jewish history, including two chief rabbis.

BEACONSFIELD WALK in Fulham, one of London's boroughs, is named for Benjamin Disraeli, who became the Earl of Beaconsfield.

BENEDICT HOUSE, 2 Manchester Square, the residence of Sir Julius Benedict, German-born composer and conductor and for many years the accompanist of Jenny Lind, is labeled as one of the city's historic homes.

BET HAIM VELHO (OLD HOUSE OF LIFE), a tiny piece of ground behind the Beth Holim Home for the Aged, at 253 Mile End Rd., in the Borough of Stepney, is the oldest Jewish cemetery in Britain and one of the most important monuments of Jewish history in England. It was acquired in 1657, and its first burial took place in 1660. Interred under the flat stones are many of the leading figures of seventeenth- and eighteenth-century British Jewry, among them Dr. Fernando Mendes, the physician who attended Charles II at his deathbed. The cemetery is no longer used, but visitors are welcome.

BET HAIM NOVO (NEW HOUSE OF LIFE), the third oldest Jewish cemetery in England, is a few hundred yards farther along Mile End Rd. (at No. 329). First used in 1733 by the Spanish and Portuguese Synagogue, it is the last resting place of such British notables as Sampson Gideon, the eighteenth-century financier; Diego Lopes Pereira, confidant of Queen Maria Theresa of Austria, and, as Baron Aguilar, the first foreign and unbaptized Jew to be ennobled by the Hapsburgs; Daniel Mendoza, father of modern boxing; and Solomon da Costa Atias, whose gifts to the British Museum (*see below*) in 1759 launched that institution's great Hebraica collection. Farther along on Alderney Road, is the second oldest Jewish cemetery, opened in 1696 by the Ashkenazi founders of the Duke's Place Synagogue. The Bet Haim Novo and the Alderney Road cemeteries are not open to visitors.

BEVIS MARKS, the Spanish and Portuguese Jews' Congregation, on Bevis Marks, a short lane, is the oldest surviving Anglo-Jewish religious building, having been opened in 1701. This synagogue, built soon after the Jewish resettlement in 1656, stands as a landmark in the commercial heart of London. Its official name is Shaar Ha-Shomayim (The Gate of Heaven).

Because the gates are frequently kept locked during the day (the synagogue is now in the center of the city's warehouse district), visitors seeking admission should call the Vestry Office, 4 Heneage Lane. The gates are on Houndsditch, the adjoining street.

Bevis Marks resembles an early Protestant meeting house, internally and externally. It was built by a Quaker, Joseph Avis, who forbade any work on the building on Saturdays and Jewish holidays. Incorporated into the roof is a mast from a British man-of-war, donated by Queen Anne. Seven massive, hanging, many-branched brass candelabra—symbolizing the days of the week—are still used to light the building with candlelight on holy days after dark. Electricity was not installed until 1929, and then only at the sides. The central chandelier was brought from Amsterdam by Dutch Jews in the late 1600s. Before the polished wood Ark, and on the lectern, stand ten great brass candlesticks, symbolizing the Ten Commandments. The twelve columns supporting the gallery on three sides signify the Twelve Tribes of Israel.

Among the treasures preserved in the upstairs vestry room are old Torah mantles, a painting entitled "Moses, Aaron, and the Ten Commandments," which came from the *First Synagogue after the Resettlement* (*see below*) by the founders of Bevis Marks. Some benches from the earlier synagogue are still in use in Bevis Marks.

B'NAI B'RITH CENTRE, 1-2 Endsleigh St., is a nine-story building that houses London's Hillel Foundation, a memorial to the 6,000,000 victims of the Holocaust, a library, a synagogue and meeting rooms.

BRITISH MUSEUM, Great Russell St., houses in its Manuscripts and Oriental Printed Books departments one of the world's greatest collections of Judaica, including 2,500 Hebrew manuscripts and 30,000 books in Hebrew and other languages. Among the literary treasures are: a mid-fifteenth-century illuminated Haggadah, said to be the finest ever created by a Jewish artist; two manuscripts of the Mishna Torah of Maimonides and, in Maimonides own handwriting, his answers to two legal questions; an Old Testament manuscript in Syriac, dated C.E. 464, the earliest dated Biblical manuscript in existence; priceless Torah Scrolls, including the one made for the now vanished Jewish community in Kai-Feng Fu in China; illuminated Bibles of great rarity and beauty, dating from the earliest days of printing; and the famed Gaster collection of Hebrew and Samaritan manuscripts.

The Hebrew collection had its beginning in 1759, the year the Museum opened, with a gift of three manuscripts and 180 Hebrew printed books by Solomon da Costa, a Dutch Jewish immigrant, as a token of his esteem and affection for the British people. (King Charles II had wanted these volumes, but he never took possession because he failed to pay for them.) The first Hebrew book acquired by the Museum at its inception was the earliest edition of the Babylonian Talmud, published in Venice in 1520, and originally the property of Henry VIII.

In 1963, the Museum acquired 300 Yiddish volumes as an addition to its already rich Yiddish collection. The additions are devoted mainly to the extermination of the Jews of East and Central Europe and to its vanished communities and personalities.

In the Assyrian Room there can be seen ancient Palestinian signets. Coins depicting the Herodian and Maccabean dynasties of Palestine and the Bar Kochba revolt are on display in the Coin and Medal Room. Jewish wedding rings are shown in the King Edward VII Gallery. Rembrandt's etchings of Jewish types and of Biblical scenes, including one of Manasseh ben Israel, who had a key role in persuading Cromwell to agree to Jewish resettlement, are displayed in the Department of Prints and Etchings.

Hebrew deeds of English Jews before 1290 are in the Department of Manuscripts. In this department is preserved the Balfour Declaration, one of the most important documents in Jewish history. The typewritten letter from Foreign Secretary Balfour to Lord Rothschild, dated November 2, 1917, contains Britain's promise to facilitate the establishment of a national home for the Jewish people. An inkspot in front of Balfour's signature looks very much like the geographical map of the State of Israel. In the Magna Charta Room the original Magna Charta can be seen, with its tenth section containing clauses directed against the Jews. The Duveen Gallery, named for the famous Jewish art patron, Lord Duveen (*see* National Gallery *and* Tate Gallery *below*), who donated it, houses the Elgin Marbles.

CENTRAL SYNAGOGUE, Great Portland St., W.1, is one of the newest Jewish houses of worship in England. It stands on the site of an earlier building, destroyed by Nazi bombs in the blitz of 1941.

CONGRESS HOUSE, 55 New Cavendish St., W.1, is the headquarters of the British section of the World Jewish Congress.

DISRAELI HOUSE, 22 Theobalds Rd., has a memorial tablet affixed by the London County Council to mark the birthplace of Benjamin Disraeli on December 21, 1804. The records of Bevis Marks note Disraeli's circumcision on Dec. 29. At 93 Park Lane there is another memorial plaque identifying the house where Disraeli lived from 1839 to 1873.

GEORGE ELIOT HOUSE, Holly Lodge, 31 Wimbledon Park Rd., was the home of the nineteenth-century novelist (Mary Ann Evans Cross) who wrote not only *Silas Marner, Adam Bede, The Mill on the Floss,* and other noted books, but also *Daniel Deronda,* the first English novel to treat the Jew sympathetically. This work is credited with creating the intellectual climate that ultimately led to British political support for a Jewish homeland in Palestine.

FIRST SYNAGOGUE AFTER THE RESETTLEMENT established in 1657 on the upper floor of a house in Creechurch Lane, a stone's throw from Bevis Marks, is commemorated by a plaque on the rear of the Cunard Building. It reads: Site of First Synagogue after the Resettlement–1657-1701. Spanish and Portuguese Jews' Congregation." This was the synagogue to which Samuel Pepys referred in his *Diaries*.

FOREIGN OFFICE, No. 10 Downing St., one of the most famous addresses in Britain, has an Israel citrus tree growing just outside the window of the office of the Deputy Under-Secretary of State. It was planted by Sir Francis Rundall in 1959 when he returned from Israel after two and a half years as British ambassador there.

FREUD HOUSE, 20 Maresfield Gardens, Hampstead Borough, is memorialized by a London County Council plaque as the house where Dr. Sigmund Freud, father of psychoanalysis, lived the last fifteen months of his life. Freud came to England in 1938 after being smuggled out of Vienna when the Nazis took over Austria. The house contains the library, manuscripts, and an art collection that belonged to Freud. An urn with Freud's ashes can be seen at the Golders Green Cemetery in London.

FREUD STATUE, corner of Fitzjohn's Ave. and College Crescent, the only statue to the father of psychoanalysis, was dedicated in 1969. Nine feet tall, the bronze sculpture, by Oscar Nemon, shows Freud seated, elbows out and hands on hip. Nemon is also the sculptor of the Winston Churchill statue in the House of Commons.

LORD GEORGE GORDON GRAVE in St. James Churchyard, Hampstead Rd., is the last resting place of the eccentric Scottish-born nobleman who created a great stir in the closing years of the eighteenth century when he became a convert to Judaism after he had precipitated the Gordon Riots during his struggle against the political emancipation of Catholics. In his latter years he returned to Protestantism.

GREAT SYNAGOGUE WALLS on Duke's Place, a continuation of Bevis Marks Lane, is all that remains of the once famous "Duke's Place Schul," which was founded in 1690. Destroyed by Nazi bombs during World War II, the wall facing the roadway is still there, and so is the name "Great Synagogue," over the walls. Plans are under way for permanently memorializing the synagogue.

GUILDHALL which is London's city hall, has inscribed on a large glass panel the names of all of London's Lord Mayors. Seven Jews have been elected to this largely honorary but exalted office since 1855, when Sir David Salomons first held it.

HEINE HOUSE, 32 Craven St., bears a memorial plaque marking the house where the poet Heinrich Heine lived during his stay in England in 1827.

HENRIQUES STREET, the former Berner St., memorializes the late Sir Basil Henriques, member of an old Anglo-Jewish family, who founded a number of settlement houses and was widely known for his philanthropies.

HOUSE OF COMMONS in Parliament Square, which has echoed for generations with the words of parliamentarians protesting outrages against Jews and where many Jewish M.P.s have served in the last century, has in its so-called Treasury Box, before which Cabinet ministers deliver speeches, three Bibles. One of these is the Hebrew Bible, used when a Jewish M.P. has to take the oath.

On the terrace staircase of the House of Commons are reproductions of murals describing "The Story of the Jews," the originals of which were painted on instructions of Henry III (1207-1272) for the walls of the old Palace of Westminster but which were lost in a fire of 1834.

In the Square, facing the Houses of Parliament, stands a bronze *Statue of Benjamin Disraeli*, whose first address in the House of Commons in 1837 was such a failure that he was openly booed. An M.P. for more than thirty years and leader of the Conservative party from 1847 until his death in 1881, he obtained control of the Suez Canal for England, had Victoria crowned Empress of India, scored a great diplomatic success at the Congress of Berlin in 1878 and attained such immense popularity that when he died he was honored as no Englishman had been since

Wellington. Victoria wanted to bury him in Westminster Abbey but he had left instructions to be buried at Hughendon (see HIGH WYCOMBE above). Victoria lamented "the death of my dear Lord Beaconsfield" as a "national calamity." April 19, the day of his death, is still celebrated as Primrose Day by Conservative party members because the primrose was Disraeli's favorite flower. His father was a member of Bevis Marks Synagogue but resigned following a quarrel and had Benjamin baptized at the age of thirteen.

Also in Parliament Square is the *Statue of Oliver Cromwell,* the "Lord Protector" of England, whose oral assurance enabled the Jews to resettle openly in England. The statue was presented anonymously, but it is now known that the donor was Lord Rosebery, Prime Minister of England and son-in-law of Meyer Nathan Rothschild, the youngest son of the original English Rothschild.

In Parliament Square, too, is Sir Jacob Epstein's bronze *Statue of Field Marshal Smuts,* the South African soldier and statesman who, as a member of the British War Cabinet in 1917, was one of the authors of the Balfour Declaration.

ISRAEL EMBASSY, 2 Palace Green, W.2.

ISRAEL HOUSE, 5 Crediton Hill, West Hampstead, is London's first permanent centre for Israeli students.

JEWISH CHRONICLE BUILDING, 25 Furnival St., is the headquarters of the famous Anglo-Jewish weekly, which was founded in 1841.

JEWISH FREE SCHOOL SECONDARY SCHOOL, Camden Rd., cor. Torriano Ave., has two tablets commemorating the final victory in 1858, gained by Baron Rothschild in his long struggle to obtain for Jews full political rights.

JEWISH MUSEUM, Upper Woburn Place (see Woburn House below).

JEWISH WAR MEMORIAL in the garden in front of the Willesden Jewish Cemetery, Beaconsfield Rd., is the first national memorial to Jewish servicemen in the British forces in World Wars I and II. Erected in 1961 by the Commonwealth War Graves Commission, the memorial is an eleven-foot-six-inch-high stone inscribed in Hebrew and English.

JEWS' COLLEGE, 11 Montagu Place, W.E., is the oldest rabbinical seminary in the British Commonwealth, having been founded in 1855. The present six-story building was dedicated in 1957. In addition to classrooms, a synagogue, offices, recreational facilities, and residential quarters for seventeen students, the College has a famous library, which is one of the most important repositories of Jewish books in the world.

In the library is a two-story Jewish mural.

JEWRY STREET, opposite Duke's Place, was a Jewish neighborhood in pre-Expulsion times before the Jews were forced to move eastward from the Old Jewry area during the anti-Semitic riots at the time of Richard I's coronation.

CHARLES JORDAN HOUSE, Finchley Rd., opened in 1958 as a rehabilative mental center for former refugees from Nazi persecution or their children, is a memorial to Charles Jordan, director of the American Jewish Joint Distribution Committee, who was found dead in Czechoslovakia in 1967 under mysterious circumstances.

KANNE GRAVESTONE in Brompton Cemetery, Fulham Rd., was erected by Queen Victoria and the Prince of Wales, "to mark their appreciation of the long and valued services of Joseph Julius Kanne—1889 . . . for nearly 40 years one of Her Majesty's most devoted servants." Kanne, a German-born Jew who became an English citizen, was Queen Victoria's courier and made all arrangements for her European travels. He served in the Crimean War and received twenty-one foreign decorations. He died in 1888 after thirty years in Victoria's service.

KOSHER RESTAURANTS: M. Bloom, 90 Whitechapel Rd., E.1; Folman's, 24 Noel St., W.1.; Bloom & Sturgess, 114 Baker St., W.1.; Kedassia, 69 New Oxford St., W.C.1; Goody's, 55 Berwick St., W.1; Aviva, 1 Platts Lane, Finchley Rd. N.W.3.

LIBERAL JEWISH SYNAGOGUE, 28 St. John's Wood Rd., N.W.8. The Union of Liberal and Progressive Synagogues has its headquarters here.

LONDON MUSEUM, Kensington Palace, W.8, displays in its collection on Parliament and the Premiership (Room 7) a unique array of costumes, documents, portraits, and personal relics associated with Britain's Prime Ministers from the eighteenth century. The nucleus of the collection was brought together through the generosity of Ernest S. Makower, a Jewish industrialist and art and music patron.

LONDON UNIVERSITY was founded in 1836 as University College by Isaac Lyon Goldsmid, a prominent banker, who purchased the University's first site. In 1841 he became the first Jew to be created a baronet. His son led the secession from the two pioneer Orthodox synagogues that brought the Reform movement to England. The Hebrew Department, created by the elder Goldsmid in 1828, when Hyman Hurwitz was appointed to its Jewish chair as the first Jewish holder of such a professorship on either side of the Atlantic, was expanded into a comprehensive center for Jewish studies in 1966 with the aid of a grant of $125,000 from the Memorial Foundation for Jewish Culture.

The *Percival David Foundation of Chinese Art,* 53 Gordon Square, W.C.1, part of the University's School of Oriental and African Studies, was established in 1952 through Sir Percival's donation of his priceless collection of Chinese art consisting of 1,400 pieces.

THE IMPERIAL COLLEGE OF SCIENCE AND TECHNOLOGY, Prince Consort Rd., South Kensington, contains the Wolfson Laboratory, named for Sir Isaac Wolfson, whose $1,000,000 gift made possible this noted research institute. It is presided over by Dr. Ernst Chain, who was one of the codiscoverers of penicillin and a co-winner of the 1949 Nobel Prize in Medicine.

The *Sterling Library,* a special collection in the University of London Library, Senate House, Malet St., is a million-dollar assemblage of 4,000 rare volumes illustrating the work of the greatest English writers from Chaucer to the moderns. It was a gift from the late Sir Louis Sterling, American-born philanthropist and industrialist, who grew up on New York's East Side and made a fortune as head of the British phonograph industry. A painting of Sir Louis hangs in the Sterling Library.

University College, on Gower St., one of the largest of the colleges, schools, and institutes that make up the University of London, has a number of places of special Jewish interest: *Mocatta Library and Museum,* in the south junction of the main building, specializes in material on the history of British Jewry. Founded in 1905 through a bequest from Frederic David Mocatta, philanthropist and bibliophile, the library contains many Jewish book and art treasures of historical importance. Some were lost when the library was destroyed in an air raid in 1940. It was rebuilt in 1954. Many of the art objects and some of the books from the former Montefiore Museum at the Judith Lady Montefiore College, in Ramsgate, are now housed in the Mocatta Library.

Just above the Mocatta Library, which is also the home of the Jewish Historical Society, is the Gustave Tuck Theatre, a gift of a president of the Jewish Historical Society. The theatre too was rebuilt in 1954 after being wrecked during the blitz.

The *Warburg Institute,* on Woburn Square, founded in Hamburg by Abby Warburg, noted art historian, as Warburg Bibliothek, and transferred to London when the Nazis took over in Germany, contains more than 350,000 books, reproductions, and photographs dealing with the history of the religions, arts, and literatures of the Mediterranean civilizations.

MACAULAY HOUSE, 5 The Pavement, Clapham Common, was the home of Thomas B. Macaulay, statesman, historian, and essayist, whose maiden speech in Parliament in 1830 advocating the removal of Jewish civil disabilities, and famous essay on the same subject, set the stage for the ultimate political emancipation of English Jewry.

MACCABI STADIUM, Hall Lane, N.W., a Jewish sports pavilion, opened in 1959, has a bronze plaque with the likeness of the first Lord Melchett, who fathered the idea of the Maccabiah Games in Israel. As Alfred M. Mond he was the founder of the Imperial Chemical Industries, served as Minister of Health and Minister of Public Works in two British Cabinets. Although not born a Jew (his father was a prominent German-Jewish chemist who converted to Christianity after he settled in England), he was one of the most active Zionist leaders of his time and when he died was buried in a Jewish cemetery. His son, the present Lord Melchett, and daughter, Lady Reading, were converted to Judaism.

MARBLE ARCH SYNAGOGUE, 32 Great Cumberland Place, in the West End, is the successor to the historic Great Synagogue on Duke's Place, a continuation of Bevis Marks Lane. Founded in 1690 by Jews from Germany, the Great Synagogue was *the* synagogue of British Jewry, where all the community's major celebrations took place. Erected in 1772 and enlarged in 1790, it was destroyed by Nazi bombs in May 1941. In 1943 a temporary synagogue was erected behind the remaining wall of the fire-gutted sanctuary.

The new synagogue is architecturally unique in that, unlike other London synagogues, it is not a detached structure with a character of its own, but part of a semicircular terrace of houses forming the east side of the street. Outwardly there is little indication that one of these beautiful houses is a synagogue. But once you are inside you find it a lavishly and tastefully furnished synagogue in Orthodox style. The *bimah* is in the center of the main floor, the hallmark of all London Orthodox synagogues. Located in the area of London's leading hotels, the Marble Arch Synagogue is attended by tourists and servicemen. It holds weekday and Sabbath services throughout the year.

The decision to erect the new synagogue (it was dedicated in 1961) in the West End instead of rebuilding the Great Synagogue on its historic site in the East End was dramatic evidence that the old and colorful Jewish quarter in the East End had ceased to be the heart of the London Jewish community. The masses of East European Jews who migrated to England between 1880 and 1906 had mostly settled in the East End parish of Whitechapel (*see below*) in the Borough of Stepney, and in the adjacent areas of Mile End and Bethnal Green. Once 80,000 Jews lived in these neighborhoods; today there are fewer than 15,000. The rest have moved to other areas of London or into the suburbs, following the impact of wartime dispersion and social and economic changes.

KARL MARX HOUSE, 22 Dean St., is marked with a round blue plaque in commemoration of the house where the father of Communism wrote "Das Kapital." Marx lived there from 1851 to 1856. The site, in the Soho district, is now occupied by an Italian restaurant.

KARL MARX TOMB in Highgate Cemetery, has a monument to the founder of Communism, who was a baptized Jew.

MEMORIAL TO VICTIMS OF NAZISM in the Liberal Jewish Cemetery, at the junction of Pound Lane and Harlesden Lane, Willesden, N.W., was the first memorial erected in Great Britain to the millions of victims of Nazism. Designed by the eminent sculptor Benno Elkan (*see* Westminster Abbey), the memorial consists of a plain stone monument inscribed in Hebrew with a verse from the Lamentations of Jeremiah. Above the inscription is a bronze figure of a kneeling man. This plaque had been designed by Elkan for a monument in Germany, but it was ordered removed by the Nazis, and Elkan brought it with him when he left Germany. There is another memorial to Nazi prisoners of war and concentration camp victims in Gladstone Park, Cricklewood, Willesdon, in northwest London. Designed by Frederick Kormis, the sculpture depicts a group of five life-size figures representing the differing moods of suffering, despair and hope.

MILK STREET, north of Cheapside, was formerly spelled Melecstrete, and since this street is in the neighborhood of Old Jewry, it was obviously named for the Hebrew word for 'king'—melech. King Street is parallel to Milk St.

MONTEFIORE HALL, Ashworth Rd., W., is in the courtyard of the Lauderdale Synagogue of the Spanish and Portuguese Congregation, one of seven under the jurisdiction of the Sephardic chief rabbi (another of these is Bevis Marks). It is named for Sir Moses Montefiore, the beloved nineteenth-century philanthropist.

JUDITH LADY MONTEFIORE COLLEGE, 4 Ashworth Rd., W., which trains rabbis and teachers for Jewish communities in North Africa, was moved in 1960 from Ramsgate, where it had occupied the country home of Sir Moses Montefiore since its establishment in 1865 as a memorial to Sir Moses' wife. Originally it trained Sephardic rabbis for British Jewry.

NATIONAL GALLERY on the north side of Trafalgar Square, which houses some of the greatest works of art, had its beginnings in 1824 with a collection of thirty-eight paintings bought from John Julius Angerstein for $250,000. Angerstein, a Russian Jew, was one of the founders and builders of Lloyd's, world-famous insurance writers. A painting of Angerstein hangs in the Gallery.

Among the Gallery's greatest patrons was the late Lord Duveen, in his time the most famous art dealer in the world. To him the National Gallery owes a wing devoted to Italian art which is housed in the Duveen Room, as well as many notable masterpieces. The Ludwig Mond Room recalls the gift of forty-two priceless Italian paintings by Dr. Ludwig Mond, noted chemist and industrialist.

The National Gallery also owns a number of Rembrandt's paintings of Jewish characters.

NATIONAL PORTRAIT GALLERY, 2 St. Martin's Place, W.C.2, which exhibits portraits of British notables, has among the more than 3,000 artistic representations of famous people pictures of twenty-two British Jews. Inclusion in this gallery is determined by the importance of the person rather than the caliber of the art. The twenty-two Jews represented are: Solomon Hirschell, chief rabbi from 1802 to 1842; Sir Jacob Epstein, the controversial American-born sculptor; Benjamin Disraeli (who is represented thirteen times) and his father, Isaac; Baron Lionel Nathan de Rothschild, the first Jew seated in the House of Commons; Sir Moses Montefiore; Baron Ferdinand Rothschild; Alfred Rothschild; John Zoffany, eighteenth-century portrait painter; Solomon J. Solomon, artist and the father of camouflage in World War I; Solomon Hart, nineteenth-century painter; Ludwig Mond and Raphael Mendola, eminent chemists; Sir Ernest Cassel, international banker and friend of King Edward VII; Sir Aurel Stein, explorer; Sir William Rothenstein, painter; Israel Zangwill, author; Lord Duveen, art patron; Sir Landon Ronald, orchestra conductor; Isaac Rosenberg, soldier-poet; Lord Reading, who was viceroy of India and Lord Chief Justice; Max Beerbohm, caricaturist; and Lucien Pissarro, painter, who was the father of Camille Pissarro.

NEW LONDON SYNAGOGUE, 33 Abbey Rd., N.W.8, which for over 80 years housed the St. John's Wood Synagogue of the United Synagogue and was the house of worship of two Chief Rabbis, Dr. Joseph H. Hertz and Israel Brodie, has since 1964 been the synagogue of Dr. Louis Jacobs, who formed the congregation after the refusal of the Chief Rabbi to reappoint him to the pulpit of the New West End Synagogue. Rabbi Jacobs' congregation is Orthodox but independent of any synagogal body.

OLD BAILEY (Central Criminal Court Building) on Old Bailey, has along the walls of the gallery, about twenty feet above the floor after you mount a broad flight of marble steps, a painting of "Moses Gave unto the People the Laws of God," and another showing Moses descending from Mount Sinai with the Tablets of the Law.

OLD JEWRY, first street on the right going along Poultry to Cheapside, was once the heart of the pre-Expulsion Jewish community. Once there was a synagogue at the southwest corner of Old Jewry. Close by the northeast corner, at Gresham St., where Gresham College now stands, was the site of the home of Cresse fils Moses, which was also used as a synagogue in 1263.

PUBLIC RECORD OFFICE, 9-21 Chancery Lane, W.C.2, stands on the site of the Domus Conversum, the house for converted Jews founded in 1232 by Henry III. It was torn down in 1896. In the Museum of the Record Office is a treasure trove of English-Jewish history. Among the hundreds of documents, many dating back to the eleventh, twelfth, and thirteenth centuries, are Hebrew deeds, charters, writs, and receipts; records of early Jewish converts; state papers dealing with secret Jews, including Queen Elizabeth I's physician, who was hanged; official records relating to Lord George Gordon (*see above*), the election of Lord Rothschild to the House of Commons, and the naturalization of Jews in the eighteenth century; and the original data relating to Manasseh ben Israel and the return of the Jews in 1656. Among the latter is his petition to Cromwell, the official report on his plea by the Council of State, his safe conduct from Amsterdam to England to meet with Cromwell to urge on him the lifting of the ban of expulsion of 1290, and a "Remonstrance Against the Jews," addressed to Charles II in 1660, when there was an abortive effort to bar the Jews again.

N.M. ROTHSCHILD & SONS, New Court, St. Swithin's Lane, in the heart of the city, headquarters of the House of Rothschild in England, is a new building erected in 1965 to replace the former palazzo-like structure that occupied the same site since 1867. The Rothschilds' principal London office has been at New Court since the bank was founded in 1804 by Nathan Mayer Rothschild, the first member of the family to settle in England. Since then the Rothschilds have been closely identified with every aspect of Jewish life, as well as with British industry, politics, science, art and literature. The board room, covered with photographs and portraits of members of the Rothschild family, was for generations the scene of important Jewish gatherings.

ROYAL EXCHANGE, at the corner of Cornhill and Threadneedle Sts., displays a painting of Nathan Meyer Rothschild, founder of the British branch of the Rothschild family. The pediment shows people from all corners of the earth, standing on a hill which bears the words of Psalm 24. In the Exchange there is a "Jew-ellers Walk," which replaced "Jews Walk" when the Exchange was rebuilt after a fire destroyed the old building. The change of name was effected at the instigation of Moses Mocatta and Sir Moses Montefiore, who felt that "Jews' Walk" was unnecessary.

REX HOUSE, 4-12 Regent St., S.W.1, is the headquarters of the English Zionist Federation, the Jewish Agency for Israel and many other Israel-related organizations. For 44 years until 1964 the principal Zionist address in London was 77 Great Russell St., W.C.1, where some of the greatest personalities in Zionist history worked.

ROYAL FUSILIERS WAR MEMORIAL, in Holborn Bars (where the Gray's Inn Rd. enters the borough of Holborn), honors the Royal Fusiliers of World War I. The 38th, 39th, and 40th Battalions of this regiment were all-Jewish units comprising the Jewish Legion, which took part in the liberation of Palestine from the Turks.

ST. JOHN'S WOOD SYNAGOGUE, Grove End Rd., St. John's Wood, N.W.8. Opened in 1964, this is Britain's largest synagogue.

CHURCH OF ST. LAWRENCE JEWRY on King St., Cheapside, is so named because it stands on the site of the old Jewish quarter where Jews lived from the eleventh to the thirteenth century. The earlier church on this spot was previously a synagogue, but it was destroyed by fire and rebuilt in 1671 by Christopher Wren.

ST. MARY COLECHURCH on the west side of the intersection of Old Jewry and

Poultry, was in the late twelfth century the private synagogue of Abraham fils Rabbi (Son of the Rabbi).

ST. PAUL'S CATHEDRAL, the city's cathedral church, has in its American Memorial Chapel an enduring tribute to the 8,000 Jews who died during World War II while stationed in or en route to Britain. In a large red-covered vellum book encased in a gilded casket is an honor roll of nearly 50,000 names, and as you turn the pages you read the Jewish names. Among the emblems that decorate the wrought-iron rails in the Chapel, which is behind the High Altar in the restored East Wing, are two 18-inch-high panels dedicated to the Jewish war dead in the United States forces. One depicts the Burning Bush which summoned Moses to the service of Israel. The second shows an outstretched hand holding one of the Tablets of the Law, on which is inscribed in Hebrew the Second Commandment. The entire Chapel is a gift of the British people.

ST. STEPHEN'S CHURCH on Coleman St., bombed out during the war, occupied the site of a thirteenth-century synagogue.

SAMUDA WALK, a street in Poplar's Isle of Dogs, is named for Joseph D'Aguilar Samuda, a leading engineer and shipbuilder of the nineteenth century, whose family came originally from Spain. He served in Parliament and founded the Institute of Naval Architects.

HERBERT SAMUEL HALL, a communal center adjoining the New West End Synagogue, St. Petersburg Place and Bayswater Rd., was named for the late Lord Samuel, eminent Jewish statesman, philosopher, and communal leader, on his ninetieth birthday in 1960. Lord Samuel was for many years the leader of the Liberal party. As Postmaster-General he was the first professing Jew to serve in the Cabinet. Later he became the first British High Commissioner to Palestine.

SAPERSTEIN HOUSE, Flower and Dean Sts., off Commercial St., E.1, is marked with a plaque by the Borough of Stepney as the building where Abe Saperstein, the London-born American Jewish sportsman who founded the famed Harlem Globetrotters basketball team, lived as a child in the late 1890s.

TATE GALLERY, Millbank, S.W.1, has many evidences of the generosity of Lord Duveen. These include the Turner Gallery, the gallery of modern foreign art, the Sculpture Hall, and the Duveen Wing, which contains the most famous works of Sargent. Some of the early Sargents were presented to the Tate Gallery by the widow and family of Asher Wertheimer, an eminent antique dealer.

Also in the Tate Gallery is the original of Sir Jacob Epstein's head of Dr. Albert Einstein. Epstein works abound in London and in other British cities. His *Madonna and Child* in Cavendish Square, *Majestas* in St. Paul's Cathedral, *Rima* in Hyde Park, *Visitation* in the Tate Gallery, and *Mother and Dead Son*, a war memorial, at the Trades Union Congress headquarters are among his best known. Epstein's most controversial works, *Genesis, Adam, Eve,* and *Jacob and the Angel*, were for many years on exhibit at Louis Tussaud's Waxworks in Blackpool.

MADAME TUSSAUD'S, Marylebone Rd., adjoining Baker St., N.W., the famous waxworks, contains the likenesses of a number of well-known Jewish personalities: David Ben-Gurion, Lord George Gordon (*see above*), Benjamin Disraeli, Danny Kaye, and Lt. Col. A. C. Newman, winner of the Victoria Cross in World War II. Capt. Alfred Dreyfus, Baron Lionel de Rothschild (to whom the Balfour Declaration was addressed in 1917) and Sir Moses Montefiore were at one time also represented.

BEN URI ART GALLERY, 21 Dean St., W.1, maintains a permanent exhibit of the works of modern Jewish sculptors and artists. The gallery is in the same building as the West End Great Synagogue.

VICTORIA AND ALBERT MUSEUM, South Kensington, S.W., exhibits in Room 84 an important collection of Hanukkah Menorahs going back to the 12th century and silver spice holders from the 17th and 18th centuries. In Room 91 there is a collection of Jewish wedding rings from sixteenth-century Italy. In the Textile Dept. there is displayed an array of synagogue appurtenances from Italy and Holland.

WEST LONDON SYNAGOGUE, 34 Upper Berkeley St., W.1, (Reform). This is the oldest Reform congregation in England, having been founded in 1842 by Sephardic Jews from Bevis Marks. Erected in 1872, the synagogue is one of the finest examples of synagogue architecture in Britain.

WESTMINSTER ABBEY

Candelabra (two), near the Tomb of the Unknown Soldier, each six feet high and seven feet wide. One of the two bronzes shaped like an oak tree has nestling in its branches thirty-two characters from the Hebrew Bible. This unique sculpture is the work of the late Benno Elkan, a Jewish refugee from Germany, who completed it in Germany and brought it with him to London. It was dedicated in the Abbey in 1940 as the gift of Lord Lee. In 1942 Elkan's second candelabrum, of the same shape but adorned with figures in the life of Jesus, was also dedicated in the Abbey. Elkan was the sculptor of the towering Menorah, depicting in panels among its branches the spiritual history of Jewry, which stands in the Knesset Building in Jerusalem.

The Stone of Scone, a prized heirloom of Britain, which rests under the Coronation Chair in the Abbey, has by a curious legend been linked to the Biblical patriarch Jacob. According to this legend, the stone, also known as the *Lia Fail,* was the very stone on which Jacob rested his head at Bethel, on his flight from the vengeance of his brother Esau. Later the stone found its way to Jerusalem, where it was incorporated in the first Temple. When Nebuchadnezzar destroyed the Temple in 586 B.C.E., the Prophet Jeremiah, it is said, and some other Jewish refugees rescued this stone and fled with it to what is now Ireland. The early kings of Ireland supposedly sat on this stone upon being crowned. Subsequently, it came into the possession of the Scottish kings, who used it for their coronation rites. Edward I, the king who expelled the Jews from England, acquired the stone in 1296 and removed it to Westminster.

Disraeli Statue stands in the Abbey's Statesman's Corner, near the monuments to Peel and Gladstone.

Above the Poets' Corner in the Abbey is a collection of ancient triple-locked chests which contain the minute records of Jewish business transactions, estates, and inheritances in England for more than one hundred years prior to the expulsion of 1290. Known as *archae*, these chests were the depositories of the so-called Exchequer of the Jews. Jews were the personal property of the king, and he saw to it that debts owing to Jews were carefully recorded lest the Crown be the loser. Branches of the Exchequer were set up in six cities. The bonds attesting the debts to Jews were called *starrs* (from the Hebrew *shetaroth*). One part of the bond was retained by the Jewish lender and the other was deposited in the chest. Frequently the bonds were in the form of tallies, or pieces of wood split asunder, each bearing the Jewish lender's name in Hebrew or Latin. It is these *starrs* that are locked in the Abbey's *archae*. Some of the bonds are said to indicate that Jews were forced to contribute toward the construction of the Abbey. The Abbey's library has two 13th century Hebrew manuscripts, nine Hebrew Bibles, including the first Rabbinical Bible in four volumes printed in Belgium by Daniel Bomberg in 1517.

WESTMINSTER BANK, 52 Threadneedle St., stands on the site of a synagogue erected in 1231.

WESTMINSTER SYNAGOGUE, Rutland Gardens, Knightsbridge, S.W.7, houses more than 1,000 Torah Scrolls brought to England in 1964 from Prague where they had been collected by the Nazis from synagogues all through Czechoslovakia. The Nazis had stored them in a warehouse as the nucleus of a proposed museum. The Scrolls filled five freight cars on the trip across Europe. They will ultimately be housed in a museum to be built as part of the synagogue.

WHITECHAPEL, the old Jewish quarter of London in the East End, is but a shadow of what it used to be, but it is still the home of a plethora of interesting Jewish institutions and remains of the historic past.

Opposite Duke's Place, where the Great Synagogue once stood, in Aldgate, *Jewry Street* is a reminder of the medieval Jewish settlement. On Sundays, Middlesex, Wentworth and half a dozen adjacent streets become the famous *Petticoat Lane Market*, where you can buy almost anything from Jewish merchants. Yiddish is the lingua franca, and Yiddish and Hebrew signs still abound. The whole atmosphere is a reminder of the most picturesque days of the open-air markets of New York's Lower East Side. During the week, Wentworth St. is a Jewish marketing area. Shops and warehouses occupy the remains of the bombed-out Jews' Free School at the end of Aldgate St. This is the school which such notables as Israel Zangwill—whose stories and novels immortalized Whitechapel—Lord Reading, and Samuel Gompers, founder of the American Federation of Labor, began their education. The *Jews' Temporary Shelter*, 63 Mansell St., Aldgate, was the temporary haven for thousands of Jews from Eastern Europe who arrived in London between 1880 and 1906 friendless and often penniless. Only recently it has again served as a refuge for Jews fleeing from Hungary and Egypt. At 59 Brick Lane is the famed Orthodox Spitalfields Great Synagogue (Machzikae Hadath). The Etz Chaim Yeshiva is on Thrawl St.

The whole area still has synagogues and other Jewish institutions that serve the remaining Jewish residents—occupants of the new housing development erected by the London County Council; shopkeepers who prefer to live near their businesses; aging Yiddish-speaking Jews who could not break with the past; newcomers from India, Egypt, and Iran; and refugees from behind the Iron Curtain. Many leading industrialists and merchants whose names are now household words in England got their start in humble shops in Whitechapel and other East End neighborhoods.

STAMFORD HILL DISTRICT in the East End, is dotted with many small Chassidic congregations and yeshivas, as well as a number of Persian, Indian and Bokharan synagogues. The latter are at 7 Amhurst Park, East Bank.

WIENER LIBRARY, 4 Devonshire St., W.E., is probably the most important single center outside of Israel for research and information on Nazi Germany from the day when Hitler first appeared on the scene. Its more than 40,000 books and pamphlets and its nearly 750,000 newspaper clippings constitute a primary source of basic data about every phase of Nazism. It had its beginnings in Germany as part of the archives of the Centralverein, the largest defense organization of German Jews. The late Dr. Alfred Wiener, an official of the Centralverein, removed what was left of the archives after 1933 to Amsterdam. The day the Nazis invaded Poland in 1939, he moved his collection to London, where it has since been used by governments, historians, newspapermen, and researchers. The library is officially known as the Institute for Graduate Studies in Contemporary History and is now associated with University of Reading.

WOBURN HOUSE on Upper Woburn Place, W.C., is the organizational and administrative heart of British Jewry, many of whose principal national institutions are housed in this seven-story building. The famous *Jewish Museum*, on the first floor, is a treasure house of English-Jewish history for the last three centuries. It also has exhibits of synagogue ritual objects from old synagogues in Europe. The Board of Deputies of British Jews, the official representative body of British Jews, now more than two hundred years old, which speaks and acts for English Jews in all matters involving the government, has its headquarters on the fourth floor. On the floor above is the office of the Anglo-Jewish Association, which intercedes on behalf of Jews abroad.

ZANGWILL HOUSE, 202 Old Ford Road, Bethnal Green, is marked as the house where Israel Zangwill, teacher, journalist, and novelist, who immortalized Jewish life in the East End in his famous novel, "Children of the Ghetto, " lived from 1884 to 1887 while a student at London University.

MANCHESTER

The present community of 32,000 Jews, founded about 1780, maintains a vast network of synagogues and communal, educational, cultural, and fraternal organizations.

CENTRAL SYNAGOGUE, Heywood St.

GREAT SYNAGOGUE, Cheetham Hill Rd., is the oldest Jewish institution in the second-largest Jewish community in the United Kingdom. The Great Synagogue is classed as a historic building, having been built in 1857.

KOSHER RESTAURANT (Fulda's), Corporation St.

MACCABI HOUSE, Middleton Rd.

PUBLIC LIBRARY, St. Peter's Square, has a notable Jewish Section, which contains current Jewish works as well as a valuable collection of Hebrew manuscripts and books, including many from the library of the late Dr. Moses Gaster, Sephardic chief rabbi of England.

REFORM CONGREGATION, Jacksons Row, Albert Square.

CONGREGATION OF SPANISH AND PORTUGUESE JEWS, 190 Cheetham Hill Rd.

MARGATE

SYNAGOGUE, Godwin Rd., serves Jewish vacationists in this popular east-coast resort community. Some of the kosher hotels also sponsor religious services.

MARKET JEW

Sometimes called Marazion (*Mara Zion*—"bitter Zion"), this little port (1,100 inhabitants) in Cornwall, near Land's End, supposedly got its name from an ancient settlement of Jews who came with the Phoenicians to trade for Cornish tin.

NEWCASTLE

GOSFORTH AND KENTON HEBREW CONGREGATION, Great North Road (Gosforth).

JESMOND HEBREW CONGREGATION, 2 Eskdale Terrace.

OLD HEBREW CONGREGATION, Leazes Park Rd., is the oldest of four synagogues in this community whose history has been traced to 1234. The modern community dates from the 1830s.

REFORM SYNAGOGUE, Derby Street.

NORWICH

CASTLE MUSEUM displays two 13th century green and black stone pitchers, a water jug and a stone synagogue pillar, remnants of the 13th century ghetto, which were recently dug up in the heart of the city.

CENTRAL LIBRARY ANNEX, a gift of members of the 2nd Division of the United States Air Force who subscribed $56,000 for an American war memorial in Norwich, has a huge scroll on which are inscribed the names of 6,000 American airmen, among them many Jews, who died in World War II.

JEWISH CEMETERY, Quaker Lane, between Pitt and Oak Sts., dating from 1813, and containing 10 graves, has been preserved by the municipal authorities in the midst of a former slum area that now has been rebuilt.

MUSIC HOUSE, one of the oldest buildings in the city, is said to have been the home of Jurnet the Jew, a twelfth century banker. The eerie structure's walls are hung with shields and pikes and the antlered skulls of long-dead stags. An early Jewish community here was the subject of the first recorded attempt in medieval

Europe to accuse the Jews of blood ritual murder. It happened in 1140, when the Sheriff of Norfolk, charged with the safety of the King's Jews, found himself appearing as their protector against the libelous accusation.

SYNAGOGUE, 3 Earlham Rd.

NORWICH CATHEDRAL which is linked with Europe's first blood ritual canard, still has on sale booklets repeating the ancient calumny, but Cathedral officials refute it when showing visitors around.

SYNAGOGUE STREET recalls an 1840 synagogue on this site, which was destroyed by Nazi bombs in 1942.

SAMSON AND HERCULES BALLROOM is built on the remnant of an 1828 synagogue. An arched cupboard in the coke store room can be identified as an arched cupboard which was once the Ark.

NOTTINGHAM

LIBERAL JEWISH SYNAGOGUE, Friends Meeting House, Clarendon St.

NEWSTEAD ABBEY, nine miles north of the city on the main Nottingham-Mansfield Rd., the former home of the poet Lord Byron, is now also associated with the name of Sir Julien Cahn, local philanthropist and sportsman, who in 1931 presented to the city of Nottingham the historic parts of the Abbey and its gardens. A memorial plaque on the wall of the west front of the Abbey tells of the gift. Byron's poems included a number extolling Judaism and advocating the return of the Jews to Palestine.

SYNAGOGUE, Shakespeare St.

OLD SYNAGOGUE, Shakespeare St.

OLD JEWISH CEMETERY, near Sherwood Road, in the heart of the city.

OXFORD

FIRST COFFEEHOUSE IN ENGLAND, opened in 1650 as the earliest resort of this kind by Jacob the Jew, is memorialized by a plaque in the headquarters of the Oxford and District Co-operative Society, 85 High St.

OXFORD SYNAGOGUE, Richmond Rd., entered through a stone Gothic doorway over which is inscribed in Hebrew, BETH HA-KNESSET, is of comparatively recent origin compared with the tradition that the synagogue, erected in 1227, stood opposite what is now St. Aldate's Church and that the ancient Jewish cemetery occupied the site of the Botanical Gardens opposite Magdalen College on the riverbank. At least three of the University's oldest buildings—Jacob's, Moyse's, and Lombard Halls—are believed to have been Jewish homes in the twelfth century. A new synagogue will shortly be erected on the site of the present house of worship. In addition to a sanctuary it will contain a student centre and kosher restaurant which will replace the small centre at 1 Nelson St.

OXFORD UNIVERSITY, in its world-famed Bodleian Library—housed in the Old Bodleian and in the new Sir Giles Gilbert Building—has what scholars regard as the second-greatest collection of Hebrew manuscripts, handwritten Bibles, and other priceless Judaica, which constitute a microcosm of Jewish contributions to culture. Among its 3,000 Hebrew manuscripts and more than 30,000 volumes in Hebrew are a collection of poems by Moses Ibn Ezra and the Elephantine papyri, the oldest known Aramaic manuscript, which dates from the fifth century B.C.E., and which describes life in a Jewish settlement in Upper Egypt in the days of Nehemiah.

Sir Thomas Bodley, for whom the library is named, was a student of Hebrew, and a copy of a Hebrew work he deciphered may be seen at Merton College. Opened as the first public library in Great Britain in 1602, the Bodleian owned 150 Hebrew works by 1629. Its greatest acquisition came in 1827, when it bought the magnificent collection of Rabbi David Oppenheimer, of Prague.

In the main reading room of the Bodleian Library is displayed the Bodleian Bowl, whose French design and Hebrew inscription indicate it was a gift from the son of Rabbi Yehiel of Paris, a thirteenth-century scholar. The bowl, made of bronze and weighing eleven pounds, stands on three hoof-shaped feet and has two handles. It was found in Norfolk in 1696. Historians say it was originally an alms bowl used to collect funds for needy Jews and scholars.

ISAAC WOLFSON COLLEGE, the new name for Iffley College, created in 1965 but which never started to function, was re-named for the famed Jewish philanthropist in 1967 when he gave $5,000,000 toward the new post-graduate college. The cornerstone was laid by Queen Elizabeth II. The college's first master was Sir Isaiah Berlin, the second Jew to be master of an Oxford college. The first was Prof. L. H. Goodhart, master of University College.

PENZANCE

GOSPEL HALL, a Christian evangelical center, is a former synagogue. In the early 18th century there was a Jewish community in this Cornish port town. Remnants of an old Jewish cemetery also survive.

PLYMOUTH

SYNAGOGUE, Catherine St., erected in 1761, is the oldest house of Jewish worship in England—except for Bevis Marks in London—still being used for its original purpose. The Jewish community here goes back to the 1750s.

POLPERRO

JEWS' HOUSE in this little Cornish town is more than a century old, but the origin of the name is unknown. The Hebrew word *Shalom* is on the door, and over one doorway is a chimney. The last known resident was the local Methodist minister.

PORTSMOUTH

JEWISH CEMETERY on Jews Lane, is more than two hundred years old. The local Jewish community, once one of the largest outside London, dates from the 1740s. The cemetery is the oldest Jewish burial ground still in use in England outside of London.

SYNAGOGUE, The Tickets, erected in 1936, is the successor to a sanctuary built in 1780s.

RAMSGATE

MONTEFIORE ESTATE (EAST CLIFF LODGE), until 1962 the home of Judith Lady Montefiore College (*see* LONDON), was originally the country home of Sir Moses Montefiore, the most beloved Jew of the nineteenth century, who became a legend in his own lifetime. A typical Victorian red-brick mansion, its large main gate is flanked by a synagogue and mausoleum. In the latter, Sir Moses, who died in 1885 at the age of 101, and Lady Judith are buried. The synagogue, built in 1833 by Sir Moses as a replica of the one in Leghorn, Italy, is the only synagogue in the world which has an exterior clock. Montefiore was born in Leghorn. Lady Judith's tomb is an exact copy of the Tomb of Rachel on the road between Jerusalem and Bethlehem.

The synagogue's interior walls are of white marble from window level to ceiling and of brown marble down to the floor. Sir Moses' chair in the pulpit is occupied only by members of the Montefiore family when they visit this now rather shabby seaside resort on the Kentish coast. Along the central staircase of the mansion the walls are lined with paintings of Lady Judith and Sir Moses and testimonials to his good works. The beautiful grounds surrounding the estate are known as King George VI Park, recalling the Montefiores' close ties with the royal family. South of the estate's main gate is a nine-room millhouse which stood empty until the 1960s when the Lubavitcher Chassidim leased it for 21 years as the site of weekend seminars, summer camps and other youth activities.

Queen Victoria knighted Montefiore in recognition of his philanthropies and his efforts on behalf of persecuted Jews in Russia, Palestine, and Rumania, to which he traveled frequently to intercede with kings and caliphs. At the age of forty-two he retired from business, to devote the rest of his life to helping less fortunate Jews throughout the world. He was honored by London when it elected him sheriff. Montefiore's one-hundredth birthday was the occasion for world-wide celebrations.

PUBLIC LIBRARY has a large painting of Sir Moses Montefiore and a number of other historic items from the Montefiore estate.

ROCHESTER

MAGNUS MEMORIAL SYNAGOGUE, High St., is named for Sir Philip Magnus, who was at the same time a rabbi and professor of mechanics at the Catholic University, as well as a member of Parliament and of a royal commission for technical education.

ROCHESTER CATHEDRAL contains artistic representations of two female figures—one, crowned and with triumphant bearing, symbolizing the Church, and the other, dejected and rejected, blindfolded and with shattered staff, the Synagogue. This piece of art is a remnant of the medieval anti-Jewish sentiment in England and differs from more modern representations of the Synagogue in Church architecture (*see* CAMBRIDGE).

SALISBURY

SALISBURY CATHEDRAL, a 13th century shrine, has in its octagonal chapter house remarkable sculptures illustrating scenes from the Book of Genesis and Exodus.

SHEFFIELD

HILLEL HOUSE, 16 Collegiate Crescent, is a community and students' center.
NEW CENTRAL SYNAGOGUE, Brincliffe Crescent.
UNITED SHEFFIELD HEBREW CONGREGATION, 11 Wilson Road.

SOUTHBOROUGH

DAVID SALOMONS HOUSE on Speldhurst Rd., now a convalescent home of the Kent County Council, but once the residence of the Salomons family, has a memorial hall which houses a variety of mementos of this eminent Jewish family. The most interesting object is the bench on which Sir David Salomons sat briefly as member of the House of Commons in 1851 while the House debated his right to the seat in view of his refusal to take the oath "on the true faith of a Christian." Salomons lost this fight and was even fined for his refusal to leave his seat until he was escorted out by the sergeant at arms.

Salomons' first cousin, Baron Lionel de Rothschild, who had started a similar fight for his civil and political rights in 1847, when he was elected an M.P. from London, ultimately became the first professing Jew to be seated in the House of Commons when the oath was changed in 1858. Salomons, who obtained the bench on which he had sat briefly by acquiring it after the House of Commons' furniture in use in 1851 was sold, had it placed in the Salomons House. It is inscribed: "Sir David Salomons—born 1797, died 1873—sat upon this bench when he asserted the right of a Jew to sit in the House of Commons, after he had been returned for Greenwich, 1851."

On display in the memorial hall are four hundred items related to the Salomons family, including books, paintings, medallions, awards, and letters. Also there is the silver-plated spade Salomons used in breaking ground for the Reading, Guildford and Reigate Railway in 1847, and the model of the automatic signaling system invented by his son, Sir David L. Salomons.

SOUTHAMPTON

SOUTHAMPTON UNIVERSITY was founded in 1908 as Hartly University College by the late Claude Montefiore, grandnephew of Sir Moses Montefiore. He served as president from 1908 to 1934, during which time he built dormitories, athletic fields and other facilities. One athletic field is named for him. He also helped create the college library where his bust, by Sir Jacob Epstein, and a portrait, by Sir William Rothenstein, are exhibited. Claude Montefiore, unlike his great-uncle, who was an Orthodox Jew, became one of the leading spirits in the creation of Liberal Judaism in England, serving as president of the World Union for Progressive Judaism.

SYNAGOGUE, Albion Place and High St.

PARKES LIBRARY, a permanent part of Southampton University, is a collection of some 7,500 books and pamphlets dealing with the relations between the Jewish and non-Jewish worlds. It was assembled over a period of 50 years by the Rev. Dr. James Parkes, a noted philo-Semite.

SYNAGOGUE, Mordaunt Road and Inner Ave.

SOUTHEND

LIBERAL SYNAGOGUE, 851 London Rd. (Westcliff-on-Sea).

NEW SYNAGOGUE, Finchley Road (Westcliff-on-Sea).

TAMAR

TAMAR RIVER, a Devonshire waterway that empties into the English channel at Plymouth, is named for the wife of the Hebrew king, Rehoboam (937-920 BCE), successor to King Solomon.

TORQUAY

SYNAGOGUE, Old Town Hall, Abbey Road. Tourists arriving at this English Channel resort community by train or car will find themselves officially welcomed by Hebrew greetings posted on official billboards which express welcome in several languages. There is a street here called Berachah Road, which in Hebrew means "Blessing Road."

TRING

TRING PARK, the former mansion of Lord Lionel Walter Rothschild, to whom the British government addressed the Balfour Declaration in 1917, is now a public museum. It was presented to the government by his nephew, Lord Nathaniel Charles Rothschild, after he had disposed of his uncle's fabulous bird museum, which had been housed in Tring Park for forty years. Lord Lionel was a world-famous naturalist.

WALLINGFORD

CARMEL COLLEGE, Mongewell Park, a secondary school for Jewish boys and girls founded in 1948 by the late Rabbi Kopul Pinson, is a unique institution that provides secular and Jewish education on a par with the best British preparatory schools.

WINCHESTER

JEWRY STREET is the only vestige of the medieval Jewish community which was located between North Walls and High Streets.

WINDSOR

SYNAGOGUE, 22 The Grove, serves the tiny Jewish community here and in nearby Slough, where the synagogue is located. The St. George's Chapel is now known as Wolfson Hall, a dormitory for students at the famous Eton College.

WING

ASCOTT, a former Rothschild mansion presented to the National Trust by Sir Anthony de Rothschild in 1949, is part of a 350-year-old estate. The mansion contains a famed collection of pictures, Oriental china, and furniture.

YORK

CLIFFORD'S TOWER, now only a stone ruin, but once the central tower of a medieval castle built on a Norman mound, was the scene of the massacre of the city's Jews in 1190. Sir Walter Scott describes this massacre in *Ivanhoe*. The entire Jewish community took refuge in the castle when a mob attacked the Jewish quarter.

SYNAGOGUE, Aldwark St., has nothing but a traditional link to the medieval Jewish community in what was once England's second-most-important city.

YORK MINSTER has five windows officially described as "The Five Sisters" but often referred to as the "Jewish Windows" because they were paid for by extortions from Jews. The Chapter House of the Minster has on its ceiling an artistic representation of the "Jewish Church, blindfolded, the crown falling and the reed broken on which she leans."

NORTHERN IRELAND

BELFAST

BELFAST HEBREW CONGREGATION, 49 Comerton Rd., the only synagogue in Northern Ireland, is one of the city's showplaces. Dedicated in 1962 to replace a building that dated from 1904, the new synagogue has an unusual circular design and a huge Star of David configuration on the ceiling.

Jewish settlement in Northern Ireland began about 1770, but the congregation dates from the 1850s, when Jewish settlers arrived from Germany. A second congregation formed in 1890 by refugees from Russia merged with the older group in 1904. There are 1,400 Jews in Belfast and a scattering in other cities. During the Catholic-Protestant riots in 1969 and 1970, the Jewish community made its Community Centre available as a neutral locale for peace meetings.

JAFFE MEMORIAL, Cliftonville Rd., originally a free school built and endowed by Sir Otto Jaffe in 1907, is now a training school for unemployed teenagers. Portraits of Sir Otto and his wife which once hung in the building are now in the Jewish Institute. Jaffe's father, Daniel, was one of the founders of the Jewish community and one of Belfast's leading citizens. Otto Jaffe created the linen industry, gave large contributions to various philanthropies, endowed laboratories in Belfast University, and was Lord Mayor of the city in 1889 and again in 1904.

Contemporary with the elder Jaffe was Gustav Wilhelm Wolff, who also came from Hamburg, one of the pioneers of the Belfast ship-building industry.

JEWISH INSTITUTE, 33 Ashfield Gardens, Glandore Ave., is a Jewish educational institute and cultural center.

NORTHLEIGH on Somerton Rd., is the Jewish Community Center.

SCOTLAND

ABERDEEN

HEBREW CONGREGATION, 74 Dee St., is the only synagogue in Scotland's third-largest city.

AYR

HEBREW CONGREGATION, 52 Racecourse Rd., is a tiny synagogue in the Invercloy Hotel, a kosher establishment.

DUNDEE

HEBREW CONGREGATION, 15 Meadow St., was founded in 1874 by German Jews who came here in the late eighteenth century as buyers of linen, flax, and packing cloth. Among these settlers was Daniel Jaffe, who moved his linen business from Hamburg in 1840. In 1851 he opened a branch in Belfast, Northern Ireland, later settling there permanently. One of these pioneer German Jews established the Polack Prizes, still offered at Dundee High School, and another, Victor Fraenkel, founded the Trinity College of Music.

EDINBURGH

The Highland Scots believe they are descended from the so-called ten lost tribes of Israel, but the first known Jews in Scotland were converts from England and Germany who were invited to Edinburgh University to teach Hebrew. There is an intriguing account in Aberdeen, in the north country, of the arrival of a shipload of Jews in 1665 bound for Amsterdam, but no record of their departure. Between 1691 and 1717, several professing Jews were given permission to trade in Edinburgh. The first of these was David Brown. By 1780 Shadrach Moyse was so well established that he was able to serve as a customs officer. There is a record of his having lent the town council substantial sums. The city directory of 1794-96 lists Herman Lyon as practicing chiropody. In the Edinbrugh University Library the visitor can see a book published by Lyon on the treatment of corns. His name is given in English and in Hebrew on the title page.

Early settlers established the Jewish community around 1780. The first synagogue in Scotland was opened in 1816 in a lane off Nicholson St. This sanctuary was succeeded by another on Richmond Court, which in turn was replaced by the present synagogue on Salisbury Rd.

Jews from Eastern Europe who began arriving in the 1880s helped expand Scottish industry, particularly in tobacco, clothing, furniture and whiskey, but most of them settled in Glasgow. Edinburgh has only 1,100 Jews.

In 1963, Manuel Kissen, a Jewish barrister from Edinburgh, was appointed the first Jewish judge in Scotland.

HEBREW CONGREGATION, 4 Salisbury Rd., is the oldest Jewish congregation in Scotland, having been founded in 1816. The synagogue building dates from 1932.

OLD JEWISH CEMETERY at the foot of Calton Hill in Scotland's oldest burying ground, is said to be the oldest Jewish cemetery in the country. Although there is a record of a plot there having been bought in 1790 by Herman Lyon, no Jewish graves are visible.

OLDEST JEWISH CEMETERY right next to a police station at 8 Braid Pl., is a small square piece of land with no sign on the gate. There are about two dozen tombstones, many of which are badly faded. The oldest that can be read is dated 1832.

HOUSE OF JOHN KNOX on The Royal Mile, a corner house, has a figure of Moses kneeling in supplication to God.

GLASGOW

GARNETHILL SYNAGOGUE, 29 Garnet St., opened in 1879, is the oldest Jewish house of worship in Scotland's largest city, and is the third-biggest in Great Britain. The congregation was founded in the early 1800s, and a synagogue was opened in 1823 in the Old Post Office Court. The present site was occupied in 1877. Sir Isaac Wolfson, the late Lord Greenhill, the first Jew in Scotland to be made a peer; the late Sir Maurice Bloch, whiskey-maker and philanthropist; Chaim Bermant, the author, and Prof. David Daiches, literary critic, were all members of this synagogue.

In 1958 the Lord Provost of Glasgow was Sir Myer Galpern, the first Jew to occupy this office in Scotland.

The largest maker of kilts is Denis Bonchy Cohen of Glasgow. One of the leading sculptors is Benno Schotz, head of the Glasgow School of Art.

CHEVRA-KADISHA-BETH JACOB SYNAGOGUE, Buchan St., is in the Gorbals area.

GIFFNOCK AND NEWLANDS HEBREW CONGREGATION, Maryville Ave., Giffnock.

GLASGOW NEW SYNAGOGUE, 147 Ayr Road, Newton Mearns, is the only Reform synagogue in Scotland.

GREAT CENTRAL SYNAGOGUE, 95 South Portland St., is one of the few Jewish institutions left in the Gorbals district, once the hub of Glasgow's Jewish life, since a massive re-development program got under way in this neighborhood. Only a handful of Glasgow's 15,000 Jews live in the Gorbals.

JEWISH DAY SCHOOL, 28 Calderwood Rd.

JEWISH INSTITUTE, the oldest Jewish social club in Scotland, having been founded in 1889, is a community centre at 67 Albert Road.

JUDAICA EXHIBIT, 244 Great Western Rd., is a private collection assembled by Archibald Hemphill, a non-Jew.

MACCABI CLUB, Kilmarnock Rd., Giffnock.

MUNICIPAL CHAMBERS displays in its gallery of portraits of the city's ex-Lord Provosts a painting of Sir Myer Galpern, the first Jew in Scotland to occupy the office of Lord Provost or mayor. He served from 1958 to 1960.

OLD JEWISH CEMETERY in the city's Necropolis, near the Cathedral, was opened in 1831 and is Glasgow's oldest Jewish landmark.

ROYAL FACULTY OF PHYSICIANS AND SURGEONS has a lecture theatre donated by and named for Sir Maurice Bloch, the first Jew in Scotland to have been knighted and the first Jew in the country to own a distillery. Sir Maurice was identified with every important Jewish institution in Scotland.

WOLFSON RESIDENCE HALL on campus of Glasgow University is a mixed student and faculty dormitory erected through the generosity of Sir Isaac Wolfson, who was born in Glasgow.

HEBRIDES ISLANDS

FINGAL'S CAVE, an unusual cavern on the island of Staffa made famous by the composer Felix Mendelssohn-Bartholdy in one his works. In 1969 a postage stamp with the composer's portrait against a background of the cave was issued.

SHETLAND ISLANDS

LERWICK has a number of permanent Jewish residents.

WALES

BANGOR

BIBLE GARDEN, near the Town Hall, groups in chronological order of their appearance in the Bible well over 100 different flowers, shrubs and trees.

CARDIFF

CARDIFF UNITED SYNAGOGUE, Cathedral Rd., was founded in the 1840s. It represents a merger of the Cathedral Road and Penylan Synagogues. The latter is on Ty-Gwyn Rd. The Jewish community here dates from 1780. Most of the 4,000 Jews in Wales live in Cardiff.

NEW SYNAGOGUE, Moira Terrace, opposite the Howard Gardens School, is the only Reform congregation in Wales.

SHERMAN THEATRE, on the campus of the University of South Wales and Monmouthshire, is named for Harry and Abe Sherman, local philanthropists.

LLANELLI

SYNAGOGUE, Queen Victoria Rd., which is seldom used, now houses a Chassidic yeshiva.

NEWPORT

HEBREW CONGREGATION, at Queens Hill, was founded in 1859.

SWANSEA

HEBREW CONGREGATION, Ffynone, is the oldest Jewish institution in Wales. It traces its origin to a community founded here in the 1760s, and some Jews lived in Swansea as early as 1730. Its first synagogue was erected in 1780. The present sanctuary was built in the 1950s to replace the synagogue on Goat St. which was destroyed in a Nazi air raid in 1941. There are 500 Jews in Swansea.

There are also synagogues in Bangor, Brynmawr, Colwyn Bay, Llandudno, Merthyr Tydfil, Pontypridd, Porthcawl, and Rhyl.

CHANNEL ISLANDS

ALDERNEY on the Island of Guernsey, to which the Germans deported some French and other Jews during the Nazi occupation of the islands, has, on the corner of Corblets Rd., a simple memorial plaque with inscriptions in Hebrew, French, English and Russian commemorating those who died on the island between 1940 and 1945. The plaque is located in a garden of remembrance erected in memory of those who died after the Germans turned the islands into a concentration camp.

ST. HELIER on Island of Jersey, has a mid-19th century synagogue that is now an X-ray center. A Sephardic Jewish community existed here from the early 1800s. A new community sprang up after World War II and it holds services for the High Holidays and major festivals in the church of the St. Brelades Parish for the 60 Jewish residents.

A number of old Jewish cemeteries can still be seen in St. Helier. In 1970 the leader of the Jewish community was W. H. Krichefski, Tabor Drive, St. Brelades.

ISLE OF MAN

CASTLETOWN

WITCHES HILL MUSEUM has on display some rare cabalistic works. One is entitled *Miftach Shlomo* ("Key of Solomon"). On the cover it is identified as a "Hebrew manuscript newly discovered and now described by Hermann Gollancz, Goldsmith Professor of Hebrew at the University of London." The book was published in 1903.

DOUGLAS

HEBREW CONGREGATION has no synagogue, the handful of Jews who live in Douglas and Port Erin worshiping in the Douglas Masonic Hall. The secretary of the congregation, Samuel Coplan, who was born in Glasgow, has lived on the Isle of Man for thirty-five years. There are perhaps 30 Jews on the island, and Coplan is their rabbi, teacher, and leader.

PORT ERIN

REMAINS OF TWO INTERNMENT CAMPS where German-Jewish refugees who fled to England in the 1930s were interned during World War II as enemy aliens, can still be seen. There were nearly 1,600 Jews here at that time, and a busy Jewish community was established. Today there are only two Jewish residents.

GREECE

Archaeological discoveries confirm the existence of colonies of Palestinian Jews on the Greek islands a century after the destruction of the first Temple in Jerusalem in 586 B.C.E. Greek and Roman writers tell of well-established Jewish settlements in the first century B.C.E. in Attica, Argos, and Macedonia. The New Testament mentions the synagogues of Corinth and Thessaly, where Paul of Tarsus "reasoned every Sabbath," and to whose worshipers he addressed his Epistles to the Corinthians and to the Thessalonians. In Salonica, the ancient Thessalonica, Jewish history goes back at least to 50 C.E.

Under the tolerant Greek and Roman rulers, the Jews of Hellas lived in peace for eight centuries. Their situation became difficult after the fifth century C.E., when Greece became subject to the Christian rulers of the Byzantine Empire. Conditions improved in the waning years of Byzantium during the twelfth and thirteenth centuries, when the Jews introduced the silk and dyeing industries to Greece. The Turkish conquest in the fifteenth century ushered in a golden age for Greek Jewry when the migration from Spain and Turkey overwhelmed and absorbed the older Byzantine communities.

In the sixteen and seventeenth centuries, Salonica, then part of Turkey, became the great center of Sephardic Jewry, known throughout the world for its famous rabbinical scholars and seminaries, Hebrew printing presses, and Jewish libraries. Until 1820, when Greece won its independence, the story of Greek Jewry was identical with that of the Jews of Turkey. Because Salonica remained a Turkish city until 1912, there were only small Jewish communities within the present borders of Greece until after the Balkan Wars.

The deep-seated spiritual disillusionment that followed the collapse of the Sabbatai Zevi movement at the end of the seventeenth century was the first major setback suffered by the Jews of Greece in modern times. During the nineteenth century they experienced periodic anti-Semitic outbreaks inspired by religious animosity, economic rivalry and the backwash of natural disasters.

By the end of the nineteenth century, 80,000 of Salonica's 120,000 people were Jews. Ladino, the Spanish-Hebrew dialect of the Jews, was a lingua franca. Much of the city's trade and industry was controlled by Jews. They also provided most of the city's artisans, dockworkers, mariners, and even its domestic servants. Because the Sephardim were strict Sabbath observers, the port of Salonica, once the second-most-important in the Balkans, was virtually shut down on Saturdays.

Greek reoccupation of Salonica after the first Balkan War led to enforced Hellenization, which marked the beginning of the end for the Jewish community's economic prosperity and cultural hegemony. The catastrophic fire of 1917 that destroyed the Jewish quarter razed many synagogues, wiped out valuable literary collections, and left 50,000 Jews homeless and impoverished. The exchange of populations between Turkey and Greece in the 1920s and 1930s resulted in economic upheaval that led to anti-Semitic agitation and further impoverishment for the Jewish community.

On the eve of World War II, there were 75,000 Jews in Greece, more than two thirds of whom lived in Salonica. The massacres and deportations that followed the

German occupation of the country almost wiped out the whole Jewish community; 60,000 died in death camps or at forced labor; 4,000 emigrated to Israel. Today there are 6,500 Jews in Greece. The largest Jewish community is now in Athens (3,500) whose prewar Jews were saved by the heroism of the Greek underground and the Greek Orthodox clergy.

Funds from the American Jewish Joint Distribution enabled Greek Jewry to rebuild after World War II. The Central Board of Jewish Communities of Greece and the associated Organization for the Administration of Jewish Heirless Property are engaged in rehabilitating smaller Jewish communities with funds accruing from the liquidation of Jewish property in abandoned communities.

AEGINA

MOSAIC PAVEMENT containing two inscriptions referring to a fourth-century synagogue in the harbor area of the town on this Aegean island, an hour's boat ride from Piraeus, can still be seen. Found by archaeologists in 1811, the structural remains of the synagogue were later explored by Jewish scholars, who identified the synagogue as having been built by Jewish tanners and dyers who fled with other Greeks from Athens and Corinth when the barbarians invaded the Greek mainland in the late Roman Era.

ARGOSTOLI

ISRAEL STREET, one of the main thoroughfares in this chief town of the Ionian island of Cephalenia, honors the State of Israel in appreciation of the efforts of Israeli seamen who helped rescue local earthquake victims in 1953 and brought food, water, and medical supplies.

ARTA

SYNAGOGUE here is one of the oldest in the country, having been opened in the seventeenth century. There are 50 Jews living here.

ATHENS

AMERICAN JEWISH JOINT DISTRIBUTION COMMITTEE (JDC) OFFICE FOR GREECE, 4 Nikis Street.

ATHENS JEWISH SCHOOL, Kameleon and Antheon Sts., in Psychico, one of the city's most fashionable suburbs, is the newest Jewish communal building in Greece, having been opened in 1960. The school, which accommodates 250 children, was made possible through a grant from the JDC.

BETH SCIALOM SYNAGOGUE, 5 Odos Melidoni St., was completed after World War II (construction had begun before the war) with the aid of a JDC grant. This is the city's chief synagogue.

CENTRAL BOARD OF JEWISH COMMUNITIES, 6 Georgiou Karitsi Place, is the national organization of all Jewish communities.

ISRAELI DIPLOMATIC REPRESENTATION, 4 Rue Koumbaria, Kolonkai.

JEWISH COMMUNAL CENTER, 6 Georgiou Karitsi Place, has a library, a restaurant, a lecture hall, and a chapel.

JEWISH COMMUNITY OF ATHENS, 5 Melidoni St., adjacent to the Beth Scialom Synagogue, houses the community's archives, the chief rabbi's office, and the headquarters of all communal services.

JEWISH YOUTH CENTER, 46 Piraeus, serves as a cultural and community center for the entire Jewish community.

MARTYRS MEMORIAL in the Jewish cemetery at Kokinia, a post-war burial ground just outside the city, is a marble monument designed like an altar. The center is a pyramid on which is listed the number of Jews killed by the Nazis in each Greek city. The pyramid is flanked by two large Menorahs mounted on marble pedestals. Nearby is another memorial commemorating the martyrdom of 14,000 Jewish children of Salonica who were gassed in Poland.

OLD SYNAGOGUE, 8 Melidoni St., now used only during the High Holy Days, has a medical center on the ground floor. After the war the synagogue was used as a shelter for concentration camp survivors.

CANDIA

SYNAGOGUE in this main city (also known as Heraklion) of the island of Crete, dates from the 15th century but is now unused and bare of ritual appurtenances. A Hebrew inscription over the front door is all that identifies it with the once flourishing Cretan Jewish community, whose origins went back to the second century B.C.E. The building is rented out as a residence by the O.P.A.I.E., the agency charged with liquidating property of heirless Jews and using the proceeds to rebuild Jewish life elsewhere in Greece. The medieval Jewish cemetery, plundered by the Nazis, no longer exists. Since 1948 the site has been used as a soccer field by Ofi, a local athletic club. Compensation has been paid to the Central Board of Greek Jewish Communities. The last Jewish family left in 1968.

CANEA

SYNAGOGUE remains in this western city of Crete consist of an empty and neglected building whose foundations go back to the fifteenth century. A few Hebrew inscriptions can still be made out.

CORINTH

HISTORICAL MUSEUM here preserves part of the door of an early Christian Era synagogue. The remnant has a Greek inscription reading, "This is the synagogue of the Hebrews." Identified as from a third-century synagogue, the remnant was uncovered in what used to be the Jewish quarter on the northern edge of the city's main area.

DELOS

"SEAT OF MOSES," a fragment of a pre-Christian Era synagogue, can be seen on this smallest of the Cyclades Islands, the legendary birthplace of Apollo and Artemis. Uninhabited except for the custodians of a museum, the island was the seat of a flourishing Jewish community between the fourth and second centuries B.C.E. Archaeologists in the nineteenth century who uncovered the sanctuary of Apollo also unearthed tiled fragments identified by some scholars as the remains of a synagogue that stood near the stadium on the shore. The so-called "Seat of Moses" is believed to have been the chair of the head of the synagogue. Other fragments include part of the synagogue roof and pieces of marble columns and bases inscribed in Greek. An inscription among the remains of the Delian theatre indicates that the ancient Jews had seats reserved for them.

DELPHI

LIBERATED JEWISH SLAVES are mentioned among the many inscriptions to be found in the ruins of this town, once the seat of the Delphic Oracle. Dated 170-158 B.C.E., the inscriptions are believed to refer to captives of the Maccabean war.

IOANNINA

SYNAGOGUE, 17 Volmoundo St., serves 40 Jewish families in this 1,000-year old community, once a thriving center of Jewish learning and industry. Jewish ritual objects in silver are still made here by Jewish silversmiths.

KAVALLA

SYNAGOGUE, 25 Pavlou Mela St.

KERKYRA (CORFU)

SYNAGOGUE, 4 Rue Palaiologou, a white stone structure with dome and Corinthian marble pillars, is the only Jewish institution left in the main city of Corfu, the most northerly of the Ionian Islands. Jews lived here in ancient times, but the modern community dates from the twelfth century. Before the war there were several synagogues and a Jewish population of more than 2,000. After the Nazi occupation the Jewish community was dispersed and today there are only 35 families here. The ancient Jewish cemetery, located in the heart of the city, was badly damaged during the war. Recently, the ground was sold and bones from unidentified tombs were reburied in a marble mausoleum in a new cemetery. Graves and tombstones that were intact have been removed to the new cemetery. To reach the synagogue, you go through a network of narrow lanes lined with shops on both sides.

KHALKIS

Khalkis was the home of Colonel Mordecai Frizis, one of Greece's most celebrated World War II heroes, whose family has lived here for thirteen generations. A captain in the Greco-Turkish War of 1922-23, Frizis was in the van of the Greek forces in driving the Italian invaders back into Albania in 1940. In command of a battalion of Greek mountain cavalry, he was leading his men across a bridge when Italian planes zoomed in for a low-level strafing. Ordering his men to dismount and take cover, Frizis remained mounted and was killed with his feet still in the stirrups. He died near the Albanian village of Bessantchi during the Battle of Tepelene, and the Greeks renamed the village Frizisville. When the area was returned to Albania, Frizis' name disappeared from the map, but the story of his heroism has become a legend.

JEWISH CEMETERY in this principal city of the island of Evvoia, has tombstones bearing out the fact that Jews lived here early in the Christian era. An old synagogue here was recently restored. This is believed to be the oldest Jewish community in continuous existence in Greece.

JEWISH COMMUNITY CENTER, 30 Kotsou St., also houses a small synagogue built in 1849 on the foundation of a 17th century structure.

The old synagogue here was restored in the 1960s. On its walls are a number of ancient slabs inscribed in Hebrew, which are tombstones removed from the Jewish cemetery when the Castle of Khalkis was demolished in 1890. Khalkis is believed to be the oldest Jewish community in continuous existence in Europe. Old records indicate Jews first came here two generations before Christ. The community treasures a letter from Philo of Alexandria, the famed Jewish philosopher, written in 50 B.C.E., in which he mentions the Jews of Evvoia.

KOS

Jews lived here on this Dodecanese island off the western coast of Turkey from the days of Alexander the Great without interruption until 1502, when they were banished. They returned in 1522, after the Turkish occupation. Thereafter, they survived wars and earthquakes, but the community of 250 Jews that lived here before World War II disappeared during the Nazi occupation. Today, only one Jew lives here.

SYNAGOGUE, 4 Alexandrou Diakou St., which is not far from the famous Tree of Hippocrates, was originally built in 1747, but only the foundation remained after the 1936 earthquake. It was rebuilt as a modern structure amid a setting of palm trees, flowering hibiscus, and bougainvillea. It is usually locked and bolted.

LARISSA

SYNAGOGUE AND JEWISH COMMUNITY CENTER, 2 Kentavron St. A housing development to care for Jews who lost their homes during the 1955 earthquake has been erected by the JDC.

PATRAS

SYNAGOGUE, 34 Pantanassa St.

RHODES

The Jewish community here goes back to Biblical times. Benjamin of Tudela found 400 Jews here in the twelfth century. Today only 40 Jews live here.

JEWISH CEMETERY on the outskirts of the modern section of the principal city of the Island of Rhodes in the Dodecanese Islands, is entered by a triple-arched gate. Beyond the entrance, as far as the eye can see, are rows upon rows of neat white above-ground crypts with inscriptions dating back many centuries. A marble monument inscribed in French, Greek and Hebrew memorializes the 2,000 Jews of Rhodes and Kos murdered by the Nazis. On one face of the memorial are inscribed in alphabetical order the family names of those who died in the crematoria.

SHALOM SYNAGOGUE, 1 Symmiou St. is the only one of four synagogues that once stood in the walled Jewish quarter. Originally erected in the 17th century, the synagogue was restored in 1731 and again rebuilt after World War II. It is open to tourists daily from 10 to 11 A.M. and from 5 to 6 P.M.

The other three synagogues were wrecked by the Nazis, who deported the entire Jewish population of 2,500. The handful of Jews who live here now are Greek Jews who left Egypt. Two yellow Stars of David, probably painted on by the Nazis, identify the remaining synagogue.

SQUARE OF THE MARTYRS is the name given to a large open area surrounded by debris which marks what was once the Jewish quarter. In the center of the Square is a fountain dominated by a sea horse topped by the Star of David. It was erected by the government in memory of the murdered Jews. The synagogue is in a little lane near this square. There is a legend that the Colossus of Rhodes, one of the seven wonders of the ancient world, a one-hundred-foot bronze statue of Apollo which was thrown down by an earthquake in 224 B.C.E., was sold in 656 C.E. by the Turkish caliph to a Rhodesian Jew who cut up the remaining pieces and sold them for scrap metal.

SALONICA

JEWISH CEMETERY in the suburb of Stayrouplis, has an imposing monument to the 60,000 Jews killed by the Nazis. The cemetery was established after the war to replace the fifteenth century burial ground east of the old Roman triumphal arch, which was expropriated by the Nazis and became a public quarry. Tombstones of great historical value were removed regardless of age. Today many of them can be seen as paving stones, as building blocks, and as parts of walls—the tell-tale Hebrew inscriptions being reminders of the tragedy that destroyed this once great Jewish community. The bones of a few of Salonica's Jewish scholars were recovered from the old cemetery and have been reinterred in a special mausoleum.

JEWISH COMMUNITY CENTER, 32 Nea Megalou Alexandrou St.

JEWISH COMMUNITY HEADQUARTERS, 24 Vassileo Irakliou St.

MONASTERIOTES (SEPHARDIC) SYNAGOGUE, 37 Syngrou St., the city's principal synagogue, is one of three that survived the Nazi occupation. Before the war there were nineteen. A second surviving synagogue, the noted Beth El Synagogue, was sold in 1952. The following year the community disposed of the Baron Maurice de Hirsch Hospital. The Baron de Hirsch housing development, a community built by the famous French-Jewish philanthropist near the railroad station in the 1880s, vanished during the war when the Nazis converted it into a ghetto. Later, it became the site of the expanded Salonica University.

PLASAO (ASHKENAZIC) SYNAGOGUE, 24 Vassileo Irakliou St., occupies the same building as the Salonica Jewish Community.

TRIKKALA

SYNAGOGUE, Diacou St.

VERROIA

SYNAGOGUE, built in the sixteenth century, stands by the side of a little stream in what used to be a ghetto. The two old ghetto gates can still be seen. There is also an old Jewish cemetery here. Still to be seen on the corners of many houses in the former ghetto are expressions in Hebrew cut into the stone blocks.

VOLOS

JEWISH COMMUNITY CENTER, 5 Moisseos St., is quartered in a wooden barracks erected in 1955 by the JDC as temporary housing for Jews who were made homeless as a result of the 1955 earthquake. Fewer than 500 Jews of the four-hundred-year-old community survived the Nazi massacres. In 1957 the JDC completed four two-story buildings at No. 62 24th St. as a model low-cost housing development for the Jewish community. The synagogue is housed in the Center.

HUNGARY

Jews have lived in Hungary for more than seventeen hundred years. When Pannonia and Dacia were Roman provinces under Emperor Alexander Severus (222-235 C.E.) there was a Jewish community and a synagogue at Dunapentele (now Dunaujáros). There was a Jewish settlement at Sopron before the Magyars under Arpad conquered the country in 895. Under the Arpad kings, who welcomed the commercial aid of the Jews, a Jewish community grew up in the twelfth century in Buda, now part of Budapest.

The new dynasties that followed the Arpads in the fourteenth, fifteenth, and sixteenth centuries subjected the Jews to varying degrees of intolerance and persecution. Conditions improved during the Turkish occupation, but when the Hapsburgs drove the Turks out at the end of the seventeenth century, Jewish residence and economic rights were again in constant jeopardy.

Hungary became the seat of important Jewish religious institutions during the eighteenth century because of the migration of large numbers of Jews from Moravia and Polish Galicia. Many Jews fought with Louis Kossuth in his unsuccessful struggle for Hungarian independence in 1848, and thousands followed him into exile. Not until 1867, when Hungary became an independent kingdom within the dual Austro-Hungarian monarchy, were the Jews granted complete political equality.

For the next fifty years the Jews contributed enormously to Hungary's economic growth and cultural expansion. Some of the nation's greatest poets, novelists, playwrights, artists, and musicians—among them Goldmark, Joachim, Molnar, Földes, Lazslo, Kaufmann, and Körmendi—were Jews. Budapest was the birthplace of Theodor Herzl and of his successor to the Zionist leadership, Dr. Max Nordau, as well as of Dr. Stephen S. Wise. Herzl's nephew, Ferenc Haltai, was mayor of Budapest, in 1913, and General Marton Zoeld distinguished himself during World War I.

Since the end of the World War I the Jews have suffered heavily from shifting political tides. The collapse of the Austro-Hungarian monarchy in 1918 brought into being a republic whose national council included fourteen Jews. This short-lived government was overthrown by a Bolshevist regime led by Bela Kun, a renegade Jew. In the ensuing counterrevolution thousands of Jews were murdered. Anti-Jewish legislation during the 1920s and 1930s undermined the economic status of the Jews and curtailed their opportunities for higher education and advancement in the professions.

In 1938 there were 400,000 Jews in Hungary. To these were added 330,000 more when Hungary, as an ally of Nazi Germany, annexed large slices of Czechoslovakian and Rumanian territory in 1938 and 1940. In 1941 many of these alien Jews were either deported to Poland, where they died in the death camps, or conscripted into labor battalions. When the Nazis occupied Hungary in 1944, the native Jews were herded into ghettos and extermination camps. About 100,000 survived the war.

The Communist take-over in 1948, the role of some Jews in the Communist regime, the government's anti-Israel stand, and the abortive anti-Communist uprising of 1956 seriously hampered efforts to rebuild the Jewish community. There are 100,000 Jews in Hungary, 80 percent of whom live in Budapest. The capital city has 34 synagogues, a Jewish high school and Talmud Torah, the only rabbinical seminary in the

Communist world and a matzoth factory operated by the government. Scattered Jewish communities are found in 60 different cities and towns.

Emigration to Israel has been halted since 1967 when Hungary adhered to the official Communist anti-Israel line. While the Israeli embassy has been closed, Israel still buys Hungarian beef and Hungary imports Israel citrus. In the windows of many food shops and on restaurant menus one sees huge Jaffa orange signs despite the continuing anti-Israel propaganda. Two Jews serve in the Communist Party Politburo, Deszo Nemes and Georgy Aczel, chief of propaganda, who replaced another Jew, Istvan Szirmai.

BUDAPEST

CENTRAL SYNAGOGUE, Dob Utca 35.

EÖTVOS-TÉR, to the south of Ferenc Jozseftér, is the site of a statue of Baron Jozsef Eötvos, the Hungarian statesman who played a leading role in the emancipation of Hungarian Jews in 1867. Eötvos, a non-Jew, was Minister of Public Worship and Instruction.

GHETTO MEMORIAL, marking the site of Budapest's World War II ghetto, is a simple tablet affixed to a side wall of what was formerly a Jewish school at Wesselenyi Utca 44, at the corner of Kertescz Utca. The plaque was dedicated in 1955 on the tenth anniversary of the liberation of the ghetto by the Soviet Army.

GOTHIC SYNAGOGUE RUINS, in the block of buildings at 23 Tancsics St., in the medieval quarter of Buda, were unearthed in 1966. Scholars have deciphered Hebrew inscriptions that indicate the synagogue was erected in 1366 and was in use until 1686 when it was destroyed during a war with the Turks. One hundred Jews died in a massacre and the remains of the martyrs as well as a cannon ball fired into the Jewish quarter have been found in the ruins.

A more recent synagogue, with eight Corinthian columns, standing on the site of a 17th century synagogue, still stands in the old city of Buda but the imposing building is now deserted. The Budapest City Council has marked the structure as an historic landmark.

GREAT SYNAGOGUE, Dohány Utca 2, now more than a hundred years old, is the largest synagogue in Europe. The huge structure has four balconies, a seating capacity of more than 3,000, and a giant organ with over five thousand pipes, on which Franz Liszt and Saint-Saëns played some of their compositions. During the Nazi occupation the synagogue was surrounded by a wooden fence, thus creating the Budapest ghetto. The synagogue itself became a concentration camp as well as the spiritual focus of the beleaguered Jewish community. In the courtyard of the synagogue there is a memorial plaque to Hanna Szenes, a Hungarian Jewess who was shot as a spy by the Nazis. In 1943 the twenty-two-year-old heroine, who was living in Palestine, volunteered for the British Army as a radio operator. The following year she was parachuted into Yugoslavia, assigned to rescue prisoners and organize Jewish resistance in Hungary.

HUNGARIAN JEWS' CENTRAL BOARD, Sip Utca 12, is the headquarters of the official national organization of Jews.

HUNGARIAN ACADEMY OF SCIENCES, Roosevelt Terrasz 2, has in its Oriental Section the famous Kaufmann Collection of illuminated Hebrew manuscripts and printed Hebraica. Among the items is a magnificent fourteenth-century hand-illustrated Hagaddah. The collection was assembled in the nineteenth century by David Kaufmann, a professor at the Jewish Theological Seminary of Budapest, and was donated to the Academy in 1905 by his mother-in-law.

JEWISH CULTURAL CENTER, a new wing of the Great Synagogue, has a spectacular Moorish-looking arcade.

JEWISH MUSEUM, housed in the Jewish Cultural Center, stands on the site of the house where Dr. Theodor Herzl, father of political Zionism, was born. Opened in 1909, the Museum displays photos, drawings, documents, artifacts, and religious objects dealing with the history of Hungarian Jewry. The exhibits include material depicting Jewish life during the Nazi occupation, a letter by Louis Kossuth to a Jewish soldier, recently discovered sermons preached in the fourteenth-century synagogue at Sopron, memorabilia of Jewish heroism in the 1848 war of independence, and a rich collection of synagogue appurtenances. On the second floor are a picture gallery and a permanent display of the works of Hungarian Jewish artists. Perhaps the most interesting objects on display are three ancient Jewish tombstones dating from the third century. A Moorish arcade connects the Great Synagogue with the Museum.

Behind the Museum is a cemetery where 2,000 martyrs who died in the Budapest ghetto are buried in a mass grave. There are many small tombstones, each about 1½ feet square memorializing community leaders.

JEWISH THEOLOGICAL SEMINARY OF HUNGARY, Jozsef-Körut 27, has for more than eighty years been a great center of Jewish scholarship. In 1944 the Seminary was converted into a detention center, through which 20,000 Jews passed en route to concentration camps or deportation. In the Seminary's assembly hall is a memorial plaque honoring those who died. The Seminary building also houses the Jewish Library, which has more than 60,000 volumes. Dr. Sandor Scheiber, dean of the Seminary, is also director of the Jewish Museum.

KOSHER RESTAURANT, Revay Utca 14, is said to be the only public eating place in Hungary that is not State-controlled. The Jewish community maintains a kosher kitchen for the needy at Kertescz Utca 32.

MARTYRS' MEMORIAL in the Jewish Cemetery at Kozma Utca 6, contains the names of more than 10,000 Budapest Jews who perished during the Nazi occupation of the city. The *Monument to the Unknown Jewish Forced Laborer* is in the Rakoskeresztur Jewish Cemetery.

MUNICIPAL LIBRARY is named for Ervin Szabo, the pioneer Hungarian librarian, who was the son of an Orthodox Jew, Gyula Schlesinger.

NATIONAL MUSEUM preserves a Hebrew inscribed stone found at Dunapentele where there was a synagogue during the Roman occupation in pre-Christian times.

ORTHODOX CENTRAL SYNAGOGUE, Kazincy Utca 16.

ORTHODOX JEWISH CONGREGATION, Dob Utca 35. In the same building there is a Yeshiva, a Hebrew school, and the headquarters of the Orthodox Rabbinical Council.

ROMBACH STREET SYNAGOGUE, a Conservative congregation.

TEMPLE OF HEROES, an imposing domed structure at the end of the arcade that leads from the new wing of the Great Synagogue, was erected as a memorial to the more than 10,000 Jews who died fighting for Hungary in World War I. The entrance is at Wesselenyi Utca 5.

WALLENBERG UTCA in the city's XIIIth district, memorializes Raoul Wallenberg, an intrepid Swedish Christian who undertook an incredible and gigantic humanitarian task during the Nazi occupation of Budapest when he saved thousands of Jews from deportation. An attaché of the Swedish embassy, he had volunteered for his mission of mercy. He rescued over 600 Jews by recruiting them as members of the embassy staff. He foiled the Nazis again by distributing thousands of "protective passports" identifying their holders as being under the protection of the King of Sweden. Wallenberg was so daring and resourceful that he was able to get advance copies of the daily list of Jews to be deported so that he could provide them with his protective passports. Repeatedly he was shot at, run down by tanks and trucks, but he always escaped. Four days before the Russians seized full control of Budapest he disappeared while on a mission to the Soviet commander. His fate is still a mystery.

DEBRECEN

SYNAGOGUE, Bajcsi Zsilinaty Utca 26.

EGER

GREAT SYNAGOGUE, Hibay Karol Utca, off Kossuth Lajos Utca, still stands but is now unused.

GYÖNGYOS

SYNAGOGUE erected at the end of the eighteenth century. The Jewish community here dates from the fifteenth century.

GYÖR (Raab)

SYNAGOGUE here is a large prewar structure with most of its windows still shattered.

KESZTHELY

GOLDMARK HOUSE, where the famed composer Karl Goldmark was born in 1830, is preserved as a national shrine. There is a memorial tablet on the building's outside wall.

MISKOLC

SYNAGOGUE, Kazinczky Utca 7.

PÉCS (Fünfkirchen)

EPISCOPAL MUSEUM OF LAPIDARY FINDS has preserved from the twelfth-century Cathedral of Pécs three sculptured scenes depicting the story of the Biblical Samson. The pieces once adorned the passages leading to the Cathedral's crypt and are considered notable examples of monumental sculpture.
SYNAGOGUE, Furdo Utca.

SOPRON (Ödenburg)

MEDIEVAL SYNAGOGUE which was buried for more than four hundred years after the Jewish community was expelled early in the sixteenth century, was accidentally discovered in 1954 while the government Commission on Public Monuments was surveying another building in preparation for its restoration. In the courtyard of a building at Uj Utca 11, which until 1440 was known as Judengasse (Jews Street), excavators found what Jewish scholars identified as a room that had been the Sopron synagogue from 1350 to 1526. The eastern wall, with the niche where the Torah stood, is still intact. The National Inspectorate of Museums has restored this first medieval synagogue to be unearthed in Europe and converted it into a museum.

Another old synagogue, dating from the 13th century was discovered here in 1968 opposite the one previously uncovered.

The second synagogue, founded by Sephardic Jews, has the names of its founders inscribed in Hebrew inside the entrance.

There is a more modern synagogue here, too.

SZEGED

SYNAGOGUE, regarded as the most beautiful in Hungary, is built on cathedral-like proportions, and at first glance it looks something like a cathedral from the outside. Built in 1903, the synagogue was the rallying point for Jews who took a leading part in organizing the counterrevolutionary government that overthrew the Bolshevik regime of Bela Kun in 1919. An imposing memorial in the synagogue honors Jewish heroes of World War I.

UJPEST

A northern suburb of Budapest and one of Hungary's largest industrial centers, Ujpest was founded in 1835 by Izsak Lowy, a Jewish leather manufacturer. Denied admission to the city of Pest, which barred Jews, Lowy and his brothers leased uninhabited land on the east bank of the Danube from Count Karolyi. A street named for Lowy was renamed in 1941.

Plate 1. Old-New Synagogue, Prague.

Plate 2.   Crucifix surrounded by gilded Hebrew letters on Charles Bridge, Prague.

Plate 3.

Rabbi Loew's tombstone in Old Jewish Cemetery, Prague.

Plate 4.   Names of Jewish martyrs on wall of Pinkas Synagogue, Prague.

Plate 5.

Statue of Anne Frank next to the St. Jans Church, Utrecht, Netherlands.

Plate 6.   Giant Menorah with Hebrew Bible characters, in Westminster Abbey, London.

Plate 7.   *One of the three so-called Jews' Houses, among the most ancient surviving relics in Great Britain, Lincoln.*

Plate 8.   *Moyses Hall, one of the oldest surviving Norman buildings in England, which is believed to have been an eleventh-century synagogue, Bury St. Edmunds.*

Plate 9.

God's name in Hebrew on Round Tower, Copenhagen.

Plate 10.

Exterior of synagogue, Iasi, Rumania

Plate 11.   *Monument to Ghetto Uprising, Warsaw.*

Plate 12.

Bergen-Belsen Concentration Camp Memorial, Bergen, West Germany.

Plate 13. Exterior of Great Synagogue and Jewish Museum Wing, Budapest.

Plate 14. *Interior of Santa Maria la Blanca, Toledo, Spain.*

Plate 15.

View of street in old Roman ghetto, Rome.

Plate 16.   Ancient Jewish tombstone found in Jewish catacomb, Rome.

Plate 17.

*Mass grave of
concentration camp victims
at Dachau, West Germany*

Plate 18.   Medieval Jewish cemetery, Mainz, West Germany.

Plate 19. Great Synagogue, on the Lungotevere Cenci, Rome.

Plate 20.

*Memorial on site of
18 Mila Street, Warsaw,
headquarters of 1943
Ghetto Uprising.*

Plate 21.   Old Jewish cemetery, Split, Yugoslavia.

Plate 22. Interior of synagogue, Florence.

Plate 23.

One of the two panels honoring
Jewish war dead, behind the high
altar of the east wing
of St. Paul's Cathedral, London.

Plate 24.   Reconstructed eleventh-century synagogue, Worms,
West Germany.

Plate 25.   View of bridge leading to entrance to Ghetto, Venice.

Plate 26.   View of eleventh-century Jewish cemetery, Worms, West Germany.

Plate 27.   Interior of Choral Synagogue, Moscow.

Plate 28.   Crypt of Memorial to the Unknown Jewish Martyr, Paris.

*Plate 29.   Holy Ark in the Italian Synagogue, one of the five ancient
houses of worship in Ghetto, Venice.*

Plate 30. Old Jewish cemetery on Moellegade, Copenhagen.

Plate 31.

Ancient tombstone uncovered in Remo Cemetery, Cracow.

Plate 32.   East wall of excavated fourteenth-century synagogue, Sopron, Hungary.

Plate 33.   Remnant of medieval ghetto, Judengasse, Trier, West Germany.

Plate 35.

Library of the Tour de Montaigne, where Miche de Montaigne wrote his essays, Bordeaux.

ICELAND

Not more than a dozen Jews live in this island republic in the North Atlantic near the Arctic Circle. There is no record of any Jewish settlement before the twentieth century, although Jews from Norway and Denmark, with which Iceland was linked for centuries, probably traded here in the nineteenth century.

The tiny Jewish settlement in Reykjavik consists of the remnant of a colony of fifty German refugees who came here early in 1940, after the British occupied the island as part of the Atlantic security zone in World War II.

The first Jewish religious services were held on Yom Kippur in 1940 in a rented hall by the refugees and soldiers in the British garrison, with a Church of England chaplain officiating. When American troops landed, the Jewish GIs organized regular services, with the aid of a Jewish chaplain. Iceland had its first *bar mitzvah* service during this period.

There is an Israeli consulate in Reykjavik, the capital and principal city. Sigurgier Sigurjonsson is the honorary consul.

IRELAND

The earliest authentic mention of Jews in Ireland is a fleeting reference dated 1062 in the *Annals of Innisfail*, a chronological record of events in medieval Eire, which notes that "five Jews came to Ireland from over the seas, bringing gifts to the Tordelbach, but were sent back over the sea." These five unknown Jews probably came from Norman England, which a century later began its conquest of Ireland under Richard Strongbow, whose expedition of 1170 was in part paid for by the Jews of Gloucester.

A Jewish settlement is mentioned for the first time in 1232 in a document of that year recording that Henry III gave his Irish viceroy, Peter Rivall, "the custody of the King's Judaism in Ireland." Expulsion of all Jews from the English domains in 1290 undoubtedly applied to the "King's Judaism" in Ireland, for there is no further reference to a Jewish community until 1655. Only individual Jews are mentioned in connection with Ireland in the intervening centuries: Francis Anes, a soldier, who commanded a British garrison in County Cork in 1583 and served as mayor of Youghal; Abraham Yarner, quartermaster of the forces sent by Oliver Cromwell to put down a rebellion in 1641; David Sollom, a merchant who acquired property in Meath in 1620; and Isaac Pereira, quartermaster general of the Duke of Schomberg's British army which defeated the Irish at the Battle of the Boyne in 1690.

Soon after Cromwell permitted the Jews to return to England in 1655-56, Marrano Jews from London settled in Dublin. In 1661 they organized a synagogue in a private house in Crane Lane, which elicited a complaint in 1662 from the Inquisition in the Canary Islands that Portuguese "Judaizers" were practicing Judaism openly in Ireland. Dublin's rabbi in 1703, Aaron Sophair, became the first chief rabbi of England in 1713.

By the middle of the eighteenth century, Dublin had 200 Jews. The first Jewish cemetery was opened in 1718, and a synagogue was established in 1746, English vetoes overruled the Irish parliament which between 1745 and 1780 passed four bills to naturalize the Jews. Until the Russian Jews arrived a century later, the Jews of Dublin led a precarious existence. They dwindled to a handful between 1790 and 1822, and the synagogue was closed for lack of worshipers. Immigration from Germany in the 1830s revived the old congregation. Baron Lionel Nathan de Rothschild of London helped raise the status of Irish Jewry in 1846, when he contributed the then princely sum of $50,000 to relieve suffering caused by the tragic potato famine in Ireland. Ralph Bernal-Osborne represented Waterford in the British House of Commons in 1870, and Alderman Lewis Harris, when he died in 1876, was slated to be named Lord Mayor of Dublin.

The coming of the Russian Jews after 1882 firmly established the Jewish community and led to settlements in Cork, Limerick, Londonderry, and Waterford. Throughout its three-hundred-year history, Irish Jewry never experienced any kind of anti-Semitism. The leaders of the struggle for Irish political equality and religious freedom championed Jewish emancipation in Great Britain. While the Jewish community maintained neutrality during Ireland's fight for independence, Dublin Jews sheltered many Irish revolutionaries, and individual Jews took a leading part in the rebellion. Chief among these were Robert Briscoe, who smuggled arms for the

Sinn Feiners, and Michael Boyk, a lawyer who repeatedly risked his life to defend Irish patriots. When the Irish Free State was established, the first woman appointed to the Irish legislature was Countess Desart, a Jewess, who was Ireland's most beloved woman.

The Irish Republic's constitution gives official status to the Jewish religion and equality to Jewish schools, which receive state support, and it exempts Jewish children from Catholic religious instruction where such training is given. No one was prouder than the Irish when the late Dr. Isaac Herzog, chief rabbi of Ireland, was appointed to a similar post in Palestine in 1936, and when Briscoe was elected Dublin's first non-Catholic Lord Mayor in 1956. Briscoe's son now serves in the Irish House of Commons while another former Chief Rabbi of Ireland, Dr. Immanuel Jakobivits, is now Chief Rabbi of the British Commonwealth.

Although Ireland has recognized Israel, they have not exchanged diplomatic or even consular representatives. The late Michael Carr (born Cohen), a Dublin-reared Jew, wrote the music of some of the most popular Irish songs, including "Did Your Mother Come from Ireland?" and "Everybody's Got a Touch of Irish."

Today there are 6,000 Jews in Ireland. Most of them live in Dublin, but there are small communities in Cork, Waterford and Limerick.

CELBRIDGE

N. ELZAS & SONS manufactures the parchment used in Torah Scrolls in a factory twelve miles from Dublin. Founded in 1830 in Borculo, Netherlands, by Nathan Elzas, a Talmudic scholar, the firm was moved to Ireland in 1951. In addition to parchment for Torah Scrolls, the firm makes material for bookbinding, drumheads, and lamp shades. Visitors are welcome.

CORK

HEBREW CONGREGATION, 10 South Terrace, founded in the 1880s by immigrants from Russia, is now the only synagogue in the Irish Free State outside of Dublin. The present Jewish community has dwindled to about thirty families. An earlier Jewish settlement by Sephardic Jews from England in the late seventeenth century established a cemetery, which has now completely disappeared. It was located where Lunham's bacon-curing factory, in Kemp Street, now stands, in the vicinity of the present synagogue. A Jewish member of the City Council is seeking permission to excavate the foundations of the factory in the hope of unearthing the cemetery.

DUBLIN

ADELAIDE ROAD SYNAGOGUE, Ireland's principal synagogue, was dedicated in 1892; it is the direct descendant of Ireland's first synagogue opened in 1660. The city's second synagogue (1746) was in the same block where the famed Abbey Theatre stood.

BALLYBOUGH JEWISH CEMETERY, oldest extant Jewish monument in Ireland, Fairview Strand Rd. (in Drumcondra, near Ballybough Bridge), was opened in 1718. The third-oldest Jewish burial ground in the British Commonwealth, the cemetery is on the site of the Battle of Clontarf, where the Irish defeated the Danes in 1014. Leased at an annual rental of one peppercorn for one thousand years, the quarter-acre plot was used until 1899, when a new cemetery was established at Dolphin's Barn. Among those buried there is Barnaby "Pencil" Cohen, who is said to have invented the lead pencil; "Chocolate" Phillips, who pioneered the manufacture of chocolates in Ireland; Benjamin d'Israeli, a Christian Huguenot and a sheriff of County Carlow (who was no relative of the statesman of the same name); and the Spanish consul at Holyhead, England, ostensibly a Catholic but actually a Marrano, who asked to be buried among Jews.

Few people in Dublin know of the existence of the cemetery because it is hidden behind a two-story structure at No. 67 Fairview Strand Rd. and can be reached only through the room on the ground floor and then into what appears to be the backyard of the house.

JEWISH LITERARY AND SOCIAL CLUB, 3 Harrington St., at South Circular Rd.

LENNOX STREET HEBREW CONGREGATION.

MACCABI SPORTS CLUB AND PLAYING GROUNDS, Kimmage Rd., is the headquarters for all Jewish community athletic events.

MACHZIKEI HADASS SYNAGOGUE, 22 Terenure Rd. West.

MANSION HOUSE, Dawson St., where the city's Lord Mayors preside, has on permanent display a portrait of Robert Briscoe, the only Jew ever elected Lord Mayor of Dublin. One of the founders and leaders of the Irish Republican Army, on whose behalf he repeatedly risked his life to run guns and ammunition through the British blockade, Briscoe, whose parents came from Lithuania, was a practicing Jew. When Eamon de Valera refused to accept England's offer of a partitioned Ireland and launched the Irish civil war, Briscoe became his most faithful adherent. For many years Briscoe served as a member of Dublin's City Council and also as a member of the Irish parliament. He was elected Lord Mayor in 1956.

In the Oak Room of the Mansion House, where the coat of arms of every Lord Mayor hangs, there is the unique escutcheon which Briscoe designed for himself. The motto and first word is "Freedom." The second word is "Justice." He could find no Gaelic word for *tolerance* and so he chose the word nearest to it in meaning, "Patience." For the shield, he drew the arms of Dublin, the three gates of which look like small castles, with tiny crosses on each side of the gate. Recalling the emblem which his coreligionists had been obliged to wear in Nazi Europe as a badge of contempt, he adopted the Star of David and superimposed it on the arms of Dublin.

MARTELLO TOWER, at Sandycove, a seaside area near Dublin, is the focal point for the annual observance of "Bloomsday" on June 16th, in memory of how Leopold Bloom, a Jewish advertising salesman who is the hero of James Joyce's famous novel, "Ulysses," spent that day on June 16th, 1904. From this tower Bloom began his odyssey, as described in the opening scene of Joyce's book.

NATIONAL MUSEUM OF IRELAND, Kildare St., displays the noted Bender collection of Oriental art presented by the late Albert Bender, Irish-born American art collector and bibliophile. Bender, who spent his adult life in San Francisco, donated the collection in memory of his mother. The donor's father, the Reverend Phineas Bender, a prominent Hebrew scholar, was the preacher at the old Dublin Hebrew Congregation in the mid-1800s. The Bender collection, housed in the Augusta Bender Room, contains temple banners from monasteries in Tibet, Mongolia, and China, Ming dynasty paintings, and a variety of Chinese *objets d'art.*

PROGRESSIVE SYNAGOGUE, 7 Leicester Ave., Rathgar, is the only Reform congregation in Ireland.

TERENURE HEBREW CONGREGATION, Rathfarnham Rd., in the suburb of Terenure.

TRINITY COLLEGE, Dublin University, across the College Green from the Bank of Ireland, preserves in its vast library a rare copy of the first Hebrew translation of the English Book of Common Prayer, the work of Abraham Judah, a Jewish convert to Christianity who taught Hebrew at Trinity College in the eighteenth century. Also in the library is an old scroll of the Book of Esther and an outsize pair of phylacteries dug up at Chester, England.

UNITED HEBREW CONGREGATION on the grounds of Greenville House, Dolphin's Farm, is the second-largest synagogue in Ireland. This building was slightly damaged in 1941 when a German bomber mistook Dublin for an enemy target. The German government reimbursed the Irish government, which in turn paid to repair the synagogue. Some Irish wags occasionally refer to it as "Hitler's synagogue." Adjoining the synagogue is Greenville Hall, a communal center.

ZION SCHOOLS, Bloomfield Ave., at South Circular Rd., is an imposing building erected in 1933 with government aid. It houses a primary school for secular education and a Talmud Torah. It is also the community's Jewish Community Center and the headquarters of the chief rabbi of Ireland.

TARA

This ancient seat of Irish kings is the focal point of a romantic Irish legend that fixes the first Jewish settlement in Ireland around 580 B.C.E. According to this story, Tea Tephi, the only survivor of the Davidic line and a daughter of Zedekiah, the last king of Judah, which was crushed by Nebuchadnezzar in 586 B.C.E. when he destroyed the first Temple in Jerusalem, escaped from Babylon with her guardian, the Prophet Jeremiah, and his scribe, Baruch, and found refuge in Ireland. At Tara, Tea Tephi married Hermon, a king of the Tuatha De Danann (people of the goddess Danu).

Among the treasures Tea Tephi is supposed to have brought with her from Palestine was the harp of David, celebrated in Irish balladry as "the harp that once in Tara's [Torah's?] halls the soul of music shed." A second was her royal escutcheon, the Lion of the House of David. Most priceless of all was the Lia Phail (or Stone Wonderful), which has a key place in the legend. Now housed in Westminster Abbey (*see* GREAT BRITAIN), this reddish stone is one of the prized possessions of the British Commonwealth, having served for generations in the coronation of Irish, Scottish and English sovereigns. Called the Stone of Scone, it is regarded by some as the pillar on which the Patriarch Jacob rested at Bethel, on his flight from Esau. Later incorporated into the first Temple in Jerusalem, it was greatly cherished by the Irish until they lost it to Fergus, King of the Scots. Half of this legendary stone is supposed to be the Blarney Stone, which can still be seen 106 circling steps up the sagging battlements of Blarney Castle, a few miles outside Cork.

ITALY

The first evidence of the appearance of Jews in Italy was the embassy sent by Simon Maccabeus to Rome in 139 B.C.E. to conclude an alliance with the Roman Senate. The ambassadors, Eupolemus, son of Johanan, and Jason, son of Eleazer, received a warm welcome from their co-religionists already settled in the city. Twenty years later there apparently was a substantial number of Jews in Rome, since a decree in that year ordered the expulsion of all Jews who had not become naturalized.

Those early Jews, punning on the name of Italy, called it *I-tal-yah* ("land of the dew of the Lord"). Jews continued to come to Rome and the community has persisted for twenty-one centuries. From Rome they spread into other parts of Italy until eventually there was no part of the country without Jewish communities. This process took centuries, and despite expulsions from one part to another, Italy was never wholly without Jews.

After the destruction of the Jewish state by Titus in 70 C.E., a large number of prisoners were transferred to Italy. Eventually, many obtained their freedom and swelled the numbers of the existing Jewish community. The attitude of the pagan Roman emperors varied; some were hostile, others friendly.

With the growth of Christianity, conditions worsened. Constantine had started his reign by advocating freedom of conscience, but after his conversion to Christianity he established oppressive laws for his Jewish subjects. These laws were abolished by his successor, Julian the Apostate, but he was succeeded by a Christian emperor who re-established the oppression. Until the fall of the Roman Empire, periods of persecution were followed by periods of toleration.

When Theodoric founded the Ostrogothic dynasty, there were flourishing Jewish communities in Rome, Mediolanum (Milan), Genoa, Panormus (Palermo), Messene (Messina), Agrigentum, and Sardinia. The popes of the period were not seriously opposed to the Jews. They were so absorbed in their struggle with the states of Italy that the Jews were left in peace. They were expelled from Bologna in 1172, but were soon permitted to return. They enjoyed great freedom in southern Italy and Sicily under the Normans. Canonical laws against Jews were frequently disregarded throughout the country.

Toward the second half of the thirteenth century there was a resurgence of Hebrew learning. There were important schools in Rome, Pesaro, Trani, and other cities. Jews wrote medical works and translated the Arabic scientific classics. Maimonides had Italian followers who influenced the religious thought of the Jewish community; one of these was the poet Imanuel of Rome, the celebrated friend of Dante. The rise of interest in poetry in Italy at the time of Dante had its effect on the Jews. The rich became patrons of Jewish writers and, in Rome particularly, a new Jewish poetry arose.

The ascension of Innocent III (1198-1216) to the papal throne had a serious effect on the political and social status of the Jews. This pope originated a series of restrictive measures, including an order that Jews must wear a distinctive badge.

Despite the restrictions on the status of the Jews, many of them violated by some of the popes themselves, Jews continued to live and work more or less at peace with their neighbors. The rise of the Renaissance in the fifteenth and sixteenth centuries stimulated the study of Biblical literature and produced a new and amicable relationship between Jews and Christians. At the time of the Medicis, Jews frequented the universities and were active in the revival of literature and the sciences. There was a renewed interest in Hebrew literature, and men such as Pico della Mirandola and Cardinal Algidius di Viterbo devoted themselves to the study of Hebrew. This period saw the growth of Hebrew printing, and the Soncino family of printers rose to fame at this time. They and others established presses, at various times, in Reggio, Mantua, Ferrara, Soncino, Brescia, Pesaro, Rimini, and a dozen other Italian cities.

The influx of Jewish refugees from Spain after the expulsion of 1492 had a stimulating effect on the Jewish community. Many of the newcomers were men of scholarship, and they obtained the protection of some of the rulers of Italy. Don Isaac Abrabanel received a position at the court of King Ferdinand I of Naples. Jews were received warmly in Ferrara by Duke Hercules I and were welcomed to Tuscany. Isaac Abrabanel and his sons maintained their relations with the great ruling families and were the pride of Italian Jewry, whom they protected wherever possible. One member of the family, Judah Leon Abrabanel, was famous as a writer under the name of Leo Hebraeus. His *Dialogues of Love* was a best seller of its day.

In 1516 Venice established the first ghetto in Italy. Although previously Jews had usually lived in separate districts in Italian cities, they were not restricted to these areas alone. The new ghetto forced Jews into special sections outside which they were not permitted to live. The area assigned to them was that of the Gietto Nuovo, or New Foundry, from which the word "ghetto" is derived. The Roman ghetto was established by Pope Paul IV, and the Jews of Rome entered it on July 26, 1556.

While persecutions at the close of the thirteenth century brought about the decline of the Jewish communities of southern Italy, those of Sicily had not been affected. Sicily was under the rule of the House of Aragon, and Sicilian Jewry had closer ties with Spain than with Italy. Jewish communities dotted the island, and the vast majority of Jews were artisans of various kinds. The long history of Sicilian Jewry came to an end in 1492, when a decree of expulsion was issued. The decree was carried out with the utmost severity; there was much suffering before the last Jews left the island in January 1493.

Sardinia was another dominion of the House of Aragon. Local Jewish history began early – the Emperor Tiberius sent two thousand Jewish youths from Rome to fight the bandits of Sardinia. Most were killed, but some survived to found the Jewish community. Sardinia was included in the Spanish decree of expulsion in 1492. Most of the Jews sailed for North Africa, whence many proceeded to Constantinople. Three boatloads are known to have gone to Italy. The expulsion ended a community which had endured for almost fifteen centuries.

The Inquisition was established in Rome in 1542, sixty years after its introduction in Spain. Although the Italian branch of the Holy Office never went to the extremes of its Spanish prototype, its implications for Jewish life were soon apparent. There were persecutions and some burnings, but the Italian Inquisition devoted itself primarily to the burning of Jewish books. The Talmud was banned, and great bonfires fed with Jewish books lit up the land.

The election of Pope Paul IV to the papal throne on May 23, 1555, was a great misfortune for the Jews. As Cardinal Caraffa he had inspired the Catholic reaction in Italy. On July 12, 1555, he issued his famous bull *Cum Nimus Absurdum*, which is one of the landmarks in the history of human persecution and Jewish martyrdom. The restrictive legislation which followed condemned the Jews to the most abject misery. The wearing of the yellow badge was enforced with the utmost severity.

With the institution of the Roman ghetto by Paul IV in 1556, this plague spread quickly to other cities. Jews forced into the ghettos had to sell their homes, vineyards, and olive groves at a ruinous loss. Many illustrious families were reduced to poverty. Throughout the papal possessions the Jewish position became one of hopeless despair. A few were fortunate enough to escape to the territories of more tolerant rulers, such as the dukes of Urbino and Ferrara.

From the Papal States the reaction spread throughout Italy. Then began a long unhappy period for Italian Jewry. The institution of the ghetto, the censorship of Hebrew books, and the long offensive against the Talmud had a deadening effect on Jewish intellectual life in Italy. The influence of the Renaissance became a mere memory. Nevertheless, a vigorous effort was made to keep Jewish learning alive, and a number of scholars continued to teach and write. One of the striking figures of the age was the famous Rabbi Leon of Modena. He was born in Venice, was an infant prodigy, and became a preacher, writer, musician, and master of twenty-six trades. While profound rabbinic scholarship was difficult to attain for lack of the Talmud, the level of achievement was far higher than might have been expected.

By the middle of the eighteenth century, the breath of emancipation could be felt in northern Europe. But Italy was a stagnant backwater of Europe, and the popes were the bulwark of reaction. The Jewish communities, which had declined tremendously through emigration, were still locked behind ghetto gates. The assault on Judaism in Italy was intensified. Many of the Italian ghettos were now places of sheer misery.

Despite the general gloom, in the second half of the eighteenth century faint signs could be discerned of the new era that had already dawned beyond the Alps. Various cities began to relax the restrictions on their Jews. In Trieste the gates of the ghetto were destroyed in 1785. However, when the news of the French Revolution and its terror arrived, the hands of the reactionaries were strengthened. Mobs attacked ghettos in various cities, and other excesses occurred.

When the French revolutionary forces invaded Italy in 1796, they were welcomed by the Jews. As the French conquered, ghetto gates were destroyed. However, this was not to last long. When Napoleon left on his Egyptian campaign, the French were gradually driven from the Italian peninsula. The Jews paid heavily for their momentary freedom. From the Alps to the Tiber, there was a wave of assaults, some accompanied by massacres in a degree never before seen in Italy. The Jews were forced back into their ghettos and gloom descended again.

The reaction was of short duration. In May 1800, Napoleon, soon to be emperor, once again led his armies into Italy. For the next fourteen years. French influence was paramount in Italy, and the equality of the Jews before the law was established. They entered the army, served on municipal councils, were free to follow any profession, and could own land.

After the fall of Napoleon in 1814, Italy came under the control of Austria. The states were reconstituted as they had been before the Revolution. Old prejudices and old restrictions against the Jews returned, but with a difference. The old order could not be completely restored. The only exception was in the Papal States, where Pope Pius VII was determined to re-establish the eighteenth-century regime down to the last detail. Once more the Jews were herded into the ghetto, and the gates were closed every night at dusk. Other restrictions were enforced rigidly.

The Jews of Italy supported the movement known as the Risorgimento ("revival") from the very beginning. They gave money freely, they joined the secret societies, they were represented among the Italian exiles in every city of Europe. They enlisted in the Carbonari, who began to work and fight for Italian freedom. After the abortive revolution of 1831, the movement of liberation was reorganized under the inspired guidance of Giuseppe Mazzini, who created the Young Italy movement. Italian Jewish youth threw itself heart and soul into it. Mazzini had many Jewish friends; his faithful companion was Angelo Usiglio; a close associate was Giuseppe Finzi, and he died in the Pisa home of Pellegrino Rosselli.

In 1848, the year of revolutions, risings occurred in many parts of Italy; in all of them Jews played a prominent part. In Venice, Daniele Manin, scion of a converted Jewish family, headed the republic proclaimed on March 23. On February 9, 1849, a republic was proclaimed in Rome under the leadership of Mazzini and Garibaldi. Jews streamed to Rome from every part of Italy, eager to play their part. The struggle continued, and individual states proclaimed freedom for their Jewish citizens. On March 29, 1848, Carlo Alberto, King of Sardinia, who had placed himself at the head of the liberal movement, signed a decree on the battlefield of Voghera, extending civil rights to all Jews and other non-Catholics and abrogating all laws to the contrary. Thus the complete emancipation of Italy's Jews came 336 years after the establishment of the first ghetto in Venice.

Italian Jewry soon entered into every avenue of life in the new Italy. Some occupied high public positions; Leone Wollemborg was Minister of Finance from 1900 to 1903; General Giuseppe Ottolenghi was Minister of War from 1902 to 1903; Sidney Sonnino, twice Prime Minister between 1906 to 1910, and Minister of Foreign Affairs from 1915 to 1919; and Luigi Luzzatti was Prime Minister from 1910 to 1911. Jews served in parliament and were generals in the army, and many were distinguished writers, scholars, scientists, and jurists.

The rise of Fascism and World War II brought new martyrdom to Italy's Jews. In 1938 a series of decrees were published restricting the rights of the Jews. These culminated in the law of November 17, 1938, in obvious imitation of the German Nuremberg Laws of 1935 but in some respects even more severe. Jews were prominent in the leadership of the opposition to Fascism in Italy, among them outstanding personalities such as Filippo Turati, Claudio Treves and the brothers Carlo and Nello Roselli.

The publication of the anti-Semitic code caused deepest despair among the Jews. Overnight, they had been reduced to the status of the ghetto days. All the rights they had won through years of struggle had disappeared. Many emigrated while there was still time. With the outbreak of war in September 1939, the Jewish position deteriorated still further. Many Jews were interned and others were drafted for forced labor. But much was yet to come.

In early autumn 1943, German SS detachments arrived in Italy. On the morning of Saturday, October 16, 1943, a great raid took place on Jewish homes in Rome, and 1,000 persons were rounded up. The deportations had begun; before they were over, 10,000 Jews had been sent to their deaths in the extermination camps. The nightmare lasted until the German surrender on April 29, 1945.

To their eternal credit, the Italian people helped many Jews survive this dark period. Many, risking dire penalties, supplied refuge to Jews, and Italian officials helped in many ways. The records indicate that there were frequent German complaints that the Italians were not co-operative enough in carrying out their anti-Jewish policies. Many Jews also found refuge in religious institutions.

Italian Jewry now numbers approximately 30,000, in some forty communities, some of them very small. The largest community is Rome, with 13,000; Milan follows with 8,500; and Turin is third with 3,000. While once again free, the Jewish community of Italy faces many problems. Small in numbers and confronted with the attrition of assimilation, it is carrying on a heroic effort to maintain its historic continuity. The oldest Jewish center of the Western world is determined to survive.

ACQUI

SYNAGOGUE, Portici Saracco 1. In 1881 the medieval ghetto, together with the old synagogue, were demolished. A new synagogue was built through the munificence of Jona Ottolenghi, after whom a street was named. The Ottolenghi family of Acqui produced several distinguished men, including two rabbis, an author, and a philanthropist, Emilio Ottolenghi, Count of Vallepiana.

ALESSANDRIA

SYNAGOGUE, Via Milano 3.

ANCONA

COMMUNAL OFFICES, Via Fanti 2 bis.
MEDIEVAL GHETTO lay in the Via di Bagno.
PIAZZA DELLA MOSTRA was the scene of the martyrdom in 1556 of twenty-four Spanish Jews, twenty-three men and a woman. A commissioner dispatched by Pope Paul IV offered the Spanish Jews of Ancona the choice of baptism or death. Sixty–three renounced their faith. The others were hanged and burnt on the Piazza della Mostra. The elegy composed by Jacob de Zano is still recited annually in the synagogues of Italy for the martyrs.
SYNAGOGUE, on the Via Astagno is a seventeenth century building with all the characteristics of the period. The lower floor houses the congregation of the Italian rite, the upper floor, larger and more elegant, the congregation which follows the Levantine ritual. Daily services are held, alternating between the two rites.

ASTI

ALESSANDRO ARTOM MONUMENT is located in the public gardens. It was erected by the city of Asti in memory of its famous son, Baron Alessandro Artom, physicist and inventor (1867-1927), member of a Jewish family which has played a distinguished part in Italian history.
PALAZZO ALFIERI on the Corso Alfieri, was given to the city of Asti by Count Leonetto Ottolenghi in 1901. The birthplace of the great Italian poet Vittorio Alfieri (1749-1803), it houses the famous Alfieri collection founded by Count Ottolenghi, the national center for Alfieri studies and the civic library.
VIA OTTOLENGHI was named in honor of Count Leonetto Ottolenghi (1829-1904), distinguished philanthropist and benefactor of his native city. In 1903, shortly before his death, he presented a statue of King Umberto I to Asti.
SYNAGOGUE, Via Ottolenghi 4, was rebuilt in 1889 by Count Ottolenghi.
The major part of the French Jews who were expelled from France in 1322 by Charles IV took refuge in Asti. They adopted the French ritual called "Rite Afm",

(from the initials of Asti, Fassano and Monclavo, where it was employed). This ritual was retained until contemporary times.

ASSISI

CHURCH OF ST. FRANCIS, built in the mid-thirteenth century, has a Star of David worked into the motif on the church altar. Apparently the artisans who carved the altar were Jews. During World War II the Germans asked questions about it, but were assured that it had no political significance.

BARI

STRADA SYNAGOGA is a reminder of an ancient Jewish community, long since vanished.

BOLOGNA

CIVIC MUSEUM, Portici del Pavaglione 2, contains several tombstones from the ancient Jewish cemetery given in 1569 to the monks of St. Peter, who were permitted to disinter and burn the bodies. In contrast to several plain medieval stones, the ornate tomb of Menahem di Abramo Daventura, with a pair of columns surmounted by an arch, dated 1555, is a fine example of the Rennaisance period.

FRANCO CESENA, the youngest partisan in Italy and probably in Europe, lies buried in the Jewish cemetery. Born September 20, 1931, he was killed in action September 14, 1944 while on a mission with his commando. It was reported that he had died while reciting the "Shema". He had promised his mother that he would return home for his bar-mitzvah. His body was delivered on his thirteenth birthday to his mother. He was posthumously awarded the Bronze Medal of the Resistance and gazetted lieutenant. His tombstone says "The Youngest Partisan of Italy". Youth groups make pilgrimages to his grave. The city of Bologna has named an elementary school in his memory.

COMMUNAL OFFICES, Via Gombruti 9.

MARIO JACCHIA, eminent lawyer, and much decorated veteran of World War I, was a top leader of the Resistance in Bologna, where he was born in 1896. Shot by the Nazis in 1944, he was posthumously awarded the Gold Medal for Valor, the highest honor of the Resistance. On April 3, 1949 a memorial plaque was placed on his house at Via d'Azeglio 58. The inscription reads, *"Mario Jacchia—faithful to the ideals of his fatherland—fought bravely for Italy—struggled tenaciously for liberty—In this house—they labored and planned—from here they set forth—to offer themselves as sacrifices—against traitorous tyranny—foreign and domestic."*

Another laudatory plaque has been placed in Room III of the Court of Appeals in the Palazzo dei Tribunali di Bologna, where Mario Jacchio had practiced as an attorney for many years, as did his father before him.

MUNICIPAL LIBRARY contains a number of Hebrew manuscripts of the seventeenth century. In the collection of Cardinal Giuseppe Mezzofanti are some Hebrew books and a number of Biblical and Talmudic commentaries.

SCUOLA D'ANTIQUARIA has on display the Renaissance period tombstone of Sabbatai Elhanan ben Isaac di Rieti—sculptured with female figures and cherubs.

SYNAGOGUE, Via Mario Finzi, was dedicated in October 1954. It replaced an older synagogue destroyed during World War II. The Italian government contributed toward the cost of building the new synagogue. A large plaque at the entrance lists the names of eighty-four members of the community who were deported to their deaths by the Germans. The list is headed by the name of Chief Rabbi Alberto Orvieto.

UNIVERSITY LIBRARY, Via Zamboni 35, has an extensive collection of Hebrew books and manuscripts, including some incunabula and twenty-seven rare editions.

VIA DE' GIUDEI leading from the two twelfth century towers in the Piazza di Porta Ravegnana, marks the site of the medieval ghetto, of which nothing remains but the name.

STREET NAMES Bologna has a large number of streets named in honor of eminent Jewish personalities, native and foreign. Some of them are:

Via Eugenio Curiel, named in honor of the Resistance leader, killed by the Germans in 1945, who was awarded the Gold Medal for Valor, the highest honor of the Resistance.

Via Alberto Einstein

Via Mario Finzi, named in honor of one of the organizers of the Resistance. Deported to his death in 1944.

Via Tullio Levi Civita, named in honor of a famous intellectual who was one of the early opponents of Italian fascism.

Via Amadeo Modigliani, honors the memory of the famous artist who was a native of Livorno and died miserably in Paris.

Via Fratelli Nello and Carlo Roselli, named in honor of the brothers Nello and Carlo Roselli, who led the struggle against fascism in Italy and who were murdered in 1937 in France by French fascists.

Via Italo Svevo, honors the memory of the famous writer who was born Ettore Schmitz in Trieste.

Via Claudio Treves, honors the memory of one of the founders of the Italian Socialist movement.

Via Filippe Turati, honors the memory of the great leader of Italian socialism, who with Claudio Treves headed the movement for many years.

Via Vito Volterra, memorializes the university professor who was an early opponent of Italian fascism.

Via Lodovico Lazzaro Zamenhof, named in honor of the Polish founder of Esperanto.

Via Della Fosse Ardeatina, honors not an individual but recalls the brutal massacre of 300 hostages in 1944 in the Ardeatine Caves outside Rome. *See* **ROME.**

For those who are interested Bologna also has a *Via da Palestina* and a *Via Gerusalemme.*

BRESCIA

There has been no Jewish community in Brescia since 1571 when the Jews were expelled from the town by order of the Venetian Senate. Brescia acquired fame since it was there that Gershon ben Moses Soncino conducted his printing press from 1491-1496. Martin Luther's Hebrew Bible was printed in Brescia in 1494 by Soncino. Heinrich Heine visited Brescia in 1844 and reported that he had seen a synagogue there.

BRINDISI

VIA GIUDEA, a street in the area of the ancient Jewish community, and an old Hebrew tombstone in the local museum are the only reminders of a long-vanished Jewish community.

BUSITO

The interior furnishings of the synagogue of this vanished community were transported to Israel in 1969 to be installed in a newly built synagogue in the Talbieh district of Jerusalem.

CARMAGNOLA

SYNAGOGUE is located on the Via Domenico Berti. There is no longer an active Jewish community in Carmagnola and the synagogue is under the jurisdiction of the Jewish community of Turin. The sectional delegate to the Turin community is Attilio Diena, Via Ferrucio Valobra 60. Permission to see the synagogue may be obtained from Mr. Diena.

CARPI

In this small town, near the notorious Fossoli concentration camp, there is a museum in memory of the deportees who perished at the hands of the Nazis during World War II. The museum is housed in the famous Renaissance castle located in the centre of the town. See **FOSSOLI.**

CASALE MONFERRATO

SYNAGOGUE, Vicolo Salomone Olper 44, was built in 1595 under a special concession to the Jews by the Duke of Mantua. It was enlarged in 1662 and underwent radical restoration in 1866. It is an impressive structure, with striking features and luxurious mural inscriptions. During the sixteenth and seventeenth centuries it was embellished with art and came to be recognized as one of Italy's architectural masterpieces. It was devastated by the Nazis during World War II, but most of the religious objects had been hidden and were saved. It was rededicated in April 1969 after ten months of restoration work by Jewish and non-Jewish volunteers under the supervision of the regional art department. Some years ago it was declared a national monument. The synagogue served a community that numbered some eight hundred Jews at its peak, but which has dwindled to fifteen since World War II.

CESENA

MALATESTIANA LIBRARY, Piazza Bufalini, has in its collection seven Hebrew manuscripts containing works of Avicenna, Maimonides, and Hanassi, dealing with medicine, philosophy, and natural science. Some are said to have come from the collection of Dr. Giovanni di Marco of Rimini, who in 1474 left his collection to the library. The manuscripts have been microfilmed for the Jewish community of Rome.

CHERASCO

SYNAGOGUE, Corso Marconi, is private property. Apply for permission to visit to Dr. Giorgio Segre, Corso Marconi. There is no active community.

CORREGIO

The Ark and interior furnishings of synagogue of this vanished community were shipped to Israel in 1957 and installed in the Hapoel Hamizrachi synagogue in Jerusalem.

CUNEO

On the Madonna del Coletto (Valdieri) near Cuneo, there is a plaque which tells how twelve citizens of Cuneo organized at this place the first armed band of the Resistance organization "Justice and Liberty". They formed the basis from which the Partisan army was created and which liberated a large part of the Province of Cuneo before the arrival of the Americans. Among the twelve names listed on the plaque are those of two Jews, the brothers Ricardo and Enzo Cavaglion.

SYNAGOGUE is located at Via Mondovi 20. There is no longer an active Jewish community in Cuneo. The synagogue is under the jurisdiction of the Jewish community of Turin. Permission to see the synagogue may be obtained from the local sectional delegates to the Turin community, Fratelli Cavaglion, Via Roma 58.

FERRARA

CEMETERY, Via della Vigne 23, dates back to 1869. The tombstones of the older cemeteries were demolished by mobs, used as building material, or placed in Christian cemeteries with new inscriptions.

CATHEDRAL OF FERRARA has an interesting group on the columns of the portal. It consists of four prophets, probably Moses, Isaiah, Jeremiah, and Daniel, and they are apparently relating something of importance to a twelfth-century Italian Jew.

The cathedral has been the center of a dispute that goes back more than two centuries. During the eighteenth century, two ancient columns bearing statues, which stand in front of the cathedral, were weakened by fire and in need of repairs. The authorities repaired the columns, using as material marble tombstones taken from the Jewish cemetery of Ferrara. Early in 1967, the columns again needed repair, and it was decided to remove the tombstones used two centuries ago and then replace them more securely. Upon hearing this, the local Jewish community leaders offered to supply the marble needed for the work so that the old tombstones could be replaced in the Jewish cemetery.

While negotiations were proceeding, the repairs were completed, using the old tombstones. When the Jewish Community Council complained, the municipality offered to put up a plaque recalling the origins of the marble used to effect the repairs. The community considered this inadequate and demanded that the plaque relate the story of past persecutions and desecrations. The Communist-dominated municipality refused to budge from its offer and the matter still has to be determined.

HOUSE OF RABBI LAMPRONTI, Via Vignatagliata 33, was once the residence of Rabbi Isaac Lampronti, famous physician and teacher. He was the author of one of the great classics of rabbinic literature, *Pachad Yitzchak*, an encyclopaedia of rabbinic knowledge.

The house has two memorial plaques affixed over the front door. The first plaque was placed in April 19, 1872, through the efforts of Jews and Christians who contributed to the cost. The inscription reads: "In this house lived Isaac Lampronti, born 1679, died 1756. Celebrated doctor and theologian. He honored his country. With reverence for science some citizens placed this plaque—1872." The second plaque was placed on April 7th, 1957, by the Jewish community of Ferrara, the Union of Jewish Communities of Italy and the municipality of Ferrara, to commemorate the bicentenary of Rabbi Lampronti's death. The inscription says that "Isaac Lampronti, doctor and philosopher, shed luster on his city, his country, and on Judaism."

SYNAGOGUE, Via Mazzini 95, was originally acquired in 1481 through the generosity of Samuel Melli, of Rome, a benefactor of the Jewish community of Ferrara. It was thoroughly rebuilt in 1842 and in 1867. The interior is beautiful and impressive. The paneled walls and ceiling date from the beginning of the sixteenth century, and the woodwork, the candelabra, and the Ark display the work of master craftsmen. There is a chapel for the use of worshipers who follow the Ashkenazic rite.

"The Garden of the Finzi-Continis" by Giorgia Bassani describes the life of an upper-class Jewish family of Ferrara during a period of social crisis prior and during World War II.

FLORENCE

ACCADEMIA delle BELLE ARTI contains the famous statue of David by Michelangelo, done by the artist between 1501 and 1504, when he was little more than twenty-five. The statue was transported here in 1873 from the Piazza della Signoria, where it was replaced by a copy. It is about fifteen feet tall on a marble base that is seven feet—a total height of about twenty-two feet. The heroic figure of the young athlete, which reflects one of Michelangelo's most serene moments of creation, is represented in an attitude of vigilant expectancy.

BAPTISTERY The pair of doors in the east portal (facing the Cathedral) were begun by Ghiberti in 1425, a year after his completion of the doors in the north portal, and were finished in 1452. This magnificent pair of bronze doors is considered to be Ghiberti's masterpiece. Michelangelo declared them worthy to be the "doors of Paradise." The ten panels represent ten episodes of the Old Testament. From top to bottom, the panels to the left present: the creation of Adam and Eve; the story of Noah; the story of Jacob and Esau; Moses receiving the Law; Saul and David battling the Philistines. In the same order, the panels to the right present: the story of Cain and Abel; the sacrifice of Isaac; the story of Joseph; the Israelites capturing Jericho; Solomon receiving the Queen of Sheba.

Above the northern gate of the Baptistery stands a group of three bronze statues by Leonardo da Vinci, representing John the Baptist, the Pharisee, and the Publican. The statues were made about 1508, commissioned by Rustici, in whose house the young Leonardo had shortly before come to live. The garments of the statues bear Hebrew inscriptions. The spelling and the character formation of the inscriptions reveal the almost certain Jewish origin of the man who cast the statues. Several features of the inscription have a Spanish character, which indicates that the craftsman might possibly have been a Marrano.

BERNARD BERENSON'S home for many years, Villa I Tatti, is located in Settignano, in the hills outside Florence overlooking the city. Here he created his world wide reputation as an art authority. He died in 1960 and bequeathed the villa and its famous library and art collection to his alma mater, Harvard University. Harvard has made the thirty room villa a centre for graduate humanistic and art studies. There, amid the Renaissance treasures collected by Berenson in nearly seventy years of residence in Italy, eight to ten fellows spend an academic year on scholarly projects. The fellows live elsewhere but study at I Tatti and use its library of 60,000 volumes and 100,000 photographs.

THE CATHEDRAL has a statue of Isaiah, attributed to Donatello, in the right nave. In the Cathedral Museum (Opera del Duomo) may be seen a number of statues of the Prophets, among them Habakkuk and Jeremiah, by Donatello.

CEMETERIES The cemetery in current use is located on Via di Caciolle 14. An older cemetery is located on Viale Ludovico Ariosto 14.

GHETTO Nothing remains of the ancient ghetto of Florence which was demolished to make way for the present Piazza della Repubblica and the Piazza dell'Olio. The Via Ramaglianti of today is the former Via dei Giudei (Street of the Jews).

The arch on the Piazza della Repubblica has an inscription which reads: "The ancient centre of the city—was restored from age old squalor to new life".

KOSHER RESTAURANT, Servi, is located on the first floor of Via Farini 2A, close to the synagogue.

LAURENZIANA LIBRARY, Piazza San Lorenzo 9, is known for its extensive collection of Hebrew manuscripts of notable interest. The library specializes in the study of ancient manuscripts.

DANIELE MANIN MONUMENT is to be found in the Piazzale Galileo, off the Viale dei Colli (*see* **VENICE**).

MARTYRS' MEMORIAL In the courtyard of the synagogue a large marble tablet has been affixed to the wall in memory of the 248 members of the community who died in deportation, or were shot, or died fighting with the Italian resistance. The names of all of them are inscribed on the tablet, headed by the name of the chief rabbi of Florence, Nathan Cassuto, who was deported in 1943 by the Germans. The fountain in the courtyard is dedicated to the memory of soldiers killed in World War I. Twenty seven names are listed.

MEDICI PALACE The walls of the Chapel of the Medici are covered with frescoes by Benozzo Gozzoli (1450). Here the artist has portrayed the leading figures of fifteenth-century Florence in the robes of Oriental kings. In the train of followers are many well-known Florentines, including Elijah del Medigo, Jewish member of the humanist circle of the Medicis, who taught Hebrew at Padua and later in Florence.

VIA GUSTAVO MODENA is named for a prominent Jewish citizen of Florence.

NATIONAL LIBRARY, Piazza Cavalleggieri 1, has a collection of Hebrew manuscripts and incunabula.

NATIONAL MUSEUM (Bargello) contains no fewer than four statues of David by great Italian masters. In the Michelangelo Room there is the great sculptor's *David* of 1530, a complex work of his maturity. In the Great Hall of the General Council are the two famous reliefs of the "Sacrifice of Isaac," one by Lorenzo Ghiberti and the other by Filippo Brunelleschi, which the two artists submitted for the completion for the Baptistery doors. As we know, Ghiberti was the winner.

Also in this room may be seen Donatello's famous bronze *David* of about 1430. Nearby is another *David* by Donatello in marble and an earlier work than the first. In the Fireplace Room stands Verrocchio's bronze statue of David.

OLD PEOPLE'S HOME, Via Carducci, was dedicated in September 1959. It is a new structure named for Settimio Saadun, who provided the funds to build the former "Casa di Riposo" on Via Amendola. Most of the inmates of the old home were deported by the Germans. The building was badly damaged in the destruction of the adjacent bridge by the retreating Germans. The present home houses eighty aged Jews; the Conference on Material Claims against Germany helped make the construction possible.

ORT TRADE SCCHOOL, Via Giambologna 25, specializes in fashion and tailoring.

PIAZZA della SIGNORIA displays the copy of Michelangelo's *David* placed there in 1873 when the original was removed to the Accademia.

PIAZZALE MICHELANGELO, a square on the heights above Florence, has in its center a bronze copy of Michelangelo's *David*.

PITTI PALACE In the main courtyard, overlooking a marble pool, may be seen a statue of Moses by the sculptor Corradi. Larger than life, one hand points to the pool and the other carries a tablet with the words *"En Israelis dux"* (Behold the leader of Israel). The four attendant female figures are allegories of Legislation, Charity, Authority, and Zeal, and one carries a legend in Hebrew script. Corradi's Moses, like Michelangelo's, wears horns. This curious usage stems from the mistranslation of the Hebrew word *keren* as "horn" instead of "ray of light."

VIA FRATELLI ROSSELLI is named for Carlo and Nello Rosselli, two anti-Fascist brothers who were murdered by Fascist gangsters in France. They were members of the Jewish family which had harbored and aided Giuseppe Mazzini during the Italian struggle for freedom.

SCHOOL at Via Farini 4, in the synagogue grounds, was dedicated on December 5, 1963. It was named the Nathan Cassuto School in memory of the Chief Rabbi of Florence who was deported to his death by the Germans. It is a two story building which also serves as a community centre. Nursery, elementary and secondary schools are housed in the building. Construction was financed by the local Jewish community and the Conference for Jewish Material Claims Against Germany through the Joint Distribution Committee.

SYNAGOGUE The great synagogue, Via L. C. Farini 4, took eight years in the building, from 1874 to 1882. It was dedicated on October 10, 1882. Its construction was made possible by the bequest of Davide Levi, a former president of the community, who willed his entire estate for the building of "a monumental synagogue becoming to Florence." The synagogue, large and in the Moorish style, is decorated in the interior with frescoes and Venetian mosaics. During World War II it was used as a medical warehouse by the Germans, and it was heavily damaged by mines placed in the pillars before the German retreat. The synagogue was restored with the help of the government. On the synagogue grounds are several small buildings, which house various communal institutions.

A small Ashkenazi congregation formerly located at Via delle Oche 5, a small *shtiebel* in the shadow of the cathedral, is now no more. The minyan which once used the *shtiebel* now gathers for services in a small room of the Great Synagogue.

PROF. GIULIANO TREVES is buried in the Jewish cemetery on Via di Caciolle. Prof. Treves, a leader of the Resistance movement in Florence, was shot by the Nazis in September 1943. His close friend, Commander Giuseppe Lattes, also a Jew, managed to bury his body in an old cemetery, Coventino, outside the Gate of San Frediano. After the war his body was disinterred and given honorable burial in the Jewish cemetery.

UFFIZI GALLERY contains a large number of paintings of Jewish interest. Botticelli's famous works on Judith and the death of Holofernes are to be found in Room 9. In Room 21 there are two paintings by Giorgione, "Boy Moses before Pharaoh" and "Judgment of Solomon." In Room 25 may be seen "Joseph Presenting His Father and Brothers to Pharaoh," by Francesco Granacci. In Room 26, there is Rosso Fiorentino's "Moses Defending the Daughters of Jethro." Palma Vecchio's titanesque "Judith" is in Room 28. "Esther and Ahasuerus," attributed to Veronese, is in Room 34. In Room 36 may be seen the "Sacrifice of Isaac" by Jan Lys; Piazzetta's "Susannah and the Elders" hangs in Room 37.

FOSSOLI

In this small place near Carpi there was a Nazi concentration camp where hundreds of Jews and other political prisoners were murdered and whence thousands were deported to their deaths in the extermination camps. A memorial to the victims of Nazism and Fascism has been erected on the site of the camp.

See **CARPI**

GENOA

JEWISH SCHOOL, Via Maragliano 3/4, is known as the Riccardo Pacifici Elementary School, in memory of the martyred chief rabbi.

MARTYRS' MEMORIAL In the synagogue courtyard there is a monument to Rabbi Riccardo Pacifici, a former chief rabbi of the community, who was deported by the Germans during the last war. The inscription reads: "A Rabbi who taught Divine law from the pulpit with dignity—and in the hour of peril remained at his post as teacher".

There is also a memorial tablet on the synagogue wall to the martyrs of the community. Both were desecrated by neo-Fascist vandals in 1955, 1957 and 1960. Each time the city of Genoa sent official apologies to the Jewish community and met the costs of restoring the memorials.

SYNAGOGUE, Via G. Bentora 6, a modern-style building, was erected in 1936. The synagogue may best be reached through the twin tunnels called the Gallerias Garibaldi, which end at the Piazza Corvetto. This leads to the steep Via Assorrati. The Via G. Bentora is a little way up on the left-hand side.

VIA THEODOR HERZL was named in 1968 in honor of the father of modern political Zionism. At the same time the city of Haifa named a street in the Hod Hacarmel quarter for Giuseppe Mazzini, the Italian patriot. This was done at the suggestion of Prof. Tramarollo, President of the Italian Mazzini Society and one of Israel's great friends in Italy. The exchange marked the recognition of Haifa as a great and thriving port, as envisioned by Herzl, and is now a maritime neighbor of the veteran Italian port of Genoa.

GORIZIA

SYNAGOGUE, Via Ascoli 13, follows the Ashkenazic rite. The synagogue dates to the seventeenth century, when Gorizia, or Görz as it was then known, was part of the Austrian Empire.

GRADO

MUNICIPAL MUSEUM contains several tombstones taken from the ruins of the ancient town of Aquileia nearby, which are the only relics of a community that flourished for many centuries. Aquileia was founded by the Romans, and one of the tombstones dates to the first or second century. It commemorates the death of a Romanized Jew, Lucius Ajacius Dama. Another, of the fifth century, records the memory of "Peter, called Papario, the son of the Jew Olympio, who alone of his tribe found his way to the blessing of Jesus." Another tombstone dates to the twelfth century. Some of the ruins are said to be those of a synagogue. Aquileia was destroyed by an earthquake in 1483.

IVREA

CAMILLO OLIVETTI MONUMENT, designed by Emilio Greco, was erected by the municipality of Ivrea in memory of the founder of the great Olivetti typewriter firm, whose main plant is located in Ivrea. The monument consists of an abstract metal structure and medallion set against a backdrop of flowing water from the cliff at the crossroads of the Val d'Aosta, Turin, and Milan highways. Camillo Olivetti was born in Ivrea in 1866 and died in 1944. He is buried in the Jewish cemetery at Biella.

CAMILLO OLIVETTI STATUE, by Mirko, may be seen in the Salone dei Duemilia, within the main factory. The plant is open to visitors.

SYNAGOGUE is located on Via Palma. There is no longer a Jewish community in Ivrea, and the synagogue is the property of the Turin community. Permission to visit may be obtained from the community's sectional delegate, Guido Pugliese, Via San Nazario 22.

LA SPEZIA

In 1965 the municipality of La Spezia named an elementary school in the new quarter of the town in memory of Adriana Revere, a young girl from this port on the Gulf of Genoa who was deported to her death by the Nazis.

LEGHORN

The history of the Jews of Livorno, as it is called in Italian, stands in a category of its own. Toward the close of the sixteenth century, Ferdinand I, Grand Duke of Tuscany, decided to create a free port in the little harbor of Livorno, together with the ancient and far more important city of Pisa not far away. In his famous charter of July 10, 1593, addressed to "men of the East and West, Spaniards and Portuguese, Greeks, Germans, Italians, Hebrews, Turks, Moors, Armenians, Persians and others", the third clause was particularly significant to Marranos of Spain and Portugal, and those living in various parts of Italy. The clause read: "We moreover desire that . . . none shall be able to make any inquisition, inquiry, examination or accusal against you or your families, although living in the past outside our Dominion in the guise of Christians". Jews poured in, the free port prospered.

The Ghetto, with all the degradation which it implied, was never introduced. The Jewish badge was unknown, there was barely any restriction on economic life, householders were legally permitted to carry arms. The community prospered, it grew from 1,000 in the middle of the seventeenth century to 10,000 by the close of the eighteenth. The monumental synagogue, begun in 1602 and superbly enlarged in 1789, was considered one of the sights of the town. Schools and printing presses flourished and Livorno acquired the title "Jerusalem of Italy". For a long time it was the most important Jewish community in Italy. These happy times came to an end in World War II.

CHILD WELFARE CENTER, Via Roma 234, was dedicated in October 1955 to the memory of its founder, Dr. Roberto Funaro. Dr. Funaro founded the center, *Instituto Provinciale Protezione Assistenza all'Infanzia,* with limited means and made it one of the best child care institutions in Italy. Because of the Fascist racial laws, he left for the United States in 1939. He had held a professorship at the University of Pisa and had a pediatric medical practice which included children of Leghorn's poorest families as well as some of Europe's royal families.

COMMUNAL CENTER, Via Lanzi 1.

JEWISH ELEMENTARY SCHOOL, Via dei Fanciulli.

JEWISH BOOKSHOP, Casa Editrice Belfort, Via della Madonna.

JEWISH DEPORTEES SQUARE was dedicated in May 1966 in the center of the city in ceremonies attended by leading civic and Jewish communal leaders.

SIR MOSES MONTEFIORE was born in this city on October 24th, 1784, while his parents were on a visit from England. He was born in the house of his great-uncle Moses Haim Racah, on the Via Reale, opposite the Great Synagogue. For many years a commemorative tablet marked the house, which was demolished several years ago. In March 1965 several members of the Montefiore family of England came to Leghorn to participate in ceremonies in memory of Sir Moses. A memorial plaque was unveiled on the wall of the Jewish community centre facing the site of the building where he had been born. A street was also named in his honor.

(*See* **GREAT BRITAIN**)

PIAZZA ELIA BENAMOZEGH in the heart of the old *Jewish quarter* of Leghorn, was named in honor of Rabbi Elijah Benamozegh, one of the great rabbis of Leghorn. He was a famous mystic writer whose works influenced the conversion of Aime Palliere to Judaism.

SYNAGOGUE, Piazza Grande, Via del Tempio was dedicated in September 1962. It rises on the site of the old synagogue, built in 1602, enlarged in 1789, restored in 1866, and completely destroyed by bombing in World War II together with its priceless Jewish museum. The new synagogue is of modernistic design, and will harmonize with the rebuilt heart of the city which suffered great damage in World War II. The architect, Angelo di Castro, said that his source of inspiration was the Tabernacle built by Moses in the desert. The interior of the new structure includes stones from the old synagogue. The total cost of $500,000 was shared by the Italian government which provided $350,000 from a fund for the repair of war damage, and the remaining $150,000 was contributed by the local community and the American Joint Distribution Committee.

MANTUA

ROBERTO ARDIGO LIBRARY, Via Roberto Ardigo 13, was founded in 1780 by the Empress Maria Theresa. In it is deposited the library of the Jewish community, consisting of 161 manuscripts and 1,549 volumes. The collection of Hebrew manuscripts is well known and was recently microfilmed for the Israeli Ministry of Education. There is also a Yiddish collection, quite unusual for an Italian library.

FRANCO CESENA, hero of the Resistance and youngest partisan to die in action is memorialized by a plaque on the synagogue wall. The young hero was born in Mantua, grew up in Bologna, and was killed six days before his Bar Mitzvah. (*See* **BOLOGNA**)

COMMUNITY ARCHIVES located in the synagogue building, consist of over 100,000 pages of documents. It is probably one of the largest collections of records of the history of one Jewish community in southern Europe to have survived the war years. The documents are a rich source for the varied and colorful history of the Jewish community of Mantua at the time of the Renaissance and the period following it. They owe their preservation primarily to the foresight of two men. In the early part of the seventeenth century, a Mantuan Jew donated a number of oak chests for the preservation of documents for future generations. At the end of the eighteenth century, another member of the community, Bonaiuto Levi, collected all the documents he could find, arranged them chronologically in nearly three hundred files and some fifty books, and added an index of eleven volumes. The chests were deposited in a safe place and thus the manuscripts survived.

JEWISH CEMETERY located at Viadana, near the city, has been desecrated several times by neo-fascist hoodlums in recent years.

MARTYRS' MEMORIAL A tablet commemorating the fifty-eight members of the community who were deported during the last war is affixed to the front of the synagogue.

SYNAGOGUE and COMMUNAL CENTER, Via G. Govi 11, are housed in a large, roomy building. The Scuola Grande (Great Synagogue) was demolished in the 1920s, and services are held in what was once the Tempio Norsa, the last remaining "private" synagogue. The building also houses a kindergarten and a home for the aged.

The Ark from the Scuola Grande was installed in 1956 in the Poniewiez Yeshiva in Bnei Brak in Israel. The ornamentation of this carved gilt seventeenth century Ark is all based on Temple accessories, from torches and *ephods* to *urim* and *tummim*. Another Mantuan Ark, also reclaimed from storage, was installed the same year in the Beit Yeshayahu synagogue in Tel Aviv.

MARINA DI MASSA

A medieval ritual murder cult still flourishes in this elegant seaside resort some 250 miles north of Rome, in Tuscany. The cult of Saint Domenichino is nurtured in the little parish church of Marina di Massa. Paintings inside the church depict the crucified child with blood streaming from his hands and feet. A booklet on sale tells the gruesome story of the cruel murder of the boy in Spain by Jews about the year 1240. The cult, which is celebrated every August with great solemnity, is a recent importation into Italy. In the 1950s the parish priest of Marina di Massa learnt of the "martyrdom" of Domenichino which was supposed to have taken place in Saragossa. He obtained one of his bones as a relic from the Roman Catholic hierarchy of the Spanish city and the Tuscan church was dedicated to Saint Domenichino in 1957. Despite protests by Jews and Catholics who frequent the resort and by some visiting students, the cult continues. Protests to higher church authorities are being made in the hope that this medieval slander will be discontinued. In the meanwhile postcards, key-rings and other souvenirs dedicated to the "Little Martyr" are on sale.

MERANO

MARTYRS' MEMORIAL, Via San Giuseppe, was dedicated in October 1952 in the local Jewish cemetery in memory of the 52 members of the local Jewish community who were deported to their deaths by the Nazis.

Another memorial is in honor of "Professor Boris", who helped Jews to go to Palestine. It was erected by the "Members of the Bricha".

SYNAGOGUE, Via Schiller 14, was dedicated in 1901.

This town in Italy's South Tyrol was once popular with Jews because of its "Jewish Sanatorium" which no longer exists. Peretz Smolenskin, the Hebrew writer, entered this sanatorium to regain his health but died in Merano in 1885, at the age of forty-five. Franz Kafka came here in search of a cure. Chaim Weizmann used to come to Merano on holiday. There is a large German speaking population in Merano and a number of well-known Nazis found refuge here at one time. This includes the wife of Joseph Mengele, who runs a tractor factory, Martin Bormann's daughter, and members of the Hermann Goering family.

The synagogue has been desecrated several times by fascist hoodlums. Some years ago a case of "Jewish soap" was found here, left over from German military stores. It was recovered by the then president of the community Dr. Frederico Steinhaus and turned over to the religious authorities for proper burial.

MILAN

AMBROSIANA LIBRARY, Piazza Pio XI, was founded in 1609; it contains an extensive collection of Hebrew books and manuscripts, and other Judaica.

EUGENIO COLORNI, a native of Milan, was an anti-fascist hero who was posthumously awarded the Gold Medal of the Resistance, its highest honor. Colorni was killed in Rome in May 1944, several days before the liberation of the city. His memory was honored in May 1963 when a State high school in the city was named in his honor.

ALBERT EINSTEIN was honored in November 1966 when a memorial tablet was unveiled on the house in which the great scientist had lived as a youth with his parents from 1894-1900. The inscription on the tablet says that Einstein "elected the world as his country, admitting borders only to the universe".

ANGELO FINZI, Resistance hero who was killed January 28, 1945, is buried in the Cimitero Monumentale, with a memorial depicting him as a martyr of fascism. A plaque has been placed at Quinto Romano, on the outskirts of Milan, where he was shot. His name is engraved in the Loggia dei Mercanti.

HOME FOR AGED JEWS is located at Via Jommelli 18.

JEWISH COMMUNITY OFFICES, Via Guastella 19, are located in the Central Synagogue building.

JEWISH SCHOOL, Via Soderini 16, is a remarkable institution. Dedicated in 1963, it is one of the largest Jewish schools in Europe. With its 1,000 pupils it covers ninety per cent of the Jewish school population of the city. The school encompasses all grades from kindergarten through high school, and is recognized by the government. The spacious, modern, streamlined building has 60 classrooms. It also houses a community centre and has two gymnasiums, meeting rooms and eating facilities. It also houses the Sally Mayer Foundation, named in honor of the late benefactor of the community, which organizes Hebrew courses, Biblical studies, conferences for adults, and edits publications. The school was built under the direction of Astorre Mayer, President of the community, son of Sally Mayer. The total cost was about $1,200,000, in part subsidized by the Claims Conference and the American Joint Distribution Committee, in part by contributions by members of the community.

VIA SABATINO LOPEZ was named in 1962 in honor of the well-known Jewish playwright.

MUSEUM OF MILAN has a permanent Caesarea Room dedicated in December 1968. The exhibits are from the excavations conducted by the Missione

Archaeologica Italiana of the Lombard Institute of Science, which dug for five seasons at Caesarea under the direction of Professor Antonio Frova.

VIA SALLY MAYER was named in honor of the noted Jewish industrialist and philanthropist by the municipality of Milan in 1962.

STATUE OF MOSES is to be seen in the *Palazzo Arcivescovile*. This large and imposing work by the sculptor Antonio Tantardini shows Moses with "horns". The Hebrew for "a ray of light" also means "a horn", and the Vulgate translates: "his face sent out horns of light". The medieval artists, including Michelangelo, were misled into representing Moses with horns protruding from his forehead.

NATIONAL BRAIDENSE LIBRARY, Via Brera 28, founded in 1770, is the repository of the Lattes Jewish Library. It was donated in 1888 by Mosé, Elia, and Alessandro Lattes.

ORT TRADE SCHOOL, Via Solari 16, draws students from Milan and other parts of northern Italy. The school specializes in electronics. It is located in the building of the Jewish School, of which it is part.

SCHAPIRA HOSPITAL, founded by the Milan industrialist and leader of the Jewish community for many years, is located at Busto Arsizio, near Milan.

SYNAGOGUES

The Great Synagogue, Via Guastalla 19, in the heart of the city, was built after the last war to replace the previous synagogue, on the same site, which had been destroyed in an Allied bombing raid in August 1943. It is a magnificent building of modern design. To the rear is an unusual choir loft which seems to be suspended from the ceiling. In the vestry there is a small chapel which is used by a small congregation of Sephardic Jews of eastern origin. The Ark in this chapel comes from an ancient synagogue of Pesaro.

Ohel Jacob Synagogue, Via Cellini 2, is the congregation of Ashkenazi Jews.

Persian Synagogue, Via Piatti 1.

New Synagogue, Via Eupili 8.

Beth Shelomo Synagogue, Corso di Porta Romana 8.

Beth Hamidrash "Angelo Donati," Via Sally Mayer 4/6.

CLAUDIO TREVES and **FILIPPO TURATI** were two of the founders and great leaders of the Italian socialist movement. They had both died in exile in Paris and were buried in Pere Lachaisse cemetery. On October 10, 1949 there was a great Socialist demonstration in Milan when their remains were re-interred in the Cimitero Monumentale. Their memory is honored in Italy and pilgrimages are made to their graves.

MONDOVI

SYNAGOGUE, Piazza Via Vico. There is no longer an active Jewish community and the synagogue is under the jurisdiction of the Jewish community of Turin. Permission to see the synagogue may be obtained from the sectional delegate to the Turin community, Dr. Marco Levi, Corso Statuto 27. Outside the synagogue there is a memorial for the Jews deported from this town, unveiled in June 1964.

MODENA

ESTENSE LIBRARY, Piazza San Agostino, has a large number of Hebrew manuscripts, including the Campori collection. Professor Carlo Bernheimer of Milan is compiling a complete catalogue of Hebrew manuscripts to be published by the Ministry of Education.

MUSEO DEL RISORGIMENTO has on exhibition the military tunic of Cesare Rovighi, showing the tear produced by a bullet which struck him during the battle of

San Martino and Solferino, June 24, 1859. Rovighi was a much decorated hero of the Risorgimento.

SYNAGOGUE is located at Piazza Mazzini 26. In front there is a memorial to Italy's youngest partisan, Franco Cesena, dedicated June 1963. *See* **BOLOGNA**

NAPLES

Naples is unique in having had a complete Jewish platoon of Italian Secret Police (Campagnia Ebraica) for the detection of Nazis and Nazi collaborators. It was founded by Dr. Lidya Torabin-Offrati, chief pathologist of the Naples police. In May 1948 a complete platoon, consisting of forty-two Jewish patrolmen, a sergeant, and a lieutenant, was activated. Through their efforts, more than a thousand war criminals and their collaborators were convicted.

COMMUNAL OFFICES, Piazza della Borsa 33.

KOSHER HOTEL AND RESTAURANT, Grand Hotel, Rettifilo 55.

NATIONAL MUSEUM contains a number of ancient Jewish tombstones from Pozzuoli, near Naples. The oldest epitaph, that of Claudia Aster (31-14 B.C.E.), also bears the name of T. Claudius, who provided her grave. He is described as president of the synagogue. This is probably the first definite evidence of a synagogue in Europe.

Also to be seen is a mural painting from Pompeii, apparently depicting the story of the Judgment of Solomon.

SYNAGOGUE, Via S. M. Cappella Vecchia 31, is about two hundred years old. It is undistinguished in appearance and forms part of a block of buildings. It is situated in a courtyard on the Piazza dei Martiri, the farthest outlet of the Via Chiaia.

ORIA

From the ninth to the eleventh centuries there was a flourishing and renowned Jewish community in Oria. The Jewish quarter can still be recognized in the "*Giudea*," near the Porta degli Ebrei (Gate of the Jews) still the most important entry gate to the town. In June 1965 an interesting ceremony took place in this small town near Brindisi. It was held to commemorate a famous son of the town who lived one thousand years ago. He was Shabatai ben Abraham Donnolo, born in Oria in 913, who acquired fame as a physician and astrologer. Donnolo was the earliest Jewish scholar in Southern Italy, the first Jewish writer on medicine in Europe, and the first Hebrew writer produced by European Judaism. During the ceremony the square outside the Porta degli Ebrei was named the *Piazza Shabatai Donnolo* and a memorial stone was unveiled.

ORTA

No Jewish community ever existed in this village on Lake Orta in Northern Italy. However, on a house in the village is a memorial to two Jews who found refuge there during World War II, placed by their neighbors. The marble plaque reads: "Victims of barbaric violence, Dr. Mario Levi and his son Roberto, taken from this hospitable house, torn from sweet affection, survive in perennial memory and sorrow. September 15, 1943." Under the plaque is a vase in which fresh flowers are put years after the tragedy. The good people of Orta have not forgotten the two Italian Jews who found refuge in their midst, but even there were traced by the insatiable hunters of Jews.

OSTIA

ANCIENT SYNAGOGUE During the construction of the highway from Rome to the new international airport at Fiumicino, in the spring of 1961, the remains of an ancient building with large columns and Corinthian capitals, were found on the site of the ancient seaport of Ostia, sixteen miles from Rome. A few weeks later two architraves, each with a sculptured menorah, a lulav, a shofar and an ethrog, were found, establishing beyond a doubt that the building was a synagogue.

As excavation continued it became apparent that a discovery of enormous historical interest had been made. The synagogue was a long rectangular hall, with the main entrance facing toward Jerusalem. The hall was divided into two parts. The front part has a mosaic pavement, the rear section is paved with marble inlays. At the central part there are four large columns with Corinthian capitals. On the left side there is a niche in which the Ark probably was placed.

To the left of the synagogue hall two more rooms were found. One of them, containing an oven, was probably the matzoh bakery. The second, almost as large as the synagogue hall, and is believed to have been used as a school. There are several other small rooms to the east and west of the synagogue hall. Inside the entrance on the right there is place for the ritual bath above a large cistern. The columns are 18 feet in height. The building is a little longer and narrower than the synagogue found at Capernaum in Israel.

Initially, there was controversy as to the date of the synagogue. At first it was believed to have been built in the first century of the common era. The mistake was discovered when a coin of the Emperor M.Maxentius was found in the mortar of a wall. Maxentius reigned from 306 to 312, and archaeologists concluded that the synagogue was built early in the fourth century.

Later, an earlier synagogue was found during excavations on the site. Some frescoes, materials used and the technique of construction have proven that the earlier building dates to the first century of the common era. The lower and older synagogue was smaller than the later one but it also had four columns in the main hall. Apparently the Jewish community of the time had erected a new synagogue on the ruins of an older one.

The later synagogue covered 9,350 square feet and it was probably one of the largest Jewish religious buildings in the ancient world. It proves the existence of a substantial Jewish community in Ostia Antica, then the port of Rome, busy and thriving. It is believed that that forty to fifty thousand Jews lived in Rome in Caesar's time, about 50 B.C.E.

PADUA

ANCIENT CEMETERY located on the Via Zodio, dates to the seventeenth century and is known as the First Via Zodio Cemetery, in order not to be confused with another in the same street. There are numerous well-preserved stones, some showing the coats of arms of prominent Jewish families of Padua.

CIVIC MUSEUM contains a number of fifteenth-century tombstones taken from one of the first cemeteries, closed in 1509, which lay beyond the city walls.

VIA DANIELE MANIN is named for the president of the Venetian Republic proclaimed on March 23, 1848. Part of the street touches the site of the western gate of the ancient ghetto of Padua, where it faced the cathedral.

SYNAGOGUE, Via S. Martino e Solferino, known as the "Italian Congregation," dates from 1548, when it was founded by Rabbi Johanan Treves. Through the centuries it has undergone numerous restorations. In 1910, after thorough restoration, it became the sole synagogue of the community. The "Spanish" and "German" synagogues, dating from the early seventeenth century, were closed. The interior arrangements of the synagogue are unusual. The hall is oblong and the Ark is placed midway against one of the long side walls. The *bimah* faces it against the opposite wall. The Ark is of glowing marble, and every detail of the synagogue reveals dignity and beauty.

The "German" synagogue (Scuola Tedesco) was damaged by bombing during the last war. Only the Ark escaped intact. It has been removed to Israel and is now installed in the synagogue in Yad Eliyahu, a suburb of Tel Aviv. The Italian government assisted in the dismantling and packing of the Ark. Composed of forty-five different types of marble, it filled eighty cases weighing twenty-seven tons.

The Ark of the "Spanish" synagogue (Scuola Spagnola) was also shipped to Israel and is now in the synagogue of Hechal Shlomo, the seat of the Chief Rabbinate in Jerusalem.

UNIVERSITY LIBRARY, Via San Biago 3, founded in 1629, is the oldest Italian university library. It contains the large collection of Professor Edgardo Morpurgo, dealing with the literature and history of the Semitic peoples. Padua was for many generations the only university in Europe open to Jews.

PARMA

PALATINE LIBRARY, Palazzo della Pilotta, houses the great de Rossi collection of Hebrew books and manuscripts, which it acquired in 1916. It was assembled by Giovanni Bernardo de Rossi (1742-1831), the famous Italian Christian Hebraist. Among the hundreds of Hebrew manuscripts in the library, the oldest goes back to the eighth century. It possesses the only known copy of the first book printed in Hebrew, Rashi's commentary on the Pentateuch, dated February 5, 1475, and published in Reggio de Calabria. In Casalmaggiore, a few miles from Parma, the Soncinos set up their press in 1486.

In the Palatine Library is also to be found the collection of Hebrew manuscripts gathered by Moses Benjamin Foa of Reggio, one of the great booksellers and bibliophiles of the eighteenth century.

SYNAGOGUE is located at Vicolo Cervi 4.

PISA

CATHEDRAL presents a series of Old Testament scenes on the doors, which were installed in 1602 to replace the ancient bronze doors destroyed by fire in 1595. One of the old doors survived and is now in the south transept. It was executed by Bonnanus in the twelfth century and depicts twenty-four Biblical scenes.

CAMPO SANTO the ancient burial place of Pisa, is literally an open-air art gallery. The walls carry a quarter mile of masterpieces; lining the walls are enough Greek and Roman sculpture to fill a museum. The north wall is of special interest. There are eight Biblical scenes, ranging from the Creation to the Deluge, by Pietro di Puccio, about 1390. These are followed by twenty-three scenes from the Old Testament, done by Benozzo Gozzoli, of Florence, from 1469 to 1485. It takes up with Noah, depicts the Tower of Babel, with portraits of contemporary celebrities, continues with the history of Abraham, Isaac, Jacob, and other patriarchs, and ends with Solomon and the Queen of Sheba.

The *Jewish Campo Santo* is different. While Christians buried their dead aboveground, in tiers in the old city walls, against which the Campo Santo is built, Jews interred theirs in the ground. Through a gate to the left lies the ancient Jewish cemetery. If the gate is closed admission may be obtained by applying to the *portiere* whose house lies outside the wall to the left.

There is striking contrast between the ancient and modern sections of the Jewish cemetery. The ancient tombstones lie flat, crumbling with the passing of centuries and covered by a thick tangle of weeks. The inscriptions on many are illegible but there are still enough to recall the memories of a once great community. The modern section is like modern cemeteries everywhere. Many of the tombstones are impressive. They recall many worthies of the community. Dr. Elio Arieti was president of the Jewish community; Moses Levy was a painter, born in Tunis; Cavaliere Professor Inginiere Cesare Modigliano was President of the Technical College of Piacenza; Inginiere Benedetto Luigi dei Baroni Montel was Professor at the Royal School of Engineering in Turin; and Knight of the Grand Cross Professor David Supino was Senator of the Kingdom from 1898 to 1922 and Rector of the University of Pisa where he taught law from 1875 to 1925. The largest and most elaborate tombstone belongs to the Carvaglio family, whose distinctions are not listed. Some Pisans of foreign birth are buried here such as Dr. Giuseppe Borociner born in Jassy, Rumania in 1852; Wulf Emdin born in Mohilev on the Dnieper in 1860; and Dr. Berta Emdin Brodsky born in Gomel (Russia) in 1893. The Jewish community of Pisa apparently offered a warm welcome to their foreign brethren.

PARDO ROQUES HOUSE on via Sant'Andrea, formerly the residence of Professor Giuseppe Pardo Roques for many years, bears a plaque placed by the city of Pisa. It commemorates the tragic death of Professor Pardo Roques along with seven Jewish and five Christian citizens of Pisa who were murdered with him by Nazi SS Troops in 1944. He was widely known as a humanitarian and philanthropist and was Deputy Mayor of Pisa for many years.

VIA PARDO ROQUES was named in honor of Professor Giuseppe Pardo Roques.

PIAZZA D'ANCONA was named in memory of one of Pisa's most distinguished native sons, Professor Alessandro d'Ancona, born in Pisa February 20th, 1835. He was the youngest of five brothers, all of whom achieved fame in their chosen fields. Alessandro d'Ancona was Italy's most distinguished historian of Italian literature and philologist. He created the scientific school of literary history and philology. He was also active in liberal politics. For many years he occupied the chair of Italian literature at the University of Pisa. A plaque marks the house in which he was born on the Piazza d'Ancona. It is now occupied by the Red Cross and is open to visitors.

SYNAGOGUE, Via Palestro 8, was built in 1595 and was remodelled in the nineteenth century. Although services are conducted only on festivals and Holy days, visitors are welcome at all times. It is situated very close to the Teatro Verdi.

PITIGLIANO

The small seventeenth century synagogue of this town, about sixty miles north of Rome, was reopened on Purim 1964. The synagogue, which is widely regarded as a building of great architectural merit, had been closed for many years, mainly because of the difficulty of raising the money required for its restoration. Few Jews live today in Pitigliano, which once had a flourishing Jewish community.

PIZZOLI

A plaque in memory of Leone Ginzburg, Italian writer of Russian origin, was placed on the wall of the city hall of Pizzoli on July 24th, 1960. Ginzburg was born in Odessa in 1909 and was murdered by the Nazis on Via Tasso in Rome in 1944. Carlo Levi, famous Italian Jewish writer, was the principal speaker at the dedication ceremony.

RAVENNA

Forty members of the Jewish Brigade, which served with the Allied Forces in Italy in World War II, are buried in the British Military Cemetery at Frangipane, two miles north of Ravenna. In April 1965 when the twentieth anniversary of the liberation of Ravenna was celebrated in the city, a large Israeli delegation participated including former members of the Jewish Brigade which had fought in the liberation of Ravenna. A marble stone brought from Israel was erected in memory of the Jewish dead. From time to time memorial services are held by representatives of the State of Israel and of nearby Jewish communities.

REGGIO EMILIA

ARTURO LEVI, young member of the Resistance, who was deported to his death, has a memorial to his memory in the local Jewish cemetery.

MUNICIPAL LIBRARY, Via Farini 3, has a number of valuable Hebrew items in its collection of seven thousand manuscripts and four hundred incunabula.

SYNAGOGUE, Via Monzermone 4, is a small chapel which serves the tiny community. It replaces an earlier synagogue which had been built in the second half of the eighteenth century on the site of a still older synagogue, on the Via dell'Aquila, and which was destroyed by bombing in World War II. The Ark, an elaborately carved structure of colored marble, which had come from the older synagogue, was not destroyed and was shipped to Israel; it is now in the synagogue at Kiryat Shmuel, near Haifa.

RICCIONE

Hotel Lido Mediterraneo provides kosher food during the summer season, under the supervision of the Chief Rabbi of Bologna, Dr. Cesare Tagliacozza.

RIMINI

Grand Hotel provides kosher food during the summer season, under the supervision of the Chief Rabbi of Bologna, Dr. Cesare Tagliacozza.

ROME

This oldest of Jewish communities in Europe has much to offer the Jewish traveler. Oddly enough for a community whose existence has spanned two millennia, it boasts only three modern synagogues. Communities much younger, in Italy and other countries, can do much better. However, Rome is replete with evidence of the Jewish presence from the days of the Roman Empire to the present Italian Republic. The catacombs offer mute testimony of a remote past, the museums and the churches are full of Jewish relics, the ghetto still carries some of the odor of the past, and the peddlers in St. Peter's Square, eager to offer rosary and crucifix to the faithful, are Jews, as they have been since time immemorial.

Just as Florence seems to be dedicated to the cult of David the shepherd-king, Rome has paid special attention to the towering figure of Moses the Lawgiver. Aside from Michelangelo's great *Moses* in San Pietro di Vincoli, he is to be found in fountains, obelisks, and frescoes throughout the city. Perhaps it is fitting that the city whence came law for so great a part of the world should pay special attention to the greatest lawgiver of all.

AMERICAN JEWISH JOINT DISTRIBUTION COMMITTEE, Via Piemonte 26, the agency's headquarters for Italy.

ANCIENT TOMBSTONE may be seen on the Via Appia Antica, about three miles out from the Porta San Sebastiano. On the right-hand side of the road there is a marble tablet, about two and a half by three feet, standing at the foot of a funeral monument some twenty feet high. It reads as follows:

L. VALERIUS. L.L.
BARICHA
L. VALERIUS. L.L.
ZABDA
L. VALERIUS. L.L.
ACHIBA

It may be that Baricha, Zabda, and Achiba were Jewish slaves of Lucius Valerius, who had freed them, perhaps in his will. Josephus mentions a senator named Lucius

Valerius who referred to the Senate the decree of friendship between Rome and Judaea in the ninth year of Hyrcanus the High Priest. Possibly the names of his freed Jewish slaves were recorded on his tomb as a token of gratitude for their freedom and the decree of friendship.

ARCH OF TITUS, on the summit of the Via Sacra on the Forum, was erected in the reign of Emperor Domitian (81-96) to commemorate Rome's victory over the Jews in the year 70 C.E. The structure bears the inscription: "The Senate and the people of Rome to the Divine Titus Vespasianus Augustus, the son of the Divine Vespasianus." The interior of the arch contains two bas-reliefs; to the right is one showing Titus in his triumphal chariot; on the left may be seen the procession of Jewish captives bearing the spoils of the Temple, the golden shewbread table, the seven-branched Menorah and the silver trumpets.

For centuries Jews considered it an ill omen to walk under the arch. This tradition was broken in World War II when the Jewish Brigade, composed of volunteers from Palestine, marched under it after the liberation of Rome, symbolizing the rebirth of the people whom Titus believed he had destroyed forever.

ARDEATINE CAVES MEMORIAL, off the Via Appia Antica, between the Via Ardeatina and the Via delle Sette Chiese, and a short distance from the catacombs of San Sebastian, is the moving memorial to the 335 Italians who were massacred by the Germans on March 24, 1944. This was in reprisal for a bombing attack by the resistance, in which thirty-three German soldiers had been killed or wounded. The order to execute ten for one was given by Marshal Kesselring, the German commander. Christians and Jews alike were picked up on the streets or taken from the Regina Coeli prison, and were butchered in the old Ardeatine Caves. Of the total killed, seventy-one were known to be Jews.

The impressive memorial was dedicated in 1957. In the courtyard is a monument by the sculptor Coccia which depicts three huge figures tied together, to symbolize human suffering. An inscription in the courtyard records the brutal deed. The caves, cut into the Ardeatine Hill, contain praying niches and are dimly lighted. On the brow of the hill stand a metal Star of David and a cross.

The martyrs are buried in a vast mausoleum carved out of granite and marble, open on all sides to air and sunlight, and topped by a massive granite roof. Each is buried in a stone sarcophagus, all uniform, with the stones over the Jewish graves inscribed with a Star of David, those over the Christian graves with a cross. Each slab bears a victim's name, age, and occupation, and it may be noted that several families had more than one member among the massacred. The whole effect is inexpressibly moving. Annual commemorative services are held in the courtyard by both communities.

CAPITOLINE MUSEUM, on the Capitoline Hill, contains a number of ancient Jewish inscriptions and monuments.

CHURCH OF SANT'ANGELO IN PESCARIA, just outside the ghetto, was for several centuries used for the conversion of the Jews. In 1572 Gregory XIII issued an ordinance that they be required to attend one sermon each week. Each Sunday several hundred men and women, and children over twelve, were herded into the church. Ears were examined to make sure they were not stuffed to deaden the sound, and attendants violently awakened those who dozed. On the façade of the church, in large Hebrew and Latin characters, may be seen the following verse from Isaiah 65:2: "I have spread out my hands all day unto a rebellious people, that walk in a way that is not good, after their own thoughts."

CHURCH OF ST. AUGUSTINE, Via della Scrofa, contains a fresco by Raphael depicting the Prophet Isaiah. Frescoes representing other prophets are by Gagliardi.

CHURCH OF ST. PAUL OUTSIDE THE WALLS has a Lapidary Museum, which contains a number of ancient Jewish inscriptions and monuments.

THE COLOSSEUM, an immense amphitheatre, was begun by the Emperor Vespasian in the year 72 C.E. and completed by his son Titus in 80. Jewish prisoners brought to Rome after the fall of Judaea were employed in its construction. According to legend, 12,000 prisoners were killed in the inauguration ceremonies.

FOOD AND AGRICULTURE ORGANIZATION OF THE UNITED NATIONS (F.A.O.), Viale della Terme di Caracalla, was originally the International Institute of Agriculture, founded by David Lubin in 1905. Born in Russia in 1849, Lubin was brought to the United States in 1855. While engaged in fruitgrowing in California, he became involved in the agrarian revolt against the railroads and middlemen and pioneered a fruitgrowers' organization in California. Convinced that only international co-operation would solve the farmers' plight, he obtained the support of the King of Italy, and this resulted in the founding, by forty nations, of the International Institute of Agriculture, which he headed.

The David Lubin Memorial Library of the F.A.O. contains his private papers which refer to a wide range of economic, financial, agricultural, political, and Jewish problems. In the library are a bust and a portrait of Lubin, and his desk.

THE GHETTO The ghetto of Rome, established in 1556 by Pope Paul IV, effected a radical transformation in the life of the Jewish community. Previously, they had lived in several sections of the city and their eleven synagogues were widely spread. There were 130 houses in the ghetto in the seventeenth century, divided between two large and six small streets. As the ghetto covered an area of one third of a square mile, with 10,000 people jammed into it, the atmosphere was crowded and unhealthy. The Tiber regularly overflowed its banks, leaving a residue of slime in the ghetto buildings. The original ghetto had eight gates, to which three more were added later, all locked at night.

The gates of the Roman ghetto were opened in 1870, long after the ghetto gates of every other Italian city had been destroyed. This is a tribute to the conservatism of the popes of that period, who had insisted on clinging to their ancient prejudices after other Italians had discarded them. The unification of Italy made it impossible to continue a medieval practice recognized as barbarous and inhuman. The gates are gone, but vestiges of the ghetto remain.

Close to the Great Synagogue, one enters the streets of the ghetto. The Via della Reginella has not changed; the houses are the same, tall and cramped, with laundry hanging from the windows. The narrow streets and alleys still present the same picture as they did a century ago.

Many names in the area recall Jewish origins. Piazza delle Cinque Scuole recalls the great building which housed five synagogues. Piazza della Azzimelle takes its name from the ovens where matzot were prepared for Passover. Via Catalana was so called because it was inhabited by descendants of refugees from Spain.

But the Ghetto has changed. It has become an in-place. Wealthy Italians and foreigners are discovering the charm of Rome's historic centre and are moving in. Ancient houses in the Ghetto are being renovated and rented to movie people, business men and diplomats. The old time residents are being forced out. There are practically no Jews left in the Ghetto today. Ten years ago there were 3,000 still living there, most of them poor and many of them helped by the community. Today there are perhaps 300-400 left.

HIGH SCHOOL in memory of Anne Frank was dedicated in December 1965 by the municipality of Rome. Anne Frank, the Jewish girl who wrote the diary of her suffering while hiding in an Amsterdam attic, was deported by the Nazis and died in Bergen-Belsen concentration camp in 1945 at the tender age of 15. (*See* AMSTERDAM)

JEWISH CATACOMBS

The Monteverde Catacombs were originally discovered on December 14, 1602, by Antonio Bosio, famed as "the Columbus of the catacombs." There are some references to it in the writings of various archaeologists, but they were eventually lost. In 1904 they were rediscovered, and the inscriptions were removed to the Lateran and other museums. Today the site, in the populous Monteverde Nuovo district, a quarter of a mile west of the present Trastevere railroad station, is covered by a block of modern apartment buildings.

On May 1, 1859, a second Jewish catacomb was found on the old Vigna Randanini, now Vigna San Sebastiano, on the Via Appia Antica. This was thoroughly explored, is in good condition, and may be seen. It contains many inscriptions throwing light on the Jewish community of the early centuries. While it is normally closed to the public, permission to visit may be obtained by applying to the offices of the Jewish Community, which has permission to accompany visitors to the catacombs. There are no lights inside the catacombs, visitors are given candles, and the place is very damp. But a visit is quite an experience. The keys are in the possession of the custodian of the Catacombs of San Calisto nearby. By law the Commission of Sacred Archaeology of the Vatican has custody of all catacombs.

In 1866 a small catacomb was discovered on the Vicolo di San Sebastiano, a little beyond the Church of San Sebastian. The site was cut up into building lots for suburban houses and is now lost.

In 1882 another Jewish catacomb was found on the Via Casilini, in a vineyard about a mile and a half outside Porta Maggiore. It was in very poor condition, and today even the exact site is not certain.

In 1885, a small catacomb was found on Via Appia Pignatelli. It lay a short distance beyond the Christian catacomb of Praetextatus. This too was lost, since no trace is to be seen in the cultivated ground which covers the area.

The last Jewish catacomb to be found was discovered accidentally in 1919 by workmen digging foundations for a new stable on the grounds of the Via Torlonia on Via Nomentana 70, in the northern part of the city. While this catacomb is not open to the general public, it may be visited by scholars and students.

Thus, two of the six Jewish catacombs discovered to date in Rome are still available for study.

JEWISH COMMUNITY CENTER, Lungotevere Cenci 9, is located in the ample basement of the Great Synagogue. It was opened on December 11, 1955, and contains an auditorium, a gymnasium, a social hall, meeting rooms, classrooms, and a library. The original plans had called for a new building in some outlying district, but the opinion prevailed that the center be situated in the old ghetto. The rooms are decorated with ceremonial objects from the eighteenth-century synagogue which stood on this site before the present one was erected in 1940. The American Jewish Joint Distribution Committee and the Claims Conference contributed to the cost of the construction of the center, the greater part of which was raised by the Jewish community of Rome.

JEWISH HOSPITAL is located on the Isola Tiberina, an island in the Tiber, close to the ghetto. It is housed in an old and dilapidated building which has served the community for several generations. The Home for the Aged occupies the top floor. The island is united to the ghetto side of the river by the Ponte Fabricio, built in 62 B.C.E., the oldest bridge in Rome, which has been known since time immemorial as the Jews' Bridge.

JEWISH MUSEUM located in the Great Synagogue, contains a collection of Jewish ritual objects gathered from the synagogues which once existed in the ghetto. In the gardens adjacent to the Great Synagogue may be seen tombstones and inscriptions removed from the ancient Jewish cemetery on the Aventine Hill.

KOSHER RESTAURANTS
Tenenbaum's Restaurant and Hotel, Via Cavour 266.
Bondi, Via Dandolo 19.
Luciano Camerino's, Via Portico D'Ottavia 16 (in the Ghetto).

LATERAN MUSEUM, Piazza San Giovanni in Laterano 6, a former papal residence, has a Jewish Room (Sala Giudaica). It contains an extensive collection of ancient epitaphs and sculptured sarcophagi. The Jewish decorative symbols are interesting and sometimes unusual. Most of the stone commemorative tablets came from ancient cemeteries. Some, however, were found in homes where they were kept during the period when the popes forbade Jews to mark their graves.

LUIGI LUZZATTI STATUE, commemorating the former Prime Minister of Italy, is to be found on the Pincio.

MAMERTINE PRISON in the Forum, goes back to ancient times. The prison is below street level and prisoners were hurled into it through two holes in the ceiling. The stairs are of medieval construction. An inscription records the names of famous captives. It relates that the Apostles Peter and Paul were kept there several months before their martyrdom. The Jewish King Aristobulus II (in 61 B.C.E.) was also a prisoner here. The last name on the tablet is that of Simon Bar Giora, the general who defended Jerusalem (70 C.E.). He was taken prisoner by Titus, was exhibited in his triumph in Rome, and then was cast into the Mamertine Prison, where he was killed.

DANIELE MANIN STATUE, commemorating the President of the Venetian Republic, is to be found on the Pincio. (*See* VENICE.)

MARTYRS' MEMORIAL was erected in 1954 in the Jewish section of the Civic Cemetery in Verano. It commemorates the 2,091 Roman Jews who were deported to their death by the Germans during World War II.

A second memorial, to the memory of all victims of deportation, irrespective of religious or political affiliations, was dedicated in the Verano Cemetery in November 1961. It was erected by the Rome section of the National Association of Former Deportees to Nazi Camps on the 18th anniversary of the first Nazi raid on the ghetto in Rome. Designed by Fulvio Gavarini, the memorial depicts a wall at the Mauthausen concentration camp, with an urn containing ashes of victims of the Nazis.

MICHELANGELO'S MOSES, in the Church of San Pietro in Vincoli (St. Peter in Chains), created by the great sculptor in the early sixteenth century, is part of the unfinished tomb of Pope Julius II. Moses is presented with an air of Biblical majesty, a massive and overwhelming figure. He is portrayed with horns owing to an erroneous translation in the Vulgate of Exodus 34:35, in which the Hebrew word *keren* is rendered "horns" instead of "ray of light." The statue is so lifelike that Michelangelo is said to have struck it and commanded, "Speak to me!" Vasari, in his *Lives of the Artists*, wrote that the Jews of Rome streamed out of the ghetto on Saturday afternoons to watch the artist at work. Moses is flanked on the left by Rachel, symbol of meditative life, and on the right by Leah, symbol of the active life. These were designed by Michelangelo and executed by his pupils.

In the same church, under the main altar, a Jewish grave, discovered by Cardinal Rampolla in 1896, is said to contain the remains of Hannah and her seven sons.

ERNESTO NATHAN (1845-1921), who was Mayor of Rome from 1907 to 1913, is buried in the Jewish cemetery at Verano, where a monument has been erected to his memory. A school named for him is to be found on Via dell'Olmata.

NATHAN M. OHRBACH STADIUM, Via della Pisana (near the Ponte Galeria), was a gift to the Boys' Town of Rome by Nathan M. Ohrbach, New York department store owner. The stadium bears the following inscription: "The Stadium of Boys' Town of Rome, generous gift of Nathan M. Ohrbach."

ORSINI PALACE, adjoining the ruins of the Theatre of Marcellus, outside the ancient Ghetto, was originally the fortress of the Pierleoni family, which was of Jewish origin. A Jewish banker of Rome, baptized in the first half of the eleventh century, founded the family, which was to play an important part in the history of Rome.

The banker's grandson, Petrus Leonis, from whom the family name was derived, built a fortified castle on the ruins of the Theatre of Marcellus, part of which he incorporated in the fortress. His son ascended the papal throne in 1130 as Pope Anacletus II, while a rival party chose Innocent II. The schism lasted until the death of Anacletus eight years later. The Pierleoni family made its peace with the pope and retained its power and influence.

The palace passed to the Savelli family and later to the Orsini family, which gave it its present name.

The sarcophogus of Petrus Leonis, in which he was buried in 1128, may be seen in the cloisters of the church of St. Paul Outside the Walls. One of the few Pierleoni possessions still extant, the tower known as "The Tower of Countess Matilda" stands at the end of what was once called "The Jew's Bridge", at the entrance to the *Trastevere*, Rome's medieval Jewish quarter.

OSE CENTRAL OFFICE AND DISPENSARY, Viale di Trastevere 60.

ORT TRADE SCHOOL, Via San Francesco de Sales 5.

PIAZZA NAVONA is built on the site of the Stadium of Domitian, which could hold thirty thousand spectators. Later it became the Circo Agonale, or Corso, as it was better known. During 202 carnivals (1466-1668), half-naked Jewish victims, chosen for their corpulence, were forced to race around the Corso, amid the jeers and blows of the mob. Today, Jewish travelers dining at Tre Scalini in the pleasant Roman evening little know that they are gazing upon the scene of their Italian forebears' agony.

PIAZZA DEL POPOLO contains an obelisk which was brought from Egypt by Emperor Augustus and erected by Pope Sixtus V. It illustrates the story of Moses.

PIAZZA MIGNANELLI contains the Column of the Immaculata, erected to commemorate the proclamation of the doctrine of the Immaculate Conception. At the base, among a group of statues, are the figures of Moses, David, Isaiah, and Ezekiel.

PIAZZA MINERVA contains an obelisk which stood originally in front of the Temple of Isis in Egypt. It was erected in 1667 by order of Pope Alexander VII. It illustrates the story of the Exodus from Egypt.

THE PINCIO, a beautiful garden on the Pincian Hill with a magnificent view of the city, contains a fountain which depicts the infant Moses being placed in the bulrushes on the riverside by his sister—or perhaps being discovered by Pharoah's daughter.

PIPERNO'S RESTAURANT, Monte Cenci, is located on the edge of the ghetto, opposite the decrepit Cenci Palace, where the unfortunate Beatrice Cenci conspired to murder her father. It was founded about a century ago as a kosher restaurant by Abraham Piperno and was known for many years as Father Abraham's. It was deemed worthy of mention by Baedeker. That omniscient guide recommended that tourists go there to sample the succulent *carciofi alla Giudia* (artichokes Jewish style), the creation of Father Abraham himself, obviously a chef of genius and imagination. *Carciofi alla Giudia* is probably the only dish in the extensive Italian cuisine which is of Jewish origin. For many years Piperno's has been neither kosher nor Jewish, but *carciofi alla Giudia* is still the specialty of the house.

VITTORIO POLACCO SCHOOL, Lungotevere Sanzio 12, is an elementary school named for the great jurist, the pride of Italian Jewry in his day. He was the greatest expert on Italian civil law, a former rector of the University of Padua, and a tutor of the royal family. When the Concordat with the Vatican was signed in 1929, Polacco, as a senator, had been instrumental in having a special provision made allowing Jews to open their own schools and to be given government subsidies. The school was built on ground given to the community in compensation for the condemnation of the ancient Jewish cemetery near the Circus Maximus.

PLACE NAMES

Rome has many streets and squares named for Jews. The following are a few.

Piazza Oscar Sinigaglia was named after a distinguished citizen who helped refugees after the war.

Piazza Sidney Sonnino was named for Baron Sidney Sonnino, who occupied the Finance Ministry from 1893 to 1896, was twice Prime Minister between 1906 to 1910, and who achieved his greatest fame as Foreign Minister from 1915 to 1919. His statue stands in the Pincio Gardens.

Via Francesco Crespi was named in memory of the famous leader of the Trieste irredentist movement.

Via Alberto Einstein was named in honor of the great physicist.

Via Luigi Luzzatti was named for the great economist and leader of the co-operative movement, who sat in Parliament without a break from 1870 to 1921. After having been Minister of Finance time after time, he served as Prime Minister from 1910 to 1911.

Via Gianfranco Sarfatti was named in memory of the young Resistance hero who was killed in combat February 21, 1945 at the age of twenty-two years.

Via Filippo Turati was named for the leader of the Italian Socialist movement, who was an ardent opponent of Mussolini. *(See* **MILAN***)*

Piazza San Bernardo is the site of the famous *Fountain of Moses* erected in 1587. The statue of Moses, squat, ungainly and ludicrously draped in a toga, has been the butt of humor for generations. Lionello Venturi, the famous Jewish art historian called it "the most shameful parody of Michelangioloismo in Rome". The story is told that the sculptor, Prospero Antichi, hearing the burst of laughter which greeted his creation when it was first unveiled, fell into deep melancholy and committed suicide. The strange figure of Moses holds the tablets of the Ten Commandments in one hand, but these must be advance copies since they were not given to Moses until after the incident of the striking of the stone to produce water. The bas-relief on the right depicts "Gideon and the Soldiers". Aside from the comic figure of Moses, the proportions of the fountain, the lettering of the inscription, the beauty of the angels and the rampaging lions and the perfect balustrade, make this one of Rome's great fountains.

PORTICO D'OTTAVIO, the last remaining Ghetto gate, was renovated about ten years ago as a permanent historic site. It was recently endangered again when a large section of one of the marble columns crashed to the ground in a cold spell. Repairs have been made. For centuries the statement "Born near the Portico d'Ottavio" has been used by Roman Jews to declare their proud identity as authentic members of this ancient community. Today very few Jews live in the Ghetto and few are likely to be born in future years near this 2,000 year old monument.

PRO DEO UNIVERSITY which is located at Viale Pola 12, is officially known as the International University for Social Studies. Kaufmann Hall, was dedicated on April 29th, 1965, in memory of the late Henry Kaufmann of Pittsburgh. A bust of Mr. Kaufmann was unveiled at the ceremonies. Judge Joseph Proskauer, honorary president of the American Jewish Committee, addressed an audience of Cardinals and other Church dignitaries at the dedication. A foundation established by Mr. Kaufmann contributed funds for a new building on the campus of the church sponsored university which trains priests and non-Catholics in the field of social studies.

RABBINICAL COLLEGE is now housed in a building on the Lungotevere Sanzio, dedicated in March 1964. The complex was built with funds contributed by the Joint Distribution Committee, the Claims Conference, the Italian government and the Italian Jewish communities. Several other Jewish institutions are housed here.

ROMAN LIBRARY, Piazza della Chiesa Nuova 18, founded in 1523, has a section composed of twenty-one records of "Jewish Bankers and Merchants" from 1594 to

1672. This collection contains all the deeds executed by the notaries of the ghetto of Rome, written partly in Hebrew. The library also has a special collection of books on the Jews in Rome.

ROSE GARDEN (Roseto Communale), on the slopes of the Aventine Hill, lies on the site of the medieval Jewish cemetery, which was known as *Orto degli Ebrei* (Jews' Garden). An inscription commemorates this. Two tombstones may be seen at the entrance, behind the statue of Mazzini. For centuries the Jews of Rome buried their dead here without erecting tombstones. For a long period after the Catholic reaction, Jews were forbidden to erect any tombstones over their graves. This ban continued in force until the time of the French Revolution.

ST. PETER'S contains a column reputed to have come from the Temple of Solomon. It is to be found to the right of the famous "Pietà" chapel of Michelangelo, behind an iron grill. Bernini used it as the inspiration for the design of the twisted columns which support the Baldachino of the High Altar. Jews regarded this column as one of the two sacred free-standing pillars, Yakhin and Boaz, in the Temple. After it were modeled the two sacred columns used in baroque Torah ornaments.

SISTINE CHAPEL in the Vatican, was built in 1470 for Pope Sixtus IV. The frescoes that decorate the walls were begun in 1481 and were meant to represent the life of Moses (Old Testament) and the life of Christ (New Testament). The first two frescoes, one on each side, were painted by Pinturicchio. The first fresco represents the Circumcision of Moses, with Zipporah performing the ceremony. Botticelli did the third and fourth frescoes. The third represents the story of Moses, showing various episodes in his youth. The fifth and sixth were painted by Cosimo Rosselli and Ghirlandaio, respectively. The fifth depicts the Passage of the Red Sea. Rosselli painted the seventh and eighth. The seventh shows God giving Moses the Tablets of the Law. Botticelli also painted the ninth fresco entitled "Punishment of Koreth, Dathan, and Abiram."

It is the ceiling of the Sistine Chapel, however, which is its great glory. In 1508 Pope Julius II ordered the young Michelangelo to paint the ceiling of the chapel. The gigantic task was begun in May 1508 and was finished on November 2, 1512. In 1535 he began "The Last Judgment," which he completed in 1541. The earlier work consists entirely of Old Testament subject matter. They are, to painting, what his great *Moses* is to sculpture. The artist created an architectural frame in which to place his principal subjects, and all the figures are the creation of a titanic sculptor.

Michelangelo depicted a series of nine Biblical scenes: (1.) The Separation of Light from Darkness; (2.) The Creation of the Sun and the Moon; (3.) The Creation of Trees and Plants; (4.) The Creation of Man; (5.) The Creation of Eve; (6.) The Fall of Man; (7.) The Sacrifice of Noah; (8.) The Deluge; (9.) The Drunkenness of Noah.

The Prophets and the Sibyls are all seated and are monumental figures. The Prophets are: (1) Jonah; (3) Daniel; (5) Isaiah; (7) Zachariah; (8) Joel; (10) Ezekiel; (12) Jeremiah.

SYNAGOGUES

Chief Synagogue, (Tempio Maggiore), Lungotevere Cenci 9, is a baroque-style building dedicated in 1901. It replaced the former structure, which housed five synagogues all under a single roof—to circumvent the papal ordinance banning more than one Jewish house of prayer in the ghetto. These older congregations followed various rites, including Spanish, Sicilian, and Italian. The present synagogue is large and commodious, with a rather ornate decorative scheme. It is perhaps the only synagogue extant with three Arks in the same sanctuary. When the old quintuple synagogue was torn down, some of the Arks were preserved by building them into the east wall of the new synagogue.

On the interior wall of the synagogue may be seen two carved memorial tablets, one inscribed with the names of Jews of Rome who died for Italy during World War

I, and the other in memory of the seventy-one Jews massacred in the Ardeatine Caves.

Ashkenazi Synagogue, Via Agostino De Pretis 77, was dedicated in November of 1961. This is the first Ashkenazi synagogue ever built in Rome, and is intended for the use of the Ashkenazi community of 100 families. The building was acquired through funds made available by the Rome Jewish Community, the Conference on Jewish Material Claims against Germany, and the American Joint Distribution Committee. The ritual objects came from the ancient synagogues, no longer in existence, of the Castilian, Sicilian, and Catalan communities, all of which became extinct in the last century.

Sephardi Synagogue is located on the Via Catalana.

Oratorio de Castro, Via Balbo 33, is a small Orthodox Italian synagogue, a benefaction of the Castro family.

STATUE OF BARON SIDNEY SONNINO, twice Prime Minister of Italy between 1906 and 1910 and Foreign Minister during the First World War, was unveiled in the Pincio Gardens in October 1962.

THERMAE MUSEUM contains a number of ancient Jewish inscriptions and sarcophagi.

TRASTEVERE the section "across the Tiber" was settled by Jews in ancient Roman times and for centuries they enjoyed a flourishing economic, religious and cultural life there. This ended in 1555, when Pope Paul IV ordered the Jews to live in the ghetto established on the opposite bank of the Tiber. The chief synagogue in the quarter was destroyed by fire in 1268. At one time there were fifteen synagogues in Trastevere. A famous medieval scholar, Nathan ben Yehiel, lived in Trastevere and is supposed to have established a ritual bath and synagogue about the end of the eleventh century. According to the historian Gregorovius, this synagogue may have been built on the site of an earlier one dating from Roman times. He inspected the site of the ancient synagogue in the "Alley of the Palms", which is said to have received its name from the palm trees the Jews were believed to have planted there.

The alley is now called *"Via dell'Atleta"* from the Greek statue of an athlete found there during the last century. The *ancient synagogue* was probably located in the small medieval building at number 13 and 14 Via dell'Atleta, which has many of the characteristics of the eleventh century. It is thought that this may have been the synagogue built by Nathan ben Yehiel. The column sustaining the first floor portico has two Hebrew words engraved near the base "Nathan Hai". If and when the historical authenticity of this building is ascertained, it would be the most ancient relic of Jewish religious life in Rome.

The Ponte Quattro Capi, later known as the "Pons Judaeorum" (Jew's bridge) connected the two Jewish communities on either river bank. Today the Trastevere is in process of change. Many foreigners (particularly Americans) and Italians of means, are flocking in and renovating the ancient buildings. Jews too are moving into this age-old quarter. The Jewish orphanage is still located there, as are the newly built Jewish schools, the Rabbinical College, the Bnai Brith and the offices of the Union of Italian Jewish communities.

VATICAN ART COLLECTION contains Raffaello Santi's sixteenth-century frescoes depicting various Biblical figures—Joseph being sold by his brothers; Joseph telling his brothers of his dreams and interpreting Pharaoh's dream; Moses smiting the rock; Saul being anointed king.

VATICAN LIBRARY has a vast collection of manuscripts and rare books, which include many ancient Hebrew writings. Jewish scholars and cataloguers in the employ of the Vatican have worked on this collection for years. Through a gift of Cardinal Cushing of Boston, the manuscripts are being microfilmed and will make available the Hebrew codices outside Rome for the first time. More than eight hundred volumes of manuscripts on microfilm will be placed at Brandeis University, Waltham, Massachusetts, and in the Pope Pius XII Library at St. Louis University.

VATICAN MUSEUM has a *Sala Judaica* in which are to be seen a large collection of gravestones found in the catacombs, most of them dating between the first and the sixth centuries, with Jewish symbols and inscriptions in Greek, Latin and Hebrew. They provide precious documentation of the civil and religious life of the early Jewish settlers in Rome.

VATICAN AUDIENCE HALL constructed in 1969 has a stained-glass panel designed by Marc Chagall. This is believed to be the first work designed by a Jewish artist for the Vatican.

VILLA BORGHESE has a statue of David by Bernini on view in the Second Room. The celebrated statue of David casting the sling was created by Bernini when he was only sixteen years old. The likeness of the artist can be seen in the face of David. It is related that Cardinal Maffeo Barberini, who admired the talented youth very much, used to hold the mirror for the young artist while he was reproducing his own likeness in the statue.

SALUZZO

On September 21st, 1964, the town of Saluzzo commemorated the twentieth anniversary of the Italian Resistance against the Germans with a "Deportees Day". A memorial stone dedicating a street to the memory of Jewish deportees was unveiled. During the German occupation Saluzzo was an important center of Partisan activity. Many young Jews from Piedmont fought among the Partisans and perished.

SAN SABBA

This suburb of Trieste was the site of a concentration camp, the worst in Italy. Many local Jews had been imprisoned in this camp, housed in a former factory building. This camp had the dubious distinction of possessing the only gas chamber in Italy. It is still to be seen at the end of the courtyard. On the left of the courtyard is the torture chamber. The cells in which the prisoners were held may still be seen. In July 1965 the Italian Government declared the former concentration camp a national monument. Two simple stone plaques on a wall recall that it was there that "victims of Nazi-Fascist hatred" suffered and died.

SENIGALLIA

SYNAGOGUE is located on the Via dei Commercianti.

VIA UGO MONDOLFO recalls the memory of Senigallia's famous native son, the historian and geographer Ugo Guido Mondolfo. On August 19th, 1962 the municipality of Senigallia honored the philosopher Rodolfo Mondolfo on his 85th birthday. He was awarded the Gold Medal of the city, which also named a street in honor of his brother, Ugo Guido Mondolfo (1875-1958). The Law of 1927 forbids naming a street until the person honored has been dead at least ten years. This law may be disregarded "in exceptional cases where the person honored is deemed 'Well merited' by the nation". By invoking this exception Senigallia was able to name the street only four years after Ugo Mondolfo's death.

SIENA

CEMETERY located in the Via Certosa dates back to the early sixteenth century. It was partly destroyed by bombing during the last war, but has now been restored.

STATE ARCHIVES, Via Banchi di Sotto 10, has a large collection of manuscripts and documents, many of them relating to the history of the Jews of Siena. Thus far no Jewish scholars have studied the collection, which has a wealth of material of considerable interest to Jewish historians.

STATUE OF MOSES by Antonio Federighi (1420-90), once adorned the ghetto wall. It is now in the Palazzo Municipale (City Hall).

SYNAGOGUE, Via della Scotte 14, is located in the heart of what remains of the ancient ghetto, much of which was leveled by the authorities in 1935. It was built in 1756 and was designed by the architect Giuseppe del Rosso, of Florence. It underwent extensive restoration in 1902. Several interesting items are to be seen. The columns flanking the Holy Ark are said to have been made out of marble brought from Jerusalem. The elaborately carved walnut circumcision chair dates to 1860. The split panels of the doors of the Ark recall a tragic episode of 1799. The liberating French army burned the ghetto gates in 1796. The reactionary movement against the French several years later brought misery and death to the Jews of Siena. In 1799 a mob from Arezzo plundered the ghetto and burned nineteen Jews alive in the Piazza del Campo, four of them women. The synagogue was desecrated and the ax marks are still to be seen in the doors of the Ark. The Jewish community of Siena recovered from this harrowing experience and later earned the title of "Little Jerusalem" from its sister communities.

On the wall of the synagogue is a marble tablet commemorating the fourteen members of the community deported to their death by the Nazis. The inscription reads: "They were true, these incredible instruments of human tyranny. With six million Jews there disappeared the deported of Siena, sons of a doctrine of Justice and love. May their names be remembered with charity and benediction."

SPOLETO

CHURCH OF SAN GREGORIO DELLA SINAGOGA on the Via San Gregorio della Sinagoga, was for many years regarded as a former synagogue converted into a church in the sixteenth century, when the Jews were expelled, never to return. In recent years this has been disputed. The new school of thought maintains that the church was so named to differentiate it from the churches of San Gregorio Maggiore and San Gregorio Minore. It is claimed that its name is derived from its location near the synagogue established in 1541 in the house of Alessandro di Pierangelino in the Vaita Frasanti section of the city. Nevertheless, tradition holds that this church was the synagogue of the ancient Jewish community of Spoleto.

TARANTO

MARCO GATTI COMMUNAL LIBRARY, Via Manduria, contains a number of rare Hebrew books in its collection.

MUSEUM located in the Church of San Pasquale contains a number of fourth- and fifth-century Jewish epitaphs in Latin and Hebrew.

TRANI

In the sixteenth century the four synagogues of Trani were converted into churches. Two remain in use today.

CHURCH OF SANTA MARIA SCUOLANOVA is on the Via Scuolanova (new synagogue), corner of the Via Sinagoga. The appellation "Scuolanova" would indicate that this was the last synagogue built before the Jews departed from Trani.

CHURCH OF SANT'ANNA on the Via La Giudea, was built in 1247. It contains a Hebrew inscription on a marble plaque on the wall inside the church.

THE CATHEDRAL has a number of ancient tombstones located under the main entrance.

The following are all street names in the ancient ghetto of Trani, which is so identified even today.

Via La Giudea
Via Mose di Trani, named for a famous rabbi
Via Scuolanova
Via Sinagoga

TRENT

For almost five centuries the town of Trent, in northern Italy, perpetuated the lie of a "Jewish ritual murder" dating back to 1475. In the Church of St. Peter and St. Paul the child "victim" was venerated as a saint. The mummified body of little St. Simon was displayed in a glass case, a wooden sculpture depicted a group of Jews committing ritual murder, and stained glass windows, put in only in 1954 depicted the same theme. The town's art gallery showed paintings of the "murder." A sixty-page booklet relating the "martyrdom" was on sale in the church and town and once a year a solemn procession was held in town displaying the body of the little "martyr" and the instruments used to torture the unfortunate Jews of Trent.

On October 31st, 1965, the twelve Jews who were executed for the alleged crime were declared innocent by the Roman Catholic Church and the cult of St. Simon was ordered suppressed. The Congregation of Rites forbade any further veneration of ‘relics or saying of masses in St. Simon's name. Furthermore, it was revealed that Simon had never been formally beatified by the Congregation of Rites. The chapel of St. Simon was ordered closed, the sale of books was stopped and the procession suppressed. The pictures and carvings were transferred to a museum to remind future generations of Italy's dark ages. The stained glass window depicting Simon's "martyrdom" was replaced by one of Moses. In the chapel itself, a statue of the late Pope John XXIII symbolizes the new era of Catholic-Jewish relations. The vindication was effected through the efforts of Miss Emma Volli of Trieste, who began the fight, Monsignor Rogger, professor of ecclesiastic history at the theological seminary at Trent and associate professor at Padua University, and Father Eckert of Cologne, Germany, a Dominican priest who made the study proving the innocence of the Jews at the request of Mgr. Rogger.

The *cherem* against Trent pronounced almost five centuries ago was lifted in March 1967 by the Rabbinical Council of Italy. Meeting in Rome the Council issued a statement which said, in part: "It recalls the *cherem* decreed in times past by the rabbis against the city and the territory of Trent, following the cruel persecutions against the Jews of that city, perpetrated to avenge the alleged murder by the Jews of the child Simon, which *cherem* was to be maintained as long as the cult of Simon of Trent lasted.

Having ascertained that the cult of Saint Simon has ceased in Trent, the Italian Rabbinical Council solemnly proclaims the lifting of the *cherem* from the city of Trent and its territory, and therefore allows—without any restriction—the Jews of Italy and of all countries to take up permanent residence and to perform any kind of work there.

TREVISO

COMMUNAL MUSEUM contains fourteen medieval Jewish tombstones and fragments. The names on most of them indicate German origin, probably of traders who settled in the ancient community.

TRIESTE

GREAT SYNAGOGUE, Via Donizetti 2, is a large, impressive structure built about fifty years ago. Topped by a Moorish tower, it has a Byzantine interior and Gothic windows. Like the architecture, services are also a mixture. On weekdays, services are conducted according to the Sephardic ritual; on the Sabbath and festivals, according to the Ashkenazi. The synagogue was looted and desecrated during World War II, and its windows were smashed by bombing raids which destroyed neighboring buildings. It has been restored.

There is also a small Ashkenazi synagogue at Via del Monte 7.

LIBRARY OF THE JEWISH COMMUNITY, Via San Francesco 19, has a large collection of Judaica and Hebraica.

HOME FOR AGED JEWS is located at Via Cologna 29.

RITA ROSANI is a local heroine. Born in Trieste in 1922, she was killed in action near Verona while on a mission with a band of partisans, on September 17th, 1944. She was awarded the Gold Medal of the Resistance, the highest honor. Her memory is perpetuated by a street named for her, *Via Rita Rosani*, and by a plaque placed at the entrance hall of the Jewish school where she taught. The plaque reads: "Always present among teachers and pupils—In Memory of the teacher RITA ROSANI—Gold Medal—killed while heroically fighting for the cause of liberty."

The *Museo del Risorgimento* displays a collection of relics of Rita Rosani.

STATUE OF ITALO SVEVO, the famous Italian-Jewish writer, and friend of James Joyce, which occupied for many years a prominent position in a public square, was toppled from its pedestal by Fascists in 1939. It has been replaced by the municipality. Svevo was born Ettore Schmitz in Trieste in 1861 and died in 1928. He is the greatest literary figure produced by Trieste.

FELICE VENEZIAN BUST may be seen on the façade of the City Hall. It was removed by Fascists in 1938 but was replaced by the city after the war.

VIA FELICE VENEZIAN is named for a distinguished Jewish citizen (1840-1908) who was a deputy in the Austrian parliament. In 1938 the Fascists renamed the street, but after the war its former name was restored.

TURIN

VIA EMANUELE ARTOM is named for a young leader of the partisan group "Justice and Liberty." He was arrested by the Germans on March 25, 1944, taken to the prison in Turin, and there tortured to death. His body never was found. He represented the idealism and courage of Italian Jewish youth.

VIA GRAZIADIO ASCOLI is named for the great philologist (1829-1907) who has a world-wide reputation in his chosen field.

GREAT SYNAGOGUE, Via Pio V 12, was built in 1834. It is a large and impressive building, with seating capacity for 1,500 men and 500 women. It was almost totally destroyed by aerial bombing in the last war, but was rebuilt, with the government bearing most of the cost.

JEWISH CEMETERY located in Corso Regio Parco, dates to the eighteenth century.

JEWISH SCHOOL, Via San Anselmo 7, is named for Emanuele Artom (*See* Via Emanuele Artom *above*). It is an elementary and secondary school, recognized by the government. About one third of the pupils come from Protestant families.

CESARE LOMBROSO MEMORIAL The world-famous scientist and criminologist Cesare Lombroso was buried in the General Cemetery of Turin, Corso Novara 135/37, in 1909. A native of Verona, Lombroso at the time of his death was professor of psychiatry and medical jurisprudence at the University of Turin. (*See* VERONA.) In Arcade No. 56 of the third division of the cemetery may be seen a memorial plaque with the following inscription: "Cesare Lombroso 1835-1909, who wrested from nature the secret of pellagra, which was a killer of humanity—he taught new ways of science to mankind at the University of Turin. This site was unanimously dedicated by the City Council."

VIA CESARE LOMBROSO is named for the great scientist who contributed greatly to modern knowledge of criminology. He was buried in the General Cemetery of Turin, and a monument was erected to his memory in his native city of Verona, where he was born in 1835. (*See* VERONA.)

DANIELE MANIN MONUMENT (*see* VENICE) is located in the Balbo flower garden in the Piazza Cavour.

MARTYRS' MEMORIALS A large commemorative tablet to the Jewish victims of Fascism and Nazism may be seen on the exterior wall of the Civic Cemetery. (Another memorial to the martyrs is located outside the Great Synagogue.)

THE MOLE ANTONELLIANA, the symbol of Turin as the Eiffel Tower is the symbol of Paris, was begun in 1863 as a synagogue. The Jewish community was unable to complete it and sold it to the municipality of Turin in 1882. Construction was completed by the city in 1897, as a national historical museum in memory of King Victor Emmanuel II. A masonry spire was added, reaching a height of 619 feet, which made the building the dominating structure of Turin. The spire crashed to the ground in 1953 during a cyclone. Reconstruction was completed in 1961, with a new steel spire. In the spring of 1962 the Mole Antonelliana was reopened to visitors, who are able to ascend to the top in elevators. The Museum of the Italian Risorgimento was originally located here, but was moved some years ago to the Palazzo Carignano.

VIA CORRADO SEGRE is named for the distinguished mathematician (1863-1924) who was professor of superior geometry at the University of Turin from 1888 to 1924.

SALOMONE AND AUGUSTO SEGRE HOME FOR OLD PEOPLE, Piazza S. Giulia 12, is named for these benefactors of the community.

CORSO FILIPPO TURATI, a brisk walk south from the railway station, was named in honor of the great leader of the Socialist movement in Italy. (*See* MILAN)

UNIVERSITY OF TURIN In 1946, in the Library of the Faculty of Humanities in the Carignano Palace, a memorial plaque was erected to the memory of Emanuele Artom (*see* Via Emanuele Artom). The inscription reads: "In this library Emanuele Artom from the sources of old experience found his hope of a free native land. Graduate in Humanities, fighter in the volunteer group for freedom, tortured and killed by the savage Germans April 7, 1944."

The chief university building contains a bust of Achille Loria, the eminent political economist. It was unveiled on October 19, 1955. Achille Loria (1857-1943) held the chair of political economy at the University of Turin from 1903 to 1932. He was preeminent in his field and served as a member of the Italian Senate.

VENICE

The words "Venice" and "ghetto" have been almost synonymous for centuries. Venice was the first city in Europe to establish a ghetto in 1516, an entirely new instrument for the persecution of the Jews. It spread rapidly enough and other cities outdid the Venetians in their zeal to restrict the Jews. Rome, for example, managed to pack more people into a smaller area and allowed only one building to house their places of worship. Venice permitted the building of five separate synagogues, some of them lovely structures.

The first ghetto was established on the site of the *Gietto Nuovo* (the new foundry), from which the name ghetto is derived. There are other explanations for the origin of the name, but this seems the most reasonable. Later the ghetto was enlarged by settling Levantine Jews on the site of the *Gietto Vecchio* ("old foundry"). Thus the new ghetto was known as the *Ghetto Vecchio* ("old ghetto"), an apparent contradiction.

Venice owes much to her Jewish sons and daughters. When the ghetto gates were destroyed by Napoleon in 1797, the Jews entered into the life of their city. When the Venetian Republic was proclaimed in 1848, Daniele Manin, son of a converted Jewish family, became President. Manin has been described as "one of the purest and noblest figures in the history of Italian liberalism".

Jews served bravely in the National Guard, and two served in the government of the Republic—Leone Pincherle as Minister of Agriculture and Commerce, and Isaac Pesaro Maurogonato as Minister of Finance. Rabbis Samuel Olper and Abraham Lattes were members of the Assembly.

It is interesting to note that Venice has three churches named for Old Testament patriarchs, St. Job, St. Moses, and St. Samuel, a record among Italian cities. This custom is derived from Byzantium where churches were dedicated to Old Testament patriarchs and prophets who were endowed with honorary sainthood by the church.

ACADEMY OF FINE ARTS contains, in the Eighth Room, Tintoretto's famous paintings in the nude of "Adam and Eve" and "Cain and Abel." Also his "Creation," which sets forth the idea of motion.

BASILICA OF SANTA MARIA DELLA SALUTE, the masterpiece of the great architect Baldassare Longhena, who designed the Spanish Synagogue, contains three ceiling paintings by Titian. They are "Abraham's Sacrifice," "Cain and Abel," and "David Killing Goliath."

CA D'ORO, one of the loveliest palaces on the Grand Canal, built in the fifteenth century, and now known as the Franchetti Gallery, was presented to the nation by Baron Giorgio Franchetti, member of a prominent Jewish family. Baron Franchetti, a well-known musician, acquired and restored the Palazzo Ca d'Oro and housed in it his personal art collection which he had acquired in long years of search in Florence, Venice and abroad. On May 19, 1916, Baron Franchetti gave the Ca d'Oro to the Italian government, the gift becoming effective after his death on December 19, 1922. At his expressed desire, his ashes were placed in a Roman urn under the doorway of the Ca d'Oro on the ground floor, where a porphyry column bears the name of Giorgio Franchetti with a Latin inscription which reads: "Here is he, proving himself superior, who conquered art with love—here lie his ashes, now cooled—here genius abides with safety."

The Ca d'Oro now houses an art collection of various periods, but it is particularly valuable as a documentation of the fifteenth-century Venetian patrician's way of living.

CHURCH OF SAINT MOSES on the Via San Moisé, is a glaring demonstration of Venetian baroque. Its elaborate seventeenth-century façade attracts immediate attention. Ruskin wrote that it was "notable as one of the basest examples of the basest school of the Renaissance." Inside is a gigantic altar, built of shining granite blocks, with great figures of Jehovah, Moses, and the Tablets of the Law on Mount Sinai.

CHURCH OF SANTA MARIA DEL GIGLIO contains the painting "Abraham Dividing the World," by Zanchi.

THE GIUDECCA is the large island in the lagoon where the first enduring settlement of Jews was established. Originally called Spinalunga, the island became known as the Giudecca after the Jews settled on it. The name is mentioned in a document dated 1252. Later, the Jews moved to the city proper but the name remained.

PEGGY GUGGENHEIM COLLECTION of modern art is housed in a *palazzo* on the Grand Canal. It is reputed to be the world's finest collection of twentieth-century art. The *palazzo* is both Miss Guggenheim's home and a gallery to which the public is admitted three times a week.

ISRAELI PAVILION at the Biennale was dedicated in 1954. It is located on the edge of the small canal which meanders through the grounds of the Giardini, in which the Biennale buildings are situated. Since it was opened, the pavilion has had great success in bringing Israeli art to the attention of thousands of visitors.

JEWISH CEMETERIES

The cemetery in use today is located on the Via Cipro, Lido. It includes a section dating back about 250 years.

The ancient cemetery established in 1386, is on the Lido, Riviera San Nicolo 2, at the corner of Via Cipro. It is in somewhat dilapidated condition. The keys are with the custodian of the Via Cipro cemetery.

DANIELE MANIN MONUMENT, the work of Luigi Borro (1875), is located on the Campo Manin, directly in front of the house in which he lived. It was erected by the city of Venice in memory of its great hero who was president of the short-lived Venetian Republic proclaimed on March 23, 1848. Manin was born in Venice in 1804 and died in Paris in 1857.

MANIN'S TOMB is located under the arch of the transept on the north side of the Basilica of St. Mark. Manin's remains were brought from Paris in 1858, and he lies in a marble sarcophagus, borne by lions.

MARCIANA NATIONAL LIBRARY, San Marco 7/12, contains a considerable collection of rare Hebrew manuscripts and rare books.

OLD PEOPLE'S HOME is located at the far end of the Ghetto Nuovo.

PALACE OF THE DOGES Among the thirty-eight finely carved capitals in Portico, the three most important are considered to be those in the corner near the Ponte della Paglia. They represent "Noah Drunk and His Sons," "Adam and Eve," and "The Judgment of Solomon." In the Hall of the Anti-Collegium may be seen "The Return of Jacob," painted by Bassano. In the Law Magistrates Room there is a statue of Eve, and in the following room one of Adam, both sculptured by A. Rizzo. Left of the façade, in the Piazzetta, is a statue of King Solomon.

SCHOOL OF ST. ROCCO is famous for the great cycle of paintings by Tintoretto, who painted them between 1564 and 1588. The vast upper floor has a series of canvases set out according to a definite order on the walls and on the gilded ceiling. The main scenes, in the center of the ceiling, narrate evils from which the children of Israel were delivered—hunger, disease, and thirst. They depict "The Rain of Manna," "The Miracle of the Serpents," and "Moses Causing the Water to Run from the Rocks." The other paintings around them relate stories from the Old Testament, ten in number.

In front of the altar are two paintings by Tiepolo, "Abraham and the Angels" and "Hagar Abandoned."

ST. MARK'S CHURCH In the narthex may be seen a series of mosaics covering cupolas and arches, dating to the thirteenth century, narrating Biblical stories. In order, from left to right, they represent "The Creation," "Six-winged Angels," "Cain and Abel," "Noah and the Flood," "Noah and His Sons," "The Tower of Babel," "The Life of Abraham," "The Life of Joseph," "The Life of Moses." Among the other scenes intermingled in these cycles may be seen "The Judgment of Solomon." Also to be seen is a bas-relief reputed to have been carved from the stone which Moses struck.

On the steps to the left leading to the altar, there is a stone embedded in the wall, marked with a crude Mogen David, reputed to have come from the Temple in Jerusalem.

INSTITUTE OF SCIENCE, LETTERS AND ARTS contains the archives of Luigi Luzzatti, Prime Minister of Italy, presented by his sons. (*See* ROME)

THE SYNAGOGUES In the ghetto are five synagogues, which were built by the followers of various rites. Two were established by Italian Jews, one by German, one by Spanish, and one by Levantine Jews. At the end of World War II all were in poor condition and were shored up at the expense of the American Jewish Joint Distribution Committee, which launched a drive to restore them.

The German Synagogue, known as the *Grande Scuola Tedesca*, is the oldest and was built in 1415. It was restored in 1953 by the Joint Distribution Committee and now houses the Jewish Museum.

The Spanish Synagogue, known as the *Scuola Spagnola*, was built in 1550 and designed by the great architect Baldassare Longhena, whose master work is the Church of Santa Maria della Salute. It was restored in 1840 through the generosity of Giuseppe Balterra, who gave 150,000 Austrian gold francs for this purpose. Regular Sabbath services are held in this synagogue during the summer months.

A plaque records the names of Jewish war dead of Venice in World War I. Among them is the name of Roberto Sarfatti, who was killed at the age of eighteen in recapturing an Alpine position. His mother, the writer Margherita Sarfatti, was an intimate friend and confidante of Mussolini and helped him found the Fascist party. In the vestibule is a plaque commemorating the visit of Sir Moses Montefiore on July 1, 1875, and another celebrating his hundredth birthday, October 27, 1884. On the outside wall is a tablet commemorating the martyrs of Venice. It reads: "1939-1945—200 Jews of Venice, 8,000 Jews of Italy, 6,000,000 Jews of Europe were barbarously massacred and died as martyrs." Nearby is another plaque, in Latin, and dated September 1704; it decrees dire punishment for any Catholic found entering the ghetto.

The Scuola Canton, which was of the Italian rite, was founded in 1532, and probably named for the family which established it.

The Italian Synagogue, known as the *Scuola Italiana*, was built in 1575, on a foundation supported by pillars.

The Levantine Synagogue, known as the *Scuola Levantina*, dates from the latter part of the sixteenth century. Serv-ces are conducted here during the winter.

VENOSA

The ancient Jewish Catacombs, in this typical small town of Southern Italy, are the most extensive and elaborate found thus far. Venosa was the birthplace of the Latin poet Horace who referred frequently to the Jews in his writings. The catacombs date to the third or fourth century, and are found on a hill-slope alongside the road leading to the railway station, outside the area of both the ancient and the modern town. The many earthquakes in the region caused the collapse of some of the underground galleries and blocked the entrance to others. The catacombs apparently entered the hill at different levels. In front of the entrances (of which some are ruined) are the remains of pillars, built of bricks and small stones, which apparently were the outer gate-posts for the catacomb courtyard.

Today the largest catacomb can be entered from the second level. It consists of two long, almost parallel galleries, with two interconnecting corridors; a third shorter gallery as well as further passages are blocked by fall-ins. Large burial niches as well as smaller ossuary niches are cut into the walls, and at intervals there are vaults containing varying number of burials. Inscriptions are to be seen in red paint or incised in small areas of plaster. The inscriptions found are 60% Greek and 30% Latin, with 10% Hebrew.

At some point during the eighth century the catacombs were abandoned. Recent excavations have uncovered scores of graves on top of the remains of the Roman bath-house. Not far from the bath-house stands the *Church of Santissima Trinita*, which was built in the tenth century and considerably enlarged in the thirteenth century. In the second building phase the building material was taken from abandoned ancient cemeteries in the vicinity, including a number of tombstones from the later open-air Jewish cemetery. The inscriptions may be seen to this day. Additional tombstones from this cemetery are found in the uncompleted part of the church, and in the town hall.

The *yeshiva* of Venosa, in the middle of the ninth century, was headed by Rabbi Nathan ben Ephraim, who was a noted scholar. One of the earliest known poets of the era was Rabbi Silano of Venosa. In the eleventh century Rabbi Akhimaatz relates that when the emissary from Palestine came to Venosa he preached in the synagogue in Hebrew and Rabbi Silano interpreted for him. No trace of the synagogue of the period has been found. Rabbi Akhimaatz lived in Oria on the south-east coast of Italy. (*See* ORIA). When Benjamin of Tudela visited the Jewish centres of Italy during the twelfth century, he referred to the nearby community of Melfi, but made no mention whatever of Venosa.

VERCELLI

FOA COLLEGE was established in 1829 and for many years served as a rabbinical school. Today it functions as an elementary school. There is a small synagogue in the grounds of the school.

VIA EMANUELE FOA is named for Elijah Emanuele Foa, who died July 20, 1796, and bequeathed his large fortune to the community for the support of charitable institutions and for the establishment of a Hebrew college in his house.

SYNAGOGUE, Via Emanuele Foa.

VERONA

THE CATHEDRAL The columns of the portal show a group of four prophets, similar to that on the portals of the Ferrara Cathedral. They probably represent Moses, Isaiah, Jeremiah, and Daniel.

CESARE LOMBROSO MONUMENT is located in the Cesare Lombroso Gardens, between the Ponte Garibaldi and the Porta San Giorgio. It was erected by the city of Verona in memory of its famous son, born in 1835, who discovered the cause of pellagra and who laid the foundations for the modern science of criminology. At the time of his death in 1909 he was professor of psychiatry and medical jurisprudence at the University of Turin. The city later named a street in his honor (*See* TURIN). In Verona the square which for many years bore his name is now called Piazza Santo Spirito. His monument bears the following inscription: "By casting the light of science upon the scourge of pellagra and the depths of human misery, truth serves the cause of humanity."

CHURCH OF SAN ENO On the portal columns may be seen carved Old Testament scenes executed in the early twelfth century.

CORTE SPAGNOLA is the street which marks the site of the ancient ghetto.

JEWISH CEMETERY is located on Via Badile, Borgo Venezia. Two ancient cemeteries had been demolished, and bones and tombstones had been transferred here.

JEWISH COMMUNAL CENTER, Via Portici 3.

VIA DANIELE MANIN and the PONTE MANIN commemorate the great Venetian patriot (*See* VENICE).

ROSANI MEMORIAL On the front of the synagogue there is a marble tablet commemorating Rita Rosani, a young Jewish girl, born in Trieste in 1920, who was killed fighting with the partisans in the Verona area in 1944 and who is buried in the local Jewish cemetery. Her courage has made her a legendary figure. The inscription on the memorial tablet reads: "To the memory of Rita Rosani, who was awarded the Gold Medal of the Resistance, who sacrificed her youth for the highest human ideals that these victims should not have died in vain. Despite the oppressors, the Jews of Verona have erected this tablet to exalt her sacrifice and perpetuate her memory on the tenth anniversary of the liberation, October 30, 1955." (*See* TRIESTE)

PESCANTINA is a railway junction near Verona. There is to be seen a monument to the memory of the 30,000 Italians, Jews and non-Jews, who died in Nazi concentration camps. This was the first station on Italian territory reached by the survivors at the end of the war.

SYNAGOGUE, Via Rita Rosani, was built in 1864. In a small chapel is an Ark taken from an older Sephardic synagogue which had been leveled. In the vestibule is a memorial plaque to the six men of Verona who died in World War I for "the glory of Italy and the honor of Israel."

VIA RITA ROSANI was named in memory of the heroine during the impressive ceremony when the memorial plaque was dedicated on the synagogue wall.

VIAREGGIO

SYNAGOGUE is located on the Via dei Oleandri, which lies behind the Viareggio Hospital. The Via dei Oleandri is a very short street with no numbers, and the synagogue is at the end of a narrow courtyard. It is constructed of marble, and it is very small, seating about sixty, but very attractive. It was build in 1954 by Signora Procacia as a memorial to her husband.

VITTORIO VENETO

The entire interior of this beautiful blue and gold baroque synagogue of this vanished community near Venice was moved to Israel in 1965. It has been installed in the Israel Museum in Jerusalem. It was purchased from the Italian Government by Jakob Michael, of New York, who dedicated it to the memory of his late wife, Erna Sondheimer Michael, on May 10, 1965.

SARDINIA

ALGHERO

Upon the expulsion of the Jews from Sardinia, then a possession of the Spanish Crown, in 1492, the local synagogue became the church of Santa Croce, later demolished. The tower known as La Torre di Porto Terra e degli Ebrei, recently restored, is reputed to be the tower built for the defense of the city. There is some dispute as to whether this is actually the Tower of the Jews, but it bears their name to this day.

CAGLIARI

The Church of Santa Croce is built on the site of the ancient synagogue. There is a belief that parts of the synagogue were incorporated in the new church built in 1661. It underwent a general restoration in the last century.

SANT'ANTIOCO

This is an ancient mining center where a Jewish catacomb was discovered some years ago. Today there is nothing left but the site.

SASSARI

The present Church of the Trinity is said to be the ancient synagogue of the community. In Sassari there are prominent families who bear names of obviously Jewish origin, such as Carcassona and Naitana. These are descendents of Jews who chose conversion in preference to expulsion in 1492.

SICILY

Little remains of the numerous Jewish communities which once dotted this island. Only an occasional street name serves to recall their onetime presence. Jewish life ended with the expulsion of 1492, and it never revived.

NOTO VECCHIO

Several Jewish catacombs were discovered here some years ago. They were dispersed among twelve Christian catacombs. Nothing remains but the sites, in the vicinity of the Castello or near the Casa Fiaccavento.

PALERMO

Once there was a flourishing Jewish community here which occupied the area near the Church of San Niccolo. But no trace remains of the synagogue, which, the traveler Obadiah da Bertinoro wrote in 1487, "has not its equal in the whole world." However, travelers may see in the little Piazza Bologni the spot where many crypto-Jews were later to give their lives in the bonfires of the autos-da-fé.

SYRACUSE

In this city may be found a Via Giudecca. Here may be found two Jewish catacombs, or at least their sites. They were located in the Capuchin district near the bridge which crosses the railroad, north of the medieval town and east of the Greek necropolis. Inscriptions and lamps stamped with the Menorah have been collected in the local museum. Great damage was done to the catacombs by the opening of new streets and construction in the area.

In 1962 a Jewish necropolis of considerable size was discovered submerged under the waters of Small Harbor in Syracuse. From the Hebrew inscriptions on some of the tombstones, it was identified as dating from the twelfth to fifteenth centuries.

TRAPANI

The Via Giudecca recalls an ancient Jewish community.

LIECHTENSTEIN

The 30 Jews who live in this tiny upper-Rhine principality wedged between Austria and Switzerland are concentrated in the two principal cities, Vaduz and Schaan. The only Jewish organization is the Jewish Aid Society. Religious services are held in private homes. The nearest synagogue is in St. Gallen, Switzerland, whose rabbi serves the Jews of Liechtenstein. (*See* SWITZERLAND *for address of St. Gallen synagogue*)

As recently as 1938, the Duchy of Liechtenstein had a reigning Jewish princess, whose portrait still decorates Liechtenstein stamps. She was Elsa Guttmann, of Vienna, sister of Barons Wilhelm and Max von Guttmann, coal kings of pre-World War I Austria.

In 1921 Baroness Guttmann was secretly married to Prince Francis Joseph I, heir to the throne of Liechtenstein. Although in his seventies when he succeeded to the throne in 1929, he insisted on remarrying the Princess in a public ceremony. After Austria was incorporated into Nazi Germany, Francis Joseph came under pressure to divorce his Jewish wife or give up his throne. He abdicated in 1938 in favor of his nephew, Francis Joseph II, the present ruler. Princess Elsa died in 1947.

LUXEMBOURG

A document dated 1276 contains the earliest reference to Jews living in the Territory that is now Luxembourg. The Holy Roman Emperor sought vainly to protect his Jewish subjects from being massacred in the cities of Luxembourg and Echternach during the Black Death in 1349. Luxembourg archives mention a Jews' Lane and a fortified tower known as the Jews' Gate in records of 1348, 1356, 1376, and 1477. Expelled from the whole area in 1370, the Jews were readmitted in 1443, when the duchy was united with Burgundy.

Subject to an annual tribute, Jews were permitted to live in what was then the German portion of the territory in the fifteenth and early sixteenth centuries until they were banished again in 1555 by the Spanish rulers of the duchy. A few privileged Jews were allowed, upon payment of a heavy tax, to trade at cattle fairs and to remain overnight within Luxembourg's borders during the seventeenth century. One of these was Isaac de Treybac, a Marrano, who is credited with having built the fortifications in the city of Luxembourg.

Equal rights were not won until after the French Revolution. The first permanent Jewish community was established in 1808, and a synagogue was opened in 1823. Following the Franco-Prussian War, many French Jews moved from Alsace-Lorraine to neutral Luxembourg. Immigrants from Russia and Poland between the two World Wars and refugees from Nazi Germany swelled the Jewish population to 3,500 in 1939. During the Nazi occupation the Jewish community was wiped out, but it has since been revived and now numbers 1,200. Most of the Jews live in the city of Luxembourg. There are small communities in Esch, Ettelbruck and Mondorf-les-Bains.

Luxembourg was the place where the Federal Republic of Germany in 1952 signed a pact with the Conference on Jewish Material Claims against Germany and the State of Israel for the payment of $715,000,000 in goods and machinery to Israel and $107,000,000 for the rebuilding of Jewish cultural and religious institutions destroyed by the Nazis in Europe.

Prince Charles, younger brother of Prince Jean, the reigning Grand Duke of Luxembourg, was married in 1967 to Joan Douglas Dillon, daughter of C. Douglas Dillon, a former U.S. Secretary of the Treasury and one-time American ambassador to France, whose paternal grandfather was a Polish Jew by the name of Sam Lapowski. Lapowski, who ran a clothing store in San Antonio, Texas in the 1860s, later adopted his French mother's maiden name. The Dillons of course have been Christians for two generations.

ESCH-SUR-ALZETTE

SYNAGOGUE, Rue du Canal, was opened in 1954. Built with funds provided by the Luxembourg government, it replaced a sanctuary dating from 1899 which the Nazis had destroyed. A number of important European Jewish industrialists and economists worship here, among them René Mayer, former Premier of France, who heads the High Authority of the European Coal and Steel Community, which has its headquarters here.

ETTELBRUCK

JEWISH CEMETERY has a monument memorializing the Luxembourg Jews deported to death camps during the Nazi occupation.

SYNAGOGUE was badly damaged by the Nazis but it has now been restored.

LUXEMBOURG CITY

GREAT SYNAGOGUE, 45 Rue Monterey, opposite Radio Luxembourg, Europe's most powerful long-wave radio station, is one of the most modern in Europe. It was erected in 1953 at a cost of more than $400,000 by the Luxembourg government. It replaced a Moorish-Byzantine structure built in 1894 and leveled by the Nazis in 1943. The Grand Duchess of Luxembourg attended the 150th-anniversary celebration of the emancipation of the Jews at services in this synagogue in 1959. The Consistoire Israélite de Luxembourg has its headquarters in the synagogue.

HEINESTRASSE is named for the beloved German-Jewish poet, Heinrich Heine. No. 4 is the residence of Dr. Henry Cerf, head of the Jewish community.

ISRAELI CONSULATE-GENERAL, 44 Avenue Guillaume.

RUE DES JUIFS (No. 30) is the site of Luxembourg's first synagogue, which was destroyed by a mob during the Black Death. The city's second synagogue was put to the torch by the Nazis.

Relics of that synagogue are preserved in the Judaica Section of the Alsace Museum.

UNITED STATES MILITARY CEMETERY AND MEMORIAL on the edge of the city, contains many graves marked with the Star of David among the tombstones of the 5,076 American dead who fell in the Battle of the Bulge and the advance to the Rhine in the winter of 1944-45.

WAR VICTIMS MEMORIAL in Belle Vue Jewish Cemetery, is a granite shaft memorializing the 2,000 Jews deported by the Nazis. On it is inscribed this verse, in Hebrew, from the Book of Lamentations: "Behold and see if there be any pain like unto my pain!"

MONDORF-LES-BAINS

SYNAGOGUE, Rue du Moulin, is a small, one-story, one-room structure which escaped destruction during the Nazi occupation. It stands on a sort of precipice, almost jutting into the air, beside the main road leading into the city. The synagogue is filled to capacity during the summer by guests from the city's kosher Hotel Bristol, 4 Avenue de Klein.

MALTA

The first Jews on Malta are believed to have been mariners from the Israelite seafaring tribes of Zebulon and Asher who accompanied the Phoenician traders when they colonized this Mediterranean island off the coast of Sicily about 1000 B.C.E. Five of the famous catacombs in which the Maltese took refuge during World War II, when the island was the target of more attacks by Nazi bombers than any other spot in Europe, have been identified as being of Jewish origin. In Roman times, many prisoners taken in the Jewish rebellions were exiled to Malta.

A Jewish community existed here under the Romans, the Byzantines, the Moslems, and the Normans until 1438, when the Sicilians segregated all Jews in a ghetto known as the *Giuerucca*. Expelled in 1493, they returned half a century later as slaves. When Malta became an outpost of Christendom from which the Knights of St. John waged maritime war on the Moslems, all Jews and Turks captured by the Knights were sent to Malta. Until the middle of the eighteenth century, the Maltese Jews were a community of slaves. In Venice and Amsterdam, Jewish charitable bodies raised funds to ransom them and engaged resident agents to look after their religious needs while they were in captivity.

The present Jewish community, numbering fewer than 60, was founded after 1800, when the island became a British possession, by free slaves and Jewish merchants from Italy and North Africa.

RABAT

HEBREW STONE outside the Roman Villa Museum, Museum Road, is an old Jewish tombstone whose Hebrew inscription has been partly defaced. All that can now be read are these words: "This is the tomb of the lady Rachel, spouse of Yeshu'a the ... May her soul be bound up in the bond of life." No date can be made out. Among the Museum's decorations is a mosaic depicting Delilah shearing the locks of Samson.

VALETTA

JEWISH CATACOMBS in the St. Agata Cemetery, near the Church of San Paolo, in the suburb of Citta Vecchia, have Menorahs engraved on the walls, reminders of the ancient Jewish settlement here. There is another catacomb with Jewish inscriptions near the Old Capital.

JEWISH COMMUNITY HEADQUARTERS, 3/4b MacIver Flats, in Sliema section.

JEWS SALLY PORTE is the name of a stretch of shore near the quay nearest to what was once the Malta Ghetto. You reach it just before St. Elmo Bay.

KIBUR EL LHUD (Burial Place of the Jews) is still the name of the site of a Jewish cemetery from the Middle Ages when the Moslems ruled Malta.

SLIEMA, the Maltese version of the Hebrew word "Shalom" is the name of a major suburb of Valetta where an Israeli company has erected a 12-story hotel.

SYNAGOGUE, 9 Spur St., houses some relics of the old Jewish community.

MONACO

The Jewish population of this ancient and independent principality on the southern coast of France numbers 600. Most of the Jews live in Monaco City and Monte Carlo. Some of them have communal and business ties with the Jewish communities of Nice and Cannes on the French Riviera. The Monaco Jewish community dates from the years after World War II.

From 1880 to 1902, Monaco had a reigning Jewish princess, the former Alice Heine, of New Orleans, a cousin of the German poet Heinrich Heine. In 1880 she became the second wife of Prince Albert I, great-grandfather of Prince Rainier (husband of Grace Kelly), who made her his consort. As Princess Alice she shared the throne of Monaco until Albert divorced her in 1902. Two yachts built by Albert for his oceanographic expeditions were named for Princess Alice. They recently appeared as illustrations on Monacan postage stamps. Another postage stamp, issued on the centennial of Monte Carlo, shows the portrait of Rene Blum, brother of the late Leon Blum, one-time premier of France, who was for many years director of the famous Ballet Russe of Monte Carlo.

During World War II, Monaco defied the Nazis and Vichy France by refusing to enact anti-Jewish laws and by permitting Jewish refugees from Italy, France, and Austria to remain in the principality.

MONTE CARLO

SYNAGOGUE, 14 Quay Antoine, 1er, is located in an apartment house called La Ruscino. The community maintains a rabbi and a Hebrew school.

NETHERLANDS

The Jewish connection with the Netherlands can be traced to the thirteenth century, when Jews from Germany settled in the northern provinces and exiles from England and France found a haven in the south. Periodic expulsions and persecutions in the thirteenth and fourteenth centuries prevented the establishment of a permanent Jewish community for two hundred years. But even before the Inquisition reached into the Low Countries in the first half of the sixteenth century, there were secret Jews in many cities of the Netherlands.

The Inquisition in Spain and Portugal substantially increased the Jewish population in Holland when Marranos began trickling into the country. Expelled later, in 1550, by Emperor Charles V, they were welcomed back in 1579 by the newly created Union of Utrecht, which drove out the Spaniards and for the first time anywhere in Europe established a climate of religious tolerance.

A tiny group of practicing Jews founded a permanent settlement in Emden about 1580. Later arrivals from Portugal also came to Emden and then moved on to Amsterdam, where in 1597 they opened Holland's earliest synagogue in the home of Samuel Pallache, the Sultan of Morocco's consul. By 1610 there were also Jewish residents in The Hague, Rotterdam, Haarlem, Amersfoort and Alkmaar, and in a number of towns in the provinces of Friesland and Groningen.

The growing Jewish population impelled the parliament in 1619 to ask Hugo Grotius, the eminent legal scholar, to draft rules governing the treatment of the Jews. This document, extraordinarily liberal for its time, lifted all degrading medieval restrictions on the Jews and accorded each city the right to accept or exclude Jews from its borders. Only Utrecht and Maastricht barred them. In 1657 the Jews were declared subjects of the State.

Enjoying freedom of movement as well as of religious practice, and encouraged to engage in trade and commerce, the Jews from Spain and Portugal employed their valuable economic connections and their substantial wealth in the interest of their new homeland. They introduced the diamond, tobacco, and silk industries, opened sugar refineries, and played a key role in developing Holland's overseas commerce. They helped oust the Portuguese from the East and West Indies, had a hand in organizing the Dutch East and Dutch West India companies, and did much to promote trade with the New World, Genoa, Leghorn, and the Near East. Welcomed in the Dutch colonies in Brazil and the West Indies, the Jews had a big hand in developing Surinam and Curaçao and the Dutch settlements in Brazil. From among these Dutch Jews came the first Jewish settlers in the New World and the founders of the re-established Jewish community in England.

Success in commerce and industry was paralleled by impressive accomplishments in literature, philosophy, and the arts. Noted rabbis, scholars, poets, and scientists helped usher in a golden age in the seventeeth century, when Amsterdam became known as the New Jerusalem. After Manasseh ben Israel set up Holland's first Hebrew printing press in 1636, Amsterdam became a leading center of Hebrew book publishing. In 1678 the *Gazeta de Amsterdam,* the world's very first Jewish-owned periodical, appeared.

The community was greatly enlarged after 1630 by the arrival of large numbers of

Ashkenazic Jews from Germany, Poland, and Lithuania. Within one generation they outnumbered the Portuguese Sephardim. It was Manasseh ben Israel, renowned scholar and chief rabbi of the Sephardic community, who in 1655 set the stage for the readmission of the Jews to England when he submitted his famous petition to Oliver Cromwell and then went to London with a delegation of Amsterdam Jews to intercede with the Lord Protector (*see* GREAT BRITAIN).

For a time the Sephardic and Ashkenazic communities in Amsterdam developed separately. The former created three congregations, starting in 1608, which were merged in 1639 as a prelude to the erection in 1675 of the historic Portuguese Synagogue. Now a national monument, it is the last remnant of the Portuguese community. The Ashkenazim founded their first congregation in 1635. When the Thirty Years' War and the Chmielnicki pogroms in Poland gave impetus to further immigration from Germany and Eastern Europe, the first large Ashkenazic house of worship, the Great Synagogue–the so-called "Hoog Duitsch"–was built in 1671. The second "Hoog Duitsch," was erected in 1677. This was succeeded by the third "Hoog Duitsch," the Third Synagogue, a few years later and was supplemented in 1730 by the New Synagogue, adjacent to the "Hoog."

In the environs of these synagogues Rembrandt lived and worked for seventeen years, steeping himself in Jewish law and lore, befriending Jewish beggars and refugees, and finding many of his models among the Jewish savants, from whom he gained an insight into the cabala. It was the elders of the oldest congregation, the Portuguese Synagogue, who twice excommunicated eminent Jewish philosophers charged with heretical views: Uriel da Costa in 1623 and Baruch Benedict Spinoza in 1656.

By the middle of the eighteenth century, Amsterdam had the largest Jewish community in Western Europe. It expanded even more after 1795, when, under the rule of Napoleon, the Jews were granted complete civil equality and Holland became the first country in Europe to elect Jews to its parliament. Further growth ensued when the Netherlands, once more independent, made Jews equal citizens and accorded Judaism parity with all other faiths in 1815. While the community grew and prospered, however, it declined as a center of Jewish learning, owing to the rise of other major Jewish communities in Eastern and Central Europe.

In the nineteenth and twentieth centuries, Netherlands Jewish statesmen, scientists, artists, dramatists, professors, and labor leaders gained international recognition, while the Dutch economy was materially enlarged by the pioneering enterprises of Jewish industrialists. At the same time there was a large Jewish proletariat of dock workers, peddlers, diamond cutters and clothing workers. Until 1940, the General Diamond Workers' Trade Union was predominantly Jewish in membership.

On May 10, 1940, when the Nazis invaded the Low Countries, there were 140,000 Dutch Jews in Holland, half of them in Amsterdam, plus several thousand refugees from Germany. At first the fierce resistance of the Dutch balked the Nazis in their attempt to exterminate the Jews. The daring revolt and general strike of February 1941 in Amsterdam was a valiant but futile protest against the deportation of Jews. Christians risked their lives daily to hide Jews, and when the Nazis forced the Jews to wear a yellow Star of David many gentiles followed suit. Ultimately, 110,000 Jews were deported to the death camps from the Westerbork concentration camp. Only 6,000 Dutch Jews survived. Today there are 30,000 in The Netherlands; nearly half of them live in Amsterdam. Because of their deep roots in the country's economic, social, cultural and political life, they have made an astonishing recovery. Jews again live in nearly 60 different towns and cities, although in recent years more than a dozen old Jewish communities have been dissolved because they lacked enough Jews to maintain a synagogue.

Dr. Ivo Samkalden, who twice served as minister of justice, was elected mayor of Amsterdam in 1967. Dr. Nico Pollak, descendant of an old Jewish family, was a member of The Netherlands Supreme Court in 1970. In 1965, when Princess Margriet, third daughter of Queen Juliana and Prince Bernhard, married Pieter Van Vollenhoven, no one raised any complaint at a story in the publication of the Royal Netherlands Genealogical Society to the effect that the royal son-in-law had maternal and paternal Jewish ancestors.

ALMELO

SYNAGOGUE AND COMMUNAL CENTER, 20 Molenkampspark.

AMERSFOORT

SYNAGOGUE AND COMMUNAL CENTER, 2 Drieringensteeg.

SINAI HOSPITAL, opened in 1960 by Queen Juliana when she presented a silver Menorah to the institution, was the first Jewish mental hospital built in Europe after World War II. It replaced the Appeldoorn Bos, destroyed by the Nazis after they deported its 1,150 patients and doctors. The new hospital was erected by the Dutch Jewish Mental Health Association, with the aid of a grant from the Conference on Jewish Material Claims against Germany.

TOWN HALL, a three-story eighteenth-century mansion, was the ancestral home of the family of Sir Bernard Waley-Cohen, Lord Mayor of London in 1961. The house was originally built by Ezekiel Cohen, who founded the local synagogue in 1727. In the building are portraits of Ezekiel's son, Benjamin, and his daughter-in-law, whose descendants played an important role in Dutch history.

AMSTERDAM

AMSTERDAM BIBLE MUSEUM, 137 Stadthouderskade, displays many Biblical antiquities from Palestine, Egypt, and Mesopotamia, as well as a model of the Temple in Jerusalem.

AMSTERDAM MUNICIPAL ARCHIVES, 67 Amsteldijk, preserves many historic Jewish documents, including the archives of the Portuguese Synagogue, whose leaders turned them over to the municipality for safekeeping during the Nazi occupation. In these archives are the original petitions from the Jews of New Amsterdam in 1656 to the Dutch West India Company in Amsterdam protesting Governor Peter Stuyvesant's action in refusing to grant them civil and economic liberties.

AMSTERDAM MUNICIPAL MUSEUM, Paulus Potterstraat, exhibits a number of the more important paintings of Josef Israels, who is considered the most important figure in Dutch art since the seventeenth century. Some of his best works are on Jewish themes. Also on display here are works by Isaac Israels, his son, as well as a large collection of etchings and lithographs by Marc Chagall, including his famous Bible illustrations.

ASHKENAZI COMMUNITY CENTER, 13 de Lairessestraat.

ASHKENAZI GREAT AND NEW SYNAGOGUES (*see* p. 229) stand empty and unused on Jonas Daniel Meyerplein (square), in the heart of what used to be the old Jewish quarter. Damaged beyond repair by the Nazis, the historic sanctuaries were further wrecked during the last winter of the war when hungry and freezing Dutchmen, seeking firewood, tore apart many old buildings. What was once the

Jewish quarter, embracing the area covering Jodenbreestraat, St. Antonilebreestraat, Muiderstraat, Weesperstraat, and Rapenburgerstraat is gradually being rebuilt and modernized by the municipality. The Portuguese Synagogue (*see below*) remains. The fate of the two Ashkenazic synagogues remains in doubt; the municipality, which has acquired the property, is thinking of converting them into museums. Most of the Jewish peddlers and traders who once filled the stalls in the famed Waterlooplein Market are gone. A few fading shop signs indicate they once belonged to Jews.

ASHKENAZIC SYNAGOGUES (modern), at 61 Lekstraat; on Jacob Obrechtplein; at 238 Gerard Dousstraat; at 70 Swammerdamstraat; 26 G.v.d. Veenstraat; and 149 Nieuwe Kerkstraat.

BEGIJNOF, an ancient grouping of 16th century alms houses, within view of the Kalverstraat, one of the city's busiest shopping centers, has imbedded in a blind wall a gable stone depicting Abraham about to slay Isaac as the angel of mercy appears.

BLESSTRAAT, near the Josef Israelskade (quay), is named for David Josef Bles, nineteenth-century painter, etcher, and lithographer, who specialized in scenes of domestic life.

DE DOOFPOT on Rembrandtsplein, corner of Utrechtschestraat, is a popular Jewish cabaret. Another is the *Li-Lalo,* on De Clercqstraat, corner of Agatha Dekenstraat, in Amsterdam-west. Jews also frequent *Le Grand Café* on Leidscheplein, *L'Extase, Les Trois Mousquetaires,* and the *Kuil.*

M. S. VAS DIAS BRIDGE, a new drawbridge on Weeperstraat, memorializes the founder of the first Dutch news agency. Nearby is a sculptured representation symbolizing communication channels, news gathering and news distribution.

THE DOCK WORKER, the statue commemorating the general strike of dock workers in protest against the deportation of Jews, stands on Jonas Daniel Meyerplein between the hulk of the Great Ashkenazi Synagogue and the Portuguese Synagogue. Erected in 1952, the monument portrays a heavyset, determined stevedore, typical of those who defied the Nazis on February 25 and 26, 1941, by walking off their jobs to demonstrate against the roundup of 435 young Jews from the old Jewish quarter. Later, transport workers and others joined the strike. For this heroic act of resistance former Queen Wilhelmina added the words "Heroic–Resolute–Merciful" to the Amsterdam municipality's coat of arms. The strike is commemorated annually with excercises at the foot of the statue, which is the work of Mari Andriessen.

DUNNER BRIDGE, one of three new bridges on the rebuilt Weeperstraat, once one of the main streets in the Jewish quarter, but now a trunk highway, memorializes rabbis who died in Auschwitz concentration camp. The bridges are named for Dr. J. H. Dunner, one-time chief rabbi of Amsterdam, Meir de Hond and Lodewyk H. Sarlouis, a former chief rabbi of the Netherlands.

FAN CABINET, 1083 Prinsengracht, is a unique exhibit of several hundred fans collected by Felix Tal, kinsman of a former chief rabbi.

ANNE FRANK HOUSE, 263 Prinsengracht, where from July 1942 to August 1944 Anne Frank and her family hid from the Nazis, and where she wrote her famous diary, is now a museum. The two adjoining houses have been converted into the International Youth Center of the Anne Frank Foundation. The restored Frank house and the youth center are maintained from royalties from the play and the book based on the diary and were built with contributions from many countries, including Germany. Thousands of people visit the house annually, among them many Germans. It faces a canal on the edge of the old Jewish quarter. Here are the original bookcase that hid the secret staircase to the attic in the converted warehouse where the Franks found refuge, the bulletin board on which Anne posted clipped photos of movie stars, cooking utensils used by the Franks, and the original diary which has made Anne Frank the symbol of all the millions of Jews done to death by the Nazis.

The diary was found on the floor amid a pile of old books, magazines, and newspapers when Otto Frank, Anne's father, returned to Amsterdam after the liberation. He alone of the family survived.

ANNE FRANK SCHOOL, 41 Nierstraat, was renamed for the famous martyr. This is the elementary school she attended before the Nazis occupied the city.

GEUZENVELD, one of the city's many "garden towns," or modern housing developments, has streets named for Teixeira de Mattos, nineteenth-century graphic artist, and Mendes da Costa, nineteenth-century sculptor.

HEIJERMANSWEG, near the Apollohal, is named for Herman Heijermans, who is regarded as Holland's greatest dramatist. His plays in the latter half of the nineteenth century gave Dutch drama international status. In addition to twenty-three major dramas, he wrote eighteen novels and twenty volumes of short stories. A bust of the playwright stands in a public park.

HEIMANSDIORAMA, 53 Plantage Middenlaan, part of the Zoological Museum of Amsterdam, is a memorial to Eli Heimans, beloved teacher, naturalist, and author of standard books for children on birds, flowers, and animals. *Heimansweg*, a street in the northern part of the city, also is named for him.

HOLLANDSCHE SCHOUWBURG on Plantage Middenlaan, a former theatre which was used during the Nazi occupation as an assembly center for Jews destined for the death camps, has been converted into a Jewish memorial by the municipal authorities. Most of the original building was torn down but the jagged stone walls of the former stage were left intact. In front of the walls a grass-covered rectangle is the site of a stark stone monument on whose base is a Star of David and inscriptions in Dutch and Hebrew which reads: "In memory of those who were deported from here. 1940-1945." A small chapel at the right of the memorial entrance has an eternal light with a carved Hebrew message. Three symbolic tombstones of different sizes, representing Man, Woman and Child, are topped by grey stone representing war.

ISRAELI CONSULATE, 26 Johan Vermeerstraat.

JOSEF ISRAELSKADE, one of the city's quays, is named for the distinguished nineteenth-century painter and etcher (*see* Amsterdam Municipal Museum), whose work revived the Dutch art tradition created by Rembrandt. This quay is mentioned in *The Diary of Anne Frank*, which notes: "We are allowed on the ferry and that is about all. There is a little boat from the Josef Israelskade, the man there took us at once when we asked him."

JEWISH HISTORICAL MUSEUM occupies two floors of the Amsterdam Historical Museum in De Waag (old weighing house), on the Nieuwemarkt, close to the old Jewish quarter. It has a unique collection of ritual and religious objects, paintings by Jewish artists, and valuable manuscripts, including a handwritten thirteenth-century prayer book, assembled over the centuries from many parts of Europe. Many of the mementos of the history of the Netherlands' Jewish communities were carried off to Germany after 1940, when the Nazis closed and plundered the museum. After the war it took ten years to reassemble these treasures.

A new department is devoted to a photographic record of the Nazi reign of terror as it affected the Jews of Holland. There are photographs and facsimiles of some of the anti-Jewish decrees, various letters of protest against these measures—such as the one signed by all the Dutch churches against the sterilization of Jewish partners of mixed marriages—and specimens of the underground press of the occupation era.

JEWISH PRODUCE DEALERS' MEMORIAL, in the central market place, Jan van Galenstraat, honors the Jewish fruit and vegetable dealers who perished under the Nazi occupation. It depicts a group of people behind barbed wire, with the inscription "Remember the grief, but do not stand silent."

KOSHER RESTAURANTS, Sal Meyer, 13 Nieuwmarkt; Elburg's, 14 J. W. Brouwerplein, near KLM terminal; I. Mouwes (sandwiches), 73 Utrechschestraat.

LIBERAL SYNAGOGUE, 8 Graafschapstraat, is a new building opened in the late 1960s. The recreation hall is named for Anne Frank.

MARTYRS' MEMORIAL at the Weesperplein, erected by the Jews of Amsterdam, in gratitude to those who helped them during the Nazi occupation, honors the Jews who died in concentration camps.The monument is a high marble wall topped by a Star of David. Set into the wall are five bas-reliefs depicting Pity, Suffering, Gratitude, Hope, and Fortitude. The inscriptions are all in Dutch.

JONAS DANIEL MEYERPLEIN the principal square in the old Jewish quarter, is named for one of Holland's most distinguished jurists. The first Dutch Jew admitted to the bar, Jonas Meyer was only twenty when King Louis Napoleon appointed him editor of the royal *Gazeta*. In 1815 he became chairman of the commission that drafted the constitution for the new kingdom of the United Netherlands, which then included Belgium. Meyer also served as head of the council of Dutch Jewish communities.

MIRANDABAD, a municipal swimming pool on the Rivierenlaan, honors Samuel Rodriguez de Miranda, who championed a variety of municipal improvements while serving on the city council from 1919 to 1939.

MONTEFIORE PARK, a short street that dead-ends at the Plantage Muidergracht, opposite the Physical Laboratory of the University of Amsterdam, is named after the famous English philanthropist Sir Moses Montefiore (*see* GREAT BRITAIN).

ORNSTEINSTRAAT, in the eastern section of the city known as Watergraafsmeer, near the Nieuwe Oosterbegraafplaats (New Eastern Cemetery), is named for Dr. Leonard Salomon Ornstein, a distinguished physicist and president of Groningen University, where he taught for thirty-two years. President of the Dutch Zionist Federation and a prime mover in the creation of the Institute of Physics at the Hebrew University in Jerusalem, Ornstein died during the Nazi occupation and his funeral was turned into an anti-Nazi demonstration.

ORT SCHOOL FOR JEWISH GIRLS, Jonas Daniel Meyerplein.

OSDORP, one of Amsterdam's garden towns, has a street called *Osstraat*, named for S. F. van Oss, renowned journalist. This neighborhood also has the *Bamberghof*, named for Eduard and David Bamberg, Jewish musical comedy stars; *Colnot en Poonshof*, named for two theatrical impresarios; and the *Boas en Judelshof*, named for two Jewish actors.

HENRI POLAKLAAN, street in the section known as the Plantage, memorializes Henri Polak, founder of the General Diamond Workers' Trade Union and of the Dutch Labor Party. A trained diamond cutter, he was one of Holland's earliest labor leaders, having organized the Jewish diamond cutters after a strike against Jewish diamond dealers. Polak, who served in the Dutch parliament, was one of the Jews who died in a Nazi concentration camp.

PORTUGUESE SYNAGOGUE, 197 Rapenburgerstraat, at the far end of Jodenbreestraat, facing the gutted remains of the old Ashkenazic synagogues on Jonas Daniel Meyerplein, is the most important relic of the old Jewish quarter. The tall, imposing building, which can seat two thousand people, dates from 1675 and historically is one of the most famous synagogues in the world. It escaped destruction during the Nazi occupation when the Dutch authorities proclaimed it a national monument. Its monumental Ark and its *bimah* of Brazilian rosewood, its twelve mammoth columns, its sandstrewn floor, and its 613 tapers, one for each of the Mosaic Commandments (there is no electricity in the sanctuary), have inspired artists and writers for generations.

This was the congregation whose elders excommunicated Baruch Spinoza for his unorthodox views, which were believed to threaten the whole Jewish community. The writ of excommunication is still in the synagogue archives. The rite of excommunication was not carried out in this synagogue, however, despite a legend to the contrary; the ban was imposed twenty-one years before the synagogue was consecrated. Spinoza's *Defense* against the writ of excommunication is a book which exerted a profound influence on European thought for two hundred years. In 1954 David Ben-Gurion, Prime Minister of Israel, who was then in temporary retirement, wrote an article in which he proposed that the excommunication be revoked. This suggestion was rejected by the Portuguese Synagogue in Amsterdam, and concurred in by its rabbi.

Adjoining the synagogue, in the *Sephardic Community Center*, is the *Ets Haim Library*, which dates from 1620. It was named for a seventeenth-century rabbinical school where Spinoza studied. Now maintained by the Sephardic community, the library contains much valuable manuscript material. In this library in 1650 Manasseh ben Israel wrote his famous tract, *Hope of Israel*, which played a decisive role in enabling the Jews to resettle in England. Ben Israel was the rabbi of the Portuguese Synagogue.

REMBRANDT HOUSE, 4-6 Jodenbreestraat, was the home of the immortal painter, who was a friend of the seventeenth-century Dutch Jews and lived in the Jewish quarter. It was the Jewish painter Josef Israels (himself known as the nineteenth-century Rembrandt) who saved the Rembrandt house from destruction. It was falling into ruins early in the twentieth century and was about to be torn down, when Israels mobilized public opinion and saved the house, which has since become a national shrine.

Among the original etchings and reproductions of Rembrandt paintings on exhibit in the house are a few of Jews, including one of Manasseh ben Israel. Of Rembrandt's two hundred oil portraits of men, thirty-seven are of Jews, including Rabbi Saul Levi Morteira, Spinoza's first teacher. Many of Rembrandt's models were Jews from seventeenth-century Amsterdam. He was the first master to portray Jews as people endowed with human dignity.

RESISTANCE FIGHTERS MEMORIAL, 95 Appollalaan, near the new Hilton Hotel, honors three young Dutch Jews shot during a Gestapo roundup. Nearby is a plaque memorializing Gerhard Badrian, a Jewish hero of the Dutch resistance.

RIJKSMUSEUM (National Gallery), on the Stadhouderskade, corner of the Hobbemakade, one of the world's great art galleries, has nineteen of Rembrandt's oil paintings, including two of his most celebrated Jewish works–the portrait of Dr. Ephraim Bueno (1599-1665), Jewish doctor and literary man, and "The Jewish Bride." There are also two of Rembrandt's Biblical paintings on view. Also exhibited here are ten oils by Josef Israels and his son, Isaac; Josef Israels' water color "The Rabbi"; Emanuel de Witte's oil "Interior of the Portuguese Synagogue at Amsterdam"; and a large collection of Biblical paintings by many of the seventeenth-century Dutch masters.

BIBLIOTHECA ROSENTHALIANA, 421 Singel, one of the world's largest libraries of Judaica, is housed in the library of the University of Amsterdam. The Rosenthaliana owes its origin and name to Leeser Rosenthal, a nineteenth-century Polish teacher and rabbi who undertook to assemble a library that would include everything written by Jews on the Bible, on Hebrew philology, and on Jewish theology. The library was presented by Rosenthal's children to the Amsterdam municipality in 1880 on condition that it be kept intact under the name Bibliotheca Rosenthaliana. The original collection numbered 5,200 volumes. Today it totals 60,000 and covers every phase of Jewish history, philosophy, religion, belles-lettres, music, art, and rabbinics.

SARPHATIPARK in the Plantage Middenlaan, is named for the nineteenth-century physician and civic reformer Dr. Samuel Sarphati, who was a pioneer advocate of modern sanitation methods, commercial education, and a palace of arts and sciences. His statue stands in the park. There is also a *Sarphatistraat* nearby.

SLOTERMEER, a garden town, has many streets named for Jewish resistance fighters who were executed by the Nazis: *David Vosstraat, Hans Katanhof, Joop Eijlstraat, Leo Frijdahof, Robert Cijferstraat, Jaap Nunes Vaszstraat, Maurits Kannstraat, Jacob Melkmanstraat, Sieg Vaz Diasstraat,* and *Badrianhof.*

In this same neighborhood are *Marianne Philipsstraat, Jacob Israel de Haanstraat, Carry van Bruggen de Haanstraat, Israel Queridiostraat,* and *Eduard Vetermanstraat,* all named for distinguished Jewish figures in Dutch literature. Nearby is *Tobias M. C. Asserstraat,* named for the eminent jurist who won the Nobel Peace Prize in 1911.

SLOTERVAART, garden town, has streets named for two of Holland's best-known women, both of whom were Jewish: Aletta Jacobs and Esther de Boer van Rijk. Dr. Jacobs, the first woman physician in the Netherlands, was a pioneer feminist and birth control advocate, who as early as 1882 sought to win women the vote in her country. In 1915 she convened the Hague Congress of Women, out of which grew the Women's International League for Peace and Freedom. Esther de Boer van Rijk was for years the queen of the Dutch stage. Her role as Kniertje, the old seaman's wife in Herman Heijermans' *Good Hope,* made her world-famous. Her portrait hangs in the lobby of the Municipal Theatre of Amsterdam.

SPINOZA'S BIRTHPLACE, 41 Waterlooplein, where the great philosopher was born in 1632, has been torn down. On the site is a gasoline station. Spinoza lived here until his excommunication on July 27, 1656 (*See* Portuguese Synagogue above).

SPINOZA CLINIC, on Spinozastraat, is a major ophthalmology hospital named for the philosopher because he earned his living for a time as a lens grinder.

SPINOZALYCEUM, on Peter van Anrooystraat, is one of the city's modern schools.

JOHAN VERMEERSTRAAT, Nos. 18-26, in a more modern section of the city, is the official headquarters of the Amsterdam Jewish community. In four adjoining buildings are the offices of the Jewish Social Welfare Bureau and of various Zionist organizations and cultural societies. The Israeli Consulate is next door.

VISSER SQUARE, in front of the new Town Hall, is named for the late Dr. L. E. Visser, Zionist leader and president of The Netherlands Supreme Court in 1940 when the Nazis deposed him.

WILHELM WEINBERG HOUSE, 51 Oranje-Nassaulaan, was bequeathed by the late banker and art collector to the Amsterdam municipality as a memorial to his wife and two sons, who died in Nazi gas chambers. It is now the home of the School of Education of the University of Amsterdam.

A. C. WERTHEIMPARK in the Plantage Middenlaan, is named for a nineteenth-century Jewish banker and philanthropist. The fountain in the park was erected in his memory.

APELDOORN

SYNAGOGUE, 76 Zutphensestraat, erected here in 1960 to replace one that was destroyed by the Nazis, seats eighty people. It is close to the royal palace, Het Loo.

ARNHEM

JEWISH COMMUNAL CENTER AND SYNAGOGUE, 17a Pastoorstraat.

BREDA

SYNAGOGUE, 77 Franklin D. Rooseveltlaan.

BUSSUM

JEWISH YOUTH CENTER, 1a Kromme Englaan.

DELFT

NATHAN STRAUS HUIS, 9 Koornmarkt, a housing and recreation center for Jewish students at Delft Technological University, was established in 1957 by Nathan Straus, New York philanthropist, as a student residence in appreciation of the aid given by the Dutch people to Jews during World War II.

DEVENTER

SYNAGOGUE AND COMMUNAL CENTER, 19 Lange Bisschopstraat.

EINDHOVEN

SYNAGOGUE AND JEWISH COMMUNAL CENTER, 23 H. Casimirstraat.

PHILIPS KONZERN, the great industrial complex manufacturing electric products of all kinds, was founded by the grandson of a rabbi. The internationally known Unilever Company, which first industrialized the manufacture of margarine, was created by the Van den Berghs. The Hartogs pioneered the manufacture of silk, and Van Leer is famous for its barrels and kegs.

ENSCHEDE

JEWISH COMMUNAL CENTER AND SYNAGOGUE, 16 Prinsenstraat.

GROET

OLDEST JEWISH CEMETERY in the Netherlands was established here in 1602 by the Jewish settlers at Haarlem.

GRONINGEN

JEWISH COMMUNAL CENTER AND SYNAGOGUE, 16 Folkingedwarsstraat.

HAARLEM

JEWISH COMMUNAL CENTER AND SYNAGOGUE, 7 Kenaupark.

THE HAGUE

TOBIAS ASSER STATUE, at the top of the main staircase of the Peace Palace, Carnegieplein, where the International Court of Justice sits, recalls a now forgotten Dutch statesman and international jurist, who in 1911 shared the Nobel Peace Prize with another Jew, Alfred H. Fried of Austria. Asser, who taught international law at the University of Amsterdam from 1862 to 1893, was one of the first judges appointed to the Permanent Court of Arbitration when it was established at The Hague in 1899. (This court, the predecessor of the International Court, was a direct outgrowth of the Hague Peace Conference convened in 1899 at the call of Czar Nicholas II of Russia, who was influenced by the works of the Russian Jew Ivan S. Bloch, an economic adviser to the Czarist government.) There is also an avenue here named *Tobias Asserlaan*.

ISRAELI EMBASSY, 12 Klatteweg.

JOSEF ISRAELSLAAN is an avenue named for the celebrated painter (*see* AMSTERDAM *above*).

JEWISH CEMETERY on the Scheveningseweg, was opened at the end of the seventeenth century.

JEWISH YOUTH CENTER, 13 Nieuwe Molstraat.

KOSHER RESTAURANT (*see* SCHEVENINGEN *below*).

LIBERAL SYNAGOGUE, 12 Stadthourdenlaan.

MADURODAM, a typically Dutch town scaled down to one-twentieth normal size, which is one of the city's most popular tourist attractions, is named for Capt. George Maduro, member of an old Dutch-Jewish family, who was one of Holland's World War II military heroes. He died in a concentration camp and in his memory his family created the miniature town, whose six hundred homes, shops, offices, taverns and churches, complete to the last letterbox, are scale model size. Crown Princess Beatrice is the honorary mayor of the town. All revenue from admission charges is contributed to the Netherlands Students Sanitarium to aid tuberculosis victims. A model of the historic Portuguese synagogue in Amsterdam is among the displays in Madurodam.

THE MAURITSHUIS on the Hofvijver, a museum of classical Dutch art, exhibits Rembrandt's famous painting "Susannah and the Elders."

MUNICIPAL MUSEUM, 41 Stadhouderslaan, displays in the main hall on the first floor a "Portrait of Spinoza" by an unknown master. On the same floor is Van Hove's painting "Interior of a Synagogue."

SPINOZA HOUSE, 72-74 Paviljoensgracht, is the house where Baruch Spinoza lived his last seven years (1670-77), earning his living as a lens grinder. Erected in 1646 in the oldest quarter of the city, the house is now a national shrine and contains a small Spinoza Museum.

SPINOZA MONUMENT, a few steps from the Spinoza House on the Paviljoensgracht, was erected by a committee of Spinoza admirers. Identified only by the name "Spinoza," the statue shows the philosopher as a young student sitting pensively with eyes lowered. During the Nazi occupation, the Dutch stubbornly defied orders to raze the statue. Saw marks can still be seen where a Nazi tried to decapitate the statue.

SPINOZA TOMB in the churchyard of the Nieuwe Kirk (New Church) on Spuistraat, main thoroughfare of the old part of the city. Spinoza was buried in this Christian cemetery in 1677 because his excommunication barred him from interment in a Jewish cemetery. His tomb is inscribed: "Benedictus Spinoza—1632-1677." The headstone placed there in 1927 on the 250th anniversary of his death is now behind a monument erected in 1956.

This memorial consists of a low brick wall cut in half by a sandstone block about five feet high. Atop the block is a carving of Spinoza's head under which is inscribed the word *Caute* ("prudently") over the philosopher's signet ring. At the bottom of the block there is a black basalt stone from Israel on which is inscribed the Hebrew word *Amcha* ("your people").

Actually, no one knows where Spinoza's bones lie. The memorial is at the site of his grave but his remains are no longer in the grave. A century after Spinoza's death, the church authorities disinterred the bones of the poor and reburied them in a common grave elsewhere; this is done at hundred-year intervals to make room in the small churchyard for the newly deceased. In 1956, on the tercentenary of Spinoza's excommunication, the Israel Spinoza Society sent a block of Galilee black basalt to be placed on his grave. The stone bears the Hebrew word "amcha".

SYNAGOGUE, 103 Wagenstraat, consecrated in 1726 by Sephardic Jews, has been marked as a protected monument. It is no longer used as a house of worship because the number of Sephardic Jews has dwindled to a handful. The building now belongs to a real estate company but it cannot be demolished and may be used only for public purposes. The religious appurtenances, including the Ark, have been sent to Israel.

HERTOGENBOSCH

SYNAGOGUE, 8 Prinz Bernardstraat.

HILVERSIUM

SYNAGOGUE AND COMMUNAL CENTER, Laanstraat.

LEEUWARDEN

JEWISH COMMUNAL CENTRE, 19 Sacramentstraat. The beautiful old synagogue in this north Holland city, which was erected in 1805 by a community that goes back to 1645, has been dismantled and all its ritual objects, including the Ark, Torah Scrolls and interior and moved to the Children's Village of Kfar Batya at Raanana, in Israel. Copies of the Scrolls are in the archives of the city whose citizens protected the originals during the Nazi occupation.

LEIDEN

SYNAGOGUE, 8 Levendaal. Its Torah Scrolls were saved from the Nazis by being hidden in the Leiden Town Hall.

MAASTRICHT

SYNAGOGUE, 2 Capucijnergang, is now a protected historical monument. Erected in 1842 by a community that traced its history in Holland back to the early 17th century, the synagogue was almost entirely destroyed by the Nazis. After the war it was restored with government funds. The interior contains the appurtenances removed from the synagogue in the neighboring village of Meerssen where there are no longer any Jews.

MIDDELBURG

JEWISH COMMUNAL CENTER, 24 Nyverheidsweg.

NIJMEGEN

SYNAGOGUE AND COMMUNAL CENTER, 25 Gerard Nootstraat.

OSS

RABBI JACOB GOLDSMIDSTRAAT is named for the last rabbi of Oss; he was deported by the Nazis in 1943.

SYNAGOGUE AND JEWISH COMMUNAL CENTER, 12 Oude Kerkstraat, near the edge of this town twenty-two miles from the German border, was opened in 1959 to replace one built in 1831 and torn down by the Nazis. Seating only sixty-five people, the synagogue was paid for through contributions by the Dutch government, private subscriptions, and a grant from the Conference on Jewish Material Claims against Germany. The synagogue is in an area where the municipality is creating a civic center. Among those present at the dedication was Sidney van den Bergh, former Dutch Minister of Defense, who was president of the Jewish community when the old synagogue was erected. Jews have lived here for more than three hundred years.

OUDERKERK

PORTUGUESE JEWISH CEMETERY, one of the oldest landmarks of Dutch

Jewry, is located in this picturesque village five miles south of Amsterdam along the Amstel River. Buried here are members of Spinoza's family as well as many eminent scholars and rabbis. The oldest tombstone, dated 1616, is over the grave of Samuel Pallache in whose Amsterdam house a synagogue was opened in 1597. The cemetery was established in 1614. Also buried here is Abigail da Penha, the model of Rembrandt's famous painting "The Jewish Bride." Some of the tombstones have fine carvings depicting Biblical scenes.

The best-known tombstone here is that of Manasseh ben Israel, poet, historian, scholar and rabbi, who had much to do with persuading Oliver Cromwell to readmit the Jews to England. Of Portuguese origin, Israel had become widely known among European scholars and even royalty because of his writings and Hebrew printing press. In 1650 he wrote a small book called *Hope of Israel*, published in Spanish. Dedicated to the British Parliament, the book sought to trace the remnants of the Ten Tribes of Israel and pleaded that the time had come for the restoration of the Jews in Palestine. Actually, the book was a thinly-veiled plea for their readmission to England, which reached Cromwell through an English translation. Israel's tombstone, resting on a row of weather-beaten bricks, is inscribed in Hebrew and Portuguese. The epitaph reads: "He is not dead, for in heaven he lives in supreme glory, while on earth his pen won him immortal remembrance." The grave was restored in 1960 by a committee of British Jews headed by Dr. M. Godfrey of London. New tablets recording this restoration and the name of Israel in English and Hebrew were affixed to the tomb. Israel died in 1657. Interred in the oldest part of the cemetery are an estimated 18,500 Sephardic Jews. The unique and elaborately carved tombstones are rare examples of sepulchral art reflecting a wide variety of Biblical allegory and baroque ornamentation.

RIJNSBURG

SPINOZA HOUSE, 2 Spinozalaan, is the residence where the philosopher spent his three most creative years (1660-63) during which he wrote *On the Improvement of the Understanding* and *Theologico-Political Treatise*. The Spinoza Society of The Hague, which owns the seventeenth-century house, has lovingly re-created Spinoza's library, including some Hebrew books, and assembled some of his personal belongings, including the tools he used as a lens grinder. There is also a large collection of literature on Spinoza. In the garden is a bust of Spinoza. Annually, the Spinoza Society meets in the Rijnsburg town hall for a Spinoza lecture and a pilgrimage to the house.

ROTTERDAM

KOSHER RESTAURANT (F. Weyl-Kuyt), 96a Walenburgerweg.
PROGRESSIVE SYNAGOGUE, 21 G. Bokellaan.
ROTTERDAM HISTORICAL MUSEUM, 31 Korte Hoogstraat, displays a carved wooden transom from an eighteenth-century British vessel depicting the Biblical story of the two spies who came back with a favorable report on the Promised Land.
ST. LAWRENCE CHURCH has an eternal light burning in its grotto in commemoration of Dutch Jews murdered by the Nazis. At the base of the light is inscribed the Hebrew word "neshoma," meaning soul.
SYNAGOGUE AND JEWISH COMMUNAL CENTER, 23 Bentincklaan, was opened in 1954 to replace all the Jewish houses of worship destroyed in the German bombardment of May 14, 1940. One of these dated from 1725. A sandstone wall at the left of the entrance to the modern structure symbolizes the Western Wall in Jerusalem. Before the war there were 11,000 Jews in Rotterdam. Today there are about 1,000. The plain geometric lines of the modern sanctuary are relieved by the

diagonal pattern of window grilles incorporating the Star of David. A memorial consisting of three reliefs, in the small garden in front of the synagogue, honors the 10,000 Rotterdam Jews killed by the Nazis.

WAR MEMORIAL, in the center of the city overlooking the harbor, which memorializes the city's martyrdom during the war, is a stark piece of giant sculpture by Osip Zadkine, noted Jewish sculptor. The great bronze stands in agony, its arms upraised and a jagged hole to indicate where its heart has been ripped out, to commemorate the afternoon in 1940 when German bombers destroyed the heart of the city.

Another war memorial, on the Stadthuisplein, located on a white brick plaza, depicts two men departing for a German work camp, with a woman and child left behind.

SCHEVENINGEN

SYNAGOGUE, 44 Harstenhoekweg, serves worshipers in this popular seaside resort which is a suburb of The Hague. The *Tel Aviv Kosher Restaurant* is in the same building.

TILBURG

SYNAGOGUE AND JEWISH COMMUNAL CENTER, 20 Willemstraat.

UTRECHT

ANNE FRANKPLEIN, a square in a new section of the city called Kanaleneiland, will ultimately have homes for 30,000 people. The square named for Anne Frank forms part of a network of streets honoring former Queen Wilhelmina and members of the Dutch resistance in Utrecht who were killed during World War II. Anne Frank's name was chosen as a symbol of the national resistance. A statue of Anne Frank stands in the Janskerjof, near the Gothic St. Johannes Church.

SYNAGOGUE AND JEWISH COMMUNAL CENTER, 164 Springweg.

VEENDAM

MARTYRS MEMORIAL, erected by the town council in memory of the town's 200 Jews deported by the Nazis, includes two stones with Hebrew inscriptions from the synagogue demolished by the Germans.

WESTERBORK

This is the site of the World War II concentration camp outside of Amsterdam, through which more than 100,000 Jews passed on their way to the extermination camps. On the 25th anniversary of Holland's liberation, Queen Juliana unveiled a memorial tablet on the site of the old concentration camp.

ZALTBOMMEL

ANTON PHILIPS MEMORIAL is a plaque on the former home of Anton Philips, founder of the world-famous Dutch industrial firm, who was an uncle of Karl Marx. The house is near the canal.

ZANDVOORT

SYNAGOGUE, 75 Haltestraat, has a kosher restaurant (Carmel) attached to it. The synagogue replaces the one the Nazis destroyed in this resort city.

ZWOLLE

SYNAGOGUE, Schoutenstraat.

NORWAY

Jews were barred from Norway until 1851, when its parliament repealed a clause of the constitution of 1814, which had excluded Jews and Jesuits when Norway broke with Denmark and was united with Sweden. The lifting of the ban was due largely to the efforts of Henrik Arnold Wergeland, Norway's greatest poet, during the first half of the nineteenth century.

His pamphlet appealing to the Norwegian people to drop the bar against Jews led to the creation of a parliamentary commission to study the question. Wergeland was invited to submit data to the inquiry, and his findings won wide popular support, but the parliament defeated a bill to admit the Jews. For four years Wergeland worked and wrote feverishly to win reconsideration for the proposal, but he died six years before the legislative body repealed the discriminatory provision.

Jews began arriving in Norway in the fall of 1852 from Lithuania, and Norway's first Jewish cemetery was opened in Oslo in 1876. Until 1880, however, there were not more than 50 Jews in all of Norway. Immigration increased more rapidly after 1880, under the stimulus of the Russian pogroms. A congregation was founded in Oslo in 1892 and another in Trondheim in 1905. Norway's first synagogue was erected in Oslo in 1920. By 1940 the Jewish population numbered 1,450, including refugees from Nazi Germany.

Anti-Semitism was virtually unknown in Norway until the Nazi invasion in 1940. During the first two years of the German occupation, the Norwegian people risked their lives to protest vigorously against anti-Jewish legislation. In 1942 the Nazis arrested 650 Jews and deported them to extermination camps in Poland. The rest of the Jews were smuggled out of the country with the aid of the Norwegian underground, in which many of them served.

After the war only thirteen of the deportees returned. In 1947, the Norwegian government arranged for the admission of 500 displaced Jews from the refugee camps in Germany. These newcomers were given housing, jobs, and ultimately citizenship. Today there are 1,000 Jews in Norway. Most of them live in Oslo. The second-largest community is in Trondheim. There are also Jews in Narvik and in Bergen. Since 1929 the practice of shechita has been banned on the ground that it is inhumane.

HURUM

JEWISH MEMORIAL PARK on the Kjerregrav Hill overlooking the Oslo Fjord, is a grove of Norwegian spruce trees planted in 1961 by Norwegian Boy Scouts from Romerike County on the spot where twenty-seven Jewish children from North Africa died in a plane crash in 1949. The victims were part of a group of two hundred Jewish youngsters from Morocco and Tunisia invited to Norway for eight months by the Norwegian Relief for Europe. The crash occurred a few moments before the plane was due to land at Oslo, thirty miles away. Isaac Allal, the only survivor, returned to Norway in 1961 with the suggestion that trees from Israel be planted on the spot. The Boy Scouts took up the idea but planted Norwegian spruces because Israeli trees wouldn't grow here. The grove contains thirty-four trees, one for each of the twenty-seven children who died here, and one for each of the three social workers and four members of the plane crew who perished in the disaster. A copper plaque inscribed in Norwegian is affixed to a large boulder in the grove.

OSLO

HOME FRONT MUSEUM, a small building next door to Norway's war memorial in the Akershus Fortress, is a tribute to the Norwegians' war effort. A copper plate lists the names of every concentration camp to which Norwegians, including many Jews, were deported. The efforts of the Norwegian underground to rescue Jews are also depicted.

ISRAEL EMBASSY, 5 Meltzergate.

JEWISH COMMUNAL CENTER, 15 Bjergstien, opened in 1960, is the headquarters of the Jewish community and the focal point for all Jewish cultural activities. The $225,000 building adjoining the synagogue was financed by the Conference on Jewish Material Claims against Germany.

JEWISH YOUTH CLUB, 15 Kirkegt, founded in 1909, was the initial unit in what is now the Scandinavian Jewish Youth Federation, with branches in Sweden, Denmark, and Finland. The club maintains summer camps and sponsors cultural and recreational programs.

JEWISH WAR VICTIMS MEMORIAL in the Jewish Cemetery, an enclave in the Ostre Gravlund (municipal cemetery), at Helsefyr Gravlund, is a monument to the 620 Norwegian Jews who either were killed by the Nazis or died in concentration camps. The memorial is designed like a Star of David; on its stone panels are engraved the names of all the martyrs. From the center of the star rises a column shaped like a sawed-off tree trunk; to it is affixed a memorial plaque. King Olav and the royal family attended the dedication of the memorial.

Tombstones in the older section of the cemetery are inscribed with traditional Hebrew texts like those on Jewish tombstones in Lithuania, whence the first Jewish settlers in Norway came.

SYNAGOGUE (Det Mosaiske Trossamfund), 13 Bjergstien, Oslo's only synagogue, was founded in 1892, and the sanctuary was erected in 1920. A second synagogue was opened in 1921, but it was leveled by the Nazis. The synagogue the Nazis left untouched was reconsecrated after the war at a service attended by Crown Prince Olav, now King Olav V, marking the first time a member of the royal family entered a synagogue in Norway.

OSLO TOWN HALL on Pipervika, perpetuates the memory of Nazi atrocities against the Norwegians by large and poignantly vivid frescoes on one of its walls. The frescoes depict executions, people being dragged from their homes as their families look on, and the pillage and plunder by the invaders.

HENRIK WERGELAND MONUMENT in the Var Frilser's Cemetery, was erected by the Jews of Denmark and Sweden in honor of the great poet who initiated the struggle that ultimately led the Norwegian parliament to lift the ban on the admission of Jews to the country. The monument consists of a bust of Wergeland on a stone pedestal. On one side it is inscribed: "To the indefatigable fighter for freedom and the rights of man and citizen." On the other side the wording says: "Grateful Jews outside the frontiers of Norway erected this monument to him." Annually on May 17, Norway's Independence Day, the monument is the focus of public gatherings while Jewish youth organizations decorate it with flowers. When the monument was first commissioned, it was unveiled in Stockholm, since Jews were then excluded from Norway. Wergeland fought for freedom everywhere, but he was particularly moved by the injustice of the bar against Jews in his own country. He enjoyed great personal popularity and his two collections of poems, one entitled *The Jew* and the other *The Jewess,* were widely read, but he died in 1845 believing he had failed in his fight for the admission of the Jews.

There is another Wergeland monument—this one a life-sized statue—in the Studenterlunden, a park across the way from Oslo University on Karl Johansgate, the city's main thoroughfare. It was erected in 1881 by the Oslo Students Society.

TRONDHEIM

JEWISH WAR VICTIMS MEMORIAL in the Jewish Cemetery, consists of three stark granite slabs on which are inscribed the names of the Jews murdered by the Nazis.

SYNAGOGUE (Det Mosaiske Trossamfund), 1 Arkitekt Christiesgaat, a few doors from the huge Nidaros Cathedral, is the northernmost synagogue in the world. Situated three degrees below the Arctic Circle, Trondheim has 120 Jews, about half its prewar Jewish population. The synagogue was once the railroad station on the main line from Oslo. Outwardly it still looks like an old-fashioned European railroad station—a square building with windows arched at the top. During the war the Nazis used it as a warehouse and barracks. In 1955 the synagogue was enlarged by adding to it a Jewish Communal Center, which also houses a Hebrew school. The funds came from the Conference on Jewish Material Claims against Germany.

RINGVE MUSEUM OF MUSICAL INSTRUMENTS on the Ringve, has a special section devoted to Israeli instruments. There are also a number of shofars on display.

POLAND

Jews reached the Polish lands from Byzantium, the Moslem East and the Judaized Khazar kingdom in southern Russia before the western Slavonic tribes united to create the Polish state in the tenth century. According to an old legend, a Jew named Abraham Prochownik declined the rulership of the tribes in favor of the peasant Piast. Prochownik was probably one of the Jewish merchants who came from the east and from the west to trade with the pagans of the Oder and Vistula basins in the ninth century before some of them settled there permanently. There is another legend that ascribes the first Jewish settlement in Poland to a heavenly command to wandering Jews, *"Po lin"* (Rest here).

In 932, a generation before the Piasts accepted Christianity, German Jews bearing Spanish names turned up at Wronki, where their thousand-year-old synagogue was uncovered in the 1920s. German Jews also settled at Gniezno, the Piasts' capital, in the tenth century, at about the same time that Bohemian Jews appeared in Cracow. The earliest written reference to Mieszko I, who ruled Poland between 963 and 992, is contained in a tenth-century report by a Jewish traveler from Spain.

Hebrew inscriptions on some of the oldest existing Polish coins indicate that Jewish mintmasters and fiscal agents were employed by the Polish kings in the eleventh and twelfth centuries. Hebrew literature of that time in France and Germany mentions Polish Jews, probably part of the stream of immigrants from Germany and Bohemia, where the flames of bigotry were fanned by the Crusades.

To restore the economy after the devastation caused by the Tatar invasion of the Ukraine in 1240 and to populate its eastern provinces, the Piast kings encouraged extensive immigration from Germany. This brought in large numbers of Jewish and Christian merchants, moneylenders, traders, artisans, and craftsmen, who laid the foundation for a middle class in the primitive society of nobles and serfs. The Jews brought with them their Judaeo-German dialect that became the Yiddish of Eastern Europe, as well as a devotion to Jewish learning and a passionate piety. The German Christians introduced Jew-baiting by inciting the Polish masses against Jewish competitors, with the active backing of the clergy. But the protection of the kings and powerful nobles enabled Polish Jewry to escape the martyrdom suffered by their coreligionists in Germany, Austria, and Bohemia between the eleventh and fourteenth centuries.

In 1264 Prince Boleslav granted the Jews a charter of privileges that guaranteed their economic rights, protected their lives, property and synagogues, and gave them an extraordinary degree of communal autonomy. Casimir the Great defied church hostility and the bigoted German merchants when he confirmed and extended this charter in 1344 and invited large numbers of German Jews fleeing from pogroms in the west to settle in his territories.

Casimir's tolerance is reputed to have been a by-product of his secret marriage to a Jewish girl. Actually, however, he had the foresight to see that the Jews were a valuable asset in building up the country's trade and commerce because of their ties with distant lands and their ability to create credit and make loans. The sharp increase in the Jewish population between 1348 and 1370 brought into being the historic Jewish communities in Cracow, Lvov (Lemberg), Kalicz, Poznań (Posen), Gniezno, Lublin and Plock.

The new dynasty that succeeded Casimir gradually yielded to the pressure of the Church and to the German-controlled trade and artisan guilds at the end of the fourteenth and the start of the fifteenth century. Anti-Jewish restrictions became more widespread, and periodic outbreaks of violence, inspired by accusations of blood ritual murder, set the stage for a systematic effort to undermine the Jewish economic position.

The zeal of the anti-Semitic clergy during the Counter-Reformation and the determination of the Christian burghers to get rid of Jewish competition caused new persecutions in the sixteenth and early seventeenth centuries and led to legislation aimed at excluding Jews from all business in the principal cities. This in turn caused a major shift in the Jewish population from the cities of the west to the towns and villages of the sparsely settled east, particularly the Ukraine, and a radical change in the Jews' socio-economic structure. In the eastern provinces they became artisans in unprecedented numbers, as well as innkeepers, agents for the landed gentry, and middlemen between the city and village economies and between the nobles and the peasants.

At the end of the sixteenth century, Polish Jewry numbered 500,000. With economic opportunities circumscribed by a hostile society to which they sought no admission and in which they found no welcome, Polish Jewry created its own rich inner life and strong communal organization and clung to Judaism more tenaciously than ever. As printed books became more available, houses of Jewish study sprang up in every town and village. Calamities in the west that barred Jewish students from going abroad for higher Jewish education led to the establishment of famed rabbinical seminaries and academies in Poland under the leadership of such sixteenth-century rabbinical giants as Shakhna, Isserles and Luria. They and other great scholars and rabbinic authorities of that day became the architects of the tradition of Jewish learning that was the hallmark of Polish Jewry. Under their inspiration, Talmudic study became not only a search for religious truth but a way of satisfying deep intellectual urges. In this era, too, Yiddish became the common language of Jewish life in every corner of Poland, from whence it spread to all of Eastern Europe.

Their internal autonomy, which the kings encouraged in order to facilitate the collection of taxes, enabled the Jews to build a compact communal structure around the *kahals*, which regulated every phase of Jewish life. The *kahals* developed into a national conference known as the Council of Four Lands—Greater and Lesser Poland, Galicia and Volhynia—which served as a Jewish parliament entrusted with major state functions affecting the Jews. With the full sanction of the government, this body exercised enormous influence on Jewish life from 1592 until it went out of existence in 1764.

In 1648 a major disaster overwhelmed Polish Jewry when the Ukrainian peasants, terribly oppressed by absentee Polish landlords, whose overseers and renters often were Jews, broke into revolt. Taking advantage of internal strife and the absence of strong central authority in the overextended Polish empire, the Ukrainians, led by the Cossack Bogdan Chmielnicki, ravaged vast areas of Poland and slaughtered 200,000 Jews in the southern and eastern provinces. Pogroms by Poles in the regions left untouched by the Ukrainian horrors following the defeat of the Cossacks and the invasions by Prussia, Russia, and Sweden, magnified the excesses. In ten years, more than seven hundred Jewish communities were wiped out.

Crushed by this calamity, the Polish Jews sought escape from reality first in the mysteries of the cabala and then in the siren calls of pseudo messiahs in the closing decades of the seventeenth century. Disillusioned by the collapse of the messianic movements, and oppressed by mounting disabilities and continuing violence in the eighteenth century, they eagerly embraced the comforting ecstasy of Chassidism, founded in Poland by Israel ben Eliezer (the Baal Shem Tov) and the discipline of piety and Talmudic study advocated by Elijah, the Vilna (Wilna) Gaon.

Between the first partition of Poland in 1772 and the establishment of the Polish Republic in 1918, the history of Polish Jewry became linked to the story of Jews in Russia, Germany, and Austria. The vast majority of Polish Jews in the late eighteenth century lived in the Ukraine, in Lithuania, and in parts of what is now White Russia. When these regions were annexed by the Czar in 1772, 1793, 1795, and 1815, the Jewish settlements there became the core of Russian Jewry. The partitions also altered the nationality of other large segments of Polish Jewry; those in Silesia became subject to Prussia, while those in Galicia came under the rule of the Hapsburg monarchy.

In 1794, when Tadeusz Kosciuszko led the first revolution against Russia, a Jewish regiment commanded by Colonel Berek Joselowicz, distinguished itself in the futile struggle. The Jews also played a prominent role in the second and third Polish insurrections in 1830 and 1863, as they did later in the Pilsudski Legion of World War I. But there was little change in the status of the Jews who remained in western Poland under Napoleon's short-lived Duchy of Warsaw or in the vassal kingdom of Poland which the Russians maintained as part of their realm until 1863. When Poland was completely submerged after the suppression of the 1863 revolt, the Jews were beset by Russian oppression and embittered Polish nationalists and their middle class allies.

The latter resented the rising class of Jewish professionals and the success of Jewish industrialists who had done much to establish new industries. The growing city proletariat saw a threat in the increasing number of Jewish factory workers. But in the towns and villages the Jews remained largely economically depressed, living by petty trade, innkeeping, and home industries. New pogroms in 1881 set off a wave of Jewish immigration to the United States, England, Canada, Latin America, and South Africa. Simultaneously, Zionism, the Jewish labor movement, the Hebrew revival, and the Jewish cultural renaissance took deep root among the Jewish masses who remained. Between 1880 and 1914, when Warsaw occupied a commanding position in Jewish life, Polish Jewry produced a galaxy of renowned men of letters—among them Peretz, Asch, and Frischman—and a host of others who were to play decisive roles in later Jewish history.

Concentrated in the areas of the fiercest fighting on the eastern front during World War I, Polish Jewry suffered heavy casualties and huge property losses from both sides as the tide of battle shifted. Pauperized, ravaged, and decimated by four years of war, the Jews in Russian Poland and Galicia were further victimized by postwar pogroms carried out by bands of Slavic guerrillas that sprang up after the collapse of the Czarist and Hapsburg monarchies.

The Versailles Peace Treaty's special provisions for the protection of the Jewish minority in the reborn Polish State quickly became scraps of paper. The government's program of state economic control excluded Jews from trade, commerce and industry. Powerless to cope with a rising economic crisis, the government deflected the hatred of landless peasants, the bitterness of unemployed workers and the frustrations of the middle class into anti-Semitism. This encouraged boycotts, discrimination in the professions and civil service, and violence in the schools and universities; and it resulted in the impoverishment of half the 3,500,000 Jews.

On the eve of World War II, one out of every three Polish Jews was dependent on assistance from American-Jewish relief agencies, especially the Joint Distribution Committee and ORT, which created credit organizations, co-operatives, vocational retraining schools, and a network of health and educational institutions. Large numbers of Polish Jews eked out a miserable existence amidst a population obsessed with varying degrees of hatred toward them. When the Nazis overran Poland in 1939, they found all of its political parties except the Socialists and Communists committed to anti-Jewish programs.

Nevertheless, Polish Jews fought gallantly with the outmanned Polish forces. The German General Staff reported 35,000 Jewish soldiers killed and 61,000 taken prisoners before the fighting ended in Poland. When Poland was conquered, many Jews who had escaped via Russia, joined the Polish legions in Russia, Norway, and Italy, and later served with the Polish army that fought its way back into Poland at the side of the Russians in 1944.

Under the Nazi occupation, Polish Jewry suffered final martyrdom as part of the greatest holocaust in modern Jewish history. The ghettos, concentration camps, and gas chambers of Auschwitz (Oswiecim), Treblinka, Lublin, Warsaw, Lodz, Chelmno, Majdanek, Sobibor, Bialystok, and many other places, claimed the lives of nearly 3,000,000 Polish Jews as well as vast numbers of other Jews sent to Poland from Nazi-occupied Europe for extermination. Desperate acts of courage such as the revolt in the Warsaw ghetto, and the little-known exploits of tiny bands of Jewish partisans behind the German lines, harassed the Nazis but could not halt their total destruction of the thousand-year-old Polish Jewish community, which had been the fountainhead of Jewish religious and cultural life in Europe.

In the first months after Poland's liberation from German occupation, thousands of Polish Jews who had found refuge in Russia were repatriated. On their return to Warsaw, Wroclaw, Cracow and Lodz they found co-religionists who had survived the Nazi years in deep forests, caves, attics, cellars or as members of partisan forces. Several thousand also were found alive in the Auschwitz and Lodz concentration camps. There were also those who escaped death with forged Polish identity papers. About 15,000 of the latter continued to hide their Jewish origin.

By 1960 emigration to Israel had reduced the known Jews to 35,000. Until 1956 the Communist regime sought to stamp out the remnants of anti-Semitism but thereafter an internal political struggle in which the Jews became the scapegoats developed into a purge of Jewish officials. The gradual "de-Judaization" of the state and party apparatuses and the steady elimination of Jews from all but the most minor positions gained headway in the 1960s.

At the time of the Six-Day War in 1967, the Jewish population was reported to be around 30,000. An estimated 3,000 left Poland in 1968 with the beginning of the government's anti-Israel policy. Another 8,000 departed in 1969 as the anti-Jewish sentiment became increasingly militant. Scores of Jewish leaders of the Communist Party were ousted and Jewish intellectuals were blamed for anti-government student demonstrations. By 1970, the Jewish population was down to 7,500 and it appeared that the last chapter in Polish Jewry's 1,000 year history was being written. About a fourth of the departing Jews, who had to leave with virtually nothing but the clothes on their backs, went to Israel. A high proportion of others went to the United States and about 3,000 found refuge in Denmark and Sweden.

What Jewish life there still is in Poland revolves around the Union of Religious Communities and its affiliated synagogues in a dozen cities, and the government-controlled Social and Cultural Union of Polish Jews. Through this organization, the government maintains a number of Yiddish schools, a Yiddish theatre, social centers, a Yiddish publishing house and a few social welfare agencies. The government also supports the Jewish Historical Institute in Warsaw and helps restore major Jewish cemeteries.

In 1971, the largest remaining Jewish communities were in Warsaw, Lodz, and Wroclaw, with smaller settlements in Cracow, Czestochowa, Katowice and a dozen other places. Virtually no Jews live in the smaller towns and villages. Everywhere there are wrecked or neglected Jewish cemeteries, ruins of synagogues and other Jewish communal buildings that have been converted to other public or private uses, and scattered memorials to victims of the catastrophe which has left Poland a vast Jewish graveyard.

AUSCHWITZ-BIRKENAU

See OSWIECIM-BRZEZINKA

BIALYSTOK

GHETTO CEMETERY on Zabia Street, holds the graves of Jews who died in the Bialystok ghetto during the first years of the Nazi occupation. Two large monuments, one a memorial to the ghetto's dead, and the other honoring Jewish partisans who led a heroic resistance movement, dominate the grounds.

POGROM MEMORIAL, a tall marble shaft in the old Jewish cemetery, contains the names of 105 Jews killed here in a 1905 pogrom. The bottom of the monument is inscribed with a poem by Zalman Shneour, famed Hebrew poet.

SYNAGOGUE MEMORIAL on the site of the city's historic synagogue, was erected in 1963, 22 years after the Nazis locked 3,000 Jews in the building and then set fire to it.

ZAMENHOF MONUMENT honors the memory of Dr. Ludwig Zamenhof, founder of Esperanto, who was born here in 1859. A school and a street are also named for him.

BIELAWA (Langenbielau)

JEWISH SOCIAL AND CULTURAL ASSOCIATION, 38 Dluga Street.

BIELSK

LEWARTOWSKI STREET is named for Josef Lewartowski, a Jewish hero of the Warsaw Ghetto revolt.

BOCHNIA

CASIMIR THE GREAT STATUE, in the center of the city, was erected at the turn of the century by the Jewish community in honor of the Polish king of the 14th century who protected the rights of Jews. Reliefs on the monument portray this historic event. The Nazis wiped out the Jewish community but the statue escaped unscathed.

BRUDNO

JEWISH CEMETERY in this suburb of Warsaw was wrecked during the Nazi occupation, but there are plans to restore it in the form of a rotunda with a lake in the center. The rotunda will cover a mausoleum containing several thousand tombstones from the destroyed cemetery.

BYTOM (Beuthen)

JEWISH SOCIAL AND CULTURAL ASSOCIATION, 38 Dluga Street.

CHELM (Khulm)

JEWISH CEMETERY is all that survives of this community celebrated in Jewish folk humor as the habitat of simpletons. Only two Jews now live here.

CHELMNO

MONUMENT TO NAZI VICTIMS on the site of the Chelmno camp, the first murder camp set up in occupied Poland by the Nazis, memorializes 340,000 Polish Jews and 20,000 from other countries. Another monument in front of the main Catholic church honors the Jews who staged an unsuccessful revolt against the Nazis.

CHRZANOW

SYNAGOGUE that survived Nazi occupation is now a warehouse.

CRACOW (Krakow)

MORDECAI GEBIRTIG CULTURAL CLUB, 35 Slawkowska St., near the Old Market Place where thirteenth-century Jews had their places of business, is a gathering place for Jewish intellectuals.

JEWISH COMMUNITY BUILDING, Krakowska St., houses a kosher kitchen where three hundred meals daily are served with funds provided by the American Jewish Joint Distribution Committee. A number of other former Jewish communal buildings have been converted into factories, warehouses, and residences, including the *Isaac Jacobowicz Synagogue*, dating from 1640, and the *High Synagogue*, built in 1663. The well-known Hebrew primary and secondary school at 5 Brzozowa St., is now a state school. During the Nazi occupation, the pharmacy owned by Tadeusz Pankiewicz, a Christian who voluntarily remained in the ghetto, was a clearing house for information about planned Nazi raids. Because Pankiewicz was responsible for saving many Jewish lives and because he stayed in the ghetto until it was demolished, recording the tragedy of the Jews, all Jews have patronized only his shop. When his drugstore was nationalized, he went to work in a co-operative pharmacy, but the Jews continue to buy their drugs only where Pankiewicz works.

JEWISH SOCIAL AND CULTURAL ASSOCIATION, 38 Dluga St.

ISAKA STREET in the ancient Jewish quarter, is named for Rabbi Isaac of Prossnitz, who in 1530 founded the first Jewish printing shop in Poland in Cracow.

JOSELOWICZ STREET is named for Berek Joselowicz, who commanded a Jewish regiment in Poland's first revolt against Russia in 1794 (*see* KOCK *below*).

MEDIEVAL GHETTO WALL REMNANT in the Kasimierz quarter, is the last vestige of the ghetto established in mid-fifteenth century, when the Jews were driven out of Cracow and allowed to live only in the nearby town of Kasimierz. All the major institutions of the six-hundred-year-old Jewish community were in this section, including the two historic synagogues and the ancient cemetery. The entire ancient Jewish quarter is to be rebuilt as a museum in memory of the martyrdom of

European Jewry. Reconstruction plans call for re-creating the medieval ghetto wall as well as the red-brick wall the Nazis erected.

MEISELS STREET is named for Dob Berush Meisels, a mid-nineteenth-century rabbi, who served in the senate of the independent Republic of Cracow as one of the leaders of the Polish liberation movement. Later, as a rabbi in Warsaw, he rallied Jewish support for the 1863 insurrection against Russia and was imprisoned after the uprising was crushed.

MICKIEWICZ MONUMENT on the Rynek Glowny, the city's main square, in front of the huge fourteenth-century Cloth Hall, is a bronze statue of Adam Mickiewicz, Poland's national poet, who was the greatest champion of Jewish rights in Polish history. In his *Pan Tadeusz*, the national epic of Poland, he paid tribute to the heroism and patriotism of Polish Jewry. In 1845, he addressed an open letter to the Jews inviting them to join in the Polish liberation movement. During the Crimean War, Mickiewicz organized a Polish-Jewish legion, which he hoped would lead the western powers to grant Poland her independence after the defeat of Russia.

MUSEUM OF JEWISH HISTORY, 24 Szeroka St., in the heart of the Kasimierz ghetto, occupies the Alte Shul, the oldest existing synagogue in Poland, which dates back to the second half of the fourteenth century. Badly damaged and looted during the Nazi occupation, the historic structure was restored by the government's Fund for the Preservation of Monuments and then converted into a museum. One section is devoted to the history and culture of Polish Jewry and the other depicts the martyrdom of Polish Jewry at the hands of the Nazis. Built like a fortress, the Romanesque-type building is partly below street level. Over the *bimah* is a striking wrought-iron canopy of sixteenth-century workmanship which rises in an octagonal dome over the reader's platform. Although it is no longer used for worship, the synagogue's religious appurtenances have been fully restored. Among the exhibits are hundreds of Torah crowns, Hanukah Menorahs and candlesticks that belonged to synagogues throughout Poland, and paintings on Jewish themes by Jewish artists who died in the concentration camps.

NEW JEWISH CEMETERY on Miodowa St., has a number of memorials to Jews murdered by the Nazis in various parts of Poland. The Nazis removed hundreds of tombstones from this burial ground and used them as paving blocks.

OLD JEWISH CEMETERY, adjoining the Remo Synagogue on Szeroka St., oldest existing Jewish burial ground in Poland, dates from the sixteenth century. Nazism, war, and vandalism almost completely destroyed the cemetery, where the most venerated of Poland's Jewish religious authorities were buried. After the war it was found that the only tombstone that had survived virtually unscathed was that of Rabbi Moses Isserles, sixteenth-century sage whose grave was for generations a place of annual pilgrimage for thousands of devout Jews. Most headstones have been leveled or have disappeared. Thousands of graves were broken into and the corpses were scattered, but the tombstone of Rabbi Isserles, famed as a codifier of Jewish law, escaped with only a piece chipped off its top. It still stands erect, surrounded by an iron fence. Also intact within the fence is the gravestone of Rabbi Isserles' brother. The epitaph on Rabbi Isserles' tomb, reads: "From Moses to Moses, there was none like Moses." Rabbi Isserles (1510-1572) is remembered particularly for his commentary on and supplement to Joseph Caro's *Shulhan Aruk*, a code for daily living which has shaped religious observance of Orthodox Jews for centuries.

With the financial support of the American Jewish Joint Distribution Committee, the Cracow Jews have been slowly restoring the cemetery, rebuilding its breached walls, and excavating and re-erecting surviving headstones that were buried under debris and weeds. Among the more than 360 tombstones already renovated are 60 in black-and-red marble, richly decorated in Renaissance style. Among these are the stones of Jewish doctors who served as personal physicians to Polish kings in the sixteenth century.

REMO SYNAGOGUE, 40 Szeroka St., one of two still used for worship purposes in Cracow, was originally built of wood in 1553 by Rabbi Isserles' father, and rebuilt in stone and brick in 1557. Its name is a contraction of Reb Moses Isserles, who preached and taught in this synagogue. His chair is still intact. The small synagogue has only one aisle and is renowned for its remarkable wood-carved Torah Ark and entrance door and its casklike interior ceiling arch. Government experts engaged in restoring the historic sites of Cracow are also collecting inscriptions found on the walls of the Remo Synagogue.

THE TEMPLE, 26 Miedow St., is the second synagogue still being used, but it is usually open only on Saturdays and holidays

CZELNO

MICHELSON MONUMENT honors Albert Michelson, famed American scientist, the first American to win a Nobel Prize, who was born in 1852.

CZESTOCHOWA

JEWISH CEMETERY, now surrounded by the huge Bierut foundry and thus inaccessible to visitors, contains four monuments to various groups of Nazi victims.

JEWISH SOCIAL AND CULTURAL ASSOCIATION, 36 Jasnogorska St.

SYNAGOGUE REMNANT, is being rebuilt to house local symphony orchestra.

DROBIN

JEWISH CEMETERY, whose tombstones were ripped up and used as paving blocks by the Nazis, was personally restored by Rabbi Abraham D. Feffer, of New York, a native of this town one hundred miles west of Warsaw. He persuaded the Polish authorities to remove a co-operative store erected on the site of the cemetery and to co-operate in reclaiming the gravestones.

DUKLA

SYNAGOGUE which escaped Nazi destruction, is now a market hall.

DZIERZONIOW (Reichenbach)

JEWISH SOCIAL AND CULTURAL ASSOCIATION, 11 Krasickiego St.

GDANSK (Danzig)

JEWISH CLUB is the only Jewish institution in this Baltic port city. The club occupies quarters in a modern new building erected after the war.

GER

GERER REBBE'S SYNAGOGUE, once the seat of a famous Chassidic dynasty, still stands but it is now a warehouse and barn. Only the metal framework of a Mogen David still to be seen in a circular air hole high up on the outer wall recalls its original role in Jewish history. What was once the residence of the Gerer Rebbe and the adjacent yeshiva have been converted into tenements. On the old Jewish cemetery there is a monument to the 5,000 Jews who perished in Ger at the hands of the Nazis.

GLIWICE (Gleiwitz)

JEWISH SOCIAL AND CULTURAL ASSOCIATION, 11 Zwieciestwa St.

HALICZ

KARAITE COMMUNITY still exists here, made up of descendants of Jews who rejected all Jewish teachings except those in the Bible.

JOZEFOW

GREAT SYNAGOGUE in this town near Lublin is still intact, but it has been converted into a large wheat silo. Unprotected Jewish tombstones may be seen in the nearby fields.

KALISZ

ESTHER WALL remains of one of the palaces built in the fourteenth century by King Casimir the Great for Esterka, his secret Jewish bride, is pointed out to all visitors. There are those who insist that the ghost of Esterka, daughter of a tailor from Opoczno, returns nightly to the wall, waiting for her royal lover, at the spot where she was supposed to have affixed a mezuzah. Most historians put no stock in the story of Casimir's Jewish consort, but the legend of Esterka is widely mentioned in Polish literature. Esterka is supposed to have borne Casimir two sons, who were raised as Catholics, and two daughters, who were brought up as Jews. Jewish folklore claims that Esterka built three synagogues and died in an anti-Jewish riot after Casimir's death in 1370.

KATOWICE

JEWISH SOCIAL AND CULTURAL ASSOCIATION, 2 Wawelska St.

KISIELICE

JEWISH CEMETERY in this once-time East Prussian town of Freystadt has been virtually effaced. Only a pile of stones bearing Hebrew letters in a meadow a few paces past the old Catholic cemetery remain.

KLODZKO (Glatz)

JEWISH SOCIAL AND CULTURAL ASSOCIATION, 6 Slowackiego St.

KOCK

JOSELOWICZ MEMORIAL in a forest on the edge of town, is an irregular granite slab, inscribed in Polish, honoring Colonel Berek Joselowicz, the greatest Jewish military figure in Poland until the days of the Warsaw Ghetto Revolt. A few feet back of the stone is Joselowicz's grave, over which there is another slab bearing his name and the dates of his birth (1760) and death (1809). The inscription on the memorial stone extols him as one who won fame "not by trading or huckstering, but as a brave knight who wrought glorious deeds for Poland, for which he gave his blood." A business agent for the Archbishop of Vilna, Joselowicz accompanied his master to Paris, where he became imbued with the ideals of the French Revolution. He was a merchant in Warsaw when Tadeusz Kosciuszko led the Poles in revolt against Russia in 1793-94. The latter named Joselowicz colonel of an ill-armed, largely untrained legion of Jewish volunteers, most of whom were killed in the battle of Praga. When Napoleon created a Polish legion in his war against Austria in 1808, Joselowicz volunteered again. He was killed on May 5, 1809, in a battle in the market place of Kock. His heroism is still cited in Polish literature and in Polish history books. When the Nazis were driven out of Poland in 1944, the forces fighting against them included a detachment of Jewish partisans that bore the name of Joselowicz. This outfit had been actively harassing the Nazis in the woods around Kock and Lublin. Joselowicz's son Joseph repeated his father's exploits in the 1830 rising against Czar Nicholas I.

KOTZKER REBBE'S HOUSE once the seat of the celebrated Chassidic Rabbi Menahem Mendel, who in the early nineteenth century was widely regarded as a miracle worker, still stands. The odd-shaped wooden building, with a cupola at the corner, is now the headquarters of an agricultural co-operative. The *sukkah* used by the rabbi and his followers is still well preserved but there are no Jews left here to occupy it. The Kotzker Rebbe was an active participant in the 1830 revolt against Russia.

KOLAKE

NAZI VICTIMS MONUMENT was erected by townspeople of nearby Zambrow to memorialize the 1,000 Jews "done to death by the Hitlerite murderers."

KONIN

SYNAGOGUE here survived Nazi occupation but it is now abandoned. A memorial stone in the Catholic cemetery honors the memory of Jews slain by the Nazis. This town was the birthplace of Michel Goldwasser, grandfather of Barry Goldwater, who was the Republican presidential nominee in 1964.

KUTNO

ASCH HOUSE, 16 Mickiewicz St., where Sholem Asch, the noted Yiddish novelist was born in 1880, is now the headquarters of the local housing authority. A plaque to the right of the entrance marks the house as Asch's birthplace. There is also an *Asch Street* here, where only two Jews now live.

SYNAGOGUE building still stands, but it is now a store. What used to be the women's gallery is now a club. The Jewish cemetery on the edge of town is a shambles, all the tombstones having been broken or stolen. The outlines of graves can still be seen and local residents point out the one where the mother of Asch is buried. Asch's novels of Jewish life in Eastern Europe were widely read in English translations that gave non-Yiddish-reading Jews and non-Jews a graphic picture of the life of the Jews in prewar Poland.

LESKO

16th CENTURY SYNAGOGUE here has been restored by the local authorities and converted into a museum. They have also restored some historically significant tombstones in the Jewish cemetery which, together with the synagogue have been designated as historical monuments.

LODZ

BERLINSKI STREET is named for Hirsch Berlinski, one of the Warsaw Ghetto fighters, who was a native of Lodz.

HOME FOR JEWISH AGED AND INCURABLES.

JEWISH CEMETERY, on Strykowska St., one of the three principal Jewish burial grounds in Poland (the others are in Warsaw and Wroclaw) being restored under the auspices of the American Jewish Joint Distribution Committee, has a huge monument memorializing the 200,000 Jews from Lodz and neighboring towns who were killed by the Nazis. The monument is a tall, obelisk-shaped piece of masonry, to the right of which is inset a large inscribed plaque. To the right of the plaque is a large stone Menorah. The monument stands in the middle of a paved plaza. The inscription, in Yiddish, Hebrew, and Polish, reads: "To the sacred memory of those who perished in the destruction of the great Jewish community at Lodz and Jewish communities in the vicinity. They died a martyr's death at the hands of the Hitlerites in the ghettos and concentration camps between 1939 and 1945. Your memory will live forever." The first ghetto in modern Europe was established in Lodz by the Nazis in 1939, but they left the cemetery and its marble tombstones and mausoleums untouched. Since the war, many of them have been smashed by hooligans. Nine empty pits intended as mass graves for Jews to be killed by the Nazis have been preserved as grisly memorials. The pits were never used because the Red Army reached the outskirts of Lodz shortly before the Nazis planned to provide occupants for the mass graves. On this cemetery there are also memorial stones over the ashes of concentration camp victims.

JEWISH PEOPLE'S LIBRARY, 32 Wieckowskiego St., is in the headquarters of the local branch of the Jewish Social and Cultural Association.

JEWISH STATE THEATRE BUILDING, 15 Wieckowskiego St., was erected in 1951 on the ruins of the Jewish Scala Theatre, destroyed by the Nazis in 1941, but it is used for general theatrical purposes since the Jewish Theatre group moved its headquarters to Warsaw.

SYNAGOGUE, 28 Poludniowa St., a small but comparatively modern structure hidden away in a courtyard, was the only Jewish house of worship in the city to escape destruction. On the site of the Great Synagogue there is now a gasoline station. Lodz, which once had 250,000 Jews, now has 3,000.

YIDDISH SCHOOL here has a playground named for Yitzhak Leib Peretz, the famous Yiddish writer.

LUBLIN

JEWISH CEMETERY on the outskirts of the city, contains the graves of many eminent rabbinic authorities of the sixteenth, seventeenth, and eighteenth centuries, including that of Solomon Luria (1501-1573). Known as the Maharshal, Rabbi Luria and his contemporary Moses Isserles (*see* CRACOW) were the two major influences on sixteenth-century Jewish life in Poland. Also buried here is Rabbi Meier Lublin (1558-1616), known as the Maharam.

LUBLINER TALMUDIC ACADEMY once the center of Jewish scholarship in Poland, where the Maharshal, the Maharam, and other celebrated scholars taught, no longer exists, but the last building of this historic institution is now occupied by the Lublin University school of medicine.

MARTYRS' MEMORIAL, a monument to the 46,000 Lublin Jews and more than 250,000 from other places, murdered by the Nazis, stands in Sawicka Square, in the heart of the city's new section near the old royal castle. At the base of the monument are buried urns containing ashes of Jews killed at the death camps of Sobibor, Piniatow, Krempiece, Belzec and Zamposcz. The monument, a bronze statue, bears the inscription in Polish and Yiddish, "I seek my near ones in every handful of ashes." Where the monument stands was the ghetto during the Nazi occupation. From this spot Jewish deportees from many countries were assembled before being sent to the nearby concentration camps and extermination centers at Majdanek, Piaski, Liepowa, and Sobibor. The old Jewish quarter, established in the early sixteenth century around the castle, was destroyed by the Nazis. The portal that led to the Jewish quarter was known as Jews' Gate. At nearby 19 Szeroka St. was the house in which the Council of the Four Lands met annually during the sixteenth and seventeenth centuries. In the Krenfitzer Forest, between Lublin and the Soviet border, there is a memorial honoring 300,000 Jews killed there by the Nazi and buried in mass graves.

I. L. PERETZ SCHOOL which was opened just before World War II, is now an office of the government health ministry.

SYNAGOGUE, a tiny upstairs room at 3 Wyszynskiego St., is the only Jewish institution left. The *Saul Wahl Synagogue*, on Podzmancze St., named for a Jewish banker who, according to legend, was king of Poland for one night, and the *Maharshal and Maharam Synagogues* on Jateczna St., are gone.

LUKOW

MARTYRS' MEMORIAL, erected by the handful of Jews in this town to those who died at Treblinka concentration camp, is a huge pyramid made of gravestones from the Lukow Jewish cemetery. Topping the pyramid is a Star of David.

MAJDANEK

MAJDANEK CONCENTRATION CAMP SITE, almost at the edge of Lublin, has been preserved by the Polish government as a grim monument. Here 250,000 Jews from the ghettos of Warsaw, Lublin, and surrounding areas were gassed or shot, and their bodies were burned in the crematorium. The core of the memorial is a 4,429-cubic-foot mound of ashes from the bones of the victims. The twenty-four barracks where prisoners were housed, the "disinfection" chamber where they were gassed, and the crematorium where corpses were burned, have all been kept intact as a reminder of man's inhumanity to man. In the center of the camp's parade ground is a stark monument in the form of a tall, circular plinth. A museum in the camp contains exhibits in the form of diagrams, statistics, and pictorial panels depicting the Nazi extermination center in action.

MINSK MAZOWIECK

MARTYRS MEMORIAL in the local Jewish cemetery, honors the memory of the 220 Jews who were burned alive in the town synagogue by the Nazis.

OLSZTYN (Allenstein)

JEWISH CEMETERY in this former East Prussian town still has a chapel designed by the late Eric Mendelsohn, noted German-Jewish architect, who was born here. This building was the first commissioned work by one of the pioneers of modern architecture. The so-called "wolf's lair," or supreme command post of Hitler, has been preserved by the Polish authorities as a tourist attraction. It was here that the abortive attempt to assassinate Hitler took place on July 20, 1944.

ORLE

STONE SYNAGOGUE, dating from the sixteenth century, still stands in this town in eastern Poland, near the Soviet frontier. It is now used by the local agricultural co-operative as a warehouse, but you can still make out the murals on the inside walls. Five miles south of here, in the village of Bielce, there was until recently the oldest Jewish cemetery in Poland, dating from the eleventh century. One of those buried here was a daughter of Rashi, the famous Talmud commentator.

OSWIECIM-BRZEZINKA

AUSCHWITZ-BIRKENAU (the German names for Oswiecim-Brzezinka) concentration camp, now preserved as a museum by the Polish government, was the most infamous murder factory in history. In this twenty-five-square mile area two hours by car from Cracow, the Nazis gassed, shot, tortured, or starved to death 4,000,000 people, of whom 3,000,000 were Jews, between 1940 and 1945. The Poles are keeping the camp site in a state of desolation and barrenness so that the millions who view it will get some understanding of the grisly things that happened here. Even the sixty miles of barbed wire that encircle the camp and that the Nazis had electrified are intact. The camp received its first transport of victims from Cracow on June 4, 1940, and thereafter as many as twenty trainloads a day arrived from all parts of Nazi-occupied Europe. Auschwitz and its half-dead 60,000 survivors were liberated on January 27, 1945, by a Russian detachment commanded by Colonel Grigori Davidowich Elishawetzki, a Jew.

The millions killed here arrived by train at Birkenau, a few miles from Oswiecim, where a railspur led to the gate of the death camp. When the Nazis retreated, they blew up the underground gas chambers and the crematoria and tore up the railroad tracks. The twisted rails are still there, however, together with huge chunks of concrete from the roofs of the gas chambers, protruding gas vents, and pieces of the concrete siding where the victims were sorted out, either for immediate murder by gas or slow death by starvation and torture. One of the crematorium ovens is intact. From its rear ran the tracks on which carts containing ashes and bones were pushed to a dump pit, now covered by a pond, a few miles from the main camp building. Daisies grow in the wreckage of the former Nazi death camp.

At the spot where the railway line ended, there is a stone monument which says, simply, "Oswiecim 1940-1945." Where the incinerators and gas chambers did their grisly work there are a number of plain monuments. One is devoted to the Jewish martyrs and is inscribed in Yiddish, Hebrew, and Polish. In 1967, the Polish Government dedicated a mammoth granite monument in the former death camp of Birkenau. At the end of the ramp where trains entered the Auschwitz complex to discharge their load of the doomed from all over Europe, a series of huge hewn stones, the work of Polish and Italian sculptors, has been deployed. The stones suggest tombs scattered there by a giant hand, the tombs of Auschwitz's unburied dead. At the foot of the monument are 18 memorial plaques in 18 languages, but none in Hebrew or Yiddish, which proclaim: "Four million people suffered at the hands of the Nazi murderers between the years 1940 and 1945."

In 1968 the government opened a pavilion at Auschwitz in memory of Hitler's 6,000,000 Jewish victims. At the entrance is a rough granite slab inscribed with a verse from the fourth chapter of Genesis: "And the Lord said unto Cain, Where is Abel thy brother?" At the exit a similar slab is inscribed: "And He said, What hast thou done? The voice of thy brother's blood crieth unto Me from the ground."

The two-story pavilion, housed in a red brick barracks known as Cell Block 27, where 3,000,000 Jews and a million non-Jews were killed, displays photographs tracing the history of anti-Semitism.

In the main camp area at Auschwitz, about a dozen huts, 60 by 40 feet, each of which housed 1,200 people, have been preserved just as they were. You enter the camp through a wrought-iron gate over which is inscribed the Nazi motto, *"Arbeit macht frei"* (Work makes one free). Just inside the gate is the great oak tree beneath which the prisoners' band was compelled to play Strauss waltzes when the work parties stumbled back into camp carrying on their backs those who had died on the job. In these huts there is the Auschwitz Museum, one of mankind's grimmest mementos.

In some of the huts are huge glass-enclosed showcases of death. Behind the glass are great bunches of human hair, piles of shoes, stacks of eyeglass frames, heaps of gold teeth and silver fillings, a tangled mass of crutches and artificial limbs, a jumble of dishes, pots, and brushes, and mounds of valises, prayer shawls, books, phylacteries, and clothing—the pitiful possessions of the former inmates. In other cases are displayed tattoo needles for putting prison numbers on the victims, uniforms, rations, insignia, letters written by forced laborers and never mailed, communications from camp officials boasting of their brutality, models of the gas chambers and crematoria, pieces of skin, whips, instruments of torture, and sticks with bloodstains still on them.

One long corridor is given over to photographs of thousands of the victims, whose dates of arrival and death are listed from records the Nazis kept. Above all the display cases are explanatory signs and charts giving a statistical picture of history's most sanguinary extermination facility. Also preserved is the straw-covered wall against which prisoners were shot. On either side of this wall are the huts used as a suffocation cell and a laboratory where sterilization experiments were carried out on women prisoners. In the museum's library are the resolutions adopted by the inmates and buried by them for future historians, official Nazi records, protocols of the war criminals' trials, thousands of books and pamphlets about Auschwitz, albums of family portraits, and the complete lists of the death transports.

One hut has been converted into a reception room where visitors are asked to write their reaction to what they have seen in a thick volume already filled with messages in scores of languages. Just opposite this hut stands the gallows the Poles built to hang Rudolf Hoess, Nazi commandant of Auschwitz. It was designed so that the last thing he saw was his own death camp.

OTWOCK

MARTYRS' MONUMENT in the forest outside this town, is a memorial to the 5,000 Jews murdered here in 1942.

PIORTKOW

MEDIEVAL SYNAGOGUE that was badly damaged by the Nazis, has been rebuilt by the Polish Ministry of Art and Culture and converted into a museum of art and history.

PLASZOW

REMAINS OF GHETTO established here by the Nazis can still be seen.

PLOTSK

MEDIEVAL SYNAGOGUE ruins are being explored by Polish archeologists who have already uncovered the remains of an 11th century Jewish settlement.

PODGORZE

REMNANTS OF GHETTO WALL erected here by Nazis can still be seen.

PONIATOWO

TRAWNIKI CONCENTRATION CAMP MEMORIALS stand in the forest outside this village, over a mass grave, and in the village itself. A third and much larger monument is being planned.

PRZEMYSL

GREAT SYNAGOGUE survived the Nazi occupation, but it is now used as a warehouse.

JEWISH CEMETERY has several memorial stones to various groups of Jews murdered by the Nazis.

RABKA

MEMORIAL TO NAZI VICTIMS stands in a forest near this village, where they were killed.

RADOM

DOM ESTERY now a museum, is one of the palaces built by King Casimir the Great for his secret Jewish bride, Esterka.

RADOMSKO

JEWISH CEMETERY here is one of the few in Poland that escaped any damage at the hands of the Nazis. The tombstones of the Radomsker dynasty of Chassidic rabbis are all intact. The chapel, which suffered some damage, has been rebuilt with the help of the American Jewish Joint Distribution Committee.

RYMANOW

SYNAGOGUE, survivor of Nazi era, is now a house of culture and public library.

SIEDLCE

MEMORIAL TO NAZI VICTIMS stands in the town's main square. A memorial to Jewish victims of the Nazis, in the form of a pyramid of 2,000 Jewish tombstones collected from other cemeteries, stands in the local Jewish cemetery where 11,000 Jews were shot.

SOBIBOR

NAZI VICTIMS MEMORIAL is an eight-foot high monument in the form of an imposing sculpture of a mother and child that stands in the Jewish cemetery.

SOSNOWICE

NAZI VICTIMS MEMORIAL is a granite monument on the site of the Sosnowice ghetto where 90,000 Jews were murdered.

SWIDNICA (Schweidnitz)

JEWISH SOCIAL AND CULTURAL ASSOCIATION, 19 Bohaterow Getta.

SZCZECIN (Stettin)

JEWISH CEMETERY in this former East Prussian city of Stettin is intact.
JEWISH SOCIAL AND CULTURAL ASSOCIATION, 2 Slowackiego St.
SYNAGOGUE, 4 Slavodski St.

TARNOW

JEWISH CEMETERY here has a memorial to Nazi victims.
SYNAGOGUE REMNANT, a solitary pillar, still stands and will be permanently preserved by incorporation into a new building to be erected on the site.

TREBLINKA

CONCENTRATION CAMP SITE, halfway between Warsaw and Bialystok, where 800,000 Jews were murdered by the Nazis, is marked by a huge stone sculpture shaped like a mausoleum topped by a large Menorah. Surrounding the monument, which stands on the spot where the gas ovens once operated, and beneath which the Nazis buried the ashes of hundreds of thousands of Jews, are thousands of huge stone slabs which make up a symbolic cemetery. The stones are engraved with the names of all cities and villages from which the Jews were rounded up. At the entrance to the monument inscriptions in six languages, including Yiddish, read: "On this site, between July 1942 and August 1943, stood a Hitlerian extermination camp where 800,000 Jews from Poland, the Soviet Union, Czechoslovakia, Yugoslavia, Bulgaria, France, Belgium, Germany and Greece were done to death. On August 2, 1943, the surviving inmates in the camp revolted. The revolt was ruthlessly and bloodily suppressed by the Hitlerian executioners. Two kilometers from here, the Hitlerites murdered 10,000 people in a forced labor camp."

Near the monument the government's Committee for the Preservation of Monuments to Nazi Martyrs in Poland, maintains an office where visitors can buy books and pamphlets on the fate of the Jews under Nazi rule and postcards bearing a stamp about the death camp.

TUREK

SYNAGOGUE still stands, but it has been converted into a store on the street level and into a social club where the women's gallery used to be. Cattle graze in the old Jewish cemetery amid broken tombstones on which names can still be made out.

WALBRZYCH (Waldenburg)

JEWISH SOCIAL AND CULTURAL ASSOCIATION, 38 Wyzwolenia St.

WARSAW

ANIELEWICZ STREET, between the former Nalewiki St., once the heart of the Jewish quarter, and Zamenhof St., is named for Mordecai Anielewicz, commander of the Jewish fighters in the heroic revolt of the Jews of the Warsaw Ghetto in 1943. He was barely twenty when he was arrested by the Soviet authorities in 1939 for organizing the emigration of Jews from the Russian-occupied areas of Poland to Palestine. Released in 1940, he became the leader of Jewish underground groups in Vilna and Czestochowa until his appointment in 1942 as commander in chief of the Jewish Fighters Organization. He was killed in the ghetto uprising.

FUNDAMANSKI STREET is named for Ephraim Fundamanski, one of the organizers of the Ghetto revolt.

GHETTO MONUMENT commemorating the revolt of the Jews in the Warsaw ghetto against the Nazi occupation forces, at the corner of Anielewicz and Zamenhof Sts., stands on the site of the central command post where the first Jewish fusilade was fired at dawn on April 19, 1943, the first day of Passover. Erected by the Polish government on the fifth anniversary of the beginning of the only open battle in which Jews succeeded in fighting the Nazis, the monument has been described as a symbolic gravestone to the 3,500,000 Jews of Poland and as a single tombstone for the thousands of Jews whose remains lie unmarked and unhallowed beneath the rubble that was the ghetto.

Designed by Nathan Rapaport, the thirty-six-foot monument is a bronze statue group mounted in front of a towering granite wall. The granite had been imported from Sweden by Hitler for a projected victory monument. The wall represents the burning side of an underground bunker where the ghetto heroes fulfilled the vow of the Jewish underground in its last appeal to the outside world: "Be it known to you that every threshold in the ghetto will remain to the end what it is now—a fortress. We may all perish in this fight, but we will not surrender . . . . We are fighting for your freedom and ours, for your human and national pride—and ours . . . . We will take revenge for the crimes committed at Oswiecim, Treblinka, Belzec and Majdanek . . . ."

The words of this pledge are incorporated in the bronze central portion of the monument, which depicts the ghetto in flames, the fighters, led by Anielewicz, surrounded by men, women and children in tattered clothes, facing death fearlessly, and armed only with stones, sticks, and naked fists. On the back is a bas-relief showing the contrasting visages of fear and despair worn by those herded off to the gas chambers. Two huge Menorahs, symbolic of Judaism and the State of Israel, flank the main part of the monument. The inscription, in Yiddish, Hebrew, and Polish, at the base contains these words: "To the Jewish People, Its Heroes and Its Martyrs."

This monument, symbolizing one of Jewry's greatest agonies, stands in a square surrounded on three sides by blocks of new apartment houses erected since 1951. The area around the monument is set aside as a park. Beneath the eight-story apartments lie the bones and ashes of tens of thousands of the Jews who died in the Warsaw ghetto.

The only remnant of the ghetto still standing is the grim ruin of the *Judenrat Building*, where the Nazis processed Jews for the gas chambers and where the Jewish puppet government of the ghetto had its headquarters. This building, with its dread reminders of the Nazi terror, faces the new apartments in the ghetto square, but it is planned to rebuild it and convert it into a museum.

Now one of the great shrines of world Jewry, the Ghetto Monument immortalizes the fighters who for forty-two days and nights held out against incredible odds in a struggle that has been compared to the siege of the Alamo and the defense of Thermopylae. In the early hours of the first day of Passover, 1943, Nazi troops who had marched into the ghetto to clean out the remaining Jews, were met with a barrage of homemade fire bombs thrown from roof tops. This began the desperate battle of a handful of young people—fewer than 1,000 Zionists, students, Jewish Socialists and Communists—against the might of an entire corps of SS troops.

When the uprising began—it had been preceded by two earlier Jewish revolts—the ghetto, covering one hundred square blocks and sealed off by an eight-foot brick wall, had been reduced to 60,000 people by starvation, disease, and deportation to the death camps. Originally, 500,000 had been jammed into this area. Armed only with fifty ancient rifles, two hundred pistols and a supply of handmade fire bombs, the tiny force of Jews seized the ghetto, ousted the Jewish puppet government, and challenged the Nazis to "come and get us." When the Nazis had shelled the ghetto into a smoking shambles, barely 80 of the Jewish fighters managed to escape via the sewers. Two of them, Isaac Zukerman, Anielewicz's co-commander, and Zivia Lubetkin, now Mrs. Zukerman, live in Israel, where there is a monument to Anielewicz.

The bunker where Anielewicz and his chiefs of staff met their death was in the building at 10 Mila St., but since the area has been rebuilt the site now faces 1 Mila St., where there is a memorial marker. On the house next to the notorious *Umschlagplatz*, where the Nazis carried out their "selections" for deportation, three simple plaques inscribed in Polish, Hebrew, and Yiddish, affixed to the wall on Stawki St., tell the tragic story. A circular memorial stone in front of the Judenrat Building marks the manhole cover exit from the sewer used by the ghetto fighters. At *Mila 18*, headquarters of the Ghetto revolt command, there is a mound surrounded by a granite memorial.

JEWISH CEMETERY on Okopowa St., at the end of Gesia St., not far from the Ghetto Monument, miraculously survived the destruction of the ghetto. The remarkable tombstones and mausoleums, with their unique carved and painted artistic representations, make this one of the most celebrated Jewish burial grounds in the world. Here rest some of the most distinguished personalities in the history of Jewry. In a literary pantheon are the tombs of Isaac Loeb Peretz, the beloved Yiddish and Hebrew poet and author of immortal folk tales; S. Ansky, who wrote the famous play *The Dybbuk*; Jacob Dinesohn, the Yiddish novelist; Hirsch D. Nomberg and Moses Broderson, authors. Nearby is the mausoleum of Ludwig Zamenhof, founder of Esperanto; the tomb of Berek Sonnenberg, the grain magnate whose grandson was Henri Bergson, the Nobel prize winner; the tomb of Osias Thon, rabbi, Zionist pioneer, and leader of Polish Jewry; and simple stones marking the collective graves of the Jewish resistance heroes whose remains were dug out of the ghetto bunkers and places of execution.

JEWISH COMMUNITY HEADQUARTERS, 6 Krajowej Rady Narodowej, is located in a kind of compound, which includes a Hebrew school, a kosher kitchen, ritual bath, residences of officials, and an ORT workshop. This is also the national headquarters of the Union of Jewish Religious Communities.

JEWISH HISTORICAL INSTITUTE, 79 Swierozewskiego St., off Dzherzhinsky Square, a State-supported institution that is part of the Polish Academy of Science, occupies the former building of the Institute of Judaic Studies, next to which the *Great Synagogue* stood on Tlomacki Place, until its destruction by the Nazis. Here can be seen one of the most remarkable collections of Judaica in the world as well as a museum and library that tell the story of the Warsaw ghetto and the Ghetto Revolt.

The Judaica collection was assembled from the remnants of Jewish libraries and museums looted by the Nazis throughout Europe and then abandoned in a long line of freight cars on a railroad siding in Silesia. The rescued materials include manuscripts, books, and documents from the Jewish Theological Seminaries in Wroclaw, Berlin, and Vienna, as well as the famed rabbinic library of the Lublin Yeshiva. Among the rare items on exhibit are a letter from Spinoza's teacher; contemporary records of the Sabbatai Zevi messianic movement in the seventeenth century; the minutes of the Council of the Four Lands in the seventeenth century; a ninth-century parchment diary of a Jewish traveler to Poland, and Jewish communal archives from many Polish and Silesian towns.

The two upper floors, known as the Martyrs' Museum, are entirely devoted to the story of the Warsaw ghetto and the other Polish ghettos. The most unusual exhibit consists of two rusty milk cans in which Dr. Emanuel Ringelblum, the archivist of the Warsaw ghetto, hid the daily record of the life and death of Warsaw Jewry from 1939 to 1943. Above the cans hangs a portrait of Dr. Ringelblum, who was shot by the Nazis after the ghetto was destroyed. The cans were dug up from under the ruins of a building on Nowolipie St. in 1946. In these cans were diaries, reports, and documents which survived because the cans were sealed behind an armored, concrete-reinforced door. In another case are an old hunting rifle and two pistols, part of the weapons used by the ghetto fighters. Elsewhere are collected the records of the Jewish councils in the ghettos established by the Nazis; files of ghetto newspapers, execution orders, statistics of arrivals and departures from the Warsaw ghetto, files of the Warsaw branch of the American Jewish Joint Distribution Committee up to December 1941, and a large gallery of photographs of life in the Warsaw ghetto and of paintings by ghetto artists. Also on display are portraits of World War II statesmen and leaders, including Dr. Chaim Weizmann, Moshe Sharett, David Ben Gurion, Stalin, Churchill, Roosevelt, and Eisenhower.

JEWISH CULTURAL HOUSE, Grzybowski Square, in what was once the old Jewish quarter, was opened in 1966 as the headquarters of the Social and Cultural Union of Polish Jews, a government-sponsored organization which maintains libraries, Yiddish schools and cultural centers in 20 cities.

In this building is also located the $1,250,000 Jewish State Theatre of Poland, which was opened in 1970 as the home of the Yiddish theatre made famous by its star performer and director, Ida Kaminska, who moved to New York in 1968. Plays in Yiddish are presented three times a week by a permanent company supported by the government.

The same building also houses the editorial offices of a Yiddish publishing house, of the Folkstimme, Poland's only Yiddish newspaper, and two Jewish cooperatives.

JEWISH HOME FOR THE AGED, 6 Wojtowska St., a four-story structure opened in 1963, is the first erected in Poland since the end of World War II. The funds were provided by the American Joint Distribution Committee and the Central British Jewish Fund. It has a small synagogue and a kosher kitchen. Some of the residents were moved from an older home in Lodz which had survived the Nazi occupation.

KORCZHAK SCHOOL, an elementary school, is named for Dr. Yanush Korczhak, physician and educator, who, together with the children from the Jewish orphanage he directed, was killed by the Nazis. The school is located in the same building from which the Nazis marched Dr. Korczhak and his charges to their death.

LEWARTOWSKY STREET, between Gesia and Anielewicz Sts., memorializes Joseph Lewartowsky, a Communist, who was one of the top leaders of the ghetto revolt.

PERETZ STREET, the former Ceglana St., is named for Isaac Loeb Peretz, one of the giants of Yiddish literature, who lived and worked in Warsaw from 1887 until his death in 1915. His stories and poems describing the hardships of Jewish life in the East European *shtetl* have become classics because they reflected the strivings of the oppressed, the poor, and the idealistic. The street bearing his name adjoins Grzybowska St., which ran through the heart of the prewar Jewish community.

SHTERN STREET is named for Abraham Shtern, a pioneer of the Haskalah movement in Poland, a director of the Rabbinical Seminary and inventor of an early 19th century adding machine.

WARSAW SYNAGOGUE, 6 Krajowej Rady Narodowej, is tucked away in the compound of the Jewish Community Headquarters. This is the only synagogue left in Warsaw.

ZAMENHOF MEMORIAL, a plaque in front of the building at 5 Zamenhof St., honors Dr. Ludwig Zamenhof, the Bialystok physician and eye specialist who invented Esperanto in 1887 as an international language, which he hoped would lead to world peace. The plaque was dedicated in 1959, on the centennial of his birth, by the International Congress of Esperantists to replace a monument erected in 1928 but destroyed by the Nazis. Zamenhof lived in Warsaw most of his adult life. *Zamenhof Street* is world-famous as the site of the Ghetto Monument.

WEGROW

JEWISH CEMETERY has been restored and fenced in by the local authorities who erected a monument in memory of the Jews killed here by the Nazis.

WROCLAW (Breslau)

SHOLOM ALEICHEM SCHOOL on Peretz St., a State-supported lyceum for Jewish children, is named for Sholom Aleichem (Solomon Rabinovitch), the beloved Yiddish humorist and teller of folk tales, who has been called the "Yiddish Mark Twain." On the walls of the school's corridors are scenes depicting incidents and characters in Sholom Aleichem's stories.

JEWISH CEMETERY which survived the Nazi era, although badly damaged, contains the tombstones of Heinrich Graetz, the celebrated Jewish historian, and Ferdinand Lassalle, the philosopher and organizer of the German Socialist party. Graetz taught at the Jewish Theological Seminary in Wroclaw when the city was known as Breslau. Mrs. Graetz, also buried here, was a kinswoman of Sir John Monash, the Jewish general who commanded the Australian Army Corps in World War I. Lasalle's tombstone had been smashed by the Nazis and the pieces of white marble were still lying about when a new one, of black marble, was erected in 1947. The name on the stone is spelled "Lassal," which is the way his father spelled it. There is also a memorial here to the Russian soldiers who liberated Breslau in 1944, among them a Jew named Joseph Bumagin.

JEWISH CLUB, 14 Dubois St., also houses the Isaac Loeb Peretz Yiddish Library.

JEWISH COMMUNAL HEADQUARTERS, 5 Wlodkiewicza St., occupies the building of the famous Breslau Jewish Theological Seminary, which was founded in 1854 and became the model for rabbinical seminaries throughout the western world. For several generations this seminary was the theological center of Reform Judaism. Until the Nazis came to power, Breslau was the third-largest Jewish center in Prussia. Today it is one of the three largest Jewish centers in Poland. Adjoining the communal building, which houses a school and an ORT workshop, is the city's only surviving synagogue at 11 Wlodkiewicza St. (the former Wallstrasse). The seminary was closed by the Nazis and has never reopened. Part of its library was saved and is now in the Jewish Historical Institute in Warsaw.

JEWISH STATE THEATRE, 28 Swidnica St., is in the building which houses the local branch of the Jewish Social and Cultural Association.

KORCZAK MUNICIPAL ORPHANAGE honors the memory of Dr. Yanusz Korczak, the Jewish physician who looked after the children in the Warsaw Ghetto during the Nazi occupation, and perished with them.

ZAMOSZCZ

I. L. PERETZ BIRTHPLACE still stands and is the site of cultural and literary meetings.

ZARY (Sorau)

JEWISH SOCIAL AND CULTURAL ASSOCIATION, 3 Zaulek Klasztorny St.

ZASLOW

NAZI MARTYRS MEMORIAL honors the 10,000 Jews, Poles and Gypsies murdered by the Nazis in the nearby Sanok Concentration camp.

PORTUGAL

The earliest reference to Jews in Portugal mentions them as winegrowers in 900 C.E., when the Moslems still controlled the Iberian Peninsula. In 1147, when the first Christian king was crowned, he found synagogues in Santarem and Beja, and Jewish settlements in Lisbon and in many villages. Portugal's rulers between the thirteenth and fifteenth centuries were unusually tolerant of the Jews, permitting them to open a synagogue in Lisbon, to organize as a quasi-autonomous minority, and to hold the highest offices. John I not only kept anti-Jewish violence in Spain from spilling over into his realm but welcomed Jewish refugees from the Spanish massacres of 1391.

One of these, Judah Abrabanel, became the royal treasurer. His son, Isaac, scholar, statesman, Bible commentator and the greatest Jewish figure of his time, served Alfonso V in a similar capacity. Abrabanel fled to Spain in 1483 because Alfonso's successor suspected him of being involved in a court intrigue, but until 1497 no profession or occupation was barred to Portuguese Jews.

They established the country's first printing press. Joseph Vecinho, court physician and counselor to John II, represented the king at a royal congress of astronomers convoked to further Portuguese voyages of exploration. Vasco da Gama, whose discovery of the sea route to India began the golden age of Portuguese history, was counseled by Jewish savants, financed by Jewish enterprise, and used maps and instruments of Jewish manufacture. As the wealth of the Indies began to reach Europe via Portugal, Jewish merchants and entrepreneurs helped make Lisbon the commercial mecca of the Continent. Garcia da Orta, physician to the Portuguese viceroy of the Indies in 1542-45, authored the pioneer study of Oriental plants and drugs. Pedro Teixeira was employed by Portugal to explore its South American territories early in the 17th century.

Large numbers of the Jews expelled from Spain in 1492 poured across the frontier to Portugal. A huge bribe persuaded John II to let the 600 wealthiest families remain permanently. Artisans and craftsmen were eagerly welcomed. Another 100,000 Jews were also admitted upon payment of a stiff head tax. Their stay was limited to eight months, after which they were to head for North Africa. Crowded into unseaworthy vessels manned by unscrupulous crews, few reached more tolerant shores; they either perished in shipwrecks, were robbed and thrown into the sea, or were stranded on uninhabited islands and left to die. Many more who were impoverished by extortions and overstayed the deadline, were given the choice of conversion or slavery, while their children were forcibly baptized and deported to the Portuguese colonies.

A week after John's successor, Manuel I, was betrothed to the daughter of Ferdinand and Isabella, he decreed the banishment of all Jews and Moslems within eleven months unless they accepted Christianity. Hoping to retain the advantages of Jewish diligence, business sagacity, and scholarship without alienating his powerful in-laws, Manuel promulgated another edict, which banned all emigration and stipulated that no one should be molested for twenty years because of his religious practices. The king expected that ultimately the unwilling converts would become genuine Christians, but the Marranos only practiced Judaism with considerably less secrecy than their contemporaries in Spain.

Gradually, the Marranos became concentrated in the northern provinces of

Tras-os-Montes, Beira Alta, and Entre-Douro-e-Minho, which became virtually a Marranoland when refugees from the Lisbon massacre of 1506 fled north. Introduction of the Inquisition in 1531 only intensified the Marranos' crypto-Judaism. The handful who managed to resist conversion and escaped from Portugal at the end of the sixteenth century founded the Jewish settlements in Holland, in North and South America, and in England.

The pseudo messiahs of the early sixteenth century brought temporary hope to the Marranos when David Reubeni was welcomed at the court of Portugal as the alleged emissary of a mythical Jewish kingdom in Asia who sought an alliance with the Christian world against the advancing Turks. His most faithful follower was Diego Pires, a Portuguese Marrano. Convinced that Reubeni was the advance agent of the messiah, Pires openly returned to Judaism under the name of Solomon Molcho and proclaimed himself the messiah. Both men created a great stir among Jews and Christians before they came to tragic ends.

The reforms of the Marquês de Pombal, himself of Marrano descent, ended all the disabilities of the Marranos in 1773, but this did not create any great manifestation of Judaism among the isolated Marranos. Cut off from the main stream of Jewish life for so long, they had come to regard the remnants of secret prayers and ceremonies which remained to them as the only true Judaism and their underground worship as a fundamental element of Judaism as they understood it.

About the middle of the eighteenth century, British Jews from Gibraltar, whose foreign nationality protected them from the Inquisition, established the modern Jewish community in Lisbon. By 1820 there was also a congregation in Faro, where a synagogue existed for more than sixty years. In the 1860s, Jews from Morocco and Tangier also settled in Faro and Lisbon. Just before World War I, the first Russian and Polish Jews arrived.

While working mining properties in the Serra da Estrella region in 1917, Samuel Schwartz, a Jewish engineer from Poland, stumbled on the forgotten Marrano communities and obtained avowals of Judaism from many of them. Further exploration turned up whole villages near the Spanish frontier inhabited almost entirely by Marranos. Since 1925, efforts have been made to further their return to Judaism.

History repeated itself in the early years of World War II, when refugees from Nazi-occupied France found Portugal their last escape hatch from Western Europe. Portuguese consuls in France were generous in providing transit visas that enabled the exiles to live in coastal villages, with the support of international Jewish relief agencies, until they could be moved elsewhere. Few remained after the war. The present Jewish population is about 800, not including Marranos, and most of them live in Lisbon.

Visitors to Lisbon will notice that the policemen wear Magen David badges. The city's famous Sintra pastries are packed in white and blue paper decorated with a Magen David.

BELMONTE

MARRANO JEWS, descendants of Jews who were forcibly baptized in 1496 but maintained a crypto-Judaism for more than four hundred years, still exist in isolated pockets in and around this mountain town of Beira-Baixa Province. There are similar groups of Marrano Jews, who practice a curious kind of Judaism, in the neighboring towns of Guarda, Covilha, and Monsanto. Their existence came to light in 1917 through the discoveries of the late Samuel Schwartz, a Polish-Jewish mining engineer, who vainly sought for remnants of the Belmonte synagogue of 1297 which stood in the Rua das Lages. In recent years Anita Novimsky, a Brazilian scholar, has engaged in extensive research into the history of the Marranos. With the support of the Portuguese government she has assembled ancient records and conducted taped interviews.

In 1928, some of these Marranos organized what was then the second Jewish congregation in Portugal since 1496 in Bragança. Their synagogue, which no longer exists, was located on Rua Direita, the city's main street. It was known as Communidade Israelita de Bragança. The building was identified by a sign that read: "The unity of God and the truth of the Law of Moses." Prime mover in the creation of this congregation was the late Captain Arture Carlos de Barros Basto, who was born of a Marrano family in Porto in 1887. A professional soldier, Barros Basto was the first to raise the flag of the Republic on the Porto town hall when the monarchy was overthrown in 1910. He served with distinction in the Portuguese Expeditionary Force in France during World War I, after which he embraced Judaism publicly and began a new career as the advocate of a movement that sought to persuade thousands of Portuguese descended from Marranos to accept Judaism. These efforts coincided with Schwartz's discoveries around Belmonte. Basto launched a Jewish newspaper, made contact with Jewish leaders in London, and established small Jewish communities in half a dozen cities.

CASTELO BRANCO

MUNICIPAL MUSEUM, in the heart of this little village, preserves the cornerstone from the thirteenth-century synagogue at nearby Belmonte.

ÉVORA

PUBLIC LIBRARY owns many Hebrew manuscripts dealing with the thirteenth- and fourteenth-century Jewish community here.

REGIONAL MUSEUM, Largo Marquez de Marialva, the most important in the south of Portugal, preserves an old Hebrew-inscribed tombstone as well as the cornerstone from the fourteenth-century synagogue in Évora.

FARO

MEDIEVAL JEWISH CEMETERY, dating from about the fourteenth century, still exists here. This city was a famed center of Hebrew printing in the fifteenth century. The first printed book in Portugal, a Hebrew edition of the Pentateuch, was issued here in 1487 by Samuel Porteira. A later Jewish burial ground dates from 1820. The synagogue established here in 1850 by Jews from Gibraltar and North Africa no longer exists.

GOUVEIA

MUNICIPAL MUSEUM, next door to town hall, has on display in its courtyard a polished granite stone with Hebrew inscriptions. Uncovered in 1968 during the demolition of ancient houses on the Rua Nova (a street name often encountered in Portugal and which recalls the 'New Christians'), the tablet has been identified as part of a synagogue dedicated in 1497. The inscriptions are lines from the Hebrew Bible.

LISBON

ASHKENAZIC SYNAGOGUE, 110 Rua Elias Garcia (first floor).

CEMETERIO ISRAELITA on Avenida Alfonso III, is hidden by a tall stone wall with no visible markings on the shabby wooden gate. Beyond the wall are terraced rows of man-sized horizontal tombstones.

CHURCH OF THE CARMO on the Largo de Carmo, atop the hill of Santa Justa, a shattered sanctuary ruined by the earthquake of 1755, contains three old Hebrew-inscribed tombstones, one of which dates from the sixth century. There is also an inscribed stone from a synagogue built in 1307 on the Judiaria Velha, now known as the Rua dos Fanqueiros.

ISRAELI CONSULATE GENERAL, 6 Avenida Poeta Mistral.

JEWISH COMMUNITY CENTER, 10 Rua Rosa Araujo, is the focal point for all Jewish communal activities. Opened in 1948, it links the older Sephardic Jews and the newer Ashkenazic Jews, who came here as refugees from France and eastern Europe in the late 1930s and early 1940s.

JEWISH COMMUNITY HEADQUARTERS, 16 R/C Rua do Monte Olivete. The honorary head of the community in 1971 was 78-year old Dr. Moses Bensabat Amazalak, a native of Lisbon, who is chancellor of Lisbon's Technical University and a world-famous scholar in history, Oriental languages and philosophy.

NATIVE ARTS MUSEUM displays a large mural depicting all the people of Portugal, including Jews who are shown wearing Stars of David on their clothing.

NATIONAL MUSEUM OF ART displays a large painting by Verdes showing a circumcision scene, which includes the mohel, the godfather holding the child, a rabbi holding a prayerbook and the mother with her face turned away. Another painting by Gonzales shows Moses holding the Tablets of the Law.

ROSSIO SQUARE was the site of the auto-da-fes where Jews were burned at the stake.

RUA DA JUDIARIA (Jews' Street), is the only remnant of what was once one of the great Jewish communities of Europe. There used to be four Jewish quarters in Lisbon. The largest was located in the Da Madalena quarter. A second was in the old Pedreira section outside the city walls. The third was in the Alfama area. The fourth, known as the Petite Juiverie (Little Jewry), was in the block of houses which now extends between the Church of San Julião and the Bank of Portugal building.

SEPHARDIC SYNAGOGUE, 59 Rua Alexandre Herculano, an imposing structure, was dedicated in 1902, although the present Jewish community dates from the middle 1800s. The synagogue houses a wealth of historical documents and religious objects dating back to the fourteenth and fifteenth centuries. A Moorish-type structure, Sinogogu Shaare Tikvah is hidden behind a 20-foot iron gate that encloses a courtyard in the center of which stands the synagogue.

PORTO

KAHAL KODOSH MEKOR HAIM SYNAGOGUE (Kadoorie Synagogue), 340 Rua Guerra Junqueiro, was the first synagogue built by and for native Portuguese Jews in over four centuries. It was opened in the 1920s under the leadership of Captain Barros Bastos, with the aid of funds provided by the Kadoorie family of Bagdad, Iraq. It is registered as British-owned property. Barros Bastos was "president, *hazan*, treasurer, secretary, and general fairy godmother" of this synagogue for more than twenty years, when he undertook his one-man campaign to bring his fellow Marranos back to Judaism.

TOMAR

ANCIENT SYNAGOGUE on the Rua Nova (once the city's Jewish quarter), is the only surviving monument of medieval Jewry in Portugal. Now classified as a national monument, the tiny, cell-like structure, with Gothic vaulting upheld by four central columns, is a real museum piece. It is redolent of port and Madeira, Portugal's famous wines, because it was for many years used as a wine cellar.

AZORES

ANGRA DE HEROISMO

PORTO JUDAEO, an ancient port on the outskirts of this town on the island of Terceira, was named for the Jews who first landed here in 1497 when the Azores were owned by the Dutch. There is also an old Jewish cemetery at Angra de Heroismo.

HORTA

JEWISH CEMETERY in this principal town on the island of Fayal, dates from the late 16th century.

PONTA DELGADA

SAAR HA-SAMAIN SYNAGOGUE (Gate of Heaven), at 16 Rua de Brum, in this chief town of the Island of San Miguel, is a beautiful sanctuary of Victorian architecture in the rear of an old-fashioned apartment occupied by two aged sisters. It was erected in 1836, more than three and a half centuries after Jews first arrived here as refugees from the Portuguese inquisition. The handsome religious appurtenances will ultimately be housed in a small museum in Temple Beth Shalom, Peabody, Mass.

SAAR-HA-SAMAIN CEMETERY behind a high brick wall, has a large number of flat tombstones, some dating from the late 16th century.

MADEIRA ISLANDS

MADEIRA

The handful of Jewish residents in this principal city of Portugal's Madeira Islands in the North Atlantic is the remnant of those who came here as refugees from Gibraltar during World War II.

RUMANIA

Jews first settled in Rumania, the Dacia of the ancient world, in pre-Christian times, probably as part of the same migration from Persia and Palestine that created Jewish colonies along the coasts of the Black and Caspian Seas and in the Caucasus in the sixth century B.C.E. This nucleus was enlarged by settlers the Romans brought in after they conquered Dacia in 107 C.E. The existence of a Jewish community in Dacia in the fourth century is confirmed by written references to a synagogue there and by the discovery of Hebrew inscriptions among Greek and Latin artifacts.

Dacia was well known to Jewish merchants from Germany, Poland, Bohemia, and Constantinople in the ninth and tenth centuries, since this region extended along the main east-west commercial route. Among the early settlers here were the Khazars, the people of the Jewish kingdom of Khazaria that ruled southern Russia between the seventh and tenth centuries.

When the principalities of Moldavia, in the north, and Wallachia, in the south, emerged out of the warring and mixed tribes of Dacia in the thirteenth and fourteenth centuries as the nuclei of what was to become Rumania, well-established Jewish communities already existed in both regions. Subjugated by the Turks in the sixteenth century, the two principalities continued to be ruled by Christian princes, whose Jewish subjects were under constant harassment. Nevertheless, the Jewish population grew steadily.

Jews expelled from Hungary in 1349 and 1360 found a haven in Wallachia. Refugees from Ukrainian pogroms poured across the border into Moldavia in 1648 and 1649. Spanish-speaking Jews from Turkey settled in both principalities between 1500 and 1700. Late in the eighteenth, and early in the nineteenth century, Jewish merchants and artisans from Poland, Germany, and Hungary were invited by the Rumanian nobles to create new towns in Moldavia and to transform the feudal system into a modern economy. Jews fleeing nineteenth-century Czarist oppression in Poland and the Ukraine sought greater freedom in Moldavia.

Attacked by both sides during the sporadic Russo-Turkish wars (1769-1812) that were fought largely on Rumanian soil, and plundered and massacred by native Rumanians in eighteenth- and nineteenth-century pogroms, the Jews hoped that the unification of Moldavia and Wallachia in 1859 and the creation of the kingdom of Rumania in 1861 would lead to their emancipation. A brief interlude of tolerance was soon ended by an official government policy of anti-Semitism. The new constitution branded Jews as aliens and vagrants and thus denied them rights of residence and occupation. Arbitrary expulsions from towns and villages and anti-Jewish excesses became so widespread that the great powers of Europe and the United States lodged official protests. In the hope of ameliorating the plight of the 200,000 Jews, the United States sent as its consul general to the new government in 1876 Benjamin N. Peixotto, a distinguished newspaper editor and a former president of B'nai B'rith.

Granted complete independence by the Treaty of Berlin in 1878 on condition that all inhabitants be accorded equal political and civil rights, Rumania deliberately evaded and violated these provisions through discriminatory legislation and regulations aimed only at Jews. Deprived of many sources of livelihood, barred from schools and universities, excluded from the professions, made the scapegoats for peasant misery, subject to a special poll tax, and denied elementary civil and political rights, the majority of Rumanian Jewry was a downtrodden minority from 1878 to the time of World War I.

Most of the Jews lived in villages and small towns, subsisting as artisans and petty traders. For the most part ultra-Orthodox, they spoke Yiddish, dressed in the traditional garb of East European Jewry, and maintained a network of religious schools and yeshivas and supported many Chassidic rabbis. Some Jews, however, particularly in Bucharest and Galati, contributed enormously to the growth of industry and commerce in the second half of the nineteenth century. They organized the country's credit, brought in French, German, and Austrian capital, developed mines, and built railroads.

In 1899 there began the unparalleled movement of the "walkers"—an organized march of thousands of Jews across Rumania to Austria and Hungary on their way to the United States, England, and Palestine. More than 70,000 left Rumania between 1900 and 1906 to escape pauperization and terror. In 1902, John M. Hay, President Theodore Roosevelt's Secretary of State, sent a note to the signatories of the Treaty of Berlin, denouncing Rumania's treatment of the Jews as "an international wrong." But neither this protest nor those made during the Balkan Wars that preceded World War I were able to alter Rumania's traditional anti-Jewish policy.

World War I added more than 500,000 Jews to Rumania's Jewish subjects as a result of the annexation of Bukovina and Transylvania from Austria-Hungary and Bessarabia from Russia. Although the postwar treaties contained safeguards for the hard-won rights of the Jewish minorities in the new territories, the discrimination and legal obstacles from which the Jews of Old Rumania had suffered were extended to all of the 1,000,000 Jews in the vastly enlarged country. New laws and regulations created crippling disabilities against Jews in trade, commerce, industry, education, and the professions. Fanned by the fascist Iron Guard and encouraged by church prelates, the anti-Jewish offensive became more intense after 1930, when King Carol returned with Magda Lupescu, his Jewish mistress. When the Nazis took over in Germany, the Rumanian anti-Semites became their allies, and in 1937 they established a fascist dictatorship of their own. The Nazi-like curbs against Jews, and the massacres that ensued, paved the way for the extermination of 385,000 Rumanian Jews under the Nazi and fascist regimes in Bessarabia and northern Bukovina and Transylvania during the war years. Fewer Jews were killed in Old Rumania and southern Bukovina and Transylvania. Nearly 400,000 Jews survived World War II. Half of these migrated after the war, most of them going to Israel. In the 1950s and early 1960s, the authorities discouraged emigration to Israel. Nevertheless, by 1970, 18 percent of Israel's population was of Rumanian origin. Today there are an estimated 100,000 Jews in Rumania, half of whom live in Bucharest. The rest are scattered in 75 other cities and towns.

Next to Russia, Rumania is the Communist country with the largest Jewish population. The Jews are recognized as a national minority, and they have equal civil, political, and cultural rights. Unlike the Soviet Union, the government of Rumania boasts of its support for Jewish cultural and religious life. The State assists synagogues and its functionaries, allows the distribution of matzoth and kosher wine, supports a Yiddish theatre, and subsidizes the religion-oriented Federation of Jewish Communities. Functioning under the supervision of the Ministry of Culture, the

Federation is managed by both Communist and non-Communist Jews. The Federation represents all Jewish communities where there are still over 100 synagogues, a score or more of Hebrew schools, and a state-created summer resort (at Borsa) for Jewish religious and educational officials. The Federation sponsors cultural events, maintains and restores cemeteries, administers Jewish education, conducts research in Jewish history, regulates kosher meat production, administers the distribution of matzoth, Passover wine and oversees the publication of Yiddish and Hebrew books issued by the state publishing house. The Federation also publishes a tri-lingual fortnightly journal, operates kosher canteens and communal kitchens.

Chief Rabbi David Moses Rosen, a native Rumanian, who is also president of the Federation, editor of the journal and a member of parliament, is trusted by both the Communist government and the Jewish community at home and abroad. He has visited and spoken in the West a number of times and has joined the Conference of Orthodox European Rabbis. Rabbi Rosen is one of only three rabbis in the country. The government pays part of their salaries but the community supports its activities from the sale of kosher foods and matzoth, burials and voluntary contributions.

The well-organized community, however, requires extensive financial aid from the American Joint Distribution Committee which cares for thousands of sick and aged poor through a network of social services, cash grants and clothing and food packages.

Since the ouster of the pro-Stalinist leadership of the Rumanian Communist Party, the regime has expanded its economic and cultural ties with Israel. An Israeli trade exposition was held in Bucharest in 1968. Rumania remains the only Iron Curtain country that refused to sever relations with Israel after the Arab-Israeli war of 1967. Several thousand Torah Scrolls from scores of unused Rumanian synagogues were sent to Israel by Rabbi Rosen with the consent of the Rumanian authorities.

The destruction of the merchant class after World War II struck hardest at the Jews, who are now largely small tradesmen, factory workers, technicians and professionals. Some Jews attained considerable influence in the Communist regime. The late Ana Pauker was foreign minister from 1947 to 1952 when she was ousted in a party purge. Gheorghe Gaston-Marin, the architect of Rumania's recent economic upsurge, was deputy prime minister until 1969 when he was demoted to the post of president of the state committee for prices. At the same time, Leonte Rautu, the party's chief ideologist, was elevated to deputy prime minister. Simeon Bughici, minister for food industry in 1970, was formerly foreign minister and deputy prime minister and a one-time ambassador to Moscow. The director of the National Theatre is Moni Gelehrter. Vassily Rausser is an influential economist and Aurel Baranga is the country's most popular playwright.

The devastating floods of 1970 obliterated the remnants of Jewish life in Satu Mare (Satmar), once the seat of the famous Satmarer dynasty of Chassidic rabbis, and in other once populous Jewish centers.

ARAD

GREAT SYNAGOGUE, Bela Farsa St.
KOSHER CANTEEN housed in the former Yeshiva building. There are 3,000 Jews in this city.

BACĂU

CERIALISTILOR SYNAGOGUE, 20 Stefan Celmari St.
MARILIS SYNAGOGUE, 15 Alexandru Celbin St.
SYNAGOGUE, 18 Aurel Marcus St.
SYNAGOGUE, 18 Jerni St.

BOTOSHANI

GREAT SYNAGOGUE, Marchian St., was founded in the sixteenth century by Jews from Poland.

BRASOV

SYNAGOGUE, 27 Poarta Scheiului.

BUCHAREST

STRADA DR. J. BARASCH is a street named for Julius Barasch, a mid-nineteenth-century physician and philanthropist. He taught at the University of Bucharest, established Rumania's first children's hospital in 1858 and was one of the leaders in the Jewish community's struggle for freedom.

CITY MUSEUM has a Jewish section containing a collection of Yiddish and Hebrew manuscripts and books. A Hebrew-inscribed tombstone in the museum is believed to be from the grave of Simon Frug, Hebrew poet.

FEDERATION OF JEWISH COMMUNITIES, 9-11 Sfantul Vineri St., government-supported body representing all Jews, is housed in its own two-story building. In the building is a library of 70,000 volumes, a large collection of religious articles from the many synagogues closed in other parts of the country, a small Jewish museum and the historical archives of Rumanian Jewry. The upper floor serves as a community clothing store to which the poor come to choose garments and from which clothing parcels are sent to the needy in the provinces.

STRADA GASTER is a street named for Dr. Moses G. Gaster, a Bucharest-born scholar, rabbi, and bibliophile, who was expelled from Rumania in 1885 because of his vigorous protests against the treatment of his fellow Jews. He settled in England, where he became chief rabbi of the Sephardic community. His great library of Judaica is now in the British Museum.

GREAT (Mare) SYNAGOGUE, 11 Adamache St.

ISRAELI EMBASSY, 5 Rue Burghelea.

JEWISH CEMETERY on May First Blvd., has in its newer section on Giorgiu Road, a concrete representation of the ill-fated S.S. *Struma*, the tiny refugee ship that hit a mine in 1942 off the Rumanian coast and sank with the loss of 769 lives. The *Struma* had tried to dock at Istanbul but was turned back because its passengers had no visas for Palestine. The monument in the Jewish cemetery contains an inscription blaming capitalists for the death of the refugees.

KOSHER CANTEEN, 51 Callea Cilaren, operated by the Federation of Jewish Communities, offers free hot meals to the indigent, and at 42¢ for those who can pay. There are eight similar canteens in other cities.

MALBIN SYNAGOGUE, 4 Bravilor St., is named from the Hebrew initials of Meir Lein ben Jehiel Micharl, a mid-19th century chief rabbi of Bucharest.

MAMULARI STREET SYNAGOGUE, also known as the Tailors Synagogue, and the Beth Hamedresh Dov Moshe Zusso, named for an eminent Chassidic rabbi. These are among the 18 synagogues still being used. Most of them are in the Vacaresti section, the city's East Side.

CHIEF RABBI'S OFFICE, 17 Maria Rosetti St.

REVISTA CULTULUAL MOZAIC, fortnightly cultural and religious magazine published by the Federation of Jewish Communities, has its headquarters in a decaying rococo 19th century mansion at 24 Poparusu St., where there is also a museum and library. The trilingual journal (Rumanian, Hebrew and Yiddish) advertises kosher hotels, tells where to obtain kosher meat and Passoyer foods, lists candle-lighting time for the Sabbath and Jewish festivals and the schedule of regular half-hour Yiddish programs over the Rumanian broadcasting service.

SCOALA PEDAGOGICA, 16 Lucaci St., is one of the three government schools in which Yiddish is the language of instruction. The other two are in Iasi (Jassy) and Timisoara (Temesvar). All three are housed in modern buildings.

SEPHARDIC SYNAGOGUE, 9 Strada Niko Belioannis.

SYNAGOGUE, 13 Strada Sticlari, an unused building, has a kosher butcher shop in its courtyard.

TEMPLUL CORAL, the chief synagogue of Bucharest, 13 Sfantul Vineri St., is where the chief rabbi officiates, garbed in a purple robe embroidered with a golden Star of David, and with the golden chain of office on his breast. Opened in 1866 and nearly destroyed by a mob that same year, the synagogue accommodates nearly four thousand worshipers. It is classified as a national monument and is under the protection of the Rumanian Academy of Arts and Sciences. In a separate wing of the synagogue building are housed the Niemerower Archives, a collection of documents on Rumanian Jewish history, named for Dr. Jacob Isaac Niemerower, chief rabbi of Rumania before World War II.

TEMPLUL UNIREA SFANTUL (Temple of the Sacred Union), 19 Sfantul Jon St., is the second of the city's major synagogues. In this building there is a community center. This synagogue is also classified as a national monument.

YIDDISH STATE THEATRE (Theatru Everisk is the way it reads on billboards), 15 Dr. J. Barasch St., is housed in its own modern six-hundred-seat theatre. Each seat is equipped with earphones tuned to a simultaneous-translation system. Attached to the theatre is a dramatic school. The conductor of the theatre's orchestra doubles as director of a synagogue choir. The theatre has an open-air site at 5 Mirca Voda for summer productions. A bust of Abraham Goldfaden, father of the Yiddish theatre, stands in the theatre lobby, having been moved there from Iasi when the Yiddish theatre there was closed and combined with the one in Bucharest. *Goldfaden Street* was named for him on the 80th anniversary of the establishment of his theatre in Iasi.

CLUJ (Klausenburg)

GREAT SYNAGOGUE, Mikes Keleman St., serves needs of 350 Jewish families. It has one of country's three rabbis. The state-supported matzoth factory has been closed, not because of official discrimination but for lack of business. Matzoth and Passover wine are now imported from Israel and The Netherlands.

CONSTANZA

ASHKENAZIC SYNAGOGUE, 7 Strada C. A. Rosseti.

SEPHARDIC SYNAGOGUE on Strada Mircea, was badly damaged by the Nazis and is no longer in use.

GALATI

SYNAGOGUES on Rosetti St. There are three synagogues on this street.

IASI (Jassy)

GOLDFADEN MONUMENT on Goldfaden Square, is a bronze bust of Abraham Goldfaden, a Russian-born editor, teacher and composer, who in 1876 established in

Iasi the first permanent Yiddish theatre. The bust stands on a granite pillar to which is affixed a plaque inscribed with the dates of Goldfaden's birth and death (1840-1908) and a tribute to his literary creativity. He presented Yiddish plays in Russia too, until they were banned. He then came to the United States where he edited the first illustrated Yiddish periodical in 1887. Goldfaden was also the father of Yiddish opera and the author of many Yiddish plays and operettas. The arias from some of them (*Rozhinkes mit Mandlen*, for example) became folk songs, and some of his characters (Shmendrick and Kuni Lemmel) passed into popular Yiddish speech.

GREAT SYNAGOGUE, Sinagogilor St., is believed to be the oldest existing synagogue in Old Rumania. It was originally built late in the seventeenth-century. The government treats it as a national monument. There is a tablet in the synagogue recording the fact that Abraham Joshua Heschel, a late-eighteenth-century Chassidic rabbi known as the "Apter Rav," worshiped here in 1820.

JEWISH CEMETERY which overlooks the city on the brow of a hill, contains some tombstones from the fifteenth century, when the Jewish community here was established. In one section set aside for chief rabbis of the city are massive black granite and marble tombs. Nearby, two perpetual lights burn in memory of the great sages. In another section is a mass grave for the 14,000 Iasi Jews exterminated by the Nazis in June 1941. A roughhewn stone wall with plaques inscribed in Hebrew and Rumanian constitutes their memorial.

NEUSCHOTZ SYNAGOGUE, Zugrev St., was built in 1865 by Jacob Neuschotz, banker and philanthropist, who devoted his fortune to educational and charitable activities.

(There are also Jewish communities in Timisoara, Roman, Suceava, Oradea, Dorohoi, Ploesti, Sinaia, Resita, Focsani, Pietra-Neamt, Stalin, and Baia-Mare.)

SPAIN

Because "Sfarad" is the Hebrew word for Spain, the Bible's reference to "the captivity of Jerusalem that is in Sfarad" has been interpreted to mean that Jewish captives were exiled to Iberia after the destruction of the first Temple in Jerusalem in 586 B.C.E. Some scholars believe there were Jews with the Carthaginians when they conquered the Iberian Peninsula and founded Barcelona in the third century B.C.E. Jewish settlements in Spain under Roman rule were visited by the Apostle Paul.

After the Visigoths overran Spain in 412 C.E., the Jews lived there in comparative peace for two hundred years, but a century of oppression began in the sixth century when the Visigoth kings embraced Christianity. Many Jews found sanctuary in North Africa, but those who remained suffered enforced conversion, expropriation, and enslavement. When the Moslems invaded Spain in 711, they had substantial help from Jews on both sides of the Mediterranean. Toledo capitulated to a Berber army led by Kaulan al-Yahudi, son of the queen of a Jewish tribe in North Africa. Córdoba, Málaga, and Seville were taken with the aid of Jews who welcomed the Arabs as liberators.

During the seven centuries of Moslem rule over all or part of Spain, the Jews acquired great wealth and rose to positions of influence. Under the caliphs, the Jews produced a remarkable galaxy of distinguished poets, philosophers, scientists, scholars, statesmen, financiers, and royal advisers, who helped bring about an amalgam of Jewish and Moslem culture. This in turn created Spain's literary, philosophical, scientific, and architectural renaissance.

Perhaps the most enduring contribution of the Jewish savants of this golden age was their role in spreading classical thought and literature to Christian Europe. Their Hebrew and Latin translations and interpretations from the Arabic of the Greek writings and Arabic works in mathematics and astronomy preserved much of this ancient culture for Western civilization.

Simultaneously, Spain became the center of Jewish learning in the Western world because of its noted Talmudic academies and scholars and the genius of such men as Solomon ibn-Gabirol, Judah ha-Levi, Moses ibn- Ezra, Bahya ibn-Paquda, Hasdai Crescas (ibn-Shaprut), and Nahmanides.

The civil wars that convulsed the Moslem dynasties in the eleventh, twelfth, and thirteenth centuries undermined the position of the Jews in the south of Spain, but in the north they rose to even greater prominence under the expanding Christian kingdoms. In their internecine struggles and in their crusade to drive out the Moors, the Catholic rulers welcomed the aid of Jewish financiers, statesmen, and scientists.

By the end of the fourteenth century, however, even tolerant rulers were unable to withstand the growing anti-Jewish feeling. The nobles were envious of Jewish aristocrats who had the royal ear; the Church was increasingly hostile to Judaism; and the masses hated the Jews because some of them were royal tax collectors. Mob attacks on the Jewish quarters in Seville, Barcelona, Córdoba, and Toledo in 1391 annihilated those Jewish communities.

So many Jews sought safety in conversion while secretly remaining adherents of Judaism, that the Church declared public war on these secret Jews, or Marranos. The Inquisition, established in 1478, sought to destroy the Marranos with every conceivable weapon, including death by torture. The clergy regarded the "new Christians" as heretics, while the "old Christians" were jealous of their success in commerce and politics. Ultimately, the Church prevailed upon King Ferdinand and Queen Isabella to expel all Jews on the ground that they were encouraging the Marranos in their disloyalty to Christianity.

Two months after Granada, the last Moslem outpost, fell, the decree expelling the Jews was promulgated on March 31, 1492. Given till August 1 to complete their departure, the 150,000 Jews were theoretically permitted to take their wealth with them. Actually, however, they were driven out with very little, since the export of gold, silver, and jewels was forbidden. The last of them left August 2, which was Tisha b'Ab, the fast day marking the destruction of the first and second Temples in Jerusalem. It was also the day that Columbus sailed for America with a crew that included a number of Marranos. Columbus's ships passed those taking the exiles to North Africa and the Balkans, where the outcasts were to lay the foundation for new Sephardic communities. Many other Spanish refugees headed for Portugal, Italy, and northern Germany, whence their descendants in later generations departed, to become the founders of the Jewish communities in Holland, England, Scandinavia, and North and South America.

After 1492 no professing Jews lived in Spain for nearly four hundred years. An auto-da-fé of the Inquisition occurred in 1720, when an underground Marrano synagogue was discovered in Madrid. As late as 1826 a "Judaizing" Marrano was burned alive in Valencia. The Inquisition had been abolished in 1813, restored one year later, abolished again in 1820 and reinstated in 1823; not until 1834 was it finally abolished. In 1868, when the edict of expulsion was rescinded, Moroccan Jews began trickling into Seville. Some refugees from Czarist pogroms reached Madrid in the 1880s. The upheaval in the Turkish domains during World War I brought Sephardic Jews from Salonica and Istanbul to Barcelona and Madrid. By 1917, Ignacio Bauer, an influential businessman and an adviser to King Alfonso XIII, was able to organize the first post-expulsion Jewish community in Madrid.

The Primo de Rivera dictatorship's grant of Spanish citizenship in 1924 to all the descendants of the exiles of 1492, regardless of where they lived, stimulated a slow but steady return of Sephardic Jews to Spain. Immigration increased in the 1930s, when the short-lived republican government decreed complete religious toleration, welcomed Jews who had fled from Nazi Germany, and converted medieval synagogues into national monuments. Córdoba was the scene of the first public Jewish religious service since 1492 when Spain, in 1935, sponsored a national celebration of the eight-hundredth anniversary of Maimonides's birth.

The civil war of 1936 and 1937 drove out most of the newly arrived Jews, but the Jewish population increased again during the early years of the Franco regime when large numbers of refugees from Nazi-occupied France fled across the Pyrenees. Most of them were interned but were not deported. Early in World War II, General Franco instructed Spanish consuls in Nazi-occupied Europe to issue Spanish passports to Jews of Sephardic origin and intervened with Hitler to rescue some Sephardic Jews in concentration camps. Many who acquired Spanish papers were not Sephardim.

After the war, Sephardim from Europe and North Africa began settling in Spain in considerable numbers. Jewish worship in private homes and hotels and later in synagogues established in apartment houses and office buildings were tolerated but were not permitted to be identified as such. A new law in 1964 that legalized the status of non-Catholic religions enabled Jews to worship publicly and paved the way for the erection of synagogues.

In 1965, Franco received the heads of the Jewish communities of Madrid and Barcelona, the first direct meeting of the head of a Spanish government with Jewish spokesmen since 1492. The following year the government participated in a public Jewish ceremony in the Transito Synagogue in Toledo. With the public dedication of a new synagogue in Madrid in 1968 and the formal rescinding of the 1492 edict of expulsion, a new era began for the Jews in Spain. While Spain still does not have diplomatic relations with Israel, the Spanish foreign minister in 1970 said that "the fact that we are friends with the Arabs does not make us the enemy of Israel."

Meanwhile, the Franco government and the church furthered research into Jewish history and promoted Jewish culture and Christian-Jewish relations. Books, pamphlets and scholarly monographs on the contribution of Jews to Spanish culture appeared with great frequency. In 1971 there were 8500 Jews in Spain. The largest communites are in Madrid and Barcelona, with growing settlements in Malaga and Vigo and smaller numbers in Seville, Marbella, Bilbao, Gijon, Valencia and Orense.

ARANJUEZ

WAKSMAN PLAQUE, the only memorial to a living Jew in Spain, honors Dr. Selman A. Waksman, the Russian-born American Jew who received the Nobel Prize in Medicine in 1952 for his discovery of streptomycin. The plaque was dedicated in 1957 in Dr. Waksman's presence while he was in Aranjuez, a Madrid suburb, to participate in the opening of a plant manufacturing streptomycin. Affixed to the outside of the building, the plaque is inscribed as follows: "To Selman A. Waksman on the Xth anniversary of the discovery of streptomycin on the occasion of the inauguration of this plant."

AVILA

DOMINICAN MONASTERY OF ST. TOMAS in this ancient walled city, was the place from which Torquemada prevailed upon King Ferdinand and Queen Isabella to order the expulsion or conversion of the Jews of Spain in 1492. Torquemada, who made his home in a cell in this monastery, is buried in the chapel of the monastery. In the adjoining auditorium, on April 4, 1966, Max Mazin, president of the modern Spanish Jewish community, addressed 200 Dominican friars on Judaism in a lecture sponsored by the Association of Jewish-Christian Friendship.

CHAPEL OF MOSEN RUBI on the Plaza Mosen Rubi, at intersection of Calle Bracamonte and Calle de Lopez Nunez, was originally built in 1462 as a synagogue, according to Don A. Halperin in "The Ancient Synagogues of the Iberian Peninsula." The chapel acquired its name from Mosen Rubi de Bracamonte, a French Jew who settled in Spain after Jews were expelled from France in 1396. Halperin speculates that Rubi's daughter, Juana, built the synagogue.

BARCELONA

CALLE DEL CALL, a street in the oldest part of the city, recalls the ancient Jewish community, "Call" being the Catalan equivalent of the Hebrew *kahal* community. A fragment of the old ghetto wall is built into a Gothic house at No. 5 Calle del Call. An archway at the northwest corner of the Plaza de la Constitucion is said to be the gateway of an old synagogue. The Hebrew-inscribed tombstone of "the martyr Rabbi Samuel of Sard" can be seen plastered next to the doorway of the corner house at Calle Marlet and Arco San Roman del Call.

CASA SEFARDITA, 24 Calle Porvenir, near Aribau Blvd., is both a synagogue and a Jewish Community Center. Erected in 1954 as the first synagogue built on Spanish soil since 1492, it has since been rebuilt with the aid of the JDC and Conference on Jewish Material Claims Against Germany. In the entrance lobby of the five-story white structure, just beyond the outside iron gates, is a tablet in Hebrew and Spanish dedicating the building to Moses Maimonides. Until you enter the downstairs lobby, this plaque is the only sign that the building houses a synagogue or is in any other way a Jewish institution. From the outside, the building looks like a residence much like those around it.

There are actually two synagogues in the building. On the lower floor is the synagogue of the Sephardic Jews, while the third floor is used as a synagogue by the Ashkenazic Jews. The rest of the building is given over to classrooms and facilities for cultural and recreational activities. Photos of General Franco and Theodor Herzl hang side by side in many of the rooms. The Sephardic and Ashkenazic Jews separate only for ritual purposes. For all other activities they constitute one community.

MONTJUICH, the slope overlooking the western section of the city, is so named because it was the site of extensive Jewish property holdings in the eleventh and twelfth centuries when the Jews helped establish Barcelona's commercial greatness. "Montjuich" is Catalan for "Mountain of the Jews." Along the slope is a one-thousand-year-old cemetery containing a special section set aside for Jewish graves. The flat Hebrew-inscribed stones in this section made good building materials after the Jews were massacred in 1391.

PROVINCIAL ARCHAEOLOGICAL MUSEUM in the Palacio Nacional at Parque de Montjuich, preserves a number of tombstones from the old Jewish burial ground on Montjuich, including some dated as early as the eleventh and twelfth centuries.

BÉJAR

DUCAL PALACE, a famed landmark, preserves a Hebrew-inscribed stone which is believed to be a fragment from a thirteenth-century synagogue. The inscription reads: "Dona Parvena—resplendent is the daughter of the king in her household."

BESALU

MIKVA, dating from 14th century, is now preserved in this village near the Costa Brava after it was unearthed during the demolition of a house in the ancient Jewish quarter.

BURGOS

COFFER OF THE CID, an old iron-bound box which the hero of the reconquest of Spain from the Moslems in the eleventh century left filled with sand in the hands of two Jews as a guarantee for loans to finance his war against the Moors, is displayed in the Chapel of St. Catherine in the Burgos Cathedral on the Plaza de la Catedral. In the Cathedral proper there is a stained-glass window that tells the story of Joseph and his brothers and of Joseph in Egypt. The old Jewish quarter of the city covered two areas in the thirteenth century which are now linked by the Calle Fernán Gonzales.

CACERES

CHAPEL OF SAN ANTONIO CHURCH on the outskirts of the town, is a former 13th century synagogue. The *Juderia* still exists in the town itself.

CASTELLÓN DE AMPURIAS

JUDERIA or ghetto, from the thirteenth century, including Calle Jueus (Street of the Jews), is still intact in this Catalonian town near Figueras.

CASTRILLO DE MATAJUDIOS

"*Kill the Jews*" is the literal translation of the name of this village in Valladolid Province, a throwback to ancient days. (Matar means 'to kill' and Judios means 'Jews.')

CORDOBA

ALMODÓVAR GATE, a massive Arabic arch erected when the Moslems ruled in Andalusia in the ninth and tenth centuries, used to be known as Bab-al-Yahud (Gate of the Jews) because it was the entrance to what was then the Jewish quarter.

AL-ZAHRA, about four miles west of the city, now a heap of broken columns and crumbling walls and scattered pieces of pottery and mosaics, was once the magnificent palace of Caliph Abd-er-Rahman II in the ninth century, the Moorish ruler whose court physician, counselor and diplomat was Hasdai ibn-Shaprut, the most celebrated court Jew of medieval times. In this palace Hasdai ibn-Shaprut received ambassadors from Byzantium and the Holy Roman Empire.

CALLE JUDA LEVI in the old ghetto, is named for Judah ha-Levi, medieval poet, whose verses have found their way into Jewish liturgy. He was born in Toledo but lived most of his life (1075-1141) in Córdoba.

MAIMONIDES STATUE on Plazuela de Maimonides, a square a short distance from the Calle Juderia, at the northwest corner of the Cathedral (the former Great Mosque), is directly opposite the statue of Seneca. Located in a courtyard paved with pebbles, the statue's base is a series of random-sized brown rocks fixed into a cube on which rests a plain marble bench containing the seated figure of a man wearing robes and a twisted turban of the desert. Holding a book in his lap is the sad-visaged likeness of Maimonides.

PLAZUELA DE MAIMONIDES, a little square in the old ghetto, is named for the greatest Jewish figure of medieval times, Moses ben Maimon, or Moses Maimonides, who is known to Jews as the Rambam. He was born in Córdoba in 1135, but his theological, philosophical, and medical career was lived in Palestine and Egypt. His family fled from Córdoba when he was thirteen, to escape persecution. At No. 5 Calle Judios is the *Casa Maimonides*, which guides point out as the house where Maimonides was born. A plaque is affixed to the door of the whitewashed building, which is now the home of twenty Spanish families, but the house was actually built two or three centuries after Maimonides left Córdoba.

PLAZUELA TIBERIAS, a new square was named for the ancient city in Israel where Maimonides is buried in a reciprocal gesture of friendship between Córdoba and Tiberias. The central town square in Tiberia is now named Kikar Córdoba.

RAMBAM SYNAGOGUE, 20 Calle do los Judios, built in 1315, is now a national monument. In 1935 the Spanish government sponsored the Maimonides octocentennial here, during which Jewish delegations from abroad held worship services in the remains of the synagogue, the first of their kind in 443 years. At the same time the municipality of Córdoba erected in the synagogue courtyard a plaque which, translated, reads: "On the occasion of the eight-hundredth anniversary of the birth of Rabbi Moses ben Maimon, the Spanish government, in the name of the entire nation, expresses its recognition of that immortal Jewish spirit. Córdoba, his birthplace, honors his memory."

The small Moorish building is almost bare, but it is recognizable as a synagogue. On the east wall is the vacant niche once occupied by the Ark of the Law. On the south wall are the remains of the women's gallery. On all the walls can be seen intricately designed Hebrew inscriptions, symbols, and prayers, which the government is now carefully restoring as part of a program of re-creating the synagogue as it was when first built. On the west wall there is visible the outline of a cross that once hung there when the synagogue was converted into the Church of St. Crispin, at the end of the fifteenth century. The Hebrew dedication giving the year the synagogue was erected and the name of its builder, Isaac Moheb, can be clearly seen.

ELCHE

SIXTH-CENTURY SYNAGOGUE RUINS can still be seen in this ancient city southwest of Alicante. In the remains of an old Roman colony there are the niche for the Ark of the Law and vestiges of the synagogue walls inscribed in Greek with the names of the Jewish community's officials.

EL ESCORIAL

MONASTERY OF SAN LORENZO, one of Spain's showplaces, is well worth a long climb to see the huge library, which contains many medieval Hebrew Bibles and manuscripts. As one enters the library one of the first things to be seen is a magnificently illuminated volume of the Book of Genesis, with the Hebrew word "Bereshit" in large letters.

In the Patio of Kings are sculpted effigies of six Kings of Judah by Juan Bautista Monegro.

ESCALONA

This Castilian town, is said to have been named by the early Jewish colonists after the ancient Palestinian city of Ascalon.

ESTELLA

CHURCH OF SANTA MARIA JUS DEL CASTILLO, built in 1262, was originally a synagogue and the center of the Jewish quarter. When Ferdinand and Isabella decreed the expulsion of the Jews in 1492, Estella refused to abide by the edict and gave its Jews sanctuary.

GERONA

CALLE DE LA FORSA was known as Calle del Call Judaic (Street of the Jewish Community) in the fourteenth century, when one of the town's two synagogues stood halfway up the narrow, winding street paralleling the banks of the Onar River. Another synagogue, now a private dwelling, was on the Plaza del Correo Viejo. A stone with part of one synagogue's dedicatory inscription can be seen in the *Provincial Museum* in the cloisters of San Pedro de Galligans.

MONTJUICH (Jews' Mountain), is a slope in the old Jewish quarter where the medieval Jewish cemetery was located. A number of tombstones from this cemetery are preserved in the Provincial Museum.

JUDERIA in this town in northwest corner of country, can still be seen. It was the birthplace of Nachmanides (1194-1270) and an early center of Kabbalistic studies. A synagogue dating from the Middle Ages is being restored here by the authorities.

GRANADA

ALHAMBRA, Spain's most famous castle, built by the Moors in the last years of their reign, is the place where on March 30, 1492, King Ferdinand and Queen Isabella signed the decree expelling the Jews from Spain. In the Hall of the Ambassadors, the royal pair put their names in that year to the agreement that enabled Columbus to sail westward across the Atlantic. Here, too, the Spanish rulers received Don Abraham Senior and Don Isaac Abrabanel, leaders of Spanish Jewry, for a last and futile plea to stay the fatal edict. Senior had been the marriage broker who united the Kingdoms of Aragon and Castile through the marriage of Ferdinand and Isabella.

The oldest sections of the Alhambra have recently been identified by scholars as the remnants of a fabulous palace built by Joseph ibn-Naghdela, the Jewish prime minister of the Caliph Badis. Joseph was the son of Samuel ibn-Naghdela, scholar, statesman, head of the Jewish community and soldier who led the armies of Granada for ten years on behalf of his master, Caliph Babbus. Samuel established a famous Jewish academy in the eleventh century in Granada where Solomon ibn-Gabirol and Moses ibn-Ezra taught.

Joseph built a palace of Solomonic proportions and grandeur midway in the eleventh century, only to see his influence destroyed and himself and his fellow Jews murdered in 1066. Later kings built on the foundations Joseph had laid in his palace as they enhanced the Alhambra. Among the present structures of the Alhambra, the twelve lions supporting the alabaster basins in the Fountain of Lions are patterned after the twelve oxen of King Solomon's Temple, which Joseph had copied for his palace.

In a room off the Courtyard of the Lions, there is a large six-pointed star over a grilled archway.

In name, and even in origin, the ancient city of Granada has Jewish links. Earliest mention of this region by Arab historians refers to a place called Elvira near a town named Gharnatha al-Yahud (Gharnatha of the Jews). These writers gave the pronunciation of Gharnatha as Granata, which means "pomegranate." The Jews, who had settled here in Roman days, called the same place Rimmon, which is Hebrew for "pomegranate," claiming it was founded by Tubal, son of Japheth (one of the sons of Noah), and named for Grana, a daughter of Noah.

Side by side with Alhambra is an ugly palace erected by Carlos V, in one of whose halls hangs Emilio Sada's painting, "The Expulsion of the Jews," showing Ferdinand and Isabella being told by Cardinal Mendoza and Torquemada, head of the Inquisition, that the Jews must go.

IBN TIBBON INSTITUTE at the 16th century University of Granada, is named for an illustrious family of Jewish scholars and translators, hailing from Granada, who flourished in the 12th and 13th centuries.

HERVAS

CALLE DE LA SINAGOGA in the town's oldest Roman section downhill from the main town, just outside the city wall, marks the site of the old Jewish quarter.

LA CORUÑA

CALLE DE LA SINOGOGA in the suburb of La Palloza recalls the site of a medieval synagogue. At No. 4 on this street is a well which is believed to have been part of a Jewish ritual bath. *Arroyo de los Judios*, a nearby brook, flows past the site of what used to be a Jewish cemetery.

LEÓN

PROVINCIAL MUSEUM in the Convent of San Marcos, preserves a number of eleventh- and twelfth-century tombstones from the now vanished Jewish cemetery in León.

LÉRIDA

KING SOLOMON'S SEAL, the six-pointed Star of David, is a prominent feature of one of the windows in the oldest section of the Cathedral of Lérida. The window is in a wall that connects the octagonal tower with the main section of the cathedral. The fact that the design is called King Solomon's Seal rather than the Star of David leads scholars to believe its origin is to be found in the considerable number of Moslems who worked as stonecutters and carvers in the building of cathedrals in the Middle Ages.

MADRID

INSTITUTE OF SCIENTIFIC RESEARCH, 4 Calle de Medinaceli, has a special section called the Arias Montana Institute, which since 1940 has specialized in studying the history of the Jews of Spain and in preserving examples of their art and culture. The institute (closed in August) has a library of more than 16,000 volumes and publishes a semiannual journal known as *Sfarad*, which is the Hebrew word for Spain.

MUSEO SEFARDITA DE MADRID, 18 Calle Zorrilla, one block from the American Express, has an interesting display of Jewish historical documents, art replicas and other objects related to the history of the Jews in Spain.

MUSEUM OF MODERN ART, 20 Paseo de Calvo Sotelo, part of the Palacio de la Biblioteca y Museos Nacionales, exhibits a painting of Torquemada, head of the Inquisition, pleading for the expulsion of the Jews before Ferdinand and Isabella in 1492.

NATIONAL ARCHAEOLOGICAL MUSEUM, 13 Calle de Serrano, displays, in the south wing, the upper part of a pillar from a thirteenth-century Toledo synagogue inscribed in Hebrew and Arabic, as well as the casts of Hebrew inscriptions from other medieval buildings.

PALACIO DE LIRIA, Calle de la Princesa, houses one of Spain's rarest manuscripts, "La Biblia de la Casa de Alba," (the Bible of the House of Alba). This is a handwritten Spanish translation of the Scriptures prepared by Rabbi Moses Arragel in 1422 at the request of Don Luis de Guzman. The manuscript contains 334 illustrations of Bible events, a synagogue interior, and, on the frontispiece, a picture of Rabbi Arragel presenting the completed work to Don Luis.

THE PRADO on the Paseo del Prado, Spain's national museum of painting and sculpture, has a number of works of special Jewish interest. Among these are Titian's famed "Moses Saved from the Waters" (Room VII); Murillo's painting of "Rebecca and Eliezer," and two works depicting an auto-da-fé.

RESTAURANTE SINAI, 33 Principe, the only Jewish (kosher) restaurant in Spain, has been in business since 1968. Paintings of Biblical and medieval Jewish scenes hang on the walls between portraits of Moshe Dayan and Golda Meir and Israeli tourist posters.

SPANISH NATIONAL LIBRARY, Paseo de Recoletos and Plaza de Colon, houses many medieval Hebrew manuscripts. In 1959 the Library was the scene of a unique exhibit of Sephardic religious objects, manuscripts, and art work.

STREET OF THE FAITH (Calle de la Fe), facing the San Lorenzo Church, is the ancient Juderia.

SYNAGOGUE, 3 Calle Balmes, dedicated Dec. 17, 1968, 476 years after the Jews were expelled from Spain, is the first Jewish house of worship erected in the Spanish capital since the 15th century. Present at the dedication, which was interpreted as an official revocation of the edict of 1492, were the Archbishop of Madrid and representatives of the Foreign and Justice Ministries. An earlier synagogue was housed in an apartment house. The new synagogue also houses a school, a community center, a meeting hall and mikveh. Under the school's auspices, the community sponsors a summer camp for children outside of Madrid. The new building was made possible through the aid of a grant from JDC.

STREET OF PROFESSOR WAKSMAN (Calle del Professor Waksman), the only street in Spain named for a modern Jew, bears the name of the Nobel prize winner and discoverer of streptomycin. The municipality honored Dr. Waksman on his visit here in 1954.

MALAGA

SYNAGOGUE, 6 Calle Alhondiga, on the sixth floor of an apartment building, was founded in 1966 when a new Jewish community came into being in the city famed as the birthplace of Solomon Ibn Gabirol, great Hebrew poet of Spain's Golden age. Some 300 Jews, mostly from Morocco and Tangier, have settled here.

MANRESA

LA FOSSANA DELS JUEUS, site of the former Jewish cemetery, and *Grau dels Jueus* (Jews' Street), a little alley, are Jewish historical vestiges in this town.

MEDINACELLI

CALLE DE LA SINAGOGA was the site of a synagogue in this mountain-top town in the province of Soria.

ANCIENT SYNAGOGUE near Calle de la Sinagoga, a low brick structure that has fallen into ruins since the Spanish Civil War, is now being restored by the state as a national monument. Since 1492 it was known as the Convent of Jeronimos and was used by nuns from a nearby convent.

MONTBLANCH

CALLE DE LOS JUDIOS, (Street of the Jews) can still be seen in this Catalan town dating from the 12th century.

ONDA

PLAZA DE LA SINAGOGA was once the site of a synagogue.

PALENCIA

PROVINCIAL ARCHAEOLOGICAL MUSEUM preserves a Hebrew-inscribed tombstone dated 1097, recording the death of Samuel ben Shealtiel, who died when his house caved in on him.

PAREDES DE NAVA

IGLESIA CRISTO DE LA BELLA CRUZ (Church of Christ of the Beautiful Cross), located in the old Juderia on an unpaved street near an unpaved square has been identified by Don A. Halperin in "The Ancient Synagogues of the Iberian Peninsula" as having been originally a synagogue, erected some time before 1391 when all the Jews of the town were forcibly converted to Catholicism.

RIBADAVIA

PLAZUELA DE LA MAGDALENA, the historical hub of this 14th century town which is an artistic monument, was the centre of the old Jewish quarter.

SADABA

SYNAGOGUE WALL, a large stone segment of what has been identified as the interior side of the eastern wall of a synagogue built about 250 C.E., is believed to be the oldest relic of Jewish settlement in ancient Spain.

SAGUNTO

JUDERIA (Jewish quarter), in this ancient town on the Valencia-Barcelona highway, can be seen from the eminence on which an old castle stands.

SANTIAGO DE COMPOSTELA

CATHEDRAL has twenty-four statues of prophets from the Hebrew Bible framed in the so-called "Holy Door." The right side of the door represents the Christian Church and the left represents "the Church of the Jews."

SEGOVIA

ALCAZAR has high on its crag a sixteenth-century structure called "The Tower of the Jew" because a Jew was once imprisoned there when he refused to abandon his Judaism. He died in the tower, still a Jew.

CALLE DE LA JUDERIA VIEJA AND CALLE DE LA JUDERIA NUEVA recall the old and new Jewish quarters of old Segovia. The old quarter is between the cathedral and the city's walls. On the side of Cuesta de Los Hoyos, a road cut out of the rock and so situated that the whole city can be seen from it, is the medieval Jewish burying ground, with tombs hewn into the rock.

CATHEDRAL OF SEGOVIA has the tomb of Maria del Salto, a Jewess whose miraculous escape from death when she invoked the name of the Virgin of Fuencisla and survived a fall from the towering Pena Grajera (Crow's Cliff) is memorialized in a fresco in the northwest corner of the cloisters. Maria fell in love with a Christian, and, as punishment, her husband threw her from the cliff. Her invocation of the Virgin was supposed to have saved her. Maria, whose Jewish name was Sarah, later became a Christian, and in 1558 she was canonized and her remains reinterred in the cathedral.

Records in the cathedral tell of an annual tax of 30 dineros imposed on the Jews of Segovia in 1302 by Ferdinand IV of Castile in "commemoration" of the Jewish role in the crucifixion. Other archives in the cathedral give the dates of the erection of two Segovia synagogues, a large one that became the Hospital of Our Lady of Mercy, and a smaller one, erected in 1410, that was converted into a church in 1419.

CHURCH OF CORPUS CHRISTI on Calle Juderia Vieja, near the Cathedral, was formerly a large synagogue erected before 1389. It became a church in 1419. Rebuilt in 1899 after a fire, the interior is a virtual reconstruction of the 14th century synagogue. There are a plaque and a bas-relief that explain that the synagogue was confiscated because the Jews allegedly desecrated the Host.

FROMKES PLAQUE, high above a modern building in newer section of the city, memorializes, the Polish-born Jewish painter who lived in this house for many years until his death in 1931. He was greatly beloved in Spain for his portraits of Spanish intellectuals and peasants.

SEVILLE

EL BARRIO DE SANTA CRUZ, between the Alcazar walls and the Murillo Gardens, is the present name of what used to be the Jewish quarter and is now one of the oldest sections of the city. A cluster of squares, alleys, and lanes, the Barrio was the home of 20,000 Jews until the massacre of 1391. A stroll through the Barrio leads through streets named "Juderia" and "Calle de los Levies." Not far from the latter street is the *Church of Santa Maria Blanca*, formerly a synagogue, which was a gift from King Alfonso the Wise to the Jewish community of Seville. The *Convent of Madre de Dios* and the *Church of Santa Cruz*, both in El Barrio, are also former synagogues.

CALLE SUSONA, between the Calles Pimienta and Vida, in El Barrio, recalls an ancient legend as well as history. The story is that Don Diego Suson, a Marrano Jew whose ancestors ostensibly accepted Christianity in 1391, organized an underground group of secret Jews who were fighting the establishment of the Inquisition. Don Diego's daughter, known as the "beautiful Susanna," knowingly or unknowingly betrayed the secret meetings of the Marranos to her Christian lover. As a result, Don Diego and his associates were burned to death as Judaizers. Susanna then retired to a convent but repented on her deathbed and instructed her heirs to hang her corpse in front of the house she had betrayed. For years the street was known as Calle de la Muerte (Street of Death) until it was given its present name.

CATHEDRAL OF SEVILLE preserves in its treasury two keys to the city presented to Ferdinand III by the Jews when he captured the city from the Moors in 1248. The Hebrew inscription reads: "The King of Kings will open, the king of earth will enter." A Hebrew epitaph for Ferdinand's tomb, devised by the Jews of Seville, has faded.

Christopher Columbus's tomb in the nave of the cathedral recalls the explorer's relations with Jews and the growing volume of literature indicating that Columbus may have been the grandson of a Marrano. Columbus's principal backer at the court of Spain was Luis de Santangel, himself a Marrano, who was the chancellor of the royal household and controller general of finance in Aragon. Don Isaac Abrabanel, leader of Spanish Jewry, was another Columbus supporter. Luis de Torres, also a Marrano, was Columbus's interpreter on his historic 1492 journey, and one of five Jews among Columbus's crew.

COLUMBUS ARCHIVES (Archives of Indies), 3 Avenida Queipo de Llano, preserves the account books of Luis de Santangel, financier to King Ferdinand and Queen Isabella, who prevailed on Isabella to recall Columbus, after the Spanish court had broken off negotiations with the navigator concerning his plan for a voyage across the Atlantic to find a short route to the Indies. Columbus's first letter describing his discovery was written to Santangel, dated February 15, 1493. Santangel's publication of this letter was the first printed record of the epochal discovery.

The Archives at one time owned one of the fifteen extant copies of the *Almanac Perpetuum*, written in Hebrew in 1473 and later translated into Spanish and Latin, in which form it was used by Columbus on his later voyages to America. This astronomy book was the work of Abraham Zacuto, a Spanish-Jewish astronomer, whose writings were well known to Columbus. The *Almanac Perpetuum* was translated by Joseph Vecinho, physician and cartographer to the court of Portugal. Columbus blamed this Portuguese Jew for the decision of Portugal not to back the voyage which led to the discovery of America. Columbus's copy of the *Almanac Perpetuum* is preserved in the *Naval Museum* in Madrid.

ARCO Y TORREON DE JUDERIA in the old Calle de la Juderia, was the gate connecting the Alcazar and the Jewish quarter. It is now a passageway between the Patio de Banderas and the Callejon del Agua.

JEWISH CEMETERY, part of the city's Christian burial ground in the Macarena district, has many unusual tombstones dating from the thirteenth and fourteenth centuries and an artistically unique entrance gate.

PROVINCIAL ARCHAEOLOGICAL MUSEUM at the Plaza de America, preserves the tombstone of Rabbi Solomon ben Abraham Yaish, who died in 1345. The epitaph indicates he was also a physician and a "reader of omens."

SYNAGOGUE, 5 Calle Torres, a tiny room six feet wide by nine feet long, serves the 19 Jewish families in this former capital of Spain.

TARIFA

Tarif ben-Malik, "a Jew of the tribe of Simon," who was one of the Berber-Jewish chieftains with the Moslem invaders when they landed in this ancient town on the Strait of Gibraltar to begin the Moorish conquest of Spain from the Visigoths in 711, is immortalized in this town's name. According to legend, Tarif was the first invader to set foot on Spanish soil.

TARRAGONA

CATHEDRAL OF TARRAGONA, Calle de Escribanias Viejas, has in its cloister a seventh-century stone inscribed in Latin and Hebrew commemorating "Isidora, daughter of Jonathas and Axia," who were probably among the settlers responsible for this town's having once been known as "the city of Jews." The upper window-sill on the house at No. 6 on the same street, next to the cathedral, contains two Hebrew inscriptions, indicating that it is made of the tombstones of Hayim ben-Isaac (died 1300) and Hanan ben-Simon Arlabi (died 1300). Some very old Jewish coins are preserved in the Archaeological Museum.

ORIGINAL ARCH which was the gate to the medieval Juderia still stands at the entrance of Calle de Talavera, behind the Church of the Trinidad, on the eastern side of the Plaza del Rey.

"PORTELLA DELS JUEUS" (little gate of the Jews), was the name given to one of the two Iberian gates on the Paseo de San Antonio.

TOLEDO

CASA DEL GRECO on the Calle Samuel Levi, an old ghetto lane, is the last remnant of one of the historic Jewish mansions of medieval Europe. It was built in the fourteenth century by Samuel ben-Meier Halevi Abulafia, treasurer and adviser to King Pedro the Cruel of Castile. Abulafia not only managed Pedro's finances, but arranged his marriage to the daughter of the Duc de Bourbon, fought for and with him, engineered his escape from prison, and negotiated for him with Portugal. His reward was the King's permission to build a new synagogue in contravention of existing laws and in the face of the clergy's bitter opposition.

The fortresslike palace, with virtually no windows, and with long galleries and halls, had vast cellars where Abulafia purportedly hid his wealth. He was also said to have bored long tunnels that linked his palace to the banks of the Tagus River. Abulafia's treasure was a tempting plum to the enemies of the Jew and his king. Ultimately, the latter turned against his adviser under the influence of rumors that Abulafia was cheating the royal exchequer. Abulafia was imprisoned and tortured. He died in 1361 after his fortune had been confiscated.

The legends of Abulafia's secret tunnels and the rumors of witchcraft and alchemy practiced in the palace by its later occupant, the Marqués of Villena, persisted until 1585 when El Greco, the gifted Greek painter, moved into the house. Today it is a museum containing notable examples of El Greco's work.

CATHEDRAL OF TOLEDO, a Gothic structure completed in 1477, has on an interior wall a huge plaque memorializing the expulsion of the Jews in 1492.

LA GALIANA, the pleasure garden outside Toledo created by Alfonso VIII for the Jewess Raquel, his mistress, is gone except for one of its gates which still stands. The late Lion Feuchtwanger told Raquel's story in his novel of the same name.

PLAZA DEL CORRAL DE DON DIEGO is noted for a wall next to a bakeshop in which there is emplaced a tombstone of a Jew named Joseph al-Naqauah. Above the doorway to No. 9 Calle de la Plata is a Hebrew-inscribed tombstone turned upside down.

PLAZA DE LA JUDERIA, halfway between El Transito and Santa Maria la Blanca (*see below*) was part of the city's two ancient Jewish quarters where many houses and streets are still much as they were five hundred years ago. One Jewish area was called the Alcana, and the other the Juderia. There is a legend that Toledo was founded four thousand years ago by direct descendants of Noah. The city may have gotten its name from *Toledot*, Hebrew for "generations." By the seventh century C.E. the city had a large Jewish population, which helped the Moors take the city from the Visigoths. Because of its learning, piety, scholars, poets, splendid schools, and translators, Toledo was known as "the second Jerusalem" in the medieval ages. Under the Catholic kings it was the center of Spanish Jewry.

POSADA DE LA HERMANDAD, a church in a narrow alley in a remote section of the city, is a former synagogue. Here Spanish Jewry received its deathblow in 1492. When the tribunal of the Inquisition transferred its operations from Seville to Toledo in 1485, it chose La Hermandad as its headquarters and from there it issued the orders that marked the end for Spanish Jewry.

PROVINCIAL MUSEUM, in the Hospital de Santa Cruz, just off Zocodover at the Sala II, preserves a number of fourteenth-century Hebrew-inscribed sarcophagi, some cabalistic medals, a piece from one of the decorative friezes in El Transito Synagogue, and a Spanish translation of some of the mural inscriptions from this ancient landmark. There are also a wooden beam containing a Hebrew inscription dated 980, and a stone identifying an eleventh-century "Inn of the Esquina." The Hebrew words, "food and lodging," can still be read.

SANTA MARIA LA BLANCA, the oldest Jewish monument in Toledo, stands in a quiet garden in what was once the heart of the ghetto, not far from the edge of the Tagus River gorge. No one knows exactly when it was built, estimates ranging from the tenth to the thirteenth century, with the latter date regarded as the more likely. Even the builder is not known, although it was believed to have been Joseph ibn-Shoshan, a friend of Alfonso VIII. Unimpressive on the outside, like all medieval synagogues, the inside is a forest of thirty-two pillars, supporting a long vista of horseshoe-shaped arches. The octagonal columns are richly decorated with designs of Moorish-Jewish motif. The rambling building was converted into the Church of Santa Maria la Blanca in 1405. Later it became a military barracks, a warehouse, and a dance hall. Now it is a national museum. But the inside is crumbling to dust.

EL TRANSITO SYNAGOGUE, built by Abulafia in 1357, is directly opposite Casa del Greco. This is probably the most beautiful Jewish building to survive the medieval era. Located on a steep, narrow street, flanked by cobblers' shops, the austere white structure towers over the city's roof tops. The interior is bare except for three rows of benches and several tombstones, Christian and Jewish, encased in the ground. The Christian tombs are of members of the Knights of Calatrava, a military order, to whom the building was given in 1492. The Inquisition transformed it into the Church of Notre Dame, hence its name "Transito" (Transition).

Only its walls remain, but these bear exquisite plaster friezes, now considered the most perfect in all Spain. The ceiling, made of cedar of Lebanon, is ornamented with delicate Hebrew letters. The filigreed plaster decorations on the walls and cornices are replete with Hebrew inscriptions and quotations, mostly Psalms. The arched recess on the east wall, where the Ark of the Law once rested, is covered on either side with long inscriptions in Hebrew containing praise of King Pedro and Abulafia. The dedication below the east frieze says, "Behold this sanctuary dedicated to Israel and the house that Samuel built." On the right-hand side facing the niche for the Ark is a remnant of the women's gallery.

The building receives light through narrow windows near the roof; their remarkably beautiful design has been imitated in many modern synagogues. In 1550 the building became an asylum. It was converted into a barracks in 1798. At the end of the nineteenth century the Spanish government declared it a national monument. In March, 1964, the Franco government issued a decree establishing the synagogue as a museum of Sephardic culture. A 21-member international board administers the museum containing a rich collection of historical and artistic material in Spanish Government archives as well as Sephardic museum pieces and documents from other parts of the world. One wall of the museum section displays 69 framed reproductions of the famed Sarajevo Haggadah (*See* YUGOSLAVIA), a large map of medieval Spain showing places of Jewish settlement, 24 fragments of columns with Hebrew inscriptions from various Spanish Juderias and a plaque recording that the museum was opened in 1966. That same year the Spanish Ministry of Posts issued a stamp depicting the Transito Synagogue.

There is a modern link with Abulafia, builder of El Transito Synagogue. Charles Joelson, a former United States Congressman from Paterson, New Jersey, is married to a daughter of Raphael Abulafia of Jerusalem, a direct descendant of Pedro's adviser. Raphael's parents were among the founders of the city of Tel Aviv.

TORTOSA

MUSEUM OF SANTO DOMINGO CONVENT preserves the sixth-century gravestone of "Meliosa daughter of Judah of blessed memory," inscribed in Hebrew, Latin, and Greek, thus indicating that the Jews then used all three languages.

REMOLINOS, one of the old steep narrow streets in this Catalan town, was the ancient Jewish quarter.

TUDELA

BENJAMIN OF TUDELA MEMORIAL, a terra-cotta plaque erected in 1960 by the citizens of the ancient Moorish town on the right bank of the Ebro River, honors the famous 12th century Jewish traveler whose remarkable record of his visits to 300 places in Europe and Asia between 1165 and 1178 became a major source of Jewish historical writing when it was first published from the original Hebrew notes in 1543. The plaque, 12 feet above street level, is on a prominent square not far from the Cathedral of Tudela.

CATHEDRAL OF TUDELA, the town's most notable landmark, includes in the northern portion of its cloister a chapel that was once part of a synagogue. You can still see six-pointed Stars of David in the corners of the mosaic floor and the women's balcony. In the Cathedral archives and libraries are many bilingual volumes in Hebrew and Latin as well as a copy of the Hebrew statutes of the Tudela Jewish community dating from 1305.

VALENCIA

BAÑOS DEL ALMIRANTE on the Calle de Baños del Almirante, 800-year old baths decorated with Stars of David and Arabic inscriptions, is believed to have been the mikveh attached to an ancient synagogue.

CATHEDRAL OF VALENCIA has the Seal of Solomon, a six-pointed star, worked into the design of the window over its main entrance.

VITORIA

MONUMENT TO JUDIZ-MENDI on the Campo de Judiz-Mendi, memorializes the ancient Jewish cemetery here. In 1492, when 2,000 Jews left here, the city fathers pledged that the Jewish cemetery on Judiz-Mendi (Jewish Hill) would never be "touched, wounded, or tilled." This was in appreciation for the heroism of the city's Jewish doctors who in 1484 tended the sick and dying when Christian doctors fled from the bubonic plague. The promise was kept for more than four centuries while the city grew up around the Jewish burial ground.

In 1939 the Jews of Bayonne, France, to which the exiles from Vitoria had fled in 1492, realized that one day Vitoria would have to break its pledge because the expanding city had halted at the edge of Judiz Mendi. The Jewish community of Bayonne offered to release Vitoria from its pledge if the city fathers would erect a small monument on the site of the Jewish cemetery and re-inter on the spot any bones found after the site was excavated for building. The war prevented the acceptance of the offer, but in 1952 a delegation from Vitoria came to Bayonne and signed such an agreement. The monument now has been erected. The inscription, in Spanish, reads: "On this spot stood the Jewish cemetery which the Jewish community of Vitoria deeded in perpetuity to the city on June 27, 1492. The city and its officials adhered loyally to the terms of the deed for 460 years, until June 27, 1952, when Vitoria was relieved of its pledge by an agreement signed on the same date with the Consistoire Israélite de Bayonne (France)."

MAJORCA
(Balearic Islands)
PALMA

HOTEL DE MAR, at Illetas, a few minutes from Palma, offers a strictly kosher cuisine supervised by a mashgiach, Alex Kesselman. The wedding of his daughter in March 1969 was described as the first Jewish wedding on Majorca in over 400 years. Religious services are held at the hotel on Rosh Hashanah, Yom Kippur, Sukkot and Simhat Torah.

MONTEZION CHURCH, which in the fourteenth century was the Great Synagogue of this capital city of Majorca, largest of the Spanish-owned Balearic Islands in the Mediterranean, is the church most frequented by the Chuetas (pronounced *chooayta*), people of unmixed Jewish stock but strict Catholics. The Chuetas are descendants of Jews who settled here in 49 C.E. Virtually every tourist who comes to Palma goes shopping for articles of gold and silver on the Street of the Jewelers (Calle de la Plateria). Most of the shops here are owned by Chuetas. Until the middle of the fourteenth century the Jews were among Majorca's most influential merchants, map-makers, navigators, artisans, and explorers. Then the Inquisition reached Majorca and the Jews were given the choice between exile and conversion. Many who accepted baptism were treated as outcasts, barred from all but a few occupations, and completely isolated from the rest of the population.

Other Catholics shunned intermarriage with them. Even when the Inquisition ended in 1834, they were still regarded as pariahs and derisively called Chuetas, which, according to one version, is diminutive for "a little Jew," and, according to another, is derived from *Chuya* (a pork eater) because the Chuetas ate pork publicly to demonstrate their adherence to Christianity.

From time to time there have been reports of a revival of Judaism among the Chuetas. In 1960, Isabel Elisheba Munoz, a wealthy Chueta, publicly reconverted to Judaism in Jerusalem and returned to Palma with a plan for establishing the first synagogue there in 500 years. But the authorities refused her permission. In 1966 four Chueta families went to Israel in the hope of settling there but when they found rabbinical objection to their conversion, they came back to Palma.

American and British tourists occasionally attended worship services in private homes but the first public Jewish service was not held until July 29, 1962 when Rabbi Leon Fram of Detroit officiated at a Friday evening service in the Anglican Church, a small room hidden away in back of a courtyard.

The 300 permanent Jewish residents, mostly British and Moroccans, are planning to establish a synagogue and have acquired a Torah and other appurtenances. The leader of the community, who conducts services at the Anglican Church, is Benito Roth, of Casa Benito, Son Vida.

PALMA CATHEDRAL, erected in 1239, is still lighted by a giant candelabrum from the Great Synagogue of Palma. It contains 350 lights, and there are those who say it was brought from Jerusalem by the first Jewish settlers. In the Cathedral's sacristy there is a unique pair of Spanish-Jewish *rimonim* (ornaments for the rollers of the Torah Scroll). These are carried by Christian worshipers in annual processions through the streets on holy days. The original Ark of the Law and Eternal Light from the Great Synagogue are incorporated into the cathedral's design. Efforts were under way in 1970 to buy the rimonim and have them transferred to Israel.

SANTA CLARA CHURCH stands on the site of a pre-Inquisition synagogue.

CANARY ISLANDS

LAS PALMAS on the island of Gran Canaria, has a permanent Jewish settlement of eight families. Religious services are held Friday evenings at 7:30 P.M. in the homes of residents. The first recorded circumcision here in half a millenium was officiated at by a mohel flown in from Morocco in 1969.

SANTA CRUZ on the island of Tenerife, has a colony of 15 Jewish families who worship in private homes.

SWEDEN

Sweden has the largest Jewish community in Scandinavia; except for Israel, it is the only country whose Jewish population has more than doubled since World War II. In 1933 there were 6,000 Jews in Sweden. At the end of 1970 there were 14,000.

More than half of this increase consisted of refugees from Germany and Austria in the 1930s and survivors of the concentration camps who were settled in Sweden after World War II. Thousands more found temporary haven in Sweden before migrating to Israel or returning to Denmark and Norway, from which they had been rescued with the aid of the Swedish authorities. In 1969 and 1970 1800 Polish Jews were admitted to Sweden when their native land launched a violent campaign of anti-Semitism. Most of the Polish Jews settled in southern Sweden.

Before 1933 the Jewish community consisted of immigrants who had come from Russia between 1880 and World War I and the descendants of the German Jews who founded the community in 1774. Before that time only Jews who accepted baptism were admitted to Sweden. Nevertheless, there were Jewish paymasters in the army of King Charles XII (1697-1718), and until recently there could still be seen on the island of Marstrand, in the Kattegat, remains of a synagogue hewn out of rocks in a cave said to date back to the Middle Ages. King Frederick I invited Portuguese Jews from Amsterdam and London to come to Stockholm in 1745, but none of them would agree to conversion.

King Gustavus III was more successful in 1774 when he permitted Aron Isaak, an engraver and merchant from northern Germany, to live in Stockholm. Isaak not only was granted trading rights but was allowed to bring with him enough of his coreligionists to enable him to conduct public worship and to establish a synagogue. Similar rights were extended in 1779 to Jews in Göteborg and Norrkoping. Three years later they were given the right to reside anywhere in Sweden but were not permitted to own land, to vote, or to hold office. A decree abolishing these restrictions in 1838 created so much opposition that complete emancipation was delayed until 1870. By then there were also Jewish communities in Lund, Uppsala and Malmö.

Descendants of the first settlers contributed much to Sweden's intellectual life. Among them were Oscar Ivar Levertin, poet and professor of Swedish literature at the University of Stockholm; Karl Johan Warburg, member of the Riksdag and head of the Nobel Library of the Swedish Academy of Literature; Martin Lamm, who served as one of the eighteen members of the Swedish Academy of Literature who choose the Nobel prize winner in literature; Herman Lamm, vice-president of the Swedish senate; Henrik Schuck, literary historian and rector of Uppsala University; Ernst Josephson, Sweden's greatest painter; Ludwig and Ragnar Josephson, directors of the Royal Theatre; Gunnar Josephson, who now heads the Jewish community; Albert Bonnier, literary patron of Strindberg and Lagerlöf, and Professor Hugo Valentin, the historian.

More than half of Sweden's Jewish population lives in Stockholm (8,000). Other good-sized Jewish communities are in Göteborg (1,700), Malmö (1,500), Boras (350) and smaller numbers in 23 other cities and towns.

GÖTEBORG

JEWISH COMMUNITY CENTER, 12 Ostra Larmgatan, a $300,000 three-story modern structure erected in 1962, houses club and recreational facilities, community offices, a kosher restaurant, a Jewish school and a small synagogue used by the Orthodox. Half of the 2,000 Jews in the community are refugees from the post-World War II era. The Center adjoins the Liberal Synagogue.

LIBERAL SYNAGOGUE, Ostra Larmgatan 12, alongside one of the canals of Sweden's second-largest city, is the oldest existing synagogue building in Sweden, having been dedicated in 1855. The Jewish community here dates from 1780.

ORTHODOX SYNAGOGUE, Andra Langgatan 6.

HALSINGBORG

SYNAGOGUE, 1 Algrand.

KRISTIANSTAD

SYNAGOGUE, 18 Ostra Storgatan.

LANDSKRONA

SYNAGOGUE, 9 Skolallen.

LUND

SYNAGOGUE, 5 Lilla Sodergatan.

MALMÖ

JEWISH COMMUNITY CENTER, 11 Kamrergatan, houses a home for the aged, a mikveh, a library, a kindergarten, and the headquarters of the Jewish community. A new settlement of Jews from Poland who began arriving in 1969 publishes a mimeographed paper in Polish called "Spojrzenia" (Views).

JEWISH REFUGEE MEMORIAL, "Flight with the Torah Scroll," is Willy Gordon's monument to the refugees from Denmark and to those who died at the hands of the Nazis. It stands in the Jewish Cemetery. The bronze sculpture on a granite podium is inscribed in Hebrew, "Am Yisrael Chai," with the dedication "to the holy martyrs who gave their lives for God." The sculptor is one of Sweden's leading artists.

SYNAGOGUE, Foreningsgatan corner Betaniaplan, is over sixty years old. Here, on Yom Kippur eve, in 1943, occurred one of the most dramatic incidents of World War II. That was the night when the Danish underground, with the aid of daring Swedes, completed the rescue of 6,000 Danish Jews threatened with deportation to concentration camps by ferrying them across the Kattegat to Malmö in a fleet of fishing boats. As many of the refugees as could crowd into the synagogue joined Cantor Israel Isaac Gordon, father of the sculptor Willy Gordon, in the traditional Kol Nidre service.

NORRKOPING

SYNAGOGUE on Braddgatan, is the second-oldest in Sweden, having been opened in 1858. The Jewish community is so small that the synagogue is used only on Rosh Hashana and Yom Kippur.

SKARA

JACOBOWSKY LIBRARY OF JUDAICA, a great private collection, at Harlungdagatan 1, is owned by Dr. C. V. Jacobowsky, librarian of the Skara Municipal Library.

STOCKHOLM

ADAS JESHURUN SYNAGOGUE (Orthodox), St. Paulsgatan 13.

ADAS YISROEL SYNAGOGUE (Orthodox), Nybrogatan 16.

GREAT SYNAGOGUE, Wahrendorffsgatan 3, the main synagogue of Swedish Jewry, was erected in 1870. It is administered by Chief Rabbi Morton H. Narrowe, an American, who formerly served as a chaplain in the U.S. Army.

Attached to the synagogue is an office building used as headquarters of the Jewish community. The Jewish Community Library, established in 1860, is also here. Among its collections are the books of the late Chief Rabbi Marcus Ehrenpreis.

INSTITUTE FOR JEWISH CULTURE AND INFORMATION, Valhallvagen 104, is directed by Daniel Brick, whose wife, Anna Rivkin-Brick, was one of Sweden's greatest photographers. Brick also edits *Judisk Kronika*, Stockholm's monthly Jewish journal, whose offices are at the Institute.

ISRAELI EMBASSY, Torstenssongatan 4.

JEWISH CEMETERY at Hagaparken, in the suburb of Solna, on the Uppsala Highway, the newest of the city's four Jewish cemeteries, has an interesting memorial to Jewish victims of Nazism. It is a simple T-shaped sculptured monument, with a Hebrew inscription on the front reading, "In memory of our martyrs who were killed and annihilated under the domination of Evil." The Hebrew lettering is copied from that on the oldest grave in the Sephardic cemetery at Ouderkerk-on-the-Amstel, outside of Amsterdam, Holland. The inscription on the back of the monument, in Swedish, reads "In memory of our martyrs during the time of persecution 1933-1945." Here are buried many of Sweden's most famous Jews, including the painter Josephson, the historian Valentin and the founders of the Bonnier publishing house.

At Igeldammsgatan, Alstromergatan and Kronobergsgatan, all in the Kungsholm section of the city, are the three oldest Jewish cemeteries in Sweden, both dating from the late eighteenth century.

JEWISH HOSPITAL AND HOME FOR AGED, Lodosevagen 9, was opened in 1959 with the aid of funds from the Conference on Jewish Material Claims against Germany.

JUDIKST FORUM, Norr Malarstrand 32, is a small liberal congregation.

JUDAICA HOUSE, 19-21 Nybrogatan, is a Jewish Community Center that also houses the Hillel School, a Jewish day school which has government financial support; the Mendelssohn Library, and the headquarters of most Jewish organizations. There is also a dairy restaurant.

KOSHER RESTAURANT (Arne Cohen), 28 Rorhalsgade.

NICOLAI POLISSTATION, 19 Sjalagardsgatan (which means Soul Protection St., because it was once the religious center of the city, is a police station that was originally Stockholm's first synagogue. The women's balcony is still there but all vestiges of Hebrew inscriptions were wiped out some years ago during a repainting of the interior.

UPPSALA

UPPSALA UNIVERSITY, in the Caroline Library's collection of more than 1,000,000 volumes and manuscripts is a famous collection of Hebrew manuscripts.

VASTERA

SYNAGOGUE, 1 Svardsliljegatan.

SWITZERLAND

The first Jews in Switzerland were merchants from Germany who crossed the Rhine to trade in Basel in 1213, nearly eighty years before the formation of the Swiss Federation. Before 1300, others had come over the Alpine passes from France, Austria, and Italy and settled in Bern, St. Gallen, Zurich, and Lucerne. So long as the Swiss cities gave nominal allegiance to the Holy Roman Empire, the Jews were under imperial protection. For this they paid stiff head and body taxes. When the Swiss threw off the Hapsburg rule, the cities and cantons continued the heavy levies while excluding Jews from commerce and handicrafts, limiting their residential rights, and compelling them to wear the *Judenhut*, or Jew's hat.

During the Black Death – 1348-49 – persecution of the Jews became so violent that it included burning at the stake as the result of accusations of ritual murder and well poisoning. For two hundred years the Swiss had confined the Jews to moneylending, but even this source of livelihood dried up when Christians began displacing them at the end of the fourteenth century. Between 1427 and 1543 the Jews were expelled from the cantons of Bern, Zurich, Fribourg, Schaffhausen, Thurgau, and Basel. In 1622 they were banished from the rest of the country. Only Jewish physicians were permitted to remain.

After 1648 some Jews began trickling in from the Rhineland, Poland, and Alsace. Most of these settled in the canton of Aargau, which didn't join the Swiss Federation until 1803 and hence was not bound to respect the ban on Jews. For more than 150 years the Jews in Switzerland were virtually segregated in the villages of Lengnau and Endingen. They had freedom of worship and movement but were forbidden to own land or work as artisans. This compelled them to turn to itinerant trading, buying and selling at fairs, and cattle dealing. Lengnau was the birthplace of Meyer Guggenheim, founder of the celebrated family of industrialists, mining tycoons, and philanthropists. A scattering of Jews also lived in Carouge, a suburb of Geneva, while it was governed by the Dukes of Savoy, in the late eighteenth century.

Napoleon's short-lived Helvetic Republic repealed the humiliating head and body taxes on Jews in 1798. In 1843 Geneva became the first canton to naturalize a number of Jews, but most of the cantons maintained their policy of exclusion, even against Jews who were citizens of other countries, for another quarter of a century. When England, France, and the United States negotiated new commercial treaties with Switzerland between 1840 and 1860, their insistence on equal rights for their Jewish nationals who lived or did business anywhere in Switzerland ultimately led to the total emancipation of all Swiss Jews. An amendment to the Swiss Federation's constitution in 1866 gave all Jews full residential and commercial rights, and eight years later complete religious freedom was achieved. There were then 5,000 Jews in the country.

History thrust the Swiss Jewish community onto the world stage in 1897 as the host to the first World Zionist Congress, which met in Basel. Nine of the first twenty-one Zionist Congresses also convened in Basel and four more were held in other Swiss cities. Many of the Congress delegates returned to Switzerland as permanent residents between 1900 and 1920, when immigration from Eastern Europe doubled the Jewish population.

In the 1930s the Swiss ignored Nazi threats and gave shelter to tens of thousands of refugees from Germany, Austria, and Czechoslovakia. Despite its sensitive position as a neutral in the heart of Nazi-controlled Europe, Switzerland sheltered 120,000 war refugees, including 40,000 Jews. Many of the latter arrived illegally and were interned in work camps, where they were supported by the American Jewish Joint Distribution Committee. All but 2,500 left after the war.

Today there are 20,000 Jews in Switzerland. Of the twenty-five organized Jewish communities, the largest are Zurich, Geneva, and Basel. Geneva is the European headquarters of a number of major international Jewish agencies.

Since 1894, shechita has been forbidden anywhere in Switzerland by a federal law. Jews have not been very prominent in public affairs. Only six have been elected to the National Council (the lower chamber) but none has ever sat in the States Council (Upper Chamber) or the Federal Council (Cabinet). A number have served in the cantonal parliaments. In 1963, Dr. Samuel Teitler, the only Jewish member of the Federal High Court, a former president of the St. Gallos Jewish Community, was appointed the country's chief justice.

ANIERES

CENTRAL ORT TEACHERS' TRAINING INSTITUTE, Chemin de l'ORT, seven miles outside Geneva, trains Jewish students from a score of countries to become instructors in various trade schools maintained by ORT in France, Israel, Tunisia, Morocco, and Iran.

BADEN

SYNAGOGUE, 17 Parkstrasse.

BASEL

BASEL ART MUSEUM, 16 St. Albangraben, has a number of paintings of Jewish interest: Konrad Witz's "The Jews" and "Esther Before King Ahasuerus"; and A. Boeklin's "King David."

BASEL HISTORICAL MUSEUM, Barfuesserplatz, preserves a number of thirteenth- and fourteenth-century Jewish tombstones found in the first Jewish cemetery opened on Swiss soil.

DREI KÖNIGE HOTEL, 8 Blumenrain, is known to millions of Jews because the best-known and most widely published photo of Dr. Theodor Herzl shows him on one of the hotel balconies dreaming of the Jewish state.

FREY-GRYNAEUM, 33 Heuberg, has in its courtyard two gravestones from the thirteenth and fifteenth centuries, each with Hebrew inscriptions. This three-hundred-year-old building was established as the home of a University of Basel professor of theology through a bequest by a pair of theologians, the Reverend Frey and Reverend Grynaeus.

THEODOR HERZL STREET leads to the Jewish Cemetery.

JEWISH COMMUNAL CENTER, 24 Leimenstrasse. As part of the complex of community facilities there is a kosher restaurant on the premises, Cafe Hess.

JEWISH MUSEUM, 8 Kornhausgasse, has an excellent collection of three centuries of ceremonial and ritual art.

KAHN'S KOSHER RESTAURANT, 18 Aeschengraben.

STADTCASINO, 14 Steinenberg, is the historic building where Dr. Theodor Herzl convened the first World Zionist Congress in August 1897. Here, at the first modern Jewish parliament, was launched the political movement that led to the establishment of the State of Israel in 1948. In the Music Hall there is a plaque inscribed in Hebrew and German memorializing the first Zionist Congress. It was dedicated in 1960 during the Herzl centennial year. The plaque is on the wall near the right-hand aisle.

STATE ARCHIVES, 2 Martinsgasse, has an interesting collection of material about the early Zionist Congresses, including pamphlets, delegates' credentials, press tickets, badges, printed speeches, picture postcards, pamphlets, and other memorabilia.

SYNAGOGUE (Orthodox), 24 Ahornstrasse.

SYNAGOGUE, 24 Leimenstrasse.

UNIVERSITY OF BASEL LIBRARY, 20 Schönbeinstrasse, has an important collection of sixteenth- and seventeenth-century Hebrew books and manuscripts.

VESALANIUM, 1 Vesalgasse, one of the institutes of the University of Basel, occupies the site of the thirteenth-century Jewish cemetery. Skulls from this cemetery used to be on display in the institute but were subsequently interred in the new Jewish cemetery together with the remains of other Jewish bodies found during excavations for new university buildings.

BERN

BERN HISTORICAL MUSEUM, 5 Helvetiaplatz, has in its collection what some Jewish writers have described as a flag of the Jewish shoemakers' guild dating from 1540. Actually, the emblem is something of a mystery, and the museum preserves it under the name of "Ratselfahne"—mystery flag. The banner has the design of a boot on it together with some Hebrew letters, but they spell nothing that makes any sense. Apart from the Hebrew letters, the flag has no Jewish connection.

ISRAELI EMBASSY, 27 Marienstrasse.

KOSHER RESTAURANT, H. Rottenberg, 21 Gutenbergstrasse.

MOSES STATUE, Munsterplatz, in front of the Bern Cathedral, shows the Hebrew lawgiver on a pillar holding the Tablets of the Law. The monument was erected in 1791 to replace one that had stood on the same spot in the sixteenth century. The latter replaced an even earlier wooden statue that dated from medieval times. In the portico of the Cathedral is a statue of King Solomon.

OGRE-FOUNTAIN (Die Kindelfressbrunner), on Koonshausplatz, is a stone image of an ogre crowned with a horned hat commonly worn by 16th century Jews in Switzerland that depicts an old libel that Jewish 'monsters' sacrificed Christian children on Good Friday.

SYNAGOGUE, 2 Kapellenstrasse. A front row pew covered with an embroidered cushion faces a small plaque inscribed, "this seat is reserved for the Minister of Israel."

SYNAGOGUE (Reform), Postfach Transit 827 (post office address).

BIEL (Bienne)

JEWISH COMMUNAL HEADQUARTERS, 21 Kontrollstrasse.

SYNAGOGUE, 3 Ruschlisstrasse.

BREMGARTEN

JEWISH COMMUNAL HEADQUARTERS AND SYNAGOGUE, 53 Antonigasse.

DELEMONT (Deisberg)

JEWISH COMMUNAL HEADQUARTERS, 10 Avenue Sorne.

SYNAGOGUE, Route de Porrentruy.

ENDINGEN-LENGNAU

EIGHTEENTH-CENTURY CEMETERY, about halfway between these two rural villages near Zurich and quaint nineteenth-century synagogues, one in each village, are remnants of the Jewish community established in the seventeenth century when Endingen and Lengnau were the only places in Switzerland legally open to Jewish settlement. There are still a few Jewish families in both villages.

The Lengnau Synagogue is directly across from the Dorfplatz, a triangular-shaped park. The clock high on the synagogue facade shows 16 minutes to 3, as it has for nearly 80 years. Some of the older houses in town still have mezuzahs affixed to their doorposts even though they are inhabited by Christians.

FRIBOURG (Freiburg)

SYNAGOGUE, 9 Avenue de Rome.

CHAIM WEIZMANN MEMORIAL, commemorative plaque in the lobby of the University of Fribourg honors the first president of Israel who received his doctoral degree here in 1899. The plaque was dedicated in 1966.

GENEVA

Geneva has become an international Jewish center because many United Nations agencies maintain European headquarters here. Among the Jewish agencies with European or international headquarters here are: World Jewish Congress and World ORT Federation, 1 Rue de Varembe; and World OSE Union, 11 Rue du Mont Blanc.

AMERICAN JEWISH JOINT DISTRIBUTION COMMITTEE, one of the principal beneficiaries of the United Jewish Appeal, has its European headquarters at 64 Rue de Stand.

ENGLISH-SPEAKING JEWISH COMMUNITY, 52 Rue Moillebeau, holds Friday evening services.

GREAT SYNAGOGUE, Place de la Synagogue, has a large bronze monument in its front courtyard to the 6,000,000 Jewish victims of Nazism.

JEWISH COMMUNAL CENTER, 10 Rue St.-Léger.

KOSHER RESTAURANT (Galil), 19 Rue Merle d'Aubigne.

MACHSIKE HADASS SYNAGOGUE, 31 Blvd. Helvetique.

SYNAGOGUE (Sephardic), 10 Rue St.-Léger.

UNIVERSITY OF GENEVA has in its main entrance hall a bust of Dr. Liebmann Hersch, for more than forty years the head of the University's department of demography and statistics. Professor Hersch was the founder and president of the Jewish Cultural Association and also president of the International Union for the Scientific Study of Population. During the Nazi occupation of most of Europe, Dr. Hersch was the key figure through which the Jewish Labor Committee in the United States sent assistance to suffering Jews and to the labor underground.

KREUZLINGEN

SYNAGOGUE, 42 Hafenstrasse.

LA CHAUX-DE-FONDS

JEWISH COMMUNAL HEADQUARTERS AND SYNAGOGUE, 63 Rue de Parc.

LAUSANNE

JEWISH COMMUNAL CENTER, 101 Galeries du Commerce.

SYNAGOGUE, 1 Avenue Juste Olivier.

LENGNAU

(*See* ENDINGEN)

LUCERNE

GUTTMANN'S KOSHER RESTAURANT, 13 Gibraltarstrasse.
SYNAGOGUE, 51 Bruchstrasse.
YESHIVA, 20 Brambergstrasse.

LUGANO

MEIEROWITZ'S KOSHER RESTAURANT, 20 Viale Franscini.
SYNAGOGUE, 11 Via Maderni.

MONTREUX

GOLDSCHMIDT'S KOSHER RESTAURANT, 4 Avenue Riviera.
SYNAGOGUE, adjoining Jewish Old Folks Home in nearby village of Vevey.
SYNAGOGUE, Ave des Alpes 25.

MUMPF

RACHEL COMMEMORATIVE PLAQUE in front of the Zur Sonne hostelry, in this village on the main road about halfway between Basle and Zurich notes the fact that the famous 19th century French-Jewish actress, Elisa Rachel Felix (*See* Paris) was born in this village.

PREGNY

ROTHSCHILD CASTLE here was bequeathed to canton of Geneva by Baron Maurice de Rothschild together with funds to maintain it and its surrounding park. Geneva will take possession when Baron Maurice's son Edmond dies.

ST. GALLEN

SYNAGOGUE, 18 Frongartenstrasse. The Jewish communal headquarters is next door.
STATE LIBRARY, 6d Klosterhof, has a substantial Hebraica collection.

VEYRIER

JEWISH CEMETERY on outskirts of Geneva, has a monument to the memory of the Jews slaughtered by the Nazis.
BERGES DU LEMAN, Jewish Home for the Aged.

WINTERTHUR

SYNAGOGUE, 5 Rosenstrasse.

YVERDON

SYNAGOGUE, 26 Rue Valentin.

ZURICH

B'NAI B'RITH HILLEL HOUSE, 14 Spyristrasse.
CENTRAL LIBRARY, 6 Zahringerplatz, houses the Heidenheimiana, a collection

of Hebrew prayer books from the eighteenth-century Hebrew press of Wolf Samson Heidenheim, a German-Jewish scholar. His Hebrew prayer books were regarded as the best in Europe.

ISRAELI CONSULATE GENERAL, 3 Stampfenbachstrasse.

ISRAELITISCHES WOCHENBLATT, Switzerland's Jewish weekly journal, is published at 14 Florastrasse.

JEWISH COMMUNAL CENTER, 33 Lavaterstrasse.

JEWISH SKI CLUB (inquire of M. H. Marksitzer, 127 Asylstrasse).

KOSHER RESTAURANT (Hadar), 12 Lowenstrasse.

SWISS INSTITUTE OF TECHNOLOGY, where Dr. Albert Einstein taught theoretical physics from 1912 to 1914, has a bust of him in its main lobby. Einstein became a Swiss citizen in 1894 and worked and taught in Bern and Zurich until After World War I, when he resumed his German citizenship.

SYNAGOGUE (Orthodox), 37 Freigutstrasse.

SYNAGOGUE (Orthodox), 8 Erikastrasse.

SYNAGOGUE (Conservative), 10 Löwenstrasse.

UNION OF SWISS JEWISH COMMUNITIES, 10 Olgastrasse, is the national body of all Swiss Jewish communities.

TURKEY

When the Ottoman Turks overran the Balkans in the fourteenth century, they found old established Jewish communities dating from Greek and Roman times in what is now European Turkey, Bulgaria, Greece, Yugoslavia, and Rumania. In Thessaly there was a Jewish colony founded in the days of Alexander the Great. The Roman Emperor Hadrian settled Palestinian Jews at Edirne (Adrianople). Istanbul (Constantinople) had a Jewish congregation in the reign of the Emperor Constantine.

Embittered by persecution under the Byzantine emperors, the Jews welcomed the Turkish conquest. Edirne became a haven for oppressed Jews from France, Hungary, and Silesia, after the city was captured by the Turks in 1361. In 1428, one of Edirne's leading rabbis sent a circular letter to the oppressed Jews of Christian Europe urging them to migrate to Turkey. When the Turks took Salonica in 1430, Jews flocked to the city and helped to make it the leading commercial center of the Balkans (see GREECE). The fall of Constantinople (Istanbul) to the Turks in 1453 enabled thousands of Jewish refugees from Spain and Portugal to find sanctuary within the borders of Turkey after 1492.

Under Turkish rule, the Jews experienced long periods of religious tolerance, prosperity, and cultural creativity, alternating with eras of discrimination, poverty, and intellectual decadence. Izmir (Smyrna), Salonica, Sofia, and Istanbul became noted centers of Jewish life and scholarship. Joseph Nasi was the Sultan's grand vizier in the sixteenth century. Nasi's mother-in-law, Gracia Mendes, persuaded the Sultan to threaten a boycott of Italian ports unless the Pope ceased his persecution of the Jews.

Under Turkish benevolence, Halachic and cabalistic study flourished. Joseph Caro compiled his great work, the *Shulhan Aruk*, the Orthodox code of religious practice, in the Ottoman Empire. Sabbatai Zevi, who proclaimed himself the messiah in the synagogue of Izmir in 1665, won large segments of the Jewish masses to his side, and then went to Istanbul to challenge the Sultan himself. Faced with death or conversion, Sabbatai Zevi ultimately became a Moslem, but his hard-core adherents continued to believe in him. Their descendants, still to be found in Istanbul, are called Donmehs, and are regarded as a Moslem sect.

By the middle of the nineteenth century, 900,000 Jews lived under Turkish rule from Asia Minor to the Arab Middle East and the Balkans. Palestine was Turkish territory until 1917. It was with the Sultan that Theodor Herzl negotiated in a futile effort to obtain a charter for Jewish colonization in the Holy Land. When the Turkish Empire began disintegrating in the nineteenth century, many Turkish Jews found themselves subjects of Bulgaria, Greece, Serbia (Yugoslavia), Rumania, and Albania.

The spirit of nationalism and anti-foreignism inspired by the Young Turk Revolution of 1908 and by Turkish territorial losses in the Balkan Wars and World War I reached a peak under Kemal Ataturk. In the 1930s and 1940s the Jews encountered serious economic and cultural setbacks. Some were temporarily deported from Thrace and the Dardanelles area. Government jobs were closed to them, and their religious and educational institutions suffered. A heavy capital levy—the Varlik—imposed on all minorities in 1942 nearly bankrupted the Jewish community. In the 1930s, however, Turkey welcomed Jewish scientists, scholars, and artists who had fled from Nazi Germany and Austria. Turkey was also a way station for many Jewish immigrants en route to Palestine via the Balkans.

Conditions improved after World War II, when Turkey became an ally of the West in the cold war. Zionist activities were barred, but the government permitted nearly half the Jewish population to leave for Israel, with which Turkey maintains diplomatic and economic ties. The migration to Israel reduced the Jewish population of Izmir from 15,000 to less than 5,000, leaving many synagogues unused, and shrank the Jewish community in Ankara from 1500 to 800. The Jewish communities in Adana, Bursa, Canakkale, Antalya, Iskenderon, Urfa, Diabekir, Aintab, Mersin, Gaza, and Tekirdag also dwindled. In Van, in the easternmost corner of Turkey, a two-thousand-year-old community of Kurdish-speaking Jews has almost vanished, most of its residents having migrated to Israel.

The 1965 census gave the Jewish population as 39,000. Of these, 32,000 live in Istanbul and 4,000 in Izmir and a few hundred in Ankara. Although there is no anti-Jewish discrimination of an official nature, the Jewish status is often affected by international events. Turkey's relations with Israel became strained during the Cyprus crisis in 1964 when Israel appeared to support the Cypriotes against the Turks. Closer ties between Turkey and other Moslem lands in the Near East have created some concern as the Arab-Israel conflict became more critical.

ADANA (Seyhan)

SYNAGOGUE here serves about 100 Jews. The rabbi lives at Yag Camii.

ANKARA

ISRAELI LEGATION, 43 Farabi Sokak.
KAHAL KADOSH SYNAGOGUE, 8 Birlik Sokak, is located in what used to be the ghetto area. Built in 1907 on the site of a much older house of worship, the synagogue is surrounded by a high iron and stucco fence. Located just off Anafartalar, the main thoroughfare of the Ulus shopping and residential area, the synagogue is reached by winding steps leading to a series of alleys.

MT. ARARAT

SNOW-CAPPED 17,000-FOOT PEAK, not far from where Soviet and Iranian borders meet Turkish frontier is believed by some scholars to be the Biblical mountain on which Noah's Ark landed. Some explorers claim to have seen 'remnants' of the Ark.

BURSA

ETZ HAIM SYNAGOGUE in the Alti Parmak neighborhood, a short walk from the Park and Celik Hotels, is a two-hundred-year-old square-shaped structure used by most of the 120 families in the historic but dwindling Jewish community, which was founded in the first century before the Christian Era. On the synagogue's outer gate is a Turkish crescent and star. There is another synagogue here, but it is not used regularly.

EDIRNE (Adrianople)

SYNAGOGUE, a comparatively modern building dating from the early 1900s, is the only synagogue here, although the Jewish community's history goes back to the first century of the Christian Era. All thirteen of the city's older synagogues were destroyed by fire, which in 1903 wiped out almost all of what was then known as Adrianople. A commanding edifice seating 600, the synagogue has a plaque on one wall recalling that "this structure was completed in the spring of the year 5669 after the creation of the world."

ISTANBUL (Constantinople)

ASHKENAZIC SYNAGOGUE, 37 Yuksek Kaldirim, the only synagogue in Istanbul that is not Sephardic, is in the Galata section, the principal commercial quarter of the city, at the foot of Beyogulu, on the northern shore of the Golden Horn. Most of the major Jewish institutions are located in the Galata area. The bulk of the Jewish population now lives in the more modern northern sections of the city.

BALAT QUARTER, in the old city on the European side of the Bosporus, is one of two historic, ghettolike Jewish sections of the city. Balat is on the southern shore of the Golden Horn; Haskoy is on the northern shore, directly opposite Balat.

CHIEF RABBINATE, 23 Yemenici Sokak, is the official body representing all Turkish Jews. Its Religious Council is responsible for religious matters, and the Lay Council administers all other communal affairs.

BETH ISRAEL SYNAGOGUE, No. 41 Effesok, Osmanbey, which traces its origin to 1453, is a more modern Sephardic house of worship located in the newer Sisli residential area in northern Istanbul to which many Jews have moved.

BETH YAKOV SYNAGOGUE on the Island of Heybeliada, one of the Princes Islands in the Sea of Marmara.

CINILI KIOSK on the grounds of the Topkapi Museum, is a famed art museum, in whose collections are preserved inscriptions in Greek, warning Jews not to set foot in the pagan temples erected by King Herod of Judaea. From the Topkapi Palace, Gulhane Parki St. leads to the Kiosk, which, like all the city's museums, is in the old city not far from Balat.

ETZ HAIM SYNAGOGUE, 38 Muallim Naci Caddesi, is in the Ortakoy section.

GRAND BAZAAR in the old town near University Square, is one of the most fascinating shopping areas in the world. Here you encounter Jewish merchants who come from all parts of the Balkans and the Levant, and who offer wares of all kinds in shops side by side with those owned by Greeks, Turks, and Armenians. Most Istanbul Jews speak Ladino, a Spanish-Hebrew dialect, but some also understand French and German. In existence since 1461, this sprawling, rooftopped city within a city, has had Jewish merchants for centuries. Only a few of them live in the vicinity.

HASKOY CEMETERY, oldest Jewish burial ground in European Turkey, has tombstones dating from the fifteenth century. One of the most unusual tombs holds the remains of Abraham de Camondo, who was head of the Istanbul Jewish community for fifty years in the middle of the nineteenth century. He designed the tomb himself. The cemetery is almost at the very tip of the Golden Horn.

HEMDATH ISRAEL SYNAGOGUE, 35 Izzettin Pasa Sokak, is in Haydarpassa, on the Asiatic side of the Bosporus.

HOME FOR THE AGED, 4 Zurefa Sokak, in Galata.

ISRAELI CONSULATE, 10 Buyuk Ciftlik Sokak.

ITALIAN SYNAGOGUE, 29 Okcu Musa Caddesi, near Tutsak Sokak, in Galata.

JANEA SYNAGOGUE, 184 Vodina Caddesi, organized by Jews from Greece, is over three hundred years old.

JEWISH COMMUNAL CENTER, 61 Buyuk Hendek Sokak, in Galata.

JEWISH HIGH SCHOOL, Mektep Sokak, in Galata.

JEWISH ORPHANAGE, 35 Yildiz Mahalesi Palanga Sokak, in Ortakoy.

LAURA KADOORIE OR-HAYIM HOSPITAL, 162-54 Dibbek Caddesi Karabas Mahalesi, is a Jewish hospital founded by the Kadoorie family of bankers and philanthropists from Bombay and Baghdad.

KARAITE SYNAGOGUE, 3 Mahlul Sokak, is the central synagogue of the Karaite sect in Haskoy. Its founders came to Turkey in Byzantine times. There is another Karaite synagogue, the *Bene Nihia*, at 1 Kececi Peri Mahlul Sokak. The synagogue entrances are below street level because the Karaites favor synagogues in low places, taking their guidance from Psalm 130, "Out of the depths have I called thee."

KENESET ISRAEL SYNAGOGUE, 79 Buyuk Hendek Caddesi, in Galata, is an all-children's congregation.

KOSHER RESTAURANTS: Vitali Levi, on 2d floor in Riza Pasa Yokusu Caddesi, and on Sabuncu Han, near the Misir Garsi bazaar. Both eating places are in the Eminonu district, not far from the Sirkeci railway station.

MAYOR SYNAGOGUE, 4/2 Aziz Sokak.

MERKEZ SYNAGOGUE, 8 Icadiye Caddesi, and **VIRANE SYNAGOGUE,** 8 Yakup Sokak, are in Kuzguncuk, on the Asiatic shore of the Bosporus, where there is a sixteenth-century Jewish cemetery as well as a cemetery of the Donmehs, followers of Sabbatai Zevi.

MUSEUM OF ANTIQUITIES, Gulhane Parki Caddesi, has among its historic artifacts original inscriptions from the Siloam water tunnel built in the eighth century B.C.E. by King Hezekiah of Judah to provide water during the siege of Jerusalem by the Assyrians. Here, too, are a number of marble tombstones of Byzantine Jews who lived in Turkey centuries before the Turks captured Istanbul.

NEVE SHOLOM SYNAGOGUE, 67 Buyuk Hendek Caddesi, is the largest and most important synagogue in the city and a much more modern congregation than those whose synagogues are in Balat and Haskoy.

OCHRIDA SYNAGOGUE, 15 Kurtci Cesmesi Sokak, in the Balat quarter, is one of the four synagogues in the city that are more than three hundred years old and whose congregations existed in Byzantine days. There is a tradition that Sabbatai Zevi preached in this synagogue. Like all the old synagogues in Balat and Haskoy, the Ochrida is named for the community from which its founders came—Ohrid (Okhrida; also Lychnidus), an ancient Macedonian town, in what is now Yugoslavia.

RABBINICAL SEMINARY, 10B Kececi Peri Mahalesi Mektep Sokak, the only such institution in Turkey, is in Haskoy. It was opened in 1955 on the site of an older institution of similar name that was closed half a century ago.

YAMBOL SYNAGOGUE, 1 Ayan Caddesi, founded by Jews from Yambol, Bulgaria, is over three hundred years old.

IZMIR (Smyrna)

BET ISRAEL SYNAGOGUE, 265 Mitat Pasa Caddesi, in the Karatas section is the principal synagogue and one of two still in use (there are three others) in this community where Sabbatai Zevi was born, in whose synagogue he first proclaimed himself the messiah in 1665, and where he won his first followers. The second synagogue, the *Havra Synagogue* is on Havra Sokak. At 18 Alsancak Sokak is an *ORT School*. A *B'nai B'rith School* is located at 410 Mitat Pasa Caddesi. Nearby, at 65 Mitat Pasa Caddesi, is the *Jewish Hospital* (Karatas Hastenasi) and the *Jewish Old Age Home*. In the latter building is the local Jewish Communal Center. The building of the Chief Rabbinate is in the same street, which is one of the oldest sections of the city, near the central market. The Jews call it Juderia, and the Turks know it as Havra, a corruption of the Hebrew word *chevrah*. Not far from this place archaeologists have uncovered the market place (*agora*) of Hellenic times.

On the same block with all these Jewish communal institutions, on a little hill, stands a crumbling stone building which has been identified as the house in which Sabbatai Zevi was born and lived in his early years. On its roof top he met secretly with his first followers. The building is now occupied by gypsy squatters who light candles periodically in memory of the "holy man" who, they have heard, once lived there.

KIRKLARELI

MUSEVI HAVRASI (Synagogue of House of Moses), is located on a little side street off the main avenue of this little town northeast of Edirne. Only 12 years old, the tiny unpretentious structure facing a small courtyard replaced a 200-year old synagogue. There are only 25 Jewish families here.

SARDIS

ANCIENT SYNAGOGUE RUINS, remnants of a synagogue that dates from between 220 and 250 C.E., according to the Harvard and Cornell archeologists who discovered them in 1962, are located about 35 miles east of Izmir on the Izmir-Manisa road. The first finds in the fabled city that was the capital of King Croesus of Lydia revealed a marble block in which were slightly incised a menorah, a lulav and a shofar. Later discoveries turned up artifacts that establish the synagogue as having been a beautiful structure approximately 300 by 60 feet. Reconstruction of the synagogue is still under way.

UNION OF SOVIET SOCIALIST REPUBLICS

The world's oldest Jewish settlements, next to those in Israel, are in the Soviet Union's Caucasian republics of Azerbaijan, Dagestan, and Georgia, and in her Central-Asian republics of Tadjikistan and Uzbekistan. Jews first reached these regions in the seventh and sixth centuries B.C.E. They came first as traders from Persia and then as refugees from Palestine after Nebuchadnezzar destroyed the first Temple in Jerusalem in 586 B.C.E. The Persian Jews founded the exotic Bukharan Jewish community that spread through Central Asia, while those who came directly from the Holy Land became the ancestors of the Mountain Jews of the Caucasus.

Later Jewish exiles from Palestine, following the destruction of the second Temple in 70 C.E., settled along the Caspian and Black Sea coasts and in the remote regions of the Caucasus Mountains where earlier settlements existed. Immigrants from Constantinople, whose Christian rulers were harassing the Jews in the sixth and seventh centuries C.E., greatly enlarged the Caucasus Jewish colonies.

One of the pagan Asian tribes with whom the Caucasian and Crimean Jews traded was the Khazars, who dominated the Caspian and Black Seas regions after the seventh century. Sometime during the eighth century, the Khazar King Bulan, his family, and large segments of his people became converts to Judaism, presumably under the influence of the Caucasian Jews and rabbis from Constantinople. Bulan's successors founded synagogues, opened Hebrew schools, invited Jewish scholars from the East to instruct his people in the Hebrew Bible and rabbinic literature, and adopted the Hebrew alphabet.

The existence of this Jewish kingdom stimulated further Jewish immigration to the Caucasus and the Crimea from Mesopotamia, Persia, and Byzantium when the Moslems began sweeping westward. From Khazaria the Jews pressed north and west into the Ukraine, Poland, Muscovy, Lithuania, and Hungary, where they became the nuclei of the later Jewish centers in Eastern Europe. In Kiev, where the Russian Orthodox Church had its beginnings in 988, the Jews antedated the Russians. In 986 they tried but failed to persuade Prince Vladimir of Kiev, then a pagan, to accept Judaism. But they succeeded in introducing Greco-Byzantine culture among his people. When the prince chose the Greek Orthodox faith of his ally, the Byzantine emperor, the Hebrew alphabet was utilized in the conversion of the Russians to Christianity.

The Khazars were conquered by the Muscovites in 1083, and Khazaria vanished after the Tatars swept over Russia in 1237-40. Some surviving Khazars either stayed in Russia or moved west, but most of them joined their coreligionists in the Caucasus, where they mixed with the native Jews and became the descendants of the Mountain Jews of Dagestan and Azerbaijan.

By the middle of the twelfth century there was also a substantial Jewish community in Kiev, then part of the Polish Ukraine. Twelfth- and thirteenth-century rabbinic literature refers to Jewish students from Russia studying at the Talmudic academies of the West and also mentions Jews from southern Russia who spoke Russian and read the Bible in that tongue. But in the expanding Muscovite empire of central and northern Russia, Jews had been denied the right of domicile since the fifteenth century because of the hostility of the Orthodox clergy and native merchants. Until late in the seventeenth century there was only a handful of Jews in the Muscovite territories. They were traders from Poland and Lithuania who came to the fairs at Novogorod, Moscow, and Smolensk and decided to stay; doctors and merchants from Germany and Poland brought in secretly by the nobles; prisoners taken in the war with Poland in 1665-66; Khazars; Karaites, members of a heretical Jewish sect; and residents of the Kiev district, which Russia annexed in 1668.

After the partitions of Poland at the end of the eighteenth century, nearly 1,000,000 Jews came under Russian rule when the Czars acquired the Ukraine, Lithuania, and White Russia. At the instigation of Russian merchants and the bitterly anti-Semitic Church, Empress Catherine II in 1791 confined all her new Jewish subjects to the provinces of their origin, the so-called Pale of Settlement. Later, they were expelled from the villages of the Pale and driven into the crowded towns and cities, where they were in competition with Christian tradesmen and artisans, and with each other.

In the first half of the nineteenth century Russia's Jewish policy was a mixture of forced assimilation and economic oppression. Violence and pressure were employed to compel the Jews to alter their garb and language and to break with their traditional way of life in the hope that they would abandon Judaism. To wean children away from Jewish learning, a government network of secular schools was established. A brutal system of military service dragged boys in their early teens away for twenty-five years of army duty at remote barracks where they were subjected to barbaric tortures aimed at forcing them to become Christians. Simultaneously, arbitrary expulsions that drove thousands from their homes, exclusion from all but a few petty trades and occupations and from the universities and professions, and the imposition of discriminatory taxes created widespread destitution among the Jewish masses. A few privileged Jews were exempt from these disabilities and were allowed to live in the big cities, but the bulk of the Jewish population was condemned to social degradation and economic pauperism.

Some restrictions were temporarily lifted in the reign of Czar Alexander II (1856-1881). Jews were admitted to secondary schools and universities; military service for Jewish children was abolished; the interior of the country was opened to selected merchants and artisans; and the insulting features of the oath imposed on Jews in the courts were modified. It was during this period that Jews entered the professions, many of them becoming prominent lawyers, doctors, and even judges, while Jewish industrialists built railroads and factories and Jewish bankers expanded the country's economy.

Alexander's assassination intensified the anti-Semitic phobia of the ruling circle, who suppressed the rising clamor of the lower and middle classes for greater freedom and economic opportunities by attributing all of Russia's deep-seated problems to the Jews. They numbered 5,000,000 when Alexander III became Czar in 1881. The new regime began with widespread pogroms, new curbs on Jews in trade and business, renewed exclusion from the universities and the professions, contraction of the Pale of Settlement, and strict enforcement of every anti-Jewish regulation. The announced objective was to persuade one third of the Jews to emigrate and another third to accept baptism, while the rest would be starved to death.

The brief era of liberalism under Alexander II coincided with the beginning of a great cultural renascence among Russian Jews. This movement, known as the

Haskalah (Enlightenment), spread modern European education among the Jewish masses by integrating Jewish thought with secular learning and stimulating a literary revival of Hebrew. The influence of such Haskalah leaders as Isaac Baer Levinsohn, Solomon Judah Rapoport, and Nachman Kohen Krochmal nurtured the generation of Jewish intellectuals, writers, and editors that fathered modern Hebrew and Yiddish literature and the Hebrew and Yiddish press. A remarkable galaxy of poets, novelists, essayists, journalists, scholars, and historians was produced by the Haskalah. Among them were such distinguished figures as Abraham Mapu, Mendele Mocher Sforim, Judah Loeb Gordon, Peretz Smolenskin, Leo Pinsker, Sholom Aleichem, Isaac Loeb Peretz, Chaim Nachman Bialik, Ahad Ha'am, Zalman Shneour, Abraham Harkavy, and Simon Dubnow. They and their contemporaries created the intellectual climate in which Jewish nationalism, Jewish Socialism and Zionism were able to capture the imagination of an entire generation and to influence the future of Jewish history.

Despite their desperate economic privation, the vast masses of Russian Jews were little affected by the Enlightenment. Cultural changes that threatened religious traditions or undermined established customs and practices were resisted by the rabbis who presided over distinguished academies of Jewish learning. The bulk of the Jewish populace held fast to the old ways, so graphically depicted in the stories and novels of Sholom Aleichem and Sholem Asch, because they sensed that these gave them the inner strength to resist and survive Czarist oppression.

The pogroms of 1881 turned the majority of Jewish intellectuals to Jewish nationalism (which sought the recognition of the Jews as one nationality in a Russian federation of ethnic groups) or to Zionism. Youthful idealists from Russia established the first Jewish agricultural colonies in Palestine in the 1870s and 1880s, and the Hebrew and Yiddish writers of Russia paved the way for the outpouring of enthusiasm that greeted Theodor Herzl in Russia when he founded the Zionist Organization in 1897. A minority of the intellectuals embraced the radical political movements in the belief that liberty for all Russians would also emancipate the Jews.

While Zionists, nationalists, and socialists competed for the support of the Jewish masses, a historic tide of Jewish migration began to roll out of Russia. From a trickle of 30,000 between 1870 and 1880, it became a flood after 1881. By 1900 more than 600,000 Russian Jews had reached the United States and another 250,000 had found their way to England, France, Canada, Australia, South Africa, and Latin America.

Nevertheless, at the beginning of the twentieth century, there were still 6,000,000 Jews in the Russian Empire. New anti-Jewish riots, carefully organized by government-sponsored bands of hoodlums, swept the country in the early 1900s. To allay the rising tide of hatred for the autocratic regime, Jews were deliberately made the scapegoats for Russia's defeats in the Russo-Japanese War. The mounting anti-Jewish violence and their own innate idealism made the Jewish youth natural allies of the reform and radical parties, but the Czar's ministers then found it easy to blame Jews for the revolutionary movement which was gaining strength. In the first legislative assembly, convened in 1905 when Nicholas II temporarily granted the country a limited constitution, the co-leader of the Liberal Constitutionalist party was Maxim Vinaver, a Jewish lawyer. In the reaction that followed the dismissal of the assembly, Jews were again the prime targets. Russia horrified the world in 1911 by staging a blood ritual trial against Mendel Beilis. Two years later, the United States abrogated its commercial treaty with Russia because American Jews were also being discriminated against in the Czar's territories.

When World War I began, half of the 14,000,000 Jews in the world lived in the Russian Empire. Because the biggest battles on the eastern front raged in areas where the Jewish population was thickest, the Jews suffered from both sides. Although 700,000 Jews were fighting for the Czar, the guilty conscience of the Russians prompted them to deport hundreds of thousands of civilian Jews to the interior for fear that they would support the Germans. The March 1917 revolution that overthrew the Czar immediately abolished all legal disabilities against the Jews. After the democratic Kerensky government was deposed by the Bolsheviks, the ensuing civil war brought new tragedy, since it was fought in the areas most heavily populated by Jews. The anti-Bolshevik armies pillaged and murdered Jews whom they regarded as Bolsheviks; the Communist forces were less murderous, but they treated Jewish communal and religious leaders as part of the middle class and therefore foes of the new regime. Between 1919 and 1921, 1,200 pogroms in 900 towns and cities of the old Pale of Settlement claimed 75,000 Jewish lives. Over 500,000 Jews fled the country. Another 2,000,000 found themselves citizens of Poland, Lithuania, Latvia, Estonia, Rumania, Finland, and Czechoslovakia as a result of postwar territorial changes.

The Communist regime immediately outlawed anti-Semitism and accorded Jews equal social, economic, and political rights. But, as part of the State's war on religion, many synagogues were closed, Jewish religious observances and instruction were severely restricted, the Hebrew language and the Hebrew Bible were prohibited, Zionism was declared illegal, communal and cultural organizations were disbanded, and contacts with Jewish communities abroad were broken off. The Yiddish-speaking section of the Communist party led the relentless assault on every vestige of Jewish life except secular Yiddish culture.

In the first years after the revolution, 70 per cent of the Jews were reduced to penury, because their traditional occupations of small tradesmen, shopkeepers, and middlemen—imposed on them by Czarist tyranny—were made superfluous by the new economic system. Having radically altered the economic base of most Russian Jews, the Soviet government first sought to normalize their position by settling them on the land. With the support of American Jewish relief agencies, who provided cattle, tools, machinery, and technical help, compact colonies of Jewish farmers were created in the Ukraine and the Crimea.

As the country became more industrialized, the Soviets retrained Jews for factory jobs and gradually absorbed them into all facets of the economy. By 1934 their economic status had been so completely changed that the majority consisted of trained artisans, factory workers, officials, white-collar workers, professionals, scientists, and collective farmers. This re-stratification also caused substantial shifts in the Jewish population from the towns and villages of the old Pale of Settlement to the big cities of central Russia and the new industrial centers in the Urals and in Central Asia.

At the outset, the Communists recognized the Jews as a separate nationality, gave the Yiddish language official status, and, in 1934, created Biro-Bidjan as an autonomous, Yiddish-speaking Jewish region in Siberia. While the organized Jewish community in Russia ceased to exist in 1917, a Jewish cultural life of sorts was encouraged and supported through a network of Yiddish clubs, schools, newspapers, book-publishing houses, theatres, and scientific academies.

In the early 1930s the Jewish section of the Communist party and the Society for

Spreading Agriculture and Industry among Jews were abolished, because the Soviets felt they had completed the economic and social restratification of the Jewish population and had won the war against Judaism. Though many of the leading Jewish Communists, including early associates of Lenin and Trotzky, were liquidated in the purges of the late 1930s, anti-Semitism had been largely neutralized because the regime fought it as counterrevolutionary.

Just before the Hitler-Stalin Pact of 1939, there began a quiet elimination of Jews from many branches of the Soviet public service. When hundreds of thousands of Polish Jews sought safety from the Nazis in Soviet-occupied Poland, they were arrested and deported to Siberia. Many others were forced back into German-occupied Poland, where they were exterminated in the death camps. Soon after the Nazis invaded Russia in 1941, active anti-Semitism reappeared there at the very time that the Soviets were sponsoring a Jewish Anti-Fascist Committee to mobilize world Jewish support for the U.S.S.R. Although the Nazi invasion struck first and hardest at the Ukraine and White Russia, where most Russian Jews still lived, the government made little effort to halt the spread of Nazi-stimulated anti-Jewish violence or to evacuate all of the Jews in time.

The 1939 census had listed 3,100,000 Jews in the U.S.S.R. Another 2,000,000 were added by the annexation of Lithuania, Latvia, Estonia, part of Poland, and the Rumanian provinces of Bukovina and Bessarabia. The Germans slaughtered 1,300,000 Jews on Russian soil. Yet, Soviet Jewry was the largest in Europe to survive the holocaust. The 1959 census counted 2,268,000 Jews, more than in any country except the United States.

With the onset of the cold war and Soviet hostility to Israel (which the U.S.S.R. had helped to establish by its surprising vote at the United Nations and its early diplomatic recognition), a new anti-Jewish trend asserted itself. It began in 1948 with a crusade against Zionism and broadened into an assault on Jews as Jews, who were branded "rootless cosmopolitans" and "bourgeois nationalists" unable to adjust to Communist society. The leaders of the Jewish Anti-Fascist Committee and hundreds of prominent Jewish writers, artists, and intellectuals were liquidated. Jewish government administrators, diplomats, army officers, and factory executives were either dismissed or demoted. Thousands of Jews lost their jobs and their homes, and many others disappeared. The Jewish leaders in Biro-Bidjan were purged as spies, thus dooming this project, which had already been downgraded. Simultaneously, every facet of secular Jewish cultural life was eliminated, and new difficulties were made for the existing synagogues.

As Stalin became more violently anti-Semitic, the press and the courts accused Jews of every crime, from embezzlement to medical malpractice and from sabotage to treason. The anti-Jewish terror reached its climax in 1952 with the fantastic "doctors' plot" hatched by Stalin and his associates, who claimed that a group of prominent Jewish physicians in Russia had killed two leading Soviet officials and was planning to murder others as part of a world Jewish conspiracy against the Soviet Union. Only Stalin's death in 1953 prevented the planned deportation of all Jews to Siberia.

The anti-Jewish violence ended with Stalin's death in 1953, but under Khrushchev and his successors Jews as a group have continued to suffer special disabilities. While those exiled by Stalin have been released and the families of the Jews he had exterminated have received pensions, anti-Jewish sentiment expresses itself in other forms of discrimination.

Few Jews are to be found in the higher levels of Soviet public service. In 1971 Veniamin E. Dymshits was a deputy premier. They are excluded from the diplomatic service and from key jobs in the press, the universities, and the armed forces. There is a systematic limitation on the number of Jews admitted to higher institutions of learning. Particularly galling is the deliberate obliteration of the Jewish record in World War II. Three per cent of all who earned the title of Hero of the Soviet Union were Jews, second only to the Great Russians and Ukrainians, while 11 per cent of all Soviet scientific workers are Jews. Gen. Hirsch Plaskov, a Jew, wrote in his memoirs that there were 47 Jewish generals and admirals in the Soviet forces in World War II and more than 500,000 Jews in uniform.

In 1963 Khrushchev told a meeting of Moscow writers that it was better for Jews not to hold top positions because "this only provokes popular resentment." In a five-page letter to Lord Russell, Khrushchev bitterly denied that the executions of economic culprits in 1962 and 1963, who numbered many Jews, including some synagogue officials, were aimed at Jews alone. Thinly veiled anti-Semitic gibes in the press and embittered attacks on Israel that aroused feelings against all Jews were climaxed in 1963 by the publication of a vicious anti-Semitic book by a notorious Ukrainian anti-Semite, Trofim K. Kichko. This volume, which bore the imprint of the Ukrainian Academy of Sciences, and was later denounced by the Ideological Commission of the Soviet Communist Party, gave rise to several instances of blood ritual accusations against Jews as well as sporadic incidents of anti-Jewish violence. The ideological debate engendered by Yevgeny Yevtushenko's poem 'Babi Yar' focused worldwide attention on Russia's refusal to recognize that Jews had shared in vast numbers in the martyrdom suffered by Russians at the hands of the Nazis. Government policy appears aimed not only at eradicating Judaism as a religion but at bringing about forced assimilation and the elimination of the Jews as a distinctive group. As a nationality, the Jews are denied most of the rights enjoyed by other national minorities. They have no literature, no theatres, no press, and no schools of their own. For 470,000 Jews who declared in the last census that Yiddish is their mother tongue, there is only one Yiddish newspaper (in Biro-Bidjan) and a national Yiddish monthly literary review called *Sovietish Heimland,* which made its debut in August 1961. During the 1960s a number of Yiddish books and some translations from Yiddish appeared, as well as an anthology of Israeli writers and a Russian-Hebrew dictionary. A number of travelling Yiddish theatrical companies and Yiddish vaudevillians and musical artists appear from time to time in the larger cities.

Official tribute to Sholom Aleichem on his centennial in 1959 through the publication of his collected works in Russian and a slim edition in Yiddish, publication of Russian translations of the works of some of the executed Yiddish writers, and occasional concerts by Yiddish artists constitute the totality of permitted Jewish cultural life.

The Jews are considered a nationality and are so designated on the individual passport every citizen carries, but, alone among the Soviet Union's many nationalities, they are deprived of cultural institutions and are isolated religiously.

Every major religious group in Russia but the Jews has a central organization. In the absence of any other Jewish institutions, the synagogues are the only places where Jews can and do gather in groups, not only for worship, but also to identify themselves with fellow Jews and to exchange information about Jewish life in Russia and abroad. Synagogues declined from 450 in 1956 to 100 in 1963 and 65 in 1970 chiefly through forcible closings. Synagogue vandalism was reported from a number of cities and attacks on Jews were stepped up in the guise of anti-religious propaganda. Publication of religious literature is banned. Not a single Jewish prayer book appeared in the USSR until 1958, when a limited edition of 5,000 copies was published. Another limited edition was edited in 1968 by Rabbi Yehudah Leib Levin of Moscow. The manufacture or importation of religious appurtenances is prohibited, and even the baking of matzoth is not permitted in some cities. The one rabbinical seminary, located in Moscow's main synagogue, no longer has any students. The ban on Jewish schools and societies remains firm. There are perhaps 40 to 50 rabbis left in the whole country, and their average age in 1971 was over 60.

No other ethnic group—not even the Volga Germans, who were once deported and dispersed by Stalin—is denied the right to corporate and ethnic existence. Yet, Soviet spokesmen and Moscow Radio broadcasts have repeatedly denied the existence of a Jewish problem and a pattern of anti-Jewish policies. The Soviet leaders claim that because the Jews are not territorially concentrated, it is not possible to provide them with facilities for their own national life, but there are other ethnic groups similarly dispersed in the USSR that do have such rights. The Soviets also insist that the Jews do not want Yiddish literature, newspapers, schools, and institutions, because they are fully assimilated to the life and culture of the peoples among whom they live. This too has been challenged. Periodically, the Russians point to Jews who hold prominent positions in the Soviet Union to contradict charges of anti-Semitism. Emigration, even for purposes of uniting families, is barred. On Dec. 3, 1966 Premier Alexis Kosygin promised to further family reunions, and in fact, in the 18 months preceding the Six-Day Arab-Israel war emigration to Israel increased slightly. But since 1967 all but a handful of Russian Jews seeking to join their families in Israel have been denied exit permits. In the wake of the Six-Day War, following which Russia broke diplomatic relations with Israel and began building up the military forces of the Arab lands, Moscow launched a sustained propaganda offensive against Israel and Zionism that quickly assumed an overt anti-Jewish character. Anti-Israel cartoons portrayed Jews in hook-nosed caricatures, anti-Jewish speeches and articles became widespread and the press, radio and TV and public meetings furthered a campaign of vilification against Israel that made Zionism a euphemism for Jew. All Soviet citizens carry passports stamped with their nationality. Jews' passports bear the letter 'Ye,' for Yevrei or Hebrew. Since Israel is the only Hebrew state, and Soviet official policy is that Israel is its enemy, the Jews of Russia are thus identified with and linked to a foreign and enemy state. The thin line between attacks on Israel and Zionism and on Russian Jews confronts the Jews of the USSR with a tragic dilemma. In 1969 several score prominent Jews appeared at a government-sponsored press conference in Moscow to pledge loyalty to Moscow's anti-Israel policy and to denounce Israel and Zionism. Simultaneously, Jews began to assert themselves as Jews by a series of petitions to the United Nations and leading Soviet authorities demanding freedom to go to Israel. Appeals, songs, interviews, transcripts and documents revealing a resurgence of Jewish exuberance among the younger generations began reaching the west through the underground and foreign correspondents. A number of Jewish poets and novelists were active in the growing resistance of Russian intellectuals to cultural repression. Arrests and imprisonment of Jews seeking to emigrate from the USSR were part of an increasingly bitter anti-israel and anti-Zionist campaign that gave rise to worldwide protests and the organization of militant efforts to persuade Moscow to end the oppression and repression of its 3,500,000 Jewish citizens and to let those who wanted to go to Israel do so.

During the celebration of the 50th anniversary of the Russian Revolution, a number of Jews received high honors, many posthumously. Among the latter was Jacob Sverdlov, first president of the Soviet Union. The government also paid high honors to Peretz Sternberg, a Russian Jewish astronomer, by issuing a postage stamp bearing his portrait on the centennial of his birth; to the late Dr. Lev Landau, world-renowned scientist who won the Nobel Prize in physics in 1962; to Prof. Arye Shternfeld, whose pioneer studies earned him fame as one of the fathers of the Sputniks; Gen. Jacob Kreiser, a World War II hero; and Lt. Boris Volynov, commander of the Soviet spaceship Soyuz-5, which in 1969 achieved the first link-up in space. Although many Jewish factory workers have settled in the new industrial cities, 82 per cent of the present Jewish population still resides in the three Slavic republics: 875,000 in the Russian Soviet Federated Socialist Republic; 840,000 in the Ukrainian Soviet Socialist Republic and 150,000 in Byelorussian (White Russian) Soviet Socialist Republic. The 1959 census also reported 95,000 in Moldavia; 94,000 in Uzbekistan; 52,000 in Georgia; 37,000 in Latvia; 25,000 in Lithuania; and 5,000 in Estonia. Unofficial estimates indicate a Jewish population of 55,000 in four republics of Central Asia and two in the Trans-Caucasus, and 40,000 in Biro-Bidjan. The largest Jewish communities are, in this order, in Moscow, Leningrad, Kiev, Odessa, Kharkov, Dnepropetrovsk, Chernovtsy, Minsk, Bobruisk, Tashkent, Alma-Ata, Kishinev, Lvov, Vilna, Tbilsi, Kovno, and Riga. A 1969 study by the government press agency indicated that there were 3,000,000 Jews in the USSR, dispersed through all the 15 republics.

AZERBAIJAN SOVIET SOCIALIST REPUBLIC

BAKU

ASHKENAZIC (East European) and BUKHARAN SYNAGOGUE, 171 Pervomayskaya St., is used by Yiddish-speaking Jews who settled here in the nineteenth century, and by the Oriental Jews from Bukhara (*see* UZBEKISTAN *below*).

MOUNTAIN JEWS' SYNAGOGUE, 39 Dmitrova St., is one of the world's oldest Jewish congregations, having been founded by descendants of settlers from Palestine who came to the Caucasus in the sixth century B.C.E.. There are about 30,000 Mountain Jews in Azerbaijan and in the neighboring Dagestan region of the Russian Soviet Federal Socialist Republic. They worship in Hebrew but speak a Judaeo-Tat language. Until recent years they wrote in Hebrew characters. Most of them are collective farmers, but some are employed in the Baku oil refineries.

KOBI

SYNAGOGUE

ARMENIAN SOVIET SOCIALIST REPUBLIC

BATUMI

SYNAGOGUE, 6 Ninth of March Street.

KAZAN

SYNAGOGUE, Pravokabannaya St.

BYELORUSSIAN (WHITE RUSSIAN) SOVIET SOCIALIST REPUBLIC

MINSK

HEADQUARTERS OF WHITE RUSSIAN UNION OF WRITERS has affixed to its wall a plaque memorializing 4 Yiddish poets who died heroically during the Nazi invasion. They are Reuben Reisen, Leib Talalei, Eli Kahan and Hennech Shwedik.

HISTORICAL MUSEUM OF WHITE RUSSIA houses a rare literary treasure in the form of more than 1,000 Hebrew books in many languages that date to the 15th and 16th century. The volumes were found in 1961 in the cellars of an old monastery in Budaslav.

SYNAGOGUE, 109 Tsnianskkaya St., a 20-year old wooden building, was acquired by the Jews of this city in 1964 after the last synagogue that once served 230,000 Jews was demolished on government orders. The former synagogue was over 250 years old. Half of Minsk's pre-war Jewish population was murdered by the Nazis. The present population is 40,000. Yiddish is still heard in the streets. Jewish residents are returned wartime evacuees and former inhabitants of nearby towns and villages who survived the Nazi invasion by fleeing to the forests and fighting the Germans as partisans.

(There are still substantial Jewish settlements in Mogilev, Grodno, Velikie Luki, Bobruisk, Brest Litovsk, Vitebsk and Baranovichi. The synagogues in the latter four cities were reported closed in 1961.)

GRANITNY

RABINOVICH-KOVALEV SCHOOL in this village memorializes Sasha Rabinovich-Kovalev, a 16-year old sailor's apprentice who was killed while trying to use his own body to block a hole in a Soviet warship hit by a Nazi shell on May 9, 1944. A museum in the school contains documents describing the young hero's exploit.

KRONSTADT

GRIGORI FEIGIN STREET is named for a hero of the Soviet Civil War.

PINSK

SASHA BERKOWICH ST. was named in 1967 for a Jewish resistance hero who during the German occupation of the city was secretary of the underground committee. During a clash between his partisan unit and a Nazi detachment, he killed himself with his last bullet.

JEWISH MARTYRS MEMORIAL was dedicated in 1964 on the 20th anniversary of the liberation of White Russia from the Nazis.

SYNAGOGUE, a prayer house in a private home, was closed by the authorities in 1966. The last synagogue here was shut down in 1961.

PERETZ MARKISH MEMORIAL, a corner of the Municipal Museum, contains manuscripts and other mementos of the life and works of the famed Yiddish poet and literary figure who was born here in 1895. He was executed during Stalin's anti-Jewish purges.

PUKHOVICHI

SMUSHKEVICH BUST in this town honors General Iakov V. Smushkevich, a self-educated former student at a Lithuanian yeshiva, who became head of the Soviet Army's air force in 1940. The bust was to have been erected in Rakiski, Lithuania, where he was born in 1902, but in 1939 his birthplace was not in Soviet territory, and so his friends selected Pukhovichi where he had been stationed in the 1920s and where he escaped death in a plane crash. In 1937 he was named a Hero of the Soviet Union.

ROGACHEV

SAMUEL GALKIN STREET is named for a World War II hero.

ROSSLAVEL

MEMORIAL TO JEWISH COMMUNITY, which was wiped out by the Nazis in 1941, was erected in 1968 by a committee of private individuals that included Helena Ivanova, a great-granddaughter of Fyodor Dostoyevski.

RUDNY

MONUMENT TO JEWS murdered by Nazis, is in local cemetery. The inscription is in Russian.

TROTYANETCH

NAZI EXTERMINATION CAMP SITE in this village east of Minsk has an obelisk erected by the Soviet government in memory of the 150,000 Soviet and West European Jews shot here by the Nazis. Their bodies were burned in pits.

VITEBSK

BUMAGIN STREET is named for Yosif Bumagin, a hero of the Soviet Union.

WINCHEVSKY AVENUE in this rebuilt city that was virtually destroyed by the Nazis is named for Morris Winchevsky, Yiddish poet and essayist, who was one of the founders of Yiddish socialist literature.

ESTONIAN SOVIET SOCIALIST REPUBLIC

TALLINN (Revel)

MARTYRS' MEMORIAL on the sandy area outside the city, marks the mass graves of Jews murdered by the Nazis at the death camp near Tagala. The dead included Jews from Poland, Russia, Germany, and Czechoslovakia.

HISTORICAL MUSEUM includes in its permanent exhibition on the Nazi occupation of Estonia documents and photographs dealing with the annihilation of the Jewish community. Among the items are several pages in Yiddish found in a field near the Tagala death camp, a school certificate in the name of Jacob Noah Lew; a half burnt medical diploma of Dr. Aaron Bernstein and a deportation order in the name of Sheppsel Pruzshan.

SYNAGOGUE, 9 Lasteaya St., is on the second floor of a small building. The local authorities planned to demolish the building in 1967 but yielded to protests and permitted it to remain.

GEORGIAN SOVIET SOCIALIST REPUBLIC

BATUM

SYNAGOGUE, Adsharskaya St.

GORI

SYNAGOGUE in the Gorinsky region.

KULARZ

SYNAGOGUE in this town thirty miles from Tbilisi is the spiritual center of the Georgian Jews whose forebears came here from Palestine 2,500 years ago. The area around Kularz is known as "Little Jerusalem" among Jews and non-Jews because of the deep religious fervor of the Jewish population. It is the seat of a rabbinic sage whose authority is recognized by all Jews in Georgia, who speak Georgian. Most of the students at the U.S.S.R.'s only rabbinical seminary, located in Moscow, come from this neighborhood.

KUTAISI

SYNAGOGUES (three), serve the religious needs of an estimated 15,000 Jews in and around this city, where Jews have lived for more than 2,000 years. Each synagogue has its own *haham*, or wise man. The main synagogue is at 47 Shaumyan St.

MAKHLACHHALA

SYNAGOGUE, 103 Lenin Street.

MTSHKET

KERKI, a section in this ancient capital of Georgia, thirteen miles from Tbilisi, was the site of the first colony of Jews from Palestine established in this vicinity after the destruction of the Temple in Jerusalem in 586 B.C.E. A Jewish delegation from the Holy Land obtained permission to settle here from the princes of Mtshket in return for paying a double tax. *Kerki* means "tax" in Georgian. No Jews live here now.

ONI

SYNAGOGUE

POTI

SYNAGOGUE

SUKHUMI

SYNAGOGUE, 48 Sovietskaya Street.

SURAMI

SYNAGOGUE, Internationalnaya Street.

TAKHAKHAYA

SYNAGOGUE badly damaged by a fire set by anti-Semites in 1962, it was painstakingly rebuilt by the Jewish community of 2,000 artisans and farm workers.

TIBILSI (Tiflis)

EAST EUROPEAN SYNAGOGUE, 3 Kozhevni Tupik, a few blocks' walk through winding streets from the Georgian Jews' house of worship (*see below*), is a one-story structure converted into a synagogue by Yiddish-speaking Jews who came to this city in recent years from other parts of the Soviet Union.

NATIONAL MUSEUM OF GEORGIA contains many of the exhibits formerly housed in the now closed Jewish Ethnological Museum, which was founded by the late Lavrenti Beria, Soviet Minister of the Interior. These displays included paintings depicting the rites and customs of the Georgian Jews; Bible scenes; reconstructions of ancient Georgian synagogues; photographs of Jewish women being sold as harem slaves by the various tribes who ruled Georgia; photographs describing the life of Sholom Aleichem; a collection of material devoted to Albert Einstein; and records of Jewish generals in the Red Army and Jewish heroes in World War II. In 1957, the Soviet ambassador to Israel presented photostatic copies of ancient Hebrew books owned by the museum to the Ben Zvi Institute in Jerusalem. Beria has been blamed by the Soviets for the violent anti-Semitism of the last years of the Stalin era.

SEPHARDIC SYNAGOGUE, 71 Leselidze St., is the principal gathering place of the Georgian Jews. The three-story red-brick building, in the old part of this ancient city that used to be known as Tiflis, towers over most other buildings because it is situated on a small hill near the Kura River. The synagogue's Star of David is a well-known landmark. In daily use, the synagogue is spick-and-span, and all its appurtenances are in good condition. Prayer books and scholarly tomes fill the cases in its meeting halls. Attached to the synagogue are a ritual bath and a study hall. Most of the worshipers are descendants of the historic community of Georgian Jews, founded here 2,500 years ago. They still speak Sephardic Hebrew, as well as Georgian, but do not understand the Yiddish of the East European Jews. On the upper floor there is a second and smaller synagogue, a replica of the one on the main floor. Intourist guides include this synagogue in their tour of the city. They do not include the East European synagogue, which is reached through an alley; but you can't miss it because of a Star of David on its main window.

KAZAKH SOVIET SOCIALIST REPUBLIC

ALMA-ATA

SYNAGOGUE, 48 Tashkent St., is a small structure set in a large open courtyard. It is the only one in the capital of the Kazakhstan Republic. There are some 6,000 Jews in this city, located about a hundred miles from the Chinese border, and 4,000 more elsewhere in the republic. There is another good-sized Jewish community, in Karaganda, whose synagogue was reported closed in 1961.

CHIKMENT

SYNAGOGUE, 7 Svoboda St.

LATVIAN SOVIET SOCIALIST REPUBLIC

DAUGAVPILS (Dvinsk)

MASS GRAVE OF JEWISH MEN, WOMEN AND CHILDREN shot by the Nazis during World War II, was uncovered in 1966 during excavations in a moat of a fortress used as a concentration camp.

MIKHOELS MEMORIAL, a marble plaque on the house at No. 4 Molodyozhnaya St., marks the birthplace of the noted Jewish actor. The inscription, in gold letters, reads: "Solomon Mikhoels, People's Artist of the USSR, was born in this house on March 16, 1890."

MUNICIPAL MUSEUM has a room named for Solomon Mikhoels, famed Russian-Jewish actor who was murdered in 1948 during the Stalin purges of Jews. Mikhoels, who was born here, was head of the Jewish State Theatre in Moscow and during World War II was chairman of the Jewish Anti-Fascist Committee of the USSR. The room contains many memorabilia associated with his stage career.

SYNAGOGUE is still in use in this city. Before World War I, Jews constituted a majority of the population. The 11,000 Jews who lived here before World War II were deported to Zolotaya Gorka by the Nazis and murdered in 1941.

JEKABPILS (Yekabpils)

MARTYRS' MEMORIAL in the local cemetery, marks the mass graves of Jews exterminated by the Nazis.

LIEPAJA (Libau)

JEWISH CEMETERY which the Nazi occupiers overlooked, has a memorial over the remains of several hundred Jews shot in the early days of World War II. The bodies were found in a mass grave on the shores of this Baltic port formerly known as Libau. Only a handful of Jews still live here.

RIGA

JEWISH CEMETERY badly damaged by the Nazis, has been rebuilt by the local authorities, who replaced the richly adorned headstones over many of the graves.

RUMBOLD WOOD outside Riga, has six giant mass graves where the Nazis exterminated 85,000 Jews in 1941, among them the great historian, Simon Dubnow. Each grave is marked by a memorial erected in 1964 by the city council.

BIKERNIK WOOD outside Riga, has a memorial to some 40,000 Latvians, Russians and Jews murdered here by the Nazis.

SYNAGOGUE, 8 Petevas St., near the Municipal Opera House, is the only one in the city, which has 10,000 Jews. Fewer than 200 of them are natives, the others having moved here since the end of World War II. Most of Riga's prewar Jewish population of 30,000 was wiped out by the Nazis. The synagogue's library is packed with patched and stitched prayer books and Torah Scrolls salvaged after the Nazis were driven out. There is also a Jewish Home for the Aged here.

LITHUANIAN SOVIET SOCIALIST REPUBLIC

JONAVA (Yeneva)

JEWISH CEMETERY, a 300-year old burying ground near Kovno, was taken over in 1968 by the municipal authorities for a housing site. Most of the tombstones were moved to a corner of the site.

KAUNAS (Kovno)

MARTYRS' MUSEUM on the site of the 9th Fort, a former Czarist fortress, where the Nazis murdered 70,000 people, displays records, photographs, and memorabilia of the martyrs. Nearby is a monument to the victims, most of whom were Lithuanian Jews from the Kaunas (Kovno) area, but also many from Czechoslovakia, Austria, Belgium, and Holland. Before World War II, Kovno had 40,000 Jews and was a noted center of Jewish life; today it has 5,000. The Nazis liquidated the Jewish community on October 23, 1943. The name of one of Kovno's greatest Jewish scholars, Rabbi Isaac Elchanan Spector, has been memorialized in the Isaac Elchanan Yeshiva, the rabbinical seminary of Yeshiva University in New York. Kovno was also the seat of the renowned Slobodka Yeshiva. The grave of Abraham Mapu, father of modern Hebrew literature, who was born here, vanished with the destruction of the Jewish cemetery.

SYNAGOGUE, Krasnoarmeyska Street.

PONARY

MARTYRS' MUSEUM in the Ponary Forest near Vilna, houses a collection of documents and other material recording the extermination of Lithuanian and Byelorussian Jewries and of Soviet war prisoners in camps situated near Lithuania. Near the museum are the mass graves of 100,000 Jews murdered by the Nazis. A Yiddish inscription on the monument at the grave-site was excised out some time in 1965. Also gone is the six-pointed star at the top of the monument. It has been replaced by the Soviet red star. The only legend left on the monument, in Lithuanian and Russian reads: "To the victims of Fascist terror."

SHAULIAI (Shaval)

KALINIUKAS STREET is now paved with tombstones from an old Jewish cemetery which was torn up in 1970 and replaced by a housing development.

SYMILOSK

CEMETERY in this town 55 miles from Vilna, has a stone slab with a plaque memorializing the 1,260 people, including many Jews, killed in this vicinity by the Nazis. The monument marks a mass grave in a flower-bordered area.

TROKI

KARAITE COMMUNITY, a handful of survivors of the ninth-century (C.E.) Jewish sect, still exists in this village south of Vilnius, where they settled in the fourteenth century. The Karaites were founded in Babylonia by heretical Jews who rejected all teachings except those of the Bible. They did not recognize the Talmud nor any of the post-Biblical rabbinic writings. Until World War II there was a Karaite synagogue in Troki and another in Vilna.

VILNIUS (Vilna)

GAONA STREET is named for the celebrated rabbinical sage known in Jewish history as the Vilna Gaon (a *gaon* is an exceptionally brilliant rabbinical scholar), who in the eighteenth century was the dominating Jewish religious personality in Lithuania. Until the beginning of World War II, picture postcards showing his grave in the old Jewish cemetery were sold at all kiosks. Born Elijah ben Solomon Zalman, the Vilna Gaon was a vigorous opponent of Chassidism, whose commentaries and decisions exercised a vast influence on his own and succeeding generations. When the old Jewish cemetery was converted into an athletic field after World War II, the remains of the Vilna Gaon, whose grave had been a Jewish shrine for generations, were removed to a new Jewish cemetery. Here a small mausoleum has been erected to house the remains of the Gaon and five of his disciples. On the stone wall behind each grave is imbedded the original stone grave marker from the older cemetery.

JULIAN KLACZKO STREET recalls a mid-nineteenth-century Vilna author, editor, diplomat, and fighter for Polish independence, who was educated in a local Hebrew school but later became a Catholic.

RUDININKAI FOREST outside the city, has, for the benefit of tourists, reconstructed replicas of half a dozen log-walled dugouts in which the Lithuanian partisans, led by Genrikas Zimanas, a former Yiddish school teacher, made their headquarters. Zimanas is now editor-in-chief of Tiesa, the Lithuanian-language newspaper of the Lithuanian Communist Party.

STRASHUN STREET memorializes Mathias Strashun, Talmudist, scholar, patron of Hebrew letters and founder of a noted private Jewish library, which the Nazis destroyed. He was one of the many personalities, lay and rabbinical, who made this city the "Jerusalem of Lithuania." Before World War II, Vilna had 100,000 Jews and was known as the cradle of modern Hebrew and Yiddish literature, the home of noted Hebrew publishing houses, the birthplace of the Jewish Socialist movement and of the Yiddish Scientific Institute, whose rich collections of Jewish life in Eastern Europe are now housed in New York. The Yiddish monthly, Sovietish Heimland, published in Moscow, and the Birobidjan Shtern, are displayed on newsstands. But the 400-page official guidebook to Vilnius makes not the slightest mention that the city was once a flourishing Jewish religious and cultural center.

SYNAGOGUE, Komsomolskaya St., is the only one here. It occupies a shabby building with boarded-up windows. Yiddish is widely spoken among the 17,000 Jews in the city. An amateur Yiddish theatrical group gives performances here.

DRUSKININKAI

TOWN PARK now has stone steps made of tombstones from the old Jewish cemetery in this one-time well-known spa where many Zionist conventions took place.

MOLDAVIAN SOVIET SOCIALIST REPUBLIC

KISHINEV

SYNAGOGUE, 8 Yakimovskiy Pereulok, is the only one left in this once historic Jewish community. There are 50,000 Jews here now, more than half of the Jewish population in Moldavia, which embraces the former Rumanian provinces of Bukovina and Bessarabia. Before the war, the Jews constituted 60 per cent of the population. Over 10,000 of them were murdered during the Nazi occupation. This city was the scene of a notorious Czarist pogrom in 1903, which first called world attention to the plight of the Jews in Russia.

(There are also Jewish communities in Orgeyev, Rezeni, and Tiraspol, but the synagogues there were reported closed in 1961.)

RYBNITSA

SYNAGOGUE, Vokkov St.

RUSSIAN SOVIET FEDERATED SOCIALIST REPUBLIC

ASTRAKHAN

SYNAGOGUE, a converted house, is at 30 Babushkin St. The city has some 6,000 Jews.

BIRO-BIDJAN

SYNAGOGUE, 9 Chapayev St., in the capital of the Jewish Autonomous Region of the same name, is used by a tiny fraction of the 14,000 Jews left in this Siberian city of some 60,000. A wooden shack on a muddy lane, a fast 12-minute walk from the center of the city, it is not recognizable for what it is since there are no markings on the outside and the building looks exactly like the wooden houses of dozens of farmers all around, except that it is somewhat larger. Covering 13,800 square miles, the region was established in 1934 as a center of national Jewish life for all of the U.S.S.R. But it never attracted the masses of Russian Jews. Today Biro-Bidjan, which is near the Manchurian border, is a Jewish region in name only. It has no Yiddish schools but a Jewish People's Theatre stages Yiddish plays at the Palace of Culture. Yiddish culture is represented by a triweekly paper, the Biro-Bidjan *Shtern*, and a few street signs in Yiddish. There are Yiddish and Russian signs over the central movie house, the collective farm market and the post office and on street signs. Another street is named for the late Yiddish writer, Emanuel Kazakievitch, who lived and produced literary works in Biro-Bidjan for three years. There are some Yiddish books in the local library and a few Jewish items in the local museum. There is also a street named for Sholom Aleichem, which crosses October Street.

BRIANSK

SYNAGOGUE, 29 Uritsky Street.

BUINAKSK

SYNAGOGUE in this third-largest city of Dagestan Republic is used by the 11,000 Mountain Jews of this north Caucasian region on the west shore of the Caspian Sea. They are kin to the Jews of neighboring Azerbaijan and have lived here for more than two thousand years. In 1960, the local Communist newspaper published a blood ritual accusation against the Jewish community.

CHUFAT-KALE

"FORTRESS OF THE JEWS" is the English meaning of the name of this ruined city two miles east of Bakhchisarai, in the south-central part of the Crimean Peninsula. The oldest tombstones in the Jewish cemetery are dated 1203 C.E., but Jews settled in the Crimea in the sixth century B.C.E. The oldest surviving Jewish communities are at Yepatorya, Kerch and Simferepol and Karasu Bazar. A copy of an ancient Hebrew prayer book from the latter community is preserved at the Jewish Theological Seminary of America in New York. There are also more modern settlements at Yalta, Russia's Riviera, and at Sevastopol. In the latter, the Jewish cemetery has a monument to Jewish soldiers in the Czar's army who died in the Crimean War. The present Jewish population in the Crimea consists of the descendants of the earliest settlers—Karaites, who arrived about 1200 C.E.; Khazars; refugees from the seventeenth-century pogroms in the Ukraine; and the survivors of Jewish farmers who were established here in the late 1920s.

IRKUTSK

SYNAGOGUE, 17 Liebknecht St. here has been partly diverted for use as a residence for local medical students. Only the upper story is still used for worship.

KALININ

SYNAGOGUE, 21 Solodovaya Street.

KUYBSHEV

SYNAGOGUE, 84 Chapayev St.

KLINTSY

SYNAGOGUE, 84 Lermontov St.

LENINGRAD

ANTI-RELIGION MUSEUM on the Newski Prospekt, contains an immense variety of exhibits and photographs, including many of synagogues and Jewish ritual objects. This museum is not included in the itinerary of Intourist because it is intended primarily to promote atheism among the Russian population.

CHORAL SYNAGOGUE, 2 Lermontovski Prospekt, one of the largest in Europe, is an imposing Moorish-style stone structure erected in 1884. The synagogue proper seats about thirteen hundred, but with the huge women's gallery and five smaller chapels, all linked by a modern loudspeaker system, more than four thousand can be accommodated. During the High Holy Days the loudspeaker system also reaches outdoors because the street in front of the synagogue is thronged with worshippers.

There is an impressive entrance gate of wrought iron inscribed with Hebrew mottoes. Beyond the gate is a large lobby, with stairways on either side leading to the women's gallery. The Ark is under a canopy, above which is a neon-lighted Star of David. The two large Menorahs flanking the Ark are also neon-lighted. On the lower level are the chapels, one of which contains a permanent *sukkah*; a sumptuous wedding hall; a library containing thousands of Hebrew books, sets of the Talmud and a large collection of Torah Scrolls; a ritual bath for women; and a ritual slaughterhouse for preparing kosher meat. There is also a smaller synagogue on the main floor. The prayer books used in the synagogue are all pretty old and worn.

During the siege of the city in World War II, when most of the civilian populace was evacuated, one of the synagogue officials risked his life when he moved into the abandoned synagogue and occupied it until the siege was lifted. Under Soviet law, title to evacuated and abandoned buildings reverts to the government. Thus, the official's heroism avoided the probability that the synagogue would have been forfeited when the war was over. The building on the left of the synagogue entrance is a state children's hospital which was formerly the community's Hebrew secondary school. In addition to the Choral Synagogue, Leningrad has sixteen private prayer houses, one for each of the city's sixteen districts.

HERMITAGE between the Palace Square and the Neva River, one of the world's richest art museums, has in its Rembrandt Gallery such famous works of the Dutch master as "The Sacrifice of Abraham" and "The Parting of David and Jonathan."

INSTITUTE OF THE PEOPLES OF ASIA, 18 Dvostovaya Neb., a branch of the Soviet Academy of Sciences, preserves two notable collections of Hebraica and Judaica. The Friedland Collection, presented by Aryeh Leib Friedland, an army contractor and philanthropist, contains 300 volumes in parchment manuscripts and more than 10,000 printed books. Two of the rarest items are a Torah Scroll made in 941 C.E. and a Hebrew calendar from 847 C.E. The second collection is named for

Jonah Guinzburg, the scholar who assembled it. Parts of the Friedland Collection are available on microfilm at the New York University Department of Hebrew Culture and Education.

JEWISH CEMETERY, about five miles beyond the city's limits, which is entered through a massive arch, contains a monument to the 7,000 Jews who were killed by bombs or died of starvation during the siege of Leningrad. They are all buried in a mass grave. Many of the gravestones contain inscriptions in the Russian language but written in Hebrew characters. About one out of every forty graves is marked by a wooden headstone crowned with a red star, the symbol of Communist party membership. One of the most notable tombstones of the pre-Soviet era is that of the eminent sculptor, Mark Antokolski, who died in 1902. The cemetery chapel is a miniature replica of the Great Synagogue in Paris. Tombstones with Hebrew or Yiddish inscriptions are hard to find among those erected in the last 20 years. Most of the inscriptions are in Russian. Because the cemetery, dating from 1750, is filled up, a new one has been opened five miles away.

BELA KUN STREET is named for the head of the short-lived Hungarian Communist government in 1919, who fled to Russia after his regime was overthrown during an anti-Semitic bloodbath. Shot during the Stalin purges, he was posthumously rehabilitated after Stalin's death and the street, as well as a school, were named for him on the 45th anniversary of the first Hungarian red government.

LENINGRAD MUSEUM, the second largest in the Soviet Union, has in one of its 31 halls an exhibit of documents and pictures related to the role of Jews in the revolutionary struggle against the Czar. None of the Jews are identified as such but anyone familiar with Russian-Jewish history can identify people like Akselrad and Deutsch at the first Geneva conference of Anti-Czarist Activists; a painting of L. Wilenski among the delegates to the 2d London conference of the Social Democratic Party; M. Gubelman (later Lyaroslavsky), who is shown among the editors of the newspaper Iskra, together with Israel Piasnicki and Rosa Luxembourg. In another part of the hall are pictures of Jacob Sverdlov, first president of the Soviet Union; W. Vlodarski (Moshe Goldstein), Moshe Uritsky, M. Nahamson and Jacob Drapkin.

LENINGRAD STATE LIBRARY, 18 Sadovaya St., has in its rare-book rooms a number of priceless collections of Hebraica and Judaica. One is the celebrated Abraham Firkowitch Collection assembled in the mid-nineteenth century by a Jewish traveler and scholar who was a specialist in the lore of the Karaites. This collection includes early Karaite, Samaritan, and Hebrew manuscripts, molds of ancient Jewish tombstones in the Crimea and the Caucasus, and more than 1,500 manuscripts from the Cairo Genizah. The latter are fragments of Hebrew Bible manuscripts going back to 929 C.E. They were part of the treasure trove located in the hiding place (genizah) for worn-out or defective sacred books in the seventh-century synagogue near Cairo. The most exotic item in the Firkowitch Collection is a leather-bound, fifty-two-page volume of parchment letters exchanged between the ruler of the Jewish kingdom of Khazaria and Hasdai ibn-Shaprut, spokesman for and financial adviser to the Spanish caliph in the tenth century. The letters are in Hebrew. Firkowitch's materials were acquired by the Imperial Library in 1859.

Another collection of Genizah fragments, put together by Father Antonin, a Russian monk from Jerusalem, in the 1860s, contains many responsa handed down by the great sages of the Babylonian academies as far back as the ninth century C.E., as well as material dealing with the Babylonian and Jerusalem Talmuds, cabala, liturgy, medicine, and philosophy, Dr. Abraham Katsh, president of Dropsie College, Philadelphia, who uncovered the continued existence of these materials, has had them microfilmed and they are now available to scholars in New York. The oldest complete Bible extant in the world today, the Codex copied in Cairo in 1008, is displayed in an airtight glass showcase in the State Library.

MOSCOW

CHORAL (Central) SYNAGOGUE, 8 Arkhipov St., a fifteen-minute walk from Red Square, is the main synagogue of Moscow. The handsome, white stone, Byzantine-style building was opened in 1891 in the midst of a violent anti-Semitic campaign, climaxed by an imperial decree ordering the gradual expulsion of all Jews from Moscow. Soon after, the synagogue was closed and its dome was removed. Instructions to convert it into a hospital or charitable institution were never carried out, but the synagogue remained closed for long periods until after the 1917 revolution. Since then it has never been closed, not even when the German army neared the city in the fall of 1941. Synagogue officials were evacuated to Uzbekistan, but for those who remained worship services continued.

Located on a small, cobblestone-paved street, the synagogue has an exterior series of Greek columns. The main sanctuary seats more than one thousand. A women's gallery that overhangs the synagogue on three sides accommodates almost as many more. On festivals and the High Holy Days, the throngs outside the synagogue overflow the street, and traffic has to be diverted. The electric-lighted altar is adorned with two 3-foot-high tablets inscribed in Hebrew and Russian with the words: "Our Father who are in Heaven, blessed be the government of the U.S.S.R., bulwark of peace." There are also other tablets in Hebrew and Russian and a large plaque containing the words of the Kaddish prayer.

Prayer books used by worshipers are limited and worn, and it is not unusual to see one book shared by two or more people. Prayer shawls are also scarce and those in use are worn thin. Information about the synagogue and how to reach it is available at the principal hotels. Services are held daily, morning and evening. In the tiny study of Rabbi Yehudah Levin there is a visitors' guest book containing such well-known names as Eleanor Roosevelt, Estes Kefauver, Jan Peerce, and Samuel Reshevsky, and the signatures of the Jewish leaders from the West who have visited Russia in recent years.

There are two other, smaller synagogues in the suburbs. One is at 70 Lermontovskaya St., in the Tsherkizovo section, and the other is at 3-5 Vtoroy Vysheshlavtsev Pereulok, in the Marinaroscha Rochtsha neighborhood.

HOTEL METROPOLE has at its entrance a plaque listing the names of prominent founders of the U.S.S.R., including that of Jacob Sverdlov. There are also memorials here to Russia's World War II heroes. If you can read Russian you will be able to identify many Jewish names.

INSTITUTE OF MARXISM-LENINISM, a four-story building opposite the Moscow City Soviet (city hall), is a repository for the papers of Karl Marx.

KREMLIN SENATE TOWER WALL has a bas-relief honoring the revolutionaries who died during the battle for Moscow in 1917; 500 of them were buried in a mass grave along the Kremlin wall between the Nicholas and Saviour Gates, and ultimately it became the custom to bury there important deceased Communist leaders, famous writers, explorers, and other notables. Among those buried in this Pantheon of the Communist great are Jacob Sverdlov, first chairman of the Central Committee of the Communist party (see SVERDLOVSK below), and Clara Zetkin, an early leader of the German Communists. The Communist notables are interred in graves on a grassy strip along the wall or in urns enclosed in the wall.

LENIN STATE LIBRARY, 3 Kalinin St., houses the famous Baron David Guinzburg Collection of Hebraica and Judaica. It contains 6,000 rare manuscripts and fragments dealing with a wide variety of subjects. The collection was assembled by David Guinzburg, a well-known scholar and industrialist, whose grandfather had been made a baron by the Prince of Hesse, a brother of the Czarina. Microfilms of much of this material and of a catalogue describing it are available at Dropsie University, Philadelphia.

LAWOTCHKIN STREET, one of the city's new streets, was named for Simon Lawotchkin, a Jewish plane designer and wartime test pilot, on the 20th anniversary of the end of World War II.

KARL MARX MONUMENT on Sverdlov Square, opposite Bolshoi Theatre, was dedicated by Nikita Khrushchev in 1961. The first monument to Marx in Moscow, the 25-foot statue is carved from a single block of gray granite. The foundation stone was laid in 1920 by Lenin.

MIKHOELS MONUMENT in the Moscow Crematorium grounds, is a bronze bust of Shloime Mikhoels, actor and director of the Moscow State Yiddish Theatre, who was murdered during the Stalinist purge of Jews in 1948. Mikhoels was an Honored Artist of the Soviet Union and, as head of the Jewish Anti-Fascist Committee, was sent abroad immediately after World War II to enlist support for the Soviet Union among Jewish communities of the West. His death signaled the suppression of Yiddish cultural activities and institutions. The bust was dedicated in 1959 by the All-Russian Theatre Society. A plaque on the bust's pedestal is inscribed with Mikhoels' name, in Russian and Yiddish, and the dates of his birth and death (1890-1948).

NOVODYEVICHY CEMETERY behind the Novodyevichy Cloister Museum, on Bolshaya Pirogovskaya St., contains the graves and buried ashes of many noted Russian artists and writers as well as revolutionaries. Not far from the grave of Anton Chekhov is the last resting place of Isaac Ilyich Levitan, Russia's greatest landscape painter. Son of a Lithuanian rabbi, Levitan was repeatedly expelled from Moscow because he had no permit to live beyond the Jewish Pale of Settlement. In 1960, the centennial of his birth was widely observed in Russia. Levitan had been buried in the Jewish Dorogmilov Cemetery on the edge of the city in 1900, but in Soviet times his remains were exhumed and reburied amid those of Russia's great literary and artistic figures. In this same cemetery there are dozens of niches containing the ashes of Jewish revolutionaries. Also buried here is the late Ilya G. Ehrenburg, one of Russia's most prominent and most controversial writers, who often defended the USSR's policies on Jews. There is a memorial stone here to Nadezha Alliluyeva, the Jewish woman who was Stalin's second wife.

PAPERNIK STREET is named for Lazar Haimovich Papernik, a former Jewish watchmaker who died while serving as a member of a Russian partisan unit.

SOVIETISH HEIMLAND, 17 Kirov St., the offices of one of the only two Jewish publications in the Soviet Union (the other is in Birobidjan) is now pointed out to visitors who ask to see Jewish institutions. What began as a Yiddish bi-monthly in 1961 has since become a monthly with a circulation of some 25,000, much of which is distributed abroad. The editor is Aaron Vergelis.

STATE LITERARY MUSEUM, 38 Dimitrova Lilitsa St., preserves the original manuscripts of the great Russian writers, including the works of the late Ilya Ehrenburg, the best-known Jewish writer in comtemporary Russia.

SVERDLOV MONUMENT, between the Lenin Museum and the Metropol Hotel, close to the Kitaigorodskaya Wall, is a life-size sculpture of Jacob Sverdlov, first president of the Soviet Union (*see below*). It was erected in 1970. Sverdlov Hall in the Great Kremlin Palace is named for him, as is one of the central districts of Moscow.

SVERDLOV SQUARE opposite the Hotel Moskva, near the Bolshoi Theatre, is named for Jacob Sverdlov. The building that houses the Soviet Council of Ministers is on this square.

TOLSTOY MUSEUM on Kropotkin St., displays a collection of Israeli-printed Hebrew translations of the works of Leo Tolstoy.

YESHIVA KOL YAACOV housed in the Choral Synagogue, is the only rabbinical seminary in the Soviet Union.

NALCHIK

SYNAGOGUE, on 3 Osetinska Street, serves the Orthodox 'mountain Jews' from the Caucasus who have settled in this capital city of the Kabadrin-Balkar Autonomous Republic. Known as "Dag Chufut," the mountain Jews used to live in Dagestan and Azerbaijan where their history goes back to the 6th century B.C.E.

NOVOSIBIRSK

SYNAGOGUE

PEREDELKINO

GRAVE OF BORIS PASTERNAK, in a fenced-in, tree-shaded corner in this village outside Moscow, has become a pilgrimage site for intellectuals who come here annually on the anniversary of his death, May 30, 1960. Pasternak, who lived much of his life as a Jew, became a convert toward his latter years before he won international fame for his novel, "Doctor Zhivago". In 1958 he was awarded the Nobel Prize in literature but the Soviet authorities forced him to decline it because his poetry and fiction were regarded as highly critical of the regime.

SARANSK

MONUMENT TO SOVIET SPACE PIONEERS, memorializes three scientists, Pavel Fedoseyenko, Andrei Vasenko and Ilya Usyskin, a Jew, who died near here in Jan. 1934 when their stratospheric balloon crashed after reaching the then record height of 22,000 meters. Records found in the balloon were credited with breaking new ground in space research. All three men are buried beside the Kremlin Wall in Moscow's Red Square.

SVERDLOVSK

Capital of the autonomous region of the same name, and the principal industrial and commercial city of the Urals, Sverdlovsk is named for Jacob Mikhailovich Sverdlov, a Jewish revolutionary who was born in Nizhni Novgorod (now Gorki), in the Ukraine, in 1885. An organizer of underground political groups, he was imprisoned five times and twice exiled to Siberia. An early associate of Lenin, Sverdlov was elected chairman of the All-Russian Executive Committee of the Soviets after the Bolshevik revolution in 1917. Later, he became secretary of the Central Committee of the Communist party, which in effect made him the first president of the Soviet Union. Sverdlov died of typhus in 1919. The city that bears his name has a good-sized Jewish community. Formerly known as Ekaterinburg, the city was renamed in 1924. The last Czar and his family were shot here.

SHENKMAN STREET is named for Yakov Shenkman, a hero of the Soviet Civil War.

SYNAGOGUE, 14 Kuibyshev St. (There are also synagogues in Derbent (Dagestan), Gorki, Kuibyshev, Makhachkala (Dagestan), Novosibirsk, Chkalov (Orenberg), Orel, Rostov-on-Don, and Saratov and substantial Jewish communities in Chelyabinsk, Tula, Smolensk, Kirov (Vyatka), Voroshilovsk (Starropol), Volgagrad (Tsaritsyn, until recently Stalingrad), Kursk and Voronezh. The synagogues in Tula, Chelyabinsk, Chkalov, and Voronezh were reported closed in 1961. In the latter city the walled-up synagogue is used as a lumber warehouse, but it is still recognizable for what it was.)

TADJIK SOVIET SOCIALIST REPUBLIC

DUSHANBE (Stalinbad)

SYNAGOGUE, 26 Dekhanskaya St., is a complex of four synagogues built around an open courtyard. The largest is the principal synagogue of the Bukharan Jews, who originally came to this region from Persia in the sixth century B.C.E. They still speak a Persian dialect. There are about 15,000 of them in Dushambe. At right angles to the main Bukharan synagogue is a smaller Bukharan prayer house. Facing these two are the synagogues of the East European Jews who first settled here in the early years of World War II as refugees from the Ukraine, the Crimea, and White Russia. They number 800.

UKRAINIAN SOVIET SOCIALIST REPUBLIC

BAR

SYNAGOGUE, 37 Eighth of March Street.

BERDICHEV

GRAVE OF RABBI LEVI ISAAC, venerated by Chassidism as the Compassionate One, who was born here in 1740 and died here in 1809, has been preserved in the old Jewish cemetery of this once famous center of Jewish learning.

SYNAGOGUE, 8 Sverdlov Street, serves 7,000 Jews in city once famed as the seat of the Chassidic Rabbi Levi Isaac of Berdichev. The 40,000 Jews who lived here before the war were wiped out by the Nazis. The present Jewish community owns a number of Torah Scrolls that escaped burning by the Nazis in 1941.

BERSHAD

SYNAGOGUE, Narodnaya St.

CHERNOVTSKY (Czernowitz)

SYNAGOGUE, 53-L, Kobyiltsky St., is the last synagogue open in this city of some 50,000 Jews. The synagogue at 55 Russkaya St. was closed in 1961 and turned into an elementary school. The Great Synagogue, a Moorish-style structure dating from 1877, when this city was known as Czernowitz and was part of the Austro-Hungarian Empire, was previously reported shut down. Two small, hutlike buildings on the outskirts of the city are now used for Jewish worship.

CHORTKOV

CHORTKOVER SYNAGOGUE, once the seat of the famed Chassidic Rabbi of Chortkov has been converted into a restaurant and the surrounding grounds have become an athletic field.

DNEPROPETROVSK

CHUDNOVSKY STREET is named for Grigori Chudnovsky, an early Russian revolutionary.
SYNAGOGUE, Kotsivbinsky St.

KHARKOV

MARTYRS' MEMORIAL, a small monument over the mass grave of 100,000 Jews murdered by the Nazis, stands on the edge of the city on the spot where the extermination occurred in a single day. The inscription says: "Here lie victims of Nazi oppression."

SYNAGOGUE here has been closed since 1947, but there is a small prayer house still in use. Kharkov was the birthplace of the first Palestine pioneer group, the Bilu, in 1882.

KIEV

BABI YAR MEMORIAL, a simple marble stone set in a grass-covered site, where on Sept. 29-30, 1941, Nazi executioners shot 33,171 Jewish men, women and children and dumped their bodies in the then abandoned lime-and-sandpit known as 'grandmother's ravine.' The memorial, erected in 1966, has an inscription in Russian that says "victims of Fascism" lie below, with nothing to indicate that the victims were Jews. For years the Soviet authorities refused to recognize this tragic symbol of Jewish martyrdom and tried to prevent visitors from seeing Babi Yar. Some years ago the ravine itself was filled in and made the site of a major housing development. The massacre was vividly described in the novel by the Russian writer, Anatoly Kuznetsov, who saw it happen as a boy of 12. It is also memorialized in Yevgeny Yevtushenko's poetic protest against Soviet anti-Semitism, 'Babi Yar,' which was set to music in Dmitri Shostakovich's 'Thirteenth Symphony.' The victims of Babi Yar, who had failed to leave Kiev before the Germans occupied it on September 21, were lined up on the edge of the ravine and mowed down by machine guns, ostensibly in retaliation for an explosion on September 24 that had wrecked the headquarters of the Fourth German Army in the Continental Hotel. The commander of the execution squad was tried and convicted at the Nuremberg War Crimes Trials and hanged. Tourist guides are still reluctant to show the place, which was behind the Lubyanovka Cemetery, once the oldest Jewish burial ground in Kiev. The memorial can be reached by taking trolley No. 4 to the end of the line and Bus No. 14.

CHMIELNICKI SQUARE has an imposing monument to the Cossack leader, Bogdan Chmielnicki, whose forces murdered 200,000 Jews in Poland during an Ukrainian uprising in 1648-49 against Poland which then included the Ukraine.

LUBYANAKA JEWISH CEMETERY where some tombstones go back to the middle of the 17th century, and which was badly damaged during the Nazi occupation, was cleared in 1963-64 to make way for new buildings. The remains were removed to a new Jewish cemetery but the families of the dead were permitted to transfer the remains of their kin to Israel or anywhere else they desired. One of those whose remains were transferred to Israel was Dov Ber Borochov, founder of the Socialist Zionist Party, whose leaders played a decisive role in the birth of Israel.

SHOLOM ALEICHEM HOUSE, 5 Krasnoarmieskaya St., where the beloved Yiddish author lived for some years, is marked by a plaque whose inscription, in Ukrainian, states that the famed writer lived there from 1897 to 1904. There is nothing to indicate that he was a Jew or that he wrote in Yiddish.

SHOLOM ALEICHEM STREET in a new housing development in the Darnista district, was named for the beloved Yiddish writer in 1966 on the 50th anniversary of his death. The street is a continuation of Zhdanov and Kirov Sts., and which is known to tourists for the Oktyabr Theatre and Dnieper Restaurant, has been renamed Constantinov Street. A Sholom Aleichem stamp, issued on his centennial in 1959, bears his name, in Russian, and his portrait; unlike other stamps in a series honoring illustrious figures of various national cultures, it omits any reference to his Jewishness.

SYNAGOGUE, 29 Shchekovitskaya St., a ramshackle building in the suburb of Podol, is in the prewar ghetto section. There is a smaller synagogue below this one, as well as a ritual bath. Kiev's Great Synagogue still stands, but is now a State puppet theatre. It is clearly identifiable as a former synagogue. There are over 150,000 Jews in Kiev, where they first settled in the tenth century. Kiev was the scene of the notorious Mendel Beilis blood ritual trial in 1911.

KRYZHOPOL

SYNAGOGUE in the Vinnitsa section.

LVOV (Lemberg)

GARAGE, at 23 Lenin St., has its entrance paved with Hebrew-inscribed tombstones.

SYNAGOGUE, last remnant of a historic Jewish community dating from the 12th century, was closed in 1962 and then converted into a sports hall in 1963. Two small prayer houses were also closed in 1970, leaving the 40,000 Jews without a place to pray for the second time in nearly 1,000 years. Only 150 of the 100,000 prewar Jews survived the Nazi occupation. The present Jewish community is composed of Jews who moved in after the war. Once known as Lemberg, this city was formerly the most important Jewish community in Polish, later Austrian, Galicia.

MEDZHIBOZH

GRAVE OF THE BAAL SHEM TOV (known as the Besht from the Hebrew initials), founder of Chassidism, has miraculously survived intact in the old Jewish cemetery in this town between Vinnitsa and Berdichev. It was here that Israel ben Eliezer created the movement that spread throughout the world. The Besht, who died in 1760, is buried in a grave surrounded by four posts and a concrete canopy. The graves of the Besht's grandsons and of their successors are also in good condition.

ODESSA

MENDELE MOCHER SEFORIM GRAVE in the main Jewish Cemetery, is one of the great shrines of Jewish culture, for here lies the father of Yiddish literature. His real name was Solomon Jacob Abramovich. After writing Hebrew essays and short stories, he turned to Yiddish, in which language he both eulogized and satirized the life of the Jewish masses in nineteenth-century Eastern Europe. From 1881 to 1905 he was principal of the Odessa Talmud Torah. He died in 1917. His original tombstone, with Russian and Yiddish inscriptions, was demolished by the Nazis, but the Russians restored it in 1947. Mendele's three grandsons are on the faculty of the University of Odessa.

SYNAGOGUE, 5 Lessnaya St., in the suburb of Peressyp, a large building next to the gasworks, burned to the ground in 1968, reportedly as the result of a short circuit in electrical wiring in the matzoth baking facility. This was the last of 11 pre-war synagogues in a community that still numbers 200,000 Jews. There were reports of plans to rebuild the synagogue in 1970. The Bolshaya (Great) Synagogue has been converted into a makeshift gymnasium, with basketball backboards and nets on the main floor and various kinds of athletic equipment where the women's gallery used to be. A large portrait of Lenin is displayed where the pulpit used to be. The Brodskaya Synagogue, another large house of worship, is closed. Odessa was the birthplace of the first Hebrew newspaper, *Hamelitz*, in 1860; the locale of the first secular Jewish school in Russia (1826); and the editorial center of the first Jewish journals in Russia. At one time or another it was the home of such distinguished

Jewish literary figures as the poets Bialik, Tschernichovsky and Shneour; the philosophers Ahad Ha'am, Fichman and Klausner; the novelists Sholom Aleichem, Frug, and Isaac Babel; and Zionist notables like Leo Pinsker, Menahem Ussishkin, Vladimir Jabotinsky (founder of the Jewish Legion in World War I) and Meir Dizengoff, first mayor of Tel Aviv. A bust of Sholom Aleichem is supposed to be erected in the City Park.

PEREYASLAV–KHMELNITSKY

SHOLOM ALEICHEM STREET in this small township in the Kiev area is named for the renowned Yiddish writer, who was born here in 1859. In 1964 the township's name was changed by the addition of Khmelnitsky (or Chmielnicki), for the Cossack leader who led pogroms in Poland in 1648-49.

POLTAVA

MEMORIAL TO JEWISH VICTIMS OF NAZIS outside the city, is a modest tablet with the inscription: "Here rest the remains of 12,000 Soviet citizens who were barbarously murdered by the Nazi occupants."

SLAVUTA

SYNAGOGUE, Skolnaya St.

UMAN

TOMB OF THE BRATZLAVER REBBE, one of the revered figures of the 18th century Chassidic movement, was destroyed during World War II but it has since been replaced. The Rebbe was the great-grandson of the Baal Shem Tov, founder of Chassidism.

YARUGA

17TH CENTURY CEMETERY badly neglected, still has a number of old Jewish gravestones.

ZHITOMIR

SYNAGOGUE, 78 Dombrousky St., a small building acquired by the 20,000 Jews in this city, replaced the last synagogue demolished by the authorities in 1962. (There are synagogues in Khust, Frunze and Vinnetsa and good-sized Jewish communities in Cherkassy, Drogobych, Kherson, Khmelnitzki, Tarnopol, Chernigov, Korosten, Kremenchug, Zhdanov, Olevsk, Poltava, Rostov-on-Don, Soroka, Donetsk. The synagogues in Korosten, Kremenchug, Olevsk, Poltava, Rostov, Soroka, Donetsk, and Vinnitsa were reported closed in 1961.)

UZBEK SOVIET SOCIALIST REPUBLIC

BUKHARA

SYNAGOGUE, 20 Tsentralnaya St., one block from the leading hotel on Lenin St., is a low, one-story, dull-gray building of clay and straw on a frame of light wood. There is no sign or other identifying mark except a blue-painted door that leads to a small courtyard on whose whitewashed walls there is a blue Star of David. The synagogue is in the same neighborhood of this ancient Central Asian city where Jews have lived since the sixth century B.C.E., when they came here by way of Persia, after the Jews were exiled from Palestine. The Bukharan Jews are one of the most colorful Jewish communities in the world, with their own customs and traditions. They speak a Judaeo-Persian dialect known as Tadjiki. Decimated in the Moslem and Mongol invasions, the Bukharan community was re-established under Tamerlane, a successor to Genghis Khan, in the middle of the fourteenth century. When the independent emirate of Bukhara was annexed by Russia in the nineteenth century, Bukharan Jews began trickling into Palestine. Today there is a large Bukharan settlement in Israel, but there are still 3,000 Jews here and that many more in the surrounding towns and villages.

ANDISHEN

SYNAGOGUE, 7 Sovietskaya St.

KOKAND

SYNAGOGUE, in the Fergana District, 45 Marshall Govorov St.

MARGELAN

SYNAGOGUE, 7 Shakirdzhanova Street.

NAMANGAN

SYNAGOGUE, in the Andizhan District, Frunze St.

SAMARKAND

SYNAGOGUE, Khudzhumskaya St., is part of the oldest Bukharan Jewish community founded by settlers from Persia before the Christian Era.

TASHKENT

ASHKENAZIC SYNAGOGUE, 103 Chempionov St., serves the East European Jews who settled here after World War II.

BUKHARAN SYNAGOGUE, 24 Sagban Tupik, is the largest Bukharan synagogue in Uzbekistan. Fifty thousand Jews live in this city.

SHOLOM ALEICHEM ST. is named for the noted writer.

YUGOSLAVIA

Ruins of a first-century synagogue uncovered on the site of the pre-Christian Greek city of Stobi, near Skopje, are the earliest evidences of Jewish settlement in what is now Yugoslavia. Remains of a third-century synagogue and cemetery were found at Salona, on the Dalmatian coast. Small Jewish colonies existed in Serbia and Slovenia in the Middle Ages. In the fourteenth century, Jews from Italy, Spain, and Portugal migrated to Dalmatia by way of Salonica when that area was under Turkish suzerainty. The East European Jewish community had its origin with Hungarian Jews who began arriving in Bosnia about 1718.

The Berlin Congress of 1878 won complete civil, economic, and political emancipation for the Jews of Serbia. Similar rights were accorded to large blocs of Hungarian, Rumanian, Bulgarian, and Austrian Jews when the new state of Yugoslavia was created after World War I by adding Croatia, Dalmatia, Bosnia, Slovenia, and Herzegovina to Serbia and Montenegro.

Yugoslavia had 85,000 Jews on the eve of World War II. Almost the whole of the Jewish community was wiped out soon after the Nazi invasion in 1941 when the Croatian fascists joined forces with the Germans in killing hundreds of thousands of Serbians and Jews. Only 15,000 Jews survived the war in prisoner-of-war camps, concentration camps, and as members of Tito's partisans. More than half of the survivors left for Israel after 1948. At the end of 1970 there were 7,000 Jews left, dispersed in 36 communities. Belgrade had 1,450, Zagreb 1,400, Sarajevo 1000 and Subotica 500. There were smaller communities in Novi Sad, Rijeka, Osijek and Skopje. Under the Tito Communist regime the Jews have enjoyed equal rights and religious freedom. The government was helpful in restoring synagogues and other communal institutions, encouraged the erection of memorials to Jewish victims of the Nazis and evinced no opposition toward emigration to Israel. Jewish life is largely secular. The country has been without a rabbi since 1968. Jewish life is preserved under the leadership of the Federation of Jewish Communities which sponsors kindergartens in Belgrade and Zagreb, two Jewish choruses, a summer camp for children and, with the aid of the JDC, an old folks home in Zagreb.

While Yugoslavia broke off relations with Israel after the Six-Day War, the Yugoslav press has not been militantly anti-Israel nor overtly pro-Arab despite the country's substantial Moslem population. A number of Jews hold important posts in government and universities.

ADA

JEWISH CEMETERY on an island outside this town has many old graves.

BELGRADE

AMAR BROTHERS STREET is named for Moshe A. Amar and his cousins, Solomon, David, Josif, and Isak Amar, who were among the great heroes of Yugoslavia's two wars of independence in 1912 and in 1918.

ASHKENAZIC SYNAGOGUE, 19 Kosmajska St., the only one in the city, was rebuilt and restored by the Yugoslav government and the American Jewish Joint Distribution Committee. It had been badly damaged by the Nazis, who used it as a brothel. The older Sephardic Synagogue, on Cara Urosa, was blown up by the Nazis before they evacuated the city. The existing synagogue, a tall, white stone structure built in 1913, is at the rear of a courtyard. The building, now rather shabby, is partially concealed by trees and a wrought iron fence. When the synagogue was reconsecrated after the war, pews were contributed by the Serbian Orthodox Church and Marshal Tito and other government leaders contributed funds.

BARUCH BROTHERS STREET in the old Jewish quarter near the Danube River, is named for Isa, Bora, and Jozi Baruch and their sisters, Shela and Bela, famous Yugoslav resistance fighters who died in the underground fighting during the Nazi occupation. Their father was an impoverished tailor. Isa was an engineer, Bora was a lawyer, and Jozi was a noted painter and teacher. Isa organized an underground fighting unit and after his death was proclaimed a national hero. The *Baruch Brothers Cultural Center* is also named for them.

CHAJIMA DAVICA STREET is named for Hayim Davitcho, a prominent member of the Yugoslavian diplomatic corps, translator of Spanish novels into Serbian, and author of novels of Jewish life.

JEWISH MUSEUM, 71 July 7th St., is in the same building as the headquarters of the Federation of Jewish Communities of Yugoslavia, which represents thirty-five communities. The museum has a permanent exhibit of religious objects and material depicting the history of the Jewish community and its participation in the War of National Liberation. The Federation's monthly journal, *The Jewish Review*, published in Serbian and English, has its editorial offices here.

JEWISH WAR MEMORIALS in Jewish Cemetery on Cardak Hill, in the suburb of Pancevo, memorialize Jews who died in the Balkan Wars, in World Wars I and II, and at the hands of the Nazis. The older memorial is a huge concrete slab topped by two stone Stars of David at each end. Set into the slab are marble stones on which are inscribed the names of Jewish heroes of the Balkan Wars and World War I. The World War II memorial, erected by the Yugoslav war veterans in 1955, is a huge stone honoring the 430 Jews killed by the Nazis in Belgrade in 1941. Nearby is another memorial erected in 1952 by the government and the Jewish community. This one resembles two huge plane wings separated by an altar topped by a Menorah. Not far away is a monument erected to Bulina Baruch, mother of the Baruch heroes (*see above*), by the Association of Fighters, in 1961. Another memorial honors 1,000 Austrian Jews murdered by the Nazis at Sabac, together with the local Jews, whose remains were reburied in the Belgrade cemetery.

JEWISH YOUTH CENTER, 19 Kosmajska St., is housed in the Ashkenazic Synagogue.

PAVLE PAP STREET is named for Pavle H. Pap, one of the leaders of Yugoslavia's Communist party, who was executed by the Italian occupation forces in 1941. For his active participation in organizing the resistance against the Nazis and Italians, Pap was proclaimed a national hero in 1951.

MOSHE PIJADE MONUMENT on Moshe Pijade Square, in the heart of the city, is an immense stone statue of one of the architects of postwar Yugoslavia (*See Below*)

MOSHE PIJADE HIGH SCHOOL, formerly the First Belgrade High School, was renamed for the Jewish statesman on its 125th anniversary. Located in the pre-war Jewish quarter known as Dorcol, the school was the training ground for many prominent Jews, including Pijade.

MOSHE PIJADE TOMB in the Kalemegdan Fortress, at the juncture of the Sava and Danube Rivers, is the last resting place of the late president of the Yugoslav National Assembly, a Sephardic Jew who was one of Marshal Tito's closest associates. A painter and author, Pijade spent fourteen years in prison for Communist activities during the reigns of King Alexander and Prince Paul. During World War II he was one of the most daring of the partisan leaders, serving by Tito's side until the country's liberation. After the war, he represented Yugoslavia at the peace conference and helped draft the country's constitution. Pijade is one of five men buried in the Crypt of National Heroes. His picture hangs side by side in many public places with that of Tito. One of Belgrade's principal streets is known as Pijade Street. Another of Yugoslavia's noted Jewish war heroes is Gen. Voija Todorovic who was born Shmuel Lehrer.

BITOLJ (Monastir)

MONUMENT TO JEWISH VICTIMS OF FASCISM stands in a newly laid-out park on the spot which marked the prewar ghetto of this Macedonian town once known as Monastir. In the park is a bust of Streja Ovadija Mery, a Jewish girl who has been proclaimed a national heroine for her wartime exploits. The local *Historical Archives* has a permanent exhibit showing how the Jews of this old town lived.

BOR

NAZI VICTIMS MEMORIAL, a huge carved stone menorah, stands on the site of a former Nazi concentration camp here where thousands of Jews died in 1943 and 1944.

DJAKOVO

MONUMENT TO JEWISH VICTIMS OF NAZIS on the site of the former Croatian concentration camp, is a huge urnlike sarcophagus of marble and granite inscribed in Hebrew and in Serbo-Croatian. It stands near a mass grave containing the remains of thousands of Jews.

DUBROVNIK (Ragusa)

HEBREW FOUNTAIN at the Pile (Brsalje), outside the old city walls, is more than five hundred years old. It was one of three built in 1420, when the city's waterworks was established. Originally known as Fontana per gli Ebrai ("Hebrew Fountain"), it used to stand just outside the ghetto. The townspeople now call it the "Fontana Kosher." Above the shell into which water flows is a lion's head, and below the shell is a lion's leg.

SYNAGOGUE, 3 zulica Zudioska (Jews' Street), is the third-oldest in Europe, having been established in 1352 by families who came from Spain 140 years before that country expelled its Jews. Dubrovnik was then an independent republic allied to Venice. Emilio Tolentino, the synagogue's caretaker, whose family was one of the founders, lives in the building, which adjoins the synagogue and is connected to it. Located on a narrow lane off the city's main square, known as Stradona or Placa, the building on the outside looks much like any of the other medieval houses in the city. Inside the sanctuary is an oblong room divided by three arches and paneled in dark wood. The ceiling is painted blue with gold stars, and Florentine candelabra hang from the beams. The delicately carved pulpit in the center and the Ark, flanked by slender wooden pillars, are of Baroque design. The Torah Scrolls date from the thirteenth century. One of the unique treasures of the synagogue is a thirteenth-century Moorish carpet, a superb piece of work, which is said to have been a gift from Queen Isabella of Spain to her Jewish physician when he was sent into exile. There are also many other old tapestries and unique examples of synagogue ritual objects in silver. Mr. Tolentino will be happy to show tourists ancient documents describing the early years of the Jewish community, which was virtually wiped out during the Nazi occupation.

JEWISH CEMETERY nestling on one of the city's slopes, is more than three hundred years old, but it contains some older tombstones from an earlier Jewish cemetery. The tiny plot is planted with tall cypress trees. On one of the tombstones is carved a five-pointed crown, an emblem granted to the chief rabbi of Córdoba, Spain in 711 by the Moors and later used as a badge by the Spanish Jewish exiles. Buried in this cemetery is Jacobus Flavius, a sixteenth-century Jewish poet who wrote Latin verse under the name of Didacus Pyrrhus. Dubrovnik was also the home of another Renaissance Jewish figure, Juan Rodrigo de Castelbranco, who became a famous botanist and physician under the name of Amatus Lusitanus.

LJUBLJANA

NAZI VICTIMS MEMORIAL is in the local Jewish cemetery.

STREET OF THE JEWS on the right bank of the Ljubljana River, marks the site of the fourteenth-century ghetto in this Slovenian city where Jews settled in the thirteenth century.

NOVI SAD

SYNAGOGUE, 35 Jugoslovenske Nar. Armije St. The Jewish community's headquarters is in the same building. The synagogue, a huge structure that accommodates 1,000 people, at 35 Jugoslovenske Nar. Armije St., recently celebrated the community's 250th anniversary.

WAR MEMORIAL in Jewish Cemetery at the end of Doze Dizkdja St., honors Jewish victims of the Nazis.

OSIJEK

MONUMENT TO NAZI VICTIMS, a huge sculptured statue of an unknown Jewish mother and child, stands in the center of this capital city of Slavonia as a memorial to 1,000 Jews who died in Nazi death camps.

SYNAGOGUE, 13 Braca Radica, also houses the Jewish community's headquarters. A second synagogue, on Dimitrija Tucovica St., is unused although it was rebuilt after the war.

PODLJUBELJ

CONCENTRATION CAMP MEMORIAL, about a mile from the Austro-Yugoslav frontier, in an area of trackless peaks and inaccessible cliffs, consists of five huge monolithic cones of roughly hewn stone which encircle a small round pedestal. On the pedestal stands the stark figure of a black skeleton, with arms outstretched. Only a few low stone buildings, now almost overgrown with flowers, remain of the former concentration camp.

RIJEKA (Fiume)

SYNAGOGUE, 9 Ivana Filipovica St.

SARAJEVO

JEWISH CEMETERY, Kovacici Nevesinska St., on the Debelo Brdo Hill on the left bank of the Miljacka River underneath the Sarajevo-Uzice railway line, has been proclaimed a national monument. It contains many unusual tombstones dating from the middle of the sixteenth century, when Jewish refugees from Spain settled here under the patronage of Joseph Nasi, the Turkish Jew who was an aide to the Sultan. The old gravestones look like huge boulders on the front of which Hebrew inscriptions are carved on slabs set into the face of the stones. A marble-and-granite monument in the same cemetery memorializes the Jews of Bosnia and Herzegovina who were killed by the Nazis. There is a memorial on the cemetery to Jewish soldiers in the Serbian and Yugoslav armies who fell in the two World Wars.

JEWISH MUSEUM, adjoining Ashkenazic Synagogue, has many old Jewish religious objects, including an eight-hundred-year-old Menorah brought to Sarajevo by Jews from Córdoba.

NATIONAL MUSEUM, Marin Dvor St., has on permanent exhibit the renowned Sarajevo Haggadah, a thirteenth-century illuminated manuscript recounting the Passover story. It reached Sarajevo via Italy through Spanish Jews who brought it from Catalonia.

SYNAGOGUE, 83 Dobrovoljacka St., was originally the Ashkenazic synagogue, built by Jews from Central Europe long after the Sephardic Jews settled here. But since the Ashkenazic and Sephardic synagogues have been merged, this is the only one in use in Sarajevo. It is located in the old ghetto area.

GREAT SEPHARDIC SYNAGOGUE on Yugoslav National Army St., along the embankment of the Miljacka River, which was almost gutted during the Nazi occupation, was turned over to the city in 1966 on the 400th anniversary of the Sarajevo Jewish community. The synagogue is now known as the Djuro Djakovic Workers University. In the synagogue's main lobby stands a giant menorah as a memorial to the Jews who died during the Nazi terror. The former synagogue also houses a museum depicting the history of the Jews in Bosnia and Herzegovina.

SENTA

JEWISH CEMETERY, 18 Dubrovacka St., has a memorial to the 3,000 Jews who were killed here by the Nazis.

SKOPJE

ALBERT VAJS JEWISH COMMUNITY CENTER, 46 March 11th Street, is named for the late president of the Federation of Jewish Communities in Yugoslavia. The street is named in memory of the day in 1943 when 7,000 Skopje Jews were deported to Treblinka. The present Center building is a renovated structure that replaces an older building badly damaged in the 1963 earthquake. The Center houses a small synagogue. The old synagogue was wrecked by the Nazis.

MEMORIAL TO NAZI VICTIMS in the Jewish Cemetery, honors those who died in the death camps.

SOMBOR

MEMORIAL TO NAZI VICTIMS in this town near the Hungarian border is a large stone wall in the local Jewish cemetery. Affixed to the wall are ten plaques on which are inscribed the names of 760 Jews murdered by the Croatian Nazis.

SPLIT (Spalato)

JEWISH CEMETERY on Marjan Hill, dates from the sixteenth century, but artifacts from a first-century Jewish cemetery found in the ruins of Salona, just outside Split, may still be seen in the Provincial Museum.

SYNAGOGUE near the ruins of the ancient Diocletian palace, was restored in 1959 after being badly damaged by the Nazis. There was a synagogue in the old ruins of the palace built by the Roman Emperor Diocletian when he abdicated in 305 and settled at Solin.

RODRIGO STREET is named for Daniel Rodrigo, a 16th century engineer who built the harbor at Split.

SUBOTICA

JEWISH CEMETERY has a memorial to 4,000 Jews murdered by the Nazis. It is an obelisk-like stone surrounded by twelve mass graves.

SYNAGOGUE, 13 Dimitrija Tucovica, a centuries-old structure, was rebuilt with funds from the Conference on Jewish Material Claims against Germany and rededicated in 1961. It also houses the Jewish community headquarters.

UROSHEVAC

AMAREVO BRDO ("Amar's Hill"), in this town between Skoplje and Pristina, in southern Serbia, is named for Moshe A. Amar, one of the heroes of Yugoslavia's war of independence, who was killed near here.

ZAGREB

JEWISH OLD FOLKS HOME, 55 Bukovacka Cesta, the newest Jewish communal building in Yugoslavia, was opened in 1957 with funds provided by the American Jewish Joint Distribution Committee and the Conference on Jewish Material Claims against Germany. It cares for the Jewish aged from all parts of the country.

MIROGOJ (Jewish) CEMETERY has a memorial to Jewish victims of the Nazis in the form of a heroic statue of Moses holding the Tablets of the Law.

SYNAGOGUE AND JEWISH COMMUNITY HEADQUARTERS, 16 Palmoticeva St. The synagogue is a single upstairs room. The rest of the building is used for offices and residences of Jewish officials. The main synagogue on Prasca St. was destroyed.

ZENICA

OLD SYNAGOGUE here has been restored.

INDEX